The New Energy Paradigm

The New Energy Paradigm

Edited by
Dieter Helm

OXFORD
UNIVERSITY PRESS

OXFORD

UNIVERSITY PRESS

Great Clarendon Street, Oxford OX2 6DP

Oxford University Press is a department of the University of Oxford.
It furthers the University's objective of excellence in research, scholarship,
and education by publishing worldwide in

Oxford New York

Auckland Cape Town Dar es Salaam Hong Kong Karachi
Kuala Lumpur Madrid Melbourne Mexico City Nairobi
New Delhi Shanghai Taipei Toronto

With offices in

Argentina Austria Brazil Chile Czech Republic France Greece
Guatemala Hungary Italy Japan Poland Portugal Singapore
South Korea Switzerland Thailand Turkey Ukraine Vietnam

Oxford is a registered trade mark of Oxford University Press
in the UK and in certain other countries

Published in the United States
by Oxford University Press Inc., New York

British Library Cataloging in Publication Data

Data available

Library of Congress Cataloguing in Publication Data

Data available

Typeset by Oxford Review of Economic Policy
Printed in Great Britain
on acid-free paper by
Biddles Ltd., King's Lynn, Norfolk

ISBN 978–0–19–922970–3

1 3 5 7 9 10 8 6 4 2

Contents

Contents

Contributors

SCOTT BARRETT

Scott Barrett is Professor and Director of International Policy at the Johns Hopkins University School of Advanced International Studies, located in Washington, DC. He is the author of *Environment and Statecraft: The Strategy of Environmental Treaty-Making* (Oxford University Press, paperback edition 2005) and many journal articles on international cooperation, most recently in the field of infectious disease control. He received his PhD in economics from the London School of Economics and taught previously at the London Business School. He spent his sabbatical in 2006 at Yale University. His new book, *Why Cooperate? The Incentive to Supply Global Public Goods,* will be published by Oxford University Press in 2007.

FATIH BIROL

Dr Fatih Birol is Chief Economist and Head of the Economic Analysis Division of the Paris-based International Energy Agency. He is organiser and director of the *World Energy Outlook* series, the IEA's flagship publication. He worked for 6 years in the Secretariat of the Organization of Petroleum Exporting Countries (OPEC) in Vienna, before joining the IEA in 1995.

The *World Energy Outlook* (WEO) series is widely recognized as the most authoritative source for world energy information and medium- to long-term energy projections and analysis. In recent years, the *World Energy Outlook* has received a number of honours for analytical excellence.

In October 2006, Fatih Birol was made a *Chevalier dans l'ordre des Palmes Academique* by the French government in recognition of his distinguished services to the field of energy economics.

GERT BRUNEKREEFT

Gert Brunekreeft is professor of energy economics at the International University Bremen (Germany) and director of the Bremer Energy Institute. Before joining IUB, he held positions at the universities of Freiburg (Germany), Cambridge (UK), and Tilburg (Netherlands), and gained practical experience as senior economist for the energy company EnBW in Germany. Dr Brunekreeft holds a degree in economics from the University of Groningen in the Netherlands and a PhD and *Habilitation* from Freiburg University in Germany, both in economics.

Dr Brunekreeft's main research interests are in industrial economics, regulation, and competition policy of network industries, especially electricity markets. Current research concentrates on the relation between regulation and investment and the economics of ownership unbundling. He has published widely in a variety of policy-related academic journals, including *Utilities Policy*, *Oxford Review of Economic Policy*, *Energy Journal*, and *Journal of Regulatory Economics*.

GARETH EVANS

Gareth Evans is Technical Adviser at Ofgem and has over 30 years experience in the electricity supply industry. During his career he has worked in transmission, distribution, generation, and the development of electricity storage. He was a member of the management team that launched National Power's successful cogeneration business and during this period worked closely with the Combined Heat and Power Association to help promote cogeneration and address market barriers. Gareth Evans's role at Ofgem is focused on the challenges of developing distribution networks to facilitate the connection and operation of new and existing distributed generation technologies. He is a Chartered Engineer and a member of the Institution of Engineering and Technology (IET). He is chair of the IET's Environment & Energy Expert Group and sits on the Energy Sector Panel.

BASSAM FATTOUH

Dr Bassam Fattouh is a Reader in Finance and Management in the School of Oriental and African Studies (SOAS), University of London, and a Senior Research Fellow at the Oxford Institute for Energy Studies (OIES). He is also the Academic Director for the Masters Programme in the Management of the Middle East and North Africa at SOAS. He has published many articles on the international oil pricing system, the relationship between the futures market and spot market, the relationship between OPEC and the market, and the long-run behaviour of oil prices. His current research focuses on the IOC–NOC relationship and its implications for investment behaviour in the Middle East. Bassam Fattouh has also published extensively in non-energy-related areas, mainly in the areas of finance and growth and capital structure.

RICHARD GREEN

Richard Green is Professor of Energy Economics at the University of Birmingham, and Director of its Institute for Energy Research and Policy. Before that, he was Professor of Economics at the University of Hull, and worked for 10 years at the Department of Applied Economics, University of Cambridge. He has spent a year on secondment to the Office of Electricity Regulation, and held visiting positions at the World Bank Institute, the University of California Energy Institute, and the Massachusetts Institute of Technology. He has been a Specialist Advisor to the House of Commons Trade and Industry Committee, and is on the Academic Advisory Panel to the Competition Commission.

MALCOLM GRIMSTON

Malcolm Grimston was educated at Scarborough College and Magdalene, Cambridge, graduating in 1979 having read Natural Sciences and specialised in psychology. He worked as a chemistry teacher before joining the Atomic Energy Authority in 1987. In 1995 he joined Imperial College as a Senior Research Fellow and in 1999 became a Senior Research Fellow at Chatham House, where he is now an Associate Fellow, conducting an investigation into the future of civil nuclear energy. He is a regular media contributor on energy and nuclear matters. Among his publications are two books co-written with the late Peter Beck: *Double or Quits—The Global Future of Civil Nuclear Energy* (2002) and *Civil Nuclear Energy—Fuel of the Future or Relic of the Past?* (2000). On 6 December 2005 he launched his latest study, looking at the differences between the political and technical mindsets and how this impacts on major industries such as nuclear energy (available at http://www.chathamhouse.org.uk/pdf/research/sdp/Dec05nuclear.pdf). He is an elected Member of Wandsworth Council and has executive responsibility for environment and leisure.

Contributors

DIETER HELM

Dieter Helm is Professor of Energy Policy at the University of Oxford. He specializes in utilities, infrastructure, regulation, and the environment, and concentrates on the energy, water, and transport sectors in Britain and Europe.

He holds a number of other advisory board appointments, including the Prime Minister's Council of Science and Technology, the Defra Academic Panel (Chair), and the DTI Sustainable Energy Panel Advisory Board.

He is associate editor of the *Oxford Review of Economic Policy*. His career to date has spanned academia, public policy, and business. He founded Oxera in 1982, was a member of the DTI's Energy Advisory Panel from 1993 to 2003, and has published extensively on economic topics. He recently completed a major study of British Energy policy since 1979, *Energy, The State and the Market*, published by Oxford University Press.

CAMERON HEPBURN

Dr Cameron Hepburn is the Elizabeth Wordsworth Junior Research Fellow in Economics at St Hugh's College, Oxford University. He is also a James Martin Fellow in climate policy at the Environmental Change Institute, and a Senior Research Fellow at the Oxford Institute for Energy Studies. In the policy arena, Cameron is a member of Defra's Academic Panel, and wrote two background papers for the Stern Review on the Economics of Climate Change. He holds first-class degrees in law and chemical engineering from Melbourne University, and a masters and doctorate in economics from Oxford University.

ANOUK HONORE

Anouk Honoré is a Research Fellow at the Oxford Institute for Energy Studies. She works in the Natural Gas Research Programme with Professor Jonathan Stern, Director of the Programme. Ms Honoré's work focuses on natural gas demand, supply and power generation in Europe, Liquefied Natural Gas (LNG) in the Atlantic basin (with a special focus on the consequences of price arbitrage), and natural gas markets in Southern Europe. Her most recent major publication is 'Future Natural Gas Demand in Europe: The Importance of the Power Sector' (January 2006).

Before joining the Oxford Institute in April 2004, Ms Honoré worked at the International Energy Agency (IEA) between 2001 and 2004. Her work focused on natural gas issues in the 26 IEA member countries, but also in China and in Latin America. She contributed to several studies during her stay at the IEA. The last one published was 'Security of Gas Supply in Open Markets: LNG and Power at a Turning Point' in 2004.

Ms Honoré is a PhD candidate in Economics at Paris XI University. Her academic research concentrates on natural gas in Bolivia and in the Southern Cone in Latin America.

PAUL L. JOSKOW

Paul L. Joskow is Elizabeth and James Killian Professor of Economics and Management at the Massachusetts Institute of Technology (MIT) and Director of the MIT Center for Energy and Environmental Policy Research. He received a BA from Cornell University in 1968 and a PhD in Economics from Yale University in 1972. Professor Joskow has been on the MIT faculty since 1972 and served as Head of the MIT Department of Economics from 1994 to 1998.

At MIT he is engaged in teaching and research in the areas of industrial organization, energy and environmental economics, competition policy, and government regulation of industry. Professor Joskow has published six books and over 120 articles and papers in these areas. His papers have appeared in the *American Economic Review, Bell Journal of Economics, Rand Journal of Economics, Journal of Political Economy, Journal of Law and Economics, Journal of Law, Economics and Organization, International Economic Review, Review of Economics and Statistics, Journal of Econometrics, Journal of Applied Econometrics, Yale Law Journal, New England Journal of Medicine, Foreign Affairs, Energy Journal, Electricity Journal, Oxford Review of Economic Policy*, and other journals and books.

Professor Joskow is a past-President of the International Society for New Institutional Economics and a Fellow of the Econometric Society and the American Academy of Arts and Sciences.

ALEXANDER G. KEMP

Alex Kemp is Schlumberger Professor of Petroleum Economics at the University of Aberdeen. For many years he has specialized in upstream petroleum economics and has produced over 200 papers and books in this area. Many are on the economics of North Sea oil and gas, including econometric models of development and production (*Energy Journal*), exploration (*Scottish Journal of Political Economy*), and decline rates (*Energy Journal*). Many papers have been produced on the effects of the North Sea royalty and tax arrangements. Professor Kemp has been an adviser to many governments, the World Bank, and oil companies on the design of royalty and tax systems. In 2006 he was awarded the OBE for services to the oil and gas industries.

TANGA MCDANIEL

Tanga McDaniel is an assistant professor at Appalachian State University. Her primary academic interests include applied microeconomics and experimental economics. Her recent research uses empirical and experimental methods to analyse deregulation of electricity and gas industries. Papers related to this research appear in the *Journal of Regulatory Economics*, *Fiscal Studies*, *Utilities Policy*, and the *Oxford Review of Economic Policy*.

KARSTEN NEUHOFF

Karsten Neuhoff is senior research associate at the Faculty of Economics at the University of Cambridge, coordinating the research council funded project Supergen, on the future of the UK power system, at Cambridge University and workstream II on international cooperation on emission and technology policy of the research council funded TSEC project. He is affiliated to the German Institute for Economic Research, Berlin. Karsten holds a PhD in Economics from the University of Cambridge and MSc degrees in Economics from the London School of Economics and a Diplom in Physics from the University of Heidelberg.

He has published on electricity market design and regulation, technology policy, and emission trading in academic and policy journals such as *RAND Journal*, *IEEE Transactions on Power Systems*, *Energy Economics*, *Utilities Policy*, and *Climate Policy*, and has edited and contributed chapters to books.

JOHN SCOTT

John Scott is the Technical Director for Ofgem, the British electricity and gas regulatory body. He has held this position since 2001 and his present activities include security of supply and industry emergency arrangements, distributed generation, and asset risk management in the regulated gas and electricity companies. He takes a close interest in the engineering challenges faced by the electricity and gas network companies and has developed Ofgem's regulatory policies to incentivize greater technical innovation where this will bring longer-term customer benefits.

John Scott was Director of Engineering for the National Grid Company in the UK, and previously the manager of the National Control centre. He is a Fellow of the Institution of Engineering & Technology (IET), chairs the IET's Professional Network Executive (Power Systems & Equipment), and is a member of the Energy Sector Panel. He is vice chair of the EU Technology Platform – SmartGrids, which is addressing the Future of Electricity Networks for Europe.

LINDA STEPHEN

Linda Stephen is Research Fellow in Petroleum Economics at the University of Aberdeen, Scotland. She has co-authored many papers on North Sea economics with Professor Alexander Kemp. She specializes in financial modelling of oil and gas exploration and production, with an emphasis on the effects of royalties and taxation.

JONATHAN STERN

Jonathan Stern is Director of Gas Research at the Oxford Institute for Energy Studies; Honorary Professor at the Centre for Energy, Petroleum & Mineral Law & Policy, University of Dundee; and Visiting Professor at Imperial College's Centre for Environmental Policy in London. Since 1992 he has been Associate Fellow of Chatham House's Energy, Environment and Development Programme, which he previously headed. He is the author of several books and many shorter works on energy and natural gas issues in the UK, Europe (western and eastern), the former Soviet Union, and Asia. His most recent book, *The Future of Russian Gas and Gazprom*, was published by Oxford University Press in 2005.

PAUL STEVENS

Professor Paul Stevens was educated as an economist and as a specialist on the Middle East at Cambridge and the School of Oriental and African Studies. He spent 1973–9 teaching at the American University of Beirut in Lebanon, interspersed with 2 years as an oil consultant, and 1979–93 at the University of Surrey. Since 1993, he has been Professor of Petroleum Policy and Economics at the Centre for Energy, Petroleum and Mineral Law and Policy, University of Dundee, Scotland (for details see web page www.cepmlp.org), a chair created by BP. Professor Stevens has published extensively on energy economics, the international petroleum industry, economic development issues, and the political economy of the Gulf. He also works as a consultant for many companies and governments.

CATHERINE WADDAMS PRICE

Professor Catherine Waddams Price is founding Director of the ESRC Centre for Competition Policy at the University of East Anglia (UEA). She joined UEA from the University of Warwick in 2000. She has studied the development of utility privatization and regulation, and is particularly interested in the effect on different income groups of introducing competition to such industries, both in developed and developing economies; and in the role of consumers in competition policy. Much of her research centres on the energy sector. She has advised the World Bank and government bodies, competition authorities, regulators, and private companies in the UK and overseas, and is a member of the reporting panel of the UK Competition Commission.

Introduction: The Return of Energy Policy

Dieter Helm

1. The Re-politicization of Energy

It was fashionable in the 1980s and 1990s to treat energy as just another commodity, which could be left to market forces. The task of energy policy was to get the state out of the energy sector and the instruments were privatization, liberalization, and competition. The security-of-supply concerns which had dominated energy policy since the Second World War, and which had been 'solved' through public ownership and statutory monopoly, were deemed to be illusory. Indeed, many went so far as to argue that state ownership and monopoly *caused* security-of-supply problems, and in Britain the dependency on coal (and coal miners) reinforced this view.

Now, over halfway through the first decade of the twenty-first century, the fashion has shifted. Security of supply dominates almost all international forums, including the G8 and EU summits. Energy policy has to a considerable extent become foreign policy, as the concentration of oil and gas reserves in the volatile Middle East and Russia has continued, with state-owned national oil companies and companies such as Gazprom now having some 90 per cent of reserves in their hands (see Stevens, chapter 5). Recent developments between Russia and the Ukraine and Belarus have highlighted the foreign policy dimension with Europe. Given the international dependencies, the state ownership of reserves, and the histories of the main suppliers' governments, it is inevitable that there has been a re-politicization of energy policy, rather than the de-politicization which was the counterpart to the 'normal commodity' view of the 1980s and 1990s.

What has exacerbated the trend towards more activist energy policies has been the other dominant theme of recent years—climate change. On the one hand, there is a 'dash for reserves', and a fear that oil and gas might be running out; on the other, a strong policy imperative to avoid burning the remaining oil and gas, and limit the substitution to coal, suplies of which are much more secure.

Climate change provides a wholly new dimension to energy policy, both in the nature of the market failure and the scale of the challenges with which it confronts policy-makers. Whereas for much of the twentieth century, energy policy was primarily a national concern—especially for countries such as Britain and the USA, which had significant degrees of self-sufficiency—climate change is a global public bad, one that necessitates a global solution. Energy systems, and all the associated energy consumption activities, are overwhelmingly carbon-based. Indeed, the phenomenal economic growth of the twentieth century was fuelled by carbon-based fuels—first coal, then oil, and finally with natural gas added on. Thus, climate change policy requires a massive switch in technologies, translating carbon-intensive economies to low carbon. It is the sort of challenge that bears comparison with the conversion of peace time to war economies between the 1930s and the 1940s.

2. Living with the Consequences of the 1980s and 1990s

The contrast between the scale of the security-of-supply and climate change challenges, on the one hand, and the nature of current energy markets, on the other, is marked. It is not only that there is a big gap between carbon intensity and the low-carbon requirements. Energy assets are long-lived and, at any point in time, they reflect the embedded assumptions of perhaps decades earlier. In Britain, most of the coal power stations are between 30 and 60 years old, and much of the nuclear capacity is approaching the end of its life. Ageing assets are a feature of most developed countries' energy sectors. Oil refineries typically date back to the 1970s, and across Europe the legacy of the OPEC years of the 1970s is reflected in the asset base.

Although the 1970s encouraged investments on the basis of ever higher oil prices—and hence focused on the diversification towards coal and nuclear—they also carried with them profound implications for economic growth and industrial structure. After the last burst of oil prices with the Iranian Revolution at the end of that decade (to around $90 in current prices), much of the developed world then experienced recession. In

Britain, the manufacturing sector contracted sharply between 1980 and 1982, under the combined weight of the oil price shock and the monetarist policy which drove up the exchange rate, with the result that the economy shifted from heavy energy-intensive sectors towards more services. The steel, coal, aluminium, chemicals, cement, and car industries all suffered major contractions. These industries migrated overseas. Energy demand behaviour changed with some decoupling of economic growth and energy demand.

The result was excess supply and excess capacity. Little new investment was needed and, as oil prices fell back, returns fell back, too. The challenge of the 1980s and 1990s was to sweat the existing assets, driving down costs, and the appropriate policy instruments were privatization, competition, and incentive-based (RPI – X) regulation—a combination which worked rather well. And where private ownership and competition were already in place—in oil and upstream gas—the incentives were already there to focus on cost reductions rather than investment. Thus, in the oil sector, refineries were closed rather than built, mergers and acquisitions focused on consolidating the market, and infrastructure suffered accordingly.

The asset-sweating approach was well advanced by the end of the 1990s, and policy-makers pushed on with the commodity approach. In Britain, the new electricity trading arrangements (NETA) epitomized the voluntary, short-term, spot market approach, and the 'British model' was widely copied elsewhere, at varying speeds and with varying effects, from California to the EU member states. When coupled with the widely shared expectation that the supply of new reserves would continue to match rising demand (itself encouraged by low prices), the conditions for a major correction were gradually coming together. If oil companies expected crude prices to remain at or below $10 a barrel, and if electricity generators were to be confronted with the consequences of excess supply (resulting, in Britain, in the price collapse at the end of the decade), then the conditions were eventually ripe for a reversal. Eventually, supply and demand would come back towards tangency: demand rising as a result of low prices, and low investment and ageing plant restricting supply.

3. The Market Shift in 2000

In retrospect, as with the shock of the 1970s on the back of the cheap oil of the 1950s and 1960s, the oil shock from 2000 was an accident waiting to happen. And, as in the 1970s, it gradually unfolded. In the 1999–2000 winter, prices doubled and, contrary to the expectations of the governments and major oil companies, they did not fall back. Over the next 5 years they gradually pushed up to $70 a barrel before easing back below $60. The reason they did not fall back sharply as expected is partly to do with Iraq and international tensions, but it is also explained in part by the erosion of the cushion of excess capacity in swing producers such as Saudi Arabia (see Stevens, chapter 5, and Fattouh, chapter 6), the lack of investment in new exploration and production (E&P), and the poor state of downstream infrastructure.

The asset-sweating decades had consequences right through the energy systems. In Britain, the rapid depletion of North Sea gas left it dependent on imports, but with not much by way of storage. Low prices and NETA-type markets discouraged long-term contracts, so that in the 2005–6 winter, when gas supply conditions were tight, Britain could not import enough because Europeans serviced their long-term contract customers as their first priority.

Throughout the first half of this decade, both companies and governments underestimated the scale of the challenge of matching supply and demand. Oil companies continued to assume prices well below those in the market for their investment appraisals, and governments discounted the price levels. In the British 2003 White Paper, *Our Energy Future* (DTI, 2003), for example, $25 a barrel was assumed for the period through to 2025. But by 2006, a new consensus had emerged that, whatever prospects there might be for a short-term fall-back in prices, the medium- and longer-term trend was likely to be upwards. With the high growth rates in China and India, with the world population projected to rise from 6 to 9 billion by mid-century, and with growth prospects in the developed countries in the 2–3 per cent range, the pressures of demand are unlikely to abate. Meanwhile, conventional oil and gas reserves are depleting, and the state of knowledge about the earth's crust makes the prospect of major new finds unlikely. New reserves are increasingly higher-cost—whether in Arctic waters or from Canadian tar sands. Only a switch to other technologies and fuels is likely to change the underlying arithmetic.

4. The New Paradigm

In retrospect, 2000 marks a structural shift in energy markets. The conditions of the 1980s and 1990s increasingly look like the abnormal rather than the normal—an interval between the 1970s and the 2000s and beyond. Reserves and resources may have turned out to have been more plentiful than they were assumed to be in the 1970s, and the early fears of the Club of Rome proved unfounded. But as time has passed and the experience of the post-2000 world gets more embedded in expectations, the energy policy concerns of the 1970s are returning, and some of the policies, too. As in the 1970s, nuclear power is, for example, making a substantial comeback (see Grimston, chapter 13).

But there are differences too. In the 1970s, climate change was not a recognized problem—indeed, global cooling and the prospect of a new Ice Age were given more prominence. In energy policy terms, security-of-supply considerations may be re-emerging in a way readily comprehensible to policy-makers in the 1970s, but climate change is an altogether new phenomenon, and presents a very different challenge to energy policy design. Taking the market structural shift in 2000, which brought security of supply back on to the energy agenda, and climate change together, they represent a new paradigm (see Helm, chapter 1).

Paradigm shifts necessitate more radical policy reappraisals than gradual evolutionary changes. Security of supply and climate change, as the two key objectives in the new paradigm, cannot be met solely by the policies of the 1980s and 1990s—privatization, liberalization, and competition. Markets may contribute to the more efficient use of energy, and they encourage signalling of the value and diversity of customers' security requirements. But security of supply is a *system* property and it has public-good elements which cannot be exhausted by disaggregated individual contracting. Thus security of supply requires that excess capacity is built into electricity generation, storage, and networks, and such excess supply is not naturally created by incumbents. In the 1980s and 1990s this problem simply did not arise; now it does.

Security-of-supply considerations are not confined to countries, and hence cannot be completely solved through domestic energy policy. As noted above, since most oil and gas reserves are now owned by governments, their supply is inevitably set in a political context. For example, the Baltic pipeline project and the decision to route the Shtokman field through it rather than go down the liquefied natural gas (LNG) route are necessarily set in the context of the new relationships between Russia and Germany. Gas security has an important regional dimension, and there are a number of aspects which are better solved through an EU policy framework. Furthermore, as import dependency grows, greater interconnection increases the security of all—and hence projects such as the competition of the European electricity grid have values beyond those captured by those on the immediate sides of each new link.

If the extent to which new policies are needed to address security of supply is debatable, few would argue that climate change can be addressed without intervention, or that, given the scale of the problem, the forms of intervention are not likely to be very considerable. The concept of a global energy policy is quite new, and the sorts of responses in the 1970s, such as the creation of the International Energy Agency (IEA), provide little guidance. Climate change requires a global agreement to restrict carbon output—a sort of grand cartel. It has to include China, India, and the USA, the first two of which have no targets under the Kyoto Protocol, and the last has not even ratified Kyoto (see Barratt, chapter 15). Together these three countries will soon comprise around half of all global emissions, and China and India are on course to add around 1 billion each to their populations by mid-century, thereby making up around 4 billion out of a total world population of 9 billion. All three are expanding their use of coal, and in the case of China, one large coal station is opened per week, adding the equivalent of the British capacity every year, and plans some 1,000 GW over the next two decades. Climate change policy is therefore very much about persuading the USA to join the European efforts (although, interestingly, its emissions record in recent years is actually very similar to those in Europe inside the Kyoto targets), and engineering the industrializations of China and India (and other developed countries) without the damage their conventional coal-burning technologies will bring (see Barratt, chapter 15).

This international perspective on climate change (and to a lesser extent on security of supply) implies that national energy policies need to be designed and evaluated as to how far they contribute to the amelioration of the international public-goods problems. On this approach, British climate change policy is not really about reducing British emissions *per se*, but about making a contribution to solving the Chinese, Indian, and US problems. It is a 'leadership' exercise. And to this end, it has two components: setting credible domestic targets which are achieved at reasonable cost; and persuading others, on the basis of its domestic achievements, of the merits of them following suit. So far this has proved remarkably unsuccessful—the 2010 target of a 20 per cent reduction in carbon emissions from the 1990 level will almost certainly be missed by a wide margin, despite being in every Labour Party manifesto since 1997, and emissions have in fact been rising since 1997. Furthermore, persuading the US administration to come inside the Kyoto framework has been a fruitless exercise so far. The implication of this policy failure is that each country should adopt targets which are credible, and that policy design needs to build instruments and institutions which build up that credibility. These might include market-based instruments, such as carbon taxes and emissions trading, and a specific body charged with monitoring and reinforcing policy, such as an energy agency (see Helm, 2006*c*).

In security-of-supply terms, the contribution to encouraging international cooperation, and investing with a view to the wider regional and international public goods, are important, too. Creating European treaty arrangements with Russia (rather than falling in line with the German–Russian bilateral arrangements), promoting trade agreements about access to reserves, and building new infrastructure connections which improve the European networks as a whole are part of such a new policy framework.

5. Designing Energy Policy in the New Paradigm

Energy policy is usually well designed to address yesterday's problems (in the current context, the problems of excess supply and low prices), and at any point in time, the inherited policies come with instruments and institutions designed to meet the old paradigm objectives. Thus, it is hardly surprising that the focus of much existing policy is with completing the agenda of the 1990s—notably with unbundling the ownership of European networks, reducing the power of incumbents, and breaking up long-term contracts. It is argued that once the market structures are atomized, with common open access, security of supply will be addressed.

This agenda has much merit, but it is at best necessary. It is very far from sufficient. It does very little to address the completion of the European grid, it adds nothing to the problem of contracting with Gazprom, and its relevance to climate change objectives is limited to the greater efficiency achieved.

The search for new energy policies, therefore, has to go beyond the market approach, even if it has to take it as given and new policies are built on its foundations. The broad choice then becomes one between adding more market mechanisms to the existing policy frameworks, or focusing on more direct interventions. There is much theoretical support for the former route, and a number of readily available instruments, such as carbon taxes, carbon contracts (see Helm and Hepburn, chapter 3), and emissions trading on climate change, and capacity markets and auctions for strategic reserves on security of supply. But in practice a mix of approaches is likely to be required, and these need to reflect the combinations of market failures that typify the various sub-markets. Renewables, for example, have important R&D aspects, and are exposed to transmission and distribution problems (see Scott and Evans, chapter

2), which nuclear power is not (see Neuhoff, chapter 10). And more narrowly, within more market-based approaches, design issues are extremely important (see Green, chapter 9, and Joskow, chapter 4).

The effectiveness of the chosen instruments depends on their institutional setting. As noted above, credibility is a necessary condition if the costs of capital are to be kept at reasonable levels, especially for more marginal technologies (see Brunekreeft and McDaniel, chapter 11). The current energy policy institutions are legacies of the 1980s and 1990s, too, and designed with their priorities in mind. Thus, in the UK, the regulator, Ofgem, is well designed for the purposes of promoting competition and asset sweating, but finds its new 'sustainable development' duty much more difficult to handle.

The new paradigm thus requires three main components: the tailoring of objectives (and therefore targets) to their international context; the selection of instruments which build on the existing market-based policy framework; and new institutional structures to reflect the new priorities. Current energy policy frameworks lag these requirements, and in the history of energy policy, significant change is normally only possible in crises. Notwithstanding the security-of-supply problems witnessed in recent years in Britain, these have not been sufficiently large crises to mandate action. But there has been movement, and the 2006 European Green Paper indicates some progress (CEC (2006a), reinforced in the European Commission's Communication, CEC (2007a)). On climate change, the scale of the problem is immense, but it is by its very nature unlikely to provide a sudden crisis that facilitates a more radical change in direction. The challenge for policy-makers is to buck the historical experience: proactively to redesign the policy framework *before* another crisis.

The chapters in this volume bring out the dimensions of energy policy, both in the specific markets and in terms of specific policy interventions. Given the vast scope of this topic, they cannot be comprehensive and, indeed, it is not intended that they should meet such a demanding remit. Rather, they provide insights into the factors that need to be taken into account in designing new energy policies for the new paradigm, in the hope that policy-makers might meet the challenge of being ahead rather than behind in meeting the challenges of security of supply and climate change.

Part 1: Concepts

1

The New Energy Paradigm

*Dieter Helm**

1. Introduction

Thomas Kuhn famously described a paradigm as a coherent pattern of research organized around commonly shared theoretical propositions and models, and a paradigm shift or 'revolution' as the emergence of an alternative framework of common and shared analysis. A paradigm is, however, sufficiently open-ended 'to leave all sorts of problems for the redefined group of practitioners to resolve' (Kuhn, 1962, p. 10). As a philosopher of science, he had in mind the development of science and of intellectual ideas. But paradigm shifts happen in policy, too: events can conspire to change the historical context to a sufficient degree to make it increasingly hard to reconcile the existing mindset of policy-makers with the evidence, leading eventually to new objectives and new policy instruments. Paradigm shifts in policy typically require a change in the context and a change in ideas in response.[1]

One policy paradigm in energy has been provided by the set of ideas surrounding privatization, liberalization, and competition developed in the 1980s. It is an internally consistent view of the world, and provides a

---

* In preparing this chapter, I have benefited from discussions with Richard Green, Gareth Davies, and Chris Allsopp. Any errors remain my own.

[1] Kuhn's approach to the history and philosophy of science has been subject to fierce debate and criticism. The notable protagonists have included Popper (1968), who argued that science advances by a process of conjectures and refutations, and Nagel (1961) and others, who take a more positivist outlook, and whose incremental approach in effect reduces science to a single paradigm—the gradual approximation to an objective reality. See also Lakatos and Musgrave (1970). Newton-Smith (1981, ch. 5) provides an accessible summary.

'preferred solution' to problems as they arise. If a particular outcome is unsatisfactory in some way, the answer, in this paradigm, is more private ownership, the removal of restrictions on trading, and the promotion of competition. It worked well in the 1980s and 1990s,[2] but around the turn of the century a set of events began to take place in energy markets that put this conventional wisdom under considerable stress. These events combined with 'new' concerns, notably the issues of security of supply and of climate change. It is a central contention of this chapter that this shift in external circumstances, combined with new knowledge about climate change, cannot be adequately addressed within this paradigm of privatization, liberalization, and competition. Though these policies continue to contribute both to the context and the outcomes, they are no longer sufficient.

Towards the end of 1999, oil prices began to climb from the low levels that had characterized the last 15 years of the twentieth century, and against the expectation that they would remain low or even fall.[3] This 'oil shock' gradually unfolded over the next 4 years, with the price reaching over $70 a barrel in 2006. There was no single cause, but rather the coincidence of a variety of factors, including the consequences of asset-sweating of refineries and infrastructure in the 1990s, low investment in new exploration and production (E&P), the continued economic boom in the USA (encouraged by very low interest rates and fiscal expansions), and the increased demand from China and the Far East. These economic fundamentals were exacerbated by political developments in the Middle East. Whether the price rises represent a cyclical movement which will correct itself through investment, or whether they are structural is keenly debated in the literature.[4]

These developments in oil markets were accompanied by wider energy-market changes, many of which were also in part caused by the asset-sweating in the 1990s. In the early 2000s, there were a number of spectacular power cuts, in the USA, Switzerland and Italy, the UK, and Scandinavia. In almost all cases, these were caused by small random events—a tree falling on transmission lines in Switzerland blacked out northern Italy; the fitting of the wrong fuse caused London's power cut; and a mistake in tripping a

---

[2] Some did rather better than others as costs fell. See the chapter by Catherine Waddams Price in this volume for an analysis of the distributional consequences.

[3] See, for example, *The Economist*, 6 March 1999, which speculated that 'we may be heading for $5 [a barrel]'.

[4] See the chapter by Paul Stevens in this volume, and Barsky and Kilian (2004).

power station caused the US event.[5] Networks suddenly seemed less secure, vulnerable to such apparently trivial incidents.

The oil-price increases and the network problems signalled a change in priorities away from cost minimization and towards investment. Many assets were old, and required replacement. In addition to ageing oil refineries and networks, much of the electricity generation capacity in Europe and the USA had been built in the 1970s. The scale of the investment requirements is indicated by the International Energy Agency (IEA) forecasts.[6]

These investment requirements have coincided with other fundamental changes in the structure of global energy markets and in energy policy priorities. There has been increased recognition of fossil-fuel import dependency among developed countries (and, indeed, some developing ones, too, such as India and China). For the USA, dependency on Saudi oil will increase, and it has sought alternative supplies from Russia, Libya, and the opening up of its own Arctic reserves.[7] Europe has similar oil dependency worries, and now over gas, too. In all of these areas, where politics had been on the backburner for the surplus years, it has now returned to centre stage. The Iraqi conflict has an energy context and energy consequences, as does instability in Saudi Arabia. Russia's political interventions in Gazprom and Yukos have undermined the assumption that its resources would be developed largely by international private investment, while political events in Ukraine—through which key gas pipelines pass—have further highlighted the political dimension of Europe's gas dependency, as it switches to gas as the main source of new electricity-generation capacity.[8]

Security of supply has re-emerged as a policy concern at the same time as climate change has gradually become an overarching priority, and a host of new interventions have been developed, including carbon-related taxes, obligations to purchase specific non-carbon technologies, emissions-trading schemes, and subsidies. These new policy initiatives are likely to become increasingly important in a context in which the demand for energy at the global level will go on increasing, as the world's population continues to climb from the current 6 billion to a very likely 9 billion in this century, and

[5] Investigations following these events revealed a variety of causes. On the UK, see Ofgem (2004a). On the USA, see US–Canada Power System Outage Task Force (2004) and Natural Resources Canada and US Department of Energy (2004). On the episode in Switzerland and Italy, see Swiss Federal Office of Energy (2003), Union for the Coordination of Transmission of Electricity (UCTE) (2003a), and Commission de Regulation de l'Energie and Autorita per l'Energia Ellectrica e il Gas (2004).

[6] See, for example, IEA (2003a, pp. 72–4), and Fatih Birol, chapter 14 in this volume.

[7] See NEPDG (2001). The EU similarly focused on security of supply in its energy policy Green Papers. See CEC (2000, 2006a).

[8] Subsequent developments in Belarus in the winter of 2006–7 exacerbated these concerns. On the North Sea, see Alexander Kemp and Linda Stephen, chapter 7.

rapid economic growth in China, India, and the developed world adds to energy demands.[9]

Historians will no doubt argue at some future date about precisely when the cumulative effects of the coincidence of so many factors (the oil-price shock, the turning point in the investment cycle, the political instability in global energy markets, and the climate-change agenda) amounted to a *structural* break. However, it is hard to avoid the conclusion that, around the year 2000, such a shift took place. The scale of this structural break—and the policy responses—amount to more than a minor adjustment. Rather, it compares with the shift in the 1970s as a result of the first OPEC oil shock, and with that of the early 1980s, which ushered in the privatization, competition, and liberalization agendas. What makes this structural break a 'paradigm shift' is that it is of sufficient magnitude to require a radical rethinking of the role of privatization, liberalization, and competition in achieving the new priorities, and hence a recasting of energy policy itself. As with the earlier examples, the implications for policy design have yet to be fully appreciated and—as Kuhn would have expected as a necessary consequence of a paradigm shift—many policies remain to be worked out.

This chapter describes the main factors that lie behind this paradigm shift, and the implications for the design of energy policy for the next decade and beyond. Section 2 describes the structural break between the 1980s and 1990s, on the one hand, and the 2000s, on the other, and sets out the new stylized facts and priorities of the energy market going forward. The shift in policy objectives is described in section 3, with the two key issues for policy design identified as security of supply and climate change. Section 4 deals with the former; section 5 the latter. Section 6 then turns to how these may be brought together into a new (but at this stage necessarily incomplete) energy policy framework, and to the much neglected issue of the appropriate institutional apparatus for designing and implementing energy policy. Section 7 concludes.

2. The Structural Shifts

The coincidence of changes in the economic conditions of energy markets at the end of the twentieth century has been multidimensional. These changes have been on both the demand and the supply sides, and have been reflected through the new, market-based ways in which energy markets are coordinated.

---

[9] On population trends, see UNPD (2003).

On the demand side, there was a structural break in the early 1980s (and perhaps even earlier) from the conventional link between economic growth and energy demand. Conventionally, in the three decades after the Second World War, it was assumed as a rule of thumb that economic growth at 3 per cent translated into growth in electricity demand of around 7 per cent. The implications of this assumed relationship were spelt out in Brown (1970). As chairman of the Central Electricity Generating Board (CEGB), Brown predicted around 100 GW of capacity would be needed by 1995—in fact, not much more than half this amount was required.[10] The task of energy policy was to ensure that this demand was met, through the centralized national-ized industries and policies designed to ensure a continuous flow of oil (and later gas).[11]

This conventional assumption had a conditioning effect on what fol-lowed in the 1980s and 1990s. The demand assumptions were translated into fixed and lumpy capital—into new nuclear and coal power stations, a plan for expanding the coal mining industry, and new oil assets. As late as 1979, the incoming Conservative government announced a plan to build a family of nuclear reactors, one per year for a decade, beginning in 1982.[12] In fact, two substantive—and ultimately related—changes undermined these assumptions and, in effect, stranded part of the asset stock. In 1979 the Iranian revolution led to a further doubling of oil prices, which peaked at $39/barrel (around $90 in current prices). There followed a sharp recession, exacerbated by the new monetarist macroeconomic policy framework. The result was a structural change in the composition of the British economy, with a sharp decline in manufacturing output, and the associated decline of large-scale, energy-intensive industrial activities. From the 1980s onwards, the British economy shifted away from coal mining (an energy-intensive industry in its own right), steel, and chemicals, towards financial services and other less energy-intensive activities. The result of this was to contribute to the break in the link between economic growth and energy demand. The energy ratio (primary energy per unit of GDP) fell and by 2001 it was 57 per cent below its 1970 level.[13]

---

[10] On the general model, see Department of Energy (1989).

[11] See Helm (2004a, ch. 2, especially pp. 24–6).

[12] In the event, only Sizewell B was eventually built. However, at the end of the 1980s, the government clung on to the hope that this would be followed by Hinkley C. On Sizewell, see the Layfield report (Department of Energy, 1987) and on Hinkley, see HMSO (1990). See also MMC (1981) on demand forecasts and Helm (2004a, pp. 51–2) for a discussion of the 1979 nuclear programme.

[13] See HM Government (2004, p. 28).

Parallel with this was a benign shift in the carbon-dioxide (CO_2) intensity in GDP. This began to decline, too, with the closure of the coal industry playing a substantive part, and with the switch to gas-fired power stations (combined-cycle gas turbines—CCGTs) in the 1990s. The total volume of carbon emissions began to fall, a trend which continued up until 1997 (but not beyond).[14] This enabled the British government to set ambitious targets for CO_2 reductions and to sign up to the Kyoto Protocol emissions targets without a need actively to intervene.

The shift in demand behaviour has been associated with improvements in energy efficiency. In the literature, there are numerous studies claiming that there is considerable scope to reduce demand through more efficient techniques.[15] But the extent to which these overall trends will be continued is open to considerable debate. Offsetting further efficiency gains is the potential for growth in energy demand, with the availability of new consumption technologies, from electrical equipment to air conditioning. There is also pressure to increase energy use in transport, with substantive projected growth in air and road traffic (Department for Transport, 2004). More efficient car engines will offset some of the energy consequences of road traffic growth.

At the global level, the IEA projects that primary energy demand will grow at 1.7 per cent per annum between 2002 and 2030, with demand reaching 16.5 billion tonnes of oil equivalent (toe), compared with around 10 billion toe now,[16] with two-thirds of this increase coming from developing countries, such as India and China. The trend in global CO_2 emissions is slightly worse: the IEA estimates these to be 60 per cent higher in 2030. Levels of CO_2 are now increasing at about 2 parts per million (ppm) per annum, having risen from about 250 ppm pre-Industrial Revolution to around 380 ppm today.[17] (Thus, while Britain may have seen falling emissions, some of these may have simply migrated overseas to more competitive locations, with the gradual deindustrialization of the British economy from 1970 onwards.) This global demand growth

---

[14] The 1997 Labour manifesto introduced a domestic target to reduce CO_2 emissions by 20 per cent from the 1990 levels by 2010. For subsequent performance, see HM Government (2004, especially pp. 19–20).

[15] For a discussion of these issues, see Helm (2004a, ch. 19). The government's energy efficiency policies are set out in Defra (2004a) and updated in the *Energy Review* (HM Government, 2006).

[16] See IEA (2004) and Birol in this volume.

[17] See King (2005) for an overview of the science.

has fed through to oil, gas, and coal markets, and contributed to the volatility of energy prices.

On the supply side, there have been three trends of note: the ageing of assets and infrastructure; the changes in technology choice; and the concentration of oil supplies in the Middle East. As noted in the introduction, energy assets tend to be long-lived, and embody the economic conditions at the time of construction. In Britain, construction of the last coal-fired station began in 1974; thus, all the coal stations are now between 30 and 60 years old. The nuclear stations are of mixed vintages, with the first civil reactors, the Magnoxes, reaching closure, and the second wave of advanced gas-cooled reactors (AGRs) following in the next two decades. Unless lives are extended, by 2020 almost all except the single pressurized-water reactor (PWR), Sizewell B, will be closed, in the process taking out around 20 per cent of the baseload non-CO_2 capacity. The rest of the coal plants will come under pressure from environmental constraints, notably in meeting the EU Large Combustion Plants Directive in 2008 (CEC, 2001*a*), but also more generally from the development of emissions trading, and the placing of much of the burden for emissions reductions on the electricity industry, rather than on transport. Though there is considerable uncertainty about the precise timing, by 2020 much of the existing capacity in coal will probably have closed, too.[18]

The second trend—the technological choice—meant that new investments in the 1990s were overwhelmingly in gas CCGTs, with some 24 GW constructed since 1990, now equal to 37 per cent of England and Wales capacity (NGC, 2004). These stations are capable of providing baseload electricity, but only if supported by sufficient pipeline gas capacity. Unfortunately, the gas infrastructure has lagged the power station capacity, with many of the CCGTs on interruptible contracts, so that, at peak demand for both final gas consumption and electricity, the constraints may bind, rationing off some demand.[19]

Since 2000, there has been a ratcheting up in investment in renewables, overwhelmingly wind turbines. This has been driven by the Renewables Obligation, which requires suppliers to purchase the wind output or pay a premium price. A target of 10 per cent has been set for 2010. This wind generation capacity is being added to a network designed for large power stations, not small, embedded, and intermittent generation at the geo-

---

[18] See HM Government (2006) for further estimates.

[19] In summer 2003, hospitals found gas supplies interrupted to maintain power station supplies. New pipelines from Norway and a further upgrade of the Interconnector will begin to alleviate this constraint from 2007 onwards.

graphical fringes. As a result, it is not clear how the capacity target translates into reliable supplies.[20]

Other technologies have not fared well against the cost advantages of CCGTs. 'Clean' coal has not proved economic, and there is yet to be a demonstration plant. Tidal and other non-wind renewables are mostly still in the research and development stage, and unlikely to make much contribution before 2020. Hydrogen, fuel cells, and related technologies are even further from the market, leaving only gas, wind, and nuclear as available options.

The third supply-side trend is the concentration of oil supplies in the Middle East. The arithmetic in oil is fairly straightforward. World oil resources are well researched and, although there will be further discoveries, the historical assumption that supply was endogenous to price has probably weakened as satellite and new geological technologies have greatly enhanced knowledge of the earth's crust. It is widely assumed that, despite new discoveries, the share of the world oil market held by Middle Eastern countries will grow, with the three largest reserve holders—Saudi Arabia, Iran, and Iraq—becoming more dominant, and able to increase their market power as US production continues to decline (even if the Arctic reserves are developed), and Chinese and Indian demands increase. Outside the Middle East, Russia is the other key player, as peripheral, more expensive, sources, such as the North Sea, have been exploited since prices rose in the 1970s and rendered them economic. Since 2000, however, they have had limited impact, as OPEC has adjusted production.

The concentration of the oil market and the tightening of the supply/demand balance have been offset partially by the development of natural gas and liquefied natural gas (LNG) supplies. Much of this gas production has gone to large industrial users and to electricity generation, in the latter case displacing coal. The reserves of gas are considerable, but, as with oil, they are concentrated. Russia holds more than 30 per cent of known gas reserves, with much of the rest in the Middle East. Oil and gas naturally go together physically, with obvious political consequences.

To some, this concentration of fixed oil (and gas) supplies in few hands, faced with rising demand, spells disaster. Oil dependency on the Middle East (and in Europe, gas dependency on Russia) is equated with threats to national security.[21] Some advocate that this dependency should drive energy policy towards greater energy self-sufficiency, diversifying sources of

---

[20] See NAO (2005) for a description of the policy and its costs, and HM Government (2006) for further policy proposals.
[21] See Klare (2004), for example.

supply and reducing dependency on fossil fuels. The 1970s oil shock led to a renaissance for nuclear power, dramatically manifest in France's PWR programme. It is argued that, now, the share of gas CCGTs in electricity production should be limited, more nuclear power stations should be built, and energy-efficiency programmes stepped up. Greater reliance on domestic coal is also argued to be a priority for the USA, China, and India—though with drawbacks on environmental grounds. We return to these arguments below, but it is worth noting here that while investing in insurance—such as storage and capacity to withstand shocks—may be economically efficient, dependency is a two-way process. The Middle Eastern economies are likely to remain almost totally economically dependent on oil exports. Similarly, Russia will depend on oil and gas exports. Indeed, with the exception of wartime, and a very short embargo in the 1970s, there has been little or no threat to the physical delivery of oil or gas.

There have, however, been consequences for price and price volatility, and price levels and volatility may increase as dependency grows. This potential volatility has been exacerbated by the redesign of energy markets in the 1980s and 1990s towards more market-driven and competitive forms. In the period from the Second World War to the end of the 1970s, energy markets were planned under conditions of monopoly and market power, with activist energy policies determining: the choice of technology; the investment locations and timing, at least for coal and electricity; and the development of natural gas and the licensing of the North Sea. By contrast, during the 1980s, the state withdrew from the market.

For politicians and regulators, such markets were widely believed to be a one-way bet: prices could only go down towards marginal cost, as the sunk costs were expropriated for the benefit of customers. In Britain, the coal and nuclear industry assets were largely written off, and the long-term take-or-pay contracts of British Gas were undermined by customer switching as the market was liberalized. But such favourable conditions for customers could, in the absence of market power, only last for as long as supply exceeded demand. As electricity prices fell in Britain, the industry vertically integrated and concentrated. Then, eventually, as the assets aged and new investment slowed down, the capacity margin tightened. The result was predictable: electricity prices fell after full liberalization in 1998 by 40 per cent and then went back up by 40 per cent after 2003. The extent to which the precise market design was causally responsible is much debated.[22]

---

[22] See Richard Green, chapter 9, and Helm (2004a, ch. 17).

Again, however, we need to avoid a purely static interpretation. Increased price levels and increased volatility themselves encourage both demand reductions and supply-side technical change. As the oil (and gas) supplies first concentrate on fewer national sources and then deplete, the economic consequences will encourage a migration to substitute energy forms. In this context, it is important to bear in mind that there is no energy shortage *per se* (the sun comes up every day). Oil and gas are but particular forms. With appropriate economic incentives and energy policies, the energy sector will evolve. The current stage in its history is, however, one where significant structural change is taking place. Policy can assist or obstruct this process of market evolution.

3. A Shift in Policy Objectives

Although energy policy tends to lag market developments, the changes in the underlying structure of the markets have placed security of supply higher up the political agenda, exacerbated by the perceived instability in the Middle East, and terrorism more generally. To these traditional concerns and reactions, a wholly new objective has been added—climate change.

As a result, it is not surprising that most industrialized countries have reconsidered the energy policies of the 1980s and 1990s. There has been the US energy plan (NEPDG, 2001), the EU Green Paper (CEC, 2000), and the UK White Paper (DTI, 2003). These initial efforts have been followed up by further policy initiatives, notably the EU Green Paper 2006 (CEC, 2006a) and the UK Energy Review 2006 (HM Government, 2006). All of these highlighted concerns about import dependency and tackling climate change, with the key difference being the US focus on oil and the EU/UK focus on gas. In all three cases—the USA, Europe, and the UK—the reconsiderations have yet to produce much by way of concrete actions.

None of these reconsiderations involved a complete rejection of what had gone before. The energy policies of the 1980s and 1990s had focused on the objectives of privatization, liberalization, and competition. These market-based policies had, in turn, been a reaction to the planning approaches of the post-war years—in much of Europe, based upon state industries such as EDF and the CEGB; and in the USA based upon rate-of-return regulation. Both approaches allowed investments to be planned, in the certain knowledge that customers would pay for the consequences.

The market approach was classically set out in Britain in 1982 by Nigel Lawson, as Secretary of State for Energy, in a speech on energy policy. Lawson stated:

I do *not* see the government's task as being to try to plan the future shape of energy production and consumption. It is not even primarily to try to balance UK demand and supply for energy. Our task is rather to set a framework which will ensure that the market operates in the energy sector with a minimum of distortion and energy is produced and consumed efficiently. (Lawson, 1982)

This approach has become conventional wisdom, and was carried over by the incoming Labour government in 1997—in part, perhaps, because it contained sufficient ambiguity about what constituted a 'distortion'. But back in the early 1980s, it was a radical departure, and it was interpreted over the next two decades in a rolling programme of, first, downsizing the coal industry (with the inevitable coal strike in 1984), pruning back the nuclear programme, liberalizing North Sea licensing, privatizing the gas and electricity industries, liberalizing retail supplies, and then redesigning the electricity market (introducing the new electricity trading arrangements, NETA) and finally extending this market into Scotland (through British Electricity Transmission and Trading Arrangements—BETTA).

The reform process was lengthy (it took two decades to complete), often tortuous, and sometimes very costly. Lessons were learnt for other countries, and the underlying philosophy was adopted gradually in the USA (spectacularly in California), in Australia, and in western and eastern Europe. Many of the implications are still being worked out: France has only now edged towards an element of private ownership. The EU eventually passed directives to liberalize energy markets in this decade, and to follow up with appropriate regulation of networks and network access.[23]

The fundamental difference between the market approach and planning was actually a rather simple one: markets determined price and quantities, whereas planners fixed both. More precisely, planners concentrated on quantity first, ensuring security of supply (which was the primary objective of energy policy). The resulting costs determined the prices, moderated from time to time by explicit and implicit state subsidies (often linked to broader industrial policy objectives, and with shorter-term political considerations in mind). The market approach

[23] The key directives were: Directive 2003/54/EC concerning common rules for the internal market in electricity; Directive 2003/55/EC concerning common rules for the internal market in natural gas; Regulation (EC) No. 1228/2003 on conditions for access to the network for cross-border exchanges in electricity; and Commission Decision 2003/796/EC of 11 November 2003 on establishing the European Regulators Group for Electricity and Gas.

assumed that competition between generators and suppliers would ensure sufficient supply, but at whatever price emerged from the competitive process. Indeed, there was always a price that would clear the market (even in California, where, had the price been allowed to continue upwards, consumers would be rationed off by their inability to pay). The assumption was that the resultant price would be not only efficient but, in practice, lower than it had been under planning, as the gold-plating of excess capacity in the planned and rate-of-return regimes was reduced, and because the private sector would be more efficient than the public.

This rationale fitted the historical context. As described in section 2, there was widespread excess capacity in electricity (and, indeed, oil) markets in the 1980s and 1990s, and hence little need to worry about quantities and the security of supply. It simply was not a problem. Focus, therefore, shifted to the reduction of operating costs (given the capital stock) and to marginal rather than average costs. For customers, this was an opportunity to transfer rents from producers. In electricity—but also in many other energy activities—the capital stock tends to be fixed and sunk, and capital is relatively dominant over labour costs. Hence the gap between marginal costs (essentially fuel costs) and average costs tends to be large. With excess capacity, prices could be driven down to marginal costs, in effect expropriating *ex post* the sunk investment costs.

By moving from average towards marginal costs, very large write-offs took place. In Britain, the state wrote off most of its investments in coal mines and nuclear power stations. For coal power stations, by the time privatization occurred in 1990, much of the initial capital costs had been recovered through depreciation. Some private investors also lost out: British Gas was privatized as a monopoly, able to pass on its long-term contract costs, but liberalization undermined this, eventually forcing its break up. Investors in British Coal similarly came unstuck, as did those in British Energy, as electricity prices fell sharply after liberalization in 1998. Some electricity companies were bankrupt, too—more so in the USA than in Britain and Europe.

If the objective was cheap energy,[24] then whatever the theoretical advantages of liberalized markets over planning, the new energy policy based upon the Lawson doctrine gradually delivered the results. Moreover, it could do so without jeopardizing security of supply, by virtue of the excess capacity which pervaded almost all energy markets in the period.

---

[24] See PIU (2002, p. 3), and below.

But such an energy policy could not be assumed to deliver such a happy coincidence of outcomes permanently. Indeed, not only did exogenous events—and new concerns, such as climate change—tighten the supply/demand balance, but the policy itself contained the seeds of its own destruction. By expropriating the sunk costs through more marginal cost pricing, and being seen to allow this to happen, investment was deterred, and the credibility of the overarching energy policy framework undermined. The focus on cost cutting—sweating the assets—reduced the resilience of the system to shocks, and investment was limited to areas where there was some (typically artificial) protection. In electricity, gas CCGTs were protected during the early years by the remaining retail franchise with the costs passed through by the regulator, keen to see new entrants; and then renewables (largely wind) were added under a compulsory cost-recovery mechanism, the Renewables Obligation. In the oil sector, the fall in prices undermined the returns to investment in E&P and in refineries and, as we saw above, contributed to the oil price shock in 1999/2000 and its persistence through this decade.

The resulting tightening of the supply/demand balance and the new concern of climate change led to a rethink of policy. Objectives that had been suppressed—or were seen as largely irrelevant—came back to the surface. Strictly, objectives had not changed, but rather had been given different priority in a different historical circumstance. These objectives are, in effect, responses to market failures: if the market could, on its own, deliver security of supply, then there would be no need to worry about this objective. Similarly, on the environment and fuel poverty, the underlying trends were benign. A switch from coal to gas sharply reduced both sulphur dioxide and CO_2 emissions, without the need for much extra intervention. Lower prices automatically reduced fuel poverty.

The objectives—and the underlying market failures—are multiple, and need multiple policies simultaneously applied to address them. The more objectives, the greater the number of instruments required and, crucially, there is a need to define the trade-offs between them. By the end of the 1990s, most governments in developed countries felt the need to restate the objectives, and the British version provided an example of how the politics and the economics got muddled up. From a political perspective, it is helpful to promise to take account of *all* concerns (and their political constituencies). In a political choice model, to maximize votes, objectives should include security of supply *and* environment *and* social issues, such as fuel poverty. But the trade-offs between them are best blurred, so that voters do not perceive the implied costs. From an economic perspective, the trade-offs need to be defined if an optimal efficient solution is to be found. Failure properly to define the trade-offs raises the risk of *ex post* adjustments undermining *ex ante* sunk costs investment assumptions. Political and regulatory risk raises the cost of capital because investors are less able to diversify or manage this source of uncertainty.[25] Such considerations have, for example, greatly affected the incentives to invest in renewables, and forced governments repeatedly to harden up the policy framework.[26]

Restating energy policy objectives required that, not only had the security-of-supply objective to be defined, but the climate-change commitment needed to be met simultaneously. In 2000, the Royal Commission on Environmental Pollution (RCEP) had recommended that the British government adopt a target to reduce CO_2 emissions by 60 per cent from current levels by 2050, and, on the publication of its report (RCEP, 2000), ministers had welcomed this. However, since it was a Royal Commission, a formal response by the government was mandated, and this posed the difficult problem of explaining how it might be achieved. The problem was compounded by the 1997 Labour manifesto commitment to reduce CO_2 emissions by 20 per cent from their 1990 level (and the Kyoto target of 12.5 per cent for a basket of greenhouse gases by 2012).

The policy process began with a review by the Performance and Innovation Unit (PIU) of energy policy, resulting in a report in 2002 (PIU, 2002). To make the task of meeting the objectives even more difficult, its report was prefaced with a statement of the government's new policy by the Prime Minister as 'securing cheap, reliable and sustainable sources of energy supply' (p. 3). The PIU report eventually led to a White Paper (DTI, 2003), and by then the word 'cheap' had been replaced by 'affordable energy for the poorest' in the Prime Minister's opening remarks (p. 3), and the paper's four objectives for Britain's energy policy had become:

- to put ourselves on a path to cut the UK's carbon dioxide emissions—the main contributor to global warming—by some 60 per cent by about 2050, as recommended by the RCEP, with real progress by 2020;

- to maintain the reliability of energy supplies;

- to promote competitive markets in the UK and beyond, helping to raise the rate of sustainable economic growth and to improve our productivity; and

---

[25] Energy companies do, however, try to manage political and regulatory risk, engaging in lobbying activities, having ex-politicians and regulators on their boards, and sponsoring research.

[26] On policy credibility, see below and also Helm *et al.* (2003), and Gert Brunekreeft and Tanga McDaniel, chapter 11. On renewables, see Karsten Neuhoff, chapter 10.

- to ensure that every home is adequately and affordably heated. (p.11, para 1.18)

The White Paper went on to say that: 'We believe that these four goals can be achieved together. As far as possible we will ensure that the market framework and policy instruments reinforce each other to achieve our goals' (p.11, para 1.19). Though the 2006 Energy Review was, in effect, an admission that the 2003 White Paper was flawed, it reiterated this claimed consistency of objectives.

What these policy statements have in common is that the new priorities are dominated by security of supply and climate change. But, as we shall see in the next sections, neither yet has much by way of a worked-out set of policy instruments. The new paradigm is defined by the new historical context (and the structural break with the past), and by new priorities and objectives. However, as with the Lawson doctrine and the market approach of the 1980s and 1990s, it will take years to work out how the objectives might be achieved—in the context of the legacy which the market approach and the historical events of the last two decades has left us.

4. Policy Instruments for Security of Supply: Investment and Market Design

The discussion above indicates that security of supply is a core component of the new paradigm, and that it is multidimensional. In practical terms, the corollary is that the focus will shift from operating cost efficiency and asset-sweating, to investment in new sources of supply, network infrastructure, generation, and supply technologies in local networks and buildings. An energy policy designed to meet the new security-of-supply agenda, there-fore, has to emphasize new investment.

The starting point is the existing market arrangements in energy and the incentives to invest. In electricity, investment (outside renewables—see below) is determined by companies in the context of NETA and expectations of future movements in price. There is no separate market for capacity—NETA is a single unified market. Companies are free to enter into any contracts they wish.[27]

The central ideas of NETA are that it is voluntary and market-driven. Companies will invest as in any other commodity market, provided

---

[27] See Green, chapter 9, for a detailed discussion of market design.

expected net present values are positive. But electricity markets are not like any other market in several respects. First, there is no substantive storage, so supply must equal demand at every point in time. This means that, in the presence of demand fluctuations, capacity must be available to meet peak demands; hence some power stations will be idle for most of the time, except at peaks. There needs to be excess supply. Consumers are buying not only energy, but also the insurance that the energy will be available on demand. Such 'peaking' capacity can either be paid for explicitly and separately by some form of capacity payment, or it can be rewarded within a unified single price market by very high prices on occasion when peaking plant is run. In the latter case, occasional large payments must yield enough revenue not only to meet energy costs at the peak, but also provide sufficient compensation to investors whose plant is idle except at peak times—and compensation for the impact of excess supply on the returns to all plant on the system.

Second, electricity is complementary to the rest of the economy: the costs of excess supply and excess demand are asymmetric. Therefore, optimal capacity (the insurance against power cuts) is greater for the economy as a whole than would result from the sum of individual investment decisions. This usually requires some form of intervention—except, of course, when the system is in general excess supply, as in the 1980s and 1990s.

Third, electricity requires a network, which is a public good to the system as a whole. The value of an investment in a power station depends upon what form it takes *and* where it is located—*and* the characteristics of all the other stations on the system, *and* the design of the network itself. Thus, the value of a new wind farm in the north of Scotland depends, among other things, on whether the transmission and distribution systems are designed for embedded generation at the fringe, and on how many other (intermittent) wind farms are on the system. Given that networks have natural monopoly characteristics, it is unlikely that they will be optimally provided without intervention.

Finally, it is important to bear in mind that fossil fuel prices are heavily distorted generally. The marginal cost of oil is very different from the OPEC-influenced price, and this distortion is so large as to affect coal and gas prices, too. Policy decisions are inevitably second-best.

These characteristics of electricity markets imply that the market approach cannot be relied upon to deliver security of supply, and that some form of intervention is likely to be required unless there is the historical accident of excess supply. But how is such intervention to be grafted on to a liberalized market structure? There are several possibilities, including: the competitive market approach, with a credible commitment not to intervene when prices spike; market-based instruments, including the development of a capacity market, fixing quantities and allowing prices to adjust; an element of planning through the placing of specific obligations on the system operator or suppliers; subsidizing specific investments; and, finally, relying on market power to create an element of cost pass-through.

Let us take each of these in turn. In the first approach—competitive markets—supply will equal demand if the price is allowed to adjust freely. It does not, however, follow that the price is optimal. In many developing countries, customers are rationed off supply by the system operator at peaks, relying on their own investments in standby generation. The level of the price required at peak depends upon the perceived risks to investors: to sink capital *ex ante* in peaking plant requires an estimate of the likelihood of intervention (as, for example, in California). Put simply, the investor has to guess what the political pain threshold is of price spikes. This will influence the investor's risk calculation and the cost of capital. It is not enough in these circumstances for the government to state that it will not intervene.[28] It has to be *credible*, and this requires an investment in credibility and reputation by government. A possible solution is to delegate to some other body the price regulation functions, independent of politicians. As Helm *et al.* (2003) point out, this institutional approach to credibility is analogous to the setting of interest rates in monetary policy. As we will see below, the institutional design of energy policy is important not just to price credibility, but to climate-change objectives, too.

Given that the price-spikes approach may not pass the credibility test, and may lead to sub-optimal prices and investments in standby genera-tion, many electricity markets introduce a separate capacity element. This can take one of two general forms: an explicit payment for availability— for example, by multiplying the probability of loss of load by the value of lost load;[29] or by fixing quantity and then allowing the capacity market to determine the price. As Green points out in this volume, this links neatly to the Weitzman general rule (Weitzman, 1974) about the choice of instruments between price and quantity—pick quantity when

---

[28] The White Paper stated that: 'For markets to work, firms need to be confident that the Government will allow them to work. . . . We will not intervene in the market except in extreme circumstances, such as to avert, as a last resort, a potentially serious risk to safety.' (DTI, 2003, p. 77, para 6.7)

[29] This was the approach taken in the England and Wales Electricity Pool, eventually replaced by the uniform price in NETA.

the expected damage function is increasing at a steeper rate than the cost function under conditions of uncertainty.

A third option is to place some explicit obligation on market participants. One version places the obligation to ensure security of supply on the system operator (in Britain, National Grid—NG), and leave it to ensure that the objective is met. In practice, this will require that NG runs a capacity market, as the contractor of last resort, or builds its own standby capacity.[30] Another version places the obligation on suppliers, either for security of supply generally or to buy specified designated capacity, with some regulatory oversight mechanism.[31]

A fourth option is subsidy, either directly or by underwriting specific kinds of investment, thereby reducing the cost of capital. Subsidy-based interventions may vary from supporting demonstration plants, to taking planning risks, and adjusting transmission and distribution costs. In the case of renewables, there are subsidies from the Climate Change Levy, legislation to ease planning restrictions, guidance on network costs, and specific tax concessions—as well as an obligation. In nuclear, costs have been absorbed in the public sector, with France the main example.

A fifth option relies on market power to impose costs. Concentrated oligopolies are exposed to the threat of regulation, and the way this is manipulated is often opaque and as much political as economic. The pay-offs may be multidimensional. For example, E.ON was recently allowed to merge with Ruhrgas with the support of the German government, despite objections from the European Commission, other European regulators, and the German cartel office. Given its dominant position, the wider pay-off to government might be that E.ON plays its part in investing in sufficient capacity for the German market or in securing gas supplies—that it plays a key part in meeting the security-of-supply objective.[32] Failure to invest may otherwise result in regulatory intervention. The price of market power is investment. And with the ability that market power renders to pass through costs to final customers, the advantage of the market power model

[30] In the past NG has done both of these: it once owned the pumped storage capacity in North Wales (from privatization); and in the approach to winter 2003 it placed direct contracts.

[31] At privatization, regional electricity suppliers had a licence condition in respect of meeting all reasonable demands, and obligations in respect of nuclear and renewables have featured since. In the gas case, long-term take-or-pay contracts were embedded into the privatization structure (as mentioned above).

[32] German energy policy has given considerable priority to security of supply, given the poverty of its domestic energy resources. See Yergin (1991, ch. 17), which refers to the importance of oil resources in the military capability in the Second World War. Now its concern is for secure Russian gas supplies, with Ruhrgas's stake in Gazprom playing an important strategic role and the North Baltic pipeline providing an example of Germany's bilateral (rather than EU) approach to its own energy security.

is that it reduces the cost of capital. In principle, provided the threat of regulation stops the undue exploitation of that market power, investment should be higher in proportion to the reduction in the cost of capital. In effect, it is quasi-rate-of-return regulation by default.

What these options indicate is that there is a variety of typically complex ways in which governments can address security of supply, and that these involve intervention in the design of markets, delegation of the responsibility, and a recognition of the oligopolistic nature of the market. In almost all developed countries, interventions of *all* the above kinds are pursued. The two simplistic ways forward—pure markets and planning—have given way to a mixture of both. Before the 1980s, the sector was largely planned. In the 1980s and 1990s, the market approach was pursued because there was excess supply. Gradually, further interventions have been added in a piecemeal fashion. This grafting of security-of-supply policy interventions on to the liberalized markets is further complicated by the ways in which the climate-change problem affects not only the environmental outcome, but also security of supply.

But before we turn to the climate-change objectives, a further dimension of security of supply needs to be considered—the exposure to international oil and gas markets. It was noted above in section 2 that dependency on the Middle East will grow over the coming decades, with implications for both physical supplies and for price. The conventional policy responses have been: to increase stocks to smooth out price fluctuations and to deal with embargoes and physical interruptions; to form international coalitions, military- and trade-based, to bring pressure to bear on suppliers; and, at the limit, to rely on military power (for example, the 1980 Carter doctrine on Gulf supplies).[33] These mechanisms are largely outside the scope of this chapter, which is primarily focused on national energy policies. International security requires sharing sovereignty over energy policy and, with the exception of oil reserves, such multinational responses have been notable by their absence. Even the suggestion of EU strategic gas reserves has met with strong opposition and, in relations with Russia, Germany has notably pursued a bilateral approach.[34]

To the extent that there has been a response to these international considerations, the main focus has been to reduce exposure to international markets by appropriate choice of technology and the

---

[33] The Carter doctrine designated the secure flow of oil through the Persian Gulf as a 'vital interest' to the USA by 'any means necessary, including military force'. See Klare (2004, pp. 3–6).

[34] See Helm, chapter 16 in this volume, and the EU Green Paper (CEC, 2006a) for the proposal of strategic gas storage.

quality of supporting infrastructure. Thus, as noted in the Foreign Office paper on energy security (FCO, 2004), domestic investments in energy efficiency, renewables, and nuclear power reduce exposure to external risks. For the USA, the introduction of more fuel-efficient cars and increased taxes on motor fuels may, therefore, be an important component of international energy security. Similarly, duplicating and reinforcing gas and electricity networks may reduce the consequences of a terrorist attack.

With this growth in *ad hoc* and overlapping interventions, what can be concluded about the appropriate instruments to address the security of supply? The liberalized market context carried over from the 1980s and 1990s naturally lends itself, in general, to market-based instruments, and the greater importance of security of supply lends itself, in particular, to quantity-based instruments. In this context, a capacity market has much to recommend it. The assignment of responsibility for security of supply is also important to manage residual risks. Clarity about *who* has this responsibility is of greater importance than *where* the precise location of the obligation lies. But whoever has this obligation also has the implied duty to contract—to be the contractor of last resort. Market power is probably a fact of life and requires regulation, including for investment. The role of specific subsidies or specific support for defined technologies on security-of-supply grounds is harder to justify, particularly if the quantity is already fixed. Unsurprisingly, perhaps, policy developments to address security of supply have yet to catch up: the UK Energy Review (2006) explicitly rejects capacity mechanisms; avoids the issue of assigning responsibility; and focuses heavily on specific technologies, notably nuclear and renewables.

5. Climate Change Policies

Climate change is also very much an investment problem—it is concerned with the replacement of existing (largely carbon-based) assets with non- and low-carbon technologies, and investing in energy-efficiency technologies.[35] Fortunately, as noted in section 2 above, many developed countries' energy assets are old and reaching the end of their economic lives. In consequence, at this natural point in the replacement cycle, carbon-reducing technologies can be introduced without the costs of writing off existing plant with considerable lives left.

[35] This section draws on Helm (2005*b*).

As with security of supply, there are a number of ways of building the carbon constraint into the energy sector. These are broadly divided between economic instruments and supporting particular technologies, though, in practice, a range of interventions will be required. There will also need to be intervention to support R&D.

As noted in section 4, economic instruments can either fix price or quantity. Under conditions of uncertainty, the choice between the two is determined by the expected shapes of the marginal cost and damage functions, and, again, the Weitzman framework provides the guidance. Climate change can be characterized as having a flatter damage function than the cost function: a small increase in CO_2 emissions will not have much effect, whereas costs may be increasing quite steeply for initial small reductions in CO_2. Hence the case for a carbon tax is dominant over that for a tradable permits scheme.[36]

Not surprisingly, a number of countries have opted for forms of energy or carbon taxes. But the overwhelming emphasis has been on quantities, as reflected in the Kyoto caps and the EU emissions trading scheme (ETS). Why is this? The answer lies in part in the problem of forming an international agreement, or collusion, to reduce emissions. It turns out to be much more credible to focus on quantities (see Helm, 2005b). Indeed, future international treaties on climate change, designed to achieve a stabilization of CO_2 in the first instance, are likely to follow this course, given that caps are more credible mechanisms of compliance than taxes.[37] Producers and consumers of energy also tend to prefer this approach since it neutralizes the income effect—instead of revenues flowing to governments—through grandfathering.

In theory, as with security of supply, economic instruments should be sufficient to achieve a climate-change target. Prices of permits, or the tax, should increase to whatever level is necessary to achieve the target, signalling the efficient contributions from the supply and demand sides. In practice, however, there is a variety of reasons why they might not be sufficient: the setting of the instruments needs to be credible over the life of future investments, and the targets need to be given, too; other market failures may inhibit the supply of new investments; and other lumpy investments may distort the value of the specific investments.

Credibility, as with security of supply discussed above, is determined by the institutional structure. In a democratic system, there is no guarantee that

[36] See Parry (2003) for a fuller exposition.
[37] In principle, accepting a cap does not imply using a permits system. A flexible carbon tax can meet the target.

climate-change targets will not be revised *ex post*. The 2050 target of reducing CO_2 emissions by 60 per cent may have been adopted in the 2003 White Paper and restated in the 2006 Energy Review, but it is unlikely to survive for nearly half a century without revision. Reputation matters, and the government's credibility, even over the period to 2010, is weak. It is not clear whether the 10 per cent renewables target by 2010 will be met, and the 20 per cent CO_2 target for 2010 almost certainly will not be met.[38] Even within formal emissions trading schemes, there may be a temptation to manipulate the quantity to hold down the price.[39] It is therefore necessary to find some mechanism to reinforce the credibility of the targets, and this may take a number of forms, from an explicit guarantee to investors, or an institutional mechanism aimed at injecting a degree of independence in policy implementation. The 2006 Energy Review, for example, recognizes the importance of a long-term carbon price—and then notably fails to deliver it (see Helm, 2006*b*). As we shall see in the next section, this credibility problem creates a powerful argument for some form of delegation to an agency.

Other market failures distort the supply of capital. Market power, sunk costs, risk assignment, as well as associated regulatory mechanisms, taxes and subsidies, all affect the choice of technique and the timing of investments. Finally, some investments are sufficiently large to affect the economics of other power stations. For example, were the government to facilitate a programme of building a new family of nuclear power stations (as indicated in the 2006 Energy Review), this would almost certainly have an adverse impact on the returns to wind generation.

The alternative approach to reliance on general economic instruments is to segment the market and create a sphere—or series of spheres—exclusively for non-carbon technologies. These can then be supported through intervention mechanisms, from a formal obligation to purchase a proportion of energy from these designated sources, through to subsidies and special tax treatments. Note that there are immediately inefficiencies here. The distinction between the market segments is sharp: it rules out intermediate technologies that may emit some carbon, but not very much. Thus, in the

---

[38] This has, in effect, been admitted in HM Government (2004). On the renewables target see NAO (2005).

[39] In phase two of the EU ETS (2008–12), some countries will face very great difficulties in meeting their national Kyoto caps. They may be tempted to encourage the rules to be relaxed on purchasing emissions reductions from outside the EU, through the Clean Development Mechanisms and Joint Implementation. Post-2012, the temptation looks overwhelming. An analogy is the European macroeconomic stability pact, where rules have been revised in the light of widespread breaches as regards government borrowing.

short run, a substitution of gas for coal may be the optimal method of meeting a target, and a general economic instrument would select this outcome. A segmented market would not.

There are also problems of definition. What is a renewable source of energy? Does it include nuclear? Is coal-based methane recovery a form of renewable energy, for example? How will the definition be changed through time? Is sequestrated carbon from coal generation to be included? Or landfill gas? And, following the proposal to create a series of *bands* for renewable sources, how might each band be defined?

Once the market segmentation approach is selected, there is a tendency towards supporting particular technologies within the segment, although this is not inevitable. In principle, once the renewables technologies that qualify have been determined, a market can be established to meet the targets, through the issue of certificates. The British Renewables Obligation Certificate is one such form, but, even here, there is additional support for particular technologies. In the British case, there has been a long tradition of subsidizing nuclear power, and more recently wind and other non-nuclear renewables. Specific subsidy-granting institutions have been set up, such as the Carbon Trust, supported by tax concessions and the Climate Change Levy. On energy efficiency, subsidy is formalized through an implicit tax or levy on electricity customers, and encouraged by the Energy Saving Trust. These organizations have objectives and budgets and support careers. The 'capture' of policy towards further intervention in favour of their designated technologies is a natural strategy to pursue.

Of the existing non-carbon technologies, there is little prospect that wind and energy efficiency will be sufficient to meet the 60 per cent 2050 target. Even with a new programme of nuclear power, the gap will be hard to close. As noted above, the existing fleet of nuclear stations is in the process of closure (except Sizewell B) and hence it would require a very considerable number of new PWRs (along the lines of the French programme) in the next two decades to bridge the gap. More likely, new technologies will also be required, and policy interventions will, therefore, be needed to deal with R&D market failures. It is, however, very hard to have an R&D policy which excludes altogether the element of picking specific technologies (other than a general tax allowance). The closer policy moves towards specific technologies, the greater the influence of special interest lobbying and hence capture.[40] Thus, rather than focus on avoiding capture in each specific case, it is important in R&D policy to

[40] Arguably this has already occurred in the case of the Energy Saving Trust and energy efficiency, and in wind. On capture generally, see Dal Bó (2006) and Helm (2006a).

31

concentrate on the institutional basis for making choices. Such institutions should be independent of government.

6. Energy Policy in the New Paradigm: Instruments and Institutions

It has so far been argued that, for historical reasons, energy industries are entering into a major investment phase, both to replace existing assets and to meet new demands. This investment is occurring at a time when there has been an exogenous shock to energy prices (encouraged by the endogenous consequences of low investment and asset-sweating in the last two decades). As the supply/demand balance has tightened and prices have increased, the focus of energy policy has shifted from privatization, liberalization, and competition towards greater emphasis on the security of supply. The price increases and the shift of emphasis to security of supply have coincided with a new constraint—climate-change policy. Together, the change in the underlying balance, the price increases, and the new policy priorities of security of supply and climate change amount to a paradigm shift in energy policy, albeit an evolutionary one, rather than a radical discontinuity. But it is a structural break with the past.

Not surprisingly, energy policy has lagged events. A rethink is, however, already under way, and, as noted, almost all developed countries have published energy plans or policy statements recognizing the new priorities and concerns. But we have also noted that the shift in policy objectives and priorities has not yet been matched in terms of instruments. One paradigm does not simply get replaced by another—it is a much messier process, given the legacy assets and the institutional structures which are inevitably carried over from one period to another. Thus, there is a difficulty in devising instruments that are appropriate to liberalized markets, where the sunk costs of investments cannot be simply passed on to monopoly customers. The problem has been how to marry up the new objectives with the liberalized markets.

The obvious solution is to use market-based economic instruments and, as noted above in sections 4 and 5, this involves economic pricing of security of supply and the economic pricing of carbon. These policies can be implemented through marketable obligations and permits—capacity markets and tradable permits—or through explicit prices for plant availability and carbon.

The market-based approach has, however, to operate in the context of the time horizon of investments, and, in both security of supply and carbon policy, we noted, too, that credibility is important to reduce investment risk and thereby the cost of capital. To achieve this, either some form of explicit government guarantees are required or new institutions need to be devised. Since the former are often expensive (as in the case of renewables) and at best partial in application, it is to the latter that we must turn.

The design of institutions which can provide policy credibility to private investors has been a major preoccupation in Britain in the regulation of privatized industries and in monetary policy. The main requirements are to minimize the scope for capture by regulatees and prevent intervention based on short-term political considerations. These aims are best achieved through an element of statutory independence with an associated emphasis on technical expertise. Independence gives the formal separation of functions, while expertise enables the regulatory body to build up reputation.

But such credibility can only be gained if the separation of functions is clear and unambiguous. In Britain, in energy, these conditions are not met. There are no clear trade-offs between the objectives of policy, and the objectives of the energy regulator, Ofgem (the office of gas and electricity markets), are ambiguous and hedged around with 'Guidance'.[41] In particular, as noted in section 3 above, the 2003 White Paper—reinforced by the 2006 Energy Review—sets out a variety of objectives, and tries to graft a climate-change policy on to a regulatory regime not designed with this purpose in mind.

The consequences have been considerable. The renewables programme has been subject to considerable delay, and the failure to coordinate the investments in the networks (regulated by Ofgem) with the timing of wind farm developments has increased risk, and almost certainly the cost of capital. Lack of clarity and credibility about interventions in pricing has also influenced investment decisions and their timing.

Clarification of the interface begins with the objectives. As with the Monetary Policy Committee of the Bank of England, delegation to an agency requires clear objectives to be assigned. In the new paradigm, these are primarily security of supply and CO_2 reduction targets. By delegating these responsibilities, a separation is introduced between the *setting of the*

---

[41] The concept of 'guidance' was introduced in the Utilities Act (2000). There then followed Draft Guidance in 2001 (DTI, 2001a), which was eventually finalized in 2004.

objectives (the job of government) and the *delivery* (the job of the agency). The agency reports progress to the government, and, where targets may be missed, this encourages a policy response.

In the market-based approach, the analogy with the Monetary Policy Committee example goes further. The Committee sets interests rates to achieve the target. In energy, if market-based instruments are used, then each target has an instrument: in the case of security of supply, it is the price of the capacity margin (either set directly or revealed through a capacity market), and for CO_2 it is the price of carbon (again either set directly through a carbon tax, or revealed through emissions trading).

This neat solution is undermined, however, when there are multiple instruments for each target. As we saw in section 5, there is a host of possible interventions, some based on specific technologies and others on reserved markets. The task of the agency in such circumstances is to bring consistency to bear, and here its reputation for technical expertise would have an important role in policy design and revision. For example, taking a single number for the social cost of carbon would reveal a wide range of implicit valuations across energy efficiency and renewables policies, and give some indication of the scope for efficiency gains.[42] A further benefit from a single agency would be to reduce the number of bodies involved, and hence their lobbying power for budgets and specific technologies.[43]

7. Conclusion

It has been argued that, around the turn of the century, there was a shift in the focus of energy policy of sufficient cumulative effect to be regarded as a paradigm shift. The objectives changed, the underlying market conditions changed from excess supply to investment, and primary energy prices moved up in a sharp and sustained way. The central question in the new energy paradigm is how to design a new energy policy with security of supply and climate change at the core.

The paradigm shift in policy objectives has yet to be translated into a coherent set of policy instruments, which have to be grafted on to a privatized and liberalized market structure. In this context—the legacy of the paradigm of the 1980s and 1990s—market-based instruments have an

---

[42] On the social cost of carbon, see Pearce (2003), and the chapters by Mendelsohn (2005) and Tol (2005), in Helm (2005*a*).

[43] Helm (2004*b*, pp. 31–41) considers how such sectoral institutions might fit into the overall regulatory framework.

inherent attraction, since they have the effect of 'correcting' market prices to reflect the 'market failures' of security of supply and climate change. Rather than adding on new interventions, and ever more institutions, in an *ad hoc* way to the existing framework, the new paradigm requires a greater degree of clarity and focus. But, contrary to Kuhn's description of paradigm shifts, the new paradigm is not incommensurate with the old. The task is to build upon the strengths of the 1980s and 1990s approaches, rather than reject it wholesale.

In a context requiring substantial investment, there is an important benefit from policy credibility. Such credibility would be reinforced by a single body—an agency—which enforces consistency across interventions and, using market-based instruments, uses the price as a currency within which the market failures can be consistently reflected.[44]

However, the history of past substantive changes in the energy market—after the Second World War; in response to the OPEC shocks of the 1970s; and the response to excess supply and the collapse of fossil-fuel prices in the 1980s and 1990s—is that paradigm shifts are only recognized and acted upon once the costs and inefficiencies of past approaches become so great as to shake conventional wisdoms. This typically requires the costs to become *politically* apparent—through power cuts, physical threats to supplies, price spikes, and, now, the physical impacts of climate change. A gradual worsening of performance and increase in costs is less likely to trigger policy redesign. The climate-change problem is very much in the latter category. Bold new targets have been adopted, but performance has so far not been encouraging. Levels of CO_2 emissions have not fallen since 1997. Since there is no immediate 'crisis', however, performance may continue to be weak until the gap between the aspiration and the scale of the market failure becomes very large—and visibly so. We are probably some way from this point, and hence it is likely that the full manifestation of the paradigm shift will not become apparent for some time. Performance relative to objectives may have to deteriorate yet further before the plethora of energy policy reviews translates into substantive reforms.

[44] This would reflect the stated aim of the 2003 White Paper, quoted above in section 3, to reconcile objectives through 'the market framework'.

2

Electricity Networks: The Innovation Supply Chain

John Scott and Gareth Evans*

1. Introduction

Energy is once again centre stage both nationally and internationally.

In addition to the recognized need for secure energy supplies to support society as we know it, the evidence grows year by year that energy use is presenting us with the first man-made threat to environmental sustainability. If there was ever a challenge that required us to invest intellectual effort to find new solutions, this must be it.

It is therefore a matter of priority that we should pay serious attention to the 'innovation supply chain' in the energy sector. This involves pure and applied research, development and demonstration of new solutions and the efficient deployment of the successful candidates. These activities can simply be defined as follows:

- pure research—expanding knowledge without pre-defined objectives;
- applied research—expanding knowledge to address a defined problem;
- development—converting research outputs into practical solutions;
- demonstration—applying new solutions in an operational environment;
- deployment—commercialization of new solutions and widespread adoption.

* John Scott (Technical Director) and Gareth Evans (Technical Adviser) are employed by the Office of Gas and Electricity Markets—Ofgem. The views expressed here are their own.

For simplicity, these activities are collectively referred to as R&D in this chapter except in situations where a more specific term is required.

The dynamics of this supply chain also require the unique features of a liberalized energy sector to be considered and the key role played by individuals in their professional capacity, the regulated companies, and other independent organizations.

To review the health of the R&D supply chain across the whole energy sector presents too great a scope for a single chapter. However, there has been an increasingly lively debate on this subject in one part of the total sector which has relevance to a wider audience: this is the electricity transmission and distribution system, referred to here collectively as electricity networks.

Electricity networks are distinguished by the fact that they are regarded universally as natural monopolies. As customers we can choose our electricity supplier (retailer), but have no choice about our network provider. Networks do not deliver a tangible product in themselves and so attract much less public interest than some other elements of the energy infrastructure. Exceptions arise where, for example, proposed network assets have an impact on visual amenity or a perceived threat to health.

The low public profile of electricity networks, combined with the multiparty nature of a liberalized sector and continuous pressures for greater efficiency, create a challenging context in which to pursue R&D. This chapter examines this situation. It discusses recent initiatives to stimulate R&D activity and the encouraging response to date. It also considers pointers for the future, identifying some key issues to be addressed by companies operating in a liberalized sector.

It argues that network companies must play their part in the innovation supply chain and that the challenge of achieving this goal in an efficient way, in a liberalized environment, must be met jointly by all the involved stakeholders. Early evidence shows that this is starting to happen, but challenges lie ahead. It will require the development of new management skills and behaviours, but there is no evidence that this is beyond the capability of the sector.

The future development of electricity networks is not, at present, technology constrained. It can be argued that the R&D focus should be weighted towards development and demonstration, as opposed to pure research. This has been a suppressed area of activity and it is the responsibility of the sector to rekindle the active engagement with innovation that was evident 50 years ago—and created the networks that deliver our power today.

2. The Development of Electricity Networks

We rely on networks of different types for the basic services that allow society to function. They provide conduits for commodities and services but are not a tangible product in themselves. Networks for gas supply, water supply, communications and food distribution share many common features with electricity networks. In spite of the fact that these networks provide us with essential services, they are largely taken for granted unless they fail in some high-profile way or the cost of using them becomes material at a customer level.

Electricity networks are in a rather paradoxical position. These networks are extensive, with a total asset value of almost £20 billion; they deliver a valuable but invisible product to every premises in the country; in urban areas the networks are unseen but in the countryside they are inescapable. Furthermore, most electricity consumers are unaware of the charges they pay to use the services of these networks. Given these contrasts, it is perhaps not surprising that they attract little attention.

However, their low profile should not belie their sophistication. These networks are highly complex systems both in terms of their design and real-time operation. When electricity systems were initially developed they usually served a distinct geographic area with no interconnection to adjacent areas. They operated as 'island' systems. In the UK in the 1930s the advantages of linking these islands together was recognized. The primary benefit of doing this was to enhance security of supply in a very cost-effective way by allowing one island to support another when unplanned events, for example generator breakdown, occurred. By linking the islands to form a network the benefit of sharing generation capacity also meant that larger, more efficient, generators could be built, while minimizing the total amount of costly spare capacity necessary to achieve supply security.

These concepts can be simply illustrated as follows. Say a grid system is to be secured against the loss, at any time, of two generating units. If this criterion is applied to a single 100MW demand island employing 20MW generators, seven units would be required; i.e. there has to be a 40 per cent plant margin (generation surplus). If two identical 'islands' are connected together, the same criterion could be met using 12 generators reducing the plant margin to 20 per cent.

The creation of the grid system occurred at a time when generator unit sizes were increasing rapidly.[1] An expanding grid therefore facilitated the

---

[1] Generator outputs increased from ~50MW in the 1930s to ~500MW in the 1960s.

connection of larger units without compromising reliability. Taking our 100MW island again, it could not have made use of 60MW generators without either providing a massive plant margin or reducing supply reliability.

As the electricity networks became established, a further opportunity was exploited. Not only could the network enhance supply security and reduce the required margin of spare capacity, it could also allow the bulk transfer of electricity from one geographic area to another on a planned basis. This enabled large power stations to be located close to their fuel sources, often remote from centres of demand. It was this requirement for bulk transfer of electricity that led to the use of higher transmission voltages. The purpose of using higher voltages is to reduce the current that flows in a circuit for a given power transfer. This allows longer distance transmission and reduces the energy lost, in the form of heat created by current flow, particularly as heat loss increases in proportion to the current squared. The highest capacity overhead lines in the UK operate at 400,000 volts. The size of steel lattice tower required for higher voltage operation also accommodates larger conductors, with the net effect that such a line can transmit up to 20 times the power of a 132,000 volt line of the design used in the original grid.

These developments gave us the networks that we have today: a very high voltage transmission network providing interconnection and energy transfer across the country, supplying lower voltage distribution networks to which most consumers connect to obtain their supplies. This basic grid infrastructure has been stable for many decades now. Its original designers had in mind an upgrade path to 1,000,000 volts operation as demand increased.[2] However, the reduction in the rate of load growth that occurred in the 1970s has meant that there has been no justification for upgrading the transmission system further.

There is evidence that the present established position is set for fundamental change. As this chapter explains, the need for equipment renewal and the potential for renewable and other distributed generation technologies could reverse the trend of 50 years. The network investment ahead is forecast to be very substantial and the opportunity is immense for innovation to create capital efficiencies and to deliver customer services that have never been available before.

The historical rate of development of the UK's electricity networks can be illustrated using historic capital investment data. These data are

---

[2] The electrical research laboratories established by the Central Electricity Generating Board (CEGB) at Leatherhead in Surrey had the physical dimensions for testing equipment at this voltage.

Table 1.

Period	Annual Investment (£billion/year, averaged over period)
Transmission 1984–9	0.25
Transmission 1991–2005	0.4
Transmission 2006–11	0.8
	(Price Control Review Final Proposals)
Distribution 1986–90	0.75
Distribution 1991–2005	1.0
Distribution 2005–10 (projected)	1.5

somewhat sparse for the peak investment period of the mid-1960s. However, investment in distribution networks alone was of the order of £2.5 billion[3] per year. Table 1 summarizes the position more recently.

The investment levels, that fell continuously from the peak of the 1960s to the end of the century, are now rising again quite significantly.

Several factors contribute to the upturn in projected capital investment. A number of them deserve particular mention. First, many network assets are reaching the end of their planned operational lives. As the networks were built at a very rapid rate in the 1950s and 1960s with a nominal life expectancy of about 40 years, we appear to be facing a peak requirement for renewal on a simple age-based criterion. However, much of the equipment used in transmission and distribution is proving to last longer than 40 years and is being replaced to a programme that takes account of its condition as well as its age. Nevertheless the case for significant investment in equipment renewal is a valid one. Second, the geographic balance of generation connected to the transmission network is changing, requiring the capacity of some parts of the system to be increased. In particular, the development of renewable generation resources in Scotland has impacts on the entire north–south transmission corridor as the demand to be met is predominantly in England. At present, connection offers for some 9,200 MW of generation in Scotland have been made and a further 4,300 MW of connection offers are being processed.[4] Third, there is a growing requirement to integrate smaller, typically low-carbon, generation sources connected at 132,000 volts and below. This 'distributed generation' is requiring some distribution networks to take on a new role. The integration of generation, potentially that connecting at distribution voltage levels, brings system design and operational challenges, which in turn require new investment. At this

---

[3] 2002/3 money.   [4] National Grid data—14 February 2006.

level, the distribution companies made connection offers of 3,600 MW in 2005.[5]

With such significant sums being invested it is essential to customers' interests that this is undertaken in an efficient way, using innovative solutions where appropriate. Like-for-like replacement of time-expired assets would appear to be a lazy choice and the solutions for the technical challenges of distributed generation (such as control of low voltage networks) cannot at present be purchased as proven products. It follows that such an investment programme should be supported by programmes of R&D focused on delivering innovation and practical, sustainable solutions.

3. R&D—Retrospect

For most of the last century, the growth of electricity demand and the drive to achieve economies of scale caused there to be very significant development of power system technology. This applied primarily to generation but also to network plant and equipment. A prime example of this, in a network context, was the rapid increase in transmission system voltage from 132,000 to 400,000 volts in just a few decades. This used to be a text book example of securing economies of scale. However, the advent of renewables and microgeneration has, in just a few years, raised the possibility of a new paradigm.

The earlier grid developments required significant R&D programmes to support them. Much of this R&D was led by the manufacturing sector, which was very strong in the UK in this period. However, the state-owned industry itself also invested considerable resources in R&D. The three major research facilities owned by the CEGB, Berkeley, Marchwood, and Leatherhead, spent £224m[6] in 1987/8—some £400m p.a. in today's money—although only a small proportion of this, of the order of 5 per cent, would have been dedicated to networks.

Annual spending by all the network companies on electricity-related R&D over the last 2 years is estimated to be approximately £6m per annum.[7]

A useful yardstick for R&D activity is the R&D intensity of individual companies. This is tracked and reported by the Department of Trade and

---

[5] http://www.energynetworks.org/pdfs/Connection_Activity_DNOs_Dec2005_rev3.pdf
[6] http://www.publications.parliament.uk/pa/cm198889/cmhansrd/1988-12-13/Debate-5.html
[7] Based on the first Innovation Funding Incentive (IFI) annual reports and data from National Grid Electricity Transmission (NGET) for 2004/5.

Industry (DTI). R&D intensity is defined as the ratio of R&D investment to company turnover (sales). As would be expected, R&D intensity varies dramatically between industries, but trends are noticeable within sectors. For example, the average R&D intensity for leading global pharmaceutical companies is 15 per cent,[8] compared with only 2.5 per cent for the engineering sector.

Today's average R&D intensity for the UK is 2 per cent compared with 4 per cent in Japan and 4.5 per cent in the USA. Against this background the data for the electricity sector are interesting. Relevant companies are reported on in two categories; 'electricity' and 'utilities'. The sample of companies quoted is small and so the data must be treated with caution. The averages for UK and global utilities are 0.2 per cent and 0.3 per cent respectively. Ofgem found that the R&D intensity of the GB Distribution Network Companies in 2004 was even lower at less than 0.1 per cent.[9]

Independent analysis of the position of R&D in the sector has drawn the same conclusions. Jamasb and Pollitt (2005) identify the coincidence of a decline in R&D activities with electricity reform. They identify a number of reasons for this observed decline, including the negative impact of breaking large entities into smaller ones, the pressure to achieve short-term profitability, the impact of price-cap regulation, and the generally higher levels of business uncertainty.

It is also worth noting that the combination of events post-privatization led to an improving trend in quality of supply and a real reduction in electricity prices up until 2005. The average annual bill, based on the second quarter of 2005, could be up to 30 per cent lower than in 1990. Average annual customer minutes lost have now fallen to 70 per 100 customers. This success was achieved primarily by better management and low primary fuel prices, and almost certainly reduced the perceived need and appetite to pursue relatively risky innovation. The outcome for R&D can be seen in Figure 1. This shows the Distribution Network Operator (DNO) R&D revenue stream as seen by a large R&D service provider. The expenditure in 2003/4 is about 14 per cent of the 1989/90 level.

In summary, there can be little argument that R&D has decreased in the electricity network companies. However, there is debate as to the causes of this trend and the actions that should or should not be taken to correct

---

[8] http://www.innovation.gov.uk/rd_scoreboard/ (giving 2004/5 data).
[9] http://www.ofgem.gov.uk/temp/ofgem/cache/cmsattach/6583_RPZ_IFI_RIA_Final.pdf?wtfrom=/ofgem/work/index.jsp&section=/areasofwork/distpricecontrol

Figure 1 DNO Spend on Distribution Network R&D with One Provider

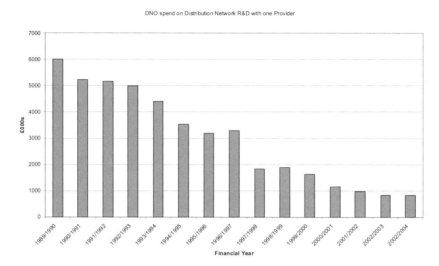

it. In any event, it is proper that the regulator should consider its impact in this area on behalf of customers and, indeed, Ofgem did this for the distribution network companies recently.

4. Development of Network Regulation

Privatization of the British electricity sector in 1990 has resulted in the most comprehensive unbundling of the electricity supply chain of any country in the world. Generation, transmission asset ownership, transmission system operation, distribution, metering, and supply are now all discrete activities. Competition has been introduced to these activities wherever this has been practical and judged to be in customers' interests. This has had wide-reaching effects and has brought many benefits to consumers, including lower prices and fewer supply interruptions.

However, consistent with all other unbundling programmes around the world, it is recognized that the electricity networks are natural monopolies and therefore require appropriate regulation. The electricity network companies have continued to invest in their assets, spending some £21.5 billion between 1991 and 2005 and with a rising trend. Forecast capital investment for the fourth distribution price control period combined with the Final Proposals for the transmission companies' fourth[10] period total some £10 billion.

The fundamental regulatory approach adopted in the UK is usually referred to as 'RPI–X' and this operates on a 5-year cycle. Each network company presents its business plan to the regulator for a 5-year period, setting out the operational and capital costs that it expects to incur. The regulator reviews these plans and judges whether the projected costs would be spent efficiently from a customer's perspective. The regulator also comes to a judgement about the return that the company should receive on its asset base—the cost of capital taking account of the risk profile of the business and the need for the business to achieve financial stability. This analysis is brought together to derive the allowable revenue for the company that is agreed for the 5-year period. This in turn allows prices to be set for the use of the networks. These carriage charges are an element of all electricity bills, but are not separately itemized for domestic consumers.

As discussed earlier, R&D investment has reduced markedly since privatization in 1990, and the regulatory framework is generally thought to be one of the causes of this trend. Regulation has certainly put substantial pressure on management to reduce costs and, in this environment, network businesses have evidently decided that the prospective returns on R&D are not sufficient to justify persisting with such expenditure—possibly because the potential benefits were not sufficiently evident, or possibly because management was not confident that the regulatory framework would allow them to retain such benefits across price-control periods, given the longer-term nature of R&D projects and their eventual deployment.

This was explored in the Regulatory Impact Assessment that Ofgem published in support of its proposals to introduce incentives for R&D in the fourth distribution price control review.[11] Jamasb and Pollitt (2005) also identified price-cap regulation as a negative impact on R&D, as did Oxera (2005). The available evidence provides a clear case for some action to correct this unintended outcome of network regulation.

---

[10] http://www.ofgem.gov.uk/temp/ofgem/cache/cmsattach/17916_20061201_TPCR_Final_Proposals_in_v71_6_Final.pdf?wtfrom=/ofgem/work/index.jsp&section=/areasofwork/transpcr

[11] http://www.ofgem.gov.uk/temp/ofgem/cache/cmsattach/6583_RPZ_IFI_RIA_Final.pdf?wtfrom=/ofgem/work/index.jsp&section=/areasofwork/distpricecontrol

5. Stimulating Efficient R&D in Regulated Monopolies

A regulator has a number of options available to stimulate a desired behaviour in a monopoly company that it regulates. For example, if an attractive risk/reward balance is attached to the activity it is likely that the company will respond. However, the challenge is to ensure that this incentivized activity actually delivers net positive benefits to the company's customers. This is particularly true for R&D, where the immediate outputs from the activity may be largely intangible and will not deliver benefits until they are deployed.

Within the RPI–X regulatory environment there are a number of approaches that could be adopted. Any company must see a reward from its investment that is consistent with the risks involved. The simplest approach is to allow the company to pass any investment costs directly through to its customers. There is no financial risk to the company and the incentive is provided by the benefits that the company might derive from the R&D, even if the regulator captures these for customers at the next price review.

An alternative approach would be to allow the company to capitalize its R&D investment and make a return on it. This was discussed in Ofgem's Regulatory Impact Assessment for the Innovation Funding Incentive (IFI) and Registered Power Zone (RPZ) incentives. It has also been proposed by Oxera more recently. This approach offers the potential to set the rate of return on the capitalized R&D investment independently from the company's cost of capital. Each company will then decide whether to invest in specific R&D projects by adding the guaranteed return it will deliver to the risk-adjusted potential benefits that will flow once outputs from the research are deployed. Capitalization of R&D also raises questions concerning accounting treatment. Ofgem has not ruled out such an approach, but decided not to pursue this for the 2005 price control review.

The regulatory challenge for both the 'pass-through' and capitalized approaches is to ensure that the resulting R&D investments are efficiently managed so that they deliver net benefits to customers.

Another way of addressing this issue is to reward outputs rather than inputs, as in the approach adopted by Ofgem to deliver better quality of service to customers. This is of course the model that applies in a fully competitive market. From the customers' perspective it has many advantages as they should be guaranteed a net benefit. However, as it allocates all the risk to the investing company it does not work well in a regulated, low-risk/return business. Perhaps more importantly, in the networks context it may be problematic to ring-fence and quantify the benefits that an

R&D project actually delivered. Quantification can be problematic in areas such as safety and environmental improvements.

Ofgem resolved these different ideas in the IFI scheme introduced in the distribution price control of last year. The approach adopted shares the risk of investing in R&D between the companies and their customers. The division of the risk between the parties is intended to reflect the sharing of the benefits that are obtained. This cannot be a precise calculation but it was estimated that the customer/company ratio would be approximately 80/20. In order to encourage early activity by the companies their 20 per cent contribution was tapered from 10 per cent to 30 per cent over the 5-year price-control period. The maximum value of IFI averages to £1–2m per distribution network company per year.

The scheme is in its second year of operation (the companies were allowed to commence IFI projects from 1 October 2004) and there is good evidence that it has achieved a step-change in R&D activity across the companies. This is demonstrated by the companies' annual reports for 2005/6. Most importantly, in many cases it has resulted in R&D being given systematic senior management attention and a strategic fit in company's plans. Figure 2 shows the overall impact of the IFI incentive. To date, none of the companies is spending to the limit of their 0.5 per cent cap, but a build-up of activity would be expected in the circumstances.

The real test for IFI is whether it delivers value to customers. With this in mind, two quality-control devices were incorporated in the scheme. First, for any major R&D investment, the company is required to assess the project costs and the potential benefits. This allows a present-value calculation to be carried out. Ofgem does not approve individual projects but does require that a company's portfolio of projects should have a positive net present value (NPV). The second quality-control device is an indirect one. Each company is required to publish an annual report of its IFI activities. Ofgem holds the view that this will encourage best practices and apply peer pressure between the companies. It will in itself help ensure that the companies take due care in selecting their IFI projects and progressing them to completion. The second annual reports were published in August 2006.[12]

Ofgem also introduced the RPZ scheme in the last distribution price control. This is targeted specifically at the challenge of deploying

[12] http://www.ofgem.gov.uk/temp/ofgem/cache/cmsattach/16054_Internetpage.pdf?wtfrom=/ofgem/work/index.jsp&section=/areasofwork/ifirpz

Figure 2 DNO Spend on Distribution Network R&D (upper figure), and DNOs' R&D Intensity (lower figure), Showing Impact of IFI Incentive

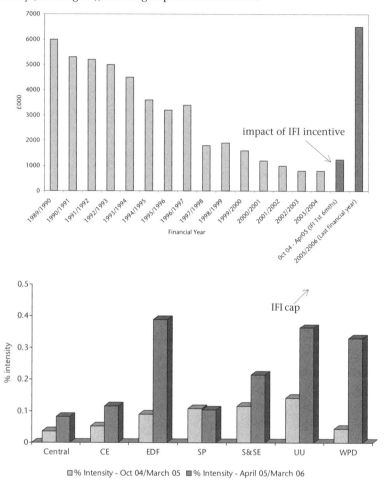

Notes: Data from 1989/90 to 2003/4 is the collaborative spending on R&D among the DNOs through a single provider. Data from October 2004 to April 2005 and the last financial year (2005/6) show reported total IFI spend. Average DNO spend on R&D in 2003 was 0.02 per cent.

innovative technology to connect generation to distribution systems. The scheme uses a different mechanism to the IFI. Ofgem was already developing an incentive mechanism to encourage the connection of distributed generation (DG). This 'hybrid' incentive combines cost pass-through for 80 per cent of connection costs with an annual return for each kilowatt of connected generation. Rather than create a separate mechanism for RPZs it was decided simply to increase the per-kW annual return by a factor of three. This enhanced return applies only for the first 5 years of a DG connection and delivers an overall return (pre-tax real basis) of about 11 per cent compared with a standard connection at about 8 per cent. The first three RPZs have been registered with Ofgem by Central Networks, Scottish & Southern Energy, and EDF Energy, and we are aware of other schemes under development. These schemes will also be openly reported.

Ofgem undertook a review of the IFI and RPZ schemes during autumn 2006, and is currently reviewing the feedback received. All the DNOs are engaging positively with these initiatives, and key issues that Ofgem will be addressing include:

- the future of IFI in the next review period;
- the level of the IFI cap on internal expenditure;
- the IFI project eligibility criteria; and
- the IFI benefit assessment requirements.

The objective in carrying out this review will be to determine what further actions should be taken to encourage the companies to optimize their R&D activities taking account of customers' short- and longer-term interests.

6. The Scope for Network Innovation

As has already been discussed, fundamental change is likely to take place in network infrastructure over the coming decades. As equipment now being installed typically has a 40-year life, today's investment decisions must be informed by a longer-term vision of network development if sub-optimal designs and stranded assets are to be avoided.

The fundamental change referred to can be summarized as follows. Until 1990, the network development model assumed ever larger power stations, centrally planned and operated, supplying 'passive' distribution networks via the transmission system. The term 'passive' here means a network that is configured to allow a known range of operating conditions with minimal manual or automatic intervention. This is a very efficient approach that is inherently dependable but is only appropriate where the operating conditions can be reliably predicted.

There is now a real prospect that in the next decade this model for distribution systems will prove not to be fit-for-purpose in many situations. The market/government pull of cleaner electricity generation combined with the technology push from novel forms of generation is leading to a future where orders of magnitude more generators will be connected to distribution networks at every voltage level including domestic microgeneration. Additionally, there is a growing potential for customers to become active parties in the electricity supply chain rather than being 'dumb' loads. These factors herald a far more organic and interactive power network (with some conceptual parallels to the Internet).

There is an ongoing debate about the relative benefits of centralized and distributed network architectures. Some argue that the transmission grid could in the medium to long term become virtually redundant and that development should concentrate on local, decentralized solutions. In all probability, both transmission and distribution systems will continue to be required as some of the best renewable resources are remote from centres of demand and some clean technologies will be best deployed on a large scale. These aspects alone mean that long-distance, high-voltage transmission will remain part of the landscape in all senses. However, it will have to operate in harmony with distribution networks that are competing to offer generator connections, and adapt to new environmental and other requirements.

It is the networks companies' responsibility efficiently to facilitate this future, not constrain it. Shared vision and effective cooperation remain important enablers of change, but single-model optimized solutions are unlikely to be fit for the future.

R&D projects are a key mechanism by which the industry can equip itself to respond to this future and the network companies have a special role in developing applications rather than products. Companies can develop a portfolio of technical solutions in conjunction with manufacturers, research providers, universities, and others. Innovation will not only bring forward solutions to new challenges but will also enable integration of new and existing systems and enable the maximum value to be extracted from existing assets without compromising security.

7. The Innovation Chain in a Liberalized Sector

Liberalization of the electricity sector has delivered real benefits to customers but has also produced a number of consequential effects. These include a significant contraction of staff numbers and reduction in specialist skills, much greater use of outsourcing, and a sector comprising many more independent parties. There is evidence of continuing cooperation on matters of common interest, such as technical standards and industry codes—the increased complexity of the sector and competitive environment notwithstanding. This situation has been greatly assisted by an underlying context of technical stability—incremental change has been accommodated and a simple philosophy of 'more of the same' has enabled management attention to be directed towards cost control and customer service. A new order of challenge lies ahead—accommodating escalating capital programmes and step-changes in technology arising from new thinking and technical innovation.

The questions to address regarding delivery of innovation are as follows.

- In a multi-party liberalized sector, who formulates the vision for change and who takes ownership of it?
- Where leadership is needed to facilitate cooperative working and to be a catalyst, who is best placed to do this?
- What is the role for parties such as government, regulators, trade bodies, and learned societies?
- How is change best enabled when business frameworks need to be adapted—e.g. legislation, technical codes, or commercial structures?
- How can technical, commercial, and regulatory matters be addressed in an integrated way?
- If specialist technical skills are needed where do they now reside?
- Is academia sufficiently incentivized to work with industry to achieve technology transfer and new commercial products?

No longer is there the simplicity of implementation that is a hallmark of a centrally planned networks sector, as it used to be under the nationalized CEGB and Area Boards. This former governance model had its strengths and weaknesses and one advantage was that when a technical policy change was agreed 'from the top' it was by and large enacted consistently across the national network. Evidence of this is that Britain's electricity networks have a familiar look wherever you are in the country—the result of common design policies being implemented by all the Boards. Two evident risks of central planning are the potential for the national roll-out of sub-optimal policies—consistent, standardized but less than best—and the tendency for bureaucracy to cause a slow response to change.

Meeting the need for a technical step change in a liberalized environment presents a new challenge. It cannot be met effectively by unilateral action by companies when multiple parties are involved. A taste of the issues can be detected from recent developments addressing renewable energy and indicates that new skills, both technical and managerial, will be called for if the changes are to be absorbed efficiently and without added risk to the security and quality of consumer supplies.

There is no simple answer here, but some of the potential pitfalls for the sector to address when contemplating expanding technical programmes are as follows.

THE BUSINESS CASE FOR STRATEGIC INVESTMENT

Developing a business case to assess costs, benefits, and risks is a fundamental part of any investment planning. Most investment decisions are made in situations where a single party can carry out this type of analysis based on its understanding of both internal and third-party risks. However, where a new initiative involves uncertain costs and benefits and material third-party risks, a single-party disaggregated response is likely to fail to find a convincing business case. If technology is unproven there is no confirmed price for it and no guarantee of how its costs will fall with widespread adoption. Also, the benefits of a new technology may be accessed by more than one party bringing commercial and regulatory complexity. Examples of this situation in the electricity supply chain include bulk energy storage and new metering technologies. Both have uncertain costs and benefits, and may require some adaptation of legislative frameworks to accommodate them. The benefits of these technologies are likely to be gained by other parties as well as the asset owner. With this range of uncertainties, a cost–benefit study will have so many assumptions in it that it can be 'made to prove whatever you want'.

So where should such projects start? Taking the metering example, the starting point has to be a shared vision—what might be achieved if the possible were to become a reality; what is judged by the experts to be within grasp and value enhancing? A vision for the future will be strongest if all relevant parties from the sector contribute to it. A shared vision is essential for achieving 'joined up thinking'—for example, gaining agreement on common technical standards that enable open systems, or identifying risks that may not be visible to a single party, such as insufficient manufacturing capacity or specialist skills.

Starting with the formulation of a vision raises some interesting questions in a liberalized sector—who initiates and facilitates the process and who is the owner of the vision so that it can be taken forward and refined? There is no single answer to this and there are examples where helpful facilitation has been undertaken by government, regulators, trade associations, and learned societies. The work of the Technology Platforms of the EU are a case in point where the Commission has acted as a successful facilitator. A recently established platform, SmartGrids, is addressing the future of Europe's electricity networks and published its 'industrial-led vision' in April 2006.[13]

Once a vision has been formulated, a staged process can be developed to go forwards: a project approach with an overall plan, defined milestones, and risk management will give the best chance of success. The project elements then become 'bite-sized chunks' and will be more amenable to cost–benefit analysis and other business techniques.

The maxim 'collaborate globally, implement locally' is helpful and points towards resolving the apparent conflict between competition and necessary cooperation. A variation might read 'collaborate strategically, compete tactically'.

REGULATIONS—FRIEND OR FOE?

The term 'regulations' encompasses many forms of rules that govern behaviour; they may be statutory (i.e. enshrined in written law) or captured in industry-governed codes and practices. The application of regulations may be commercial (e.g. contractual), technical (e.g. grid codes and international standards) or regulatory (e.g. the business framework enforced by bodies such as Ofgem). Regulations are essential enablers for business and customer protection and they need to be fully understood by those who must conform to them. Complications can arise when circumstances change and regulations are no longer fit for purpose.

This chapter has already made reference to the new financial incentives introduced by Ofgem to promote innovation and capital efficiency. This is but one example of a situation where inadvertent barriers, or perverse incentives, have unintentionally arisen in regulatory frameworks. Another example in the technical domain has been the introduction of a long-established technology from Europe (so-called fault current-limiting devices for networks). This technology has been found to be in conflict

---

[13] www.smartgrids.eu

with statutory safety regulations in the UK which prevents their application. Regulatory constraints prompt the obvious question—if the barrier is inadvertent can we get the regulations changed?

This may present itself as a daunting problem to a technical project team or developer. Mechanisms invariably exist for enabling change, some are ad hoc, some are highly structured (e.g. network code panels), but none is quick or easy. This is not for reasons of awkwardness or intentional inertia, but because achieving change involves many parties and disciplines and other competing priorities often constrain progress. Does your particular issue take precedence over others that may be in the queue? Getting the attention of those who operate the change control mechanisms is the first hurdle; there may, however, be another queue for enactment of change—for example, parliamentary time or the appropriate time window in regulatory cycles.

Unless the change processes are understood and there is shared agreement about the reasons for change, these issues may be a serious barrier to implementing innovative solutions. Four pointers can be offered here.

- **Address technical, commercial, and regulatory dimensions in a holistic manner**: do not assume that, say, regulatory matters can be resolved 'at a stroke' by calling in a specialist at a later date.

- **Research and understand the change control processes**: do not, however, assume that they are simply mechanistic processes.

- **Debate in the right language**: communicate the issues and the benefits of change in the respective professional languages of each party; for example, talk of technical vision and engineering judgement just will not cut the mustard if your audience is of a non-engineering discipline.

- **Have a plan to achieve cross-sectoral professional engagement**: use the informal as well as formal channels; understand the work queues, take advice on achieving prioritization.

This list should not be regarded as indicating the existence of excessive bureaucracy or unhelpful attitudes. It is a reflection of the complexities of the real world where simple principles nevertheless have the 'devil in the detail'. In view of the show-stopper nature of the issue, project managers will be well advised to see it as a critical-path task and act accordingly.

ALLOW TIME TO OVERCOME CORPORATE INERTIA

When any organization is working to respond to new challenges it may expose unexpected weaknesses in internal processes, absence of specialist skills, and a corporate amnesia as regards the management skills required. Time must be allowed in project plans for new learning curves to be climbed and, on occasion, prejudices and ignorance to be overcome.

Some examples will illustrate the point.

- An executive group faced with sanctioning a new technology project where none of the directors has first-hand experience of managing such a situation; this puts all parties outside their comfort zone, places unacceptable personal risk on the sponsoring director, and may result in delays or indefinite deferment.

- The procurement process for new technology can present a serious cultural challenge—if the organization has excelled in its cost control through international competitive tendering, standardized specifications, and rigorous unit-cost ranking of alternatives, how will it respond to a request to purchase a one-off item that has no recognized specification, and can only be obtained from a single source?

- If single tender action is not enough to cause delays in itself, there is the further challenge of the form of contract. Procurement departments familiar with contract forms used by major international suppliers may not recognize a contract used by a university or research institute. This will include the treatment of intellectual property, patents, licensing and so on, which the network company may lack the policy to address. It is another situation where there may be personal risks for individuals and understandable caution about proceeding.

The above examples are all issues that can be overcome, but experience has shown a potential time-lag of some 6 or 12 months before these factors are absorbed and an organization starts to address innovation as business as usual.

ACADEMIA AND THE ALIGNMENT OF INCENTIVES

Britain's academic institutions are rightly highly regarded, they are a uniquely valuable repository of the nation's skills: for example, discovery, invention, expert knowledge, and analysis. They are at the root of the R&D process.

There is a lament heard in Britain and in Europe that funding spent on research frequently results in an interesting report, but only infrequently leads to commercialization and industrial roll-out. Without roll-out there can be no benefit for companies or customers. A detailed treatise could be developed at this juncture, analysing the merits of pure and applied research, exploring the recognized difficulties of technology transfer from academia to industry and subsequent commercialization—graphically known as 'crossing the valley of death', between a working prototype and a commercial application—and reviewing the causes of low engagement between industry and academia at formative research stages.

However, Britain appears to have a further factor that is not shared with Europe. This is the comprehensive 'Research Assessment Exercise' that is used to inform the distribution of public funds for research in UK universities.[14] This league-tabling approach has many merits in principle and will be welcomed by alumni from the school of 'if you don't measure it you can't manage it'. However, incentives can be powerful tools and will influence behaviours, priorities, and policies of academic institutions, regardless of sub-optimization in a wider national context.

The RAE scoring is based on a peer review methodology that weights merit, as shown in Table 2 for engineering disciplines.

It is striking that technology transfer appears to contribute in only a small way to a department's scoring. It is part of the assessment process but makes only a very modest contribution as a sub-element of the 20 per cent category. From an observer's perspective it would not appear to be surprising that the focus of our universities is directed strongly towards academic excellence, but, particularly for applied research, it is surprising that technology transfer practices are not a key measure of excellence.

The RAE2008 policy document on Panel Configuration and Recruitment[15] states that: 'where possible and appropriate the sub-panel should include individuals with significant experience of research environments outside UK HE, including people with experience of commissioning and using research, or of overseas research organizations'.

However, an examination of the composition[16] of the six sub-panels for engineering shows that membership is predominantly academic, with

[14] www.rae.ac.uk
[15] http://www.rae.ac.uk/pubs/2004/02/rae0402.doc (para 27).
[16] Membership data are at http://www.rae.ac.uk/panels/members/members.xls (Main Panel G refers).

Table 2. RAE Weighting Methodology

Weighting	Methodology	
50%	'RESEARCH OUTPUTS'	Typically four research outputs, e.g. published papers, submitted for each member of research staff Assessment criteria include: advancement of knowledge, originality, innovation, impact on theory, influence, and take-up by academe or industry
30%	'ESTEEM INDICATORS'	External funding achieved for research Fellowships, prizes, and awards received Collaboration with industry Impact of research on practices, wealth creation, and quality of life
20%	'RESEARCH ENVIRONMENT'	Department's vision and strategy Research staff numbers Support for interdisciplinary research Promoting international activity Technology transfer practices and relationship with industry and commerce

industrial representation averaging only 13 per cent with two of the sub-panels having no industrial representatives and two achieving 21 per cent.

Some rebalancing of priorities would appear to be in order, such that academic excellence and technology transfer are treated in a more complementary way to provide incentives to those working in universities. The next assessment is due in 2008 and it is encouraging that in the last budget the Chancellor made reference to a review of this mechanism.

7.1 *Enabling the Innovation Chain*

The sector has started to explore the consequences of a new paradigm for networks. A Technical Architecture report was published in 2005[17] and work is being taken forward through an Ofgem/DTI industry committee, the Energy Networks Strategy Group.[18]

The Technical Architecture work revealed a particular and critical shortfall in the capabilities of the sector to respond to the technical challenges now emerging. This shortfall is the very low engagement in horizontal working, across teams and across companies. The report highlighted horizontal working or 'professional engagement' as the

[17] http://www.dti.gov.uk/energy/gas_and_electricity/trading_networks/index.shtml
[18] http://www.distributed-generation.gov.uk/documents/12_07_2005_ensg_info_note_2_jun_05.pdf

mechanism that enables innovative change, minimizes risks, and identifies cost-effective solutions.

Anecdotal evidence indicates that these shortcomings are generic and common to other sectors. Companies in the power sector have responded very effectively to the business challenges created by regulatory and competitive pressures; the regulated companies have, for example, reduced their costs while raising their delivered quality of supply.[19] However, they have done this against a stable engineering background and it is this background that is now changing.

Professional engagement is emerging as an issue now because the business innovation seen to date could be done largely in-house, perhaps with the assistance of consultants or IT providers, but engineering innovation cannot. None of the network companies now has in-house R&D facilities and none ever had a manufacturing capability.

7.2 *Professional Engagement*

Professional engagement[20] is a driving force behind innovation, creativity, and change. Without it, organizations fail to thrive, particularly in times of change, and risk losing business advantage.

Some causes of low engagement are as follows:

- a short-term management focus
- ingrained 'silo mentalities'
- narrow training
- continual change
- lower job security—avoidance of personal risks
- line managers seeing wider engagement as a distraction to delivering their immediate tasks.

Evidence of low engagement is shown in the depleted levels of engineering representation at events and seminars, little authorship of papers or articles for journals and conferences, and the decline to a trickle

---

[19] http://www.ofgem.gov.uk/temp/ofgem/cache/cmsattach/17905_204_06.pdf?wtfrom=/ofgem/work/index.jsp&section=/areasofwork/qualityservice/qualityofsupply
[20] Professional engagement is described by the Institution of Electrical Engineers (IEE) as 'the way people engage with their colleagues, with their organization and the organizations within an industry sector. This includes the way people communicate, e.g. face to face, e-mail etc., but it also includes intangibles such as trust and meaning—factors that help people feel part of a whole and help them commit to their work'. The IEE is now the Institution of Engineering and Technology (IET), http://www.theiet.org/

of people applying for chartered status of the professional engineering bodies. At the corporate level there has been almost no profile in the engineering domain where companies could valuably be shaping sectoral technical policy. (There are a few notable exceptions to this generalization and some signs that a change is starting to take place.) Furthermore, there has been little or no technical participation of these companies in European activities, whether the premier 2-yearly conferences of CIRED (International Conference on Electricity Distribution) and CIGRE (International Council on Large Electric Systems), or participation in European research projects. In Europe no British companies are project sponsors, even though 50 per cent funding is available, and despite the risks of not engaging with policy developments that may translate into European law or standards and become mandatory here in Britain.

7.3 *The Underlying Causes*

To understand the reasons behind this situation, it is necessary to look beyond the symptoms and to recognize that professional engagement is about more than simple 'networking'. Organizations comprise both structural and creative elements: structural elements comprise the business framework—the regulated, hierarchical, and predictable environment; creative elements are the intangibles that include creativity, trust, and engagement. In a situation where the dominant focus of organizational activity is cost control, the creative factors become subjugated, all the more so for their non-linear, non-rational characteristics. This is explored further in an Appendix to the Technical Architecture report.

The IEE[21] (now the Institution of Engineering and Technology, IET) has undertaken a survey to gather evidence about the status of professional engagement, its perceived value to businesses and individuals, and the barriers experienced. One finding that is of organizational significance concerns the attitudes to engagement at different levels of seniority. The findings from some 800 respondents show that directors believe that professional engagement is important to them and important to their companies and their sector, but this importance diminishes almost linearly by seniority and 'team members' report almost the converse response (Figure 3).

Some observations can be made: in spite of this issue being regarded as important by senior managers, this is not reflected in the priorities of

---

[21] http://www.iee.org/OnComms/sector/power/profsurvey.cfm

Figure 3 'Me' (Importance of Professional Engagement to the Individual) versus 'Others and Wider' (Importance of Professional Engagement to their Company and Sector)

Source: IEE.

their staff (this corroborates what is witnessed in the sector); professional engagement can be seen as a competence of senior managers; if junior staff have an aspiration for management it will be necessary to develop this competence. However, professional engagement is a subtle competence, best learned by apprenticeship; the opportunities for developing such skills would appear to be much restricted if line managers do not have the same view of its priority.

Other findings in the survey confirm that the focus on short-term delivery is one of the main counter pressures here, putting priority on time and costs that mitigates wider engagement.

This issue needs management attention to resolve it; solutions will be hard to find by individuals operating alone, however strong their commitment. Among all the business pressures and competing priorities it would be unrealistic to expect managers to put professional engagement to the top of their agendas—however, a place somewhere on the agenda would result in material improvements and these findings show that action can be expected to have backing from the very top.

7.4 *Engagement and the Innovation Chain*

In summary, it is evident that engineering innovation requires cross-sector engagement involving parties across a wide innovation chain. The current silo working and lack of wider engagement by engineering practitioners, while understandable in the face of business pressures, has nevertheless been identified by the sector as a potential barrier to engineering innovation. The IEE survey shows that respondents have significant variation in their attitude to this issue, corresponding to their position in company hierarchies. It indicates that the pressures on line managers may be resulting in a blocking factor. There is an issue here requiring attention within organizations; it is one of the many challenges facing management operating under competitive and regulatory pressures but one that, given focus, can be expected to be resolved. Solutions will not be found by returning to old models, but by creative approaches using modern techniques, and through leadership by example.

8. European and International Challenges

A discussion about innovation cannot be complete without reference to the international dimension. The market for electricity network equipment is now truly global. The most significant markets for this equipment are in the developing nations, particularly China and India. The Great Britain market is tiny by comparison and it would be quite unrealistic for it to adopt an island approach to the development of its electricity networks.

Cooperation with other nations is essential. In the first instance this translates to an active engagement with Europe. The record of British companies is not good in this respect. The causes of reduced R&D investment have also resulted in a lack of engagement with European energy projects under the Framework Programmes (FP).

However, there is renewed impetus coming from Europe in relation to electricity networks. The Commission's Green Paper,[22] 'A European Strategy for Sustainable, Competitive and Secure Energy', proposes that the level of interconnection between member states should be increased and that a common Grid Code could be developed by a European Centre for Energy Networks.

---

[22] http://ec.europa.eu/energy/green-paper-energy/doc/2006_03_08_gp_document_en.pdf

In parallel with this, FP7 is now being developed. Whereas in FP6, energy systems were a part of the 'sustainable development, global change and ecosystems' thematic area, in FP7 'Energy' has been elevated to be a primary theme.[23] FP7 will run from 2007 to 2013 and the indicative budget for 'Energy' is some €2.9 billion. Importantly, one of the energy sub-themes is smart electricity networks. It is vital that this major programme of work is properly focused and delivers real value to the industry and its customers. Will the UK play an active role in this work and will our network companies develop efficient ways of engaging with it?

Reference has already been made to the EC's 'SmartGrids' Technology Platform (TP) for 'Electricity Networks for the Future'. A vision document and a Strategic Research Agenda[24] have been published by the TP as key inputs to the FP7 programme. It can be hoped that part of this European activity will establish productive links internationally so that proper account is taken of developments both in the developed and developing markets.

9. Conclusions

Energy is once again high on political, industrial, and personal agendas and the global demand for and dependence on electricity supply continues to grow. Electricity transmission and distribution networks play a vital but largely unsung role in the electricity supply chain. The fundamental structure of these networks and the technologies employed has essentially been stable for a number of decades. However, there is now a real prospect that significant changes will be required in the coming decades to accommodate new, less polluting sources of generation and the needs of a more sophisticated demand side.

Capital investment in these networks has already turned a corner. In Great Britain it is now increasing strongly to replace ageing assets and accommodate new generator connections. This growth in investment is happening at all voltage levels. It is essential that investment is carried out efficiently, taking account of both immediate and longer-term network issues.

Against this background a number of related developments cause concern. The first is the reduction in R&D activity in the sector and the

---

[23] http://www.cordis.lu/fp7/themes.htm
[24] http://www.smartgrids.eu provides access to both documents.

second is the low level of professional engagement. Both of these areas need to be reinvigorated and there are promising signs that this is now happening. Ofgem takes the view that these are important issues from a customer's perspective and it is playing a part here.

The fact that these developments are taking place in a liberalized market environment presents its own challenges. The industry's stakeholders have to find a way of committing to and pursuing both short-term performance metrics and longer-term strategic goals. This is new territory for all and brings its own challenges.

All of this leads to the conclusion that there is a need to re-examine the innovation supply chain from pure research to the adoption of new technologies and solutions. In particular, there is a need to ensure that academic and industrial drivers are sensibly aligned to enhance the productivity of the total supply chain. An emerging but important challenge will be to address the international dimensions of this new paradigm for networks.

The UK has led the world in the development of a liberalized electricity supply sector. We now need to ensure that we build upon that lead by addressing the technical, commercial, and regulatory challenges created by 'renewal and renewables' and do this with a vision that sets the sails for the next 40 years of network development.

3

Carbon Contracts and Energy Policy

Dieter Helm and Cameron Hepburn

1. Introduction

Addressing climate change requires a sustained replacement of the carbon-intensive energy system with a lower-intensity one. At the global level, the task is immense: over this century the world's population may rise from the current 6 billion to 9 billion; and China and India are projected to grow rapidly, both in population and economic activity, reaching standards of living now enjoyed in the developed world, which itself is expected to triple its GDP by 2050. For the British electricity industry, this means replacing conventional coal (and eventually gas) power stations with low-carbon technologies, probably replacing the current nuclear capacity as it reaches the end of its economic life, and designing an energy policy which will facilitate this investment.

Although demand-side measures will have a significant role to play, a 'solution' to climate change will inevitably require investment in large-scale electricity generation. Such technologies already exist, and include nuclear, clean coal with carbon capture and sequestration, and fuel cells. However, none is so far competitive against conventional plant, notably combined-cycle gas-fired turbines (CCGTs), unless the economic consequences of carbon-dioxide (CO_2) emissions are taken into account. Put another way, such lower or non-carbon technologies need CO_2 to be priced into the market.

The traditional argument by technology-specific lobbyists has been for either direct government subsidy, or for subsidy from consumers, via an obligation to purchase from specific technologies. Given the time horizons, the current renewables obligation (RO), in practice, takes the latter route. Governments, in effect, 'pick winners' and then ensure that the costs are passed through to customers and taxpayers.

Such policies do, indeed, induce the desired technologies: private investors have some comfort that their costs are recovered. But they require that all the costs are passed through, not simply the CO_2 aspects. They rely on government being able to decide the market shares of specific technologies. Inevitably, the outcomes are inefficient, since some element of government failure (notably capture by lobbies) cannot be avoided.

An alternative approach is to target the source of the problem explicitly, by focusing exclusively on the CO_2 problem, leaving the other components of the investment decision to the market. Instead of supporting wind, clean-coal, and/or nuclear through obligations or subsidies, CO_2 can be directly addressed through carbon taxes or carbon contracts. Investors then internalize the expected price of carbon over the lifetime of the project, and are able to capitalize that value.[1]

The core problem facing investors is that there is no carbon market over the relevant investment period. The EU emissions trading scheme (EUETS) only extends until 2012 (coincident with the Kyoto Protocol targets).[2] There are no binding targets after 2012. Thus investors face political risk: they need to try to predict what governments will do after 2012 for the duration of their project; and they need to make that prediction now. Political risk is thereby transferred from government to the private sector—a very inefficient risk allocation, violating the principle that risk should be assigned to whoever is best placed to manage it.

These uncertainties and time-horizon problems increase the cost of capital for low-carbon investments. This often tips the balance from profitable to unprofitable, and severely reduces the likelihood that emission-reduction targets will be met. The problem is a classic 'catch-22' one: governments are limited in their ability to introduce new climate change policies because they expect business resistance over the costs, while companies are unable to invest in low-carbon solutions because of the absence of long-term policies.

---

[1] Depending upon the country, policy is generally based on price instruments (carbon taxes), quantity instruments (emissions trading schemes), or frequently a somewhat messy combination of both (Hepburn, 2006). For analysis of how to combine the two, see Roberts and Spence (1976), McKibbin and Wilcoxen (2002), and Pizer (2002).

[2] See CEC (2001b, 2002a).

Solutions to resolve this catch-22, to provide long-term incentives and to reduce policy risk, or at least shift it to the most appropriate entities—arguably the governments responsible for negotiating the next round of international agreements—are needed if climate change is to be addressed by energy policy.

This chapter proposes a novel and more efficient solution to incentivizing investment in low and non-carbon technologies, without 'picking winners', without transferring all the project risk to customers and/or governments through obligations and subsidies, and without placing political risk on the private sector. The core idea is that the government issues a longer-term carbon contract or contracts, open to any bidders, consistent with its overarching climate change policy. We show how such a contract would work, the efficiency properties, and how the liabilities to the government could be minimized, in the absence of *ex ante* credible targets after 2012.

The chapter is structured as follows. In section 2, we identify the *core credibility* and *commitment* problems which lie at the heart of the renewables, nuclear, and clean-coal investment decisions. Section 3 sets out the carbon contract concept and how such contracts might be auctioned. Section 4 shows how the carbon contract might play a wider role in helping to develop emissions trading, and encouraging governments to continue to support carbon market developments once they hold permits to sell. Section 5 outlines how carbon contracts might work in the context of a nuclear project. Section 6 concludes.

2. The Need for Commitment: Credibility and Time Horizons

2.1 *Credibility Problems*

If the national and state governments with long-term carbon targets, such as the UK[3] and California,[4] are serious about achieving them, they need equivalently long-term policy instruments. Without these, the private sector has good grounds for scepticism about the sincerity of such announcements, and will most likely conclude that such carbon targets are largely 'aspirational' and not credible.

[3] The UK Energy White Paper (DTI, 2003) aspires to a 60 per cent reduction from current levels by 2050.
[4] Californian Executive Order S-3-05 (signed by Governor Schwarzenegger on 1 June 2005) aspires to an 80 per cent reduction from 1990 levels by 2050. See www.climatechoices.org/CA_Policies_Fact_Sheet.pdf

Such scepticism would be well founded. Credibility from governments is an extremely rare commodity, because politicians have multiple objectives and parties alternate in government.[5] It is not surprising that there is a history of past default. Governments can and do 'change the rules' in a way that the private sector cannot.

The language employed to communicate these long-term targets often only heightens levels of cynicism. For instance, the UK Energy White Paper (DTI, 2003) states that 'our *ambition* is for the world's *developed economies* to cut emissions of greenhouse gases by 60 per cent by around 2050 . . . therefore . . . the UK should *put itself on a path* towards a reduction in carbon dioxide emissions of some 60 per cent from current levels by *about* 2050' (italics added). The language allows a future government to claim that this was a conditional target that the UK can legitimately renege on because other developed countries failed to fulfil their side of the bargain. Indeed, such conditionality is rational: climate change is a global public bad, with incentives for individual countries to free ride on others' emissions reductions. If the UK *unilaterally* reduces emissions, the net effect on global warming will be negligible and British competitiveness will suffer. Given this characterization of the global coordination problem, the signal to companies is that they should operate on the assumption that the target will not be met.

2.2 Time Horizon Problems

Even more pressing is the fact that most carbon policy does not even extend to long-term targets, whether purely aspirational or not. Although the international negotiations under the United Nations Framework Convention on Climate Change (UNFCCC) provide UK and European companies with a degree of security until 2012—at least they can be confident of the existence of a legal trading system for the next 6 years in the EU ETS—there is no regime to rely upon post-2012.

The lack of long-term incentives is crucial for a very simple reason. The profitability of investments made today, given time lags between design, planning approval, commissioning, and operation, depends in large measure upon the policy environment one or two decades into the future. Without a clear policy framework, or ideally a guarantee over carbon prices, for the next couple of decades, governments should not be surprised when the private sector under-invests in low-carbon technologies

[5] Other sources of 'time inconsistency' are discussed in Abrego and Perroni (2002) and Marsiliani and Renström (2000).

such that emission targets fail to be achieved. Indeed, it is hardly surprising that the UK 2010 domestic target to reduce CO_2 emissions by 20 per cent from the 1990 level is likely to fall well short.

2.3 *Traditional Solutions*

There are a limited number of policy instruments available to solve the credibility and time-horizon problems. The traditional route involves the government directly subsidizing particular technologies—nuclear, for instance—to provide low-carbon generation over several decades, or requiring customers to subsidize specific technologies through a compulsory obligation to purchase a given percentage market share.

But this traditional technology-specific approach suffers from several problems. First, the government is compelled to evaluate the competing claims of cost-competitiveness of each technology, which involves taking a view of the rate at which the technology is moving down the learning curve. In other words, government is forced to 'pick winners'. This is a classic asymmetric information problem, where firms hold better information than the government, so there is little to guarantee that the public will get value for money. The result is capture by lobbies and vested interests, with government vulnerable to picking losers rather than winners. The history of the nuclear and wind industries provide illuminating case studies (see Helm, 2004*a*).

Second, once the subsidies and obligations are in place, there is little incentive for R&D or major capital expenditure in other technologies, since these are crowded out of the market. During the 1970s and 1980s, non-nuclear R&D suffered accordingly.

Third, if subsidies are used or there is a cost pass-through to customers, the incentives to complete projects efficiently may be weak (as in the nuclear case), and, finally, if an obligation is placed upon customers and then the obligation itself is traded, there may be an incentive to limit development within the obligation category (as in the RO case, where the value of renewable obligations certificates (ROCs) depends upon the gap between the obligation target and actual delivery).

It is clear that a superior alternative is urgently needed. One possibility, outlined in Helm *et al.* (2003), is to create a credible agency, independent of the politics of government, designed along the lines of the Monetary Policy Committee (MPC) of the Bank of England.[6] The agency would be

---

[6] A formal model is outlined in Helm *et al.* (2004), including the proposal to delegate to an 'environmental policymaker', along the lines of Barro and Gordon (1983).

charged with achieving a given target or targets, and allocated a corresponding number of instruments (a carbon tax and capacity payment, for example) with which to achieve those targets.[7] Another possibility, proposed here, is to auction long-term carbon contracts.

3. The Carbon Contracts Solution

3.1 *Overview*

Under the carbon contracts scheme, the government would auction off carbon contracts for the supply of emission reductions over a long time horizon, such as 20–30 years. The contract auction (discussed in more detail in section 3.2 below) for emissions reductions (ERs) might have two phases—the first to determine the type of contract companies are prepared to bid for, the second to determine the actual prices.

As with the traditional routes (discussed above), auctioning carbon contracts provides a forward revenue stream with long-term price certainty that can be used to secure project finance (see Figure 1). But carbon contracts have several additional advantages.

First, they are technology blind, so the government is not forced to pick winners. That being so, the government can neatly side-step the messy business of evaluating and second-guessing various industry claims about which technology is cheaper, and thereby avoid technology capture. It simply lets the market decide.

Second, carbon contracts improve risk allocation by shifting policy risk in respect of carbon away from the private sector and on to the government, which is in a better position to manage that risk.

Third, the government can then diversify the policy risk by selling the emission reductions on to the market as the plant comes on stream, and as eventually emissions trading and targets emerge for future periods. Indeed, if the government can find an appropriate counterparty (or if forward markets are functioning), it could even forward sell the emission reductions to eliminate its liabilities altogether. And in the unlikely absence of either possibility, the carbon contracts costs could be assigned to electricity customers by default, through the system charges.

---

[7] For the underlying theory in the monetary policy context, see, for example, Kydland and Prescott (1977). Blackburn and Christensen (1989) provide a survey of the field and Walsh (2003) and Romer (1996) provide textbook treatments.

Figure 1 Carbon Contracts

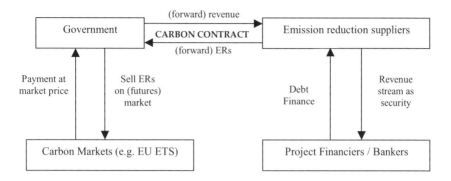

3.2 *The Contract Auction*

A central feature of the carbon contracts approach is a technology-blind contract auction. The basic idea is that the government would seek to agree to purchase a supply of (delivered) future emission reductions at the lowest possible price. Companies would bid their prices (for different quantities), and the government would write contracts with those firms who can commit to supply a future stream of emission reductions at lowest cost.

However, as with any auction of this nature, the devil is in the details. In particular, important issues include the following.

A staged versus one-shot auction
The starting point for a carbon auction is to recognize that this is a novel idea, about which the government has limited knowledge. There is therefore considerable merit in having a pre-qualifying bidding process to elicit information about the design of the contract auction itself. Such pre-bidding is common to many large-scale projects and would enable potential purchasers to reveal their preferred parameters for the definition of the full auction—for example, such matters dealt with below as the likely demand for contracts and appropriate volumes, domain, geography, and periods.

The proportion of the overall carbon target to be auctioned
While auctioning a quantity of carbon contracts equal to the overall target has the merit of ensuring that the target is actually achieved, the government need not bind itself to such a demanding policy position.

It can, in principle, choose *any* quantity between zero and the target ceiling. The lower the quantity the less the risk to the government that it might not be able to sell all its contracted position on to the market.

Indeed, there are good reasons not to auction the full target. Other policies can be assumed to make contributions (even if they are less efficient). If other countries do not take sufficient steps towards reducing their emissions, then the cost of British policy will be lower if below the desired target ceiling. Finally, if the entire target were auctioned, the government might have more difficulty selling on its contracts to counterparties, or if counterparties can be found, the government may end up making a loss on the sale.

Permitted bidders

In principle, any company which can deliver reductions in CO_2 emissions consistent with the definition of the base line for the government's preferred target or aspiration might be invited to bid in carbon reductions. This might be limited to specific sectors, or there might be separate sector auctions.

The most obvious sector to which to apply the auction is the energy sector, following on from the design of the EU ETS. However, the transport sector is also a candidate, as is the large industrial energy users group.

An interesting question is whether overseas companies and organizations might bid, too—whether within the EU, under conventional contract rules, or more generally in line with the Clean Development Mechanism (CDM) and Joint Implementation (JI) developed within the Kyoto regime. The preferred geographical domain depends upon whether the government's target is a domestic one, or a conditional international objective.

In the two-stage auction system suggested above, the first phase might be pluralistic, so that government can elucidate information, before committing in the second phase to a defined domain. If the total amount of carbon to be auctioned is well inside the target level, then it is less important if the sector and geography is narrowly defined. Thus, if, say, 20 per cent of the required emissions reductions under the overall target is auctioned, then the domain could be as narrow as the UK electricity sector.

Auction periodicity

It is unlikely that a single auction would be the most efficient: for the bidders new information of competing technologies becomes available and for government over time more is learnt about the actions of other countries, and, indeed, about the underlying science.

A pragmatic element is also important: at a time when much of the base-load electricity generation capacity is coming to the end of its life and needs replacement, it is an opportune moment to auction carbon reductions for the power sector roughly in line with the required capacity replacement and the time horizons of the competing players. If the auction is in two phases, then in phase one, initial bids could include the contract duration. This information would then help define the period and identify a future date for further possible auctions.

Auction mechanisms and pricing

There is a range of possible auction methods, notably sealed bids and dynamic auctions. There are also different pricing approaches, notably pay-as-bid, uniform pricing, and Vickrey pricing. The literature on the relative merits is considerable (see Klemperer, 2004), and it is beyond the scope of this chapter to set out a detailed recommendation. Note, however, that the merits of the carbon contracts concept are not dependent on the choice of method.

3.3 *Securitization*

The auction contract should be designed to facilitate access to project finance by suppliers of emissions reductions.[8] This means that the contracts need to be long-dated (as discussed) and be of a 'take or pay' variety with a price guarantee backed by the government. These two features would ensure that companies could use the future revenue stream as security to raise the necessary debt (and equity) for the low-carbon investment.

3.4 *Efficient Risk Allocation*

The key carbon policy risk concerns the likely international negotiating position after the Kyoto compliance period in 2012. Will the United States and Australia persist in their reluctance to accept caps and join the international trading scheme? Might they convince the Europeans and others that technology transfer without caps (and hence without a carbon price) is the best approach? If so, what form will the carbon market take?

---

[8] On the difficulties of using emissions reductions alone as securitization, see McClellan (2005).

These are clearly risks that are difficult for low-carbon suppliers to manage. The most appropriate entities to bear international negotiating risk are the nation-states themselves; they are, after all, the only entities in a position directly to shape the outcome of those negotiations.[9]

As such, it makes sense for this risk to be allocated to governments through carbon contracts. If the carbon market disappears altogether, through negotiation failure, national governments bear the cost of that failure. Governments can then choose whether costs arising in the event of negotiation failure are passed on to taxpayers or energy customers. Equally, if the carbon market thrives and tight caps are negotiated, national treasuries reap the rewards in the form of higher revenues from their carbon contracts. Increasing the efficiency of risk allocation could dramatically reform the incentives faced by the players, as discussed further in section 4.

3.5 Risk Transfer to the Market

Realistically, even if carbon policy risk is most efficiently allocated to the government, it unfortunately does not necessarily follow that governments will be prepared to stomach this risk. One might well ask how such governments expect the low-carbon companies to deal with the risk when they have very little control over international climate negotiations—but this, of course, is part of the problem.

Nevertheless, there is a partial solution to this problem, too. The government has two options. First, if carbon markets continue to exist, it can sell out the carbon contract over time to unwind its liability. For instance, suppose a contract involves paying a new nuclear plant to produce non-carbon energy. The government needs to find a counterparty to buy this benefit. Airlines or carbon-intensive manufacturers might be examples. With a functioning emissions trading market, this is a straight-forward exercise. Even without such a market, the government could still sell its credits on to companies who wish voluntarily to become 'carbon neutral' for advertising or reasons of corporate social responsibility (but after selling the credits into the voluntary market the government should no longer be able to use them to meet its own national target).

If governments cease grandfathering carbon permits—which is sensi-ble[10] and also appears to be the direction in which policy is heading—the

---

[9] As Borch (1962) demonstrated, an optimal allocation of risk between different entities involves the entities accepting risk in proportion to their ability to bear it.

[10] This is for a variety of reasons. Some concern efficiency and the double-dividend hypothesis (on this point and the marginal cost of public funds, see Ballard and Fullerton (1992) and Goulder (1995); others relate to equity considerations. See Hepburn *et al.* (2006).

periodic auction of permits provides another opportunity to unwind this liability. In a sense, the government would be acting as a crucial policy 'middleman', providing a degree of market liquidity and, at the same time, achieving its emission-reduction objectives.

The second option, if a counterparty can be found, is to forward sell its supply of emission reductions. This would provide the counterparty with a guaranteed supply of emission reductions at a fixed price, hedging the counterparty's position against the carbon price while simultaneously unwinding the government's liability before it even arises.

4. Additional Benefits of Carbon Contracts

4.1 *Reduced Carbon Market Volatility*

Carbon contracts have a number of additional advantages, notably in providing stability to carbon markets and creating incentives to protect and enhance carbon trading beyond 2012. A further advantage of carbon contracts is that the government could use its supply of emission reductions to inject liquidity and stability into the market, smoothing out volatility. By selling when prices are high, the government—as a player with a degree of market power—would be able to prevent prices from reaching levels that damage local industry. Moreover, by selling when prices are high, the government could walk away with a profit.

4.2 *Improved Negotiation Incentives*

Second, as alluded to earlier, if carbon contracts were adopted by a variety of different government entities prior to the next round of international negotiations, the incentive to find an agreement would be substantially increased. With carbon-based assets on the government balance sheet, national treasuries are unlikely to want to scrap a process that would devalue these assets—perhaps to zero. On the contrary, they can maximize the value of their carbon assets by negotiating relatively tight caps. In short, carbon contracts would likely provide the private sector as a whole— including firms which do not win a carbon contract—with increased security that the market will continue to function. After all, why would it fail if national governments have an incentive to keep it running?

5. An Example: Nuclear New Build

The carbon contracts concept is not only an efficient general mechanism to reduce CO_2 emissions, but also one which addresses some of the immediate policy problems confronting government. A pertinent example is the application to the question of nuclear new build, as promised in the 2006 Energy Review (HM Government, 2006).

Under the traditional approach, the government would address this question in two stages: first, it would try to estimate the comparative costs of nuclear as against other non-carbon or low-carbon technologies; and second, it would support nuclear by either a subsidy or a nuclear obligation.

Under the carbon contracts approach, these steps would be largely redundant. The government would focus on its carbon target, and then auction some proportion of that target. Nuclear would presumably bid against the other competing technologies, such as wind and clean coal. The bids would determine the technology choice. Hence there would be no need in a nuclear review to analyse the detailed project costs.

Note, too, that other parts of a nuclear project would not, under the carbon contract approach, need to be subsidized or otherwise paid for under a nuclear obligation. The costs of construction would be market determined, as would performance guarantees. Fuel supplies would be contracted for, and power output forward sold. The government would of course be a counterparty to a waste and decommissioning contract (via the Nuclear Decommissioning Authority (NDA)), but many of these elements of contracting are already in place for existing operating reactors, and a pension fund arrangement would be required for decommissioning. The problem to which nuclear purports to be an answer is how to reduce CO_2 emissions: the carbon contract reveals whether it is—as its advocates claim—the cheapest option.

Nuclear, of course, has other dimensions, as do competing technologies. For example, advocates claim it contributes to security of supply, and it is rightly observed that the absence of a capacity market militates against it. There are also well-known problems with the electricity market design (in particular, the new electricity trading arrangements (NETA)) which would need to be addressed. A nuclear review would need to incorporate these factors, too. But the substantive point remains: by using carbon contracts, much of the detailed project costs can be left to the market to reveal—and, in the process, the area where capture by lobbyists has been most prevalent in the past is neatly side-stepped.

6. Conclusions

Given the seriousness of climate change, it is unsurprising that governments seek ways to lower the carbon content of the energy sector and the economy more generally. But given, too, that the problem is a global one, there is an understandable reluctance by national governments to pre-commit to domestic targets, when others may not do so, and, indeed, free-rider incentives are rife.

But this reluctance by government to bind itself to the mast of carbon targets creates a major barrier to low-carbon technologies. Without credible targets, the future price of carbon cannot be estimated, and hence investors cannot capture these carbon-related benefits. Indeed, with the EU ETS only running to 2012, the uncertainty is considerable.

As a result, governments are being encouraged to intervene directly to promote particular technologies. This has already occurred in respect of the RO, and the nuclear and clean-coal interests are pressing for similar concessions.

This chapter has argued that longer-term carbon contracts not only avoid much of this traditional policy approach of 'picking winners' but will also provide an efficient method of harnessing the market, while at the same time limiting the financial exposure of the government and avoiding pre-commitments to long-term targets in the context of international negotiations. Indeed, it is quite possible that carbon contracts may make a net profit to the government.

The precise form of carbon contracts auctions is beyond the scope of this chapter. However, we have argued that a two-phase approach, with pre-bidding, would help in the contract and auction design, and that there is no need to auction quantities up to the targets in the first instance. Issues such as sectoral and geographical domains, periodicity, and auction method and pricing rules, can be resolved once the concept is adopted: it is not dependent on the precise answers to these detailed specifications.

In the nuclear example, we have shown that much of the traditional cost estimation can be avoided, and the risk of capture by vested interests is notably reduced by using auctions. These observations apply to wind, clean coal, and other technologies, too.

4

Competitive Electricity Markets and Investment in New Generating Capacity

*Paul L. Joskow**

1. Introduction

Policy-makers in many countries are expressing concerns that competitive wholesale electricity markets are not providing appropriate incentives to stimulate 'adequate' investment in new generating capacity at the right time, in the right places, and using the right technologies. These concerns are often expressed in the context of concerns about 'supply security', 'reliability', 'resource adequacy', or 'supply diversity'. In most cases the concerns have been raised as policy-makers observe growing electricity demand, shrinking reserve margins, and rising prices, but little evidence of investment in new generating capacity responding to balance supply and demand consistent with traditional metrics for generation resource 'adequacy'. Many economists and market enthusiasts dismiss these concerns as reflecting the misguided conclusions of nervous politicians and system engineers who do not understand how markets work and who have not made the intellectual transition to a world of liberalized electricity markets. Nevertheless, there is a growing number of

* This chapter builds on research discussed in Joskow (2005, 2006) and Joskow and Tirole (2006). I have benefited enormously from conversations with Jean Tirole and Steve Stoft about these issues and, in particular, the recent paper by Cramton and Stoft (2006) provides an excellent technical discussion of several of the issues discussed here. Financial support from the Massachusetts Institute of Technology (MIT) Center for Energy and Environmental Research is gratefully acknowledged. The views expressed here are my own and do not necessarily reflect the views of those with whom I have worked on these issues or of MIT.

recent situations in which state-owned entities have stepped in to contract for additional generating capacity or where policy-makers have required incumbent distribution companies to contract for new supplies to mitigate resource adequacy concerns (e.g. Chile, Brazil, New Zealand, Ontario, California).[1]

In this chapter I argue that, at least based on US experience with organized competitive wholesale power markets for electric energy and operating reserves, there are a number of market imperfections and institutional constraints that have the effect of keeping wholesale prices for energy and operating reserves below their efficient levels during hours when prices should be very high and provide insufficient net revenues to support the capital costs of an efficient portfolio of generating facilities. If this situation is allowed to persist it will in turn lead to underinvestment in generating capacity and to higher rates of power-supply emergencies and involuntary rationing (black-outs). These problems have been exacerbated in the USA by instability in the wholesale market designs and market rules that characterize these wholesale markets (continuing reforms of the reforms), uncertain commitments by government policy-makers to liberalization (calls for re-regulation), and an incomplete transition to a stable retail competition framework. At least some of these problems are likely to characterize competitive electricity markets in some other countries. That is the bad news. The good news is that these problems can be fixed with appropriate reforms to wholesale and retail market designs and credible government commitments to market liberalization.

The concerns about investment in new generating capacity reflect one or more of several interrelated groups of real or imagined problems with competitive wholesale electricity markets. First, it has been argued that competitive wholesale electricity markets for energy and operating reserves do not, and perhaps cannot, credibly provide sufficient net revenues to attract adequate investment in generation to meet conventional operating and investment economic efficiency and reliability criteria. According to this view, spot wholesale electricity market prices for energy and operating reserves will simply not be high enough to cover both the operating costs and the capital investment costs (including an appropriate risk-adjusted cost of capital) required to attract new investment in long-lived generating capacity to support a least-cost generation supply portfolio consistent with mandatory reliability criteria. Wholesale spot market prices, in turn, are reflected in forward prices for power that are too low as well through the

---

[1] For example see the chapters in Sioshansi and Pfaffenberger (2006).

normal operation of inter-temporal arbitrage behaviour. I will follow Cramton and Stoft (2006) and refer to this as the 'missing money' problem.

Second, it is sometimes argued that short-term wholesale electricity prices are too volatile to support new investment in long-lived capital intensive generating capacity without support from long-term contractual agreements between generators and wholesale or retail supply intermediaries. Retail customers, with a few exceptions, show little interest in entering into contracts of more than 2 or 3 years' duration and, for this and perhaps other reasons, a liquid voluntary forward market for longer duration contracts that investors can rely on to hedge electricity market risks has not emerged naturally. A variant on this 'uncertainty barrier' argument is that the problem is not that investments will not be forthcoming at some price level, but rather that the cost of capital used by investors to evaluate investments in new generating capacity, that will operate in competitive wholesale spot markets for energy and operating reserves, is so high that it implies electricity prices that are even higher than those that would have been experienced under the old regime of regulated vertically integrated utilities where market, construction, and generator performance risks are largely shifted to consumers by fiat through the regulatory process. This then turns into an argument against liberalized electricity sectors.

Finally, it is sometimes argued that market rules and market institutions change so frequently and that opportunities for regulators to 'hold up' incumbents by imposing new market or regulatory constraints on market prices is so great that uncertainty about future government policies acts as a deterrent to new investment. As I discuss in more detail below, this is especially problematic in electricity markets because a large fraction of the net revenues earned to compensate investors for the capital they have committed to generating capacity relies on very high spot-market prices realized during a very small number of hours each year. The potential opportunity for market rules and regulatory actions to keep prices from rising to their appropriate levels even in a few hours each year when efficient prices would be very high can seriously undermine investment incentives.

In this chapter I focus on the first set of concerns—the missing money problem, discuss empirical evidence indicating that it is a real problem in the organized wholesale power markets in the USA, and identify its causes. I do not think too much of the argument that price uncertainty *per se* deters investment, though I discuss how restrictions on the natural evolution of retail market institutions can contribute to the failure of a normal market-based risk-allocation mechanism to operate properly. The issues related to investment disincentives caused by opportunism or hold-up concerns are real and require more attention. While mandating that retail suppliers enter into long-term contracts may be a solution to this problem from the perspective of investors (Joskow, 1987), it is a solution that is not compatible with the effective diffusion of retail electricity competition and may deter further improvements in wholesale market institutions. Finally, I discuss a series of reforms built around (*a*) improvements in spot wholesale energy markets and (*b*) the introduction of forward capacity markets with particular attributes that can resolve most of the problems that have been identified and are compatible with the continued evolution of a healthy retail competition framework.

2. Background

Questions have been raised about whether competitive wholesale and retail markets for power would produce adequate generating capacity investment incentives to balance supply and demand efficiently since the transition to competitive electricity markets began. Until 2001, the wholesale market system in England and Wales provided for additional capacity payments to be made to all generators scheduled to supply during hours when supply was unusually tight (i.e. when the loss-of-load probability was relatively high).[2] The wholesale markets created and managed by the Eastern Independent System Operators (ISOs) in the USA during the late 1990s have continued their traditional policies of requiring distribution companies (or more generally 'load serving entities', or LSEs, to encompass competitive retail electricity suppliers) to enter into contracts for capacity to meet their projected peak demand plus an administratively determined reserve margin. Argentina's competitive electricity market system also included capacity payments to stimulate investment in reserve generating capacity. In Chile, distribution utilities are required to enter into forward contracts to meet forecast demand plus a reserve margin. The system in Colombia also imposes capacity obligations. California's wholesale electricity market design did not impose capacity, reserve or forward contract obligations and the California electricity crisis of 2000–1 is sometimes (erroneously) blamed on underinvestment in generating capacity. Capacity obligations are now being introduced in California in the form of generating reserve margin criteria and forward contracting obligations. On the other hand, the wholesale market in England and Wales abandoned capacity payments

---

[2] This payment mechanism was dropped when the New Electricity Trading Arrangements (NETA) system was introduced in 2001.

when the New Electricity Trading Arrangements (NETA) were introduced and Texas (ERCOT—the Electric Reliability Council of Texas) has never had capacity payments or capacity obligations. There appears to be no interest in introducing them in either market.

Questions about whether wholesale markets will bring forth adequate investments in generating capacity arise naturally from the unusual characteristics of electricity supply and demand: (*a*) large variations in demand over the course of a year; (*b*) non-storability; (*c*) the need physically to balance supply and demand at every point on the network continuously to meet physical constraints on voltage, frequency, and stability; (*d*) the inability to control power flows to most individual consumers; (*e*) limited use of real-time pricing by retail consumers; and (*f*) that even under the best of circumstances (i.e. with effective real-time pricing of energy and operating reserves) non-price mechanisms (black-outs) will have to be relied upon from time to time to ration imbalances between supply and demand to meet physical operating reliability criteria because markets cannot clear fast enough to do so.[3]

These attributes have a number of implications. First, a large amount of generating capacity that is available to meet peak demand plus the associated operating reserve requirements supplies relatively small amounts of energy during the year. For example, in New England in 2001, 93 per cent of the energy was supplied by 55 per cent of the installed generating capacity while the remaining 45 per cent of the capacity supplied only about 7 per cent of the energy.[4] Potential investors in new generating capacity must expect to cover their variable operating costs, their fixed operating and maintenance costs, and their capital costs from sales of energy and operating reserves over the life of generating capacity under consideration. The return of and on the associated capital investment in new generating capacity is the difference between the prices they receive for generation services (including capacity payments, if any) and their operating (primarily fuel) costs—what I refer to here as 'net revenues'. The profitability of generating units that are likely to operate only for a relatively small number of hours in each year ('peaking capacity') is especially sensitive to the level of prices that are realized during the small number of high-demand hours in which they provide energy or operating reserves.

---

[3] In response to questions about why demand response was not relied upon to respond to the sudden loss of 1,100 MW of generating capacity that led to rolling black-outs in Texas on 17 April 2006, a representative of the ISO is reported to have said: 'In this case, when four generators tripped, it was just bang-bang-bang-bang.' (*Electric Transmission Week*, 24 April 2006, pp. 1, 12)

[4] Sithe Energy presentation, International Association for Energy Economics, Boston Chapter, 19 February 2003.

Second, the generating capacity available to supply energy at any point in time must always be greater than the demand for energy at that point in time as a result of the physical need to carry 'inventory' in the form of generators providing frequency regulation and operating reserve services. That is, generating capacity (or, in principle, demand response) must be available that is either 'spinning' or available to start up quickly to provide energy to balance supply and demand at each location on the network in response to real-time variations in demand and unplanned equipment outages. When these operating reserves fall below a certain level because available generating capacity and demand response resources are fully utilized (e.g. 7 per cent of demand), system operators begin to take actions to reduce demand administratively according to a pre-specified hierarchy of 'operating reserve shortage' actions. The final actions in this hierarchy are voltage reductions and non-price rationing of demand (rolling black-outs). I discuss system operator behaviour during such 'scarcity' or 'operating reserve shortage' conditions in more detail below, as they play a central role in explaining the missing-money problem in the USA.

Finally, limited reliance on real-time pricing, the inability to control real-time power flows to all but the largest retail consumers, the potential for and economic attributes of a network collapse, and the attributes of system operating protocols such as voltage reductions, undermine the ability of market mechanisms alone to choose the efficient level of system reliability. Reliability has public-goods attributes and we cannot expect the market to provide the efficient level of reliability. Whether the market can choose the efficient level of reliability or not, a variety of administrative reliability rules and operating protocols have been carried over from the old regime of vertically integrated monopoly to the world of liberalized electricity markets. These reliability rules have important implications for market behaviour and performance and for assessments of the 'adequacy' of investment in generating capacity and the associated probability of rolling black-outs and network collapses.

3. Wholesale Electricity Market Behaviour and Performance in Theory

To oversimplify for expositional purposes, a well-functioning, perfectly competitive wholesale electricity market will operate in one of two states of nature. Under typical operating conditions (State 1), market-clearing prices for energy *and* operating reserves should equal the marginal (opportunity) cost of the last increment of generating capacity that just clears supply and demand at each point in time. In the case of wholesale electric energy supply, this price is the marginal cost of producing a little more or a little less energy from the generating unit on the margin in the bid-based merit order. Figure 1 depicts the spot-market demand for electricity and the competitive supply curve for electricity under typical operating conditions (State 1). Infra-marginal generating units earn net revenues or quasi-rents that contribute to the recovery of their fixed operating and capital costs whenever the market-clearing price exceeds their own marginal generation costs. In the case of operating reserves, the efficient price is (roughly) equal to the *difference* between the price of energy and the marginal cost of the next increment of generation that could supply energy profitably if the price of energy were slightly higher plus any direct costs incurred to provide operating reserves (e.g. costs associated with spinning). This price for operating reserves is equal to the marginal *opportunity cost* incurred by generators standing in reserve rather than supplying energy. Under typical operating conditions (State 1) the price of operating reserves will be very small—close to zero, and far below the price of energy.

The second wholesale market state (State 2) is associated with a relatively small number of hours each year when there would be excess demand at a wholesale price that is equal to the marginal production cost of the last increment of generating capacity that can physically be made available on the network to supply energy plus operating reserves. In this case, the market must be cleared 'on the demand side'. That is, consumers bidding to obtain energy would bid prices up to a (much) higher level reflecting the value that consumers place on consuming less electricity as demand is reduced to match the limited supplies available to the market (or value of lost energy or load—VOLL). This second state is depicted in Figure 2. In Figure 2, the area labelled R_{mc} represents the quasi-rents that would be earned by infra-marginal generators if the wholesale price is equal to the marginal generating cost of the least efficient generator on the system required to clear the market. The area labelled R_s reflects the additional scarcity rents from allowing prices to rise high enough to ration scarce capacity on the demand side to balance supply and demand. In what follows, I refer to the conditions depicted in Figure 2 as *competitive* 'scarcity' or 'shortage' conditions.[5]

Under competitive scarcity conditions the competitive market clearing price of energy will now generally be much higher than the marginal

---

[5] To distinguish it from contrived scarcity, resulting from suppliers withholding supplies from the market to drive up prices.

Figure 1 Short-run Marginal Cost Pricing

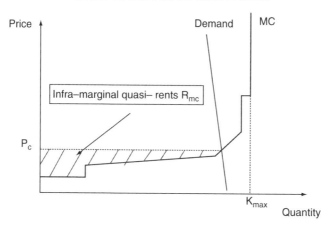

SHORT RUN MARGINAL COST PRICING

Figure 2 Pricing with Binding Capacity Constraints

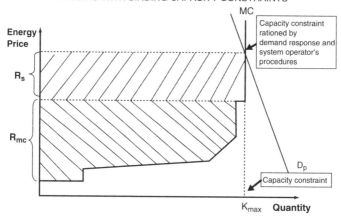

PRICING WITH BINDING CAPACITY CONSTRAINTS

production cost of supplying the last available increment of energy from generating capacity available to the network, reflecting the high opportunity cost (VOLL) that consumers place on reducing consumption by a significant amount on very short notice. Furthermore, while the price of operating reserves will continue to be equal to the marginal opportunity cost incurred by generators standing in reserve rather than supplying energy, this opportunity cost will rise significantly as well in response to the higher 'scarcity value' of energy. *All* generating units actually supplying energy and operating reserves in the spot market during scarcity conditions would earn substantial 'scarcity rents'. These scarcity rents in turn help to cover the fixed capital and operating costs of all generating facilities.

In a hypothetical well-functioning competitive electricity market, and, in particular, ignoring the market imperfections associated with the market-provision of reliability, price signals for energy bought and sold in the market not only induce the right amount of generating capacity (and associated levels of reliability), but also the right mix of generating technologies. Because electricity is non-storable and demand varies widely over the course of a year, the most economical portfolio of generating plants will include technologies with a variety of capital cost/operating cost ratios. Base-load generating facilities (typically nuclear or coal) have relatively high capital costs and low operating costs. These facilities are economical to build if it is efficient to operate them for a large fraction of the hours of each year. Intermediate load facilities (typically gas or oil fuelled) have lower capital costs and higher operating costs than base-load facilities. These facilities typically operate for 20–50 per cent of the hours during the year. Finally, peaking facilities have the lowest capital costs and the highest operating costs per unit of capacity. These facilities are expected to be economical to operate from a few hours per year up to (say) 20 per cent of the hours during the year.[6]

For base-load and cycling units, the net revenues they earn during scarcity conditions may account for a significant fraction of the total net revenues they earn throughout the year. For peaking capacity that supplies energy or operating reserves primarily during such scarcity conditions, the net revenues it earns during these periods will account for substantially *all* of the net revenues available to cover its fixed costs (capital, maintenance, and operating). The number of hours in which 'scarcity' conditions emerge depends upon the amount of generating capacity that has been installed and is physically available to operate relative to the tail of the distribution of aggregate demand realizations during the year. The quantity and type of generating capacity that is physically available to the network in a market context will then depend on investors in generating capacity balancing the costs of additional investments against the net revenues they expect to receive, including the 'scarcity' rents produced under State 2 conditions, from spot-market sales and through sales pursuant to forward contracts if suppliers choose to

---

[6] There does not exist a distribution of generating technologies that reflects a continuum of capital/operating cost ratios. However, the more options there are along such a distribution the better can be the match between generating technologies and the number of hours they will operate each year to meet demand.

hedge market price risks. The prices for such forward contracts are necessarily linked directly to expected wholesale spot-market prices for energy through intertemporal arbitrage and consumer and supplier preferences for market price risk.

This simple theoretical analysis of a well-performing wholesale market has so far largely ignored uncertainty. Uncertainty enters short-run operating (dispatch) behaviour and long-run investment behaviour in a number of ways. Electricity demand is uncertain in both the long run and the short run. From a long-run investment perspective, electricity demand depends on the average level of future electricity prices, the prices of substitute fuels, the replacement rates of appliances and equipment, and both the level and composition of aggregate economic activity. In the short run, given the stock of appliances and equipment, electricity demand is particularly sensitive to weather conditions since weather variations lead to large variations in heating and cooling demand. Short-run price and income elasticities are very low. On the supply side, from an investment perspective, there is uncertainty about future electricity prices, fuel prices, and the rates of entry of new and exit of old generating capacity. In the short run, there is uncertainty about unplanned outages of generating facilities and spot prices, reflecting the interactions of uncertain demand and uncertain supply. Uncertainty on the supply and demand side introduces volatility into spot prices over and above the natural variability in prices associated with variable demand and differences in the short-run marginal costs of operating diverse generating technologies. It will also lead to a least-cost investment portfolio that will have more nominal generating capacity (measured before taking account of forced outage rates) than the expected (mean) level of peak demand. The difference between the nominal generating capacity on the system and the expected peak demand is the system's expected 'reserve margin'.

Historically, when the electricity sector was composed of vertically integrated regulated monopolies, these aspects of uncertainty affected investment and operating decisions in important ways. From an investment perspective, long-term planning protocols reflected longer-term uncertainty on the supply and demand sides by establishing target 'reserve margins' over and above the expected level of peak electricity demand. These reserve margins were based on forecast levels of peak demand and forecast levels of capacity, assuming that all of the capacity would be available at the time of system peak. So, for example, in the USA, systems were planned to yield an average 'planned' reserve margin of 15–20 per cent. The reserve margin typically could include contracted demand response that the system operator could control but did not assume that demand would otherwise respond to rapid changes in real-time prices.

From a short-run operating perspective, the quantity of generating capacity scheduled to be available to supply electrical energy includes capacity used for frequency regulation, operating reserves and replacement reserves. In a typical system these 'operating reserves' account for an additional 10–12 per cent of generating capacity above the actual demand for energy at any particular time. Generating capacity is scheduled in this way as a result of the perceived need to have 'quick response' generation resources available to respond to short-term fluctuations in demand and unplanned outages of generating and transmission capacity, in order to keep the probability of non-price rationing (rolling blackouts) and cascading network outages (network collapse) very low. These operating and investment criteria are typically enshrined in various engineering reliability rules that have been carried over without many if any changes into the world of liberalized electricity markets.

The role of operating reserves in real electricity systems changes the static notion of a capacity constraint in real-time operations as typically reflected in simple market models (as, for example, in Figure 2). Capacity constraints are now 'soft' constraints that exceed the actual demand for energy on the system at any particular time. In normal operations, the generating capacity scheduled by the system operator to supply energy quickly through the wholesale energy and operating reserve markets will include about 10 per cent operating reserves of one type or another over and above the demand for energy. When this target level of operating reserves cannot be maintained because there is no additional generating capacity or demand response available for the system operator to call upon, an 'operating reserve emergency' or 'operating reserve shortage' will be declared. That is, the capacity constraint is effectively reached when the generating capacity available to the system operator falls below (say) 110 per cent of current demand for energy (or forecast demand for the next few hours). Accordingly, a more realistic characterization of capacity constraints (State 2 conditions) depicted in Figure 2 should include operating reserves in total capacity required to meet any given level of demand. Moreover, as I discuss in more detail presently, the 'soft' capacity constraint created by the operating reserve targets and system operator reliability protocols in the face of operating reserve constraints significantly complicates the price formation process during scarcity conditions.

4. Numerical Examples[7]

The simple economics of the efficient utilization, investment, and pricing for an electric-generating system is usefully clarified with a couple of simple numerical examples that, for simplicity, ignore uncertainty and public-goods aspects of reliability. Table 1 displays the parameters of three hypothetical electric-generating technologies with different capital cost/operating cost ratios and a hypothetical load duration curve representing the number of hours during the year the aggregate system demand or 'load' reaches any particular demand level.[8] The capital costs of a generating facility are fixed costs once the investment to build it has been made. The operating costs vary directly with the production of electrical energy from the generating facility.[9] There is a 'base- load' technology with relatively high capital costs (annualized) and low operating costs. Next there is an 'intermediate load' technology with lower capital costs and higher operating costs. Finally, there is a 'peaking' technology with still lower capital costs and higher operating costs. In the example, demand is equal to 10,000 MW for the entire year (8,760 hours) and is 22,000 MW for only one instant during the year. System demands between 10,000 and 22,000 MW are realized for between 8,760 hours and one instant during the year. For now, we will assume that the annual hourly system demand profile summarized in the load duration curve is not sensitive to prices. This assumption will be relaxed presently. We also ignore uncertainty on the demand side and the supply side for now.

Total costs (capital plus operating) per unit of generating capacity vary with the number of hours that the capacity is used to produce electricity each year. More importantly, from an investor's perspective, the comparative total costs of the three technologies depend upon how many hours each year it is anticipated that each will be economical to 'dispatch' to supply electricity. If a generating unit is expected to operate economically for 8,760 hours per year, the base-load technology is the lowest-cost choice. If a unit of generating capacity is expected to be economical to run, for

[7] These examples and the associated discussion of investment and dispatch behaviour should be familiar to anyone who has read the old literature on peak-load pricing and investment for electricity. See for example, Turvey (1968), Boiteux (1960), Joskow (1976), Crew and Kleinfdorfer (1976). Well-functioning markets should reproduce these idealized 'central planning' results.

[8] The arithmetic associated with the example is in continuous time though, for simplicity, I refer to 'hours' of load duration and generator utilization in 'hours' in the discussion.

[9] For the purposes of this example we ignore so-called fixed operation and maintenance expenses which are incurred each year simply to keep the plant available to produce electricity after the initial investment in it has been sunk.

Table 1. Hypothetical Electric Generation Technology Options and Load Duration Curve

Generation technology	Annualized capital costs $/MW/year	Operating costs $/MWh
Base-load	$240,000	$20
Intermediate	$160,000	$35
Peaking	$ 80,000	$80

Load duration curve (See Figure 1): $D = 22,000 - 1.37H$ $[0 < H \leq 8,760]$
where D = system load, and H = number of hours system load reaches a level D.

Figure 3

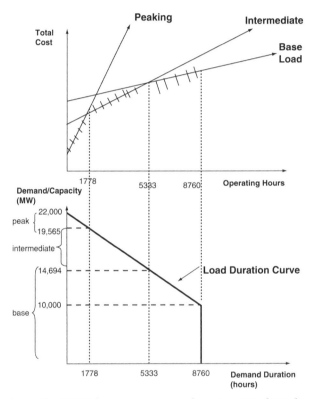

example, for only 4,000 hours per year, then intermediate-load technology is the lowest-cost choice. If the capacity is expected to be economical to run, for example, for 200 hours per year, then peaking technology is the least-cost option. These relationships for this numerical example are depicted in the top panel of Figure 3. The top panel yields the duration of demand at which each technology is economical from a total cost (capital plus operating) perspective. The lowest-cost mix of investments

Table 2. Least-cost Mix of Generating Technologies and Running Times for Hypothetical System

Generating technology	Capacity (MW)	Running hours	Total cost ($billions)
Base-load	14,694	5,333–8,760	$5.940
Intermediate	4,871	1,778–5,333	$1.385
Peaking	2,435	1–1,778	$0.366
Total	22,000		$7.694

in generating technology can then be determined by 'fitting' the total cost of building and operating each generating technology at alternative utilization rates to the load duration curve for the system (since electricity cannot be stored). This can be accomplished graphically by including the load duration curve in the bottom panel in Figure 3 and matching the technology in the top panel to the load duration in the bottom panel at which it is the least-cost technology. The quantity of capacity of each technology that makes up the least-cost generating investment portfolio can then be read off the vertical axis in the bottom panel of Figure 3 at the load duration cut-off points for each technology.

For this example, Table 2 displays the least-costs mix of generating capacity, the total costs (operating plus capital) for each technology and for the system in the aggregate, and the most efficient utilization duration (running hours) for each technology consistent with the parameters in Table 1 and the graphical representation in Figure 3. In this example, the least-cost mix includes a lot of base-load capacity, a much smaller amount of intermediate capacity, and an even smaller amount of peaking capacity.

One can think of the generating investment and utilization programme displayed in Table 2 as what an (imaginary) well-informed benevolent social planner would come up with. That is, this is a benchmark generating capacity investment portfolio against which market behaviour and performance can be compared. The question then for evaluating the behaviour and performance of a competitive wholesale market is whether and how market prices can provide incentives for decentralized decisions by profit-maximizing investors to replicate the efficient outcome.

It should be immediately obvious that except when demand reaches 22,000 MW and fully uses all of the generating capacity in the least-cost programme that the market will operate in a regime where there is 'excess capacity' as in Figure 1 (State 1) above. In a perfectly competitive market, prices will reflect short-run marginal operating costs under these 'State 1' conditions. When demand is less than or equal to 14,694 MW, base-load

Table 3. Short-run Marginal Cost Pricing Price Duration Schedule

Marginal technology	Short-run marginal cost $/MWh	Duration hours
Base-load	$20	3,427
Intermediate	$35	3,556
Peaking	$80	1,778

Table 4. Profitability of the Least-cost System with Short-run Marginal Cost Pricing of Energy Production

Generating technology	Revenues ($billions)	Total cost ($billons)	Net revenue shortfall	
			$(billions)	$/MW/year
Base load	$4.765	$5.940	($1.176)	$80,000
Intermediate	$0.996	$1.385	($0.390)	$80,000
Peaking	$0.173	$0.368	($0.195)	$80,000
Total	$5.934	$7.694	($1.760)	

capacity is marginal and the perfectly competitive market price will be $20/MWh. When demand lies between 14,694 MW and 19,511 MW the marginal unit is the intermediate technology and the perfectly competitive market price will be $35/MWh. Finally, as demand rises above 19,511 MW, peaking capacity is marginal and the perfectly competitive market price will be $80/MWh up to the point where capacity is fully utilized. Table 3 displays the number of hours that each technology is the marginal supplier. Let me defer for now a discussion of what the price would be when demand and capacity are both exactly 22,000 MW in this example.

Table 4 displays the revenues, total costs, and the difference between revenues and total costs (shortfall or net revenue gap) for each technology and in the aggregate under the short-run marginal-cost pricing scenario just discussed. It should be clear that short-run marginal-cost pricing yields revenues that are not nearly adequate to cover the total costs for any technology or total generating costs in the aggregate *at the efficient investment levels*. The shortfall turns out to be $80,000/MW of installed capacity for all technologies. Clearly, decentralized markets will not attract investment to support a least-cost generation investment portfolio under this short-run marginal-cost pricing scenario since it would be unprofitable. For investors to break even the market must somehow come up with another $80,000/MW of generating capacity or $1.760 billion (an increase in revenue of 30 per cent). Note for future reference that the required $80,000/MW of generating capacity is also exactly equal to the annualized capital charges for a megawatt of peaking capacity. Clearly

Table 5. Hypothetical Electric Generation System with Demand Response 'Technology'

Generation Technology	Annualized Capital Costs $/MW/Year	Operating Costs $/MWh
Base-load	$240,000	$20
Intermediate	$160,000	$35
Peaking	$80,000	$80
Demand response (VOLL)	0	$4,000

Load duration curve (see Figure 1): $D = 22{,}000 - 1.37H$ $[0 < H < 8{,}760]$
where D = system load, H = number of hours system load reaches a level D.

either some type of 'capacity' charge equal to the capital cost of a peaking turbine must be paid for each unit of capacity used at the time of system peak when capacity is fully utilized (effectively $80,000 per peak MWh consumed when demand is 22,000 MW), or some alternative market mechanism must emerge to increase energy prices significantly during some hours of the year.

To capture how (simplified) well-functioning competitive wholesale energy markets are supposed to function, we must introduce some demand elasticity into the example. It is convenient for the exposition here, and to capture the way system operators think about demand response, to conceptualize 'demand response' as a technology option through which demand is paid to reduce consumption. The payments reflect the marginal value consumers place on consuming less energy in the very short run—the VOLL (see Stoft, 2002, chs 2–5). Accordingly, I expand the numerical example to include an additional demand response technology which reflects a VOLL of $4,000/MWh. Table 5 expands the example reflected in Table 1 to include this fourth 'demand response' technology with a VOLL of $4,000/MWh. As I discuss presently, this value for VOLL is well within the range of available estimates used in practical applications (e.g. in the old England and Wales pool and in Australia).

We can now derive the least-cost mix of the four 'generating technologies', including demand response. The result is displayed in Table 6 which should be compared to Table 2. With the demand response option available, 28 MW of demand response is substituted for peaking capacity and demand with durations of between 1 second and 20.4 hours is now bought off the system by high 'scarcity' prices. This represents the realizations of 'State 2' conditions displayed in Figure 2. Demand response effectively flattens the very top of the load duration curve. This also leads to a change in the short-run marginal cost and distribution of the hours when each technology is marginal—see Table 7. There are now fewer hours when peaking capacity

Table 6. Least-cost Mix of Generating Technologies and Running Times for Hypothetical System with Demand Response

Generating technology	Capacity (MW)	Running hours ($billions)	Total cost
Base-load	14,694	5,333–8,760	$5.940
Intermediate	4,871	1,778–5,333	$1.385
Peaking	2,407	20.4–1,778	$0.3657
Demand response	28	0–20.4	$0.0011
Total	22,000		$7.692

Table 7. Short-run Marginal Cost and Scarcity Pricing Price Duration Schedule

Marginal technology	Short-run marginal cost $/MWh	Duration hours
Base-load	$20	3,427
Intermediate	$35	3,556
Peaking	$80	1,757
'Scarcity' (demand response)	$4,000	20

Table 8. Profitability of Short-run Marginal Cost and 'Scarcity' Pricing of Energy Production for Least-cost System

Generating technology	Revenues ($billions)	Total Cost ($billons)	Shortfall ($billions)	$/MW/year
Base-load	$5.940	$5.940	0	0
Intermediate	$1.385	$1.385	0	0
Peaking	$0.366	$0.366	0	0
Demand response	$0.0114	$0.0114	0	0

(marginal cost = 80) is marginal and as many as 20.4 hours when demand response is marginal (marginal cost = 4,000). As already noted, we refer to these 20.4 hours either as 'scarcity hours' or 'shortage hours'. Table 8 recalculates revenues, costs, and any shortfall in cost recovery using the expanded set of short-run marginal costs, associated prices, and load durations. The major difference between Table 8 and Table 4 is that *all* generating capacity now receives $4,000/MWh during about 20 hours of 'scarcity' conditions. As indicated by Table 8, with 'scarcity pricing' during only 20 hours in the year, each generating technology now covers its total costs, as does the system as a whole.

The 'scarcity price' of $4,000/MWh may seem like either a lot to pay for avoiding reducing electricity consumption or (equivalently) too small a number of hours of the year for the system to be in 'scarcity' or 'shortage' conditions. In this example, if we reduced the value of lost load to

$2,500/MWh, demand response would be triggered for about 33 hours and the maximum quantity of demand response would be 45 MW, a qualitatively similar result.[10] It is important to recognize that the VOLL in this case reflects a very short-run demand elasticity and (typically) a loss of load with little or no notice to the retail consumer and lasting for a few hours. Measuring the VOLL empirically, absent meaningful market valuation data, is a very difficult exercise. It will depend on the nature of the consumer activities interrupted, the notice that consumers are given before an interruption takes place (Joskow and Tirole, 2006), whether the interruptions are voluntary through market arrangements or involuntary through rolling black-outs, and the duration of the outage.

Nevertheless, there have been numerous efforts to measure the VOLL. Bushnell (2005, p. 14) points to a range of estimates between $2,000 and $50,000/MWh. Cramton and Stoft (2006, p. 33) suggest that conventional 'planning' reliability criteria based on keeping the probability of rolling black-outs very low imply a value of lost load of $267,000/MWh. The number of 'scarcity' or 'shortage' hours derived in the example presented here are also similar to those experienced in practice (Cramton and Stoft (2006, p. 40). Accordingly, the numbers used in this numerical example are well within the range of available estimates from customer surveys and those implied by historical electricity system behaviour and are probably on the low side.

Clearly, the availability of demand response (demand elasticity) allows supply and demand to be balanced at a price that reflects consumers' willingness to pay for more or less supply in the very short run and satisfies a break-even constraint necessary to attract investment consistent with a least-cost generation investment and operating equilibrium. For future reference, note that the revenues earned under scarcity conditions from 'scarcity pricing' of energy in this example represent a large fraction of the quasi-rents necessary to cover the capital costs of the least-cost quantity and mix of generating capacity. Table 9 displays the fraction of the quasi-rents earned from market revenues under 'State 1' short-run marginal-cost pricing conditions and 'State 2' under scarcity conditions. Both sources of rents are required to cover the capital costs of all three supply technologies that make up the least-cost supply portfolio. For base-load technologies 33 per cent of the rents come from scarcity pricing, for intermediate-load technology 50 per cent, and for peaking technology 100 per cent.

---

[10] If I had drawn the load duration curve in the example to have a higher 'needle peak' demand lasting 20–30 hours, the quantity of demand response would, of course, be larger. The cut-off operating duration would not change, however.

Table 9. Quasi-rent Distribution with Marginal Cost and 'Scarcity' Pricing for Hypothetical Least-cost System

Technology	Net revenues earned	
	Marginal-cost pricing hours (%)	Scarcity pricing hours (%)
Base-load	67	33
Intermediate	50	50
Peaking	0	100

The failure to include active price-related demand response in this way or to keep prices from rising to $4,000, for example by imposing price caps, does not imply that *no* investment will be profitable. Rather it implies that the efficient quantity and mix of generating capacity will not be profitable and, in a market context, an efficient investment programme would not be sustainable. Absent price-related demand response, the system operator will have to find some alternative way to ration demand at the time of system peak and define some default price or price cap at which suppliers will be compensated for energy and operating reserves under these conditions. This is the case because absent the availability of demand response to clear the market when demand reaches 22,000 MW, there is a vertical demand and vertical supply curve and there will be no well-defined market clearing price. Investment will adapt to whatever default pricing arrangements are chosen in this case. Assume that the system operator can implement a non-price rational scheme (i.e. rolling black-outs) when capacity constraints are reached to balance demand with the capacity constraint, and sets the default price or price cap at $500/MWh under these conditions. Under these assumptions, an equilibrium in which generation suppliers can cover their total costs is characterized by less peaking capacity, less total capacity, and nearly 200 hours of rolling black-outs each year, or ten times more hours of rolling black-outs than in the example with demand re-sponse. The lower the price cap, the less investment will be forthcoming and the more hours of shortages requiring non-price rationing (rolling black-outs) will be necessary.

While these numerical examples are static, the presence of uncertainty does not change the basic economics of investment and operation discussed above. Investment decisions would, in principle, reflect the expected values of the relevant variables on the demand and supply sides, including any risk-bearing costs borne by consumers and/or investors. The VOLL would be reflected in both investment and operating decisions. Uncertainty will also introduce volatility into both prices and profitability (quasi-rents) realized in spot energy and operating reserve markets. When peak demand is at the high end of the probability distribution peak period prices and profits will be relatively high and vice versa. However, in a least-cost equilibrium the expected net revenues earned over time during 'scarcity' conditions should still be equal to the carrying costs of a peaker, and the similar quasi-rent results for the other technologies will also hold over time. As I will discuss, however, price formation during scarcity conditions in the presence of operating reserves, related reliability constraints and discretionary behaviour by system operators can complicate significantly the market price formation process and the production of quasi-rents consistent with a least-cost investment portfolio that meets administratively determined reliability criteria.

5. Is There an Investment Problem?

At first blush, some may find it surprising that policy-makers are concerned that wholesale market mechanisms will not provide adequate incentives for investment in new generating capacity. The early experience with electricity sector liberalization during the 1990s suggested that competitive wholesale markets could and would mobilize adequate (or more than adequate) investment in new generating capacity. Substantial amounts of capital were mobilized during the late 1990s to support construction of new generating capacity in many countries that had implemented reforms. In the USA, over 230,000 MW of new generating capacity went into service between 1997 and 2005, most of it merchant capacity burning natural gas, an increase of 30 per cent from the stock of generating capacity that existed in the USA in 1996. The net summer capability of generating capacity in the USA increased over 25 per cent between 1997 and 2005, after taking account of both new entry and retirements (see Table 10). About 40 per cent of the stock of generating plants in service in England and Wales at the time its electricity sector was restructured was replaced with modern efficient combined-cycle gas-turbine (CCGT) technology between 1990 and 2002 as old, mostly coal-burning, generators were retired and replaced by what was expected to be less costly CCGT capacity. Many other countries implementing reforms during the 1990s, including Argentina, Chile, and Australia, also attracted significant investment in new generating capacity (Jamasb, 2002) after the reforms were initiated.

Table 10. US Generating Capacity Additions, 1997–2005

Year	New generating capacity (MW)
1997	4,000
1998	6,500
1999	10,500
2000	23,500
2001	48,000
2002	55,000
2003	50,000
2004	20,000
2005	15,000
Total	230,000

Total US generating Capacity (MW net summer capacity):

1996	776,000
2005	980,000

Source: US Energy Information Administration.

So, why are policy-makers so concerned now? First, we should recognize that liberalization has evolved in much of Europe during a period when there was significant excess generating capacity, Spain and Italy being the major exceptions. Capacity constraints have not been on the policy-makers' radar screen until recently. Even in England and Wales, the quantity of generating capacity in service today is not much greater than it was in 1990, with most of the investment in generating capacity during the 1990s being stimulated by opportunities to replace the inefficient stock of old generators operated by the state-owned Central Electricity Generating Board at the time of privatization, expectations that natural gas prices would stay low, long-term contracts entered into by retail suppliers early in the UK's liberalization programme, and the high prices for energy and capacity payments available in the wholesale market, inflated by the exercise of market power by the dominant generators (Wolfram, 1999). These investments were not the result of a significant need for new generating capacity to meet rapidly growing peak demand.

Second, the environment for financing new generating capacity has changed dramatically in the last few years as a result of financial problems faced by merchant trading and generating companies in Europe, the USA, Asia, and Latin America (Jamasb, 2002; Joskow, 2005; Sioshansi and Pfaffenberger, 2006). Potential investors have gone to great lengths to convince policy-makers that they will not provide investment funds for merchant generating capacity in the future under traditional project-financing arrangements without major changes in the behaviour and performance of wholesale markets. Whether they are crying wolf or signalling the reality of investor views, their arguments have increased policy-makers' concerns about 'resource adequacy' or 'supply security'.

Most importantly, as demand has grown, as older plants retire, and as wholesale market prices have risen, policy-makers in many countries see little evidence of a response to these market signals in the form of investment in new merchant generating capacity. The situation in the USA has attracted particular concern from policy-makers in those areas of the country where the electricity sectors have been liberalized and rely on merchant investment. After peaking at 55,000 MW of new capacity entering service in the USA in 2002, the quantity of new generating capacity entering service in the USA and the quantity under construction has steadily declined. In 2005, only 15,000 MW of new generating capacity entered service, most of which was built either by municipal utilities that have not been subject to restructuring and competition reforms, by traditional vertically integrated utilities in states that have not liberalized their electricity sectors, or was wind projects that benefit from special subsidies and contractual arrangements. Concerns about investment in additional generating capacity to meet growing demand have been raised in New England, New York, the PJM regional transmission organization (RTO), and California. System operators in the northeastern USA and California are projecting shortages and increases in power supply emergencies starting in 2–3 years, recognizing that since developing, permitting, and completing new generating plants takes several years, if there is little under construction today little will come out of the pipeline 2 or 3 years from now.

On the one hand, a market response that leads prices (adjusted for fuel costs) and profits to fall and investment to decline dramatically when there is excess capacity is just the response that we would be looking for from a competitive market. At least some of the noise about investment incentives is coming from owners of existing merchant generating plants who would just like to see higher prices and profits. On the other hand, numerous analyses of the performance of organized energy-only wholesale markets in the USA indicate that they do not appear to produce enough net revenues to support investment in new generating capacity in the right places and consistent with the administrative reliability criteria relied upon by system operators and regulators.

The theoretical framework and the numerical examples in the last section make it clear that in order to attract investment to balance supply and demand with traditional levels of reliability, competitive wholesale markets must produce 'rents' over and above the short-run marginal cost

Table 11. Net Energy and Ancillary Services Revenues, New Combustion Turbine Peaking Plant in PJM, 1999-2005

Year	Simulated net energy and ancillary services revenue $/MW/year
1999	64,313
2000	18,724
2001	41,517
2002	25,480
2003	14,402
2004	10,311
2005	17,989
Average	27,534

Note: Annualized 20-year fixed cost ~ $70,000–80,000/MW/year.
Source: *2005 State of the Market Report*, pp. 124–32, PJM Interconnection.

of operating generating facilities in order to provide compensation for the capital costs of these facilities. Prices and the associated revenues produced during 'scarcity' conditions when generating capacity is fully utilized are especially important. In particular, over time, wholesale prices must produce rents greater than or equal to the capital costs associated with marginal investments in new peaking capacity consistent with the least-cost quantity and mix of generating capacity to balance supply and demand. Accordingly, a common test for whether wholesale markets are providing adequate price signals is to calculate the net revenues (quasi-rents) that would have been earned by a hypothetical investment in new peaking capacity from economical sales of energy and operating reserves over a period of several years.

The experience in the PJM RTO in the USA is fairly typical. Table 11 displays the net revenue that a hypothetical new combustion turbine would have earned from wholesale energy market plus ancillary services revenues in PJM if it were dispatched optimally to reflect its marginal running costs in each year from 1999 to 2005. In no year would a new peaking turbine have earned enough net revenues from sales of energy and ancillary services to cover the annualized capital costs of a new generating unit and, on average, the net revenues contributed only about 40 per cent of the annualized capital costs of a new peaking unit.[11] Based on energy market revenues alone, it would not be rational for an investor to invest in new combustion turbine capacity in PJM based on 6 years of historical experience. Similar calculations of net energy market revenues have been performed for hypothetical investments in new CCGT capacity and pulverized coal capacity in PJM.

[11] These calculations are probably an overestimate of the net revenues that a new peaking unit would realize in practice since that assumes 'perfect' economic dispatch and does not take account of various operating constraints (PJM, 2006, pp. 128–32).

These calculations also indicate that energy market revenues alone do not come close to covering the capital costs of new investments in these technologies either (PJM, 2006, 127–32). This net revenue gap—the missing-money problem (Cramton and Stoft, 2006)—is a major deterrent to investment in new generating capacity in the organized wholesale markets in the USA today.

As I discuss in more detail in the next section, one solution to the 'missing money' problem in the USA has been to impose capacity obligations on LSEs,[12] to create a market for the associated qualifying capacity, and in this way to create another stream of revenues for generators that it has been hoped would make up for the net revenue gap in the energy market. For example, LSEs might be required to have contracts for qualifying generating capacity equal to 118 per cent of their peak load each year. The 18 per cent reflects a capacity reserve margin defined to meet reliability criteria established by the reliability authorities in the area in which the LSEs purchase power. There is then a market for qualifying capacity that defines capacity prices. Indeed, PJM has always had capacity obligations which it carried over into its competitive market design.

In theory, capacity prices should adjust to clear the market consistent with the reserve margin chosen and make up for the 'missing money' (Joskow and Tirole, 2006). However, even adding in capacity-related revenues in PJM during the 6-year period covered by Table 11, the total net revenues (energy plus capacity-related revenues) that would have been earned by a new peaking unit over this 6-year period were significantly less than the capital costs that investors would need to expect to recover to make investment in new generating capacity profitable. The average annual capacity market revenue for a combustion turbine in PJM from 1999 to 2005 was about $13,000/MW/year (PJM, 2006, pp. 230–2). Adding the capacity market revenues to the net revenues from sales of energy and ancillary services in Table 11 brings the total net revenues for a hypothetical peaking unit to about $40,000/MW/year for 1999–2005, roughly $35,000/MW/year short of the annualized capital costs of new peaking capacity. Again, similar results are revealed for CCGT and pulverized-coal technology investments.

The missing-money phenomenon is not unique to PJM. Every organized market in the USA exhibits a similar gap between net revenues produced by energy markets and the capital costs of investing in new capacity measured over several years' time (FERC, 2005, p. 60; Joskow, 2005; New York ISO, 2005a, pp. 22–5). Indeed, since 1998 there is not a

---

[12] LSEs include distribution companies with retail supply obligations and competitive retail electricity suppliers.

single year when energy market revenues covered the annualized capital costs of a peaking turbine. There is still a significant gap when capacity payments are included. The only exception to the latter result appears to be New York City where prices for energy and capacity collectively appear to be sufficient to support new investment, though new investment in New York may be much more costly than assumed in these analyses (FERC, 2005, p. 60). Moreover, a large fraction of the net revenue estimated for investment in generating capacity in New York City comes from capacity payments rather than energy market revenues (New York ISO, 2005*a*, p. 23).

One potential explanation of these results is that they simply imply that there is excess generating capacity in these systems and the low net revenue results are simply signalling that too much capacity has come into service. That is, this is an indicator of excess generating capacity. However, this result is inconsistent with the behaviour of system operators in the northeastern USA, California, and in other countries which are forecasting capacity shortages in the near term and are taking actions to stimulate more investment. For example, the New England ISO forecasts significant capacity needs beginning in 2008, but there is almost no new generating capacity under construction at the present time. Moreover, in New England the energy and capacity markets are not even producing enough net revenues to keep a significant amount of generating capacity from closing down (typically permanently). The New England ISO has found it necessary to sign special 'reliability contracts' for up to 7,000 MW of existing generating capacity to keep it in service (ISO New England, 2005, p. 80). PJM also forecasts that there will be a need for a significant quantity of new generating capacity to meet demand in the next few years. The generating capacity now under construction does not satisfy these forecast needs, which are magnified by plans for old generating units to retire. Thus, the failure of wholesale markets to provide adequate revenues is the likely cause of the failure of investors to begin to build new generating facilities to match forecasts of resource needs.

A more subtle counter-argument is that policy-makers are overestimating the need for additional generating capacity because these estimates are based on old reliability criteria that do not properly reflect consumer valuations. That is, the reliability criteria used by the reliability organizations in the USA (and other countries, since they are very similar) are inconsistent with the marginal VOLL to consumers during these periods. According to this view, the market is signalling that consumers do not want to pay for this much reliability and the market, rather than reliability organizations, should make that choice. It may very well be that reliability targets require more generating capacity than consumers are willing to pay for and that these engineering reliability criteria should be re-evaluated. However, as I discuss further below, at the present time it is unlikely that market mechanisms have yet evolved to produce the appropriate level of operating reserves or capacity margins consistent with consumer valuations of lost load resulting from potential rolling black-outs and network collapses. Moreover, reducing reliability in these dimensions is not politically appealing and, in the USA, runs counter to the provisions of the Energy Policy Act of 2005 which seek to strengthen, harmonize, and enforce traditional reliability criteria more aggressively.

6. What are the Causes of the Missing-money Problem?

The ultimate source of the missing-money problem is that spot market prices do not rise high enough during 'scarcity' hours to produce adequate quasi-rents to cover the capital costs of investment in an efficient level and mix of generating capacity. Since prices for forward contracts reflect the expected value of spot market prices (plus any risk-bearing costs) via intertemporal arbitrage, any truncation of the upper tail of the distribution of spot prices will be reflected in forward prices that are below the efficient level as well. But why do not wholesale markets produce adequate revenues? There are a number of wholesale market imperfections, regulatory constraints on prices, as well as procedures used by system operators to deal with operating reserve shortages that appear collectively to suppress spot market prices for energy and operating reserves below efficient prices during the small number of hours in a typical year when they should be very high.

To understand the sources of the missing-money problem we must examine in more detail how system operators in the organized markets in the USA balance supply and demand on real electric power networks, especially during 'scarcity' or 'operating reserve shortage' hours. In a market context, the attributes of the price formation process during these operating reserve shortage conditions is critical for understanding whether and how the wholesale market provides appropriate price signals to attract investment. If it were the case that operating reserve constraints were always met by variations in prices that kept supply and demand in balance continuously, as in simple theoretical models of electric power systems with demand response, then there would be no problem. Indeed, there would be no need for system operators to establish operating reserve and other reliability criteria. The market could be relied upon to do so. However, at least at the present time, there are a number of market imperfections that make it unlikely that markets will lead to this happy result.

(*a*) Only a tiny fraction of electricity consumers and electricity demand during peak hours can see real time prices *and* react quickly enough from the system operator's perspective to large sudden price spikes to keep supply and demand in balance consistent with operating reliability constraints. Neither the metering nor the control response equipment is in place except at a small number of locations. As a result, on a typical US network 98+ per cent of peak demand is effectively price inelastic in the time frame that system operators are looking for during scarcity conditions. Since supply is also effectively up against capacity constraints during operating reserve deficiency conditions we face a situation where we have a vertical demand curve and a vertical supply curve. Under these conditions system operators in the USA resort to non-price rationing of demand (rolling black-outs) to maintain minimum operating reserve levels and the frequency, voltage, stability, and other physical engineering operating reliability criteria.

(*b*) In and of itself, the limited availability of real time meters and associated customer monitoring and response equipment is not a fatal problem, however. LSEs could enter into 'priority rationing contracts' (Chao and Wilson, 1987) with retail consumers that would specify in advance the level of wholesale market prices at which customers would allow the system operator to implement demand curtailments. Retail customers entering into such contracts would receive a lower price per unit consumed on their standard meters (Joskow and Tirole, 2005). They would not have to monitor real time prices themselves. This would be done (ultimately) by the system operator through a parallel contract with the retail consumer's LSE. However, priority rationing contracts require the system operator to be able to control the flows of power that go to individual customers and to have the capability to curtail individual customer demand on short notice. Except for the very largest customers, control over power flows does not go this far down into the distribution system, and system operators can only curtail demand in relatively large 'zones' composed of many customers (Joskow and Tirole, 2005). That is, individual consumers cannot choose their individual preferred level of reliability when rolling black-outs are called by the system operator; their lights go off along with their neighbours' light. Zonal rationing is especially problematic in the presence of retail competition (Joskow and

Tirole, 2005, 2006) and gives reliability as reflected in the probability and duration of demand curtailments' collective-good attributes.

(c) System operators hold operating reserves for two reasons. One is to keep the probability of 'controlled' non-price rationing of demand (rolling black-outs) low. The other is to keep the probability of a network collapse, such as those that occurred in the northeastern USA and in Italy in 2003, very low. When there is a network collapse there is both excess demand and excess supply because the network infrastructure to allow demand and supply to interact has collapsed. The outages are widespread and restoring the system to operational status can be time consuming and costly. Nevertheless, since the market also collapses in these situations, prices are effectively zero. Individual consumers can do nothing to escape the consequences of a network collapse, aside from installing their own on-site generating facilities. Nor can individual generators profit from 'scarcity' during a network collapse. As a result, there is no way for market mechanisms fully to capture the expected social costs of a network collapse. Joskow and Tirole (2006) argue that this gives operating reserves public-good attributes. As a result, the efficient level of operating reserves will not be provided by market mechanisms but must be determined through some administrative process that reflects the probability and costs of a network collapse.

These three attributes of electric power networks give reliability public-good attributes. Accordingly, even if the other market, regulatory, and behavioural imperfections are resolved we cannot count on 'the market' alone to provide the efficient level of reliability.

(d) Rolling black-outs resulting from a shortage of generating capacity are extremely rare on electric power systems in developed countries.[13] Almost all of the 'scarcity hours' are realized during operating reserve deficiency conditions, when the system lies between the target level of operating reserves and the minimum level that triggers non-price rationing of demand. The value for additional scarcity rents earned under scarcity conditions is uncertain since they depend on the operating protocols implemented by the system operator during operating reserve deficiencies and the associated price-formation process.[14] Once price-responsive demand has been exhausted, the price-formation process

[13] Almost all black-outs experienced by consumers result from equipment failures on the distribution network.
[14] The sequence of events and system operator behaviour leading up to the rolling black-outs in Texas on 17 April 2006 provide an extremely informative insight into system operations during such scarcity conditions (Public Utility Commission of Texas, 2006).

during these conditions is extremely sensitive to small decisions made by the system operator and it is not evident that a market mechanism exists to produce the efficient price levels during these hours (Joskow and Tirole, 2006). And a close examination of system-operator protocols and behaviour during scarcity conditions makes it fairly clear that it is highly unlikely that efficient 'scarcity prices' will emerge during operating reserve shortage contingencies. I offer two examples here.

The last thing that system operators typically do when there is an operating reserve deficiency prior to implementing rolling black-outs is to reduce system voltage by 5 per cent. This reduces system demand and helps the system operator to keep operating reserves above the minimum level that would trigger rolling black-outs. However, reducing demand has the effect of *reducing* wholesale prices relative to their level at normal voltage and demand levels, just as the system is approaching a non-price rationing state. Moreover, voltage reductions are not free. If they were free we could just operate the system at a lower voltage. Voltage reductions lead lights to dim, equipment to run less efficiently, on-site generators to turn themselves on, etc. These are costs that are widely dispersed among electricity consumers and are not reflected in market prices. Thus, the marginal social cost (in the aggregate) of voltage reductions is not reflected in market prices. As long as voltage reductions are employed in this way, market price signals will lead to underinvestment in reliability because the social costs of voltage reductions are not internalized.

Second, markets for operating reserves typically define the relevant products (e.g. spinning reserves) fairly crudely. For example, spinning reserves may be defined as supplies from 'idle' generating capacity that can be made available to the system operator within 10 minutes. The market for spinning reserves may not have a locational dimension to it or it may reflect a very crude distinction between geographic zones. Generator attributes are typically much more differentiated within the general product definitions used in organized wholesale markets in the USA. The system operator may find it necessary to call on generating capacity that responds in, say, 2 minutes at particular locations on the network, to maintain the physical parameters of the network. The system operator typically has information about a more detailed set of generator characteristics than is reflected in product market definitions and can act upon this information when it thinks that it is necessary to do so to avoid rolling black-outs or a network collapse. When supplies from generators with more specific characteristics are needed by the system operator, it may rely on bilateral out-of-market (OOM) contracts to secure these supplies from specific generators and then dispatch the associated generating units as 'must run' facilities at the bottom of the bid-stack. This behaviour can inefficiently depress wholesale market prices received for energy and operating reserves by other suppliers in the market. The behaviour of the New England ISO during a severe cold snap in January 2004 is an example of this behaviour and its consequences (FERC, 2005, and ISO New England, 2004). Despite the fact that the New England electric power network was severely stressed during this period, prices did not rise to levels that produced market-based quasi-rents for either CCGTs or peaking turbines; the spark spreads were zero or negative.

(e) The limited amount of real-time demand response in the wholesale market leads to spot market demand that is extremely inelastic. Especially during high demand periods as capacity constraints are approached, this creates significant opportunities for suppliers to exercise unilateral market power. In the USA, the Federal Energy Regulatory Commission (FERC) has adopted a variety of general and locational price mitigation measures to respond to potential market power problems in spot markets for energy and operating reserves. These mitigation measures include general bid caps (e.g. $1,000/MWh) applicable to all wholesale energy and operating reserve prices, location-specific bid caps (e.g. marginal cost plus 10 per cent), and other bid-mitigation and supply-obligation (e.g. must offer obligations) measures.

Unfortunately, the supply and demand conditions which should lead to high spot market prices in a well functioning *competitive* wholesale market (i.e. when there is true *competitive* 'scarcity') are also the conditions when *market power* problems are likely to be most severe (as capacity constraints are approached in the presence of inelastic demand, suppliers' unilateral incentives and ability to increase prices above competitive levels, perhaps by creating contrived scarcity, increase). Accordingly, uniform price caps will almost inevitably 'clip' some high prices that truly reflect competitive supply scarcity and consumer valuations for energy and reliability as they endeavour to constrain high prices that reflect market power. They may also fail to mitigate fully supra-competitive prices during other hours (Joskow and Tirole, 2006).

If there is a significant unmitigated market-power problem, then wholesale prices should be too high. But the analysis above suggests that wholesale prices are too low, not too high, on average. As a result, many economists assume that the primary source of the 'missing-money' problem must be the price caps and related market-power mitigation procedures imposed by regulators. That is, that the efforts to mitigate market power have had the effect of suppressing energy prices too much, especially during scarcity conditions when prices should be very high.[15]

The problem with blaming the entire problem on the price caps is that when one examines the full distribution of energy prices in the organized US wholesale energy and operating reserve markets over the last 6 years it is evident that the price caps, which do in fact appear too low compared to estimates of the VOLL, *are rarely binding constraints* (Joskow, 2005; New England ISO, 2005; New York ISO, 2005a; PJM, 2006). Even during most 'scarcity hours', market prices are below the price caps. Accordingly, it is unlikely that the price caps are the only source of the missing-money problem. I believe that the effects (not the goal) of the other system-operator behavioural factors discussed above play a much more important role in suppressing prices during scarcity conditions in the organized wholesale markets in the USA than do the price caps on energy and operating reserves.

There also exist *de facto* price caps on capacity prices in those wholesale markets in the USA that have implemented capacity obligations and associated capacity markets. The way these markets have worked historically, the penalty imposed on LSEs for not contracting for adequate capacity, has been a monthly or annual deficiency charge assessed by the system operator. The deficiency charge is typically calculated based on the annualized lifetime capital cost of a new peaking turbine using a set of assumptions about the cost of capital, depreciation, plant life, and taxes. This approach appears to be consistent with the discussion of the quasi-rents that must be earned by a peaking turbine to make competitive entry financially attractive and to support least-cost investment in all technology options. In practice, however, it is not, because it assumes implicitly that capacity will earn net revenues equal to the deficiency charge in each year of its economic life.

The capacity obligations that are central to these systems have historically relied on hard reserve margin criteria (e.g. 18 per cent of peak load). Due to uncertainty on both the demand and supply sides, even if the target reserve margin is hit on average over a period of years, there will be some years when the actual reserve margin is greater than the target and some years when it is less than the target. In those wholesale markets with capacity obligations, capacity prices have tended to rise to the level of the deficiency charge during periods when supplies are tight and then drop to zero or close to it during periods when the reserve margin exceeds the

---

[15] Price caps that constrain prices to levels below competitive market prices in some periods but allow prices to rise above competitive market levels in other periods do not necessarily lead to a shortage of generating capacity. In this case, however, price caps would induce the wrong mix of generating capacity.

target. On average, the revenues are then significantly less than the lifetime carrying charges of a peaker. If the distribution of realized reserve margins is symmetrical around the target, generators will earn only 50 per cent of the capital costs of a peaker over time. Thus, by calculating the deficiency charge in this way, a *de facto* price cap is placed on capacity prices as well. This is the primary reason why traditional capacity obligations and capacity markets have not solved the missing-money problem.

7. Other Possible Deterrents to Generation Investment

While in my view the missing-money problem is the most serious deterrent to investment in generating capacity, other financial barriers to efficient such investment have also been identified by various commentators. Wall Street investment bankers routinely argue that investment in new generating capacity will not be forthcoming because prices in wholesale spot markets are too volatile and there are inadequate opportunities for investors to find counterparties willing to enter into forward contracts of 10 or more years' duration to allow investors to hedge market risks. They claim that absent long-term contracts with creditworthy buyers, it will be difficult to find financing for any merchant generating project.

I do not know of any good theoretical reason why market price volatility or price uncertainty *per se* should make it impossible to finance new generating facilities if the missing-money problem is solved. Perhaps price uncertainty will affect the cost of capital used by investors to evaluate projects, but this would just increase the prices and quasi-rents that the market would have to produce to stimulate investment. Investors finance oil refineries, oil and gas drilling platforms, cruise ships, and many other costly capital projects where there is considerable price uncertainty without the security of long-term contracts.

One attribute of electricity markets that may have implications for the efficient allocation of market price risk between investors, intermediaries, and consumers is the retail procurement framework that has accompanied the liberalization of wholesale electricity markets. In the USA and several other countries, comprehensive retail competition programmes have been created but have been slow to evolve. Large fractions of system demand continue to be served by incumbent distributors with default service obligations and who contract for power with relatively short-term

contracts. The contracting requirements are driven by regulatory requirements rather than through market-based allocations of risk. There is no
reason to believe that they are optimal. As retail competition matures and
retail suppliers with large diversified portfolios emerge, they are likely to
be more willing voluntarily to take on longer-term commitments to buy
power from generators (or build their own generating portfolios) if this
can reduce the prices they must pay to buy power over time. While
individual retail consumers may only have 1-, 2-, or 3-year contracts, a
diversified portfolio of retail customers, especially smaller customers who
are reasonably 'sticky', would provide a retail supplier with the kind of
stable demand base that it would need to make it potentially attractive
to sign long-term supply contracts.

This observation leads directly to questions about the optimal contractual, financing market structure for electricity suppliers at wholesale and
retail. The initial model for independent power producers that emerged in
the USA after the Public Utility Regulatory Policy Act (PURPA) went into
effect in the early 1980s, was based on long-term purchase contracts
between independent power producers and regulated utilities. Project
financing with high debt/equity ratios secured by these contracts was the
financing framework of choice. The next wave of investment in merchant
generating capacity beginning in the late 1990s relied on the project
financing model but without the long-term contracts. When wholesale
markets collapsed after 2001 many of those projects could not meet their
debt obligations and many went bankrupt or were subject to alternative
financial restructurings.

I believe that the merchant investment model based on wholesale
generating companies relying on highly leveraged individual project financing arrangements is likely to be poorly suited to a competitive wholesale and retail electricity market framework. Partial vertical integration
between retail supply and generation ownership (but not transmission
and distribution) combined with diversified portfolios of spot, short-,
and medium-term contracts with independent suppliers to make up for
the rest of the retail supplier's wholesale power requirements, is likely to
be a superior organizational form for financing investment and dealing
with imperfections in wholesale spot markets, including the potential
'hold-up' problems that I discuss presently. Such vertically integrated
retail supply and generation companies are likely to be large firms with
substantial balance sheets and rely primarily on balance-sheet financing
for their generation portfolios. The power supply industry will look more
like the oil and gas industry, with a relatively small number of large

vertically integrated firms, and a large number of 'small' independent generating companies. This industrial structure is gradually emerging in the USA and Europe. There need not be a conflict between competition goals and an industry with large vertically integrated power supplies as long as the firms' wholesale and retail supply businesses are sufficiently dispersed geographically that there are several competing suppliers in any region and the transmission network is owned and operated independently. However, in practice there may be a conflict between vertical integration and competition in regional markets where there is a dominant vertically integrated incumbent and associated barriers to entry of competing vertically integrated suppliers.

A final reason why it may be difficult to finance investments in new generating capacity are concerns about opportunistic behaviour by government regulators or system operators that may affect spot-market prices at critical times over the life of a new generating unit. As discussed in detail above, a large fraction of the net revenues or quasi-rents from sales of energy in spot electricity markets required to cover the costs of capital investments is produced in a very small number of hours each year when capacity is fully used. Moreover, due to uncertainty on the demand and supply sides, these hours will not appear uniformly from year to year but will fluctuate widely. One year it may be 80 hours and another year 5 hours of scarcity conditions (Joskow, 2005; Cramton and Stoft, 2006, p. 33). For a peaking plant, all of its net revenues are derived under these conditions. Accordingly, investors must be very concerned about actions by regulators or discretionary behaviour by system operators that might have the effect of constraining prices in exactly those few hours with very high prices when investors expect to earn most of the net revenues required to cover their capital investment costs. It is now widely recognized that opportunism problems, whether by counterparties or government entities, can lead to under-investment and that credible long-term contracts or vertical integration are efficient institutional responses to opportunism problems (Williamson, 1979; Hart, 1995; Joskow, 1987). From the investor's perspective, long-term power supply contracts with credit-worthy buyers can allow them to shift this risk to buyers.

8. Policy Responses

Numerous policy proposals have been made to fix what is now widely viewed in the USA as the failure of organized wholesale power markets to provide adequate incentives to stimulate investment in new generating capacity to balance supply and demand efficiently, consistent with system reliability criteria. I focus primarily on the missing-money or net revenue gap problem here. However, I also take into account related concerns about market-power mitigation, price volatility, and opportunism. The proposed policy reforms involve a combination of mechanisms to improve the performance of spot markets so that prices will come closer to reflecting the (uncertain) VOLL during scarcity conditions and a forward market for reserves that reflects the reliability targets specified by regulators. These reforms involve price triggers and quantity targets and are related to the application of a combination of prices and quantities to controlling pollution discussed by Roberts and Spence (1976).

8.1 *Improving the Performance of Organized Spot Markets*

The fundamental source of the net revenue gap problem is the failure of spot energy and operating reserve markets to perform in practice the way they are supposed to perform in theory. It is natural to focus on improving the performance of these markets. While I believe that the performance of spot wholesale energy markets can be improved, I do not believe that all of the problems, especially those associated with the market's provision of reliability, implementation of engineering reliability rules, and the associated behaviour of system operators during scarcity conditions, can be fully resolved quickly—if ever. Nevertheless, improving the behaviour and performance of spot wholesale markets for energy and operating reserves can be a constructive component of a broader set of reforms.

RAISE THE PRICE CAPS AND HIT THEM DURING SCARCITY CONDITIONS

The $1,000/MWh price cap in effect in most of the organized markets in the USA ($250/MWh in California) is a completely arbitrary number that is clearly below what the competitive market clearing price would be under most scarcity conditions (State 2). However, as I have discussed, the $1,000 price caps are rarely binding constraints in the organized US markets, so that increasing them alone would not have much of an impact on the net revenue gap problem. Increasing the price caps to reflect reasonable estimates of VOLL would also make it more attractive and profitable for suppliers to exercise market power in spot energy and operating reserve markets. Nevertheless, there are good reasons to increase the price caps to reflect reasonable values of VOLL if this is combined with changes to the wholesale market price-formation process, more reliance on other approaches to mitigating market power, and continued reliance on market monitors as in all of the US ISOs.

To make the higher price caps meaningful contributors to the net revenue gap problem, and to deal with the price-formation problems that emerge when system operators implement reliability protocols when there are capacity constraints, I would propose that whenever a system operator issues a notice that operating reserve deficiency protocols will be implemented the wholesale market prices for energy and operating reserves be moved immediately to the price cap. This is a rough and ready mechanism to get prices up to where they should be under scarcity conditions and is a practical response to the challenges of integrating reliability rules, responses such as voltage reductions which are not properly priced through market mechanisms, and various discretionary behaviour that we must allow system operators to undertake to maintain network reliability and avoid network collapses.

As with raising the price caps, this increases supplier incentives to withhold supplies as capacity constraints are being approached, and market monitors will have to focus their attention on withholding of capacity during hours when capacity constraints are being approached. However, there are mechanisms other than price caps that can help to mitigate market power. It has been widely recognized that more reliance on forward contracting for energy can help to mitigate spot energy market power problems (Allaz and Vila, 1993; Wolak, 2004) and there have been many recommendations that wholesale markets should rely much more on forward contracting. More forward contracting would be a good thing from both a market power mitigation perspective and from the perspective of those who believe that price volatility, price uncertainty, and opportunism are deterrents to investment.

One problem here is that proponents of more forward contracting provide little guidance regarding how this goal will be achieved in the context of retail competition. With competitive retail markets it is generally up to retail customers and their supply intermediaries to decide on their contractual arrangements, including contract duration. If retail suppliers are not voluntarily entering into longer-term contracts we need to understand why; and if implementing the recommendation that more reliance be placed on long-term contracts involves compelling LSEs to enter into bilateral forward contracts with generators, the implications of doing so also need to be better understood—in particular, the implications for the diffusion of retail competition. I discuss below how the creation of a forward capacity obligation and associated capacity markets can be structured in order also to hedge energy prices during peak periods and mitigate incentives to exercise market power.

INCREASE REAL-TIME DEMAND RESPONSE RESOURCES

Increasing efforts to bring more demand response that meets the system operator's criteria for 'counting on it' during scarcity conditions[16] can also help both to increase the efficiency with which capacity constraints are managed and improve the price-formation process during scarcity conditions. However, the way in which demand response is brought into the system for these purposes is important. Demand response should be integrated into the system in a way that is symmetrical to the treatment of supplies of energy, operating reserves, and capacity. Demand response should be an active component of the price-formation process and compete directly with resources on the supply side. The best way for this goal to be achieved is to structure demand-response contracts as call contracts in which curtailments are contingent on wholesale prices rising to pre-specified levels. If capacity payments are made to generators, then equivalent capacity payments should be made to qualifying demand response. It also matters exactly how capacity payments are reflected in retail prices (Joskow and Tirole, 2006). Today, demand-response resources tend to be pre-contracted, the costs partially recovered through uplift charges spread over many hours, and calls on demand response triggered by system operating conditions and reliability protocols rather than high prices. The New York ISO has done a good job improving the ways in which demand response is integrated into spot energy markets and this is the kind of reform that I have in mind (New York ISO, 2005*b*).

INCREASE THE NUMBER OF OPERATING RESERVE PRODUCTS SOLD IN ORGANIZED WHOLESALE MARKETS

Market performance would also be improved if market designs recognized that system operators need more refined 'products' than are currently reflected in the ancillary service product definitions around which wholesale markets are now organized. For example, if the system operator needs 'quick start' supply (or demand response) resources that can supply within 5 minutes rather than 10 minutes, it is better to define that as a

---

[16] This may require, for example, that demand responds to either price signals or requests for curtailment from the system operator within 10 minutes or less. Demand response times have been identified as an issue in the investigation of the rolling black-outs in Texas (ERCOT) on 17 April 2006 (see *Electric Transmission Week*, 1 May 2006, p. 2).

separate product and to create a market for it that is fully integrated with related energy and ancillary service product markets rather than relying on out-of-market bilateral arrangements and 'must run' scheduling in the bid-based supply stack. The supply of energy and various operating reserve services are substitutes, arbitrage links their market prices together, and opportunities exist to change the use and physical attributes of generating facilities in response to price incentives for specific operating reserve attributes.

REVIEW AND ADJUST RELIABILITY RULES AND PROTOCOLS

This leads to one final observation regarding the missing-money problem that affects all proposed solutions to it. Many of the policy assessments of whether or not there is adequate investment in generating capacity turn on comparisons between market outcomes (investment in new and retirement of old generating capacity) and traditional engineering reliability criteria. These reliability criteria and associated operating protocols have been carried over from the old regime of regulated vertically integrated monopolies and may have reflected in part efforts to justify excess generating capacity. It is not at all clear that even a perfectly functioning competitive wholesale market would yield levels of invest-ment and reserve margins that are consistent with these reliability rules. Indeed, Cramton and Stoft's (2006, p. 33) observation that the capacity reserve margin criterion used in the Northeast reflects a VOLL of $267,000/ MWh suggests that this reserve margin is much too high from the perspective of consumers' valuations for reliability. The criteria used for operating reserve targets may also be inconsistent with consumer valuations. At the very least, it would make sense to re-evaluate these reliability criteria and to search for more market-friendly mechanisms for achieving whatever reliability criteria are adopted.

8.2 *Capacity Obligations, Forward Capacity Markets, and Capacity Prices[17]*

The reforms to wholesale energy markets discussed above should help to reduce the net revenue gap. However, it is not at all obvious that the missing-money problem will be solved with these reforms or that they can

---

[17] The new forward capacity market framework filed in March 2006 with FERC by the New England ISO as a settlement among many parties contains many of these features (ISO New England, 2006). See Cramton and Stoft (2006) for a detailed discussion of the rationale for the provisions of the New England ISO's forward capacity market proposal.

be implemented overnight. These reforms may also increase market power problems and further increase price volatility. I believe that reforms to spot markets need to be accompanied by a system of forward capacity obligations placed (ultimately) on LSEs and the effective design of associated capacity markets. If properly designed, forward capacity markets can act as a safety valve to fill the net revenue gap and support efficient investment in generation and demand response, are compatible with the continued evolution of wholesale spot markets, are consistent with the continued evolution of retail competition, and can help to reduce investor concerns about price volatility and opportunism. If spot energy and ancillary reserve market performance improves dramatically, capacity obligations and capacity markets can also effectively fade away.

FORWARD CONTRACTS FOR ENERGY ALONE DO NOT SOLVE THE NET REVENUE GAP OR MISSING-MONEY PROBLEM

Before discussing how forward capacity obligations and associated capacity markets can be structured to do all of these good things I want briefly to discuss one type of frequently mentioned proposal that *will not* in and of itself solve the net revenue gap problem. Several proposals have been made to require LSEs (or system operators) to enter into some type of 'hedged' forward contracts for energy to cover a large fraction of their retail customers' energy demand. The proposals include fixed price forward contracts for energy between LSEs and generators as well as option contracts that specify a call price for energy *ex ante* (e.g. Wolak, 2004; Oren, 2005). It is claimed that these hedging contracts will solve the 'resource adequacy' problem. These assertions are simply wrong.[18] They are wrong because they do not deal with the underlying market imperfections and institutional constraints that lead to the missing-money problem and implicitly assume, without explanation, that the relevant market failure results from inadequate forward contracting by retail consumers and their retail suppliers. They ignore the considerations discussed above that lead to the conclusions that 'the market' cannot be relied upon to select the optimal level of reliability.[19] Moreover, policy-

---

[18] Bidwell (2005) and Singh (2000) have also made proposals that have option contract components. However, they also have components that deal with the missing-money problem by incorporating reliability criteria. See Cramton and Stoft (2006) for a more detailed comparison of these proposals.

[19] See Cramton and Stoft (2006) who discuss this issue in more detail, focusing on the implications on limited real-time pricing and the inability to control power flows to individual consumers.

makers will not allow the market to make this choice. They will continue to impose reliability standards and associated operating reserve requirements and capacity reserve requirement criteria as they do now. There may be good reasons to change these requirements and the mechanisms used to meet them, but economists are dreaming if they think that policymakers will be ready soon to leave reliability criteria to the market. The hedging contract proposals do reduce price volatility and are likely to mitigate market power. These are good outcomes. However, unless they incorporate generating capacity reserve criteria ('resource adequacy criteria') as well, they will not solve the missing-money problem. The forward contract prices will just reflect the low spot wholesale energy prices that create the net revenue gap in the first place.

IMPLEMENT WELL-DESIGNED FORWARD CAPACITY MARKETS

Recent so-called 'capacity market' proposals start with the reliability criteria established by the responsible reliability organizations.[20] The primary generating capacity-related criterion is typically a generating capacity reserve margin measured by the difference between the system peak demand (D) before any curtailments and the peak generating capability (G) of the system assuming that all installed generating capacity is operating at the time of system peak. Qualifying demand response resources are in principle included in this generating capability number. The generating reserve capability criterion (R^*) is then defined as $R^* = (G–D)/D$ and typically lies between 15 per cent and 20 per cent in the USA. The target generating capability of the system is then $G^* = (1+R^*)D$. In theory, the value for R^* should reflect considerations of demand uncertainty, supply uncertainty, and the VOLL from rolling black-outs and network collapses. In reality, the origins of these criteria are rather murky. Generating reserve criteria may be defined for the entire network controlled by the system operator and for individual sub-regions to reflect transmission constraints at the time of locational demand peaks. All LSEs then have the obligation to pay for their proportionate share of this generating capacity/demand response obligation based on their own LSE load at the time of system peak. Under the forward capacity market proposal the auctions are for delivery several years into the future and prices may be fixed, at the supplier's choice, for a few years starting with the delivery date.

---

[20] In the USA this organization would be the regional reliability council under which system operators manage their control areas and a national reliability organization provided for by the Energy Policy Act of 2005.

115

LSEs can meet their forward capacity obligations either by contracting directly with generators for capacity to be available to supply energy at the time of system peak or by purchasing this capacity through an auction process conducted by the system operator. In the latter case, the system operator runs a series of auctions for qualifying generating capacity to meet the reliability criterion for installed generating capacity G*. The auction mechanism defines the price for generating capacity for one or more future periods. All LSEs are required to pay the market clearing price in the auction for their load-based share of the system generating capacity reserve obligation, net of any generating capacity that they own or have contracted for separately outside the auction ('self-supply'). Self-supply can be easily accommodated by requiring generators with bilateral contracts to offer their capacity to the organized capacity market with a contract for differences with the LSEs with which they have pre-contracted and then including all LSE demand in the market as well. Effectively, the system operator buys capacity through the auction and bills LSEs for their share net of any self-supply by contract or ownership they have registered with the system operator prior to the auction. Owners of generating capacity that clears in the market have an obligation to offer energy to the wholesale spot market when requested to do so by the system operator, or pay a significant performance penalty if they do not.

Under the forward capacity market proposal the spot energy markets continue to operate as before, with whatever improvements are introduced as discussed above. Following the numerical examples above, in equilibrium the market clearing price (P_c) for generating capacity should equal the capital costs of a peaker (P_k) less the quasi-rents that a peaker would expect to earn (R_p) in the energy market, or $P_c = (P_k - R_p)$ adjusted for expected forced outage rates and associated penalties (Joskow and Tirole, 2006).[21] This solves the missing-money problem since the capacity price essentially acts as a safety valve to fill the gap between the capital costs of a peaker and the quasi-rents that a peaker expects to earn in the energy and operating reserve markets. Moreover, as the performance of the wholesale spot energy market improves, the expected quasi-rents produced for a peaker in the energy market will rise toward $R_p = P_k$ and the capacity price will fall toward zero.

As already noted, simple versions of capacity obligation/capacity market approach have been operating for years in several US ISOs, but

---

[21] Intermediate- and base-load capacity get the capacity price plus the quasi-rents they earn in the energy market consistent with the equilibrium conditions discussed above. In equilibrium all generating technologies that are included in the least-cost portfolio cover their capital costs.

have not solved the missing-money problem or the other problems noted above. The forward capacity market proposals on the table today include several enhancements to these older capacity mechanisms. I now discuss several of the enhancements that characterize the forward capacity market framework.

The earlier mechanisms relied on cost-based calculations of deficiency payments that effectively placed a price cap on capacity prices. This cap kept realized capacity payments below the level necessary to make up for the net revenue gap from wholesale energy and operating reserve markets. The enhanced mechanisms retain a price cap to deal with potential market power problems, but the price cap is based on an analysis of the probability distributions of demand and supply, rather than being set arbitrarily at the average annualized lifetime capital costs of a peaker, so that on average the mechanism should yield a capacity price equal to P_k before netting out any quasi-rents produced in the energy market. The proposed annual capacity price cap included in the forward capacity market proposal for New England is more than twice the old deficiency payment cap.

A second problem noted with the existing capacity obligation/market systems is that they employed a hard value for the reserve margin and implied quantity of installed generating capacity (R* and G*) required to meet reliability criteria. This approach implied that the reliability value of generating capacity slightly above G* was zero and that the value of any decrease in generating capacity below G* was effectively equal to the price cap. That is, the demand for capacity was equal to the price cap for G < G* and equal to zero for G > G*. This led to very volatile capacity prices that jumped between close to zero and the price cap from year to year. The New York ISO has introduced a reserve capacity demand curve mechanism that essentially smooths capacity prices around the target generating capacity reserve margin. The demand curve's structure is based on an assessment of the distribution of loss-of-load probabilities and the VOLL. It is similar in concept to the capacity payment mechanism that was a component of the original wholesale market design in England and Wales. A similar approach was proposed for New England. However, the initial proposal was renegotiated and, among other changes, the demand curve was replaced with an auction mechanism with caps and floors (a 'price collar') on capacity prices and an intertemporal adjustment mechanism to reflect information about capacity market values drawn from actual market behaviour over time. Together, these provisions also have the effect of smoothing out the distribution of capacity prices and better reflecting the value of capacity above and below a hard installed generating capability target.

A third problem sometimes identified with the existing capacity obligation/market arrangements is that the capacity market was effectively a short-term procurement market that did not give potential entrants an opportunity to participate in the auction, increasing the potential for incumbent generators to exercise market power in the capacity market as well as in the energy market. The reforms proposed in New England and PJM respond to this problem by turning the capacity auctions into forward markets for capacity that occur sufficiently far in advance of delivery that new entrants can participate in the auction. In the New England proposal, the capacity auction will be for capacity that is to be available to the market over 3 years in the future.

A fourth problem identified with the existing capacity market arrangements was that they provided investors considering entering the market with no way of locking in capacity prices for any time period in advance of completion. Whether this concern reflects uncertainty *per se* or potential opportunism problems is unclear. However, the New England forward capacity market proposal allows new entrants at their choice to lock in capacity prices determined in the auction for a period of up to 5 years after the forward capacity delivery date.

A fifth problem identified with the existing capacity obligation/market arrangements was that generators had poor incentives to be available during hours when capacity is constrained, because capacity payments were not tied to actual performance but rather to historical availability experience. This problem is exacerbated by the failure of energy prices to rise to high enough levels during these critical periods. The new proposals include penalties for generators who are not available to perform when they are most needed.

A sixth problem identified with the existing arrangements (and the primary initial motivation for the reforms in New England and PJM) was that capacity obligations were applied for the system operator's entire network and did not reflect transmission congestion and local reliability and associated installed capacity criteria . At first blush, this problem may seem a little surprising since the Eastern and Midwestern markets in the USA rely on locational marginal price (LMP) mechanisms for energy that yield prices that are supposed to reflect congestion (Joskow, 2006). However, the same market and institutional failures that suppress energy prices generally, also affect prices in constrained areas. To respond to this problem, the new capacity market mechanisms allow for capacity obligations and capacity prices to be determined for sub-regions where there are congestion problems (e.g. Southwestern Connecticut, New York City, Northern New Jersey).

A final criticism of the existing capacity market arrangements is that they fail to do anything about market power in the energy market or to stimulate more hedging of energy price volatility for retail customers ('hedging load'). The New England proposal has an interesting component that responds to these concerns. Each year the system operator will calculate the quasi-rents earned by a hypothetical peaking unit for sales of energy and operating reserves in the spot market ('peak energy rents' or PER) and deduct these rents from the capacity price determined in the auction. The PER is calculated based on a strike price for a hypothetical peaking unit with a high marginal generating cost.

This provision has several effects. First, it hedges load against peak-period energy price spikes since, as peak period prices increase in the energy market, the net price of capacity decreases. Second, it provides a net revenue hedge to peaking capacity that performs as expected and a partial hedge to base load and intermediate capacity. Third, it reduces incentives to exercise market power in the energy market since higher spot market prices do not benefit generators that are fully hedged in this way. Finally, it provides good performance incentives. A generator that does not meet the performance targets and parameters used to calculate PER for a hypothetical peaker will lose money on the PER adjustment (as well as from other performance incentives). A peaker that can realize better performance keeps the additional net revenues. As Cramton and Stoft (2006) argue persuasively, by hedging prices paid by load during peak hours this additional component of a forward capacity market design effectively integrates the forward contract/options/load hedging proposals discussed above within a framework that also deals with the missing-money problem.

Most of the discussion of capacity obligation/market mechanisms has focused on the supply side. To restore fully appropriate incentives to market participants, the demand side of the market should be treated symmetrically. Demand response resources that are compatible with the system operator's reliability criteria should be compensated at levels equivalent to what is paid to generators to make capacity available during capacity-constrained periods. Moreover, the price paid for capacity should ideally be reflected in prices paid by retail consumers during these same critical periods. This should be a goal of further refinements in the forward capacity market framework.

Much of the discussion of proposals for dealing with generation investment incentives has also ignored the implications for the further evolution of retail competition. The proposals that would require LESs to enter into a portfolio of long-term contracts with individual generators for supplies of energy to meet their peak loads are, in my view, incompatible with retail competition. In areas where a large fraction of the retail load has not switched to competitive suppliers, the responsible LSE would be the incumbent *regulated* distribution company. The costs of the long-term contracts signed by the LSE would then be passed through to 'default service' retail customers on a cost-of-service basis. This raises potential stranded-cost problems (again) and can distort decisions by consumers regarding switching to competitive retail suppliers or default service, as wholesale market prices will inevitably deviate from the average cost of the of the regulated incumbent's portfolio of long-term contracts at any point in time that is used to set regulated default retail prices. This approach also places additional financial burdens on competitive retailers since it will increase their credit obligations to become counterparties to long-term supply contracts. Retailers may not be able to put together a retail contract portfolio that matches their wholesale contract obligations or to recover the market value of the contractual risks that have been imposed upon them in market-based retail prices. Accordingly, requiring all LSEs to enter into long-term contracts will increase the market risk faced by competitive retail suppliers, placing an additional burden on the already slow diffusion of retail competition.

The forward capacity market mechanism is much more compatible with retail competition than are the proposals that place forward contracting proposals on individual LSEs. Capacity prices are set through an organized market process and the associated financial obligations to make the capacity payments are ultimately a collective obligation of all retail suppliers in the aggregate rather than a long-term capacity commitment of each individual retail supplier. As retail customers switch from retailer to retailer, the capacity obligations associated with their demand move along with them, along with the financial obligations (capacity prices) associated with the forward price obligations determined through forward capacity auctions. Individual retail suppliers do not have to post credit to support (say) 5-year contractual commitments since the credit is provided by the collective obligations of retail suppliers defined in the system operator's tariff.[22] Since the obligations for capacity payments are based on each retail supplier's share of peak demand and the price of capacity is established *ex ante* through an auction mechanism, movements of retail customers among retail suppliers and the associated movement in capacity payment obligations can be handled easily by the system operator.

9. Conclusion

Evidence from the USA and some other countries indicates that organized wholesale markets for electrical energy and operating reserves do not provide adequate incentives to stimulate the proper quantity or mix of generating capacity consistent with mandatory reliability criteria. Based on US experience, a large part of the problem can be associated with the failure of wholesale spot markets for energy and operating reserves to produce prices for energy, during periods when capacity is constrained, that are high enough to support investment in an efficient (least-cost) mix of generating capacity. A joint programme of reforms applied to wholesale energy markets, the introduction of well-designed forward capacity markets, and symmetrical treatment of demand response and generating capacity resources is proposed to solve this problem. This policy reform programme is compatible with improving the efficiency of spot wholesale markets and the continued evolution of competitive retail markets, and restores incentives for efficient investment in generating capacity consistent with operating reliability criteria applied by system operators. This reform package also responds to investment disincentives that have been associated with volatility in wholesale energy prices by hedging energy prices during peak periods as well as responding partially to concerns about regulatory opportunism by establishing forward prices for capacity for a period of up to 5 years. These hedging arrangements also reduce the incentives of suppliers to exercise market power.

---

[22] All retail suppliers and generators would still have to meet the system operator's standard credit requirements, and provisions for obligations incurred by suppliers who go bankrupt must be defined.

Part 2: Oil and Gas

5

Oil Markets and the Future

Paul Stevens

1. Introduction

Oil remains a key source of primary energy. Figure 1 illustrates its dominance. This pre-eminence arises because of oil's physical characteristics (Frankel, 1946; Stevens, 2000). As it is a liquid which flows in three-dimensional space all stages in the value chain attract large technical economies of scale leading to low costs relative to other fuels. Oil has a relatively high energy content compared to other fuels—some 50 per cent more than coal on a weight basis and 170 times more than natural gas on a volume basis. Oil is also a truly international business. Crude oil and refined products comprise the largest single item in international trade whether measured by volume or value (Hartshorn, 1993). It is viewed as a strategic commodity which involves it in politics and conflict on a local, national, regional, and global basis (Mitchell *et al.*, 1996; Parra, 2004). Finally, as will be discussed, the oil price remains a key economic variable to determine the health of economies.

Thus oil markets matter. This chapter examines the current and future state of oil markets and some policy implications. Since the first Gulf crisis of 1990–1, there was a tendency to leave oil to 'market forces' and to encourage governments to deregulate and liberalize (Helm *et al.*, 1988; Robinson, 1993; Newbery, 1996, 2000; Hunt, 2003; Helm, 2004*a*). How-ever, in recent years, there have been growing concerns that leaving oil to the market may produce undesirable results. Consequently, there has been a revival in the debate over the extent to which oil markets should

Figure 1 World Primary Energy Consumption, 1965–2004

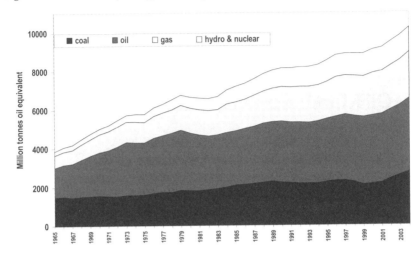

Source: BP Statistical Review of World Energy 2005.

attract policy attention. This pressure has been strongly reinforced as the high price of crude oil has fed into higher prices for transport fuels. This chapter examines what elements in oil markets may attract concern and hence policy intervention and what the nature and effectiveness of such intervention might be. A particular focus is the recent debate which has emerged between different explanations for the relatively high oil prices experienced since 2004. This rise in price has attracted considerable attention among analysts of the industry (Horsnell, 2004; Stevens, 2004a). In particular, the rise to over $70 for the OPEC basket has puzzled many observers. There are two schools of thought which explain such strength—the 'cyclical school' and the 'structural school'. The difference is crucial since if the cyclical school is believed then what goes up comes down whereas the structural school would argue that higher prices than the average of $17.68 for the OPEC basket in the 1990s will be here for some time.

Markets have characteristics which determine how they function. They have players—buyers and sellers—who have something to exchange—goods/services and money. The players have objectives which they pursue. This pursuit takes place in a context subject to legal and regulatory interventions—the rules of the game. For the oil market, the key to its operation lies in the role of market power in a strongly oligopolistic market structure. This creates very considerable rent in the international oil price, pushing crude prices far above marginal cost.

Thus, while supply and demand influence price determination, they do so in the context of a highly distorted market. This raises many policy issues for consideration.

This 'characteristics' approach to markets is used as the framework for this chapter. Sections 2 and 3 provide a brief history of recent developments with respect to the oil market and to oil price respectively. In particular, section 2.5 concentrates on the 'cyclical' versus 'structural' debate which is central to the chapter. This is because if, as this author believes, there has been a structural change in oil markets, it means we are moving to a high price world for some time to come, probably 5–10 years or longer. Obviously the policy implications for a high-oil-price world are very different from those of a low-oil-price world. Section 4 then considers future issues which arise out of the current context described in sections 2 and 3 which may have policy dimensions. Five issues are addressed: capacity levels and supply; 'resource curse' and the future of supply; market control and the role of OPEC; levels of competition in the market place; and, finally, implications for the environment. Section 5 concludes with an overview of the challenges of using policy in such an international industry.[1]

2. Recent Developments in the International Oil Market

2.1 *The Players—Consumers*

In the last 20 years, oil-importing countries have pursued three broad strands of policy—deregulation, imposition of sales taxes, and measures to address security-of-supply concerns.

There has been a strong trend of deregulation of domestic oil markets particularly relevant in the emerging market economies (EMEs)[2] (IEA, various years). State control over the supply chain together with direct pricing controls has been relaxed and private-sector involvement has

---

[1] The academic literature on the international oil industry has always been sparse and tends to lag events, although, wherever possible, references to the academic literature are made throughout this paper. However, much of the information contained comes from the trade press. To provide citations would simply swamp the paper. Therefore many of the statements remain unsupported. However, invariably they are sourced from the excellent Middle East Economic Survey and the curious reader can find supporting evidence there. The website—www.mees.com—carries weekly summaries of the Survey and often allows free access to the Op-Ed pieces. Another valuable source of information on current oil market developments and issues is the Oxford Energy Forum.

[2] Defined as South and Central America, Africa, Middle East, non-OECD Asia, and non-OECD Europe.

been encouraged. In large part, this was in response to the general views of the 'Washington Consensus' regarding the undesirability of state intervention in the economy which gained ground during the 1990s.

At the same time, consumer governments have been imposing ever higher sales taxes on oil products (Seymour and Mabro, 1994). Most recently, EME governments have moved away from protecting consumers from the oil shocks of the 1970s via subsidy, to raising final prices via sales taxes (Paga and Birol, 1994; Bhattacharyya, 1995). The motive has been the attraction of raising revenue from oil products disguised under rhetoric to protect the environment, although rising international prices have made the cost of continuing subsidy increasingly difficult to bear. Oil products have a large tax base and an inelastic demand allowing for high tax rates. They have an added attraction of involving low collection costs and are difficult to evade. They are a very attractive source of net revenue to any exchequer. The result of this policy trend has been a growing disconnect between international crude oil prices and demand. For example, in the European Union, of the final price of gasoline, only 12 per cent was accounted for by the price of crude (OPEC, 2003). Thus a doubling of international crude prices would increase the final gasoline price by only some 12 per cent.

The final policy trend in the oil importers has been growing concern about security of supply (Fried and Trezise, 1993; Mitchell, 1994; Bohi and Toman, 1996; Mitchell *et al.*, 1996; Andrews-Speed *et al.*, 2002; Leiby *et al.*, 2002). The oil shocks of the 1970s associated with the apparent supply disruptions of the Arab Oil embargo, the Iranian Revolution, and the Iraq–Iran War forced supply security to the top of the energy policy agenda. However, the aftermath of Iraq's invasion of Kuwait in 1990 convinced many governments that supply security was no longer an issue. The International Energy Agency (IEA) had in place its emergency sharing mechanisms which obliged members to maintain strategic stocks. This strategic cushion plus letting the market 'work' meant the worst-case scenario—i.e. a major military conflict in the Gulf—had been managed following Iraq's invasion of Kuwait. There was minimal disruption and a short limited price spike which the global economy weathered without difficulty. However, the tragic events of 9/11, growing import dependence in the United States, plus the deteriorating situation in the Middle East has caused oil importers to think again, and security of supply has moved back up the energy policy agenda.

This has been compounded by different dimensions of events in the region. Obviously the deteriorating shambles in Iraq has emphasized the limitations of the United States in managing and controlling situations. This has caused unease. As for oil markets, concerns over loss of Iraqi exports, or, indeed, the loss of exports for other geo-political reasons in Venezuela or more recently Nigeria or Iran in the event of an American/ Israeli military strike, have played a role in the strength of prices since 2004. In particular, they have been potent in driving paper markets by the provision of a 'fear premium'. However, for the oil market and especially the paper markets, concern over Saudi Arabia has probably dominated. In particular, attacks on expatriate workers in the Kingdom have raised the spectre of sabotage on oil installations. For the oil market such an outcome could be devastating. For example, one single facility in the Kingdom—Abqaiq—processes 5–6m barrels per day of crude oil. If it were damaged by terrorist action, the results would be serious physical shortage in the international market. In the event, February 2006 saw an abortive attempt to attack Abqaiq. The last time there was real physical shortage in crude markets was during the second oil shock in the aftermath of the Iranian Revolution of 1979. In today's dollars the price hit over $80 per barrel. Furthermore, that was in a market context where there was no paper market to encourage speculation and price data were only estimated every 24 hours by Platt's Daily Telex service. In today's context of extensive paper markets and real-time screen trading, the heights to which prices might be pushed could be unimaginable. In the autumn of 2005, Goldman Sachs was widely reported as projecting a price of over $100 per barrel in the event of further oil market disruptions.

In reality, of course, it is precisely because of their importance and their vulnerability that oil installations in the Kingdom attract very tight and effective security. However, security can be breached and in December 2004, a tape allegedly from Osama Bin Laden called upon Saudis to attack oil installations to deny oil supplies to the West. Also, even a failed attack would certainly encourage the paper markets to impose a significant premium on oil prices, as did the attempted attack on Abqaiq in 2006.

2.2 The Players—Producers

THE INTERNATIONAL OIL COMPANIES (IOCS)

The key trends which have characterized the IOCs in recent years are moves away from vertical integration, a change in financial strategies, and a bout of mergers and acquisitions.

The aftermath of the second oil shock of 1979–81 saw a significant change in structure, moving away from vertical integration to a greater use of markets. Vertical integration can take two forms (Stevens, 2003*b*). Financial vertical integration is when different stages in the value chain are owned by one holding company which controls their cash flows. Operational vertical integration is when the crude and products move between these affiliates. Operational vertical integration requires the presence of financial vertical integration, but the reverse is not true. Markets can substitute for operational vertical integration.

The IOCs, before the second oil shock of 1978–81, were financially and operationally vertically integrated (De Chazeau and Khan, 1959). Several factors explain (Penrose, 1965; Bindemann, 1999). Transactions and information costs made operational vertical integration superior to markets which were non-existent or highly inefficient. Operational vertical integration also inhibited competition since it provided significant barriers to entry. If the companies only exchange crude between their affiliates, there is no access to crude for third parties. It is possible to practise price discrimination by integrating into the low-priced market, preventing arbitrage. Finally, operational vertical integration enabled the companies to play tax games through the use of transfer prices to minimize their global tax bill.

After the second oil shock, the IOCs moved away from operational vertical integration, preferring to use markets. The nationalizations of the 1970s plus the discrediting of long-term contracts increased the number of arm's-length transactions which meant a greater number of buyers and sellers plus greater market transparency (Hartshorn, 1980). The consequent lowering of transactions costs encouraged further use of markets which created a self-feeding process of more players, more transactions, and more transparency. Barriers to entry weakened as new non-integrated crude producers entered the market and as the majors began to sell off refineries to smaller 'petropreneurs' (Bleakley *et al.*, 1997). In such a world, constraints of competition became less relevant. Finally, the tax authorities began to limit transfer pricing games. Hence operational vertical integration among the IOCs, except in certain specific cases, disappeared. Most recently the issue under discussion is the value of financial integration for IOCs given the continued poor profitability of the refinery sector (Horsnell, 1997; Stevens, 1999).

A relevant trend has been a shift in financial strategy (Stevens, 2004*a*). During the 1990s, following the general trend in corporations in the United States and the United Kingdom, the IOCs began to adopt value-based management systems. Thus, based upon capital asset pricing model methodology, if the company cannot earn a rate of return on its capital at least as great as the equities in the sector and the market more generally, then it should return funds to the shareholders via dividends or share buy-backs rather than investing itself. A consequence which deserves further discussion in section 4 is that during the high prices experienced since 2000, increased sums of capital have been draining out of the industry's investment pot. This contrasts with the aftermath of the second oil shock of 1978–81. High prices led to sharp increases in investment in the upstream, creating a large expansion of capacity which, by the mid-1980s, undermined the high oil prices resulting in the 1986 oil price collapse.

Finally, the IOCs since 1998 have experienced mergers and acquisitions which have significantly increased the concentration ratios in the upstream and downstream of the industry (Luciani and Salustri, 1998). This was triggered by the oil price collapse of 1998 which made the purchase of others' reserves an attractive proposition. Several factors explain the dash to 'merge' (Stevens, 1999). Certainly it was perceived that there would be synergies to reduce costs. It also gave an opportunity to reshuffle the new asset portfolio with a view to selling the lesser performing assets, mainly in the downstream. In addition, the well-known 'herd instinct' which has dominated the industry since 1945, may have played a role (Ollinger, 1994; Lynch, 1995). Once the first mega-merger had taken place between BP and Amoco, shareholders' expectations created a feeding frenzy forcing the others to follow. Whatever the reason, the industry became more concentrated. To be sure, various regulatory bodies in the United States and Europe forced the larger companies to divest certain key assets to protect competition, but the sense remains that the industry did become less competitive as a result. In particular, and this is relevant for later discussion, the now much larger IOCs as buyers of services became extremely powerful, forcing down profits for the service companies leading to lower investment in service industry capacity threatening the industry's ability to develop more upstream capacity.

THE NATIONAL OIL COMPANIES (NOCS)

The paths followed by the NOCs of the major producing countries were rather different from those followed by the IOCs.[3] From the 1980s, many NOCs developed a financial vertically integrated capability largely through

[3] The use of the term IOCs can be misleading since an increasing number of NOCs are, indeed, operating internationally. However, the distinction is determined basically by ownership.

buying the divested downstream assets of the IOCs. However, they opted to use operational vertical integration rather than markets (Stevens, 1998, 2003b). The official reason was to lock in market share to protect them from the new supply emerging from non-OPEC. However, an alternative explanation was to deepen the information asymmetries at the heart of the principal–agent relationship, thereby enabling greater rent capture by the NOC management. This prompted producer governments to scrutinize the behaviour of their national oil companies (Van der Linde, 2000; Stevens, 2004b; Marcel, 2006). The result has been in many cases severe restrictions of funds available to NOCs and a desire by the controlling ministries—usually finance—to force greater transparency and accountability from the NOCs. One of the options to achieve this has been by opening the domestic upstream sector to IOC investment in an attempt to create benchmarking options reducing the information asymmetries.

An important dimension of these growing restrictions relates to the relative importance of the NOCs versus the IOCs. The NOCs are increasing their role in crude supply relative to the IOCs largely as a result of their exclusive and preferential access to acreage (Luciani and Salustri, 1998). This is compounded as the NOCs of the importing countries of Asia are encouraged to move abroad in search of equity oil. If this growing dominance of crude supply is linked into the continued use of operational vertical integration, this could lead to a reduction of transactions in crude oil markets, reducing the efficiency of those markets and increasing the transactions costs associated with their use. In such a world it is feasible that the IOCs could begin to revert to operational vertical integration, moving away from the development of efficient markets which have characterized the last 20 years.

OPEC

OPEC's ability to manage the market has long been a subject of intense interest (Adelman, 1980; Seymour, 1980; Gately, 1984; Griffin, 1985; Mabro, 1992; Parra, 2004). The role of OPEC and its problems are clear and well understood. The international oil industry has generally faced excess capacity to produce crude oil. Figure 2 illustrates the pattern since 1950. Several factors explain (Stevens, 2000). The price of oil has always exceeded the cost of replacing the produced barrel. This rent, arising either from low production costs as a result of favourable geology or from market manipulation, created the incentive for the owner of the discov-

Figure 2 OPEC's Excess Capacity to Produce Crude, to January 2004

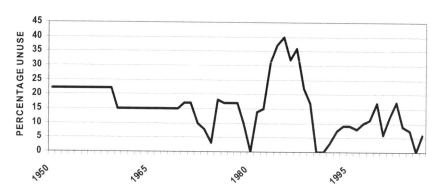

Source: 1950–70 author's estimate; 1971–91 Central Intelligence Agency, *World Fact Book* (various years); 1992–2005 author's estimate.

ered oil-in-place (normally the government) to develop the capacity to produce it. Existing producing facilities have been subject to sudden outages from accidents or political events. This required the rapid development of replacement capacity. However, once the original loss is restored, this capacity becomes surplus to requirement. As indicated earlier, the industry has always been driven by a strong sense of consensus. Everyone, following the same signals, tends to make the same investment decisions, generating a classic case of the fallacy of composition. For example at the end of the 1970s and early 1980s all the IOCs believed the price of oil would rise inexorably forever. The result was massive investment in developing capacity outside of OPEC, from which they had recently been excluded by successive nationalizations. The final explanation for the presence of excess capacity was the result of a deliberate decision by Saudi Arabia. When they decided in 1985 to maintain lower stable prices to encourage a reversion to oil by energy consumers, it was decided that stability required the maintenance of spare capacity in the Kingdom to manage potential oil shocks.

Given this excess capacity, the function of the market controller—the IOCs in the 1950s and 1960s and OPEC since 1982—has been to prevent the excess coming to market creating downward pressures on prices. Thus OPEC must estimate the call for its crude and then allocate that call among the members to ensure the market is managed. This faces two challenges—poor quality of market information and the classic cartel problem of cheating (Stevens, 2002).

131

In the 1950s and 1960s, when the IOCs controlled, their operational vertical integration and dominance of international supply gave them excellent information on supply and demand. This enabled them to orchestrate supply and (to an extent) protect prices from downward pressures. The breakdown of this horizontal and vertical integration of the industry by the nationalizations of the 1970s and the other processes described above meant that the information was simply lost. When OPEC comes to assess world oil demand, non-OPEC supply, and the consequent call on OPEC, the data are poor and unreliable. The best OPEC can do is guess and hope. Thus, for example, the price collapse of 1998 was triggered by an OPEC decision taken at the November 1997 meeting in Jakarta which grossly overestimated demand and underestimated supply outside OPEC-10.

The second problem facing OPEC is the inevitable cartel problem of detecting and deterring cheating. Thus much of the analysis of oil markets has focused upon these challenges and OPEC's ability (or lack of ability) to manage (Stevens, 2002). In particular, there has been much debate about the relative importance of OPEC versus Saudi Arabia in the literature (Crémer and Salehi-Isfahani, 1991; Dahl and Yucel, 1991; Al Turki, 1994; Gately, 1995; Salehi-Isfahani, 1995; Gulen, 1996; Al-Yousef, 1998). In the best traditions of empirical testing in economics, the results are ambivalent and contradictory. However, on balance, few would dispute the pre-eminent role of Saudi Arabia in controlling oil markets by virtue of its possession of significant quantities of spare capacity which it has been willing to use to manage the market.

Over the last couple of years (described in more detail below in section 3.2) OPEC control has been less of an issue. Strong demand, a poor performance by non-OPEC outside of Russia, and the loss of capacity as a result of geo-politics have meant that OPEC, with the exception of Saudi Arabia, has been able to produce to capacity in a market of rising prices. Thus the quota system has been less controversial and questions about OPEC's ability to control the oil market appeared to be slipping off the agenda. However, a fundamental issue remains since some members, producing over their quotas, want a formal increase. This desire for a higher formal quota is reinforced because the opening to IOCs in the upstream (described below in section 2.4) means their capacity is expected to grow in the foreseeable future. At the same time there are members (notably Indonesia, Venezuela, and Iran) who cannot produce to quota but who are unwilling to acknowledge this by giving up their share of quota. Should demand weaken, non-OPEC regain its former strength, or

Figure 3 Oil Consumption by Region, 1965–2003

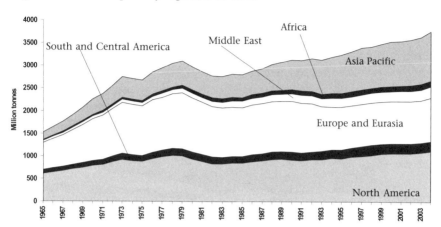

Source: BP Statistical Review of World Energy 2004.

geopolitics cease threatening supplies, this will raise concerns again about OPEC's role.

2.3 *The Exchange*

In terms of the exchange in the oil market, several clear trends have emerged. Oil consumption is inexorably moving towards the EMEs, especially in Asia. Figure 3 illustrates. Forecasts suggest this trend will continue, and if they are to be believed, will become ever more pronounced (IEA, 2002). Also much of the growth is in the transport sector (Paga and Birol, 1994; Dargay and Gately, 1995). Heavy fuel oil continues to lose ground in the static sector which requires ever growing investment to convert the heavier ends of the barrel into light ends where the demand growth will come. This 'destruction' of fuel oil has become one of the most pressing issues for the refinery sector.

Supply of traded crude has been increasingly concentrated in the Middle East, as can be seen in Figure 4. This causes growing unease among consumers who rightly or wrongly perceive the region to be politically unstable and unreliable, although such views are regarded as unjust and unreasonable within the region itself. In particular, Saudi Arabia rightly sees itself as a source of great stability and reliability in the oil market. The final trend is that reserves close to markets are dwindling and the additions to reserves are further away. The oil must travel ever greater distances to reach markets, which raises issues of the adequacy of the

Figure 4 World Oil Exports by Region, 1980–2004

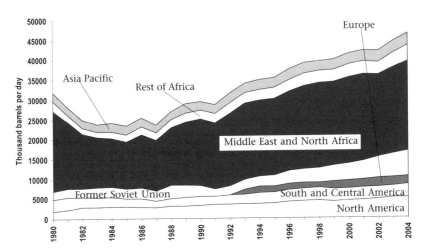

Source: BP Statistical Review of World Energy 2005.

transportation infrastructure and the security of sea lanes and transit pipelines (ESMAP, 2003).

2.4 *The Rules of the Game*

The trends of recent years have been for the legal and regulatory environment to encourage greater private-sector involvement in the industry and to deregulate the sector (IEA, various years). This has been especially prevalent in the EMEs where there has always been a history of heavy state involvement (Van der Linde, 2000).

In the downstream and midstream in the OECD, the emphasis has been on maintaining competition. For example, during the mega-mergers described in section 2.1, the competition authorities, notably in the United States and European Union, examined the implications and in most cases forced some degree of divestiture to maintain competition. Similarly, many legislative authorities have also been working to try and widen access to pipelines and other infrastructure (Stevens, 1996). In the EMEs, the emphasis has been on moving what was a largely state-controlled sector into the private sector. This has involved a combination of privatization and deregulation (MacKerron and Pearson, 1996, 2000).

In the upstream, the main change has been opening acreage for exploration and development for IOC and NOC investment. This has been driven by a desire to access capital and technology and to provide benchmarks to measure the performance of NOCs. This process has been

134

especially noticeable within the OPEC members. Some, such as Algeria and Nigeria, have been very successful. Others, such as the 'apetura policy' in Venezuela, the 'buy-backs' in Iran, and 'Project Kuwait' in Kuwait, have all proved problematical as a result of the process falling foul of domestic political disputes. Currently, only two countries—Saudi Arabia and Mexico—have ruled out such investment and, even here, Mexico is trying to remove the constitutional restrictions to upstream investment. This opening has also been encouraged by technical change, which has allowed operations in ever greater depths of the oceans. The outcome of this general opening has been a major increase in capacity over the last 10 years. One consequence of this already described in section 2.2 (OPEC) is that some in OPEC are seeking higher quotas. More recently there is growing concern that because of a resurgence of nationalism in some parts of the world, this opening process has stopped and reversed. Thus increasing amounts of exploration acreage are not accessible to the IOCs, which is one of the explanations for their relatively poor performance in terms of returns.

An area of particular interest in this 'opening' process has been the Former Soviet Union (FSU). Immediately following the break-up, there was a strong rush of IOC investment in the upstream. In the Caspian region this proved to be relatively enduring (ECSSR, 2000). In Russia, however, the early enthusiasm quickly dampened as the institutional framework proved ineffective (Considine and Kerr, 2002). More recently, Russia has come back on to the agenda for upstream investment, starting with the massive involvement of BP in the TKN joint venture. However, there remain concerns. The legal and regulatory environment remains very uncertain and unpredictable. There are also clearly signs of political tensions in relations between the Putin Administration and the oil oligarchs. Finally, there is concern that continuing production growth could lead to a severe attack of Dutch disease, whereby the inflow of revenues causes a significant appreciation of the real exchange rate. After the collapse in the value of the rouble in the summer of 1998, there has been a strong revival in the non-hydrocarbon sector. Any appreciation of the real exchange rate could halt that in its tracks. While many forecasts are projecting continuing growth in Russia's crude production, for the reasons outlined above, there must be some doubts about the validity of such forecasts.

One significant development in the rules of the game at an international level has been the Energy Charter Treaty (Waelde, 1996). This Treaty emerged from negotiations started in 1991. The initiative from Jan

Figure 5 Monthly Oil Prices, OPEC Basket, 1983 to the end of January 2006

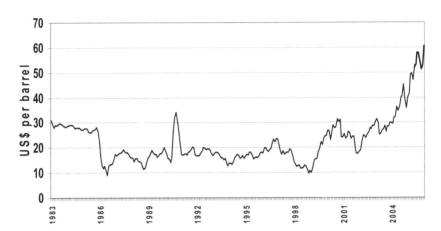

Note: In June 2005, OPEC changed the composition of the basket.
Source: Middle East Economic Survey—various issues.

Lubbers as President of the European Union was to provide a legal framework to govern investment from Western Europe into the energy sector of the FSU. Subsequently, the scope and coverage widened considerably. A particular purpose of the Treaty, which became binding in April 1998 with the 13th ratification, is to manage disputes in a way which minimizes disruption to operations. Thus member states, by signing and ratifying the Treaty, give their consent to the submission of disputes to international arbitration in the event that an investor in an energy project chooses this course. In particular, the problems associated with transit pipelines received considerable attention. However, a problem with the Treaty is that it was negotiated in a hurry and many crucial issues were finessed, leaving interpretation to the courts. Also the Russian Federation, which is clearly a key player, has yet to ratify. It remains to be seen just how effective the Treaty may prove in terms of encouraging investment in energy and influencing government policy in the member countries.

2.5 A Recent Debate

As already alluded to, the recent rise in crude prices seen in Figure 5 has attracted considerable attention. The two schools of thought which explain such strength—the cyclical school and the structural school—have each been vocal in support of their view of events, although most participants in the debate see both schools as having validity. An important dimension concerns how the difference between a cycle and a structural change is defined. Oil prices are determined by drivers which impact demand and supply and the behaviour of those who make the price. Changes to these drivers can be viewed as cyclical. A structural change is when the 'coefficients' which determine the impact of these drivers on price change. These coefficients can be quantitative, such as various price and income elasticities. They can also be qualitative, such as the price objectives of OPEC and expectations in the paper markets. One of the problems with the debate is that given this definition, a structural change is not apparent until the cycle changes, and so the outcome of the debate must await events.

The cyclical school argues that all drivers of oil prices since December 2002 have been pushing in the same direction. Thus, in the wet barrel market, demand has been exceptionally strong and for 2004 is the highest global growth in oil demand since 1978. At the same time, outside of Russia, non-OPEC supply has disappointed as projects have been delayed. Finally, geopolitics has removed physical supply, starting with the Venezuelan oil workers strike in December 2002, followed by the Iraq war, problems in Nigeria, and various other interruptions. Thus the physical market for oil has been tight, with the result that surplus capacity to produce crude oil has diminished from around 7m barrels per day (mbd) at the start of 2002 to less than 1 mbd by October 2004.

At the same time, the paper markets were also pushing prices higher. There was a widespread perception that the historically low levels of inventories signalled real physical shortage, although this was almost certainly not the case. The companies were moving towards 'just-in-time' inventory management to try and reduce working capital. Also backward-ation in the future's curve meant that those wishing to secure future supplies were better buying paper barrels rather than paying high current prices and then having to pay for storage. Geopolitics also frightened the non-commercials operating in the paper market, in particular terrorist activities in Saudi Arabia which gave the appearance of creating a serious threat to oil supplies on a grand scale. Finally, the money managers, faced with disappointing results in equity markets, moved considerable funds into commodities with the result that all commodity prices were increasing during 2004. More recently, as the markets entered 2006, inventories have been at comfortable levels, yet prices continue to rise. An obvious explanation for this apparent contradiction is that the geo-political uncertainties over Iran and Nigeria mean that users of crude oil, i.e.

refineries, are more than willing to carry physical stocks in order to protect themselves from supply disruptions.

The structural school sees the rise in prices in a different light. It argues that years of inadequate investment had caused the excess capacity prevalent at all stages in the oil industry value chain to erode and be replaced by current and impending shortages. This new view was reflected in changes to the forward curve for oil prices 6–7 years out. During the 1990s and up to 2002, while the front end of the curve had jumped around from between $10 and $35 per barrel, the back end remained stubbornly between $18 and $22 per barrel. However, since late 2002, the back-end price has been steadily rising and has reached in excess of $60 per barrel. This is seen as reflecting expectations of impending shortages. While this may indeed reflect concerns about shortage, it can also partially be explained by spread trading practices whereby speculators are buying crude 6–7 years out as part of a trading play in a very illiquid market which would tend to push up the back-end prices.

This 'structuralist' view, it should be said, is different from that espoused by the depletionists or those followers of Harold Hotelling. The depletionists argued that the world would become reserve constrained and, using Hubbard Curve analysis, predicted an imminent downturn in oil supplies (Campbell, 1997; Campbell and Laherre, 1998). The fact they had been predicting this 'imminent' demise for over 20 years did not give them much credence. Furthermore, their arguments were seriously flawed methodologically (Barnett and Morse, 1963; Adelman, 1990; Gordon, 1994; McCabe, 1998; Stevens 2004a). Three reasons explain this. First, they assume a fixed stock of 'conventional' oil reserves. This ignores the role of investment and while (as is discussed below) this is a key issue, it has no part in the depletionists' battery of arguments. An even more egregious error is that it ignores the potential from 'unconventional' oil reserves. Second, they assume future oil demand will grow without limitation. Again, there are a great many arguments which can be deployed as to why various drivers will eventually slow such growth. These range from environmental and security-of-supply concerns to consumer governments in EMEs using sales taxes on oil products to raise revenue, to name but a few. Finally, they ignore the feedback loops provided by markets. Growing shortage would increase costs and prices, which would in turn reduce the quantity demanded and increase the quantity supplied.

As for the views of Hotelling (Hotelling, 1931), these argued that because the stock of oil was 'fixed', producers maximizing wealth would produce this fixed stock in such a way that prices would rise in line with their discount rate. However, the notion of a 'fixed stock' of oil is simply not true, except in some trivial geological sense. Also the evidence fails to support the Hotelling hypothesis (Bradley and Watkins, 1994; Adelman and Watkins, 1995). Hotelling's contribution to the understanding of oil markets is controversial and much debated—most convincingly and eloquently by Adelman (1990) and Gordon (1994). One obvious contribution is the observation that scarcity would be signalled by rising costs and hence eventually rising prices. Some argue that more sophisticated models, such as Dasgupta and Heal (1979), derived from Hotelling's original model, offer insights into the nature of substitution.

As explained below in section 3.2, the structuralist school argues for shortage and higher prices arising from lack of investment rather than the reserve constraint argued by depletionists, or producer behaviour argued by Hotelling. Which school of explanation is correct, of course, will be crucial to the future prospects of oil prices and this is discussed below.

3. Recent Developments in Oil Prices

3.1 *Volatility*

Oil prices have increasingly become volatile. This is supported by casual observation of Figure 5, but is also supported by empirical studies (Plourde and Watkins, 1994). The origins go back to 1986. To avoid a return to Government Official Sales Prices and the netback pricing method which prompted the oil price collapse of 1986, OPEC adopted the use of a basket of spot oil prices to determine contract prices.[4] While it continued to try and balance the market to match supply and demand, the actual market price was left to the vagaries of the physical spot market and increasingly the newly developing paper markets (Roeber, 1993; Hartshorn, 1993; Parra 2004).

This approach suffered two basic flaws (Stevens, 2002; Lynch, 2003). The first was the poor quality of information already discussed. The second was that many of the non-commercial players have a poor understanding of the international oil market. Therefore, their reaction to information as it trickles into the market place is fickle, unpredictable,

---

[4] This is different from 'the OPEC Basket'.

and often perverse. Furthermore, their decisions to trade paper barrels are often influenced by what is happening to other elements in their financial portfolios, which have little or nothing to do with oil markets. They also have a strong herd instinct which encourages bubbles and significantly aggravates volatility, despite the assertions of some economic theory (Lux, 1995).

Thus the majority of the traded crude oil is priced off a handful of spot crude prices—some 60 per cent is priced off Brent (Horsnell, 1997). Furthermore, the physical availability of these crudes is diminishing. Resulting poor liquidity plus unpredictable behaviour by traders inevitably leads to much greater price volatility. As discussed below, this greater volatility is causing problems both for producers and consumers, leading to demands for policy intervention.

3.2 Trends

Two recent oil price trends which carry policy implications are developed in this section—the Asian Premium and the rise in oil prices since 1999.

The Asian Premium is the observed difference between the price of crude oil sold into Asia compared to the other two main consuming areas—the United States and Europe. Since 1997, the formula prices of Arabian Light into Asia have averaged a premium of $1–1.50 per barrel while formulae prices to Europe and the USA have remained roughly similar (Ogawa, 2002).

The Premium owes its origin to the aftermath of the 1986 price collapse. The Saudi formula prices (at least notionally) were determined in the market place and were based on various spot prices. Three pricing areas were introduced: deliveries to the USA based upon WTI; deliveries to Europe based upon Brent; and deliveries to Asia based upon an average of Dubai and Omani crude. However, for each formula price 'adjustment factors' were applied involving 'a little monthly ad hoc finagling, the details of which are not published and not generally known' (Frank Parra, MEES 45:38, p. D3). The significance of this price-setting process is that other OPEC prices tend to 'pretty much follow' (ibid.) these Saudi formulae prices.

The Asian Premium is understood by reference to 'discriminating monopoly' and 'limit pricing'. As part of the introduction of formula pricing, Saudi Aramco imposed destination clauses on crude sales and refused to allow spot sales. This was the key mechanism to keep markets physically separate. Without destination clauses, the Asian 'limit price' would be the European price plus any additional transport costs. Most of the other Middle East crude suppliers have limited ability to sell more crude into Asia. They are limited by the amount of crude they can shift from Europe to Asia in response to price differentials. By contrast, Saudi Arabia, with its very large excess capacity, can easily meet additional demand from Asia, albeit within the context of OPEC quotas. Thus, again, this inability to switch between markets strengthens the ability of Saudi Arabia to keep the markets physically separate.

However, the real key is the difference in demand elasticities between the Asian and the US and European markets. The USA and Europe, compared to Asia, face a variety of crude suppliers willing and able to supply crude oil. Asia is obsessed by the issue of supply security and will pay a premium for what it sees as secure supplies of crude oil. Specifically, the bulk of the crude purchased is purchased on the basis of term contracts rather than spot contracts. Asian buyers are unwilling to risk the vagaries of the spot market and fear that they will be unable to secure refinery input. In effect, the Asian premium exists because Asia is willing to pay it.

Also, there is much more scope for 'limit pricing' in Asia than in the USA or Europe. All the time when Saudi Arabia sets its formula price for Asia, it is risking that it can set it at a level which will not drive away buyers or attract competition from other sources. Asia demands term contracts. Because alternative suppliers are very few, the 'limit price' is higher than in the USA or Europe where attempts at over-pricing will produce a rapid and effective competitive response from buyers and other suppliers. The difference is the Asian Premium.

The policy dimension relates to what the Asian consumers (who understandably object strongly to the existence of the Premium) might do and how Saudi Arabia might react. These are discussed in section 4.4.

A key issue of concern over price trends is whether the recent strength in prices is here for some time. The answer depends upon which of the two explanatory schools outlined in section 2.5—the cyclical or the structural school—proves correct. Both have strengths and weaknesses. There have been cyclical dimensions to the price strength. In particular, there was strong crude stockpiling in Asia following the growing crisis in the Middle East, and exceptional demand growth in China. However, both look unsustainable, as was the bull-run in the paper market which followed the hurricane season in 2005—although after a collapse in November 2005, prices began a steady recovery as geo-political concerns began to encourage buying in the paper markets. However, fears of growing shortage as a result of a lack of investment do have some justification, as developed below in section 4.1. In addition, it seems likely that Saudi Arabia's oil pricing policy has undergone a significant change during 2003. Since 1985, Saudi Arabia pursued a policy of stable relatively low prices to encourage energy users to return to oil, thereby reversing moves away from oil following the oil shocks of the 1970s. However, it now looks likely that while wishing to maintain stable prices, Saudi Arabia wants higher prices above the $50 per barrel mark. Several factors explain. The recent devaluation of the dollar has meant that prices in the fourth quarter of 2004 were equivalent in terms of euros to the price at the start of 2002. Thus part of the 'higher' price of oil is misleading, depending upon who is trading. The growing problem of unemployment in the Kingdom is creating a major political crisis for the government which can only be solved by creating yet more public-sector jobs, which requires ever more revenue. In addition, the objectives of the low price strategy have continually been undermined by the policy of raising sales taxes on oil products, described above in section 2.1. Finally, no less a person than Alan Greenspan indicated that the global economy can comfortably live with $30 oil, although given that oil prices are now so much higher this is a view which could be controversial, as discussed in section 3.3 below.

Taken together, impending shortage and the new Saudi policy imply that prices significantly higher than those experienced in the 1990s are here to stay for some considerable time. However, as previously discussed, we will not be sure of this until the cycle changes and we can observe if the 'coefficients' have changed. As developed below, a high oil price world could well prompt calls for a policy reaction.

3.3 *Impact of High Prices on the Global Economy*

Ever since the first oil shock of 1973-4 appeared to trigger a global recession, the impact of oil prices on global economic activity has been a subject of considerable interest (Fried and Schultze, 1975; Hamilton, 1983; Heal and Chichilnisky, 1991; Mork, 1994). The general conclusion of these and other studies is that high oil prices do inhibit global economic growth. Indeed Hamilton (1983) has claimed that all but one recession in the United States since 1945 has been preceded by a period of higher oil prices.

The higher oil prices experienced since 2000 have revived interest in the subject—especially when prices went above $50 in 2004 and above $70 in

2005. The balance of recent evidence continues to support a connection (Balabanoff, 1995; Lee and Ratti, 1995; Huntington, 1998; Jones *et al.*, 2004). However, during 2004/5 there were many claims reported in the trade press from those who argued that the world had changed and could now live with higher oil prices. In particular, they cited the fact that compared to the 1970s and 1980s oil is much less important in the balance of payments in most countries and oil intensities are less. For example, the Asia Development Bank claimed that an increase in price from $30 to $40 reduces Asian GDP by 0.1 per cent, trade balance by 0.3 per cent of GDP, and consumer price inflation increases by 0.5 per cent. These are relatively small numbers. Also some have queried the direction of the relationship, pointing out that higher oil prices are triggered by strong economic growth and thus the causal relationship between higher prices and recession is spurious (Barsky and Killian, 2004). However, there are still grounds for concern. A growing number of observers are beginning to argue that GDP growth in 2006/7 will be slowed by the higher oil prices. As a result they are now downgrading their oil demand forecasts. Also, the macroeconomic models upon which many of the forecasts projecting little or no impact are based are notoriously bad at managing sudden changes in expectations of the sort that much higher oil prices can create. Thus, it is too early to determine the precise effect of the exceptionally high oil prices experienced since the third quarter of 2004.

4. Key Future Issues for Oil Markets Which Carry Energy Policy Implications

4.1 *Capacity Levels and Supply*

A matter of concern is future capacity availability at all stages in the oil industry value chain. In terms of the upstream, while the depletionists' arguments based upon reserve constraints can be dismissed, there is a danger that predictions of crude shortage may prove true. It is generally agreed that a great deal of money needs to be invested in exploration, development, and production to sustain an increase in crude oil supplies. The IEA estimated that some $2,188 billion would need to be invested in exploration and development between now and 2030 if expected oil demand was to be supplied (IEA, 2003*a*)—an annual average of $81 billion. Leaving aside issues of exaggeration in the forecast, there must be serious doubts that enough will be forthcoming from the IOCs. This is not for lack of funds. The high prices enjoyed in recent years have given the IOCs record years in financial terms. In the past, such high oil prices would have encouraged ever greater investments in exploration and production, thereby creating a self-adjusting mechanism by increasing supply (Berman and Tuck, 1994).

However, this has failed to materialize. As explained above, the IOCs in their struggle to maintain shareholder value are returning money to the shareholders. In 2005 the six largest IOCs invested $54 billion in the industry, but at the same time returned over $71 billion to shareholders in the form of dividends and share buy-backs. The danger is that the short-term benefits to share price will be at the expense of future investment in maintaining and developing crude capacity.

There are several reasons why returns are sufficiently poor to justify returning funds to the shareholders. Existing fiscal regimes have become so progressive in recent years that at prices much above $30 per barrel, the bulk of the windfall accrues to host governments rather than the IOCs. Also access to low-cost reserves, which could improve returns, is limited. Some 53 per cent of world proven oil reserves lie in four countries. Of these, Kuwait and Iran are trying to encourage IOC investment, but the process has stalled because it has fallen foul of domestic politics. Saudi Arabia refuses to allow investment from abroad in upstream oil, and Iraq is such a disaster area that no serious investment from the IOCs is likely for a long time to come. The other major opening has been in Russia, but as explained earlier there are also problems as this develops.

A consequence of the mega mergers of the late 1990s is that the IOCs have been shedding labour to cut costs. Thus they have now become managerially constrained and lack enough staff to manage new projects effectively. Also, the service industry has been squeezed as the large IOCs have increased their monopsony power and as the growing use of E-Commerce has also cut service industry margins. Thus the service industry which is losing money has not been investing in capacity and capacity is tight. This means that even if the IOCs decided to try and spend the money on new investment, there is insufficient capability in the service industry to accommodate more projects.

As to other sources of investment funds, as described above, many of the NOCs in the major producers are currently capital constrained. Governments are increasingly suspicious of their rent-seeking behaviour and in any case have locked themselves into a high-spending world. Thus the revenue is required for other things, and investing in new capacity which may bring down price makes less sense. Thus NOCs in the producer countries may not fill any gap arising from IOCs' unwillingness to invest.

This was reinforced by President Bush's State of the Union Address in January 2006 when he asserted the USA would reduce its dependence upon Middle East oil. By raising serious doubts among the producers regarding their security of demand, he has added a further impediment to investment in new capacity in the OPEC countries.

Simple economics argues that high prices produce a supply response creating a self-correcting mechanism. However, this tends to neglect the lead times. In upstream oil, the lead times for new capacity from negotiations on acreage to first oil can be between 5 and 8 years. Thus any crude shortages resulting from the current outflow of potential investment funds could be around for some time, together with their resultant high oil prices. Furthermore, this lack of investment will have an impact on all stages of the industry, including refining, transportation, marketing, and distribution. This is reinforced because a lack of investment in refinery upgrading capacity means that there is strong demand for light sweet crudes. These—specifically WTI on NYMEX and Brent on the IPE—act as the 'headline' crude prices reported in the media. Overall there is a serious danger that short-termism driven by the demands of the stock market may prove to be seriously damaging to oil supplies and prices.

The obvious question is, if there is a case of market failure, can policy help to alleviate these potential shortages? This is reinforced if there are security-of-supply concerns and concerns about the macroeconomic impact of higher oil prices.

Several policy solutions are in theory available. Home governments of the IOCs cannot order them to invest more, but they can try and persuade. This could be done by offering industry-specific tax breaks on investment. Alternatively, they could penalize returns to shareholders, although this is an extremely unlikely option since it effectively undermines the basis of a market economy. However in a global world economy, there is always the temptation for government to free ride and leave difficult solutions to others. Such policy solutions could only be effective if there was some form of collective decision by the home governments, possibly under the auspices of the G8.

Individual home governments could also ensure that there is no collusion between the IOCs to restrain capacity. The minerals industry in the 1980s went through a similar process to oil. Mineral prices were poor and company profitability weak. The industry stopped investing, capacity became tight, prices and profitability rose. However, preferring this world to the previous world, the mineral companies allegedly limited investment to keep supplies tight. There is a suspicion that this was achieved through a degree of collusion and a number of anti-trust cases are pending.[5]

An alternative option would be to bring political pressure to bear to try and improve access to upstream acreage. An obvious example would be for the United States to remove sanctions against Iran as it has done for Libya, although currently concerns over Iran's nuclear activities make this unthinkable in terms of US domestic politics. Restoring Libya to international respectability has led to a feeding frenzy by oil companies to invest in that country's upstream. Saudi Arabia might also be amenable to pressure. There has been a long history of the Kingdom sacrificing its stance on oil policy in return for perceived foreign policy benefits. International efforts to stabilize the desperate situation in Iraq might also assist. However, such a policy option smacks of a revival of the old imperialist days which many would regard as undesirable.

Consumer governments, who may also be home governments, have several policy options. If they are also producers, they could relax fiscal terms to encourage more investment in their upstream. They could also follow the example of some of the larger Asian oil importers and encourage upstream investment by their own companies abroad. This is clearly a pattern which they followed during the period of higher minerals prices described earlier, and there are signs that India and China are following suit in oil. How effective this might be is debatable and the record of Japan following such a policy is not encouraging (Koyama, 2001). One possible negative consequence of such moves, discussed below in section 4.2, is the danger that the investors pay little or no attention to the consequences for the host country. These range from promoting 'resource curse' to embedding extremely unpleasant regimes.

4.2 Resource Curse and Future Supply

There is a further threat to future crude oil supplies—resource curse—which carries important policy implications. Common sense and economic theory argue that large windfall profits from oil projects should enrich a country and its population. While money cannot buy happiness, it is a good down payment. Large inflows of foreign-exchange revenue should overcome capital shortage and lack of investment. However, there is strong evidence that the reverse is true and that large oil revenues damage the economic base of a country and tend to aggravate poverty rather than alleviate it. This phenomenon has been labelled

---

[5] The US cases have now been dropped.

resource curse. It has a long history but recently has moved up the agenda (Stevens, 2003*a*). This has been partially as the result of the World Bank's 'Extractive Industry Review', forced by a number of non-governmental organizations (NGOs) to consider the Bank's role in funding oil, gas, and mineral projects in developing countries. It is also partially a consequence of growing concern about corporate social responsibility. There is a real danger that concern about resource curse could inhibit future investment in upstream capacity by responsible IOCs, aggravating the potential capacity constraint discussed in section 4.1.

There are multiple policy issues which follow. All are geared to answering the question as to how a 'curse' can be avoided and how a 'blessing' can ensue since there is growing evidence that resource curse is not inevitable (Stevens, 2005). The answer lies in the distinction between 'developmental' and 'predatory' states (Mkandawire, 2001).

A developmental state has two components—ideological and structural. The ideological component is when the ruling élite adopts 'developmentalism' as the prime objective and legitimacy is derived from the ability to deliver development—i.e. growth and poverty reduction. The élite then establishes an ideological hegemony—via the ballot box or less desirable means—over society. The structural component involves the capacity to implement wise and effective policies to deliver development. Apart from technical capabilities, this also requires a strong state to resist pressures from powerful, short-sighted private interests. It also requires a 'social anchor' to restrain temptation to use its autonomy in a predatory manner. Key to the analysis is the realization that developmental states can still fail. While the 'right' ideology and limits to predation might be in place, the capacity of the state to implement effective policies might not be enough to manage certain problems. Such problems may be driven by exogenous shocks, mistakes, or just old-fashioned bad luck. In this context, the aim should be to try and enhance the capacity to employ policy. Clearly both the international financial institutions and the IOCs have a role in capacity building, although the primary responsibility must lie with the country itself.

A predatory state, by contrast, is one where the ruling élite is only interested in plundering the economy for its own ends. There are no counter-balancing forces, social anchors, or other constraints on its kleptocracy. Here the options to use policy to reverse the situation are limited. One option is for the IOCs not to invest. The problem with this solution is that there will be other companies, notably some NOCs, who will invest. The only other solution is for some form of coordinated and cohesive international moves to prevent investment and to seek to change the behaviour of the ruling élite—or, indeed, change the ruling élite. This is extremely complex and controversial. First, who decides who is 'predatory' and upon what criteria? Second, the history of such multilateral action is not encouraging in terms of cohesion. Equally, the sort of unilateral action we have seen in Iraq has been a disaster, and a disaster that is likely to get far worse.

However, despite these difficulties it is an issue which needs to be resolved if we are to get the levels of investment in upstream capacity that the oil markets will require in the future.

4.3 *Market Control and OPEC*

As indicated in section 2.2 (OPEC) above, at the moment, because of relatively tight markets, OPEC is insulated from its traditional problems of trying to manage the market. Furthermore, if new capacity fails to materialize, as suggested in sections 4.1 and 4.2, this could continue for quite some time. However, from this view of the future several key issues emerge which have serious policy implications.

The first issue is what policy responses are possible if current high oil prices around $70 per barrel continue and appear to be damaging levels of economic activity. Some policy solutions have already been discussed in sections 4.1 and 4.2—namely encouraging greater investment by IOCs and NOCs, preventing IOC collusion, and encouraging greater opening of acreage. An alternative possible policy response discussed concerns the reaction of the Asian countries where oil demand growth is strongest—mainly China and India. It is already apparent that the growing Asian consumers of oil will seek to put funds into developing new sources. They may also gain attractive terms, since they are much less constrained by ethical concerns when investing in certain countries. Thus there is less competition on the fiscal terms.[6] Whether this sort of investment will be sufficient to maintain and increase crude producing capacity, given the sorts of numbers being bandied around by the IEA, remains a moot point. It also raises fascinating issues to do with the geo-political consequences of such moves. In particular, the Chinese with their obsession over supply security will almost certainly seek political influence and control in the countries where they seek to develop crude producing capacity (Andrews-Speed *et al.*, 2002). It is quite feasible to imagine a world

---

[6] There is also a suspicion that China and India are beginning to collude rather than compete over terms for new upstream acreage.

some 5–10 years down the road where China and the United States come head to head in the Middle East over securing political influence to ensure oil supplies, thereby reviving a version of the Cold War.

The ability of Saudi Arabia to manage the markets will determine future levels of price volatility. If volatility increases, this will produce a demand for a policy response both in producer and consumer countries. The option of controlling paper markets, the major source of volatility, is a non-starter. At any hint of government control, the present trading arrangements can simply dissolve into cyber space outside of any jurisdiction. A more plausible option is to revive the OPEC price band. This was created in 1999 as an automatic stabilizing mechanism. If the price moved outside the $22–28 band for a specified period, OPEC would automatically increase or decrease production by a specified amount to force prices back into the band. Unfortunately, OPEC failed to honour the automatic nature of the mechanism and thus it became discredited. To further complicate its revival, there are currently demands from several members to increase the level of price bands and, in January 2005, OPEC formally announced the 'suspension' of the bands. If OPEC did decide to revive them, albeit at a much higher level, and did acknowledge that they have to be used without discretion, this could stabilize prices since it would effectively determine expectations. The problem would be to get agreement within OPEC on a new level for the bands.

A policy area which is being explored to help stabilize prices both in terms of volatility and level is the producer–consumer dialogue. This has a long history going back to the North–South dialogue of the 1970s (Fesharaki, 1990). In recent years it has been revived largely as the result of the oil price collapse of 1997–9. However, it is difficult to see how such meetings can produce any realistic option to impact price, since by definition this creates winners and losers and potential winners would be unlikely to accept loss. Also, while both sides may approve of price stability, consumers tend to favour stable low prices while producers tend to favour stable high prices.

An alternative option to manage price volatility lies in using paper markets to hedge. Certainly a number of oil producers, including Mexico and Alaska, have used such paper markets (Lindahl, 1996). There are, however, complications. In theological terms, such activities in Islam are regarded as gambling and therefore forbidden—although often such problems can be finessed by the use of language. Also, it is probably unrealistic for large producers to enter paper markets since this could swamp expectations, thus aggravating price volatility. Finally, buying such insurance inevitably costs. In particular, while spending money in such a way looks good if prices move in the 'correct' direction, if they move against the hedge, then this is seen as at best incompetence and at worst as a sign of corrupt practices.

A variation on this theme would be to create stabilization funds which have been used both by oil-consuming countries, such as Korea and Taiwan, and by oil producers. However, in consuming countries where sales taxes on oil products are very high, crude price volatility matters less since the sales tax acts as a cushion between crude prices and the final price to the consumer. Given the growing tendency described above in section 2.1 for all oil importers to increase their sales tax levels, this implies that price volatility might become much less of an issue for consuming countries. As for stabilization/revenue funds for producers, these too are controversial (Fasano, 2000; Davis *et al.*, 2001; Devlin and Lewin, 2002). The argument is that if conditions are conducive to independent and effective operation of a fund, then the problems can be managed within the existing fiscal mechanisms and a separate institution is not required. But if conditions are not conducive, then such funds are prone to corruption and mismanagement and tend to raise unreasonable expectations on spending.

A second issue in this section is the observation made in section 2.3 that supplies are becoming more concentrated in the Persian Gulf. One implication is that OPEC is likely to lose members. During the 1990s two members—Ecuador and Gabon—left the organization. Technically, Indonesia should now follow, as it has moved from being a net exporter of crude to one of net imports. In both Venezuela and Nigeria there are strong lobby groups who believe they should leave OPEC. If this were to happen, in theory it might make OPEC's ability to manage the market easier, since a smaller group might be expected to be more cohesive. However, counter to this is the observation that if market management involves pain as a result of having to close in capacity to balance the market, a smaller group implies greater pain for each member.

An implication of growing concentration relates to supply security. In 2003, 47 per cent of world oil exports came from the Middle East and North Africa. As indicated in section 2.1, the political stability in the region is perceived to be a source of concern and has begun the process of forcing governments to consider their policy response. Several broad policy areas are under consideration—reduce oil demand; develop alternative technologies; increase domestic supplies; diversify sources of oil imports; and finally build up strategic stocks.[7] While such policies can be driven by security-of-supply concerns, they carry implications for other energy policy objectives, such as environmental concerns.

The first policy option to solve security problems is to reduce the demand for oil. This, however, is more complex than it might seem. As indicated in section 2.3, since the oil price shocks of the 1970s, in the OECD oil has been pushed out from under the boiler. Thus the only realistic option to try and reduce oil intensity lies in reducing its use in the transportation sector. For example, there is undoubtedly considerable scope for further improvements in automotive fuel efficiency, especially in the United States where the spread of SUVs has effectively undermined the corporate average fuel economy (CAFE) standards. However, reducing oil use in transport by means of policy will face problems. In terms of aircraft fuel, the international nature of the industry means any individual government would be ill advised to raise the price of jet kerosene, either through sales taxes or price control. Aircraft would simply refuel elsewhere. In terms of gasoline and diesel, raising the final price to consumers remains a politically sensitive issue, as illustrated by the fuel protests in Western Europe in 2002. While there is undoubted scope to reduce gasoline and diesel use by imposing strict regulation of automotive fuel efficiency, this is often seen as unwarranted interference in the role of markets and consumer sovereignty.

One option would be to encourage alternative technologies for transport which used different fuels. This could also assist the environmental objectives to be discussed below in section 4.4. Governments could play a key role, in part through funding basic research but also overcoming market failures. A good example relates to hydrogen powered cars. Consumers are willing to buy such vehicles but only if they can be reassured that filling stations will be easily available. Oil companies are willing to invest in such infrastructure but only if there are sufficient customers. This is precisely the sort of market impasse which can only be broken by government intervention—most obviously by the use of discriminating sales taxes (as has been the case to encourage the use of unleaded gasoline) and the provision of tax incentives for companies to invest in the needed infrastructure.

---

[7] Policy responses to security-of-supply concerns are greatly complicated by the fact that there are many different perceptions of what the threat actually involves. For example, is it the threat of physical shortage, or is it the threat of the macroeconomic consequences of higher prices resulting from a shortage?

An alternative option to address security concerns, assuming the geology permits, is to increase domestic oil supplies. Several policy options are feasible. The first is to open up new areas for exploration. The most obvious example would be in the United States, where this was explicitly recommended by the Cheney Commission in 2001 with specific reference to the Alaskan Wild Life Refuge and other areas. The obvious problem here is a negative reaction from the environmental lobbies. The second option is to improve the fiscal terms for the oil upstream—in particular, in mature areas, to give tax breaks to encourage operators to increase the recovery factor on existing fields.

One other option is to try and diversify sources of imported oil. This can be achieved by allowing markets to function. In general, attempts by governments to secure supplies by attempting to promote bilateral relations with other countries have failed and proved expensive. The case of Japan presents a classic example (Koyama, 2001).

The final option is to develop strategic stocks. Since the mid-1970s, this has been achieved through the framework of the IEA's emergency stockpiling system. This was boosted by the development of the United States' Strategic Petroleum Reserve after 1977. More recently, Asian oil consumers have also been developing a strategic stockpiling capability. One of the problems with this is that there is a great temptation for countries to free ride. Given the international nature of the oil market, a release of stocks by any individual will reduce prices and this will benefit all players in the market. Thus the costs are borne by one country, while the benefits are shared by all (Leiby *et al.*, 2002).

4.4 *Competition*

Several policy issues arise in terms of competition in oil markets. One already referred to in section 2.4 is ensuring that breaking up the state control of the sector by privatization and deregulation does lead to competition in the downstream and midstream. One also concerns efforts to overcome the natural monopoly elements inherent in pipelines (Stevens, 1996). As more pipelines emerge because of the growing need for trade, as outlined in section 2.3, this may become more of an issue than at present.

A new area for competition policy consideration relates to the outcome of the mega-mergers started in the late 1990s. There are several areas for concern. The first already discussed is the fact that the mergers have increased the monopsony powers of the IOCs in terms of the service industry. Thus before 2004, the service industry was facing ever tighter margins, thereby inhibiting the willingness and ability to expand capacity. As developed in section 4.1 above, this has led to problems in developing adequate capacity to meet expected demand.

The final competition issue relates to the Asian Premium outlined in section 3.2. Asian consumers can use policy to avoid the Premium. They could develop strategic stocks to give them confidence to move away from dependence on term contracts. They could also encourage crude oil from other suppliers to enter the region, most obviously encouraging pipeline supplies from Russia. Also, improving the competitive nature of crude and product markets in Asia would further assist the process. Many national oil markets in Asia retain strong elements of regulation and government interference. Regionally, Singapore is the only spot market in Asia and, compared to its US and European counterparts, the volume of trading is small (Horsnell, 1997). Greater entry into world oil markets would further undermine the ability of the Middle East exporters to impose the Asian Premium. As for the Saudi policy dimension, the key is its willingness and ability to impose destination clauses in its sales contracts. It is not clear why they would be willing to undermine a system which is worth a very large amount of revenue. However, a key will be Saudi entry to the World Trade Organization (WTO), since it seems very likely that the WTO would have serious problems with such destination clauses (Desta, 2003).

4.5 *The Environment*

Environmental issues play a crucial role in oil markets and will remain a central dimension of policy because environmental concerns dominate all stages of the industry. In the production of crude there are issues of access to 'wilderness' areas, plus the negative impact of operations ranging from gas flaring to the disposal of drilling muds. Environmental policy outcomes in the upstream, all of which will increase production costs and reduce supply, will depend upon the extent to which other policy drivers, most obviously supply security, supersede environmental concerns. In midstream transportation, there are problems of pipeline leakages and tanker accidents. Increasingly, restrictions are being placed upon the specifications for tankers before they are allowed into territorial waters. In the downstream, there is growing regulation restricting refinery operations, notably flaring and closures. Because of the environmental costs of refinery closure, in the future, it is extremely unlikely that any refinery will actually close. Rather they will cease formal refining operations but remain designated as 'refineries'. One important consequence of this will be that statistics regarding refinery capacity will need to be treated with some circumspection.

At the same time, concerns regarding emissions as a result of burning oil products are creating serious pressures for tighter environmental policy. The most general and widespread regulations are with respect to sulphur content in diesel. Throughout the world these are being tightened, thus giving something of a boost to gas-to-liquids technology which produces a sulphur-free diesel. Gasoline specifications are also a subject of policy interest, notably in terms of the 'boutique fuel problem' in the United States. The United States Clean Air Act of 1990 allowed individual jurisdictions to formulate their own gasoline specifications. The result has been a plethora of different gasolines. In 1974, there were five gasoline specifications, today there are over 55. The result has been a fragmentation of the domestic gasoline market, resulting in very large price differentials between regions. The normal operations of arbitrage between regions—or, indeed, with countries outside the United States— have been suspended because of the growing differentiation of the product. Given the political sensitivity of gasoline prices in the United States, this problem is already attracting public attention and there are growing pressures for a rescinding of the ability to specify gasoline on such a micro basis. More generally, in many developing countries the issue is reducing the lead content in gasoline and this will continue to be an increasingly important issue, not least because the negative effects of lead are well established, well understood, and there are many feasible solutions. There are also new pressures for the lowering of sulphur content in heavy fuel oil.

Finally, there are the issues related to the emission of greenhouse gases. Based on CO_2 emissions, in a world of a true carbon tax, arguably oil would do rather well, given its lower emissions compared to coal. However, both in the United States and in the European Union, carbon tax proposals have invariably tried to give protection to domestic coal, thereby disadvantaging oil. Similarly in large coal consumers, such as India and China, it is inconceivable that a carbon tax would be imposed, resulting in significant increases in oil imports. However, the current high price oil world is likely to encourage less oil use and therefore less CO_2 emissions. Arguably, the gap between the marginal costs of producing oil and the current price levels are greater than the optimal levels that would

Table 1. Issues in the International Oil Market which are Likely to Prompt Demands for a Policy Response

Supply concerns	Insufficient investment by IOCs returning funds to shareholders
	Insufficient investment by NOCs because of rent-seeking
	Fiscal terms not providing enough incentive to invest
	Constraints upon the service industry
	Restrictions on access to upstream acreage
	Fears of 'resource curse' inhibiting investment
	Growing dependence on the Middle East and North Africa
	Fears of terrorism affecting supplies
	Fears regarding the future growth of Russian oil supplies
	Need to clean up operations in all stages of the value chain
Demand concerns	Increasing need for fuel oil 'destruction'
	Need to limit demand growth to lower prices
	Need to limit demand growth to reduce dependence
	Need to limit demand growth for environmental reasons
	Need to clean up product emissions
Market concerns	Need to improve market efficiency
	Increased industry concentration following merger and acquisition activity
	OPEC and Saudi Arabia's ability to manage the market
	Saudi Arabia's oil policy
	Higher prices and their impact on economic activity
	Growing crude oil price volatility
	The Asian premium

be set for a carbon tax. In effect, OPEC and the control of the oil market have effectively internalized the costs of the greenhouse gas externalities.

In terms of markets, other policy means to internalize all these externalities outlined above, either through regulation or some form of permit trading, all involve the industry in greater cost and a requirement for ever greater investment. This creates a serious problem in the downstream because until very recently it has experienced an extremely poor record of profitability. This problem of increased investment to meet green regulations is reinforced when it is remembered that, as explained in section 2.3, the demand for the heavy end of the barrel is on terminal decline, forcing ever more investment in extremely expensive upgrading facilities. The process of tightening environmental regulation in the downstream is likely to aggravate the growing problem of lack of refinery capacity, which in turn is encouraging higher refinery gate prices, irrespective of what is happening to the price of crude oil. This could create a public backlash against growing green legislation, especially in areas where oil product prices are already a sensitive political issue.

5. Conclusion—Challenges of Using Policy

There are potentially a large number of areas relating to the oil market that are likely to cause the sort of popular concern which will demand a policy response. Table 1 summarizes the issues which have been identified in this chapter.

In outlining these issues of concern, the chapter has tried to outline the various policy options available. However, the effectiveness of any policy response will be constrained by a number of factors.

- Following the oil shocks of the 1970s, many of the easy policy options have been already been implemented, especially in the OECD. For example, oil intensities have fallen significantly (IEA, various years). Specifications have become tighter, producing much cleaner products etc. Thus the costs of policies are certain to rise exponentially as the objectives turn to the ever harder targets.

- There is a lack of agreement over the causes of many of the issues of concern. For example, if higher prices are largely the result of cyclical factors, then the solution lies in leaving them to the market. What goes up will eventually come down. However, if, as this author believes, structural factors are more important, then this would require a policy response. Leaving it to the market would not solve the problem of higher prices except in the very long term required for the inherent time lags on both the demand and supply side to take effect. It is worth remembering that the last time the world experienced very high oil prices in the 1970s, eventually the market feedback loops of reduced demand and increased supply did lead to a fall in price in 1986. However, 1986 was 13 years after the First Oil Shock of 1973!

- The international nature of the oil market limits the effectiveness of national policy. There are two dimensions. First, there is the inevitable problem of free riding. For example, the release of strategic stocks will lower oil prices following a price shock. However, because oil is a global market, the lower prices benefit all. Thus there is no incentive to incur the very considerable costs associated with strategic stockpiling. Second, the international nature of the industry inhibits unilateral action. For example, taxes on jet kerosene to internalize the externalities associated with air travel would simply not work, except, possibly, if it were introduced into the North

American Free Trade Agreement, where alternative fuelling options would be very limited.

- However, the main constraint on any policy solution arises from domestic politics in the countries concerned. The policy options which are available are for the most part likely to be politically very unpopular. For example, in the case of the UK, proposals to introduce road pricing which would be an obvious solution to traffic congestion, increased gasoline consumption, and consequent pollution is described in political circles—but not publicly—as 'the poll tax on wheels'.[8] Thus the future faces a serious dilemma. On the one hand there are the issues listed in Table 1, which will produce domestic political pressure for policy. But on the other hand the only viable and effective policy options will be politically unpopular. In such a world, the commonest response from governments is to obfuscate and delay. However, meanwhile the very real problems in Table 1 will accumulate and are unlikely to go away of their own accord. The implication is that only a major international crisis will sweep away the political constraints upon effective policy. While the Middle East is very likely to supply this, it is a sad reflection that we must solve our problems at the expense of others' misery. Furthermore, the probable lack of a coherent and urgent policy response simply makes the crisis both more probable and more dramatic than it might otherwise be.

---

[8] For non-UK readers or young UK readers, the poll tax was introduced by Margaret Thatcher in 1985. It proved so unpopular it is widely credited with ending her term as prime minister in 1990.

6

OPEC Pricing Power: The Need for a New Perspective

Bassam Fattouh

1. Introduction

Since the 1973 oil price shock, the history and behaviour of the Organization of Petroleum Exporting Countries (OPEC) have received considerable attention both in the academic literature and in the media.[1] Many conflicting theoretical and empirical interpretations about the nature of OPEC and its influence on world oil markets have been proposed. The debate is not centred on whether OPEC restricts output, but the reasons behind these restrictions. Some studies emphasize that OPEC production decisions are made with reference to budgetary needs, which in turn depend on the absorptive capacity of the members' domestic economies (Teece, 1982). Others explain production cuts in the 1970s in terms of the transfer of property rights from international oil companies to governments which tend to have lower discount rates (Mead, 1979; Johany, 1980). Others explain output restrictions in terms of coordinated actions of OPEC members. Within this literature, OPEC behaviour ranges from classic text-book cartel, to two-block cartel (Hynilicza and Pindyck, 1976), to clumsy cartel (Adelman, 1980), to dominant firm (Salant, 1976; Mabro, 1991), to loosely cooperating oligopoly, to residual firm monopolist (Adelman, 1982), and most

---

[1] For an historical account of OPEC see Seymour (1980), Terzian (1985), and Skeet (1988). For a comprehensive review of the theoretical literature, see Gately (1984), Cremers and Salehi-Isfahani (1991), and Mabro (1998a).

recently to bureaucratic cartel (Smith, 2005). Others have suggested that OPEC oscillates between various positions but always acts as a vacillating federation of producers (see, for instance, Adelman, 1982; Smith, 2005). The existing empirical evidence has not helped narrow these different views. Griffin's (1985) observation in the mid-1980s that the empirical studies tend to 'reach onto the shelf of economic models to select one, to validate its choice by pointing to selected events not inconsistent with model's prediction' still dominates the empirical approach to studying OPEC behaviour and its pricing power.[2]

In this chapter, we examine OPEC's ability to influence oil prices. As in any other issue related to OPEC, there are divergent views regarding OPEC pricing power. More importantly, there seem to be switches in perception shifting from one extreme, where OPEC is perceived to play no role or a very limited role in pricing, to the other extreme, where OPEC is perceived to be a price setter. These switches in perception became very apparent in the events that surrounded the oil price collapse in 1998[3] and the oil price hike in 2004. In 1998, when the Dubai price approached the $10 per barrel level, many observers claimed that OPEC has lost its ability to defend oil prices, with many of them predicting its demise. This view of an ineffective OPEC, however, was reversed only few months later with many observers in the media considering the events of 1998 as inducing cooperation among OPEC members and ushering in a new era.[4] During March 1998 and March 1999, OPEC embarked on two production cuts in an attempt to put an end to the slide in oil prices. These production cuts were implemented with a high level of cohesiveness among members, which contradicts the view that OPEC is not able to implement cuts.[5] In the high oil price environment of 2004, there was another switch in perception, where doubts re-emerged about OPEC's pricing power. But unlike the events surrounding 1998, the loss of pricing power in 2004 was mainly attributed to OPEC's loss of excess capacity.

The events of the last few years highlight some important observations that are essential for understanding OPEC behaviour. First, OPEC's pricing power is not constant and varies over time. There are many

---

[2] See Smith (2005) for a more recent empirical review.

[3] See Mabro (1998*b*) for an insightful view of the 1998 oil prices.

[4] See, for instance, Stanley Reed, 'Cheap Oil? Forget It', *Business Week*, 3 August 2004, Issue 3873.

[5] This has led some observers to question how OPEC 'suddenly acquired new powers in March 1999, having been unable to force a sustained increase in oil prices since 1986, and how the same cartel just two years later seemed to be on the verge of collapse' (Barsky and Kilian, 2004, p. 125).

instances in which OPEC can lose power to influence oil prices. Second, this change in pricing power is induced by market conditions and can occur both in weak and tight market conditions. This does not imply that market participants can afford to ignore OPEC. In fact, the organization has succeeded in many instances in implementing production cuts to prevent declines in oil prices. Furthermore, OPEC (and more specifically Saudi Arabia) has succeeded in offsetting the impact of sudden disruptions of supply and in moderating the rise in oil prices.[6] Third, pursuing output policies has become more complicated with the growing importance of the futures market in the process of oil price discovery. The effectiveness of any policy depends to a large extent on the ability of OPEC to influence participants' expectations in the futures market (Fattouh, 2006a). Finally, long-term investment plans can have important implications for the long-run pricing power of OPEC. Many international organizations such as the International Energy Agency (IEA) and Energy Information Administration (EIA) project greater reliance on Middle Eastern oil in the next two decades and, hence, they predict a marked increase in the market share of Middle Eastern oil exporters. This is seen to have the effect of automatically increasing OPEC market power. However, we argue that OPEC may not have the incentive to invest. Even if member countries decide to invest, there are serious bottlenecks that may prevent this investment from taking place.[7] Finally, even if the investment materializes and OPEC market share rises markedly, its ability to influence prices does not automatically follow.

This chapter is divided into six sections. In section 2, we provide a brief account of the evolution of the international oil pricing system, emphasizing the recent shift to the futures market for oil price determination. In section 3, we discuss OPEC's current role in the market and the failure of theoretical models to take into account three major features in their analysis: the varying conduct hypothesis, the asymmetric response to global market conditions, and the signalling mechanism. In section 4, we discuss the implications of IEA and EIA projections that the world is likely to become more reliant on Middle Eastern OPEC producers. In this section, we assess whether OPEC has the incentive to increase its market share and whether the investment to meet projected demand will materialize, discussing briefly some of the factors that can hinder

[6] This was clearly evident during 1990 when OPEC offset the loss of exports from Iraq and Kuwait, and in 1979–80 when political developments surrounding Iran resulted in panic buying.
[7] See Fattouh and Mabro (2006) for a discussion on the under-investment problem in the oil sector.

investment. In Section 5 we discuss Saudi Arabia's position in the oil market. Section 6 concludes.

2. The Evolution of the Oil Pricing System: A Brief Historical Account

Since the discovery of oil in the Middle East, at the beginning of the twentieth century, until the early 1970s, OPEC member countries played no role in the production or pricing of crude oil.[8] Governments simply received a stream of income calculated on the basis of 'posted' price (Mabro, 1984). Being a fiscal parameter, the posted price did not respond to the usual market forces of supply and demand and hence did not play any signalling role. Other prices, such as spot and long-term contract prices, played a very limited role in price discovery owing to the vertically and horizontally integrated industrial structure dominated by the large multinational oil companies, known as the Seven Sisters. This meant that oil trading became, to a large extent, a question of inter-company exchange, with no free market operating outside these companies' control. Multinational oil companies used to balance their positions on the basis of long-term contracts, but the prices in these contracts were never disclosed.

By the late 1950s, changes in the oil market, such as the arrival of independent oil companies that were able to obtain access to crude oil outside the Seven Sisters' control and the arrival of crude oil from the former USSR, started to challenge the dominance of the multinational oil companies. However, these changes never posed a serious threat to the Seven Sisters' control or to the posted price system. At the same time, OPEC countries were too weak to change the existing pricing regime. Thus, the multinational oil companies maintained their dominant position both in the upstream and downstream parts of the industry for most of the 1960s (Penrose, 1968).

It is not until the early 1970s that the oil pricing system witnessed a major transformation which saw the power of price setting shift from the multinational oil companies to OPEC. This transformation was driven by an array of factors, the most important of which is the tight demand–supply oil conditions that emerged in the early 1970s. Between 1970 and 1973, global demand for oil increased at a fast rate, with most of the

[8] This section is based on Fattouh (2006a).

increase in demand met by OPEC countries. This enhanced OPEC governments' power relative to the multinational oil companies and governments began seeking higher stakes on their oil sales. In October 1973, after the negotiations with multinational oil companies to increase oil prices failed, the six Gulf members of OPEC unilaterally announced an immediate increase in the posted price of the Arabian Light crude from $3.65 to $5.119. In December 1973, OPEC raised the posted price of the Arabian Light further to $11.651. These events represented a major transformation in the oil pricing system. For the first time in its history, OPEC assumed a unilateral role in setting posted prices, while before it had been able only to prevent oil companies from reducing them (Skeet, 1988). At the centre of the new pricing system was the marker or reference price, with individual member countries setting their prices in relation to the price of the Arabian Light which became the marker crude.

Another important development in the early 1970s that had direct implications on the pricing system was OPEC governments' decision to stop granting new concessions[9] and claim equity participation in the existing concessions, with a few of them opting for full nationalization. Equity participation gave OPEC governments a share of the oil produced which they had to sell to third-party buyers on the basis of an official selling price (OSP) or government selling price (GSP) (Mabro, 1984). However, for reasons of convenience, lack of marketing experience, and inability to integrate downwards into refining and marketing in oil-importing countries, governments made it compulsory, as part of the equity participation agreements, to sell the oil back at buy-back prices to the companies that originally held the concession.

Equity participation and nationalization of oil reserves profoundly affected the structure of the oil industry. During the late 1970s, multinational oil companies lost large reserves of crude oil and became increasingly dependent on OPEC supplies. The degree of vertical integration between upstream and downstream considerably weakened, as companies no longer had enough access to crude oil to meet their downstream requirements. This encouraged the development of an oil market outside the inter-multinational oil companies' trade, and pushed companies to diversify their sources of oil supply by gaining access and developing reserves outside OPEC.

---

[9] As early as 1957, Egypt and Iran started turning away from concessions to new contractual forms, such as joint-venture schemes and service contracts. In 1964, Iraq decided not to grant any more oil concessions (Terzian, 1985).

In the early 1980s, new discoveries in non-OPEC countries responding to higher oil prices and taking advantage of new technologies meant that significant amounts of oil began to reach the international market from outside OPEC. According to the EIA (2005*a*), non-OPEC countries increased their share of world total oil production from 48 per cent in 1973 to 71 per cent in 1985, with most of the increase coming from Mexico, the North Sea, and the Soviet Union. The increase in non-OPEC supply had two main effects. First, non-OPEC countries were setting their own prices that were more responsive to market conditions and hence more competitive. Second, the number of crude oil producers increased dramatically. The new suppliers of oil, who ended up having more crude oil than required by contract buyers, secured the sale of all their production by undercutting OPEC prices in the spot market. Buyers who became more diverse were attracted by the competitive prices on offer which were below the long-term contract prices.

It became clear by the mid-1980s that the OPEC-administered oil pricing regime was unlikely to survive these competitive pressures for long. OPEC or, more precisely, Saudi Arabia's attempts to defend the marker price only resulted in a dramatic reduction in its oil exports and loss of market share as other producers could offer to sell their oil at a discount to the Arabian Light. As a result of these pressures, OPEC saw its own market share in the world's oil production fall from 52 per cent in 1973 to less than 30 per cent in 1985, with Saudi Arabia's share being the most affected. In an attempt to restore the country's market share, Saudi Arabia adopted the netback pricing system in 1986 (Mabro, 1986). The netback pricing system provided oil companies with a guaranteed refining margin since it was based on a general formula in which the price of crude oil was set equal to the *ex post* product realization minus refining and transport costs. The netback pricing system resulted in the 1986 price collapse, from $26 a barrel in 1985 to less than $10 a barrel in mid-1986.

Out of the 1986 crisis, the current 'market related' oil pricing regime was born. The adoption of the current market-related pricing system represented a new chapter in the history of oil price determination since it resulted in the abandonment of the administered oil pricing system that dominated the oil market from the 1950s until the mid-1980s.

The current 'market-related' oil pricing regime is centred on formula pricing, in which the price of a certain variety of crude oil is set as a differential to a certain marker or reference price. The emergence and expansion of the market for crude oil allowed the development of market-referencing pricing off spot crude markers such as spot West Texas

Intermediate (WTI), dated Brent, and Dubai. The declining physical liquidity of the reference crudes, however, has raised doubts about their ability to generate a marker price that reflects accurately the price at the margin of the physical barrel of oil. First, it is often argued that thin and illiquid markets are vulnerable to distortions and squeezes. Second, in thin and illiquid markets where actual deals are far apart and irregular, the number of price quotations for actual transactions is quite small. But for crude oil to act as a reference or benchmark, price quotations should be generated on a regular basis.[10]

The declining liquidity of the physical base of the reference crude oil and the narrowness of the spot market have caused many oil-exporting and oil-consuming countries to look for an alternative market to derive the price of the reference crude. The alternative was to be found in the futures market. When formula pricing was first used in the mid-1980s, the WTI and Brent futures contracts were in their infancy. Since then the futures market has grown to become not only a market that allows producers and refiners to hedge their risk and speculators to take positions, but also at the heart of the current oil pricing regime, where the price of oil is determined. Thus, instead of using dated Brent as the basis of pricing crude exports to Europe, several major oil-producing countries, such as Saudi Arabia, Kuwait, and Iran, rely on the International Petroleum Exchange (IPE) Brent Weighted Average (BWAVE).[11] The shift to the futures market has been justified by a number of factors. Unlike the spot market, the futures market is highly liquid, which makes it less vulnerable to squeezes and distortions. Another reason is that a futures price is determined by actual transactions in the futures exchange and not on the basis of assessed prices by oil reporting agencies. Furthermore, the timely availability of futures prices, which are continuously updated and are disseminated to the public, enhances price transparency.

In brief, the oil pricing system witnessed major transformations in the last 50 years or so which saw the oil market shift from the administered

[10] For a regular flow of price quotations and daily price assessments of reference crudes, markets rely on oil price reporting agencies for price discovery. In their assessment, oil price reporting agencies obtain information from market participants about the deals concluded and the bids and offers made. In order to provide reliable price assessments, reporters should observe plenty of arm's-length deals between market participants. Since market participants have different interests and different positions (short or long), it is very unlikely that they would reveal the actual price used in the deals. In a liquid market, this can be less of a problem since, by pooling information from different participants, biases could cancel out (but not necessarily).

[11] The BWAVE is the weighted average of all futures price quotations that arise for a given contract of the IPE futures exchange during a trading day. The weights are the shares of the relevant volume of transactions on that day. Specifically, this change places the futures market, which is a market for financial contracts, at the heart of the current pricing system.

oil pricing system, first governed by multinational oil companies and then governed by OPEC, to a 'market related' system, in which initially oil was priced off the spot market and where later the futures market assumed a greater role in price discovery. This had important implications on the pricing power of OPEC as is explained below.

3. OPEC, the Market, and Oil Prices

At first sight, it might seem that OPEC plays a very limited role in the formation of oil prices. OPEC members, like other oil exporters, just take the marker price from the spot market and, more recently, from the futures market and plug it into the pricing formula to arrive at the price at which they sell their oil. But this simple characterization does not provide a realistic description of OPEC's role in price formation. By changing output quotas, the organization and its dominant player, Saudi Arabia, are bound to have an influence on oil prices. But, as we discuss in this section, this process is not straightforward.

OPEC sets production quotas based on its assessment of the market's call on its supply. Oil prices fluctuate in part according to how well OPEC does this calculus. Through the process of adjusting its production quotas OPEC can only hope to influence price movements towards a target level or target zone. In a supply–demand framework, the oil price is determined by OPEC and non-OPEC supplies as well as by oil arriving to the market from OPEC members who did not abide by the assigned quotas. Since these supplies cannot be predicted with accuracy and are influenced by factors other than the oil price, OPEC can only hope that the resulting oil price is close to its preferred price. In this context, models that consider OPEC simply as a price setter that maximizes the net present value of oil receipts over time are of limited usefulness (see for instance, Pindyck, 1978).[12] As Mabro (1991, p. 13) notes,

the revenue maximization objective which theory postulates and core producers would dearly like to achieve is not credible. One has to become content with a second best: to obtain through the pricing policy more revenues than would accrue under a competitive market structure. This more may be much better than nothing but is likely to be very different from the optimum.

[12] Pindyck (1978) considers a model in which the behaviour of OPEC, as a monopoly owner of an exhaustible resource, is highly predictable: OPEC would choose prices or quantities such that the marginal revenue minus the marginal extraction cost will increase at the rate of interest (Pindyck, 1978). In Gately's (1984) words: 'even a dumb OPEC has to set its price so as to satisfy the appropriate Hotelling conditions'.

165

From a very different perspective, which emphasizes the bureaucratic nature of OPEC, Smith (2005) reaches a similar conclusion where he argues that 'OPEC acts a bureaucratic cartel; i.e. a cooperative enterprise weighed down by the cost of forging consensus among members and therefore partially impaired in pursuit of the common good' (p. 74).

Achieving the desired price level to achieve 'more' revenues has become more difficult in the current context in which prices are increasingly being determined in the futures market. OPEC's influence on prices has now become dependent on the expectations of participants in the futures markets. In principle, quota decisions can be viewed as signals to the market about OPEC's preferred range of prices. It is important to stress that this signalling mechanism may or may not succeed, depending on how the market interprets these signals. Specifically, the effectiveness of the signal will depend on whether the market believes that OPEC is able to undertake the necessary output adjustment in different market conditions.

Although OPEC has on many occasions succeeded in defending the oil price, adjusting output downward has in many instances proved to be unsuccessful. If global demand for oil falls, non-OPEC suppliers will continue to produce at their maximum potential. OPEC members, in their attempt to defend a target price, would call for production cuts. However, because of the different features, needs, bargaining power, and divergent interests of member countries, OPEC cannot usually reach agreements on allocation of production cuts. Even when agreements are reached, each member has the incentive to free ride on these decisions. Because of the absence of a monitoring mechanism, these violations are not usually detected and, even if they are, the organization does not have the power to punish and force member countries to abide by the agreed production cuts (see, for instance, Kohl, 2002; Libecap and Smith, 2004). These problems become more acute when the required cuts are significant, because the small OPEC members usually find it difficult to reduce their production on a pro rata basis—the usual system adopted by OPEC over the years. In these circumstances, market participants would doubt the credibility of OPEC's decision to cut production and may decide to ignore the signal. This especially holds if there are deep divisions and political rivalries among member countries. Lack of transparency about the decision-making processes and lack of information about production reduce further the credibility of the signal.

Adjusting output in the face of growing global oil demand can also be problematic, though for different reasons. Although agreements to increase quotas are easier to reach and implement when global demand is rising, OPEC may not respond fast enough to this upward trend in an environment of imperfect information and uncertainty about future demand. After all, the decision to wait and not to increase output is more profitable than to increase output if expectations about growth in demand turn out to be false. Anticipating this response, market participants may ignore the signal of an output increase, considering such a move as not credible.

The rise in global demand for oil can have an impact on OPEC pricing power through another channel: the erosion of spare capacity. This became very evident in 2004. Since the early 1990s, the year-to-year increase in global oil demand has outpaced the increase in non-OPEC supply in almost every year.[13] In fact, over the period 1990–2004, global demand for oil increased by around 16m barrels per day (mb/d) while the increase in non-OPEC supply amounted to only around 6 mb/d. The difference between the increase in global demand and non-OPEC supply had to be met by OPEC. During 1990–2004, OPEC supplied the additional 10 mb/d. The main impact of the increase in demand for OPEC oil has been the gradual decline in OPEC spare production capacity, a process which accelerated in the 1990s and early 2000 (Fattouh, 2006*b*). In addition to these demand and supply dynamics, the reduction in sustained capacity in some OPEC member countries contributed to the loss of spare capacity. Oil workers' strikes in Venezuela, which caused production capacity to fall, sanctions in Iraq, Iran, and Libya, which resulted in long periods of underinvestment, and Indonesia's failure to arrest production declines all contributed to the erosion of production capacity. When the majority of OPEC members produce at or close to their maximum capacity, OPEC has no influence on oil prices. This problem can be compounded by market scepticism about OPEC's spare capacity and its ability to raise production. In 2004, doubts about the ability of the dominant producer, Saudi Arabia, to supply the market with additional supplies of the required quality of crude rendered any OPEC announcements of production increases ineffective. This led *The Economist* to comment that, 'Ali Naimi, the Saudi oil minister, usually moves markets when he speaks. Yet when he promised a few days ago that

[13] Exceptions were 2000, 2001, and 2002, which saw large increases in Russian oil production.

more oil is on the way, traders ignored him and the rally continued apace.'[14]

This leads us to the analysis of the price band mechanism which OPEC adopted in 2000 as a signalling mechanism. This mechanism sets a target range for the OPEC basket price of between US$22 and US$28 per barrel of oil. If prices are below the floor for 10 consecutive days, OPEC will automatically cut production. If prices are above the upper band for 20 days, it will automatically increase production. Recently, various studies have examined OPEC pricing policies within a target price zone providing a rationale for the lower and upper bands (Chapman and Khanna, 2001; Tang and Hammoudeh, 2002; and Horn, 2004). For instance, Horn (2004) explains the floor in terms of OPEC's position as a partial monopolist in the oil market. He argues that lower prices are probable only if the OPEC cartel breaks up. As to the upper band, it is set to prevent stimulation of production of unconventional oil based on oil sand or coal. He thus predicted that crude oil prices above $30 per barrel are, therefore, not sustainable for a long period. Recent events, however, have shown the invalidity of the target price zone. Specifically, OPEC will not respond by increasing supplies if prices exceed the upper band. Further-more, in a very tight market, when spare capacity is very low, the upper band becomes irrelevant as OPEC will not be able to defend it. Thus the most important feature of the price band is the floor as, in principle, OPEC will be able to defend it by cutting production. The difficulty of managing such a price target zone in a tight market led OPEC to suspend its 5-year-old oil price band mechanism in January 2005.

Thus, although OPEC sends signals to the market about a preferred range of prices, their impact depends on participants' understanding of their implications and their perceptions of the credibility of the policy. In fact, this hypothesis has recently received some empirical support. Wirl and Kujundzik (2004) investigate whether OPEC still influences the oil market by examining whether the decisions made at the OPEC confer-ence exert any influence on oil prices. Using data for the period 1984–2001, they find that the impact of OPEC decisions on oil prices is weak and, if there is any impact, it is restricted to decisions that call for price increases. The authors argue that this result could be due to three reasons:

(i) sufficient information is leaked prior to the meeting so that the official Conference reveals hardly any new information; (ii) news shows up only in data with higher, say

---

[14] *The Economist*, 'Unstoppable? How OPEC's Fear of $5 Oil Led to $50 Oil', 21 August 2004.

hourly, frequency; (iii) the Conference lacks credibility that the agreed upon policies will be actually carried out by the individual member countries (p. 60).

As we have seen, OPEC pricing power is not straightforward. Any theoretical and empirical model should take into account the following three features. First, OPEC behaviour is not constant and can exhibit variation in conduct with important implications on price dynamics in the oil market. In this respect, the study by Geroski *et al.* (1987) represents an important but lonely contribution. Using quarterly data from 1966 to 1981, they find evidence which is consistent with the variation in conduct hypothesis.

Second, OPEC's influence is asymmetrical, depending on whether it is responding to rising or falling global oil demand. In fact, a large literature developed on whether firms find it more difficult to collude during booms or recessions (Rotemberg and Saloner, 1986; Haltiwanger and Harrington, 1991; Staiger and Wolak, 1992; Bagwell and Staiger, 1997). The main intuition behind this literature is that changes in demand conditions affect the one-shot deviation gains, the losses of future collusive profits, and the future cost of being punished, which have direct implications on the sustainability of collusive outcomes. Haltiwanger and Harrington (1991) find that, under the assumptions of constant and symmetric marginal costs, a firm's incentive to deviate is stronger when future demand is falling, because the value of the forgone collusive profits is smaller when demand is falling than when demand is rising. Thus, according to their model, it becomes more difficult to sustain collusion in weak market conditions. However, this clear-cut result is less so if capacity constraints are introduced into the picture. For instance, Fabra (2006) shows that, when firms face severe capacity constraints, demand fluctuations can also have an impact on the future cost of being punished. When firms are operating close to their maximum capacity, the future costs of being punished are low, while in the presence of large excess capacity, the future cost of being punished can be very high. This can make collusion more difficult in booms rather than in recessions. Incorporating these insights into OPEC models can prove quite useful.

Third, the shift to the futures markets for price determination has introduced a large number of players and the large variety of participants (floor traders, fund managers, refiners, producers, financial institutions, and speculators) has certainly complicated the process of decision-making within OPEC.[15] OPEC's influence on prices has become dependent on the expectations of these participants and how they interpret OPEC signals. In standard signalling models, informed agents communicate private information indirectly via choices of observable actions. Because the choices made are costly, signalling becomes credible. The signalling hypothesis has been successfully applied to a large number of issues, including banking, corporate finance, macroeconomic and monetary policy, and industrial organization.[16] These traditional models of signalling, however, may not be appropriate in this context. First, OPEC communication with the market is direct through public announcements. Second, different from traditional models of signalling, OPEC signals are costless. This raises the question whether any information can be credibly transmitted when signalling is costless and direct. This issue has been extensively analysed within the context of 'cheap talk' in game theory (Crawford and Sobel, 1982; Farrell and Rabin, 1996). The insights from this literature can be very useful in studying OPEC's relationship with the market. The main shortcoming, however, is that cheap-talk models are characterized by a multiplicity of equilibria ranging from the 'babbling' equilibrium in which recipients consider all signals to be meaningless, all the way to the more informative equilibrium. Crawford and Sobel (1982), however, show that informative equilbria still entail a significant loss of information. The literature examines some of the measures that can be used to limit information loss.

4. The Dependence on Middle Eastern Oil and Pricing Power

Many international organizations, such as the IEA and EIA, project that most of the increase in global demand for oil would be met by OPEC, especially Middle East producers within OPEC. In an exercise which focuses on Middle East and North Africa (MENA) oil and gas resources,

---

[15] The list of factors that OPEC has used to explain its decisions since 1999 has expanded to include not only the level of oil price, but also, among others, the open interest position of 'non-commercial' traders on the futures market and the level of stocks (Garcia, 2005; Mabro, 2005). See Fattouh (2007), on the dilemma that OPEC faces in the current market conditions.

[16] For early applications, see Ross (1977) and Leland and Pyle (1977). Leyland and Pyle (1977), for instance, argue that by not selling their entire project to outside investors, entrepreneurs with high-quality projects can send clear signals about the quality of their project. But this signalling act is costly since it entails risk-averse agents (who have a strong preference not to take any risk and to sell the project in its entirety) investing part of their wealth in the project.

the IEA (2005) projects in the reference scenario a rise in MENA oil production from the 2004 level of 29 mb/d to 33 mb/d in 2010 and 50 mb/d in 2030. In this scenario, Saudi Arabia will remain the largest supplier, increasing its output from 10.4 mb/d in 2004 to 11.9 mb/d in 2010 and over 18 mb/d in 2030. A second important player would be Iraq, which is expected to witness the second fastest production growth after Saudi Arabia. The IEA envisages that the MENA share of world oil production would increase from 35 per cent in 2004 to 44 per cent in 2030 with four countries (Iraq, Kuwait, the United Arab Emirates (UAE), and Libya) increasing their shares. The IEA, however, warns that this requires doubling of annual upstream investment in MENA, which may not take place because 'MENA governments could choose deliberately to develop production capacity more slowly . . . or external factors such as capital shortages could prevent producers from investing as much in expanding capacity as they would like'. The IEA claims that MENA producers would lose out by not making these investment commitments because higher revenues, owing to a rise in oil prices, would not compensate for the loss in revenues owing to lower export volumes.

Such a scenario would have important implications on oil prices and OPEC pricing power. First, it suggests that insufficient investment in the large OPEC Middle Eastern exporters can lead to sharp rises and more volatile oil prices. Second, the scenario predicts that the OPEC share in the global oil market would rise drastically. Third, the scenario implicitly assumes that the elasticity of supply outside core producers would diminish such that there will be low supply response from non-OPEC to rises in oil prices. The last two factors may have important implications on pricing power, depending on the model used. For instance, in the dominant firm model, pricing power depends on the elasticity of world demand for oil, the elasticity of the supply of the competitive fringe, and OPEC share in the world market. With predictions of increasing market share, lower non-OPEC supply elasticity and inelastic global oil demand, the model clearly predicts a greater OPEC pricing power.

Rather than focusing on the implications of the different scenarios on pricing power, we take a different approach and address the following questions. First, will OPEC seek to increase market share without any regard to price implications? Second, will the investment required to increase market share materialize? Third, assuming that OPEC decides to seek and is successful in achieving larger market share, does this necessarily imply that it would have greater pricing power?

4.1 *The Incentive to Increase Market Share*

The projections about OPEC supply made by the IEA and EIA are not based on any behavioural analysis. Rather, they are derived from a simple accounting formula that balances world demand after taking into account various factors. The following quotation from EIA (2006, p. 28) makes this idea clear:

> to develop the reference case an initial world oil price path was assumed for the 2010 to 2030 period. Future total world oil demand was then estimated on the basis of that price path and assumptions about future economic growth. The assumed price path was also used to estimate future non-OPEC production of conventional oil and production of unconventional liquids from both OPEC and non-OPEC countries, based on estimates of the total petroleum resource base. Finally, the level of OPEC conventional production that would be needed to balance world oil markets for the assumed reference case price path was calculated by subtracting non-OPEC conventional supplies and total unconventional supplies from total world oil demand.

Although this simple approach overcomes the problem of modelling OPEC's complex behaviour, it has been widely criticized. The above analysis implicitly assumes that OPEC has the incentive to increase market share without any regard to oil prices. Gately (2004) and IMF (2005) analyse whether OPEC producers have the incentive to expand oil output and increase their market share as the IEA and the EIA project. Rather than calculating the OPEC supply as a mere residual, Gately (2004) calculates OPEC's net present value (NPV) of profits for different choices of OPEC's market share and given certain paths of non-OPEC supply. His main finding is that the NPV of the discounted profits is relatively insensitive to higher output growth. In fact, aggressive expansion plans to expand output can yield lower pay-off than if OPEC decides to maintain its market share. This result is quite intuitive. Given certain assumptions about the model parameters, the increase in the discounted expected profit from higher output would be more than offset by lower prices as a result of a rapid output expansion. Gately (2004) thus concludes that projections of rapid rise in market share are implausible and 'are likely to be contrary to OPEC's own best interests' (p. 88). He notes that the incentive to increase capacity at a rapid pace might exist only under the assumptions of high price elasticity of world oil demand and if non-OPEC supply is more responsive to high oil prices.[17]

---

[17] In a separate paper, Gately (2001) reaches the same conclusion regarding Persian Gulf oil producers.

4.2 Bottlenecks to Investment

Rather than a deliberate choice to limit production capacity, there might be serious barriers that prevent some OPEC countries from expanding their production capacity to levels anticipated by the various international organizations. The underlying framework for analysing investment in many of these projections is a frictionless model in which investment decisions are made in a world of no transaction costs, perfect information, and no political constraints. The oil industry, however, is driven by its own logistics, by the lags between planning investment and production, by incomplete information and ambiguous signals, by its capital intensity, and by political and historical developments. These factors and the interaction between them imply a very complex decision-making process which may often produce less than optimal investment decisions. The failure to take these frictions into account will affect our assessment of future patterns of investments in the oil sector.

There is no scope in this paper to discuss the investment scene in MENA. However, it might be useful to make some general observations to emphasize some non-price factors that might prevent MENA exporters from increasing their capacity in the future. First, unfavourable geo-political factors and sanctions can prevent capacity expansion in many oil-exporters through creating an adverse investment climate. In the past, economic sanctions hindered investment and deferred the development of projects in Libya, Iraq, and Iran. In the near future, Iraqi production capacity is likely to be highly affected by geo-political conditions and the security situation. Expectations that once Saddam Hussein had been overthrown, production would go back to the pre-Kuwait invasion level proved to be very optimistic. The security situation has had its toll on the industry where looting and destruction, sabotage of pipelines, corruption, and smuggling are likely to limit the export capability of Iraq. More importantly, the dynamics of Iraqi federal politics and uncertainties in the hydrocarbon laws are likely to undermine the incentive for foreign oil companies to invest. In this respect, it is doubtful that the Iraqi oil capacity will expand to high levels such that it will alter the current market structure before a clear vision emerges about the future shape of Iraq—especially about the future status of Kirkuk and Southern Iraq, where most oil fields reside.

In MENA countries where the state controls the hydrocarbon sector, the relationship between the government (the owner of the resource) and the national oil company (the operator) can result in an unfavourable environment for investment. Specifically, given the competing and increasing demands for economic, social, and infrastructure projects, national companies' budgets are likely to be kept tight, preventing them from undertaking investment, acquiring technological capabilities, and enhancing their managerial expertise. This factor affects MENA exporters to varying degrees, with some national oil companies facing severe budgetary constraints preventing them from expanding capacity.

Investment is also complicated by another relationship—that between the governments and/or national oil companies and the international oil companies. Many consider that restriction of access to reserves is an important barrier to investment. However, access is not the central issue, since such access is effectively restricted only in Saudi Arabia and Kuwait, with the latter developing plans to open its sector to foreign investment through Project Kuwait. What matters most is the nature of the relationship between the two parties. Experience has shown that, even in countries where access to reserves is allowed, there may be important obstacles that could delay or prevent investment by international oil companies. As markets have tightened, the terms and conditions demanded by the owners have been hardening over time. This problem is likely to affect MENA countries to varying degrees, with countries such Iran being especially affected. Iran has very ambitious plans to increase its production capacity from the current level of around 4 mb/d to more than 5 mb/d by 2010 and 8 mb/d by 2015. These levels of production, however, cannot be achieved without attracting sufficient foreign investments and foreign expertise. However, Iran has not been able to attract foreign investment on a large scale because of the political uncertainties and unattractive contractual terms.[18]

Finally, many OPEC officials consider that uncertainty about demand for oil constitutes a very important obstacle for investment. This has led

[18] The Iranian constitution forbids granting petroleum rights on the basis of concessions or production-sharing agreements. Instead, Iran has invented a type of service contract called the buy-back contract, in which the contractor has to fund all exploration and development costs and, in case of discovery, receives remuneration from the National Iranian Oil Company (NIOC). Once the contract is completed, the foreign oil company has to transfer the assets and operation of the field back to the NIOC. Foreign oil companies find this type of contract unattractive for a number of reasons. First, the contract does not guarantee that the oil company would be permitted to develop its discovery or operate it. Second, buy-back contracts usually do not allow foreign oil companies to build a long-term interest in the country. See EIA (2006), 'Country Analysis Briefs: Iran'.

OPEC members to call for security of demand in face of concerns about security of supply. This argument has been made explicit by OPEC where it argues that

if investors are unsure about the risks and the likely returns from petroleum investments they may not make those investments. If we do not invest enough money, or do it far enough in advance, then the world could face a shortage of oil supplies and a downward spiral in the global economy. However, if oil producers continue to receive reasonable prices and stable demand, they will maintain their production and invest far enough in advance to meet the growth of demand. Thus the security of oil supplies relies upon the security of oil demand. Oil producers—and oil consumers—need to work together to ensure that the security of oil supply and demand is preserved.[19]

This argument of security of demand is highly impractical in the current market structure and the idea that uncertainty has to be resolved before making an investment is highly unrealistic. Instead, investment decisions can only be made in the context of uncertainty. As suggested in the literature of irreversible investment, uncertainty has the effect of increasing the value of the option to wait, i.e. delaying the investment until new information about market conditions arrives. For the oil industry, the option to wait is very valuable. After all, the decision to wait and not to invest is more profitable than to invest and increase production in face of falling global demand. In other words, it is more profitable for OPEC to err on the side of under-investing in new capacity as opposed to expanding capacity, because the decline in oil sales can be compensated by the increase in oil price in tight market conditions.

4.3 *Managing Capacity Expansions and Pricing Power*

The above analysis suggests that there are serious bottlenecks that may prevent rapid capacity expansion. This is likely to have long-run implications on the pricing power of OPEC. To see why, let us consider a scenario in which there is rapid expansion in capacity—for instance, the scenario in which Iraq re-emerges as a significant producer. If such a scenario materializes, there is less incentive to reach agreements on production cuts because it is much more difficult for member countries to implement production cuts to levels well below their maximum sustained capacity. Under such circumstances, the incentive to cheat becomes high, especially for those exporting countries with large revenue

---

[19] OPEC, 'Is There any Need for Security of Oil Demand?', OPEC website, http://www.opec.org/library/FAQs/aboutOPEC/q19.htm

needs. On the other hand, if capacity expansion fails to materialize and if demand continues to grow, then it is much easier to negotiate and reach agreements on the preferred utilization rates as many of the member countries would be producing close to or at their maximum capacity. In this respect, geo-political factors may have worked in OPEC's favour, in the sense that the region has been hit by many conflicts that prevented large expansions in capacity and reduced disagreement on the allocation of idle capacity. These events include among others the Iranian revolution, the outbreak of the Iran–Iraq war, US sanctions against Iran and Libya, the Iraqi invasion of Kuwait, the UN sanctions against Iraq, and the invasion of Iraq (Libecap and Smith, 2004). This does not mean that OPEC no longer faces the problem of allocating idle capacity, but the problem is less acute when many member countries are producing close to their maximum capacity.

According to the above analysis, there is an unambiguous negative relationship between levels of excess capacity and the degree of collusion (see, for instance, Scherer, 1980; and Phlips, 1995). However, this view has been challenged by various studies that argue that excess capacity has two effects on collusion. On the one hand, it increases the incentive for firms to cheat and deviate from the agreement. On the other hand, excess capacity implies a more severe punishment on the deviating firm (Brock and Scheinkman, 1985). Thus, according to this strand of the literature, the relationship between excess capacity and the degree of collusion is not unambiguous. However, as argued by Compte *et al.* (2002), these studies have focused on situations when all firms have the same maximum capacity. The authors show that the introduction of asymmetric capacities makes collusion more problematic when excess capacity is high.

The failure to enhance capacity expansion, however, creates problems of a different nature, because even moderate shocks, such as exogenous reduction in supply owing to geo-political or weather-related factors and/ or healthy demand driven by a boom, can cause the core producers to lose their spare capacity. In these cases, they can no longer act as price-makers. Thus, it is essential for core producers within OPEC to plan capacity expansion such that reasonable surplus capacity is always maintained. However, coordination on capacity expansions is very difficult if not impossible to achieve.

5. The Role of Saudi Arabia

Some observers have predicted that re-emergence of Russia and Iraq as significant oil exporters may undermine Saudi Arabia's prominent role in oil markets. These views, however, proved premature and there is little doubt nowadays that Saudi Arabia is likely to remain the most prominent player in OPEC and in the oil market, at least for the foreseeable future. Furthermore, Saudi Aramco has been investing heavily in upstream oil with the aim of increasing the Kingdom's capacity from its current level of around 11 mb/d to 12.5 mb/d in 2009. In 2004, Saudi Arabia completed two mega projects, Qatif and Safah, with estimated gross production of 500,000 b/d and 150,000 b/d in 2004. In 2006, Saudi Aramco brought on stream its Haradah III crude oil project 2 months ahead of schedule. The project is expected to produce around 300,000 b/d of Arab light crude at its peak. This expansion push is likely to continue for the next few years. Saudi Aramco is planning to bring on stream the AFK project in 2007, with estimated gross production of 500,000 b/d of Arab light. In 2008, the Shaybah (Phase 1) and Nuayyim fields are expected to come on stream with an estimated gross addition of 250,000 b/d and 100,000 b/d respectively. The largest increment of production is expected to come from the Khurais field, scheduled for completion in 2009. The gross addition from Khurais is estimated to reach a massive 1.2 mb/d.

According to Saudi Arabia's official oil policy, the reasons for embarking on such rapid expansion are twofold: to maintain a back-up capacity and enhance the stability of the world oil market.[20] Regarding the latter objective, it is important to note that stabilizing the world oil market does not mean that Saudi Arabia prefers or wants low oil prices. In this respect, it is important to make a distinction between price-takers and price-makers within OPEC. The former is a small producer with little influence on price, while the latter has market power and can influence the price by individual actions. As argued by Mabro (2003), the role of the price-maker is

to set the price not to express, in an unconstrained manner, views about its level. The view he is obliged to take will have much to do with what can be achieved, not with what one

---

[20] Saudi Arabia's official oil policy, as outlined by Ali Naimi, the Saudi Oil Minister, is based on the following five pillars: 'The first is a high level of oil and gas reserves. . . . Second is daily oil production. . . . The third is our back-up capacity. . . . Fourth is our regard for stability of the world oil market. . . . Fifth and finally, Saudi Arabia has followed a policy of acquiring and developing technology to advance its expertise.' The first two elements have been shaped by geography.

can dream about in an idealized world divorced from reality. We have, therefore, on the one hand the price-takers, who have the freedom to dream and no power to act, and the price-maker who has the unenviable task to bring the dream within the confines of real economic and political conditions. The feasible price, in most circumstances, is likely to be lower than the one price-takers talk about and would like to have. In these situations the price-maker will always appear to be a moderate. This does not necessarily characterize his 'ideal preferences'...it does certainly not mean that low prices are an objective of policy.

The aim of maintaining back-up capacity is to preserve Saudi Arabia's leadership in international oil markets which depends on managing and maintaining excess capacity without which it ceases to become a price maker. A widely held view in the literature is that Saudi Arabia has assumed the role of a swing producer on many occasions. Because of its excess capacity, Saudi Arabia can swing its production depending on the residual demand it faces, which in turn depends on global oil demand and the oil supply of the fringe producers. In fact, Libecap and Smith (2004) consider that it is this special role of Saudi Arabia that has kept OPEC afloat all these years. To provide support for their hypothesis, they examine the frequency of countervailing adjustments, i.e. output adjustment in the opposite direction to the fringe producers. Their basic hypothesis is that if the supply behaviour of the fringe is erratic, then Saudi Arabia production would also be erratic, but in the opposite direction. They find that the countervailing adjustment is higher than one would expect from a cohesive and disciplined cartel.[21]

Others have argued that, by using its excess capacity, Saudi Arabia has played the role of a discipliner which from time to time punishes members who exceed their quotas by flooding the oil market and reducing the price (Griffin and Neilson, 1994; Soligo and Jaffe, 2006). For instance, Griffin and Neilson find evidence that Saudi Arabia opted for a tit-for-tat strategy that punishes and rewards other members. Specifically, as long as Saudi Arabia earns more than Cournot profits, it will be willing to tolerate deviations. However, if cheating goes too far, the swing producer will punish the cheaters by increasing its production until everybody gets Cournot profits. The adherents of this view refer to two examples from recent years: in 1986 when Saudi Arabia increased its supply in an attempt to increase market share, and in 1998 when Venezuela embarked on a policy of increasing production and rapid capacity expansion. In both cases, it is argued that Saudi Arabia played

---

[21] Of course, there would be occasions in which the output adjustment moved in the same direction—for instance, if there is an increase in global demand for oil or if Saudi Arabia feels that residual demand facing it has fallen to very low levels and decides to embark on a policy of increasing market share.

the role of discipliner, which was important to keep the cohesiveness of OPEC, especially in the absence of a formal disciplinary mechanism within the organization.

Despite this prevailing view in the literature, the evidence has not been very supportive for the swing producer role. For instance, Smith (2005) finds inconclusive evidence and concludes that

if the Kingdom has assumed the role of Stackelberg leader, dominant firm, or swing producer, it must not have been pursued with enough vigour and continuity, either before or after the quota system was adopted to have left discernable pattern in the data.

Mabro (1998b) also argues that against all expectations, Saudi Arabia has been performing the role of a fixed volume supplier that does not vary output according to changes in oil demand, noting that from 1992 to the first half of 1997, the Kingdom maintained its production almost fixed at 8 mb/d. This suggests that further research is needed to gain better understanding of the role of Saudi Arabia in the oil market.

Regardless of the nature of its role, given the Kingdom's dominant position in reserves, production, and excess capacity, Saudi Arabia's actions are bound to influence oil prices. However, it is important to stress the following points. First, in a slack market, Saudi Arabia could be left with huge surplus capacity, a situation which it tries to avoid but cannot escape if it is concerned about the price level. Second, although the target set by Saudi Arabia could be achieved, the planned spare capacity of 2 mb/d is very thin for a system as big and complex as the world petroleum system. In any case, the rise in capacity may be absorbed by rising demand and falling supply outside Saudi Arabia. Thus, unexpected events can cause an erosion of excess capacity—in which case Saudi Arabia will cease to act as a price-maker. Third, the notion that Saudi Arabia will always have the incentive to maintain spare capacity should be critically examined. Recently, Saudi Arabia has been raising the issue of whether it should bear on its own the costs of maintaining spare capacity. It is obvious that the 'international oil order', where non-OPEC supplies much of the incremental global oil demand and Saudi Arabia provides the capacity cushion, may no longer be viable in the future.

6. Conclusions

Although there is plenty of room for OPEC to influence the oil price in the current oil pricing system, this influence is not unconstrained. In this chapter, we have argued that the recent changes in the international pricing system have diminished OPEC pricing power, especially when compared to the previous administered oil pricing system. We have also emphasized that OPEC pricing power is not constant and varies according to oil market conditions. Finally, we question the proposition that OPEC in general and the Middle East in particular are bound to have greater influence in the oil market as they develop their reserves and gain greater share of the market.

Although the chapter's focus has been on economic factors, it is important to stress that OPEC does not operate in a political vacuum. I argued elsewhere that pricing systems in the past reflected the balance of power at those times and that this present system is no exception (Fattouh, 2006a). For many, the balance of political power can have an impact on OPEC behaviour. For instance, Doran (1980) hypothesizes that there are limits on how much Saudi Arabia can increase its oil price because very high oil prices can be 'damaging to their own interests because of the danger to the world economy and to their larger commercial involvements and because of the incentive to outside military pressure by distraught consumer governments' (p. 91). He also argues that 'political and cultural similarity' has facilitated Saudi Arabia's role in forming coalitions regarding price preferences. Others have attributed important episodes in oil history to political factors. For instance, some argue that the decline in oil prices in 1986 might have been orchestrated between Saudi Arabia and the USA to undermine the financial position of the USSR.

There is no harm in incorporating some (but not all) of these ideas into the analysis of OPEC pricing power. However, it is important to stress that the impacts of such political factors are not independent of oil market conditions. For instance, the oil price rise in 1973 would not have occurred in slack market conditions and the collapse of oil price in 1986 would not have happened in tight market conditions. Similarly, the oil price shock in 1990, owing to the Iraqi invasion of Kuwait, would have had a much bigger impact if it had occurred in the tight market conditions of 2004. Similarly, imposing oil embargoes is more feasible when oil prices are low and markets are well supplied. These and other examples suggest that although oil is a 'political commodity', it is still a commodity and, like any other, in the long run its price responds in large part to economic forces.

7

UK Oil and Gas Depletion Policy with Growing Import Dependence

*Alexander G. Kemp and Linda Stephen**

1. Introduction

It is well known that the UK reverted to becoming a net gas importer in 2004, following a period from 1997 to 2003 as a net exporter. Ongoing net oil imports are frequently stated to be imminent. There are implications for depletion policy, the balance of trade, and security of energy supply. The prospective size of net imports over the longer term has often been discussed in rather alarmist terms, generally without adequate supporting information on supply and demand. The gas supply problems of the 2005–6 winter have added to concerns about the future security-of-supply situation.

Security of supply and depletion policy are clearly interrelated but in the literature they are often examined as separate issues. Depletion theory has traditionally been concerned with the optimal allocation of production through time, with emphasis on the perceived growing resource scarcity and the desire of the investor to maximize the present value of the sum of expected returns over the lifetime of the resource. While policy-makers are certainly aware of the relevance of depletion policy relating to indigenous reserves for security of supply, the relationship is by no means straightforward. Under some assumptions there may be little or no causal link. Security of supply in the UK depends on the

* The authors are grateful to Dieter Helm and an anonymous referee for very helpful comments.

actions of other participants in the international oil and gas markets, both as consumers and producers. It is also conceivable that the rate of depletion will influence overall recovery rates, a possibility not foreseen in the conventional literature.

The present chapter sets out to discuss UK oil and gas depletion within the context of impending increasing import dependence. Attention is given to security-of-supply issues and the need to encourage maximum economic recovery. There is much emphasis on gas supply and demand because of the extra complexities of peak demand and supply, and uncertainties surrounding the phasing and scale of import and storage schemes. The estimates reflect the uncertainties surrounding international oil and gas prices. Substantial attention is given to the peak winter demand issue and the summer situation of relatively low demand.

2. Historical Development of UK Depletion Policy

Following first licensing in 1964, prolific gas discoveries were made in the Southern North Sea in 1965 and 1966. Policy was to introduce North Sea gas into the energy market as soon as possible. Rapidly increasing gas utilization was desired, based on the perceived benefits of a relatively cheap indigenous fuel substituting for imported naphtha, in particular. The government and the Gas Council were both very anxious to ensure that this new fuel was available from the North Sea as cheaply as the needs to encourage exploration and development permitted. The resulting negotiations with the producers were prolonged and caused some delays to production. But production commenced in 1967 and grew at a fast pace until the early 1970s.

In the 1970s a combination of low prices on offer from British Gas, the monopsony buyer, the greater attractions of oil exploration and development in the Central and Northern North Seas, plus the signing of the huge Frigg contracts, led to a major reduction in exploration in the Southern North Sea. Production from the United Kingdom Continental Shelf (UKCS) reached a plateau and imports from Norway soared. By the beginning of the 1980s British Gas became concerned about the long-term adequacy of gas reserves for the growing UK market and offered very much higher prices for new supplies from the UKCS. Exploration interest revived. The proposed huge Sleipner import contract then created considerable controversy and uncertainty. Its cancellation led to further increases in exploration and development in Southern, Central, and Northern waters of the UKCS.

The result was a dramatic increase in production. Between 1990 and 2000 (the peak year) it grew by 138 per cent. Associated gas from fields in Central and Northern waters became increasingly important. The swing factors for these fields were much less than in those for the dry gas in the Southern North Sea, where they had averaged 1.67. The rapid expansion in the 1990s coincided with the liberalization of the UK market by the government. This contributed to the growth in output. When British Gas effectively supplied all the UK gas market it planned its gas purchases to be consistent with its estimates of gas market demand. When liberalization came along, competition in supplying consumers gradually developed. This produced a more competitive market at the upstream part of the gas chain. The end result was such a large increase in output that the evolving wholesale spot prices fell dramatically in 1995 (from around 18 pence per therm to around 10 pence). This had major consequences for the long-term contracts between producers and British Gas. They had to be renegotiated, with painful consequences for British Gas. The opening of the Interconnector between Bacton and Zeebrugge in late 1998 enabled exports to take place which led to the end of the gas bubble. Thereafter the UK and continental markets became linked.

Oil production commenced in 1975 and grew at a quite remarkable rate (even by world standards) to reach a peak in 1985 of 2.6m barrels of oil per day (mmb/d). This was primarily the consequence of the discovery of several giant fields, particularly Forties, Brent, Ninian, and Piper. They were all developed within a fairly short time of each other and accounted for a very high proportion of the aggregate. Government depletion policy was again to give priority to early production, particularly to alleviate the continuing balance-of-payments problem and to procure security of supply. This coincided with the interests of the oil companies. The pace of development around the mid-1970s was somewhat frantic, leading to substantial cost escalation. In real terms, expenditure on field investment in the UKCS reached its all-time maximum in this period.

The incoming Labour government in 1974 soon introduced an increased taxation package. Although this excited much attention at the time, the new Petroleum Revenue Tax (PRT) had several substantial allowances which ensured that field developments and exploration could proceed unimpaired. The Labour government also took powers to regulate depletion rates and established the British National Oil Company (BNOC) with an accompanying state participation policy which included existing as well as new licences. All these measures provoked great controversy with the industry. The debate did not adversely affect development plans for the first generation of oil fields. The Varley Assurances with respect to limitations on production cuts and development delays gave some comfort to investors, but still left uncertainties. The field development approval procedure, whereby production approvals were given only for part of the life of a field, with the remainder subject to later consent, also created uncertainties and controversies. Thus, on the Forties field, the performance of the reservoir exceeded expectations, and the operator sought an upward revision to his agreed production profile in 1980. This was eventually approved, but only after much debate relating to the diverging arguments for more early tax revenue and slower depletion.

The debate and negotiations relating to state participation occupied much time and effort but did not hold back production from the early generation of fields. Broadly speaking, and despite the many debates and comprehensive powers taken to control depletion, a permissive policy was adopted. The only overt intervention was the 2-year delay imposed on the development of the Clyde field. The effect of this on overall depletion was negligible, although, as BNOC was a substantial partner, it did improve the short-term public-sector borrowing requirement (PSBR).

It had become clear by the later 1970s that, on existing trends, oil production would reach a peak in the mid-1980s and then fall at a quite noticeable pace. The depletion policy debate related primarily to the pros and cons of smoothing the hump to prolong approximate self sufficiency and enhance security of supply in the later 1980s and 1990s. A further ingredient in the debate was the notion that the prospect of rising real oil prices meant that investment in oil in the ground was a serious consideration. Yet another element was the idea that rising oil revenues would push up the sterling exchange rate to undesirably high levels and thus lower depletion rates would be beneficial to the macroeconomy. In the event, by the early 1980s when major decisions had to be taken on whether field development delays and production cuts consistent with the Varley assurances should be made, a combination of the perceived needs for a repletion policy for the late 1980s and beyond, plus the short-term tax revenue needs determined the outcome. The near-term revenue requirements, in particular, determined that there would be no production cuts. Taxation policies were not designed to influence depletion policy. The many changes introduced in the later 1970s and early 1980s were certainly controversial. The introduction of the Supplementary Petroleum Duty (SPD) in 1981 and 1982 as a fourth tier of government's take possibly contributed to some field development delays. The major relaxations made in 1983 certainly incentivized both exploration and the development of smaller fields.

The collapse of oil prices in 1986 had a major negative effect on the pace of new field developments. Two years later came the Piper Alpha tragedy, resulting in 167 deaths. Priority was then given to investment in safety enhancement. Production continued to fall to 1990. Even as late as 1989 some reputable oil production forecasts were indicating continuous decline. The major upturn which took place in the 1990s was the combined result of a number of substantial discoveries, technological progress, and a cost-reducing initiative.

The achievement of a major increase in oil production to a record high of over 2.8 mmb/d in 1999 was remarkable because of the decline in the average size of new field. From a peak of around 600m barrels of oil equivalent (mmboe) in the first half of the 1970s, the average size fell to a little over 30 mmboe by the year 2000. The increase in output in the 1990s was thus achieved by the development of large numbers of fields. From the mid-1990s onwards, the average annual number of new field developments has been around 20.

Over the last few years oil and gas production have become increasingly dependent on fields of more recent vintage. This is an inevitable consequence of the depletion of the older fields. There is a worrying implication, however. Decline rates in fields of more recent vintage are generally substantially higher than those of older vintage.[1] The implication is that if the overall depletion rate of oil and gas is to be moderated, a large number of fields will have to be regularly developed and/or a major increase achieved in the recovery factor from existing fields.

3. Lessons from Principles Relating to Optimal Depletion

The conventional principles of optimal natural resource depletion played only a minor role in determining the outcome. It is pertinent to consider how these principles can inform depletion policy in the current situation. The conventional starting point is the Hotelling model, based on the proposition that the optimal depletion rate is that which

[1] See Kemp and Kasim (2005), for a detailed statistical analysis.

produces the maximization of returns through time. This involves the equalization of the present values of returns in each time period.[2] The model emphasizes the influence of growing scarcity from the exploitation of a non-renewable resource, with the optimal solution being where the resource rent (or royalty, or user cost, or depletion premium) grows through time at the rate of interest. The production volumes are adjusted in each time period to produce this result.

On this analysis the key to the optimal depletion rate is thus how it is priced through time. In any period the price should reflect its marginal social costs (including the depletion premium which is a real resource cost). The model's findings depend on a number of restrictive assumptions, particularly the existence of competitive markets (including the efficient functioning of futures markets), and information on the size of the petroleum reserves. From a national policy viewpoint, the social discount rate is the relevant interest rate in the calculation.

The petroleum industry historically has been personified by new discoveries sufficiently large to affect significantly total recoverable reserves and thus the supply curve and efficient price path. Similarly, technological progress has been such that the industry supply curve has been moved substantially to the right, and with it the efficient price path. Thus, in the UKCS the combined cost of exploration, development, and production of new oil fields (including return on investment) in the first half of the 1980s was estimated by the Department of Trade and Industry (DTI) to be around £16 per barrel whereas for the present vintage of new fields the corresponding figure is around £7 per barrel. The existence of the OPEC cartel in the petroleum market constitutes a major departure from the competitive model and greatly influences the efficient price path.

The application of the Hotelling model to the petroleum industry has been subjected to much examination, with the general finding being that, at least to date, it has not provided much illumination.[3] The depletion premium has generally been found to be fairly insignificant. Given the major market imperfections, it can be argued that, under the umbrella of the Hotelling framework, the efficient price should equal the marginal production cost plus depletion premium plus economic rent due to supply restraints (whether from OPEC quotas or other investment restrictions).[4] This can, in principle, indicate the efficient price path (and

---

[2] See Hotelling (1931).

[3] For illuminating discussions see Watkins (1992) and Adelman (1993).

[4] This is the general approach adopted by Newbery (1985) in estimating the efficient price for gas in the UK within constrained market conditions.

thus production volumes) consistent with estimates of current production costs and size of depletion and other premia. Some insights into current perspectives of oil and gas price expectations, and thus implications for depletion policy, can be obtained. But changes to investment restrictions within OPEC countries and elsewhere may occur. Technological progress to an extent not currently foreseen may also take place. Demand changes (not considered in the Hotelling model) may also occur to an extent not currently foreseen. The result of any or all of these could be significant changes to the efficient price path and thus the optimal depletion rate.

These possibilities indicate the difficulties of formulating a consistent and stable long-term depletion policy. Views have to be taken of the behaviour of actors over which the UK government has little or no influence. Further, on past experience the behaviour of these actors is liable to vary in unpredictable ways which will significantly affect the current level and future trajectory of efficient prices. The implication is that policy should be flexible in recognition of the likelihood of exogenous shocks substantially altering both current and prospective future prices.

The important elements in petroleum exploitation policies relate to licensing and taxation, both of which can influence depletion rates. A key choice lies between the awards of licences based on competitive cash auctions or on work programme bids and other criteria relating to the prospective contribution of the investment to the economy. The bonus bidding system is widely employed in the USA and Alberta but not elsewhere. The main advantages claimed for the scheme are that, given effective competition among investors, it should collect the expected economic rents to the state at low compliance costs. It is also argued that it does not distort the size of the work programmes. Proponents of the auction scheme argue that the use of work programme as the bid variable introduces a distortion to the allocation of resources and, in particular, can lead to unnecessary drilling being undertaken.

The proponents of the discretionary system are concerned that bonus bidding can only collect expected economic rents. Realized economic rents may be very different owing to factors such as field sizes and oil/gas prices varying substantially from the expected. A discretionary system of taxation is thus necessary to ensure that the nation receives an appropriate share of the realized rents. The free-market view is that the investor takes the risks at the time of the initial licence award and the returns should reflect the risks seen at that time. It is also argued that the bonus bid system reduces the exploration budget available for drilling and other work. In a mature province, such as the UKCS, where the numbers of commitment wells in recent licence rounds have been very low, it is arguable that the likelihood of 'excessive' work programmes being bid is quite remote, and that, where the priority is to mitigate the fall in reserves, the emphasis should be given to work programmes. It is, of course, possible to combine an auction system with a discretionary royalty/tax system.

The optimal tax system for collecting realized rents has been the subject of much discussion, particularly since the 1970s.[5] The economic inefficiencies of conventional royalties and the merits of special taxes targeted on the economic rent have been highlighted. Essentially the resource rent tax permits the investor to recover his costs plus a threshold rate of return after which tax relating to his cash flow is levied. A recent variant proposed by Lund (2002) provides that the threshold rate of return be given over a depreciation period rather than as soon as income from the project permits. This device ensures that taxation payments occur earlier.

The UK adopted petroleum revenue tax (PRT), a complex variant of the resource rent tax, in 1975, but, oddly, abolished it for all new fields in 1993. The current system for all new fields is essentially a cash-flow tax as far as existing, tax-paying players are concerned. This scheme was proposed as long ago as 1948[6] but never adopted until recently. A key feature of this tax is that the post-tax internal rate of return continues to equal the pre-tax rate (excluding debt capital issues). Thus a positive pre-tax return is never turned into a negative one by the tax. From the viewpoint of incentives it ensures that *all* investment risks are fully and immediately shared by government to the extent of the tax rate. (It is for this reason that governments have generally been reluctant to adopt it.) It can be claimed for the cash-flow tax that, other things being equal, it provides maximum investment incentives and even reduces the downside risks. The only issue concerns the tax rate. Returns expressed in net present values (NPVs) are obviously reduced by the tax and the only possible disincentive can arise when a high rate reduces these to unacceptably low levels.

A licensing issue which is relevant to depletion policy relates to the relinquishment conditions. These determine how speedily licensees undertake work programmes on their blocks. An extreme view is that, as the investor is the best judge of the optimal timing of his investment,

---

[5] See, for example, Garnaut and Clunies Ross (1983), Kemp (1988), and Lund (2002).
[6] See Brown (1948).

there should be no relinquishment obligations. No government in its capacity as landlord has accepted this view. Host governments throughout the world attempt to ensure that speedy exploration and development occur, while investors argue for longer periods before relinquishment obligations ensue. The supposition is that, at least in many instances, governments have higher discount rates. Investors will generally have a portfolio of assets and opportunities, and optimization of a worldwide portfolio could produce a different time pattern of investment in particular countries. In countries where depletion rates exceed discovery of new reserves, the need to reduce or eliminate the presence of fallow acreage becomes more pressing. This may also be the situation where the perceived exploration opportunities to investors are less exciting than those available elsewhere.

4. Current UK Government Policies

Current policies in the areas of licensing and taxation are directed to enhancing and accelerating activity in the UKCS through the removal of perceived barriers while ensuring that the state receives a substantial share of the economic rents. A series of licensing measures involving more frequent rounds, with large numbers of blocks being offered, and more interventionist initiatives designed to reduce the numbers of fallow blocks and discoveries are the main elements, along with a tax system which is designed to incentivize investment. The context is the continued fall in hydrocarbon production since 2000 and the decline in discovered reserves of both oil and gas since the mid-1990s.

A further consideration in current policy is the view that the total remaining potential is still very substantial. Total oil depletion to the end of 2005 was 3,090m tonnes. Proven oil reserves are officially[7] estimated at 516m tonnes, proven plus probable at 816m tonnes, and proven plus probable plus possible at 1,267m tonnes. The respective reserves: production (R:P) ratios are 6.8, 9.6, and 14.9. These figures are quite low by the standards of major producing countries. When estimates of potential additional reserves and undiscovered resources are added, the total remaining potential is officially estimated at 930m tonnes (low), 1,764m tonnes (central), and 3,271m tonnes (high), amounting respectively to 30, 57, and 106 per cent of total depletion to date.

[7] http://www.og.dti.gov.uk/informtion/bb_updates/chapters/reserves_index.htm (September 2006).

189

For natural gas, total depletion to date is 2,007 billion cubic metres. Proven reserves are estimated at 481 billion cubic metres, proven plus probable at 728 billion cubic metres, and proven plus probable plus possible at 1,006 billion cubic metres. The respective R: P ratios are 5.6, 8.5, 11.7, all relatively low for a major producing country. The ratios have also been falling in recent years with the rapid growth of production in the 1990s. When estimates of potential additional reserves and undiscovered resources are added, the total remaining potential is 775 billion cubic metres (low), 1,290 billion cubic metres (central), and 2,323 billion cubic metres (high), amounting respectively to 39, 64, and 116 per cent of total depletion to date. The potential is thus relatively more favourable for gas than for oil, though the R:P ratios are similar.

With respect to security of supply it is often argued that domestic production is more secure than imports. This is frequently an assertion rather than a scientifically tested proposition. In general it is arguable that greater diversity adds to security of supply, irrespective of whether these sources are indigenous or imports. A highly concentrated domestic source may involve substantial security-of-supply risks. With respect to the North Sea there are currently over 300 sanctioned producing fields, including over 100 gas producing ones. This diversity contributes significantly to security of supply. In fact, significant risks are more likely to emanate from the infrastructure, which is more concentrated. The discovery and development of new fields will contribute to security of supply by enhancing or maintaining diversity, though it should be acknowledged that the interdependence of production from fields through reliance on common infrastructure is increasing both offshore and onshore.

A major current policy initiative concerns fallow acreage. The problem relates principally to blocks awarded in early licence rounds where the relinquishment terms typically required the surrender of 50 per cent of the acreage after 6 years and allowed retention of the remainder for 40 years without the specification of further work obligations. The annual licence fees are also quite low (especially at today's values). These represent the holding costs of the licences. The issue was of less consequence when considerable prospective acreage was available for licensing to new and existing players. In recent years little 'new' prospective acreage has been available, particularly in the mature North Sea, and most of the blocks put on offer have been relinquished from previous rounds.

The issue was raised forcibly as long ago as 1988 by BRINDEX and since then the government has been trying to enhance the utilization of fallow acreage. A multi-pronged PILOT initiative was launched in early 2002. With respect to fallow blocks/discoveries, where there has been inactivity for 3 years after the initial term has expired (the 'official' definition of fallow), the licensee has to discuss his plans for the asset. If an acceptable work programme is produced, the block or discovery can be retained, but the DTI continues to monitor the situation. Where an acceptable work programme is not in place, the licensee has to consider and report on whether and how activity could be enhanced. This would involve consideration of partner misalignment, reassignments, and market testing, including putting the assets on LIFT (licence information for trading). For fallow blocks a total time of 1 year is allowed after which the asset has to be divested, reassigned, or relinquished. For fallow discoveries a total time period of 2 years is allowed.

A further initiative relates to pre-emption rights of partners in licence groups when one participant seeks to assign his interest. These rights have hindered transactions and inhibited new players from pursuing them. The PILOT agreement stated that pre-emption rights cannot be included in future joint-operating agreements among co-licensees. For existing licences they may remain but in a standardized form which would become generally known to potential purchasers.

The 20th Round in 2002 ushered in significant changes in licensing polices generally designed to accelerate activity levels. Blocks were awarded for an initial term of 4 years, after which 50 per cent of the acreage had to be surrendered. After a further 4 years, the remainder also had to be surrendered unless a development was under way or in prospect. In that event, the relevant part of the block could be held for a further 18 years. These changes were designed to accelerate the exploration of acreage and to ensure that unworked acreage was not held for a long time.

Another innovation in the 21st Round in 2003 was the introduction of Promote Licences. These are designed to encourage companies, includ-ing very small ones, to acquire data, work up prospects, and, where appropriate, seek resource commitment, over an initial 2-year period when the licence fees are reduced by 90 per cent. In the second 2-year period, significant work has to be undertaken. No fewer than 34 companies acquired Promote Licences in the 21st Round. Around 60 per cent are seismic contractors or small consultants/new independents.

In the 22nd Round in 2004 163 blocks were awarded, at that time the largest number since the 4th Round in 1971–2. It should be noted, however, that the majority of the blocks were in the Promote Licence category, where the initial work commitments are generally much less than with traditional licences. A further noteworthy feature of the 22nd Round was the substantial presence of new players. Of the 58 companies offered licences, 15 are newcomers.

In 2005 in the 23rd round no fewer than 254 blocks were awarded, the highest since the 4th round, with the involvement of 99 companies. Of these 24 are new entrants. Around half the licences were in the 'promote' category. The offers involved 17 commitments wells.

An issue which was examined several times in the 1990s relates to terms and conditions for access to infrastructure by third parties. These have been negotiated between asset-owners and users. The legislation established in 1975 gave the government powers to determine tariffs, but only if requested to do so by one of the relevant parties. No official requests have been made, but negotiations over terms have often been very protracted. In a free-market situation the asset owner can attempt to set tariffs at levels which are just less than the costs of alternative transport (or other services). It was this phenomenon which led the government to levy PRT on tariff incomes in 1983. There was then a concern that the economic rents from a field's production were being diverted into high tariffs.

The government investigated the sluggish operation of the tariff market in the 1990s and a voluntary Code of Practice was implemented whereby asset owners agreed to publish indicative tariffs for their transportation and processing services and to provide them on a non-discriminatory basis. The market continued to function in a sluggish manner, however. Potential new entrants expressed their concerns over the issue. The DTI led another initiative on the matter which has culminated in a revised Code of Practice being agreed with the industry under the PILOT umbrella in September 2004. Key features of the agreement are that tariff terms will be non-discriminatory and details of actual agreements will be published. The most important element from an economic viewpoint relates to the determination of tariffs. The agreement states that the parties shall negotiate in good faith for up to 6 months. If after that time no agreement has been reached, the DTI can intervene and determine tariffs in accordance with competitive market conditions. Thus local monopoly elements in tariff levels would be excluded, but elements reflecting costs and risks would be included.

In the Finance Act 2003 the Chancellor introduced a further measure dealing with tariffs. Up to then, where a host asset (such as a platform and/or pipeline) was subject to PRT, tariff income received was subject to PRT and corporation tax, producing a marginal rate of 70 per cent. Where the host asset was not subject to PRT, the tariff income received was not subject to PRT and the marginal rate of tax was 40 per cent. This situation produced a non-level playing field in the evolving tariff market and was arguably anomalous. There was a further oddity. Where the producing user field was itself subject to PRT the host asset received a tariff receipts allowance (TRA) per tied-in field. But where the producing user field was not subject to PRT, no TRA was available to the host asset. In the Finance Act 2003, PRT was removed from tariffs relating to new contracts. There was an understanding with the industry that the net economic benefits from this removal of PRT would be passed on to the user. This is not straightforward. The net economic benefit to the asset owner of the PRT removal depends on the combined effect of the reduced tax payable on the income and the reduced tax relief on the expenditures incurred in producing that income. Host assets are now commonly employed to receive some hydrocarbons where the tariffs are subject to PRT (old contracts) and some where the tariffs are free of PRT. The relevant costs have to be allocated between the two categories. This has to be done on a just and reasonable basis according to the PRT legislation.

The most recent PILOT development is the stewardship initiative. This relates to activity in mature fields. In essence, licensees may be asked to demonstrate that they are taking all reasonable steps to procure maximum economic recovery from the fields in question. Where the DTI exhibits concern that more could be done to enhance production, such as by activating idle wells or making other incremental investments, licensees are given the opportunity to respond with appropriate plans within a specified time period. If these are deemed satisfactory the evolving position is monitored. If the investors' plans are deemed not to be satisfactory the licensees could be asked to trade the assets. This initiative is still in its early stages and reflects the concern of the DTI to enhance activity in mature fields and so moderate the decline rates.

Important recent tax changes occurred in 2002. A package of measures was introduced. A Supplementary Charge of 10 per cent was added to corporation tax, capital allowances for field investment were increased from 25 per cent declining balance to 100 per cent first year, and royalties were abolished from January 2003. In December 2005 the Supplementary Charge was increased to 20 per cent from January 2006. This applies to third-party tariffs as well as production income, which is arguably inconsistent with the perceived need to make tariff levels more competitive. For existing taxpayers there is effectively a cash-flow tax for all their operations in the UKCS. The changes have been received with dismay by the industry. For fields developed from March 1993, the marginal rate is increased to 50 per cent. For fields developed before that date the top marginal rate is 75 per cent. Investors not in a tax-paying position are allowed to carry forward their allowances at 6 per cent compound interest.

5. Modelling and Methodology Assumptions

The projections of production have been made through the use of financial simulation modelling, including the use of the Monte Carlo technique, informed by a large, recently updated, field database validated by the relevant operators. The field database incorporates key, best-estimate information on production, and investment, operating, and decommissioning expenditures. These refer to 316 sanctioned fields, 112 incremental projects (76 probable and 23 possible) relating to these fields, 19 probable fields, and 23 possible fields. Those unsanctioned are currently being examined for development. An additional database contains 215 fields defined as being in the category of technical reserves. Summary data on reserves (oil/gas) and block location are available for these. They are not currently being examined for development by licensees.

Monte Carlo modelling was employed to estimate the possible numbers of new discoveries in the period to 2030. The modelling incorporated assumptions based on recent trends relating to exploration effort, success rates, sizes, and types (oil, gas, condensate) of discovery. A moving average of the behaviour of these variables over the past 10 years was calculated separately for 6 areas of the UKCS (Southern North Sea, (SNS), Central North Sea (CNS), Moray Firth (MF), Northern North Sea (NNS), West of Scotland (WOS), and Irish Sea (IS)), and the results employed for use in the Monte Carlo analysis. Because of the very limited data for WOS and IS over the period, judgemental assumptions on success rates and average sizes of discoveries were made for the modelling.

It is postulated that the exploration effort depends substantially on a combination of (a) the expected success rate, (b) the likely size of discovery, and (c) oil/gas prices. In the present study three future oil/gas price scenarios were employed as shown in Table 1. These values are below current market levels but are used to reflect values generally used by investors when assessing long-term investments.[8]

[8] In early 2006 The Royal Bank of Scotland published the results of a survey of investors regarding prices used for assessing long-term investment decisions. The median values were $33 per barrel for oil and 23 pence per therm for gas.

Table 1. Future Oil and Gas Price Scenarios

	Oil price (real)\$/bbl	Gas price (real)pence/therm
High	40	36
Medium	30	28
Low	25	24

Table 2. Exploration Wells

	2006	2030
High	50	38
Medium	38	27
Low	31	20

Table 3. Success Rates (%)

Medium effort/medium success rate	23
High effort/low success rate	19
Low effort/high success rate	24

The postulated numbers of annual exploration wells for the whole of the UKCS are as shown in Table 2. The annual numbers are modelled to decline in a linear fashion over the period.

It is postulated that success rates depend substantially on a combination of (*a*) recent experience, and (*b*) size of the effort. It is further suggested that higher effort is associated with more discoveries but with lower success rates compared to reduced levels of effort. This reflects the view that low levels of effort will be concentrated on the lowest risk prospects, and thus that higher effort involves the acceptance of higher risk. For the UKCS as a whole, three success rates were postulated as shown in Table 3. It is assumed that technological progress will maintain these success rates over the time period.

The mean sizes of discoveries made in the period for each of the six regions were calculated. It was then assumed that the mean size of discovery would decrease in line with this historic experience. Such decline rates are quite modest. For 2004 the average size of discovery for the whole of the UKCS was 34 mmboe. For purposes of the Monte Carlo modelling of new discoveries the standard deviation (SD) was set at 50 per cent of the mean value. In line with historic experience, the size distribution of discoveries was taken to be lognormal.

Using the above information, the Monte Carlo technique was employed to project discoveries in the six regions to 2030. For the whole

Table 4. Total Number of Discoveries to 2030

High effort/low success rate	221
Medium effort/medium success rate	179
Low effort/high success rate	146

period the total numbers of discoveries for the whole of the UKCS were as shown in Table 4. For each region the average development costs (per boe) of fields in the probable and possible categories were calculated. These reflect substantial cost inflation over the last 2 years. Using these as the mean values, the Monte Carlo technique was employed to calculate the development costs of new discoveries. A normal distribution with a SD = 20 per cent of the mean value was employed. For the whole of the UKCS the average development costs on this basis were \$9.45/boe. Annual operating costs were modelled as a percentage of accumulated development costs. This percentage varied according to field size. It was taken to increase as the size of the field was reduced, reflecting the presence of economies of scale in the exploitation costs of fields.

With respect to fields in the category of technical reserves, it was recognized that many have remained undeveloped for a long time, but it was assumed that, reflecting the high current costs and prospective technological progress, their development costs would be aligned with those for new discoveries for each of the regions. For purposes of Monte Carlo modelling a normal distribution of the recoverable reserves for each field with a SD = 50 per cent of the mean was assumed. With respect to development costs the distribution was assumed to be normal with a SD = 20 per cent of the mean value.

The annual numbers of new field developments were assumed to be constrained by the physical and financial capacity of the industry. This subject is currently very pertinent in the UKCS. The ceilings were assumed to be linked to the oil/gas scenarios with maxima of 22, 20, and 17 respectively, under the high-, medium-, and low-price cases. These constraints do *not* apply to incremental projects which are additional to new field developments. To put these assumptions in perspective, 13 new fields received development approval in 2005 but in the 1990s significantly higher numbers (averaging nearly 20 per year) were achieved.

A noteworthy feature of the 112 incremental projects in the database validated by operators is the expectation that the great majority will be executed over the 3 years from 2006. It is virtually certain that in the medium and longer term many further incremental projects will be designed and executed. They are just not yet at the serious planning stage.

Such projects can be expected not only on currently sanctioned fields but *also* on those presently classified as in the categories of probable, possible, technical reserves, and future discoveries.

Accordingly, estimates were made of the potential extra incremental projects from all these sources. Examination of the numbers of such projects and their key characteristics (reserves and costs) being examined by operators over the past 5 years indicated a decline rate in the volumes. On the basis of this, and from a base of the information of the key characteristics of the 112 projects in the database, it was felt that, with a decline rate reflecting historic experience, further portfolios of incremental projects could reasonably be expected. As noted above, such future projects would be spread over *all* categories of host fields. Their sizes and costs reflect recent trends.

The financial modelling incorporated a discount rate, field economic cut-off, and the full details of the current petroleum tax system including the changes in the 2006 Budget. The base case emphasized has a post-tax discount rate of 10 per cent in real terms. An important assumption is that adequate infrastructure will be available to facilitate the development of the future projects. It is also important to note that it is assumed that investment decisions are made on the basis of the oil/gas prices indicated. When the prospective investments in probable and possible fields and incremental projects were subjected to economic analysis, it was found that most were quite small and the returns in terms of NPVs were correspondingly often small on the assumptions described above. It was felt that, to reflect the relationship between the risks and rewards involved, a minimum expected NPV at the discount rates employed would be necessary before the project/field was sanctioned. For purposes of this study, minimum NPVs of £10m were employed as thresholds.

Estimates of UK gas demand were obtained from a variety of reputable sources including National Grid, Energy Contract Company (ECC), JESS Reports, and DTI.[9] A list is given at the end of the chapter. Similarly, estimates regarding the phasing and scale of gas import schemes were derived from a variety of sources. Often they gave rather different estimates and the figures shown here reflect the judgement of the authors. Estimates of the phasing and size of gas storage schemes were also derived from a variety of sources, and those presented again reflect the judgement of the authors. The results presented make a clear

---

[9] For both oil and gas the DTI UK demand projections are based on the high and low cases in *UK Energy and CO_2 Emissions Projections* (UEP26), DTI, July 2006—www.dti.gov.uk/files/file31861.pdf

distinction between new storage which is confirmed (and thus very likely to be available) and possible new storage (which is much more uncertain).

It is important to note that the data on import projects relate to the *capacity* of the scheme in question. This is clearly not the same as the likely size of the gas flows. Experience in the winter of 2005–6 showed that the capacity might not be used on the scale available, both with gas from pipelines and in liquefied natural gas (LNG) form. In the presentation of the results different assumptions are made about gas flows through the Interconnector and the LNG schemes.

6. Results[10]

6.1 *Annual Production and Demand—Oil*

Potential oil production (excluding natural gas liquids—NGLs) under the $30, 28 pence scenario is shown in Figure 1. After an increase in 2007/8 a key feature is the fairly fast decline from sanctioned fields. In the later part of the period the pace of decline moderates, such that in 2020 production from this category of field is around 200,000 b/d. Incremental projects make a major contribution to the moderation of the decline rate over the next few years.

Other features of the results are the major long-term contributions made by fields in the technical reserves category and new discoveries from 2015 onwards. In 2020 total production is around 1.2 mmb/d and the future incremental projects, technical reserves, and new discoveries contribute the great majority of the output. Oil production may exceed demand until 2010, after which the shortfall in supply grows to 600–700 tb/d by 2020.

In Figure 2 oil production prospects under the $40, 36 pence case are shown. Exploration activity and the pace and volume of new field developments are significantly higher under this scenario. Aggregate production holds up very well in the short term, but falls to 1.7 mmb/d in 2010. There is only a gentle fall after that, owing to the development of large numbers of fields in the categories of new discoveries and technical reserves. By 2020 output is 1.34 mmb/d with the great majority coming from technical reserves, new discoveries, and future incremental

---

[10] In the figures which follow, the areas of the charts may occasionally be difficult to distinguish. The legends, read from left to right and top to bottom, correspond to the areas in the charts, reading upwards from the bottom left.

Figure 1 Potential Production and Oil Demand $30/bbl and 28p/therm NPV: £10m@10 per cent Real Post-tax Discount Rate

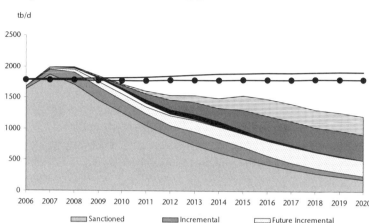

Figure 2 Potential Production and Oil Demand $40/bbl and 36p/therm NPV: 10m@10 per cent Real Post-tax Discount Rate

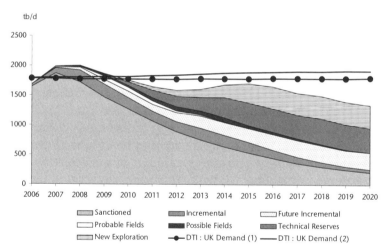

projects. Again oil production may exceed demand until 2010, after which the shortfall in supply grows to 462–584 tb/d by 2020.

In Figure 3 under the $25, 24 pence price scenario, oil production falls quickly after 2008 to a level of just over 1.6 mmb/d in 2010. By 2020 it is around 0.88 mmb/d. The longer-term contributions from technical reserves and new discoveries are very much less under this scenario. Again

Figure 3 Potential Production and Oil Demand $25/bbl and 24p/therm NPV: £10m@10 per cent Real Post-tax Discount Rate

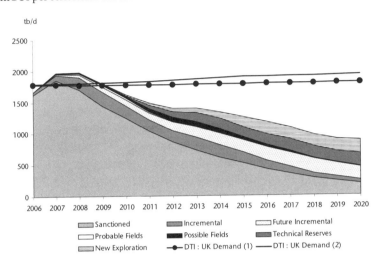

oil production may exceed demand until 2010, after which the shortfall in supply grows to 923–1,046 tb/d by 2020.

6.2 Annual UK Production and Demand—Gas

In Figure 4 prospective UK production of natural gas (excluding NGLs) under the $30, 28 pence case and potential UK demand are shown. In 2010 6.9 bcf/d is produced and 4 bcf/d in 2020. Production from the sanctioned fields falls at a fairly fast pace after 2007, but by 2013 this category of field still accounts for over 50 per cent of total output. By 2020 technical reserves and new discoveries account for around 60 per cent of total production. Figure 4 also shows estimates of gas demand based on those produced by National Grid's 10-Year-Statement (2005), the Energy Contract Company (2006), and the DTI. Under all demand estimates, production from the UKCS is insufficient to meet it. Using the National Grid or Energy Contract Company estimates, the demand shortfall may be 3,917–3,997 mmcf/d by 2010. Using the DTI estimates of gas demand, the shortfall is between 1,981 mmcf/d and 3,141 mmcf/d in 2010, rising to between 5,633 mmcf/d and 7,974 mmcf/d in 2020.

The results are that, by 2010, UKCS indigenous gas production may meet 63 per cent of UK demand according to the demand estimates of National Grid and the Energy Contract Company, or 68–77 per cent of UK demand as seen by the DTI. By 2015 UKCS production may fulfil only

Figure 4 Potential Gas Production and Demand $30/bbl and 28p/therm NPV : £10m@10 per cent Real Post-tax Discount Rate

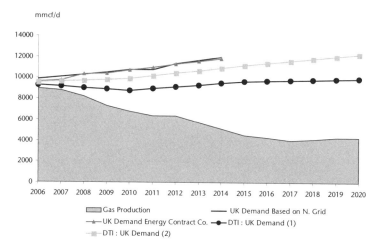

Figure 5 Potential Gas Production and Demand $40/bbl and 36p/therm NPV : £10m@10 per cent Real Post-tax Discount Rate

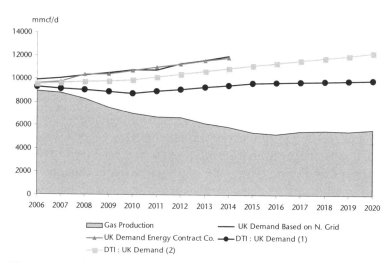

40–47 per cent of UK demand as seen by the DTI, and by 2020 35–43 per cent of demand.

In Figure 5 gas production under the $40, 36 pence scenario is shown. Output falls to around 7 bcf/d in 2010. Thereafter the development of large numbers of fields in the categories of technical reserves and new discoveries moderates the decline rate. By 2020 output is 5.6 bcf/d. Using

Figure 6 Potential Gas Production and Demand $25/bbl and 24p/therm NPV:
£10m@10 per cent Real Post-tax Discount Rate

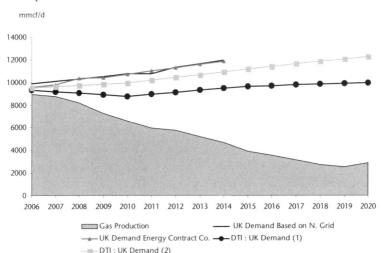

the National Grid and Energy Contract Company estimates of demand, the demand shortfall is 3,696–3,776 mmcf/d by 2010. Using the DTI estimates of demand, the shortfall is between 1,760 mmcf/d and 2,920 mmcf/d in 2010, rising to between 4,281 mmcf/d and 6,623 mmcf/d by 2020. As a consequence, by 2010 UKCS gas production may meet 65 per cent of UK demand according to the demand estimates of National Grid and the Energy Contract Company, or 71–80 per cent of UK demand as seen by the DTI. By 2015 UKCS production may fulfil only 48–56 per cent of UK demand, and by 2020 46–57 per cent of demand.

In Figure 6 UK gas production under the $25, 24 pence scenario is shown. It falls sharply from 8.8 bcf/d in 2007 to 6.6 bcf/d in 2010. In 2020 it is around 3 bcf/d. Using the National Grid or Energy Contract Company estimates of demand, the demand shortfall may be 4,118–4,198 mmcf/d by 2010. Using the DTI estimates of gas demand the shortfall may be between 2,181 mmcf/d and 3,341 mmcf/d in 2010, rising to between 7,049 mmcf/d and 9,390 mmcf/d by 2020. The implications are that, by 2010, indigenous gas production may meet 61–62 per cent of UK demand according to the demand estimates of National Grid and the Energy Contract Company, or 66–75 per cent of UK demand as seen by the DTI. By 2015 UKCS production may fulfil only 35–41 per cent of UK demand as seen by the DTI. By 2020 23–29 per cent of UK demand may be met by UKCS production.

A considerable number of import schemes, both by pipeline and LNG, have either been sanctioned or are currently being seriously examined. In addition, several storage schemes have also been implemented or are being planned. IUK capacity is set to increase in 2007 to 2,275 mmcf/d, Langeled capacity in 2007 should be 2,470 mmcf/d, Vesterled capacity should be 1,275 mmcf/d in 2007, BBL capacity should be 1,550 mmcf/d in 2008, and there may be 'other' imports from Norway in 2008 via existing pipelines, such as FLAGS, of about 900 mmcf/d. The Isle of Grain capacity is set to increase in 2009 to 1,225 mmcf/d. There could be approximately 590 mmcf/d of capacity from Milford Haven's Dragon facility in 2009, increasing to almost 800 mmcf/d in 2012, and the Milford Haven's South Hook facility could provide capacity of more than 2,000 mmcf/d by 2012 in two stages. The two schemes at Teesside (Excelerate and ConocoPhillips) are aggregated in the figures.[11]

Figures 7, 8, and 9 show expected annual average UK demand plus exports to Ireland and the Netherlands[12] alongside potential production and estimates of net imports at the $30/bbl and 28p/therm price. *Net IUK is the Bacton to Zeebrugge Interconnector at capacity minus known contracted exports*. The other import schemes show their estimated capacity.

UK potential production plus Langeled and Vesterled imports are just sufficient to satisfy UK annual average demand in 2006, according to all demand estimates shown, although the position is very tight with the National Grid estimate. After this, a substantial capacity surplus is in prospect. The Langeled pipeline officially opened in October 2006 and could initially supply 1,447 mmcf/d, increasing to 2,470 mmcf/d in October 2007. However, initially at least, because of capacity constraints the total volume of gas which will flow from Norway in the Langeled and Vesterled pipelines will be less than the total capacities. Once facilities have been upgraded to bring Norwegian gas from the Ormen Lange field into line with the gas specification required in the UK, the full joint capacity may be used.

In Figures 10, 11, and 12 the results are shown under changed assumptions whereby the Interconnector's *import capacity* is shown (rather than Net IUK). The results indicate a comfortable supply position for the UK to 2020 if the import capacities were fully employed.

---

[11] In Figures 7–24 information on all the known schemes is shown. Other schemes such as Irish Sea Offshore LNG are not shown because of lack of information on the likely capacities.

[12] Exports to the Netherlands exclude any through the BBL line.

Figure 7 Potential Production, Imports, and Gas Demand $30/bbl and 28p/therm NPV : £10m @ 10 per cent Real Post-tax Discount Rate

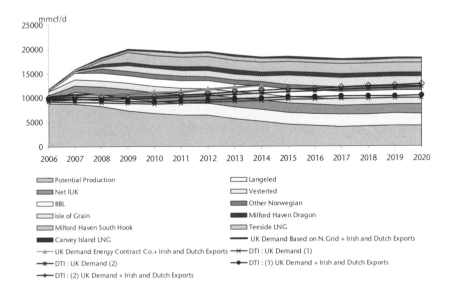

Figure 8 Potential Production, Imports, and Gas Demand $25/bbl and 24p/therm NPV : £10m @ 10 per cent Real Post-tax Discount Rate

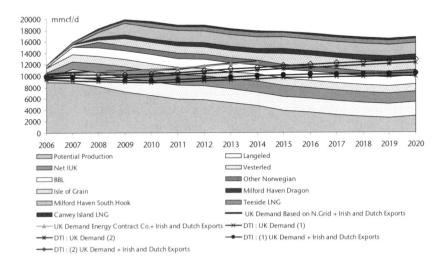

Figure 9 Potential Production, Imports, and Gas Demand $40/bbl and 36p/therm
NPV : £10m @10 per cent Real Post-tax Discount Rate

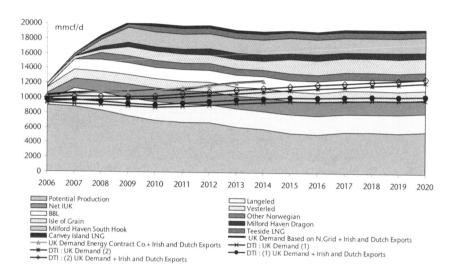

Figure 10 Potential Production, Imports, and Gas Demand $30/bbl and 28p/therm
NPV : £10m @10 per cent Real Post-tax Discount Rate

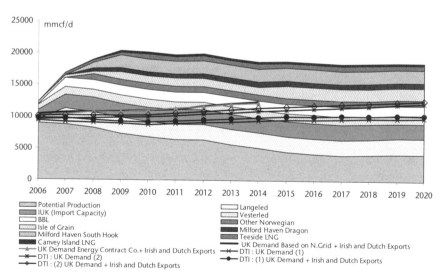

Figure 11 Potential Production, Imports, and Gas Demand $25/bbl and 24p/therm NPV : £10m @ 10 per cent Real Post-tax Discount Rate

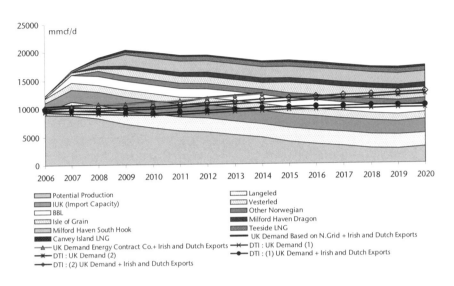

Figure 12 Potential Production, Imports, and Gas Demand $40/bbl and 36p/therm NPV : £10m @ 10 per cent Real Post-tax Discount Rate

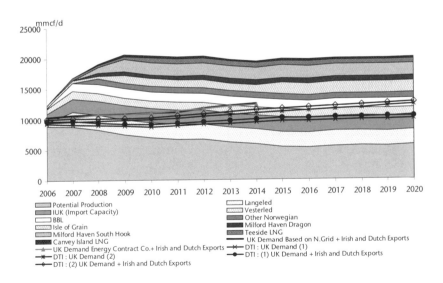

It is important to emphasize that the import capacity figures should not be equated with gas flows. The capacity could be underused. The LNG market is increasingly international in character and at least some gas is being sold on a spot or short-term basis according to the attractiveness of different markets. Further, even with pipeline gas the flows may also not correspond to the capacity and short-term price differentials. This has already happened with the Interconnector and could happen with the Balgzand–Bacton (BBL) line. Thus caution is required in interpreting the figures.

6.3 *Peak Gas Demand and Supply*

A potentially more pressing problem is whether or not gas supply, storage, and demand management (through the use of interruptible contracts) will be adequate to meet peak demand. Much of UK peak demand was historically provided for through the swing factor from SNS fields. However, because of the changing nature of contracts and the depletion of the older fields, much of this swing has gone. Newer contracts tend not to have the same requirements for swing gas, and a large proportion of UKCS gas is now extracted as associated gas where the pace of oil extraction determines the rate of gas supplied. Given that the gas price is much higher in periods of peak demand there is still some incentive for producers to attempt to increase their swing potential.

The National Grid view of peak demand shown is undiversified demand for 1 in 20 winter conditions. This means that the 1 in 20 peak demand occurs *simultaneously* in all parts of the UK. This could exceed expected or diversified demand by around 10 per cent. National Grid is obliged to use undiversified demand in the planning of its network since any element of the system has to accommodate 1 in 20 conditions. Gas customers with the ability to switch to alternative fuel sources may do so when the gas price rises. National Grid estimates that this potential to switch may reduce demand by 10 per cent. In the JESS report the concept of severe winter demand is employed. This relates to 1 in 50 winters.

Two cases of peak gas production have been employed in this study. The first case, High Swing, is based on *recent* historic performance (modest compared to earlier dates) where a field's swing factor is known, or, for future fields, is based on the average swing factor for the area and field type. The second case, Low Swing, is based on a much lower swing factor to take account of the change in contract styles and the current typical nature of new gas production.

Table 5. Potential Storage Capacity and Deliverability in 2015

	Deliverability (mmcf/d)	Number of days	Capacity (mmcf)
Current storage/LNG			
Rough	1,483	67	113,560
Hornsea	635	18	11,155
LNG	1,694	5	9,178
Hole House	106	10	988
Hatfield Moor	71	23	4,095
Humbly Grove	254	37	10,255
Confirmed new storage			
Aldbrough	1,412	11	14,826
Byley	565	10	5,825
Hole House	212	5	1,003
Caythorpe	388	18	7,060
Saltfleetby	1,906	11	21,180
Welton	318	48	15,356
Possible new storage			
Holford	251	24	6,001
Albury (1)	388	15	5,648
Fleetwood	4,024	15	60,010
Bletchingley	2,753	11	30,888
Portland (1)	953	11	10,590
Albury (2)	388	65	25,240
Gateway	1,094	31	34,241
Portland (2)	635	28	17,474
Portland (3)	635	28	17,474
Gainsborough	124	65	7,992

Table 5 shows the estimated prospective deliverability, capacity, and number of days over which the deliverability is sustainable from storage in the year 2015. The estimates are those of the authors based on information from a variety of sources (see the list at the end of the chapter). Those projects in the new confirmed category are very likely to become available. Those in the new possible category are subject to much more uncertainty. The storage in the possible category becomes significant only in 2009, building up to a plateau in 2012.

Figures 13 and 14 show potential peak supply with high and low swing factors and demand at the medium price with current and potential storage and imports. The figures for imports reflect the *capacity* of the schemes. The figures for storage reflect the *deliverability rates*. The results indicate that peak demand should generally be met, particularly after the 2006–7 winter. By 2017 the new storage capacity will certainly be required.

Figures 15 and 16 show the potential peak supply/demand position to 2024 under the higher price scenario. After the 2006–7 winter the capacities comfortably meet peak demand until 2020, when the new storage scheme will be required.

Figure 13 Potential Peak Gas Supply/Demand $30/bbl and 28p/therm NPV : £10m @ 10 per cent Real Post-tax Discount Rate (high swing)

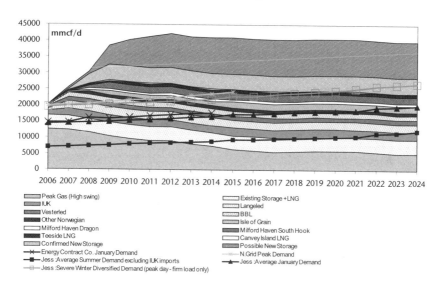

Figure 14 Potential peak Gas Supply/Demand $30/bbl and 28p/therm NPV : £10m @ 10 per cent Real Post-tax Discount Rate (low swing)

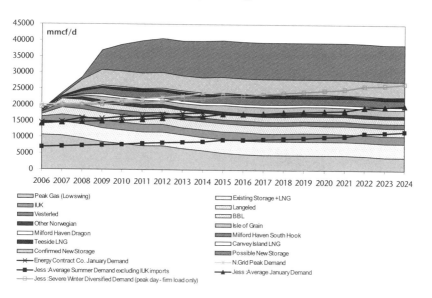

Figure 15 Potential Peak Gas Supply/Demand $40/bbl and 36p/therm NPV : £10m @ 10 per cent Real Post-tax Discount Rate (high swing)

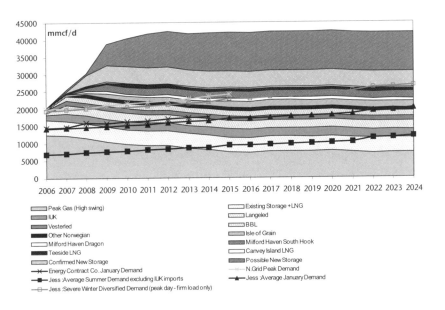

Figure 16 Potential Peak Gas Supply/Demand $40/bbl and 36p/therm NPV : £10m @ 10 per cent Real Post-tax Discount Rate (low swing)

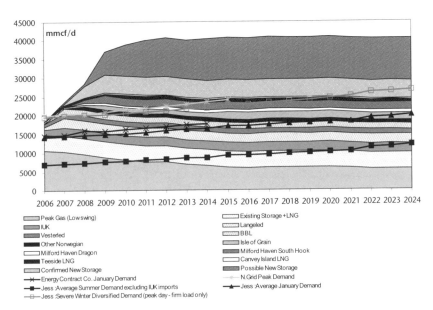

Figures 17 and 18 show the potential peak supply/demand position to 2024 under the low price scenario. The main effect of the lower UK production is to accelerate to around 2016, the time when the new storage schemes will be required.

It should again be emphasized that these comforting results depend upon the capacities of the various import schemes being substantially reflected in gas flows. If the gas flows are substantially below capacities the UK market could be much tighter.

6.4 *Summer Supply and Demand with Restrained Imports*

There is understandably much concern regarding supply security in peak demand winter periods, but very little attention has been given to the supply/demand position in the summer months. UK production is reduced in the summer months by scheduled maintenance programmes, and demand is lower as less gas is required for power generation and the domestic market. Two cases are examined here with respect to utilization of the import capacity. In the first, the gas flows are well below capacity, especially with respect to the LNG schemes. In the second, the capacity is heavily used. Specifically, in the first case it is assumed that Langeled and BBL will operate at around capacity in the summer months, but Vesterled and Other Norway will operate at only 55 per cent of capacity. It is also assumed that the Isle of Grain, Milford Haven South Hook, Milford Haven Dragon, Teesside LNG, and Canvey Island LNG schemes operate at 30 per cent of capacity in most summer months.[13] The summer production was calculated from annual production and peak swing. The production shown below assumes an *average* swing factor (between High and Low).

Figure 19 shows the summer position on the above assumptions at the $30 and 28p price. The negative portion of the production shows the gas being put into existing storage in the summer months.[14] After 2006 the excess supply potential rises rapidly to a peak of 2,750 mmcf/d in 2008. This is consistent with a fall in the summer spot price. Some gas might then be diverted to the European market. LNG can also be diverted to other markets. In the longer term (post-2015) it is clear that domestic production plus the restrained imports are insufficient to meet UK demand. The scenario is not a viable one in the longer term.

[13] The assumptions for summer capacity utilization of the Vesterled and Other Norway pipelines and the Milford Haven South Hook and Dragon, Teesside, and Canvey Island LNG schemes follow those made by The Energy Contract Company (2006).

[14] Looking ahead gas will also be put into the new storage schemes but the uncertainties on the volumes concerned are so great that this is not presented here.

Figure 17 Potential Peak Gas Supply/Demand $25/bbl and 24p/therm NPV : £10m @ 10 per cent Real Post-tax Discount Rate (high swing)

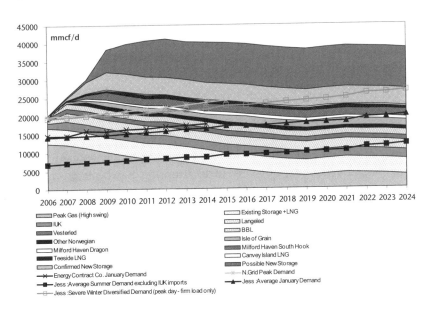

Figure 18 Potential Peak Gas Supply/Demand $25/bbl and 24p/therm NPV : £10m @ 10 per cent Real Post-tax Discount Rate (low swing)

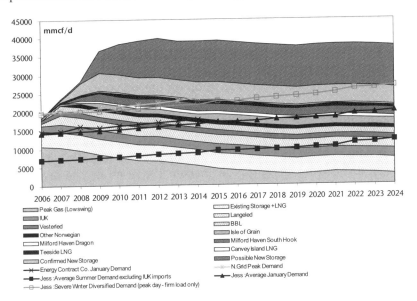

Figure 19 Potential Summer Gas Supply/Demand $30/bbl and 28p/therm NPV : £10m @ 10 per cent Real Post-tax Discount Rate

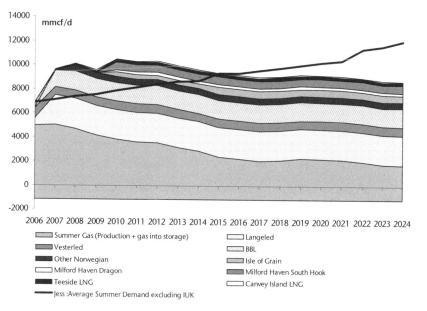

Figure 20 Potential Summer Gas Supply/Demand $25/bbl and 24p/therm NPV : £10m @ 10 per cent Real Post-tax Discount Rate

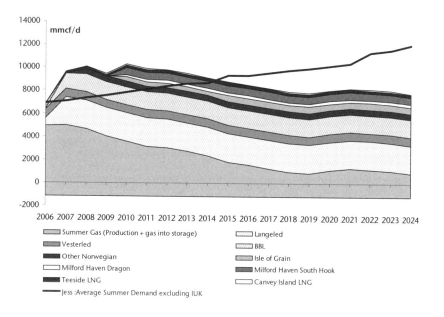

213

Figure 21 Potential Summer Gas Supply/Demand $40/bbl and 36p/therm NPV : £10m @ 10 per cent Real Post-tax Discount Rate

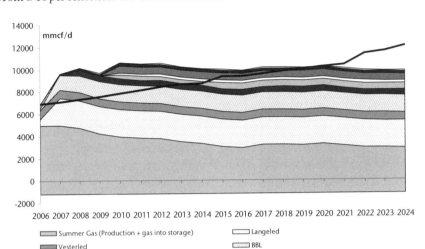

Figure 20 shows the summer position at the low price. After 2006 the potential supply excess rises to a peak of 2,696mmcf/d in 2008, which is again consistent with a fall in summer prices. There could again be diversion of gas to other markets. After 2014 domestic production plus the restrained imports fall well short of UK demand, suggesting that the scenario is not viable in the long run.

Figure 21 shows the summer position at the high price. After 2006 the potential supply excess rises to a peak of 2,795mmcf/d in 2008. This again could lead to falls in the spot summer price and a diversion of supplies to other markets. From around 2020 further imports will be required.

6.5 *Summer Supply and Demand with Imports at Capacity*

Figures 22, 23, and 24 show prospective summer supply with the import projects at around their capacities. It is seen that there is then a substantial potential surplus of gas, consistent with a fall in summer spot wholesale price. This is the case under all the price scenarios, though by 2024 the capacity would be fully utilized.

Figure 22 Potential Summer Supply/Demand $30/bbl and 28p/therm NPV : £10m @ 10 per cent Real Post-tax Discount Rate

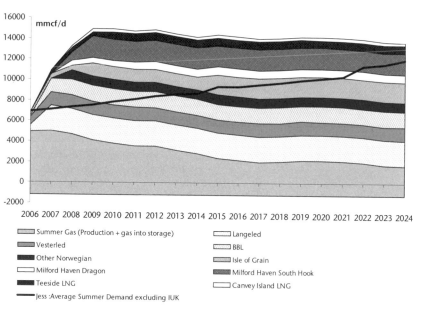

Figure 23 Potential Summer Supply/Demand $25/bbl and 24p/therm NPV : £10m @ 10 per cent Real Post-tax Discount Rate

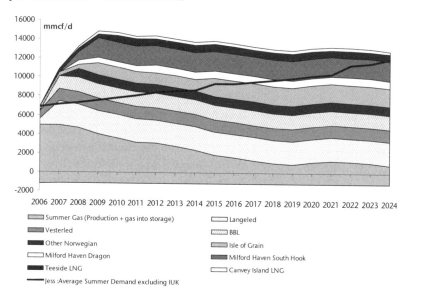

Figure 24 Potential Summer Supply/Demand $40/bbl and 36p/therm NPV : £10m @ 10 per cent Real Post-tax Discount Rate

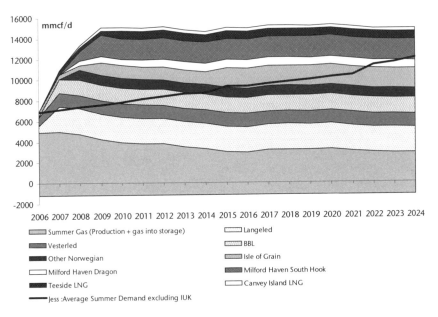

7. Implications of Recent Oil Price Increase

The recent large increase in the oil price and the related increase in gas prices have implications for future activity in the UKCS. Cash flows have increased very substantially. Investment decisions are generally made on the basis of long-term price expectations. Oil companies tend to take cautious views on this subject, but if oil prices are expected to remain at levels of over $30 per barrel for some years, more incremental projects and fields in the technical reserves category would pass conventional eco-nomic hurdles. For relatively short-lived incremental projects and pro-duction from at least some part of the life of a new field it is currently possible to contract to sell on the forward market at very high prices. There is thus an incentive to bring forward in time more projects. Further, the increased cash flows from current operations facilitate the financing of more projects.

On this basis there should be some acceleration in development projects. On the other hand, however, there are physical constraints relating to drilling rig availability and skill shortages, in particular, which limit the flexibility in the timing of projects. The current focus on reserves replacement by many oil companies could also mean that, given the relatively small size of many of the remaining prospects, additional investment is concentrated in other petroleum provinces where larger reserves are in prospect. In this context it is noteworthy that the mean size of field in the technical reserves category is only 20 mmboe and the most likely size considerably less (given the lognormal distribution). On a world basis these are quite low for investors with an international perspective. Hence the importance of the tax rate in maintaining the competitiveness of the UKCS.

So far as new exploration is concerned, there is evidence that the expected full-cycle returns are sensitive to oil and gas price behaviour. On the other hand there is also evidence that the main determinants of the exploration and appraisal effort are more strongly correlated to geological prospectivity, including expected size of discovery and full-cycle costs, than to oil/gas prices.[15] The experience of the last few years is consistent with this view. On balance, the likelihood is that the major increase in prices will result in a moderate absolute increase in the exploration and development effort. In the present circumstances even a modest acceleration in the development of new fields and incremental projects could bring a double benefit. They could help to prolong the lives of the existing infrastructure. Accelerated developments would also be likely to have a longer life because the supporting infrastructure would be available for a longer period. It is arguable that accelerating developments, and thus depletion rates, will increase the overall recovery factors because marginal projects proceed on the basis of infrastructure availability. If the infrastructure is decommissioned some incremental projects may not be viable.

8. Policy Implications

The analysis in this chapter has pointed to the advantages of enhancing and accelerating the pace of new developments. This would be optimal in the sense that it is consistent with (*a*) minimizing the resource costs of extracting the oil and gas, and (*b*) maximizing the ultimate recovery of hydrocarbons from the UKCS. Deferral of the decommissioning of platforms and other infrastructure is also accomplished by enhancement of the level of activity.

---

[15] For a fuller discussion of this subject see Kemp and Kasim (2006).

The analysis has indicated that security of gas supplies in the medium-term when the UK becomes a substantial net importer should be a manageable problem. There should be ample import capacity and sufficient storage capacity to meet the needs of the UK market. It has to be stressed, however, that import capacity should not equate with imported *gas flows*. These, via LNG schemes and at least some pipelines, will depend to some extent on relative prices on the European continent and the USA. UK gas prices may still be volatile as marginal supplies respond to opportunities in these markets. The analysis also shows that the UK will not rely *directly* on significant gas supplies from Russia for a long time ahead. But there will be *indirect* effects emanating from the knock-on impact of any changes in Russian supplies on Continental European markets.

From an overall energy policy viewpoint enhancing domestic production over the next few years enlarges the breathing space required to develop other (domestic) sources of energy, particularly for electricity generation. The continued availability of offshore infrastructure and producing facilities can also contribute to lower emissions in another way. Thus carbon dioxide from major sources of emissions, such as power stations, can be captured, transported out to the North Sea fields, and injected into the reservoirs for sequestration there and/or for use to enhance oil recovery. If this were achieved, conventional power stations could continue in operation with reduced emissions.

The government now has in place a number of licensing and regulatory measures designed to enhance activity. The fallow block/discovery initiative is now starting to bear worthwhile fruit. Some existing players and potential new entrants express concern that the assets being made available are not of great interest, and that many more blocks which existing licensees are allowed to keep are not being worked very fully, although they have passed the DTI's scrutiny. What constitutes an appropriate minimum work programme must involve some judgement, but it is arguable that it should be seen in the context of the need to procure maximum economic recovery.

It is possible to construct an argument for slowing down depletion rates. Thus, if longer-term future oil and gas supplies are to become more expensive and less secure, husbanding the remaining reserves might constitute a worthwhile national investment. Currently, there is a vociferous group which argues that peak world oil production is nigh, to be followed by decreases at a fairly sharp pace.[16] The conventional view

---

[16] See Campbell (2003) for statements of recent views and estimates.

is that world oil production can increase to 2030 or so.[17] With respect to gas this study has shown clearly that very substantial imports from diversified sources are in prospect in the medium term. For the longer term, however, further contracts become necessary when supplies from the ones in prospect start falling. It is thus possible to construct a scenario whereby, on energy policy grounds alone, slower depletion could be justified. The costs and risks of such a policy are substantial, however, and pursuing current policies should produce higher overall economic recovery through more effective use of the infrastructure in the UKCS.

The 2004 Infrastructure Code of Practice has the potential substantially to increase the efficiency of the operation of the offshore infrastructure market. Its success depends on goodwill being exhibited by the parties involved and, in the event that they fail to agree, the skill of the DTI in the practical determination of market rates for tariffs taking into account the costs and risks involved. The alternative of direct regulation of tariffs by the state was chosen in Norway. This approach can always be held in reserve if the new scheme does not operate efficiently.

There is widespread agreement that activity can be boosted by the ready trading of assets. Every investor has his own perceived range of worldwide opportunities, priorities, and also his own interpretation of the remaining prospects in the UKCS. The inevitable differences can readily lead to misalignment of partner interests within a licence group. This can hold back developments—the partner drag phenomenon. Potential new entrants are, of course, anxious to secure acquisitions in a timely manner. There are several perceived potential or real barriers to asset transactions. Those relating to the third-party use of infrastructure and the fallow block/discovery phenomenon have already been discussed. There is a market in mature fields, with some licensees willing to sell and others willing to buy. A problem can arise with respect to financial liability for decommissioning. There is joint and several liability for this in the UK. This was imposed by the government in order to protect the state's interests against a default. The effect is to encourage licensees to take steps to protect themselves against the possibility of default by their partners. On the occasion of a proposed asset transfer, the DTI decides whether in its opinion the prospective new licence group can satisfactorily meet the decommissioning obligation. If there is a concern the prospective group has to establish a Financial Security Agreement (FSA) to which the DTI can become a party. A key issue is the security required for an acceptable

---

[17] See for example, IEA (2005, Endnotes).

FSA. This should normally sum to at least 100 per cent of the likely cost. Acceptable security includes cash, letters of credit from a reputable bank, and performance bonds from such a bank. These forms of security can be quite expensive and, particularly for smaller companies, can have a material effect on their borrowing capacity. They may also lead to the premature cessation of production of fields because of the additional annual costs involved.

In the early 1990s, the concept of a Decommissioning Fund was discussed between the government and the industry. Under this scheme, contributions would be made into an alienated fund during the life of a field by all licensees. These would sum to the amount required for decommissioning when that event arrived. The concept produces financial security for all parties. The stumbling block was the refusal of the government to permit the provisions to be tax deductible on the grounds that (*a*) tax relief was generally not given for an expenditure until it was actually incurred, and (*b*) it would encourage overprovision by investors. The scheme is now employed in a number of countries, including the Netherlands, Angola, and Azerbaijan, where steps are taken to ensure that abuse does not occur, for example by subjecting overprovisions fully to tax, and for requiring independent estimates of the likely costs of decommissioning during the part of field life when provisions are being made. Another possibility is insurance-based schemes. These have recently been promoted, but again the stumbling block is tax relief under the schemes. Given the importance of incremental recovery from mature fields and the willingness of parties to trade these assets, there is a sound case for the provision of tax relief for schemes which offer to provide security for the abandonment liability at relatively low cost. There is a potentially significant positive effect on the number of desirable transactions and subsequent extra recovery from the fields.

The cash-flow taxation system generally applicable to the UKCS has highly attractive features in the context of encouraging investment. For existing players, all risks are immediately shared to the extent of 50 per cent for exploration and new developments, and on older PRT-paying fields to the extent of 75 per cent for incremental projects. The downside risks are reduced and the upside returns shared to the extent of the tax rate. While the internal rates of return remain at their pre-tax levels the NPVs at typical discount rates are reduced. In the context of small UK fields and capital-rationing on a worldwide basis, this may reduce the attractiveness of investments, especially with lower oil prices. Judgement on the appropriate tax rate is always required and should be seen in the context of capital-rationing and international opportunities. For new players for whom tax relief is not available the current interest rate on exploration, appraisal, and development cost allowances carried forward (6 per cent) does not produce a level playing field. There is a case for increasing it to reflect better the cost of capital. The cost to government would be negligible. If the exploration were unsuccessful the new investor still bears the full cost. Relief for the expenditures would only become available against future discoveries. A more radical alternative has recently been introduced in Norway. This involves the cash reimbursement by the government of a share of the exploration costs at the overall marginal tax rate for investors who do not have tax cover.

The various initiatives taken recently by the DTI are generally commendable. If they are to produce substantial benefits they need to be pursued with vigour. Slow implementation and a slow response from the industry would mean that the production profile would fall quite briskly over the next few years. The attainment of the production levels indicated in the text depends on a vigorous response to rigorously implemented initiatives.

Further Reading

Argus European Natural Gas (2006), 'UK Rules Out Strategic Storage for Now', July.

Brown, S., and Ofgem (2006), 'Moving Towards Global Energy Markets', National Grid Conference on *Transporting Britain's Energy 2006*, London, July.

Cocks, S., and National Grid (2006), 'Transporting Britain's Energy 2006', July, London.

DTI (2006), *UK Energy and CO$_2$ Emission Projections Updated Projections to 2020*, February, dti.gov.uk/files/file26363.pdf

__ (2006), *Gas Security of Supply, the Effectiveness of Current Gas Security of Supply Arrangements*, October.

__ (2006), *The Energy Challenge: Energy Review Report*, July.

DTI and Ofgem (2006), *Joint Energy Security of Supply Working Group (JESS) Sixth Report*, April.

Durkin, C., and DTI (2006), 'Securing the UK's Energy Requirements', National Grid Conference on *Transporting Britain's Energy 2006*, July, London.

Heren, P., and Heren Energy (2006), 'Trading Interactions in Europe', National Grid Conference on *Transporting Britain's Energy 2006*, July, London.

Ilex Energy Consulting (2006), *Strategic Storage and other Options to Ensure Long-term Gas Security*, April.

Kemp, A. G., and Stephen, L. (2006), 'Prospects for Activity Levels in the UKCS to 2035 after the 2006 Budget', North Sea Study Occasional Paper No. 101, Department of Economics, University of Aberdeen.

King, J., and Eclipse Energy Group (2006), 'UK Gas Prices—Short and Long-Term', National Grid Conference on *Transporting Britain's Energy 2006*, July, London.

National Grid Transportation (2006), *Winter 2006/07 Consultation Document*, May.

—— (2006), 'Development of NTS Investment Scenarios', National Grid Conference on *Transporting Britain's Energy 2006*, July, London.

Oxera (2004), *Security of Supply, Energy Investment Requirements and Cost Implications*, August.

Proffitt, E., and Major Energy Users' Council (2006), 'A Consumer View', National Grid Conference on *Transporting Britain's Energy 2006*, July, London.

Reed, T., and Centrica (2006), 'European Gas Market Behaviour', National Grid Conference on *Transporting Britain's Energy 2006*, July, London.

Stern, J., and Oxford Institute for Energy Studies (2006), 'UK Pipeline Gas and LNG Supplies from the Middle East, Africa, Caspian and Russia: Prospects and Consequences', National Grid Conference on *Transporting Britain's Energy 2006*, July, London.

Tyler, G., and Wood Mackenzie (2006), 'UK Update—From Shortage to Surplus?' National Grid Conference on *Transporting Britain's Energy 2006*, July, London.

8

A Constrained Future for Gas in Europe?

Anouk Honoré and Jonathan Stern

1. Introduction

Natural gas was virtually unknown in Western Europe until after the Second World War, when fields began to be developed in France and Italy. Dutch gas was discovered in 1959 and gas was found in the North Sea, by England and Norway, in the 1960s. In the 1970s and 1980s, gas markets developed as a consequence of the 1973/4 and 1979/80 oil price shocks, in order to substitute gas for oil products. Its uses were concentrated in the residential, commercial, and industrial sectors. The use of gas for power generation was predominantly based on domestic gas, but was limited in most countries as it was believed to be an inefficient use of a 'premium fuel'. Because of increasing environmental awareness and improvements in gas-turbine technology in the 1980s, gas for power generation developed in the 1990s with the construction of combined-cycle gas turbines (CCGTs). As a result, power generation became the most important growth sector for natural gas consumption.

In central and eastern Europe, gas industries were developed principally from Soviet supplies; once again, residential and industrial consumers—rather than power generation—were the main end-users in most countries. For countries around the geographical periphery of Europe, large-scale gas use started only in the late 1980s and early 1990s. For the Iberian Peninsula, Greece, and Turkey, gas is a relatively recent addition to the fuel balance and explains why these countries now have the fastest demand growth rates on the Continent.

Gas demand growth has been a success story for the past 40 years. Between 1965 and 1975, gas rapidly increased its market share in the total primary energy supply from 2.5 to 14 per cent and has since increased steadily to 25 per cent in 2005. From 1990 to 2005 demand increased by 50 per cent from 380 billion cubic metres (bcm) to 581 bcm. Thus, during the 1990s and early 2000s gas was the major growth area in the energy balances of most European countries, and this was projected to continue over the following two decades. In the middle of the first decade of the twenty-first century, those projections have been called into question owing to a combination of rising prices, fears about security of supply, and an uncertain regulatory and competitive environment. Commercially, the competitive position of gas in power generation has weakened—particularly outside southern Europe—because of rising oil prices.

At the same time, growing fears about rising import dependence and market power of exporters in general, and Russia in particular, is leading governments to question whether gas is a desirable fuel whose growth should be encouraged. Finally, a combination of increasing market concentration through mergers, and a reluctance on the part of major utilities and their governments to provide third-party access to infrastructure on a transparent basis, have severely limited the development of liberalization and competition. These developments have called into question the assumption of rapid growth in demand over the next decade, and raised the prospect that the future of gas in European energy balances may be constrained.

In any discussion about 'European' gas markets, it is important to be precise about the geographical region under consideration. The most common definitions of Europe are the 25 member countries of the European Union prior to 2007 enlargement, or the 23 countries of OECD Europe. However, in gas terms it is important to look at 'Europe' as a group of countries interlinked by pipelines through which gas is exchanged. In this chapter, unless otherwise stated, 'European gas markets' include 35 countries stretching from the Atlantic Ocean in the west almost to the Commonwealth of Independent States (CIS) countries in the east: Albania, *Austria, Belgium*, Bosnia and Herzegovina, *Bulgaria*, Croatia, *the Czech Republic, Cyprus, Denmark, Estonia, Finland, France, Germany, Greece, Hungary, Ireland, Italy, Latvia, Lithuania, Luxembourg, Malta, Netherlands*, Norway, *Poland*, Republic of Macedonia, *Romania, Portugal*, Serbia and Montenegro, *Slovakia, Slovenia, Spain, Sweden*, Switzerland, Turkey, and the *United Kingdom*.[1]

[1] The countries in italic are members of the European Union in 2007.

The chapter is structured as follows. Section 2 provides an outlook for demand and supply to 2015 with particular emphasis on the prospects for gas-fired power generation, the likely development of pipeline and liquefied natural gas (LNG) supplies, and import dependence. Section 3 deals with security of supply and the worsening geo-political environment for natural gas trade around Europe, with a particular focus on Russia and the Middle East. Section 4 reviews the development of competition and liberalization since 2000, not only in relation to energy legislation and regulation but also the growing importance of competition law, in the wake of market concentration. The final section draws together these different factors into a conclusion.

2. Demand and Supply Outlook to 2015

In 2005, natural gas was the second largest source of primary energy in the European Union after oil. Increases in gas demand over the next decade were expected to follow historical trends, mainly driven by power generation. Following the increase in gas prices since 2003, doubts are now being expressed regarding the likely increase in gas consumption. In early 2006, we were still expecting an average increase of 1.5 per cent per year until 2015; new analysis conducted in 2006 shows that increases in demand could be closer to 1 per cent per year up to 2015 (Honoré, 2006, forthcoming).

Gas resources are adequate and available to meet easily the projected increase in demand over the next decade, but international trade will need to expand to accommodate the growing mismatch between the location of demand and that of production. The maturity of the resource base in most European countries means that indigenous gas production will level off and then decline over the next decade and beyond, which means that an increase in gas imports will be needed to cope with increased demand. 'Europe 35' imported about 45 per cent of its consumption in 2005, but this share is expected to rise sharply, creating a new situation and challenges for many gas-consuming countries in Europe.

2.1 Demand, Prices, and Power Generation in Europe

Generalizations about 'European' gas demand hide major disparities between countries. Gas demand is mainly concentrated in north-west Europe, where gas markets developed 40 years ago, plus Italy and Spain.

Figure 1 Gas Demand in Europe 35 in 2005, in bcm

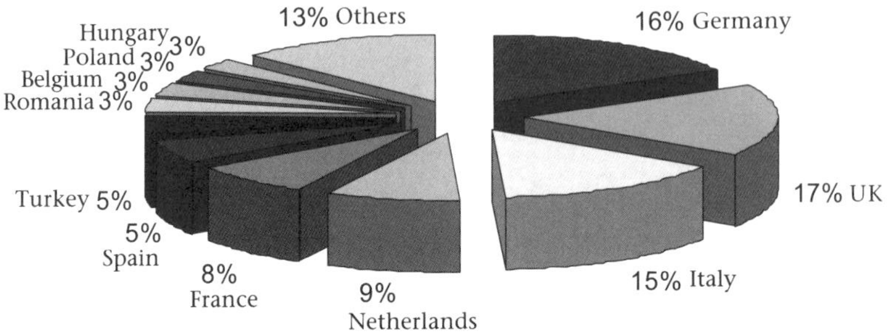

Source: IEA (2006a).

Eleven major gas markets represented about 87 per cent of the European gas demand in 2005 (see Figure 1).

Most publicly available energy forecasts and scenarios[2] predict natural gas to be the fastest growing fossil fuel source in the next 2–3 decades in Europe. This projected growth in gas demand is in line with historical trends, as shown in Figure 2.

Gas demand forecasts commonly show optimistic trends increasing gently or steeply. However, interestingly, projections of European gas demand, which has been universally expected to increase in a steep, straight line for the next 25 years, are being revised downwards, as shown in Figure 3. It is not clear whether this is a result of fundamental analysis, assuming lower demand because of high gas prices, lower gross domestic product (GDP) growth, increased role of other fuels in power generation (coal, renewables), or better energy conservation. Projections are still relatively optimistic, but certainty about future gas demand in Europe has changed over the past few years. There will be growth in all sectors but gas-to-power is projected to be the main demand driver.

In 2003, the residential/commercial sector was still the largest consumer, followed by the industrial sector. However, gas demand in these sectors will not increase significantly over the coming years, since in most countries these markets are approaching saturation. Their growth will remain relatively modest at around an 0.8–1 per cent increase per year, largely depending on historical trends and GDP forecasts. There is a slightly different story in southern Europe (Spain, Portugal, Greece, and even Italy), where demand in these sectors may grow faster, but this will have a relatively small impact on overall European gas consumption.

[2] For example, IEA *World Energy Outlook* series, EIA *Annual Energy Outlook* series, etc.

Figure 2 International Energy Agency Forecasts of Primary Energy Demand in EU25 (Reference Scenario)

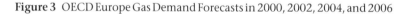

Source: IEA (2004, p. 251).

Figure 3 OECD Europe Gas Demand Forecasts in 2000, 2002, 2004, and 2006

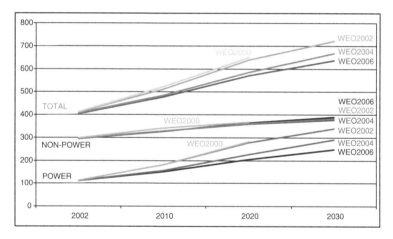

Sources: IEA: 2000, 2002, 2004, and 2006, Tables on Reference Scenario: OECD Europe, in the Appendix.

Most projections suggest that roughly 70 per cent of the projected demand increase will be coming from the power sector in the next 20 years. The reasons for this expected 'dash for gas' are well known: the economics and efficiency of the new CCGT power plants, the environmental qualities of gas, and the adaptability, flexibility, and availability

227

of gas in an open power sector. Growth in gas-fired power generation will be most pronounced in Mediterranean countries and the UK. Natural gas became the fuel of choice for new power plants during the 1990s, mainly at the expense of coal, owing to cost and environmental considerations.

The technological advantages of gas-fired plant, combined with the need to rebalance existing portfolios to permit more effective risk management, is continuing to drive investment in gas-fired plant in competitive electricity markets in the short/medium term. However, in a situation of high gas prices (at post-2003 levels), generators with old, fully amortized coal-fired or nuclear plants which continue to provide lucrative returns have a greatly reduced incentive to build new gas-fired power plants. This lack of incentive is delaying the construction of large-scale new CCGT and other gas-fired plant.

A survey of gas-fired power plants projects in Europe shows that although the use of natural gas for power generation will increase substantially, it will not increase either as much or as fast as is generally expected. Moreover, approximately 85 per cent of the increase in gas demand for power generation in Europe by 2015 will come from three countries: Italy, Spain, and the UK; and 70 per cent of all gas-fired power projects are in Spain and Italy. Both countries need new generation capacity, and building permits for coal-fired power plants are almost impossible to obtain. Italy needs to increase gas-fired generating capacity to decrease its import dependence and to move away from oil-fired generation. Spain needs new capacity to meet its growing demand and has limited connections with neighbouring France to import electricity. Several gas-fired projects are also planned in the UK, which is expected to lose coal (and oil) fired capacity after the Large Combustion Plant Directive comes into force in 2008. Germany has several new gas-fired projects, but it is hard to see them running at base or even middle load by 2015. The Netherlands, France, Belgium, Hungary, and Poland will not have much new gas-fired capacity in the coming years. Outside these nine big markets, Greece, Portugal, Norway, Austria, and Ireland have several gas-fired power plant projects at different stages of development. However, even for countries such as Greece and Portugal, which will see a huge percentage increase in gas-fired capacity, gas demand for power will remain relatively small in absolute terms.

In Continental Europe, gas prices are traditionally linked to oil prices through formulae in long-term contracts which secure the competitiveness of gas against oil products. In the UK, gas prices are generally determined by short-term prices at the National Balancing Point (a virtual hub), but these prices are influenced by oil-linked Continental European prices via the Interconnector (IUK) pipeline (Wright, 2006, pp. 87–8). Continued high oil-linked prices are expected to slow down the general level of demand, especially in the power generation sector where CCGT plants will be delayed and/or will run at lower load factors. North European power generators believe that gas prices need to be indexed to some combination of power and coal prices before gas can be used to generate baseload power. In Mediterranean countries, gas is more widely used for baseload generation owing to a different mix of power plants (less nuclear, lignite, and coal) and higher power prices. Though never mentioned in most gas demand forecasts, load factors of CCGT plants have a huge impact on gas demand. At post-2003 prices, gas-fired power plants will not run base load in either north-west or east Europe. Base-load generation is possible only in the UK and in southern European countries.

Following this reasoning, only significantly lower gas prices (compared with post-2003 levels) in the period up to 2010 can speed up plans to build new gas-fired generation and lead to the major increases in gas demand by 2015 which had been anticipated.

With a bottom-up methodology, and assuming a load factor for each country (based on historical data and future trends), we project 648 bcm (Honoré, 2006) of gas consumption in Europe 35 by 2015, with 208 bcm for the power sector, and 449 bcm for the non-power sector.

European power generation is still mainly based on domestic resources (coal, lignite, hydro, or domestic gas in the Netherlands) or on nuclear. To the extent that coal-fired generation depends on imported coal, there is a world market for this fuel. However, additional gas-fired power generation will increasingly be based on gas supplies imported from a relatively limited number of players.

2.2 Supply: Pipeline and LNG, Sources, and Import Dependence

European gas resources and production are declining. UK production, which has been the largest in Europe, is already in a decline which is projected to deepen, with the country becoming up to 40 per cent dependent on imports in the early 2010s, rising to as much as 80 per cent by 2020. Dutch production can hold level until 2010–15 with output from the Groningen field compensating for declines in the smaller fields. However, after 2015, all fields will experience accelerating decline. Else-where in Continental Europe, most countries will experience a gradual

Figure 4 EU25 Gas Supplies in 2005 (total: 536 bcm)

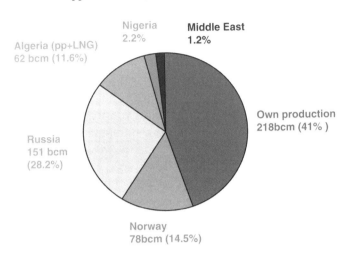

Source: Cedigaz (2006, Tables on Pipe Trade and LNG Trade).

decline in production. The only exception to the trend of declining gas production in 'Europe' is Norway, which exported 78 bcm of gas to the Continent and the United Kingdom in 2005. The Langeled and Tampen (via FLAGS) pipelines will increase export capacity to 130 bcm/year in 2010 where it will level off and, without additional resource discoveries, decline.

Traditionally, Europe has relied on four main sources of gas, two European—Netherlands and Norway—and two non-European—Russia and Algeria. In 2005, Europe imported about 45 per cent of its gas demand from Russia and Algeria (Figure 4).

Algeria exported 62 bcm of gas to Europe in 2005 (pipeline and LNG). Its two export pipelines to Europe have a combined capacity of 34 bcm. There are two new pipeline projects: the Medgaz line to Spain, 8 bcm/year, with a projected start date of 2008, and the Galsi line to Italy via Sardinia, 8 bcm/year, and a projected start date of 2009.

In 2005, Russian was the largest single supplier to Europe with more than 156 bcm gas to 22 countries—around 25 per cent of European gas demand.[3] All of this gas was exported by the dominant Russian gas company, Gazprom, via its export subsidiaries—principally Gazexport.[4]

---

[3] Gazprom (2005, pp. 54–5). These figures do not include the three Baltic countries to which Gazprom exported 5.5 bcm in 2005, but which may also have received small additional quantities of Russian gas.

[4] In November 2006, this subsidiary company was renamed Gazprom Export.

Dependence on Russian gas is not uniform throughout Europe: some central and east European countries are totally dependent on Russian gas and there is significant dependence in north-west Europe. But the Iberian Peninsula imports no Russian gas, and the UK (Europe's largest gas market) has so far only imported relatively small quantities on a short-term basis.[5] The NordStream Gas Pipelines will create an additional 55 bcm/year of Russian export capacity to north-west Europe by the mid-2010s.

In the 2000s, Europe developed a huge enthusiasm for LNG with numerous proposed projects. For many companies and governments, LNG has advantages over pipeline gas. First, the more border crossings that a pipeline needs to make, the greater the commercial and political risks. Therefore, the likelihood that new gas pipelines to Europe—such as Nabucco—will have to cross numerous borders favours LNG.

LNG can also provide supply diversification and potential competition, and, with falling costs throughout the chain during the 20 years up to 2005, seemed able to deliver profitable gas to most suppliers at a price level of \$3.50/MBtu (million British thermal units).[6] This is a huge change compared with prospects for LNG a decade ago: both long-term and traded LNG volumes are increasing, and will become a more and more important source of Atlantic Basin gas supply. In addition, LNG helps companies overcome problems of obtaining access to networks in Continental Europe.

The Atlantic Basin includes seven exporting countries (Algeria, Libya, Egypt, Nigeria, Oman, Qatar, and Trinidad) and 10 importing countries (USA, Mexico, Spain, France, Italy, Turkey, Greece, Portugal, the UK, and Belgium). Norway, Equatorial Guinea, and Angola will join the list of exporting LNG countries, while Russia is expected eventually to be a major LNG-exporting country. Brazil, Germany, the Netherlands, and Poland may join the list of importing LNG countries in the next 5–10 years.

European LNG imports jumped by almost 21 per cent in 2005 to nearly 48 bcm, helped by new Egyptian supply and restoration of Algerian capacity. There was double-digit growth across Europe, except Greece and (curiously) Belgium, where imports fell. In that year, Europe received 25 per cent of global LNG deliveries, the USA and Caribbean 10 per cent, and East Asia plus India 65 per cent (Cedigaz, 2006, Tables 3 and 4). The UK alone has four new LNG terminals in various stages of construction:

[5] Gazprom exports to the UK in 2005 were 3.8 bcm or around 4 per cent of total demand. Gazprom (2005, p. 54).

[6] Since 2005, costs have spiralled upwards owing to increases in materials (especially steel) prices.

Table 1. LNG supplies in 'Europe' in 2005

From/ to	Oman	Qatar	UAE	Algeria	Libya	Nigeria	Egypt	Malaysia	Australia	Total
Belgium				3.11						3.11
France				7.10		4.15	2.00			13.25
Greece				0.46						0.46
Italy				2.50						2.50
Portugal						1.58				1.58
Spain	1.65	4.5	0.37	5.19	0.87	4.96	3.53	0.16	0.08	14.55
Turkey				3.85		1.03				4.88
UK				0.40						0.40
Total	1.65	4.50	0.37	22.61	0.87	11.72	5.53	0.16	0.08	47.07

Source: Cedigaz (2006, Table on LNG Trade).

Grain, Dragon, South Hook, and Teesside (Excelerate). In 2005, nine countries delivered LNG to Europe. The rate of growth in the Atlantic Basin is even outpacing Asia Pacific, the historical focus of LNG marketing. New trade flows in 2005 included Egypt to France and Spain, Algeria to Portugal, Qatar to Belgium, and Australia to Spain; and, in 2006, Egypt to the UK.

LNG will become a major contributor of incremental gas supply in Europe over the next two decades. It will particularly be the case in Spain, Italy and the UK. LNG will also expand in France and Belgium. Within a decade LNG terminals are likely to be built in Germany, the Netherlands, and some central and east European countries. The numerous regasification facilities announced in 2004 and 2005 in the Atlantic Basin emphasize the rapid growth and changing market conditions within the Atlantic Basin.

FUTURE SUPPLIES[7]

Because of political concern about security of Russian gas supplies (see below), diversification of supply has become an important priority. The obvious regions from which substantial supplies could be made available are North Africa, the Middle East, and the Caspian Region. As far as the Middle East and North Africa (MENA) is concerned, the potential exists to increase exports fourfold by 2030. In absolute terms, this would require an increase in total exports of nearly 350 bcm/year, of which the majority (over 200 bcm) would need to come from the Middle East. In 2005, Middle East gas exports had reached only 58 bcm, which had been achieved 25

---

[7] The two following sections of the paper are drawn from Stern (2006c).

years after the start of exports.[8] This is not because of any lack of resources, project proposals, or interest in developing gas exports. North African projections foresee exports from that region increasing more than threefold to 200 bcm/year over the next 25 years, when around 40 years were required for exports to reach the 2005 level of 78 bcm.[9]

These levels of gas exports could certainly be sustained by known proven reserves (let alone what may be discovered in these countries over the next three decades), although a significant number of new fields will need to be developed.[10] New LNG and pipeline projects, both under construction and in advanced stages of planning, would support the projections to 2010. Cost reductions in LNG (and to a lesser extent pipeline) projects over the 20 years up to 2004 meant that the economics of any project under discussion are positive.[11] A more serious doubt is whether such a huge rate of increase in exports, sustained over a 25-year period, is realistic: institutionally, politically, and geo-politically. In a number of countries, particularly Iran, but also perhaps Algeria and Libya, increases in domestic consumption of gas (either directly or for reinjection in oil fields) may curtail availability for export (Hallouche, forthcoming).

The share of Middle East exports delivered to European markets is projected to increase to more than one-third by 2010, and to nearly one half by 2030. Out of a total of 270 bcm of MENA LNG exports in 2030, the International Energy Agency (IEA) believes that Europe will capture a minimum of 113 bcm or 42 per cent, and perhaps up to 50 per cent.[12] This suggests that Europe largely 'wins the battle' for global LNG supplies with the USA and the Pacific Basin for both Middle East and North African LNG. This is a very optimistic projection for Europe and, given developments in the North American gas market, it must be uncertain whether it is realistic.

In the 2000s, West Africa has emerged as an important LNG-exporting region with Nigeria as the major supplier and Equatorial Guinea and Angola likely to start deliveries over the next few years. After more than

---

[8] 2030 projections in this paragraph are from IEA (2005, pp. 178–9, 560, 564, 568, 580, 592, 596, 600, 604). Abu Dhabi started to export LNG in 1977 and was joined by Qatar in 1997; all other Middle East exports started more recently.

[9] 2005 figures from Cedigaz (2005). Algerian LNG exports commenced in 1964 and pipeline exports in 1987; Libyan exports only became significant with the start of pipeline trade in 2004.

[10] For example, by 2030, less than 40 bcm out of an anticipated total of 200 bcm of Algerian gas production will come from fields currently in production (IEA, 2005, Figure 9.7, p. 301).

[11] Although in the middle of the first decade of the twenty-first century a combination of increased commodity prices and pressure on manufacturing and contracting capacity to implement pipeline and LNG projects has seen costs begin to rise again.

[12] Calculated from the statements in IEA (2005) that the share of LNG in total MENA exports will not exceed 60 per cent (p. 178) and the figures in Figure 5.6 (p. 180).

30 years of discussion and disappointment, the Nigeria LNG (NLNG) project began exports in 1999. But within a decade of starting these exports NLNG will have six trains in operation, delivering more than 30 bcm/year of supplies to the Atlantic Basin. Two more Nigeria LNG trains are planned which would add a further 22 bcm of export capacity. In addition three more projects are in various stages of planning which, if realized, would see up to another 47 bcm of LNG export capacity, bringing total export capacity to nearly 100 bcm/year—in the same range as Qatar and Algeria—to make the country one of the world's leading gas and LNG exporters. In addition, Equatorial Guinea and Angola may add up to another 12 bcm of exports per year. West African gas export potential currently appears somewhat less than either North Africa or the Middle East, but additional discoveries could significantly expand current expectations.

In the early 2000s, significant emphasis has been placed on creating a new pipeline route to Europe via Turkey carrying supplies from a number of Middle East and Caspian countries: Azerbaijan, Turkmenistan, Kazakhstan, Iran, Iraq, and Egypt. None of these countries has thus far shown an inclination to commit *substantial* piped volumes to the European market and it is uncertain whether some could be considered secure suppliers. But diverse sources of supply flowing through a single pipeline would decrease the importance of any individual source. This appears to be the concept underpinning the Nabucco pipeline currently being promoted by a number of central and south-east European utilities and the European Commission.[13] Such pipelines from the Middle East/ Caspian region are strongly endorsed by governments in the USA, European Union, and south-eastern Europe, to promote diversification away from Russian gas supplies and transport routes. However, two points should be recalled in relation to pipeline gas from the Middle East and Caspian region.

- In no way can such pipelines be considered a new idea. There have been regular initiatives to create such projects for at least the past 30 years without success.

- It is not clear—given the number of borders which they will need to cross and the potential for problems within and between countries along the route—whether such pipeline routes can be considered

[13] 'Commissioner Piebalgs welcomes agreement to accelerate Nabucco gas pipeline project', Press Release IP/06/842, Brussels, 26 June 2006. This mentions a scenario in which 10–15 per cent of EU gas supplies would come from the Caspian region by 2025, suggesting 2–3 Nabucco-sized pipelines by that date.

more reliable than existing and new supplies from and through Russia which they are intended to displace.

3. Security of Supply

Security of gas supply, expressed as current and projected national or collective dependence of European countries on supplies from individual suppliers (or groups of suppliers) over the next 15–25 years, has become an increasingly important subject in the 2000s. Even before the cuts in Russian supplies to Ukraine in the first days of 2006, restricting the availability of supplies to some European countries and bringing the subject of gas security to the attention of politicians and public, the European Commission had already published a Green Paper on the subject and passed a Directive on gas security (CEC, 2000, 2004). In March 2006, the Commission published another Green Paper on security (as well as sustainability and competitiveness) in which it projected that the share of imports in EU gas demand would increase to 80 per cent by 2030 (CEC, 2006a, para 1).

Even if these projections of future dependence are believed to be correct, they form only a small part of a security environment which includes a cluster of short-term and long-term issues including resource availability, technical breakdown and accident, terrorist attack, political instability, lack of investment, and disagreements in relation to existing and future supplies, transit, and facilities.

The trend towards declining European gas production and resource discovery has been discussed above. A major question is whether—as most commentary assumes—rising import dependence should automatically be considered to be equivalent to decreasing supply security.

3.1 *Russia*

European gas security concerns have focused on the role of Russia (and, prior to 1992, the Soviet Union). This is not a new subject, but what has changed in the 2000s is the pan-European scope and the much larger volumes of Russian gas supplies.[14]

---

[14] A very brief overview of the past 25 years of this debate can be found in Stern (2005, pp. 140–4).

Irrespective of national positions, the crisis on 1–4 January 2006 which saw Russia cut gas supplies to Ukraine, with the consequence that Ukrainian consumers diverted substantial quantities of gas in transit through their country to Europe, produced a huge negative reaction from governments and commentators on both sides of the Atlantic.[15] Gazprom's imposition of steep increases in gas prices on CIS importing countries since 2005 has been interpreted both within and outside those countries as politically motivated, despite the continuing gap between those prices and the corresponding EU import price. CIS governments (as well as some in central and eastern Europe) appear to believe that, if they could only obtain access to non-Russian supplies of pipeline gas and LNG—they would be able to import such supplies on more favourable terms and improve their security of supply.

The 2 months immediately following these events saw a period of exceptionally cold weather in both Russia and many parts of Europe, Moscow experienced temperatures well below –30° Celsius for an entire week. This raised gas demand in Russia and much of central/eastern Europe to extremely high levels, placing a huge strain on Russian gas and power networks. During this period, there were again diversions of Russian gas in transit to European countries through Ukraine. These diversions—mostly not disputed by the Ukrainian government—prevented Gazprom from being able to meet the very high demand requirements of some European customers. Buyers in Poland, Hungary, Italy, and Austria reported that deliveries were between 10 and 35 per cent below requested volumes on a substantial number of days in January and February.[16]

The overwhelming conclusion of the political and public commentary throughout Europe on these episodes was that, by this action, Russia was exerting political pressure on the Ukrainian government and president in order to reassert its influence on a country attempting to make a decisive move towards the European Union and NATO and away from Russian political influence. The lack of any public official European censure of Ukraine for taking gas supplies to which it was not entitled, clearly demonstrated where European politicians believed the blame lay for this episode.[17]

[15] For details of this crisis and the subsequent reaction see Stern (2006a,b).

[16] In the Italian case, deliveries were still up to 15 per cent below nominations at the beginning of March 2006.

[17] There are indications that confidential letters were sent from both the EU and the Energy Charter Secretariat to the Ukrainian government, pointing out shortcomings in the latter's behaviour. But even if these existed they stood in sharp contrast to the harsh and very public condemnation of Russia.

236

Irrespective of the contractual situation (i.e. legal obligations in respect of entitlements, prices, and payments), the January/February 2006 episodes, and ongoing problems and uncertainties in the Russian–Ukrainian relationship, raised serious doubts in the minds of European politicians as to whether Russian gas can be considered reliable. There have been suggestions that the Russian government was—by this action—'sending a signal' to Europe that it had the power to cut off gas supplies should it choose to do so and that, should European countries act in ways which it did not like, it might so choose. This is based on an increasingly popular view of Russian foreign policy which holds that the Putin Administration sees energy trade as an important means—and perhaps the principal means at Russia's disposal—of projecting its political power and influence internationally.[18] In this view, the Ukrainian crisis is seen as a 'trial run' for what Europe might suffer in the future, particularly if there should be a significant deterioration of its political relationship with Russia.

The March 2006 EU Green Paper on energy security envisaged a deepening of the existing energy partnership with Russia and argued that the G8 should intensify efforts to secure Russian ratification of the Energy Charter Treaty and its Transit Protocol (CEC, 2006a, para 2.6). But these suggestions were not new and the failure of the European Commission to play any significant role during or after the events of 1–4 January 2006, using the institutions of the EU–Russia Energy Dialogue and the EU–Ukraine Summits, were not confidence-inspiring for its role in any future crisis management.[19]

European concern about Russian gas security was echoed by the US Administration both in January 2006 and later in the year by Vice President Cheney in a speech to a conference of European leaders in Lithuania when he noted:[20] 'No legitimate interest is served when oil and gas become tools of intimidation or blackmail, either by supply manipulation or attempts to monopolize transportation.'

The IEA subsequently made a direct connection between Gazprom's export monopoly and security, and cast doubt on Gazprom's ability to honour its long-term contracts with European customers: 'the IEA is

---

[18] Section IV.3 of the 2003 Russian Energy Strategy (*Energeticheskaya Strategiya Rossiya na period do 2020 goda*; confirmed by the Russian government on 28 August 2003) states that one of the strategic aims of gas industry development is to 'secure the political interests of Russia in Europe and surrounding states, and also in the Asia-Pacific region'. Many believe that president Putin's PhD Dissertation also supports such a policy, see Balzer (2006, pp. 31–9).

[19] For the history of the EU–Russia Dialogue and the Energy Charter Treaty in relation to Russian gas trade with the EU, see Stern (2005, pp. 134–9).

[20] http://www.whitehouse.gov/news/releases/2006/05/20060504-1.html

worried about the increasingly monopolistic status of state-controlled Gazprom. Europeans cannot import gas from Russia unless Gazprom agrees. This restriction undermines European energy security.'[21]

'Current IEA projections suggest that Gazprom could face a gradually increasing supply shortfall against its existing [European] contracts beginning in the next few years if timely investment in new fields is not made' (IEA, 2006c).

3.2 A Worsening Geo-political Environment

Just as there is a common assumption that the principal threats to European gas security are externally focused, so there is a common assumption that, within that external focus, the policies of exporting countries and/or political events which are likely to happen within exporting countries will be the principal threats to European gas security. Thus, in respect of both Russia and the Middle East, much European commentary is focused on the general political and economic policies of governments—as well as narrower (oil and) gas policy frameworks—which are believed to 'threaten' European (and possibly wider OECD) gas security. Some part of this stronger recent sensitivity towards exporting countries is the product of a new assertiveness of (oil and) gas producing and exporting countries in the wake of the post-2003 increase in prices and a widespread perception (whether correct or not) that such price levels will be at least a medium-term phenomenon. This new assertiveness—often termed 'resource nationalism'—has produced significant commercial challenges to both international oil and gas companies and OECD government policies in countries as geographically diverse as Venezuela, Bolivia, Russia, and Iran, combined with a desire and an ability to challenge the political and geo-political status quo which they see as imposed by US and EU governments.

Geo-political scenarios, such as the Clingendael Institute's 'Regions and Empires', and Shell International's 'Low Trust Globalization', have produced comprehensive storylines which are strongly negative for geo-political energy trends (Clingendael, 2004; Shell, 2005). Correljé and van der Linde (2006) have observed that under 'Regions and Empires' there is likely to be, 'a slowly emerging [gas] supply gap, as a result of lagging investments as a consequence of ideological and religious contrasts, particularly with regard to the North African suppliers, the potential supplies in the Persian gulf and the Caspian Sea region.' The middle of the first decade of the twenty-first century is witnessing a worsening of

---

[21] http://www.iea.org/journalists/topstories.asp (visited 23 May 2006).

international energy relations owing to increasing producer/exporter assertiveness and increasing concern of OECD countries which believe they are faced by a range of commercial threats including: deprivation of access to resources for international oil and gas companies (IOGCs), demands by host governments and national energy companies for increasing shares of the rent from any joint activities with IOGCs, competition for energy exploration opportunities and resources with (particularly) Chinese and Indian companies. Overlaying all of these commercial developments are trends which have potentially serious consequences for European gas supplies:

- increasing bilateral and geo-political tensions between Russia and both the US and European governments because of what the latter perceive to be weakening commitments to democracy and economic reform in Russia;

- continued deterioration of political stability in the Middle East region as well as increasing tensions between potential gas-exporting countries, such as Iran, and US and European governments. Six countries account for more than 90 per cent of MENA gas exports in the period 2010–30; two countries—Algeria and Qatar—account for 70–90 per cent of total exports.[22] Should any political or geo-political problems prevent these two countries from developing exports as anticipated, the consequences for European gas supplies and the Atlantic Basin (and global) LNG market will be significant;

- uncertainty about political stability in West African LNG-exporting countries, especially Nigeria.

3.3 Security and Import Dependence—Empirical Evidence and Legislation

The traditional inclination among politicians and the media in OECD countries is to regard energy supplies which are produced domestically as 'secure', and supplies which are imported as 'insecure'. Most security planning is predicated on disruptions of imported supplies.[23] If we summarize the security incidents which have occurred over the past 25 years in Europe, there have not been very many; those that have occurred have been divided between the three main causes (source, transit, and

[22] The other four countries are Iran, Iraq, Libya, and Egypt.
[23] For example, the EU Gas Security Directive (Article 2), which defines a major supply disruption as 'a situation where the Community would risk to lose more than 20 per cent of its supply from third countries'.

facility), but facility incidents appear to have increased over recent years. In particular, as far as the UK is concerned, the risk of facility incidents became increasingly problematic in the middle of the first decade of the twenty-first century, owing to the tightness of the supply/demand balance and the lack of storage capacity (Stern, 2004). Despite the constant references to the EU of the problems of importing gas by 'regions threatened by insecurity', it is difficult to think of any historical incident involving political instability which has prevented gas from being delivered to Europe.[24]

There is no evidence from Europe or anywhere else in the world that imported gas supplies have been—or are *necessarily* likely to be—less secure than supplies of domestically produced gas. Indeed, history suggests that all serious security incidents—i.e. where customers have lost gas supplies for a considerable period of time—have stemmed from failure of indigenous supplies or facilities. No empirical experience would lead to the conclusion that a country with substantial dependence on imported gas supplies would be *necessarily* less secure—i.e. more prone to disruption—than one which was self-sufficient. Increased security—whether for domestically produced gas or imports—requires increased diversity of sources, transportation and transit routes, and facilities. These facilities include pipelines, LNG terminals, processing plants, and storage. Clearly the higher the percentage of gas in a country's energy demand, the greater is the importance of diversity as protection against security incidents.

Exporting countries have a very strong incentive to maintain continuous and secure deliveries owing to the revenues which they earn and the importance of those revenues to corporate and national budgets. For most non-OECD gas-exporting companies and countries, earnings from gas export revenues are not only very significant in absolute terms but also as a proportion of their total revenues. Even for a company as large as Gazprom, gas export revenues in 2005 were around 55 per cent of the company's total receivables and around 17 per cent of total Russian foreign trade earnings outside CIS countries.[25] This is a long-term stream

[24] However, this may depend on the exact definition of 'political instability'. Political instability has delayed or prevented a number of contracts from being concluded, but the only example of political instability—meaning inability of central government to maintain political control over a region—which these authors can recall which has caused any protracted disruption of supplies in an ongoing contract was Indonesian LNG deliveries from Aceh (Sumatra) to Japan and Korea in 2001.

[25] However, for Gazprom, European earnings fell from around 63 per cent of total receivables in the early 2000s, which, given the huge increase in European gas prices and volumes post-2004 is significant, and shows the importance of increased domestic and CIS gas prices over the same period.

of earnings that would not be lightly jeopardized by an exporting company or government and which could not easily or quickly be replaced by any other commodity.

Two dimensions of European gas security which are only just beginning to receive the attention which they deserve are the potential problems which can be caused by infrastructure breakdown, and how to ensure adequate gas storage in liberalized markets. The fire at the Rough storage site in February 2006 deprived the UK of access to around 80 per cent of its stored gas for more than 4 months. Had the incident happened any earlier (or later) in the winter, the consequences might have been substantially more serious than the price spikes which the market experienced in the few weeks before temperatures rose and demand declined.

While significant investments in both new supplies and new storage are under way, these will arrive several years later than the market needed them. Even when all of the storage capacity which UK investors are currently seeking to build is complete, this will only equate to around 10 per cent of annual demand, substantially less than other major markets in Europe. The Italian case provides a useful comparison, where a combination of problems with Russian gas and very cold weather in the winter of 2005–6 forced the use of strategic storage. The Italian government considered that it had a narrow escape with 3.9 bcm of strategic storage remaining on 22 March 2006 (Garriba, 2006). But this volume is roughly equal to the total available storage in the UK—a much larger gas market than Italy. Both these cases, but especially that of the UK, raise important issues about the ability of liberalized gas markets to provide market-based security investments when these are needed.[26]

They also raise the issue of whether EU security standards, particularly in relation to gas storage, require more centralized coordination from Brussels. Stringent standards were proposed by the original draft of the Gas Security Directive but not accepted by either gas utilities or their governments.[27] The eventual Directive (Article 3.1) required the establishment of policies and definition of roles and responsibilities to ensure

---

[26] Van der Linde *et al.* (2006). Arguably, the UK framework will provide the supplies which the market requires, but 2–3 years later than these supplies were needed. Whether it is able to provide the storage which is needed—and whether this problem is more related to planning constraints than to market liberalization—is a question for a separate paper.

[27] 'Proposal for a Directive of the European Parliament and the Council concerning measures to safeguard security of natural gas supply', August 2002. For a sample of the opposition from industry to the original proposals see 'Eurogas Response to the Proposed Security of Natural Gas Supply Directive', February 2003.

adequate minimum levels of gas security, but nothing more specific. In relation to protection of customers, the Directive went no further than to set security of supply standards (Article 4)—which conformed to those which already existed in most countries. It encouraged (rather than required) member states to develop national storage, enter into bilateral storage agreements with other countries, and publish targets for the future contribution of storage to security. This was as far as member states were prepared to go in relation to cooperation in gas storage. The only new institution created by the Directive (Article 7) was the Gas Coordination Group—which met in January 2006 following the Russia–Ukraine crisis—but this fell somewhat short of the European Observation System with wide-ranging duties and powers in the event of a crisis, which was proposed in the Draft Directive.

4. Competition and Liberalization

EU competition and liberalization initiatives in the gas industries date back to the late 1980s when they were first introduced as part of the 'single market' agenda. In November 2005, after more than 15 years, and the passage of a huge quantity of EU and national legislation and regulation, the European Commission concluded that 'European energy markets are not yet functioning on a competitive basis and that there are a number of serious malfunctions'.[28]

A decade of negotiations were required before the first EU 'Common Rules' Gas Directive was agreed by member states in August 1998, and required the opening of markets to competition, commencing in August 2000.[29] Despite the fact that some member states passed more advanced legislation to open gas markets prior to that date, overall progress during the first 2 years of market opening was so unimpressive that the Commission almost immediately introduced a second Common Rules (Electricity and) Gas Directive—the 'Acceleration Directive' and wider market opening began in July 2004.[30]

---

[28] 'Energy: Member States must do more to Open Markets; Competition Inquiry Identifies Serious Malfunctions', European Commission press release IP/05/1421, Brussels, 15 November 2005.
[29] CEC (1998). Some member states failed to pass the legislation by the required date; it was only transposed into French law in December 2002.
[30] CEC (2003a). By the start of the first tentative market opening under the first Directive, the British market was already fully open to competition.

In June 2004, 10 new member states acceded to the European Union which meant that 25 countries were expected to operate liberalized gas markets.[31] Bulgaria, Romania, and Croatia are candidate countries, with the first two joining the Union in 2007. Most EU energy legislation and regulation also applies to the European Economic Area (EEA) countries—Norway, Iceland, and Liechtenstein—through the Treaty between the two organizations. The ratification of the European Energy Treaty in June 2006 requires another eight countries to implement the key EU Directives and Regulations by July 2007.[32] The EU energy *acquis* is therefore on the verge of becoming pan-European, encompassing virtually all European nations, stretching from Belarus in the east, to North Africa and the Middle East in the south.

The liberalization of European gas industries, in terms of:

- creating access to transmission and distribution networks;

- demonopolization of markets; and

- abolition of exclusive rights of utility companies;

has been an extremely long process which is far from completed. Table 2 shows that gas and electricity markets will be fully opened to competition by 2007, nearly 20 years after the European Commission published its first paper on the liberalization of these sectors. At virtually every stage prior to agreement in 1998, key principles of liberalization and competition were fiercely opposed by a majority of gas utilities and gas-producing companies, as well as governments of major European member states. In comparison to electricity, the depth of the opposition from the gas industry can be seen in Table 2, which shows that the first Electricity Directive was passed one and a half years prior to its gas counterpart.

As its title implies, the July 2003 'Acceleration Directive' was designed to speed up and reinforce the provisions of the 1998 Gas Directive. The latter allowed for a relatively leisurely pace for the opening up of markets which, given the opposition from member states, was all that could be agreed at that time. Negotiated—rather than regulated—access to networks was allowed, and no detailed rules for design and implementation of tariffs were established, even for the majority which had chosen regulated access. The first Directive also provided for only relatively weak

---

[31] Two of the new member states, Malta and Cyprus, do not have gas markets.

[32] The countries are: Albania, Bulgaria, Bosnia and Herzegovina, Romania, Croatia, Macedonia, Montenegro, Serbia and UNMIK Kosovo. Negotiations have also included: Turkey, Moldova, Ukraine and Norway as observers. *Treaty Establishing the Energy Community and Annexes*, http://ec.europa.eu/energy/electricity/south_east/treaty_en.htm

Table 2. European Union Gas Legislation, Regulation, and Policy Initiatives: A Chronology

1985:	Single European Act largely excludes energy sector.
May 1988:	Publication of the Commission's Paper on 'The Internal Energy Market'.
July 1990:	Price Transparency Directive comes into force.
December 1990:	Electricity Transit Directive comes into force.
May 1991:	Gas Transit Directive comes into force.
May 1994:	Hydrocarbons Directive comes into force
February 1997:	Common Rules Directive for Electricity comes into force.
August 1998:	Common Rules Directive for Gas comes into force.
September 1999:	First meeting of the Madrid Forum
August 2000:	Market opening begins under 1998 Gas Directive.
July 2003:	Acceleration (Electricity and) Gas Directive comes into force.
November 2003:	European Regulators Group for Electricity and Gas (ERGEG) established by a Commission Decision.
July 2004:	Market opening commences under the Acceleration Directive(s).
June 2005:	DG COMP launches an Energy Sector Inquiry
November 2005:	Regulation on access to natural gas transmission networks comes into force.
July 2007:	Full gas (and electricity) market opening to be achieved.

'accounting unbundling', i.e. separation of accounts of different functions within the same company.

The Acceleration Directive strengthened all of these provisions by requiring:

- that by July 2004 all non-household customers should be open to competition and by July 2007 the entire market should be open (Article 24);

- the establishing of access to networks based on published tariffs (Article 18)—or at a minimum methodologies for calculating such tariffs, i.e. regulated access, to be approved by a regulatory authority (Article 18); negotiated access remained an option only in respect of storage (Article 19);

- 'legal unbundling' of networks into separate subsidiaries (Article 9) which would be designated transmission system operators (TSOs) and distribution system operators (DSOs), although it was specifically stated that this did not constitute an obligation to separate the ownership of network assets from the supply business (ownership unbundling);

- Regulation: Article 25 of the Acceleration Directive contains a legal requirement to establish a regulator and to fix tariffs (or methodologies for calculating tariffs) prior to their coming into force. This forced the creation of a German regulatory authority, a development which both industry and government had been resisting since the start of the liberalization process (Lohmann, 2006). In November 2003, the Commission set up the European Regulators' Group for Electricity and Gas (ERGEG) to help to ensure consistent application of the Directives as a liaison both between national regulatory authorities, and between the latter and the Commission.

One major shortcoming of the liberalization process was the lack of any specific guidance regarding how to set transmission and distribution tariffs, and the rules of access to networks. The Acceleration Directive did not resolve this problem and it was left to the Madrid Forum—a twice-yearly meeting of natural gas regulators and industry representatives—to create a set of 'Guidelines for Good Practice' in September 2003.[33] These guidelines were codified into a Regulation on Access applied by the member states from July 2006, consisting of three sets of guidelines:[34]

- third-party access services;
- principles underlying capacity allocation mechanisms and congestion-management procedures;
- definition of the technical information necessary for network users to gain access; transparency requirements and time schedules for information.

4.1 Progress Towards Market Opening and Competition

Under Article 31 of the Acceleration Directive, the Directorate-General Energy and Transport (DG TREN) of the Commission is required to prepare an annual progress report on the implementation of the Directive in the member states; these are known as the 'benchmarking reports'.[35] In addition to the benchmarking reports, DG TREN also produced a 2005 report on progress towards creation of a liberalized gas (and electricity) market (CEC, 2005b). This report was published at the same time as an issues paper from the Commission's Directorate General for Competition's (DG COMP) Energy Sector Investigation, and followed up in February 2006 by a substantial preliminary report from the same investigation (CEC, 2005c, 2006a).

---

[33] The history and documents produced from the Madrid Forum meetings can be found at: http://europa.eu.int/comm/energy/gas/madrid/index_en.htm

[34] CEC (2005a). The detail is not contained within the Directive itself but in an annex containing the guidelines.

[35] Available at http://europa.eu.int/comm/energy/gas/benchmarking/index_en.htm. There have been benchmarking reports every year from 2001 to 2005 which are required by Article 28 of the Electricity Directive and Article 31 of the Gas Directive.

The conclusions of the DG TREN and DG COMP reports were essentially the same. Industries were not yet operating on a competitive basis and identified 'serious malfunctions'. While progress in some countries has been better than others, criticisms essentially fall into five categories set out in DG COMP's preliminary report (CEC, 2005c, pp. 3–4).

- Concentration in wholesale markets: there has been no significant change in the high level of concentration created in the pre-liberalization period.

- Vertical foreclosure: long-term supply contracts between producers and incumbent importers have deprived the market of liquidity. Access to networks—often owned by incumbent importers—remains unsatisfactory.

- Market integration: cross-border sales exert no competitive pressure as incumbents rarely enter other national markets and cross-border capacity is limited. The majority of primary capacity in transit pipelines is owned by incumbents based on legacy contracts which have derogations from the access provisions of the Directives.

- Transparency: there is a lack of reliable and timely information about markets. Incumbents have this information but new entrants have great difficulty obtaining it, often on the grounds of commercial confidentiality.

- Price formation: Continental European gas prices continue to be linked to oil product prices and therefore fail to react to changes in supply and demand; there is no clear trend towards market-based pricing.

In addition to these high-level measures of liberalization and competition, the 2005 DG TREN report adds several more levels of detail to the problems of, specifically, access to networks and the barriers to entry that these create (CEC, 2005b, pp. 13–14):

- Lack of liquidity in both gas and capacity owing to long-term transportation and supply contracts remains a huge problem. Capacity allocation mechanisms with first-come-first-served provisions are a major problem for new entrants in obtaining transportation.

- Network unbundling is not as effective as it should be and it is increasingly questioned whether this can be rectified in the absence of ownership unbundling. This extends to detailed issues such as balancing regimes[36] which are unnecessarily stringent because they are not market-based and not cost-reflective.

- Access to storage remains a major problem despite the adoption of guidelines for good practice in 2005 (see below).

This situation is illustrated by the relative lack of switching shown in Table 3 where only in the UK, where this process started much earlier, is the majority of the gas being sold to all end-user groups being delivered by a different supplier.[37] Outside the household sector, significant progress has been made in Ireland and Spain; some progress has been made in Denmark, Belgium, and Italy. The household sector is at the very beginning of liberalization in all Continental European countries, recalling that the Acceleration Directive does not require this sector to be opened until July 2007. Two further observations need to be made about this table:

- no data were received from Germany and very little from the Netherlands—two extremely important EU gas markets;
- in the vast majority of the new member states, the competition and liberalization process has yet to get under way.[38]

Most Continental European utilities would object to an interpretation of Table 3 which suggests that little competition has taken place. For these utilities—and particularly those in Germany—the test of competition has been price-cutting and rebates which the incumbents declare they have been required to give to customers to prevent competitors from taking away their business.[39] The problem is that lack of transparency and the confidentiality culture of the industry do not allow independent verification of this proposition, which has no support from any source other than the industry itself. The most that can be said from the price data in the public domain is that during the period 2003–5 end-user prices in north-west Europe appeared to rise more slowly than the oil product-linked import price, suggesting an inability of utilities to pass through the full impact of wholesale price increases to their customers (CEC, 2005*b*, pp. 58–63).

---

[36] A 'balancing regime' refers to the need for network users to balance, over a period of time, the volume of gas which they input into the network with the volume they extract from the network.

[37] For details of the UK see Wright (2006).

[38] Although this may be as much about lack of data as lack of liberalization, since in countries such as Lithuania there has been liberalized access to pipelines for many years.

[39] For a detailed account of German gas liberalization, see Lohmann (2006).

Table 3. Summary of Customer Switching Volume of Gas Consumption (%) having Switched by Group—Cumulative since Market Opening[a]

Country[b]	Power plants	Large and very large industrial	Small/medium industrial and business	Very small business and household
Austria		6		4
Belgium	25		9	
Denmark		30		2
France		14		0
Germany		no data		
Ireland	100		49	0
Italy	23		3	1
Luxembourg	—	2	0	0
Netherlands		no data		5
Spain		60		2
Sweden		no data		
UK	>90	>84	>75	47
Hungary		6		

Notes: [a] Data from the first half of 2005; [b] all other member states 0 per cent in all categories.
Source: CEC (2005*b*, Table 3.2).

But even allowing for the possibility that price-cutting may have taken place, the continuing dominance of incumbents—even after divestment, release gas programmes, market-share limitations, and other attempts to curtail their dominance—clearly shows the difficulties which regulators face in attempting to promote competition.

4.2 Mergers and Market Concentration

As noted above, the 2005–6 DG COMP investigation into the energy sector singled out market concentration as one of the most important obstacles to competition. In the pre-liberalization era, there was one dominant merchant gas transmission company in each European country with a *de facto* (and in some cases a *de jure*) monopoly of many of the key industry functions: purchase, transmission, storage, and imports; as well as local, regional—and, in a few cases, national—sales monopolies.

Tables 4 and 5 demonstrate the degree of market concentration in both production and imports, and supply to different groups of end-users, at the end of 2004. With the exception of the UK (where the liberalization and competition process began much earlier and was aggressively enforced), markets remain highly concentrated and, although more recent data would certainly alter the picture for Spain, the Netherlands, and possibly Italy, it is uncertain whether for other countries, figures for 2006 would show a substantially different picture.

Table 4. Market Structure in Import and Production of Gas (end 2004)

	No. of companies with 5% share of production/ export capacity	No. of companies with 5% share of available gas	Share of 3 largest gas shippers in wholesale market (%)	Liquidity multiple spot trading/ total consumption (%)
Austria	2	4	80	3
Belgium	2	2	—	229
Denmark	2	2	97	—
France	2	2	98	—
Germany	5	10	c. 80	—
Ireland	5	5	84	—
Italy	3	3	62	—
Luxembourg	1	—	—	—
Netherlands	1	1	85	5
Spain	4	4	73	—
Sweden	1	5	78	—
UK	7	7	36	10
Estonia	1	—	100	—
Latvia	1	1	100	—
Lithuania	4	—	92	—
Poland	1	1	100	—
Czech Republic	—	—	—	—
Slovakia	1	1	—	—
Hungary	2	1	100	—
Slovenia	1	1	100	—

Note: This is one of the tables in the corrigendum to the report, http://europa.eu.int/ comm/energy/electricity/report_2005/doc/2005_report_corrigendum_en.pdf
Source: CEC (2005*b*, Table 5.1, corrected version).

Over the past decade, a mixture of privatization and the threat of liberalization and greater competition has fundamentally changed the corporate structure of energy utility industries and the strategies of restructured companies. Mergers and acquisitions in the gas and electricity (and other utility) industries have created a relatively small number of very large companies which are aiming to operate on (at least) a pan-European scale. The Continental European gas utilities which created and dominated the gas business in Europe during the period 1960–2000 have been restructured, merged with/taken over by other (principally electricity) companies, although many have had their pipeline networks separated and in rare cases no longer own these networks. A brief survey of these companies illustrates this. [40]

- In the UK, the privatized British Gas has undergone several demergers (starting in 1997) of which the largest companies are Centrica, BG Group, and (the gas network of) National Grid.

[40] These utility mergers were in addition to the mergers among the international super-majors during the same period: BP/Amoco, Exxon/Mobil, Conoco/Phillips, Chevron/Texaco.

- In 2001, the Italian gas company SNAM was demerged into a network company (Rete Gas) and a supply company which became part of the ENI Group.
- In 2004, the dominant German gas company Ruhrgas merged with the giant multi-energy conglomerate E.ON.[41]
- The Dutch gas company Gasunie demerged into two companies— Gas Transport Services (owned by the Dutch government) and Gasunie Trade and Gas Supply (the latter may be further divided into companies owned by the Dutch government, Shell, and Exxon).
- The Belgian company Distrigas, with a separate network company Fluxys, became fully owned by the French multi-utility Suez.
- The Spanish company Gas Natural demerged its network company—Enagas.
- Only Gaz de France still resembled a traditional European gas company with a separate, but wholly owned, transmission company.

As this chapter was completed in late 2006, new mega-mergers were in the final stages of completion, with E.ON poised to purchase the Spanish electricity company Endesa, Suez merging with Gaz de France, and the Spanish power utility Iberdrola's takeover of Scottish Power.[42] Elsewhere in Europe dominant multi-energy and multi-utility companies have purchased large (often majority) gas industry stakes in Hungary (E.ON), the Czech Republic (RWE), Slovakia and Romania (E.ON, Gaz de France), and the Baltic countries (E.ON). In addition, Gazprom was seeking to buy equity in European utility companies—with an emphasis on the UK and, in particular, Centrica—causing additional concerns among European politicians about the potential security implications of such developments.

While the successors of the privatized British Gas looked towards North America for mergers and acquisitions, the traditional European gas companies have added significant scale in Europe (including the UK)— in terms of size and multi-energy/utility capability—to their operations in order better to compete on a Europe-wide scale and compensate for loss

[41] The other major German gas companies BEB and Thyssengas—now part of the RWE Group—have undergone similar ownership change and restructuring.

[42] The Spanish government was fiercely (and in the view of the EU competition authorities, illegally) resisting the Endesa takeover, while the Suez/Gaz de France merger arose from defensive moves by the French government to prevent Enel (the Italian electricity major) purchasing Suez.

Table 5. Structure of Gas Supply Market (end 2004)

	Companies with market shares over 5%	Market share of three largest			
		Large companies/ power plants %	Large industrial users %	Small/medium-sized users %	Small/very small users %
Austria	4	—	—	—	—
Belgium	3/5	—	90–100	99–100	99–100
Denmark	3	100	92	100	100
France	3	—	—	—	—
Germany	1	—	—	—	—
Ireland	3	91	100	100	100
Italy	5	80	54	—	33
Luxembourg	4	99	95	93	93
Netherlands	3	—	—	—	83
Spain	5	—	72	77	90
Sweden	—	—	—	—	—
UK	6	56	53	61	77
Estonia	1	85	100	100	100
Latvia	1	—	100	100	100
Lithuania	2	—	100	100	100
Poland	7	100	—	—	—
Czech Rep	7	—	54	51	57
Slovakia	1	100	100	100	100
Hungary	7	95	77	76	79
Slovenia	8	—	—	—	—

Source: CEC (2005*b*, Table 5.2, corrected version—this is one of the tables in the corrigendum to the report, http://europa.eu.int/comm/energy/electricity/report_2005/doc/2005_report_corrigendum_en.pdf)

of market share to competitors in their national markets. In particular, it became conventional wisdom among European gas utilities that it was no longer possible to survive and prosper:

- as a gas-only company; the minimum scale for a European energy utility must be gas and electricity;
- as a utility company in a single country; the minimum necessary scale for future success would be expansion to other European countries.

The energy-sector investigation by the European competition authorities, which is due to report in early 2007, is expected to recommend that gas and electricity utilities should separate the ownership of infrastructure from that of the supply and marketing business. If that recommendation is accepted, it will lead to further ownership changes in the gas (and power) sector.

5. Conclusions: A Constrained Future for Gas in Europe?

By late 2006, the future prospects for gas were much less bright than had seemed the case a few years previously, for two main reasons:

- demand is likely to increase more slowly because of the reduced attractiveness of gas-fired power generation owing to high prices;

- ongoing depletion of indigenous resources and increasing import dependence has raised serious political concerns about security of supply.

The continued strong link between gas and oil prices, guaranteed by long-term contracts throughout Continental Europe, has meant that the prices of the two commodities have risen in step since 2003. This has jeopardized the commercial future of gas-fired power generation in many countries despite its advantages in terms of carbon (and other) emissions. At the same time, while ample gas reserves could be potentially available by pipeline to Europe from CIS, the Caspian, and Middle East countries, serious uncertainties have developed around the politics of their development and transportation. While LNG will become a more important source of imports for many European countries, the latter will face competition from both North America and the Pacific Basin, especially for Middle East LNG.

These problems will not create a shortage of gas in Europe over the next 5 years—indeed, the short to medium term is more likely to see a period of surplus rather than shortage. In this time frame, at least as much, and probably more, attention should be devoted to dealing with the risk that end-users could be deprived of supply owing to a combination of domestic infrastructure failure and insufficient storage to meet extreme weather conditions. Security of domestic supplies and infrastructure, particularly for countries—such as the UK—which have limited storage capacity relative to the size of their markets, will be of paramount importance.

Weakening the link between oil and gas prices, and creating significant closer linkage between gas and power prices, could give power companies more confidence to build new gas-fired stations. One way this could happen is through increased liberalization and competition. The DG COMP Sector Investigation seems set to announce the need for ownership unbundling of networks in order to enforce competition by structural means where more than a decade of legislation and regulation has failed. However, continuing market concentration through mergers between companies which were already of a very substantial size, is not a promising omen for competition. It is difficult to be optimistic that self-sustaining competition can be created between a handful of mega-utilities which—even if they are forced to sell their networks—seem set to dominate European gas (and electricity) markets, particularly when many Continental European governments are encouraging market concentration at the expense of competition. The dominant buyers of gas in Europe and their small number of suppliers are likely to try to maintain the commercial status quo. Both sides have much to gain from the maintenance of oil-linked prices at post-2003 levels, particularly if supply-security concerns create an obstacle to substantial increases in gas trade.

However, *if* Europe requires a significant increase in gas-fired power generation, supply problems may arise after 2015 and particularly after 2020. The source of the next 50–100 bcm/year of supply for European markets is not clear because of political and geo-political problems between Europe and its principal suppliers in Russia and North Africa; and its principal potential suppliers in the Middle East, the Caspian, and West Africa. At present, there is no sign that these problems will be resolved quickly. In the middle of the first decade of the twenty-first century, European international gas security discourse was dominated by commercial and political difficulties between Russia and the CIS countries which transit its gas to Europe. It would be comforting to think that established EU institutions—such as the EU-Russia Energy Dialogue—could play some role in helping to resolve them. Whether justified or not, there is likely to be considerable nervousness in Europe about Russia for the foreseeable future. A combination of heightened European security concerns and a worsening geo-political environment, may mean that a political limit on Russian gas supplies is likely to be reached following the completion of the two NordStream Pipelines in the early 2010s.

Political developments within the main alternative gas suppliers to Russia—and relations between those countries and Europe—are similarly discouraging. Producers and exporters in the Middle East, North and West Africa, Central Asia, and the Caspian have alternatives to dedicated pipeline gas supplies to Europe; and the routes that such pipelines could take are either dominated by Russia, fraught with political complications, or commercially unattractive in comparison to pipeline or LNG alternatives.

Whether Europe faces a constrained gas future depends on two crucial judgements:

- whether Europe's suppliers—and particularly those suppliers outside Europe—are prepared to adjust prices to allow gas to compete in the power sector which is the only major growth market for the fuel over the next 20 years;

- whether the geo-political environment between Russia and Europe, and the Middle East and Europe will improve, thereby encouraging additional pipeline connections.

If the answer to either of these questions is negative then the future of gas is in doubt; and if the answer to both of them is negative then the future of gas in Europe will be severely constrained.

Part 3: Electricity

9

Electricity and Markets

Richard Green*

1. Introduction

Twenty-five years ago, the electricity industry was largely made up of vertically integrated monopolies. Smaller utilities without their own generation bought their power under contract from a larger firm, or simply paid the tariff that the generator set each year for its power sales. When the utilities with generation wished to trade power among themselves, they typically did so on a split-savings basis. Each utility would report its marginal cost, and the price would be the average of the two figures, thus giving each utility half of the gains from trade. Even where there were 'power pools' involving a large number of generators, they operated as clubs, rather than as markets.

Today, many of these monopolies have been broken up, and the electricity industry in a large number of countries has been reorganized around markets. The first wholesale market was established in Chile in 1978, but the great wave of deregulation did not get under way until the 1990s. England and Wales established a spot market, the Pool, in 1990, and Norway liberalized its own market in 1991. In 1996, this became the world's first international electricity market, when Sweden joined the renamed Nord Pool. By then, Australia and New Zealand had created

* Support from the Leverhulme Trust, through the award of a Philip Leverhulme Prize, is gratefully acknowledged. I would like to thank the Department of Applied Economics, University of Cambridge, for its hospitality, and Dieter Helm, Janusz Bialek, an anonymous referee and participants at an *Oxford Review of Economic Policy* seminar for helpful comments—the usual disclaimer applies.

electricity markets, and many others followed them. In the United States, the Pennsylvania–New Jersey–Maryland Interconnector (PJM), which had acted as a club pool since 1927, converted itself into a spot market in 1998, followed by California, New England, New York, and Texas.

While electricity spot markets attract a lot of attention, with their highly visible and frequently changing prices, any company that relies on them is taking a large risk. Most companies do most of their trading through longer-term contracts, although this now means contracts lasting not for decades but for years (or even for a single year). Depending on the design of the local spot market, these may be contracts for physical delivery of power, or they may be financial contracts for differences which hedge the spot market price, and reduce the risk of trading in that market.

Over the past 20 years, we have also become more conscious of the pollution caused by electricity generation, and of the challenge of climate change. There has also been a shift from command-and-control regulations for pollution, towards market-based incentives. The United States established a market for sulphur-dioxide emissions, a major cause of acid rain, through Title IV of the 1990 Clean Air Act Amendments. This has been followed by a number of regional markets for nitrogen oxides. The European Union still largely relies on command and control to deal with these emissions, but has created a market for carbon dioxide (CO_2) as part of its efforts to comply with the Kyoto Protocol's targets for the emissions contributing to global warming.

Even before the carbon trading scheme was agreed, most European countries were trying to reduce emissions by promoting renewable generation—wind power, hydro power, and the like. At first, these generators received direct subsidies, or sold their power at higher prices to utilities that were required to buy a set proportion of their needs from renewable sources. Schemes like these have the disadvantage that it can be difficult to set the special tariff at the appropriate level to encourage the desired amount of new construction. Some countries have adopted a different system, based on tradable green certificates. Each renewable generator obtains green certificates for its output, and each retailer must hold certificates equal to a specified proportion of its sales. We do not consider these markets further, but they can provide an important stimulus to renewable generators, over and above the impact of carbon trading.

How well are these various markets working? We shall see that a wide range of different market designs have been applied around the world.

Does the choice of market design matter, in terms of the prices and investment incentives that it will produce? Can we identify unambiguously good and bad designs, or do some designs perform well against some objectives, and badly against others? For example, does a price cap that guards against the abuse of market power when there is spare capacity make it hard to remunerate peaking plant and incentivize investment once more capacity is needed? In that case, does the choice of design depend upon the industry's current state? We should remember, however, that making significant changes to market rules should not be done lightly—the implementation costs of writing new contracts and software can be high, and each change creates uncertainty about future changes that can deter investment. It is probably better to choose, and stick with, a market design that will perform well in most circumstances, than to adopt a less robust design that happens to be better suited to the industry's current situation.

The physics of electricity provide some important constraints on the design of an appropriate market, and so section 2 gives a brief account of these. The next section shows how a spot market with constantly changing prices can allow generators to recover the full costs of all types of generating capacity in equilibrium. Sections 4–6 discuss electricity wholesale markets from around the world, concentrating on the price of energy, different ways of paying for capacity, and transmission pricing. Section 7 moves on to discuss long-term contract markets for electricity. Section 8 covers markets for emissions permits, and the chapter finishes with brief conclusions.

Before we start the main body of the chapter, it is worth defining a few terms. Generators are at the upstream end of the industry. At the downstream end, retailers sell to consumers. I use the term 'retailers' in this chapter in order clearly to distinguish between the demand and the supply side of the wholesale markets, although retailers in the UK energy markets (and some others) are known as 'suppliers'. The wholesale markets are where generators, retailers, and independent traders meet, together with a few large customers who purchase on their own account (a distinction which is not important for our purposes). In the new energy paradigm, both wholesale and retail markets can be opened to competition. Delivering electricity, however, depends upon networks which are natural monopolies, and are usually regulated as such. We distinguish between transmission and distribution networks. Most customers are connected to distribution networks where the voltage is low. The distribution networks are connected to a transmission system that works at much higher voltage. The transmission systems have to be actively managed to ensure that electricity can reach the distribution systems, whereas distribution system management can be more passive—most of the flows just go down the network to consumers.

2. Some Physics

Electricity is the extreme example of a non-storable commodity. At every moment in time, generation must balance demand, with only a small tolerance for changes in frequency to absorb fluctuations. Generation and transmission equipment alike will be damaged by excessive flows, and is protected by circuit breakers that will cut off the current if they sense a power surge. A failure in one area can thus cause millions of people to lose power, as large parts of the grid automatically shut themselves down—the northeastern United States and Ontario, parts of Sweden and Denmark, and Italy all suffered from large-scale power failures during the summer of 2003. To minimize the risk of such problems, and to contain them if possible, the electricity system must be tightly controlled. Within each area, there must be a control centre with authority to over-ride individual companies' commercial decisions, if this is necessary to protect the grid. The control centre will have to ensure that there is sufficient spare capacity to cope with the loss of any single element. Transmission investments are planned so that the system can cope with the loss of any two elements. These 'N-1' and 'N-2' rules imply that there must always be enough spinning reserve—generators that are running part-loaded—to replace the sudden loss of the largest single unit on the system. Similarly, the transmission lines must have enough spare capacity that if one circuit fails and the current flowing down it is redistributed over the rest of the system, none of the remaining lines is overloaded.

Electricity flows cannot generally be steered through the grid, and will follow every feasible route between generators and loads. This means that it is not sufficient to have spare capacity on some route between a generator and a load, in case a circuit is lost—there must be enough spare capacity on every line to cope with the uncontrollable change in flows that it might experience. Sometimes, this means that the system controller will not be able to accept all the flows that market participants would like to schedule, and so part of the transmission system will be constrained. Some generators with relatively low costs, located on the wrong side of the constraint, will have to be replaced by other generators in a better location, but with relatively high costs. In some cases, where the constraint surrounds a relatively small 'load pocket', the system operator will have no real choice about which generators to constrain on in this way. In other cases, the system operator has more well-placed plants to choose from. The system operator also has some discretion over whether a constraint exists or not, since the issue is not whether it is physically possible for any more power to flow down a line in the system's current state, but whether there is a significant risk that the system could reach a state in which the additional flow would cause a problem.

3. Some Economics

To explain how electricity prices vary over time, we must consider the costs involved. Start with the top right panel (1) of Figure 1. The two straight lines show the total cost (per megawatt) of operating two types of power station for different numbers of hours over a year. The vertical intercept represents the station's fixed costs, while the slope gives the variable cost per megawatt-hour generated. The peaking plant (which might represent an open-cycle gas turbine, or an old plant nearing retirement) has lower fixed costs but a high variable cost. The base load plant (combined-cycle gas turbines (CCGTs) have been the investment of choice in most countries where gas is available) has higher fixed costs but a lower variable cost. If the plant is needed for more than T hours a year, it is cheaper to build a base load plant, whereas the peaking plant is cheaper for less intensive use. The thicker line segments show the lower envelope of the cost function, for this efficient plant mix.

How much capacity of each type is needed? Move down to panel (2), which shows the load-duration curve. The hours of the year are ranked in decreasing order of demand, and there are T hours in which the demand is at a level of B GW or above. If the industry has B GW of base load plant, they will all be used for at least T hours a year. If there were any more base load plants, they would be used for less than T hours, and it would have been cheaper to use peaking plants instead.

What about the total capacity? At this point, we need to remember that the demand for electricity, and hence the load-duration curve, depends upon its price. The load-duration curve in panel (2) is drawn on the assumption that the price of electricity is the variable cost of the marginal plant in operation. At a price equal to the variable cost of a peaking plant, the maximum demand for electricity would be D. Peaking plants would

Figure 1 The Determination of Electricity Prices

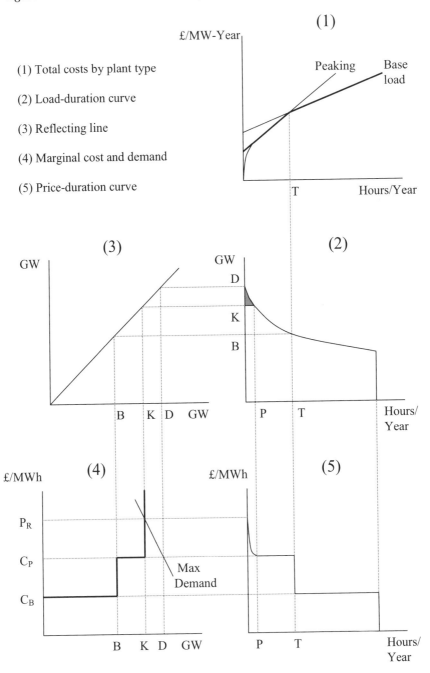

(1) Total costs by plant type

(2) Load-duration curve

(3) Reflecting line

(4) Marginal cost and demand

(5) Price-duration curve

not be able to recover their fixed costs, however, if the price of electricity never rose above their variable costs.

In an ideal electricity market, there would be a smooth demand curve for power at each point in time—some consumers have to pay the market price and would be willing to reduce their demand as the price rose. The highest of these demand curves is shown in panel (4)—panel (3) is a reflector which allows us to switch from having capacity on the vertical axis in panel (2), to having it on the horizontal axis in panel (4). The heavy line in panel (4) is the industry's marginal cost curve. There are B GW of base load plant with a variable cost of C_B, and $(K - B)$ GW of peaking plant with a variable cost of C_P. The marginal cost curve becomes vertical at K, the industry's total capacity. If the price were equal to C_P, the maximum demand would be equal to D GW, but since this much cannot be generated, the price must rise to P_R in order to ration demand to capacity.

This leads us to the price-duration curve shown in the final panel, (5). The maximum price is P_R, and the price remains above C_P for the first P hours of the year. At hour P, panel (2) shows that the demand at a price of C_P is just equal to K, there is no need to ration demand to capacity, and the price is equal to the variable cost of the peaking plants. After T hours, demand is low enough to be met by the base load plants alone, and the price drops to C_B.[1] The shaded area just under the top of the load-duration curve (2) represents the electricity that would be demanded at a price equal to variable cost but is not generated, flattening the peak demand to the level of available capacity, K. Note that in a system where rationing by price was not possible, but the available capacity was still equal to K, the shaded area would represent non-price rationing, in the form of 'unserved energy' (i.e. power cuts).

Finally, we can return to the top panel (1) to consider the question of cost recovery. The curved line in the bottom left of the panel shows the rate at which plants earn revenue in the highest-demand hours of the year—the line has a steep slope because prices are high. By hour P, this total revenue line has met the thick line giving the total costs of a peaking plant. Since all the peaking plants are in use for at least the first P hours of the year, this allows all of them to cover their fixed costs. Since the

---

[1] The step change in the price-duration curve implies that there is no demand curve passing through the vertical section of the marginal cost curve at B. We could adapt the analysis if some demand curves did pass through this section of the cost curve. In practice, a system with a large number of plants has a nearly smooth marginal cost curve, and no noticeable discontinuities in the price-duration curve.

marginal revenue for each additional hour's generation up to T is equal to the variable costs of the peaking plants, the total revenue line is superimposed on the total cost line for those plants. After T, the price drops to the variable cost of the base load plants, and so the slope of the total revenue line falls. By the definition of T, however, this is the point where the two types of plants have equal total costs, and so the base load plants will also have total costs equal to their total revenues.

This analysis has been simplified (and more detail is available in Stoft (2002)), but it shows us that if the industry has the right amount and mix of capacity, all plant types can recover their costs from market-based pricing. The key requirement is that peak prices must rise above the variable costs of peaking plant. If we have too little plant, prices will be above this level for longer, and so all types of power station will be paid more than their costs, signalling that entry will be profitable. If there is too much capacity, prices will only exceed variable costs by a small amount, and stations will lose money, encouraging exit. Similar conclusions can be drawn about the mix of capacity—if there are too many peaking plants relative to base load capacity, prices will be high for a greater proportion of the year. This raises the earnings of base load stations above their costs, sending a signal that more are needed.

We should also discuss the pricing of electricity transmission. Ignoring losses for a moment, if there were no transmission constraints, the marginal cost of power could be the same at every point in the system. If there is a binding limit on the flow along some line, however, some more expensive output from the importing side of the constraint must replace some cheaper output from the exporting side. If the price in each region is equal to the marginal cost in that region, then the difference between the two prices represents the marginal cost of the transmission constraint, and the economically correct charge for sending electricity between the two regions. In a meshed network, however, in which there are many possible routes between any two points, it is no longer correct to think of just two prices. If a node on the network is 'close' to the constraint—the resistance on the lines between that node and the constraint is relatively low—then Kirchhoff's laws imply that a relatively high proportion of any change in generation at that node would flow across the constrained line. Changes in generation at other nodes will have less impact on the constrained line. This implies that the marginal cost at a node could be thought of as depending on the marginal cost (per MWh) of the constraint, multiplied by the proportion of a 1 MW increase in demand at that node that would actually flow over the constraint.[2]

Transmission losses also lead the marginal cost of power to differ at every point on the system. As electricity flows through the network, an amount proportional to the current squared is lost in heating the wires, and there are also losses in transformers and other pieces of equipment. Because the heating losses depend upon the current squared, the marginal loss is twice the average loss. This implies that the marginal cost of meeting a demand at the importing end of a heavily loaded line can be significantly greater than at the exporting end. At the winter peak, it could be necessary to generate 106 MW in the north of England in order to meet an extra 94 MW of demand in the south-west, if no closer plants were available (NGC, 2004, table 7.4).

If the system has been dispatched in a way that minimizes overall costs, then the marginal cost at any node where a generator is running with spare capacity is the marginal cost of that generator. However, we would obtain the same number if we calculated the marginal cost of generation at some arbitrary point on the network (known as the 'swing bus'), plus the cost in terms of losses of getting the power from the swing bus to our location, plus the impact of additional demand at our location on constraints.[3] The same formula is used to calculate the marginal cost of meeting demand at all other nodes on the system.

4. Electricity Markets

There are three key questions in the design of an electricity market. First, and probably least controversial, is how to set the price of energy. Second, should there be any specific extra payments for capacity? Third, to what extent (and how) should the prices include transmission effects? This section discusses a range of answers to the first question; the others are answered in the following sections.

Why do there seem to be so many answers to these questions, and such a diversity of market designs around the world? In part, this is due to the complexity of the issues involved—we genuinely do not know the best

---

[2] Note that if the node is on the exporting side of the constraint, an increase in demand will decrease the flow across the constraint, this proportion will be negative, and the impact of the constraint is to reduce the marginal cost at this node. It is even possible for some marginal costs to be negative!

[3] This result holds, in part, because the cost of the constraint is derived from the difference in the marginal cost of generation on each side of it.

way of dealing with some of the problems. Sometimes, the equivalence between different market rules comes about because one system will be based on an expectation (particularly of the value of capacity, for example), while another will be based upon an out-turn value. Some markets choose to reward capacity based on prices (letting the market decide quantities) while others use rules based on quantities (so that the market sets the price). While the various rules can be equivalent under theoretical conditions, we do not know how they will perform in practice without experience.

When it comes to practical market design, there can be a tendency to react to perceived flaws experienced in other countries' markets, by moving away from their designs. Policy-makers also change their views on which problems are the most important—the UK's first market design used a lot of the industry's former operating procedures in order to minimize the risk of disruption. By the time that the market was re-designed, these rules were seen as encouraging gaming to raise prices, while security of supply was not regarded as such a constraint. After a few years of low prices, low investment, and declining capacity margins, however, security of supply has moved back up the political agenda—will this lead to further market changes?

Moving back to the specific question of how the price of energy is set, we should first ask which transactions it will cover. In a gross pool, all but the smallest generators are required to sell all of their output to the pool, and receive the pool's price for it. In a net pool, generators can agree bilateral trades with retailers. They have to inform the system operator, which will take them into account when drawing up its operating schedule, but they do not pass through the pool from a financial point of view.

In practice, the difference can be more apparent than real. With a gross pool, generators and retailers can sign financial contracts for differences which hedge the pool price, and then bid in a way that ensures their plant output matches the quantity covered by the contracts. As long as they maintain this output level, they face no financial exposure to pool prices. In a net pool, bilateral trades should pay transmission charges in the same way as trades made through the pool.[4]

The world's first electricity market, in Chile, was a net pool in that generators could also sign long-term contracts, and the spot market was

---

[4] Some of the support for 'trading outside the Pool' in the UK came from companies that believed it would allow them to avoid paying uplift charges (for keeping the grid stable) in the same way that self-generators (quite reasonably) did.

only used for the differences between actual and contracted deliveries. However, the economic dispatch that determined actual outputs was based on generators' bids, and the energy price was set equal to the bid of the marginal generator. The bids were not freely made, however, but had to equal the generators' (auditable) costs. Furthermore, there was an adjustment system that came into play if the price in a long-term contract differed from the average spot price by more than 10 per cent.

The second electricity market, in England and Wales, allowed generators to choose their bids freely. Each generating unit submitted a complicated bid with up to five prices and various technical parameters, and the transmission system operator used these to calculate the least-cost schedule that could meet its demand forecast. The program that it used was actually the same program that had been used when the industry was a vertically integrated public corporation, and prices had just been substituted for internal cost estimates. The energy price in each half-hour, the 'system marginal price', was based on the average cost of the marginal unit, or rather the most expensive unit in normal operation. The rules were complex and sometimes produced anomalous prices—spikes caused by the scheduling of a few high-priced MWh became common towards the end of the Pool's life (Offer, 1999).[5]

The world's third electricity market, which started in Norway and has evolved into Nord Pool, covering four countries, had a very different design. Energy prices were set by the intersection of simple supply and demand curves, in which companies just bid the price they would like to pay or be paid for a given quantity. The market is a net pool, and many companies generate their own power, or trade bilaterally. The system operators need to know about these transactions, but they need not enter the market. Elspot is the main market, which sets prices and volumes for an entire day (although separate bids can be submitted for each hour), and closes at noon on the previous day. There are separate short-term markets (Elbas, for example, covers Sweden, Finland, and Eastern Denmark) allowing participants to trade in individual hours up to one hour before delivery. After that time, the national system operators take over the task of balancing the markets, using bids for 'up' and 'down regulation'. In 2003, 118 TWh was traded on Elspot, compared to

---

[5] A price of £865/MWh was once obtained because a large unit submitted a price for starting up of around £12,000 (which was reasonable for a unit of that size) alongside an inconsistent set of technical parameters which caused the computer to attempt to run it at 5 per cent of its capacity for less than 2 hours. Dividing the start-up price by less than 20 MWh of output produced a very high price. The rules were later changed to allow such anomalous prices to be investigated and sometimes over-ridden.

consumption of 380 TWh in the four countries. The short-term market Elbas saw much less trade, just 0.6 TWh, compared to consumption of 230 TWh in the area it covered. Because Nord Pool is dominated by hydro-electric generators, the level of rainfall is a key determinant of prices. Abnormally low rainfall in the autumn of 2002, for example, sent prices to record levels in the winter of 2002/3. This provided incentives for consumers to reduce consumption, and the winter was passed without major incidents, despite low reservoir levels (von der Fehr *et al.*, 2005).

Australia established a market in Victoria in 1994, which was renamed the National Electricity Market as it expanded to cover the densely populated coastal strip in the south and east of the country. This again used a relatively simple bidding system, and set prices on the intersection of supply and demand curves. One feature was that generators could set negative prices—it costs a lot to turn off and then start up a large coal-fired unit, and so generators sometimes paid to be allowed to run overnight, when demand was low and not all the units were required. The marginal price is calculated every 5 minutes, and six prices are then averaged to get the half-hourly price used for trading (NEMMCO, 2004).

In the United States, the PJM interconnector and California both opened markets at about the same time, in 1998. California's well-publicized disaster has been covered in many other papers (e.g. Joskow, 2001) and is not discussed here. PJM has been much more successful. Like Nord Pool, it is a net pool, in that generators and retailers can trade bilaterally, although they must inform PJM's independent system opera-tor of their transactions. PJM has a day-ahead market, in which both generators and retailers can submit price-sensitive bids, and in which market-clearing prices and quantities are calculated, taking operational constraints into account. These transactions are financially firm, in that the resulting payments must be made, whatever happens on the day. In the real-time market, PJM schedules plant to meet the actual level of demand, using the cheapest resources as far as possible, and sets prices on the basis of the marginal cost of generation. These prices are used for the differences between previously scheduled transactions (either bilateral or day-ahead) and what market participants actually do. Overall, the energy passing through the spot markets is equal to 40 per cent of average demand, with four-fifths of this in the day-ahead market (PJM, 2004). Table 1 shows that average prices are higher in the day-ahead market than in the real-time market, but that they are also less volatile. Effectively, buyers are paying a premium to avoid the greater risks of real-time purchases.

Table 1. Prices in PJM, 2003

	Day-ahead	Real-time	Difference	Difference as % of real-time
Mean LMP	$38.72/MWh	$38.27/MWh	−$0.45/MWh	−1.2
Median LMP	$35.21/MWh	$30.79/MWh	−$4.43/MWh	−14.4
Standard deviation	$20.84/MWh	$24.71/MWh	$3.87/MWh	15.7

Note: LMP stands for locational marginal price.
Source: PJM (2004, Table 2-27).

Most electricity markets are therefore based upon the idea of marginal pricing—the most expensive generator in use sets the price for everyone who has not made a bilateral trade or signed a hedging contract. Great Britain, however, has moved away from this with the New Electricity Trading Arrangements (NETA) adopted in 2001.[6] To many observers, the Pool had become discredited, and some believed that allowing the marginal generator to set prices for all worsened the market's well-known problem of market power (Green and Newbery, 1997; Green, 2001). The compulsion inherent in a gross pool was also believed to be undesirable, and so NETA is based upon bilateral trading. At Gate Closure, now set 1 hour before real time, bilateral trading has to stop and companies report their contracts to Elexon, the company responsible for the Balancing and Settlement Code. The National Grid Company (NGC) is responsible for balancing the system in real time, buying and selling power to keep demand in line with supply and resolve transmission constraints. Some of these trades are made at short notice; others can be made in advance, or called in via option contracts signed in advance. NGC records the cost of all its purchases, and the revenues it receives for all of its sales.

Originally, the average cost of NGC's purchases was used to set the System Buy Price (SBP). Any company with a negative imbalance—one that had sold more than it generated, or bought less than it consumed—had to pay the SBP for its imbalances. The average revenue from NGC's sales set the System Sell Price (SSP). Companies with positive imbalances—those that had generated more than they had sold, for example—were paid the SSP. The SBP was expected to be greater than the SSP, and this was intended to give companies an incentive to balance their positions before Gate Closure, and to penalize deviations from their contracted positions.

---

[6] NETA was for England and Wales alone, but the market was extended to Scotland in April 2005, with the British Electricity Transmission and Trading Arrangements (BETTA).

In practice, the SBP was much further from the prices in the bilateral markets, and much more volatile, than the SSP. Generators could minimize their expected imbalance payments by deliberately selling less than they expected to produce, and holding plant in reserve in case they suffered an outage. An increase in the level of part-loaded plant reduces the system's efficiency (the economies from pooling reserve exceed the gains from stronger incentives to reduce outages), while NGC faced problems in managing a system where every participant wished to have a surplus of power. The rules were amended so that participants with a 'neutral' imbalance—one in the opposite direction from that in the market as a whole, which thus reduces the overall imbalance and could be seen as making NGC's life easier—now pay an imbalance price based upon prices in the short-term bilateral markets. Another recent change moves in a small direction towards marginal pricing, basing the main imbalance price only on the most expensive 500 MWh of NGC's balancing actions in the half-hour. For 80 per cent of the time, this will still be the average price of all of them, but, in a few periods, only half of NGC's actions will be used to set the price. Overall, these changes reduce the incentive to have an expected surplus of power—being out of balance in the opposite direction to the market will cost less, and being out of balance in the same direction will sometimes cost more.

How much impact does the use of pay-as-bid rather than marginal pricing in the short-term market have? Green and McDaniel (1999) show that in a perfectly competitive market with completely inelastic demand, the choice of pricing rule will not affect any generator's expected revenues. The most expensive generator with a chance of being called will bid its marginal costs under both pricing rules. Infra-marginal generators will bid their marginal cost under the marginal pricing rule, and will bid above their costs with the pay-as-bid rule. If they run, these generators will normally be paid more than their bid under the marginal pricing rule, but under NETA, they only receive their bid. The change in bidding exactly offsets the change in pricing rule. Federico and Rahman (2003) argued that a pay-as-bid rule is more vulnerable to market power when demand is price-responsive, although their model does not quite follow NETA's principles.[7] Bower and Bunn (2000) used an intelligent agent computer simulation to predict that a pay-as-bid rule would produce worse results than marginal pricing.

---

[7] They assume that all buyers pay the highest accepted bid under either pay-as-bid or marginal pricing, whereas NETA makes buyers pay the average of all the accepted bids, which will be lower.

In practice, prices were low in the first years after NETA was introduced, but the major generators had divested plant in the run-up to the change in market design, which reduced concentration in the wholesale market to very low levels. Subsequent mergers have increased concentration, somewhat, while fuel prices have also risen significantly since 2003. Evans and Green (2005) use a supply function model to simulate monthly average wholesale prices from April 1997 to March 2005. They find that the same model provides a reasonable fit to actual prices throughout the period, with no evidence of a structural break in the relationship between the simulated and the actual series. The implication is that the relationship between market fundaments (demand, fuel prices, capacity and seller concentration) and prices did not change when the market rules changed. In other words, the short-run impact of spot market rules on market outcomes is limited.

In the longer term, NETA may well make entry into the industry harder. Most electricity systems have a liquid short-term market, and because participants can always trade out their positions in this market, it is not necessary to be vertically integrated in order to compete effectively. If the short-term market is illiquid, then a physical hedge between generation and retailing becomes much more important, and unintegrated entry much harder. This would then lead to a less competitive industry and higher prices in the long term. It is certainly the case that many large companies in the electricity industry welcomed NETA (at the same time that the regulator argued that it would make the market more competitive) and that mergers in the industry led to a largely vertically integrated structure by the time the market rules changed.

What can we conclude about the choice of payment system for energy? In a transparent market, the choice between a gross pool and a net pool should be irrelevant to the market outcomes, although a net pool may allow more flexibility in the design of contracts. If bilateral trading is not transparent, however, the gross pool will give market participants more information, and may make trading and entry and exit decisions more efficient. The lack of transparency may be one of NETA's greatest drawbacks. Most other market design choices, however, will trigger offsetting responses by market participants, and so it seems that a wide range of energy payment systems are working well in practice.

5. Paying for Capacity

Section 3 showed that the price of electricity has to rise above the marginal running cost in peak hours if generators are to cover the fixed costs of keeping capacity available. This section discusses some of the ways in which electricity markets raise peak prices to pay for capacity. There are three broad alternatives. First, some markets have no explicit mechanism. Second, some market designs include a payment to capacity, which generally declines as the amount of spare capacity rises, in order to reward capacity most when it is needed most. Third, some systems include an explicit market for capacity, in which electricity retailers are required to contract with a specified amount of capacity (including a margin over their expected demand) or pay a penalty. This sets the quantity directly, whereas capacity payment systems set the price. Either could produce the same equilibrium values, but the capacity payments system is likely to produce a greater range of outcomes in terms of the level of capacity. Given the importance of avoiding capacity shortages, this could be a significant disadvantage.

Some markets have no explicit payment for capacity. Nord Pool, for example, has none because electricity production in the Nordic countries is dominated by hydro-electricity. The average hydro scheme in the Nordic countries has enough storage capacity to run (at full power) for just under half the hours in the year (Nordel, 2004). The average demand for electricity in 2003 was 73 per cent of the peak demand, however. This means that if the system is to store enough energy to meet the overall demand for MWh over the year, it will invariably have enough 'effect capacity' to meet the peak demand in MW. The implication is that market prices need to be high enough to remunerate hydro storage capacity over the year as a whole, rather than to remunerate 'effect capacity' at the system peak. The proportion of thermal plant on the Nordic system may rise in future, however, as much of the available hydro resource has been used. Furthermore, the Swedish transmission operator has been concerned by the lack of reserve capacity to cover peak demands (and water shortages) in its own system (which has a more even balance between hydro and thermal capacity). Svenska Kraftnät has signed medium-term contracts for nearly 2,000 MW of capacity (the country's peak demand is about 26,000 MW), and discussions are under way to find a long-term solution.

The UK, however, has a thermal power system, and NETA is an energy-only market with no special provision for paying for capacity. The implication is that energy prices are believed to provide sufficient reward for capacity. Bids in the balancing mechanism are made very close to real time, when it should be possible to predict accurately whether there is going to be a shortage of capacity. If a shortage is predicted, the most expensive generators will be able to make bids well above their variable costs. This will contribute towards their fixed costs. Newbery *et al.* (2004) point out that even when a few generators are receiving these very high prices, the SBP is likely to be at much lower levels. This certainly provides much lower incentives for demand-side load management that simply reacts to the market price[8] than a marginal price would, and Newbery *et al.* suggest that incentives to provide generation capacity are also muted.

It is true that the infra-marginal generators are very unlikely to be able to raise their bids to the level of the marginal generators. Green and McDaniel (1999) show, however, that with competitive bidding, no risk aversion, and full information (but random demand), infra-marginal generators will always bid slightly above their costs. Their bid will in fact be equal to the expected revenue (per MWh) that they would have got in a market based on marginal pricing. In the forward markets, arbitrage against the balancing mechanism ensures that the price is also equal to the expected price in a market with marginal pricing. In other words, if a market with marginal pricing would produce enough revenue for generators, so will NETA. The impact of imperfect competition or risk aversion on this result, however, is an open question.

Australia also has no explicit payment for capacity, but the market rules include a 'value of lost load' (VOLL), set at $5,000/MWh, and the price will be set at this level if there is ever a shortage of capacity and customers have to be interrupted. At other times, the VOLL acts as a price cap on generators' bids—if the market is getting short of capacity, they may be able to raise prices towards this level. Allowing the market to set prices at this level brings political risks, even if most of the payments would actually be covered by hedging contracts. Despite this, VOLL was raised to $10,000/MWh in April 2002 in response to fears that the lower level did not give sufficient incentives for reliability. A safety net was added to cap

---

[8] Such 'passive' load management may not be the most appropriate type under NETA, in any case. A reduction in demand below the level that the retailer anticipated and contracted for will actually increase its costs, through the unattractive imbalance price. NGC holds tenders for short-notice reserve and similar services, and a number of customers provide these in the form of demand reductions when required.

payments, however, linked to their cumulative level over a week (ACCC, 2000).

Most other electricity markets do have a specific payment for capacity. The key choice here is whether the rules should aim to set the price for, or the quantity of, capacity. The Pool in England and Wales had a capacity payment which can be seen as related to the Australian VOLL mechanism. Instead of letting the price rise to VOLL when there was an actual shortage, however, the Pool calculated the risk of a power cut at the day-ahead stage, and then paid all available generators this loss of load probability (LOLP) multiplied by the net VOLL. The latter was the VOLL set by the government at £2,000/MWh in 1990 and uprated each year by inflation, less the system marginal price (or the station's own bid, for stations that were not scheduled to operate). If the LOLP is correctly measured (and experience suggests that the Pool's figures were generally too high), the Pool's overall price should equal the expectation of prices set in the Australian way.

If the VOLL accurately measures the cost of a power cut, then these payment rules give the expected (Pool) or actual (Australian) value of capacity at the margin. In terms of Figure 1, panel (2), this is the value of the unserved energy in the shaded area of the load-duration curve. If the marginal unit of capacity can just cover its fixed costs from the payments it receives, then we would have an efficient outcome.

Capacity payments were often criticized. Some critics asked how a payment which changed every half-hour could act as an incentive for investment in long-lived power stations and thus deliver the correct level of capacity. This missed the point. Adjustments in the level of capacity for next year have to be made by bringing forward, or postponing, the retirement of existing stations, since a station already under construction is effectively committed to arrive, and a station not yet under construction will not be ready in time. It was possible to sign a contract that would hedge capacity payments over the coming year, and thus to lock in the revenues for a station considering retirement. The actual level of capacity payments would almost inevitably differ from the predicted level, but the generator did not need to worry about this when deciding whether to keep its station open. Over the longer term, new generators might expect that the closure decisions on older plant would keep expected capacity payments approximately equal to the fixed costs of such plant. They could then take these revenues into account when deciding whether to enter the market. Companies without strong balance sheets, however, would want the security of a contract before sinking large amounts of money in a new power station.

A more serious criticism was that the capacity payments could be manipulated, withholding stations from the market. This certainly happened on a small scale, as generators could find it profitable to delay returning a unit after an outage if capacity payments were high—the extra volume would be offset by a reduction in the level of the capacity payments. In the Pool's second year, PowerGen even adopted a strategy of declaring plant as unavailable, raising the level of capacity payments, and then re-declaring it as available in time to receive those higher payments (Offer, 1991)! The Pool Rules were soon changed to prevent this, and the regulator started to monitor capacity declarations. Green (2004a) shows that there is little evidence that capacity withholding affected prices to a significant extent over the years.

The final problem with the capacity payment system was that the calculated LOLP became increasingly divorced from reality, due to the way in which stations' past reliability data were used in the calculation. Towards the end of the Pool's life, very high capacity payments were being set at times when there was actually plenty of spare capacity, but some of the stations had suffered outages at unfortunate times during the earlier periods when their reliability had been assessed. In a long-run equilibrium, a capacity payment rule that over-compensates a given level of capacity will encourage the over-provision of capacity until the resulting payments are expected to equal the marginal cost of keeping capacity available. If this does not vary much with the level of capacity, there will be little impact on prices. In the short run, however, an over-generous formula for capacity payments is likely to feed through into the level of consumer prices. If the formula errs on the other side, security of supply could be compromised.

Given this, the trend in the United States has been to establish markets in which electricity companies are required to secure an appropriate amount of capacity, setting the reserve margin directly, and accepting the resulting price. In PJM, for example, every retailer must acquire a specified volume of capacity resources, based upon their forecast (annual) peak load, scaled up to take account of reserve requirements and generator reliability. Retailers who do not have sufficient capacity must make a deficiency payment, based on the annual fixed costs of a peaking plant (a daily penalty of $170.96/MW was equivalent to $62/kW-year in 2003/ 4). This gives peaking capacity an additional revenue stream, and ensures that every retailer is bearing a share of the costs of reserve capacity. The reserve margin incorporated in the capacity requirement, and the deficiency payment (which affects retailers' willingness to pay) can be adjusted to encourage the market to supply the level of capacity which policy-makers believe is desirable. If the rules are adjusted too often, of course, then companies may lose confidence in the market as a reliable source of revenue, and it will become less effective.

The choice between price- and quantity-based ways of paying for capacity can be viewed in the light of Weitzman's (1974) discussion of the choice of policy instrument in the presence of uncertainty. Weitzman showed that where costs and benefits were uncertain, a quantity standard would be preferred when the slope of the marginal benefit function was steeper than the slope of the marginal cost function. The marginal cost of providing capacity is likely to be fairly flat over the relevant ranges, whereas the marginal benefit of extra capacity rises quickly as the level of spare capacity falls.[9] This suggests that capacity markets should be favoured over price-based systems, at least as long as the evolution of demand is taken into account when the quantity required is determined.

Capacity markets are also likely to have political advantages over capacity payments. Systems based upon prices alone tend to need occasional very high prices if they are to create enough revenue, and these create financial and political risks, even with hedging contracts. Generators may not believe that prices will be allowed to rise to the necessary levels. A generator must face the risk that it will not be available during the price spike, losing the associated revenue, and will be even worse off if it has contract payments to make. The indirectness of the link between the high prices and improved security of supply is also likely to be a disadvantage as investment needs move up the political agenda. A capacity market has a direct link to security of supply, which makes it easier to justify the resulting prices. Signals to investors can be clearer when there is an obvious demand for capacity, even though the time lags involved in building plant can help to create investment cycles.

Markets with no explicit mechanism for ensuring enough capacity may work in theory, or where there are large amounts of price-responsive demand. If an energy-only market with a low price elasticity of demand encounters a season of high demand or low supply, as happened in California, it is likely to be vulnerable to power cuts and politically

---

[9] The number of hours for which the marginal unit of capacity can expect to run increases as the level of capacity falls, as can be seen from the shape of the load-duration curve in panel (2) of Figure 1.

unacceptable prices. Overall, the costs of insufficient capacity greatly outweigh those of having too much. Many electricity systems need a lot of investment over the next decades, as plant built in the 1960s and 1970s retires, and as renewable generators replace conventional stations. However, the costs and likely profitability of this investment remain uncertain. In this context, the quantity-based signal of a capacity market is more likely to produce an acceptable level of investment than the price-based signal of capacity payments.

6. Transmission Pricing

Section 2 pointed out that constraints and losses on the transmission system mean that the cost of electricity can vary significantly from place to place. The British, however, have generally dealt with geographical issues by ignoring them. The system operator could not ignore transmission constraints, of course, and had to buy more output from generators inside import constraints, while selling some of their output back to generators on the other side of the constraints. In some markets, this is known as counter-trading. The net cost of this (since the generators constrained on were paid more than the system operator received from the generators constrained off) was recovered from all customers. From 1994 onwards, the system operator was given a financial incentive to keep these costs down. Transmission losses were never used to set regional prices—a rule change to introduce this was blocked by generators who stood to lose from it. When the regulator was given more power over the market's rules, under NETA, the rules were changed to take account of transmission losses, but before this could be implemented, it was blocked by the government, which believed that it would hamper the expected (and desired) growth of renewable generation, located mainly in the north of the UK.

Nord Pool has two separate approaches for dealing with transmission constraints. When the transmission lines between two countries (or between regions within Norway) are congested, Nord Pool calculates separate prices for each side of the constraint, and cross-border flows are charged a transmission fee equal to the price difference. Congestion within a region is dealt with by counter-trading. This market-splitting procedure is well understood within the market and produces reasonable price signals, although Glachant and Pignon (2005) argue that the rules can provide perverse incentives for the system operators. Congestion within a country is dealt with by counter-trading, which forces the system operator to incur some costs, whereas cross-border congestion brings in revenue from the price differentials. The system operators clearly have an incentive to declare that the constrained lines are at the borders, even if the constraint is actually within a country.

PJM uses nodal pricing, and so prices across the network vary whenever a link is constrained, to reflect the cost of the constraint. Companies have to pay the difference in nodal prices between the point where they put energy into the system and the point where they take it out, whether they are trading in the PJM market or bilaterally. An earlier system which allowed bilateral transactions to escape the impact of congested transmission quickly collapsed when everyone switched to bilateral transactions (Hogan, 1998). Because PJM's system can produce large geographical price differences, participants can hedge these with financial transmission rights (FTRs), known as transmission congestion contracts when first proposed (Hogan, 1992). These effectively pay the difference between a nodal price and the price at the market's swing bus, and so a participant holding FTRs equal to its actual generation can ensure that it receives the swing-bus price.

Although other market designs have been tried, it looks as if most restructured markets in the United States are evolving towards the PJM model. New York and New England chose similar designs when they first restructured their markets, and California's tortuous redesign process is moving in the same direction. Texas opened a state-wide wholesale market in 2002, based primarily on bilateral trading, and using a zonal model (like Nord Pool) to manage congestion. This state, too, is now redesigning its market to adopt nodal pricing. The PJM design is also the basis of the Standard Market Design proposed by the Federal Energy Regulatory Commission (FERC, 2002). The politics of states' rights, however, mean that FERC is unable to impose this market on states that do not wish to restructure. Most of the states that had below-average electricity costs have no wish to adopt market-based prices that would probably be higher. Economic efficiency can come a poor second to practical politics.

Transmission pricing is the area where the choice of market rule most clearly makes a difference to the market outcomes. To put it most starkly, some customers and generators will gain from cost-reflective transmission pricing, and some will lose. When the losers are aware of this (and generators certainly will be) they are likely to do everything they can to prevent the imposition of these charges. The question then is whether the overall gains are worth the costs of pushing through the changes. Green (2007) estimates that the gains from adopting locational transmission prices in England and Wales could equal about 1.5 per cent of generators' revenues in a competitive market, and would be higher in the presence of market power. Whether such a policy is worth pursuing is a normative question.

7. Electricity Contract Markets

Electricity spot prices are volatile. They can accurately signal the changing marginal cost of power, but most customers do not change their consumption in response to real-time price signals—most are not equipped to receive such signals, nor motivated to change their behaviour if they did. Retailers can reduce the impact of spot price variations—on both their customers and themselves—by signing contracts lasting for longer periods. In a market with a gross pool, these have to be financial contracts for differences, while a net pool allows either physical or financial contracts. A combination of a contract and an appropriate set of bids allows a company to fix the cost of a given volume of electricity, while responding at the margin to the spot market price. Because contracts reduce the importance of the spot price for the company's profits, they can act to mitigate market power. Some markets deliberately imposed vesting contracts, with prices and volumes determined before restructuring took effect, in order to curb market power. In California, the reluctance of the major utilities to sign longer-term contracts made them more vulnerable to price increases caused by increasing costs and the exercise of market power, and contributed to the state's disaster.[10]

A successful forward market requires liquidity. In the UK, multi-year contracts related to coal purchases and to the construction of new gas-fired power stations took up much of the market, so that most companies had little need for additional contract trading until the second set of coal contracts expired in 1998. This discouraged outsiders from entering the markets, and liquidity was low. While the contracts were meant to be hedges on the underlying market of the Pool, they had a significant

---

[10] It is fair to write of the utilities' reluctance, because the California Power Exchange did create a market for forward contracts, and the Public Utilities Commission did agree that the utilities could treat the cost of buying a proportion of their power on this market as an allowable expense for regulatory purposes. Southern California Edison made much more use of this market than Pacific Gas and Electric, and it was the latter company that declared bankruptcy (Blumstein et al., 2002).

impact on the way that the generators bid their plant there. Although developments in the Pool were often driven by the contract market, it was perceived as complicated and vulnerable to exploitation by the dominant generators. This also made independent traders reluctant to enter the contract market. Nord Pool, in contrast, has a simple price-setting mechanism and a much more competitive market structure. This creates confidence and liquidity, producing a virtuous circle, so that the volume traded in forward and futures markets is now several times the annual electricity output of the member countries.

Liquidity could be a problem in a market with volatile transmission prices. Companies might be concerned to trade for delivery at their own location, since trading elsewhere would not provide an adequate hedge, but this would then fragment the market. PJM's approach to this problem is to create a number of trading hubs at different points on the network, at which liquidity can be concentrated. The hub price is a weighted average of the prices at a number of nearby nodes, with pre-specified weights. Physical market participants can then use financial transmission rights to hedge the difference between the price at the trading hub and at their location.

The other problem facing contract markets is that if generators are to use them to finance investment in new power stations, the contracts will need to last for many years. Retailers can be willing to sign such contracts if they are reasonably sure that they can pass on the costs to their consumers, and this was the case when retailers had monopoly franchises. Once retail markets have been opened to competition, however, retailers face the risk that retail prices will be closely linked to the current wholesale prices. If wholesale prices fall, this will leave companies unable to pass through the cost of their contracts. This would then make them reluctant to sign long-term contracts with generators, enhancing market power in generation both directly and by making entry harder (Newbery, 2002). Furthermore, Green (2004b) shows that a quantitatively significant effect can occur, even if retail markets are relatively uncompetitive, which seems to be the case at present, as argued by Waddams Price in this book.

8. Emissions Markets

Many types of electricity generation can cause pollution. The risk of radioactive pollution from nuclear power stations was probably the first to be recognized. Acid rain, caused by emissions of sulphur and nitrogen oxides, came to prominence in the 1980s. In the 1990s, the world became increasingly aware of the problem of global warming and the impact of carbon emissions.[11] Reducing these emissions is now a major policy aim in the EU.

Traditionally, environmental regulation has taken a 'command and control' approach. Regulators have decided on an appropriate level, or rate, of emissions, or a technological standard for emissions reduction equipment, and ordered companies to comply with it. The problem with this approach is that the regulators will almost always know less about each company's cost of reducing emissions than the company itself does. If, as is very likely, this cost varies significantly between companies, then a uniform standard will not minimize the cost of achieving a given total level of emissions. Regulators may try to take costs into account when setting their standards (the UK used to require the 'best available technology not entailing excessive cost', for example) but the problem of asymmetric information remains.

Emissions trading uses a market to reveal which companies can reduce their emissions at least cost. After unsuccessful experiments in the 1970s, the US Environmental Protection Agency allowed refineries to trade the lead content in petrol between 1983 and 1987, helping them to phase in a reduction in the average content from 1.1 grams to 0.1 gram per leaded gallon. Refiners that were able to reduce their lead content ahead of schedule could sell their spare permits to others, allowing them more time to reach compliance. The cost of meeting the new standard was reduced, without using more lead on average than the standard implied.[12]

In 1990, Congress passed Title IV of the 1990 Clean Air Act Amendments, which established a market for sulphur-dioxide emissions from power stations. The market started in 1995, covering the largest stations (Phase I), and was extended to all stations in 2000 (Phase II). Annual emissions, 16m tons in 1985 and 14m tons in 1994, had to fall to under 10m tons in 2000, and about 9m tons by 2005. Emissions from the affected stations fell by more than one-third in the programme's first year, and were roughly one-third below the limit over the five years of Phase I. This meant that nearly 12m tons of sulphur dioxide had been banked by the start of Phase II. This gave generators more time to adjust

[11] Climate change policy is discussed at length by Helm (2003) and the other papers of Vol. 19, No. 3 of the *Oxford Review of Economic Policy*.

[12] To the extent that a refinery was already ahead of the standard, allowing it to sell its spare permits does increase emissions, compared to business-as-usual for that refinery and no access to permits for would-be buyers. The earlier schemes had involved bureaucratic mechanisms that attempted to prevent companies from getting spare permits 'for nothing', but this complexity had been one reason for their relative failure (Ellerman *et al.*, 2003)

to the tougher cap in Phase II. Ellerman *et al.* (2000) calculate that trading between plants within Phase I saved $1.8 billion (discounted to 1995), and that trading between plants within Phase II will save $17 billion by 2007. Banking permits between Phase I and Phase II will have saved a further $1.3 billion. Overall, the cost of reducing emissions was cut by 57 per cent.

Plants were allowed to opt in to Phase I, and the rules for allocating permits were clear enough to allow rational decisions to be made. Some plants opted in because their abatement costs were low and so they could profit by reducing emissions ahead of schedule. Their participation will not have raised total emissions over the life of the market. Other plants opted in because their emissions were already below their potential allocation of permits, and so they would have a surplus to sell, even if they did nothing. Allowing these plants to join the market does raise total emissions when they sell their spare permits, but Montero (1999) estimates that the effect was less than 2 per cent of total predicted emissions between 2000 and 2009. Offsetting this is the clarity produced by having simple rules for allocating the permits. In particular, the allowances given to generators were based upon their past behaviour. This is equivalent to a lump-sum transfer, and does not affect their future behaviour.

The European Union (2003) has adopted an Emissions Trading Scheme (ETS) to help it reduce emissions of carbon dioxide. This covers all plants in some industrial sectors (coke ovens, oil refineries, and the manufacture of iron and steel, pulp and paper, cement, glass, and ceramics) and all plants with a thermal input of more than 20 MW. Affected plants must surrender allowances equal to their emissions of carbon dioxide during a calendar year within 4 months of the year end, or pay a penalty. The first phase runs from 2005 to 2007, the second phase from 2008 to 2012, and subsequent phases will be for 5-year periods. As with the acid rain programme, the first phase has something of the nature of a lead-in, since member states can exclude some of their plants from the scheme, and the buy-out payment for non-compliance is €40/tonne, rather than €100/tonne in Phase II. Banking is automatic between the second and subsequent phases, whereas the Directive allows member states to choose whether to convert unused allowances from the first phase into second-phase allowances.[13]

[13] Some member states are allowing this, which would create an incentive to transfer unused allowances to organizations in that state, unless conversion is only allowed for the difference between an organization's original allowance and its actual emissions.

The allocation of allowances is left to the member states, subject to Commission approval, and a requirement that at least 95 per cent (90 per cent) are given away free of charge in the first (second) phase. In practice, most member states have given away all of their allowances,[14] apart from a reserve for the use of new entrants. If entering an affected industry (almost) automatically endows a firm with valuable allowances, while shutting a plant means that it has to give up all future allowances, this could distort decisions on whether to open and shut plants. The scheme should still ensure that operating decisions at the margin take the new cost of emissions into account, however.

How large is that cost? Ratcliffe on Soar, a large coal-fired station, emits 0.9 tonnes of CO_2 for each MWh that it generates, while Connah's Quay, a CCGT from the mid-1990s, emits 0.4 tonnes per MWh (PowerGen, 2001). If CO_2 allocations cost €20/tonne, then this will add about £12/MWh to the marginal cost of the coal-fired plant, and about £5.50 to the marginal cost of a CCGT. The impact on the price of electricity in any half-hour depends upon which plants are marginal, and whether the ETS changes this. (If a low coal price offsets the higher thermal efficiency of CCGT plants, then coal plants might be cheaper without the ETS, but their higher emissions could make them more expensive than gas plants once the ETS starts.) It also depends upon how competitive the market is—oligopolies typically absorb part of any increase in costs. Electricity generation in Great Britain is reasonably competitive at present, however, and predictions of cost pass-through included 90 per cent (Carbon Trust, 2004) and 100 per cent (Ilex, 2004). In 2005, prices in Germany and the Netherlands rose by between 60 per cent and 117 per cent of carbon costs (Sijm *et al.*, 2006).

What will this imply for generators' profits? Keats Martinez and Neuhoff (2005) suggest that gas-fired generators will gain, even if they have to buy all of their allowances. First, they will run more. Second, in the hours for which they are infra-marginal, the price will normally be set by generators with higher emissions levels, and so the ETS will raise prices by more than their costs. When the plants are marginal, the ETS affects the market price by just as much as their marginal costs, and so they do not lose.

Efficient coal-fired generators could win or lose, in principle, if they had to pay for all their allowances. Keats Martinez and Neuhoff assume

[14] At the time of writing (August 2006), only some member states have announced their proposed allocations for Phase II—the UK plans to auction 7 per cent of its allocation, but others will continue a completely free allocation.

that these generators would have been infra-marginal in medium-demand hours, in the absence of the ETS, when the price would have been set by gas-fired stations. This price, therefore, rises by less than the coal-fired stations' costs: either the gas-fired stations are still on the margin in those hours, and the price rises by their marginal emission costs, or the coal-fired stations are now on the margin, losing their infra-marginal rent entirely. Offsetting this, there will be some high-demand hours when generators with even higher emissions are setting the price, and so the ETS raises the efficient firms' margins. A priori, we cannot tell which effect will dominate. Simulations in the paper, however, show that the coal-fired generator's margin over fuel, emissions, and operations and maintenance costs would more than halve, from £27.5/kW-year to £12.4/kW-year, if it had to buy all of its allowances. If the plant was allocated two-thirds of the allowances it needed for free,[15] however, its margin would rise to £35.3/kW-year. The gas-fired plant's margin would rise from £27.2/kW-year to £32/kW-year with no free allocation, or £48/kW-year with an allocation based on past emissions.

What about the long-run impact, once capacity can adjust fully? Figure 2 shows the analysis for an example in which peaking plants have higher emissions than base load plants. Panel (1) is a repeat of the top panel of Figure 1, showing the total costs of the two types of plants, for different numbers of hours of operation. In panels (2) and (3), the higher marginal costs imposed by carbon permits imply that the slope of the total cost lines will increase. If the permits are auctioned, then the lines will pivot around their previous vertical intercepts. An alternative is that some permits are given to plants free of charge, as long as they remain on the system.[16] In this case, the intercept will shift down by the value of the free permits. The break-even point is where the two lines cross. In panel (2), base load plants are given enough free permits to run for about $2T$ hours (T being the highest number of operating hours for which it would be economic to build a peaking plant). In panel (3), peaking plants are given enough free permits to run for about $T/2$ hours. Assume that the system of giving away permits means that any new plant is given the same allocation as an existing plant, and that any plant that closes receives no

---

[15] Note that this hypothetical allocation is equal to the plants' average emissions in an earlier period when its output was lower, and does not depend upon its actual emissions in the modelling exercise.

[16] This might be described as 'grandfathering' (although that could imply that permits would still be given to the owners of plants, even after those plants had closed) or 'updating'. Updating schemes, however, include those in which future permit allocations would change in response to current emissions, greatly reducing the incentive to cut emissions.

Figure 2 The Impact of a Carbon Trading System

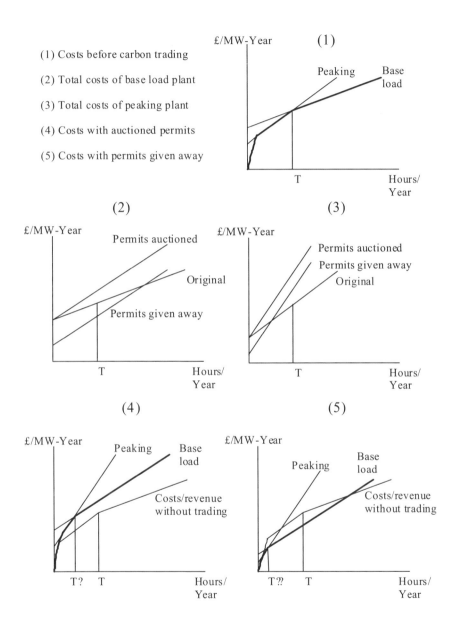

more allowances—this is the general thrust of most national allocation plans under the ETS.

The thick line in panel (4) shows the envelope of efficient costs if permits are auctioned. In a sustainable competitive market, these must also equal the plants' revenues, as described in section 3. The panel therefore also shows the original cost envelope from panel (1) of Figure 1 (the thin line with a kink at T), which should be interpreted as the revenue required without carbon trading. Without carbon trading, it was efficient for peaking plants to run for up to T hours a year. With carbon trading, these carbon-intensive plants should run much less, for T' or less. The price in each hour is given by the slope of the cost/revenue line. Prices are clearly higher for the peak hours to the left of T', and the off-peak hours to the right of T. In the intervening hours, prices might rise or fall, depending on a comparison of the cost of a peaking plant without permits (originally marginal) and a base load plant with permits (marginal now).

In panel (5), the impact of a free allocation of permits is shown, on the assumption that the base load plants are given more free permits than the peaking plants. (The value of the free permits is equal to the vertical distance between the 'permits auctioned' and 'permits given away' lines in panels (2) and (3), and the base load plants clearly get more permits in this example.) The free permits offset so many of the fixed costs of a base load plant that it is only efficient to use a peaking plant if its running time is very short—T'' is close to the origin. The peaking plant's net fixed costs, that have to be recovered from prices above its marginal running cost, are also very low. This means that fewer hours of very high prices are required, although prices are higher than before in the next group of hours, when they are equal to the running costs of the peaking plant. As panel (5) is drawn, however, it should be clear that for plants running for around T hours, the revenues that they need are well below the revenues needed without carbon trading. In other words, the price averaged over the highest T hours of the year will be lower in the presence of carbon trading. Over the year as a whole, however, time-weighted average prices will be higher, since the free allocation to a base load plant is not sufficient to allow it to run for the entire year without having to buy some permits, raising its total costs.

The specific predictions of this example depended upon the peaking plants having a higher carbon intensity, and a smaller free allocation, than the base load plants. Change these assumptions, and the results will change. The aim, however, is to show that the ETS will affect entry and exit decisions, and is quite capable of reducing electricity prices in some periods, even though we can expect generators' overall revenues to rise.

How has trading in the ETS worked in practice? For much of 2005 and the first part of 2006, prices were higher than initially expected, at around €25/tonne. In May 2006, however, prices fell sharply as the first audited emissions figures became available, showing that there had been an over-supply of permits compared to emissions in 2005. Prices did not fall to zero, for the market is likely to become tighter as economic growth raises emissions in the later years of Phase I, and there may be scope for banking allowances into Phase II. The emissions data did show that most member states had been relatively generous in the number of permits that they had allocated, and would need to be more restrictive if Phase II was to lead to significant cuts in emissions. There is an obvious incentive to be generous, since each country's allocation will have a direct impact on the profitability of its own companies. The impact on the price of permits and on overall emissions will be muted, since most countries issue only a small proportion of the total number of permits. The European Commission will need to take harsh decisions on draft national alloca-tion plans to offset this incentive.

The marginal cost of permits has been largely passed through to the wholesale price of electricity, as predicted by economic models, even though most companies received many of the permits that they needed for free. In countries such as Germany, this led to political problems for the electricity industry, amid accusations that consumers had been 'ripped off' (Gabriel, 2006). While the analysis above shows that in a long-term equilibrium, giving away permits without charge should mute the scheme's effect on prices, in the short term, emissions trading will always raise the price of power, for a given capital stock. Since reducing the demand for power will also reduce emissions, it may be best to auction all the permits, allowing the price of electricity to rise in a transparent manner, and using the revenue to reduce other taxes.

Is the ETS an efficient response to the problem of climate change? Pizer (2002) uses Weitzman's (1974) results on the choice between quantity- and price-based regulation, and the fact that the marginal damage function of carbon emissions is almost horizontal (although its level is uncertain),[17] to argue that a tax-based scheme would be more efficient. He does point out, however, that a permit scheme allows governments far

---

[17] The damage from climate change is related to the stock of greenhouse gases in the atmosphere, and the flow of emissions of carbon dioxide only changes this very gradually. I am indebted to an anonymous referee for directing me to this reference.

more flexibility in allocating the costs and rents involved in reducing carbon emissions, and avoids the political baggage of a new tax. He also suggests that the best policy would combine a permit system with a buy-out charge. This would allow agents to exceed the permitted level of emissions if the out-turn cost of reductions proved to be too high, while letting the government distribute rents when it allocated permits. The ETS does, indeed, include such a buy-out price, although at a level (€100/ tonne of CO_2 in Phase II implies €367/tonne of carbon) which is far above the tax levels that Pizer considers optimal for the first decades of this century. The ETS is probably best seen as a reasonable response to political constraints. Its full effectiveness may well depend upon the way in which permits are allocated after Phase II.

9. Conclusions

Electricity companies have been participating in an ever-growing number of markets over the past 15 years. The motivation for this is that price signals created in a competitive market are believed to give better incentives than vertically integrated companies have had in the past. The analytical results in this chapter show that markets are capable, in theory, of signalling the marginal cost of power and of providing the right incentives to build capacity. The examples from around the world show that many different market designs have been used in the attempt to translate these results into practice.

In the United States, there seems to be a consensus that an energy market based upon nodal marginal cost prices, coupled with a market for capacity, is the best structure for a liberalized electricity industry. (There is no consensus about whether to liberalize or not, however.) In Europe, there are few capacity markets, and transmission pricing is much less sophisticated. Europe has moved ahead of the United States, however, in implementing markets for emissions of CO_2, and for supporting renewable generators.

How much do these choices matter? We do know that choices about transmission prices can have large impacts on how (and whether) prices vary over space, and can lead to large transfers between agents. There are worthwhile efficiency gains from implementing prices that signal marginal costs, but they are almost always much smaller than the transfers.

In advance of real time, electricity can be traded in a variety of ways, but real-time operation must be delegated to an operator who can keep the system stable. The way in which these real-time operations are paid for will affect all the other electricity trades through arbitrage, since waiting until real time and paying the prices determined then is always an option for demand. Almost all electricity markets set real-time prices upon the basis of the marginal plant in operation, which should send transparent and efficient price signals through the market. In the UK, the designers of NETA believed that agents should be deterred from real-time trading, and that creating a less transparent market without marginal price signals would produce better results. It is hard to believe that this could be the case. The biggest impact of NETA is probably not in short-term trading, but in the trend towards vertical integration between generators and retailers, which is a response to the lack of transparency in the market, and likely to make independent entry much harder. That will affect the long-term structure of the market, and the evolution of capacity.

Theoretical arguments suggest that getting the right level of capacity does not depend upon having a capacity market, and that price-based systems can send the right incentives. The length of an investment cycle, relative to the few years since most countries liberalized their electricity markets, means that we do not have enough experience to be sure that these arguments will work in practice. Many OECD countries started their reforms with a surplus of generation capacity, ensuring that it would be some time before much investment was needed—although some experienced investment booms in any case. With the correct incentives, demand response can act as a substitute for at least some spare capacity, at a rather lower cost. Given the importance of electricity to the modern economy, however, we need to ensure that the system operators can expect to have enough capacity available to them. A well-designed capacity market is likely to produce more reliable results than using energy prices alone.

10

Large-Scale Deployment of Renewables for Electricity Generation

*Karsten Neuhoff**

1. Introduction

Using renewables on a large scale to replace fossil-fuel electricity generation offers two principal advantages. Environmentally, renewables offer a means to reduce significantly greenhouse-gas emissions. This is a priority, given the need to minimize the risks of climate change resulting from rising concentrations of greenhouse gases, caused in large part by the burning of fossil fuels. Renewable energy sources can also help to diversify energy supplies in most countries. Reducing dependence on energy imports reduces the exposure of economies to international fuel-price fluctuations and potential interruptions caused by political instability and resource constraints. In addition, most renewables are cleaner, thereby providing ancillary benefits to the environment and to human health.

A variety of studies show that renewables have a large technical potential. Yet, currently they only supply 13.5 per cent of global energy demand, and nearly all of this is from established sources of hydropower

* I would like to thank Joanna Ellis, Tim Foxon, Michael Grubb, Robert Gross, Daniel Kammen, David Newbery, Nic Rivers, Annette Schou, Rick Sellers, and Simon Upton for extensive discussions and comments on various versions of the chapter. I would like to thank Jun Arima, Thobjon Fangel, Anna Marie Fitzpatrick, Norbert Gorissen, Jan Losson, Joachim Nick-Leptin, Chris Mottershead, Stefan Klinski, Mark Radka, Maya Papineau, Till Stenzel, Piotr Tulej, and Nicole Wilke for valuable insights and discussions. Most of all I would like to thank Lucy Butler for a lot of help and the survey of renewable resources. Financial support from the OECD round table on sustainable development and UK research councils ESRC/EPSRC project Supergen Futurenet is gratefully acknowledged.

and small-scale wood fuel and other biomass combustion, which are limited in their potential expansion. The reason why renewable energy technologies contribute so little to global energy demand differs between three groups of technologies. The mature generation includes hydropower, biomass combustion, solar thermal hot water, and geothermal technologies. These technologies are already cost-competitive with conventional forms, provided the renewables plant is located in a high-quality resource area, and where there is low-cost access to the grid. The challenge to expanding these markets relates to high up-front costs and to local site issues. The emerging generation of technologies includes wind, several advanced forms of bioenergy, and solar photovoltaic (PV). These technologies are proven technologically, but still need substantial cost reduction through market experience. The third group are the technologies still in the R&D phase, including concentrating solar power, ocean energy, and even more advanced forms of bioenergy, such as lignocellulose processing. These technologies will require substantial public research, development, and demonstration (RD&D) support in order to prove them on a market scale, and to begin entry into commercial markets.

This chapter does not address the optimal mix of different renewable and conventional generation technologies to supply future energy demand. It only asks whether individual renewable technologies are capable of supplying more than a small percentage of our energy demand. After renewable technologies are developed and society is accustomed to their use, markets can then determine what fraction of energy to supply from individual technologies. This chapter discusses the potential for new renewables and addresses the economic issues associated with their deployment in three main parts.

- Section 2 summarizes the resource potential for renewables, concluding that fundamental technological and resource constraints are *not* the major obstacle to large-scale deployment (section 3).

- The core of the chapter looks in depth at the economic barriers to renewable energy: the impact of competition in an uneven playing field (section 4) and the specific obstacles associated with market structure (section 5) and non-market (section 6) barriers. The main argument for active technology policy is presented in section 7. The nature of the product and markets structure requires government intervention to overcome technology lock-out in the energy sector.

- Finally, the chapter considers the potential policy responses. It is argued that the key is for programmes of strategic deployment (section 8) to accelerate the pace of improvement through market experience (learning). Given the strong feedback loops between research and market experience, R&D as a supporting, but not unique, element of renewable energy technology policy is discussed (section 9). The specific instruments available are then reviewed (section 10), and the chapter takes a brief look at the international dimension of renewable technology policy (section 11).

2. Renewable Market Share and Potential

Currently, only bioenergy and hydropower make significant contributions to meeting energy demand (IEA, 2003c), followed by geothermal energy and wind power. Africa and Asia are the biggest users of bioenergy, but this will only be sustainable if active replanting complements the collection of firewood. Renewables supply only 19.6 per cent of global electricity and 13.5 per cent of global energy demand (IEA, 2004).

Several studies show that this is only a small part of their technical resource potential. These estimations take account of a range of constraints; for example, WBGU (2004) assumes that only 4 per cent of land with significant wind resources or 1 per cent of all land will be used for electricity production. Figure 1 shows the estimated energy that can be produced per year with solar, wind, tidal, wave, geothermal, hydro, and biomass resources, translated to a common tonnes-of-oil unit. This potential is compared to current global electricity demand. Current energy systems require 2.5 units of primary energy to produce 1 unit of electricity— renewable energy in the form of electricity would, therefore, not only replace the electric energy but also eliminate the corresponding transformation losses.

The figure assumes that all renewable-resource potential is allocated to electricity generation. If biomass is used for heating or cooking, then transformation losses (assumed to be 65 per cent) can be reduced. In the medium term, the highest value application of biomass will be through bio-fuels. Storage and safety requirements for fuels in the transport sector can be better and more cheaply addressed by bio-fuel than by hydrogen. Space and water heating can be provided by solar and geothermal energy. In this case, the transformation losses to electricity are avoided and local resources can be used up to five times more efficiently.

Figure 1 Achievable Electric Energy from Renewable Sources

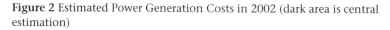

□ Bonn TBP (2004) △ WEA (2000) ■ RIGES (1993)
✕ Shell (1996) ○ Greenpeace (1993) ◆ WBGU (2004)
◇ Fischer & Schrattenholzer (2001) − IEA (2002) - WEC (1994)
● IPCC (1996) ✕ Hall & Rosillo-Calle (1998) ⊗ Hoogwijk et al (2004)
- Grubb & Meyer (1993)

Note: Detailed references in Neuhoff (2004).

Figure 2 Estimated Power Generation Costs in 2002 (dark area is central estimation)

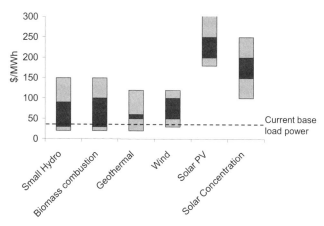

Note: Based on NET Ltd. Switzerland. This assumes a discount rate of 6 per cent for all technologies, amortization periods of 15–25 years and technology specific operation and maintenance costs.
Source: IEA (2003c).

Figure 1 also demonstrates the large range of estimated global resource potentials of wind and solar power, and underlines the need for discussions about an appropriate level of land-use restrictions. For tidal, wave, and geothermal energy, technological uncertainty is high. It is difficult to predict what fraction of the theoretical potential can be tapped. Therefore, the resource assessment is less certain.

Figure 2 presents estimates for costs of electricity produced with current renewables technologies. Costs are above costs for conventional technologies—one reason why they contribute so little to satisfy current energy demand, despite the large resource potential identified in Figure 1. Small hydro, bio-power, geothermal, and, recently, wind generators are only competitive with current power prices of conventional generation capacity if local resource potentials are exceptionally good. Solar PV and solar concentration generators are not competitive in the wholesale markets. If intermittent renewables contribute large shares of electricity, then their value might be reduced as they require additional storage or demand management.

Finally it should be noted that renewable energy sources are not the only means of tackling the problems associated with current fossil-fuel dependency. The single most promising approach is improvement of energy efficiency in all sectors. The European Commission estimates that demand reductions of up to 18 per cent are currently cost effective, and reductions over 40 per cent are typical in the field (EU Commission, 2000). Taking into account economic and population growth, promoting energy efficiency, without further development of renewable energy sources, is unlikely to address adequately the need for energy security and carbon dioxide (CO_2) emission reductions (Hoffert et al., 2002). Equally, the reverse is true, and the ideal approach would comprise both policies.

Switching fuel sources from coal to gas would reduce CO_2 emissions if gas resources remain adequate. Carbon sequestration could capture CO_2 from coal and gas power plants. This would require new technologies for sequestrating and storing CO_2, storage facilities with low leakage rates, and deployment both of new power plants and of CO_2 transport networks.[1] Nuclear energy could provide for up to 40 per cent of global electricity demand. Assuming that proliferation risks continue to necessitate open fuel-cycles, the global uranium resources would at this level only last for 50

[1] Carbon sequestration involves the capture of CO_2 produced during the use of fossil fuels, and its storage. For example, CO_2 from the oil and gas production process is reinserted into wells and enhances oil recovery. For large-scale application, new infrastructure must be built to generate electricity with sequestration, to transport and store CO_2 underground. Cost-effectiveness and leakage of stored CO_2 back into the atmosphere are still widely debated.

years and therefore the demand for renewable energy technologies would not be affected.[2]

3. Technological Barriers

Research to date does not point to fundamental technological barriers to renewable energy technologies. This assessment is robust for technologies such as onshore wind, geothermal, and solar PV (Alsema, 2000), where deployment experience is significant. The assessment is also valid for technologies that have been applied in demonstration projects, such as offshore wind (Neumann *et al.*, 2002; EWEA, 2004; Musial and Butterfield, 2004) and solar concentration. More demonstration projects for wave and tidal energy are needed to assess potential technical barriers.

Typical concerns about renewable energy relate to its intermittency. It can be assessed on the following three time frames.

First, 3–4 hours before production, average regional output can be predicted with a high degree of accuracy. Remaining uncertainty is mainly due to sudden wind bursts shutting down turbines or cloud fronts covering solar panels. Transmission networks are already designed to cope with larger output changes caused by sudden shutdowns of large fossil or nuclear power stations (Grubb and Vigotti, 1997). Currently, the heavy and fast-rotating conventional generators provide the inertia to drive the system through the critical first moment after a failure. If wind and solar replace most or all conventional generation, their power electronics will have to be improved so they can drive the system through the critical moment. Network tariffs do not (yet) reward such capabilities. At the distribution level, sudden output changes from large shares of renewable generation capacity can result in voltage swings. Recent developments of power electronics or active management of distributed generation offer solutions.[3]

Second, during the 24 hours prior to production, the accuracy of output predictions for wind, solar, and wave generation increases. With improving predictions, the operation schedule for power plants and the

---

[2] An interdisciplinary research group at MIT concluded: 'over at least the next 50 years, the best choice to meet [cost, safety, proliferation and waste management] challenges of nuclear generation is the open, once-through fuel cycle' (Ansolabehere *et al.*, 2003). At twice the current uranium price, the known uranium resources suffice to fuel a global fleet of 3,000 reactors of 1 GW for 50 years. Apart from nuclear operational and transport risks in this large-scale scenario, nuclear will provide less than 40 per cent of global electricity demand.

[3] See recent EU research projects: www.sustelnet.net, www.dispower.org, www.clusterintegration.org and http://www.ecn.nl/docs/library/report/2004/rx04078.pdf

transmission network must be adjusted to make efficient use of all resources. Current electricity market designs do not provide the flexibility or trading liquidity for such adjustments. For example, in Germany deviations from the rather inaccurate 24-hour predictions of wind output are compensated for with last-minute balancing activities. This requires flexible and, therefore, expensive plant operation. Germany's system operators have an incentive to retain this scheme, because they own most of the generation assets and benefit from selling balancing services. Furthermore, they can reduce political support for further wind deployment by pointing to (artificially) high balancing costs[4] and thereby reduce competition for their existing fossil and nuclear generation.

Third, for system-planning purposes no power plant can be assumed to produce with 100 per cent availability. Repair, maintenance, constraints on fuel and cooling water, and availability of wind and solar energy can reduce or inhibit production from all technologies. Statistical models are used to calculate the risk that multiple plants are not available simultaneously. This determines how much back-up capacity is required to ensure reliable electricity supply. Availability of output from wind, solar, wave, and tidal generators is far lower than that of conventional power stations. If they contribute only a small share of total electricity generation (<5 per cent), the system benefits from the increased diversity and renewable output is of similar value to conventional generation output.

With increasing market shares, the lower availability implies that individual renewable technologies contribute less towards peak demand and, therefore, that wholesale value of their output is reduced (by approximately 10 per cent, with market shares below 20 per cent, according to Smith *et al.* (2004); see also Strbac (2002)). If individual intermittent renewables contribute large shares of electricity, then they require significantly more back-up and storage capacity than conventional power stations. Retaining old power plants was historically the cheapest option for provision of back-up capacity for periods of peak demand or power-station outages. This could also prove a low-cost way for initial support of larger market shares of intermittent renewables. In the long term, if intermittent renewable resources dominate electricity generation, new back-up capacity or storage technologies must play an important part.

The 20 per cent quoted above is not a fixed number; it is subject to current research and a function of at least four system characteristics. (i) Spatial diversity reduces the correlation of output of renewable generation

---

[4] E.ON Netz *Wind Report 2004*, at www.eon-netz.com

and therefore increases the value. This provides a strong argument for integrated networks rather than micro-grids and closely coordinated operation of these networks. (ii) Mixing different renewable technologies provides uncorrelated output—once again increasing the value.[5] (iii) PV output is, in many regions, correlated with peak demand from air conditioning and can, therefore, significantly reduce system costs (Herig, 2000). (iv) Demand-side response and demand shifting reduce the need for peak capacity and increase the value of intermittent generation.

The discussion shows that individual renewable energy technologies can contribute a significant share of electricity production. This makes them valuable for our electricity systems. The uncertainty about availability and costs of generation, network, storage, and control technologies makes it difficult to predict the maximum market share or optimal future mix of individual renewable energy technologies.

4. Uneven Playing Field

In liberalized energy markets, investors, operators, and consumers should, in theory, face the full costs of their decisions. This applies to access to resources and capital, and the social and environmental impacts of energy consumption. However, current practice falls short of this ideal. In the first place, impacts may be hard to quantify. Second, even if potential impacts can be quantified, any decision on the extent to which they should be internalized will be a highly politicized judgement. This can be difficult enough with new technologies (for instance, opposition to the detrimental impact on landscapes by windfarms). But where impacts have previously been tolerated, seeking to change what are perceived to be existing rights is even more difficult. The same holds for those energy producers whose commercial viability has relied on a variety of financial and social subsidies. Not surprisingly, operators want to protect any benefits they have been granted and avoid any new constraints that would limit environmental impacts. Levelling the playing field to enable renewable energy to compete on a more equal footing involves tackling these unpriced 'advantages' for conventional technologies.

The most obvious influences on markets are direct and indirect subsidies (see Pershing and Mackenzie (2004) for a recent survey). It is estimated that OECD countries alone still spent US$20–30 billion on

---

[5] See http://www.eci.ox.ac.uk/lowercf/intermittency/summary.html

energy subsidies in 2002 (OECD *et al.*, 2002; see also de Moor, 2001). The level of subsidies in developing and transition economies is much higher. These subsidies often include cheap domestic rates, which are intended to benefit people on low incomes, but usually benefit well-off households that tend to consume much more energy. The effect of such energy subsidies is increased consumption by 13 per cent (IEA, 1999) and delayed investment in energy efficiency and renewable energy provision.

In many developing countries, traditional energy technologies also benefit from export credit guarantees extended by OECD government agencies. In the late 1990s, export credit guarantees facilitated US$17 billion annual investment in fossil energy and only US$0.8 billion investment in renewables (G8, 2001). In 2003, the World Bank allocated only 13 per cent of its energy loan portfolio to renewable projects. The nuclear-energy sector illustrates a more subtle type of subsidy, rooted in the role governments played in the development of the industry. A government underwriting of accidents means that private insurance cover for only €700m is required for nuclear power plants.

The failure adequately to 'internalize' environmental impacts in prices is the other obvious source of 'subsidy' that makes it difficult for clean energy technologies to make headway. Traditional environmental regulation sets emission limits and requires firms to invest in improved combustion or exhaust-clearing technology. Emissions below the emission limits also cause environmental damage, but firms are not exposed to these costs and will not include them in the energy price. Estimates for these damages, excluding the costs of global warming, range from an additional €8.7–25/MWh for modern coal power plants.[6] Most of this damage relates to human health problems. These unpriced externalities will obviously rise if some account is taken of CO_2 emissions and their contribution to climate change. Averaging over a large set of studies for the cost of climate change suggests that the CO_2 impact of electricity produced by coal can be conservatively estimated at €10–23/MWh (Tol, 2003).[7] The true costs are likely to be higher, as current studies compare

[6] *Source*: Externalities of Energy, A Project of the European Commission, http://externe.jrc.es. Roth and Ambs (2004) estimated externality costs of modern coal plants in $/MWh as NO_x 12.96, SO_2 1.68, PM (particulate matter) 0.24, N_2O 0.15, upstream 2.57, land use 5.26, water related 1.3 (best estimates quoted). All externalities are based on coal power plants. They have the highest emissions levels (apart from peaking oil plants) and are, therefore, most likely to set the marginal electricity price if externalities are priced.

[7] Roth and Ambs (2004) estimated global warming externality costs of $26.38/MWh. ExternE (http://externe.jrc.es) calculated a range of €3–111/MWh. Increasing the implied rate of time preference from 2 to 3 per cent will reduce the weight on people in 100 years from 37 to 5 per cent of today's population and thereby reduce the marginal cost of CO_2 emission. Equity weighing of global population leads to a higher estimate of the marginal costs (Yohe, 2003).

snapshots of future outcomes and ignore extreme weather events and the costs of changing infrastructure, agricultural practices, and living patterns (Tol, 2003).

Cap-and-trade programmes aim to internalize the costs of SO_2, NO_x, and, most prominently, CO_2, and might in the long run ensure that electricity prices reflect the true environmental costs. The experience gained in using emission-trading schemes is less promising. In political negotiations, emission-reduction targets, and therefore scarcity price of emission certificates, are frequently set below the levels suggested by scientific evidence. To ensure the support of the power sector, a large fraction of the allowances are usually handed out for free. As a one-off windfall payment, based on historic output, this would not affect prices and investment decisions. The national allocation plans for CO_2 allowances in Europe, however, show that politicians are reluctant to grant such large one-off payments. They insisted that free allocation is conditional on future output or availability. This reduces the opportunity costs of allowances and the resulting electricity prices. Some national allocation plans also grant free allowances to new power plants. This distorts technology choices (Keats Martinez and Neuhoff, 2005). As a result of these political processes, electricity prices will only gradually come to reflect environmental externalities.

The recent debate on security of supply has highlighted a different way in which traditional energy pricing does not accurately reflect the social and economic risks many societies run. The dependence of many economies on imported fossil fuels means that they are vulnerable to serious disruption if geo-political events disrupt supply. The same risk applies to the disruptions of fossil-fuel use in the case of future stringent action to slow global warming. Macroeconomic and technology models show that it is socially rational to diversify technology options when confronted with such supply uncertainties (Gruebler *et al.*, 1999). For example, a study of the UK electricity system showed that wind power reduced the risk of power shortages during gas supply interruption, thus increasing the value of small shares of wind power by €7.60/MWh (Oxera, 2003). Further studies are required to put a price tag on the value of energy and technology diversity.

If the political influence of incumbent energy companies is likely to hold back moves to eliminate subsidies and internalize environmental impacts, there is a strong case for subsidizing renewable energy, to prevent an ongoing distortion in the choice of technologies that figure in future investment decisions.

5. Marketplace Barriers

The electricity sector has been liberalized gradually to ensure that security of supply will be maintained. As a result, the electricity market has been designed to replicate the historic operation of centralized power plants and favours their operation. For example, solar PV can reduce peak loads on the distribution network in summer peaking systems, and combined heat and power—whether gas or bioenergy—can do likewise in winter peaking systems (Hoff and Cheney, 2000). Frequently, however, network tariffs do not reward this kind of system service (Alderfer *et al.*, 2000). Another example of inherited market design is provided by mechanisms that accommodate the inflexible operation of some fossil and nuclear power plants, while few markets are optimized to provide flexibility for intermittent generation.

The main market concern for renewable energy technologies is that wind, solar, and wave output cannot be predicted with sufficient accuracy at the time of the liquid day-ahead market. By the time the prediction accuracy improves (about 4 hours before final production), most international electricity transmissions have been allocated and liquidity in energy markets is low. This is despite the fact that transmission flows can be adjusted within seconds, most power plants can be started and stopped, and all power plants can change their output within this time frame.[8] As a result, the electricity system is operated inefficiently and wind, solar, and wave generators selling their output in the general energy market receive lower than justified prices.

In most countries, electricity generation companies have high market shares in their regional markets and can influence prices in day-ahead and intra-day markets. Currently, they sell most output on longer-term contracts and therefore profit little and will typically refrain from influencing short-term prices. With higher penetration by renewables, trade in the short-term market will increase. At times of low renewable output, it is profitable for conventional generation to sell additional output in the short-term market above cost. At times of high renewable output, it is profitable for conventional generation to buy back energy sold on longer-term contracts, but below cost. This market power will reduce the revenue of intermittent renewables below their fair value and can result in production inefficiencies.

[8] This effect is enhanced if, in systems like the English and Welsh NETA, renewables generators balance their output if they want to avoid high imbalance prices. As individual output is relatively more volatile than aggregate output, this results in higher levels of flexible plant that must be kept running, creating energy and capital costs.

Vertically integrated companies face additional incentives to obstruct the entry of renewable energies, if this takes market share from their conventional generation assets, or if it results in changes to the transmission system, which reduce the value of some of their existing assets (Alderfer *et al.*, 2000). However, inexperienced or inert companies can also increase project costs for decentralized generation and cause unnecessary delays, if they have not established procedures for interconnections, or if they request technical assessments and insurance cover that are only appropriate for large central power plants. If the market share of a technology is at or below 1 per cent, niche applications or specific regulatory provisions dominate its economies, even when they are economically competitive in a technology-to-technology comparison (Kammen, 2004). Regulatory intervention can reduce this effect or compensate initial investors for these costs.

Most renewable energy sources are small relative to the expansion scale of transmission and most distribution capacity. If a project developer has to pay large fractions of the lumpy network expansion costs required for its turbines (deep connection charging), then these costs are likely to inhibit the project. Coordination among project developers to build in the same area and to share the cost would resolve the issue. Such coordination is difficult as each project hinges on funding, planning permits, and energy contracts. Conventional technologies do not require coordination as they are of the same scale as network expansion projects. To avoid delays, countries have shifted towards charging shallow connection charges. Only the cable from the last distribution point to the turbine is paid directly by the project. Of the lumpy investment costs within the network, only the fraction used by the individual generator is allocated to the specific generator (e.g. the British energy regulator, Ofgem, is discussing locational differentiated access tariffs to the distribution network). The remaining costs are socialized among all users until additional generators pick up the tab. This obviously creates the risk of stranded assets, but is a common approach on the demand side: costs of excess network capacity to accommodate for potential demand growth have always been socialized.

A different set of questions relates to the regulatory and market risk of investment in electricity generation capacity. It is currently widely debated whether the risk might prevent timely investment in new generation capacity. This risk could be eliminated by long-term contracts between final consumers or consumer franchises and electricity generation companies. However, current regulators prevent such long-term contracts in an attempt to foster retail competition. This exposes investors to electricity price risk and induces them to charge a risk premium on their capital. The risk premium, created by artificial regulatory constraints, affects capital-intensive technologies more than technologies with high fuel costs and therefore biases against nuclear and renewables (Neuhoff and De Vries, 2004).

Regulators are concerned about the implications of investment risk, because it could postpone investment, causing unpopular power shortages. But instead of reducing market and regulatory risk, they typically implement financial payments for available capacity. Regulators not only retain the bias against capital-intensive technologies but might reinforce that bias, if the (small) contribution which intermittent generation offers towards supply during peak demand is not rewarded. Furthermore, short-term contracting in electricity markets can reinforce cyclical investment patterns. This can hinder development of small industries with less scaling opportunity and restrict their opportunities for continuous research and production improvements.

Financial markets face difficulties in providing risk-management instruments for new renewable technologies (United Nations Environment Programme, 2004). First, historical actuarial data are not available to assess risk (Sonntag-O'Brien and Usher, 2004). Conventional technologies have never faced these difficulties, because they were already deployed before liberalization. Historic records from these times have allowed risk assessment since liberalization. A second disadvantage faced by renewable energy projects is their small scale, which results in disproportionately high transaction costs for risk management tools, complex financing arrangements, or export credit guarantees. Large institutions such as the World Bank have little track record with efficient administration of small-scale projects (below $15m).

6. Non-marketplace Barriers

The complex interactions between the public, administration, private sector, and electricity system operators can create non-marketplace barriers for new energy technologies.

Administrative frameworks were developed for existing technologies and are not yet tailored to the needs of renewables. While spatial planning traditionally envisages specific zones for industrial development, local plans must frequently be revised to allow for the location of wind or bioenergy plants. This creates uncertainty and costly delays for project developers, for European wind projects between 1.5 and 4.5 years

(Admire Rebus, 2003). The small scale of renewable energy projects multiplies the relative costs incurred through multiple administrative processes. For example, biogas plants in Germany required several parallel permit processes designed to address issues such as EU regulations to prevent the spread of bovine spongiform encephalopathy (BSE), while large power plants only require a single general permit process (Klinski, 2004).

Reliable and comprehensive information about the motivation and benefits, as well as the costs and externalities, of renewable technologies must be shared with involved and affected citizens. While early investors in renewable energy technologies require technical and economic information upon which to base their decisions, subsequent groups of adaptors might have to familiarize themselves with the technology through trial and error and learning through experience (Kaplan, 1999). Citizen support has been seriously affected by concerns about wind turbines killing birds, that since seem to have been addressed by the design and siting of new turbines, or by unease about the excessive energy-intensity of solar PV production, based on prototype figures (Alsema, 2000). In contrast, German project developers report that if they involve citizens and local councils in the early planning stages, they are more likely to obtain planning consent. In addition, polling in Europe shows that support for wind energy tends to strengthen after plants have been installed and in operation for some time.[9] This illustrates that some time is required to allow stakeholders to adjust to and accept new technologies.

The successful deployment of wind turbines in Denmark is a result of long-term thinking, local community involvement, benefits to incumbent energy companies, public and private R&D support, and government support (Ministry of Economic Affairs, 2004). Over time, Denmark has developed domestic industries to design, finance, insure, manufacture, install, and maintain renewables systems, using local equipment and labour (Sawin, 2004). Countries cannot simply rely on adopting an internationally developed technology. Even in the rapidly developing and uncontroversial field of the telecoms industry, some countries experienced significant delays in adopting new technologies (Dekimpe *et al.*, 2000). Active technology policy must give population, industry, and administration a chance to get used to a new technology and learn how

---

[9] According to a 2003 survey in Scotland, among people living close to the ten largest wind farms, 82 per cent of respondents want an increase in electricity generated from wind, and 54 per cent support an increase in the number of turbines at their local wind farm (Braunholtz, 2003).

to deal with its new characteristics (Duke *et al.*, 2002; Sonntag-O'Brien and Usher, 2004). Because of this 'institutional learning' process (Espejo *et al.*, 1996), countries benefit if they support the deployment of renewables before they are fully cost-competitive. This will remove non-marketplace barriers for subsequent use in competitive markets and accelerate their future growth.

7. Technology Lock-out

Technology 'lock-in' and 'lock-out' refer to processes which favour conventional, established technologies at the expense of innovative technologies. In this section it is discussed how learning by doing can result in a 'lock-out' of new technologies. The previous sections illustrated how an uneven playing field, marketplace, and non-market barriers and adoption costs can also deter new renewables (Sanden and Azar, 2005). Because a combination of barriers causes the technology 'lock-out' it might not suffice to remove one barrier to resolve it. For example, a lack of full internalization of negative externalities on our climate from CO_2 emissions creates an uneven playing field for carbon-free energy sources. However, even if an effective CO_2 trading scheme would internalize externalities of CO_2 emissions, it will not remove the other barriers. Therefore it does not eliminate the need to assess and pursue active technology policy carefully (Jensen and Skytte, 2003).

Figure 3 shows how new renewable technologies have consistently reduced their costs with increasing market experience. The fact that the cost of new technologies falls with increasing deployment has been established in a large set of studies on energy technologies (Watanabe *et al.*, 2001) and in other industry sectors (Isoard and Soria, 1997; IEA, 2003*b*). Consequently, without large-scale applications, the cost of new technologies can stay high and investors will continue to use established technologies. As a result, new technologies can be 'locked out'. This is sometimes described as path dependency—what seems economic in the future depends on previous patterns of investment (Arthur, 1989; Kline, 2001; Unruh, 2002).

The strength of technology lock-out varies across industries. The energy sector exhibits three basic characteristics that result in a strong technology lock-out. First, new technologies produce the same basic product: electricity, in the case of most renewables. Hence, they have to compete mainly on price, making them immediately more vulnerable to lock-out. This is in sharp contrast to the IT, telecoms, and other sectors, where product

Figure 3 Learning Curve for Energy Technologies

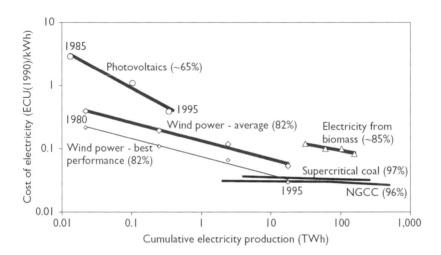

Source: IEA (2000).

differentiation is a prime instrument of marketing and innovation and the innovator can charge more for enhanced functionality or reduced size of a new device. This surpasses tendencies to lock out. Some high-value applications also exist for renewable energy technologies. But both the individual project size and the total market volume are probably too small to support significant learning by doing and research efforts. For example, PV cells are far more valuable in off-grid applications, but in 2002 this market segment contributed less than 10 per cent to global PV sales (PVPS, 2003).

Second, perhaps because they involve transformation and delivery of large quantities of energy, the technologies and systems tend to involve large-scale engineering products that last decades. This greatly increases the scale and time horizon of financial investment, and multiplies the risks associated with innovation; it also means that new energy technologies compete with incumbents that have gained market experience over several decades and large quantities of global investment, often drawing on prior public R&D.

Third, both the above factors make it far harder for individual private firms to appropriate the full benefits of learning and R&D in the energy sector than in other sectors. Dasgupta and Stiglitz (1988) show in a model that oligopolistic firms might be prepared to incur initial losses by expanding their production if learning effects would reduce their future costs, thereby allowing for larger future market shares and profit margins. However, technology 'spillover' allows other companies to copy the initial learning at a fraction of the costs (Irwin and Klenow, 1994; Watanabe *et al.*, 2001). As more producers compete, the benefits of the invention are split among several producers who share the market and consumers who pay lower prices (Duke and Kammen, 1999). This problem has been resolved in the pharmaceutical sector by granting patents for inventions, and companies spend 15 per cent of revenue on drug development. But the monopoly position granted by patent rights also results in inefficient markets. Profits account for 30 per cent of sales volume in the pharmaceutical industry, with marketing and administration accounting for a further 30 per cent.[10]

For at least two reasons it seems unlikely that patents will play a major role in promoting innovation and improvements of renewables. First, pharmaceutical patents protect a specific, distinct drug; it is far harder to define engineering patents in ways that cannot be circumvented over time.[11] There is even the risk that enhancing intellectual property rights protection impedes innovation and diffusion of new knowledge (Alic *et al.*, 2003). Second, renewable energy technologies consist of a large set of components and require the expertise of several companies to improve the system. A consortium will face difficulties in sharing the costs of 'learning investment', as it is difficult to negotiate and fix the allocation of future profits. Firms are, therefore, reluctant to invest for the benefits of consortium members (the hold-up problem). At the same time the scale, expertise, and time horizon of 'learning-investment' tends to exceed the funds of individual companies and the patience of the venture-capital markets.

Despite all these challenges to innovation in the energy sector, the oil extraction industry is relatively innovative. The example of deep-water oil drilling shows that government support was instrumental. Initially, costs were significantly higher than for onshore or shallow water fields. Oil companies preferred to develop cheaper fields, as they had to sell output

---

[10] Based on SEC filings, annual reports, Hoovers.com, and company presentations for Abbott Laboratories, Johnson & Johnson, Novcartis, SmithKlineBeecham, Merck & Co, Bristol-Myers Squibb, American Home Products, AstraZeneca, Pfizer, and GlaxoWellcome for the year 1999.

[11] First, successful drugs targeting is guided by scientific knowledge but requires a lot of luck. Therefore, it might take time for a competitor to find a substance with similar characteristics. Second, the new substance requires the same extensive clinical trials, which are the most expensive part of drug R&D. The substance will only be accredited if it has better features than the existing drug. Third, the follower must decide whether all these costs will be recovered with lower market share in a lower-margin duopoly market.

on a global oil market at a homogeneous price. Governments reduced extraction taxes to compensate private oil companies for higher field development costs of deep-water oil fields. With improvements through market experience, costs for deep-water drilling fell and governments could reduce the scale of incentives. In the next section the economics of such strategic deployment are discussed.

8. The Economics of Strategic Deployment

These diverse barriers to deployment and impediments to innovation underpin the case for 'strategic deployment'. Diverse policy options must be applied to foster large-scale investment in renewable energy technologies before they are commercially competitive in current energy markets. The existence of barriers obviously does not imply that a technology will be cost competitive if the barrier is removed; this suggests that both technology appraisal and some experimenting is required to guide policy decisions.

The experience with onshore wind power is a good example of the success of strategic deployment. R&D-led attempts in Germany, the USA, and other countries to build multi-megawatt wind turbines in the early 1980s failed both on engineering and cost grounds (Norberg-Bohm, 2000; see also Bergek and Jacobsson, 2003). At the same time, private and subsequently public initiatives supported the deployment of small wind turbines in Denmark (Jensen, 2004). Through application experience, the turbine manufacturer learned how to address design challenges, and turbine size gradually increased (Grubb and Vigotti, 1997). Today's commercial turbines have reached the size of the ambitious experimental turbines of the 1980s. A combination of public and private R&D, market feedback, operational experience, and incremental improvements achieved cost reductions and allowed an increase of turbine size. At windy locations, wind power is now as cheap as new conventional capacity, and it may approach competitiveness in other locations, depending on competing fuel cost and the extent to which policies reflect environmental costs. The wind power market is burgeoning, with growth sustained at 20–30 per cent/year since the early 1990s. Strategic deployment of wind energy cost Denmark an estimated US$1.4 billion in subsidies over 1993–2001; meanwhile, annual revenues of Danish wind companies by 2001 were $2.7 billion, the vast majority from its dominant position in export markets (Carbon Trust, 2003).

Figure 4 Learning Investment and Future Benefits of a New Technology

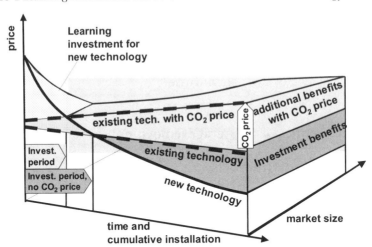

Figure 4 illustrates the basic idea of strategic deployment. Initially the costs of a new technology exceed the costs of existing technologies (y-axis). With increasing cumulative experience in the market, costs of the new technology fall (x-axis). To allow for this increasing experience, the market volume increases (z-axis). Thus, despite decreasing costs of the technology, during the initial years the costs of strategic deployment increase because of the increasing market volume. We refer to extra costs of deploying the new technology during the initial years multiplied by the market volume as the 'learning investment', required to get the technology to a cost-competitive level.

After the new technology reaches the cost level of the existing technology, the strategic deployment programme is no longer required. Instead, society can harvest the benefits of the new technology. Their value is the cost savings relative to the conventional technology times the market volume. Thus, even if the per-unit cost savings are relatively small, a large market volume can create significant benefits. To the extent that the new technology sets the market price, consumers will capture the benefits of the learning investment and the benefits from learning investment are a public good.

Costs also fall for established technologies, but at a slower pace. This is because, for established technologies, doubling of global installed capacity takes much longer, and therefore further cost reductions are slower.

Environmental externalities influence the viability of strategic deployment of low carbon technologies. As illustrated in the graph, if CO_2 prices

Table 1. Public Learning Investment (Billion Euro) Required to Make PV Cost Competitive at Wholesale Level

Rate at which technology improves with market experience	Future wholesale electricity price level		
	€40/MWh	€50/MWh	€60/MWh
Slow	110	55	29
Historic	38	20	12
Rapid	17	10	6

are internalized, then the cost of conventional technologies increases (coal, gas). This has two effects. First, the funding required to cover the extra costs of the new technology during the early years is reduced and the new technology reaches the point at which it is cost competitive with the existing technology earlier. Thus the learning investment is reduced. Second, the benefits of the new technology are higher, because they are accrued earlier on and the reference price relative to which they are calculated is higher. Price internalization of CO_2 externalities thus has a big impact on the benefit–cost ratio of technology policy—it increases the benefits and reduces the costs.

This illustrates the link between technology policy and policies that internalize CO_2 externalities into the product price. Price internalization on its own will usually not increase the costs of the conventional technology sufficiently to make the new low-carbon technology cost competitive at the early stages. Technology policy on its own might not exhibit a sufficiently high benefit–cost ratio to be credible for technology investors.

For technologies with some market experience, such as wind and solar PV, historic data can be used to estimate costs and benefits of such an active technology policy (IEA, 2000; McDonald and Schrattenholzer, 2001). Cost predictions for offshore wind, solar concentration, and marine technologies rely on engineering assessments, which are more detailed but also more subjective as a specific technology evolution has to be assumed. Table 1 shows the public learning investment that may be required to create sufficient market experience for PV to make it cost competitive with existing technologies. Neuhoff (2004) provides more details and comparison with the similar calculations of IEA (2000) and Duke (2002). In the base case, €20 billion of public subsidies are required, spread over the period 2005–23. The calculations assume that PV is applied both in markets for high-value off-grid and distributed PV and in centralized installations to gain sufficient scale.

Table 2. Ratio between Net Present Value (NPV) and Learning Investment

Rate at which technology improves with market experience	Future wholesale electricity price level		
	€40/MWh	€50/MWh	€60/MWh
Slow	0	2	9
Historic	4	15	38
Rapid	17	44	92

Two uncertainties drive the prediction. The first uncertainty is the future costs of conventional generation, including the extent to which environmental and security externalities are internalized; this determines the wholesale price against which PV needs to compete. Second is the rate at which PV costs decline with increasing market experience. Slow improvements through market experience correspond to cost reductions of 17 per cent with each doubling of cumulative installed capacity, 'historic' to 20 per cent and 'rapid' to 23 per cent. IEA (2000) assumes learning rates between 18 and 22 per cent. A survey by McDonald and Schrattenholzer (2001) suggests 20 per cent.

These uncertainties influence the benefits that society will obtain from strategic deployment. Table 2 shows the global 'strategic benefit–cost' ratio. In the base case the benefits until 2040, at a 5 per cent discount rate, would be 15 times the costs of learning investment. However, if both learning rates and the reference electricity price were at the lower end of the assumed distribution, the 'learning investment' would not be recovered by 2040. This type of technology risk is unavoidable (Alic *et al.*, 2003). It requires continuous evaluation of technology progress in order to stop unsuccessful programmes. It also requires support of several technology options to ensure that future energy security is not jeopardized if one technology does not satisfy expectations.

Of course, the real picture is complicated by the diversity of resources and potential applications. For example, PV electricity in very sunny regions is obviously cheaper than in others. In addition, there are issues of international competition: learning is likely to be partly domestic and partly generic, and many different actors and countries could contribute to learning, and in turn, recoup benefits of component or machine exports (as with Danish wind energy). But the fundamental point is that there is a clear economic case for government action to build markets for advanced deployment of emerging clean-energy technologies.

In such strategic deployment, policy determines the subsidy volume and therefore the growth rate. The previous calculations assumed a growth rate of 35 per cent, slightly above recent development of 32 per cent (PVPS, 2003) and slightly below the growth rates of the semi-conductor industry.[12] If the growth rate is reduced, more learning takes place in high-value off-grid and distributed markets. This reduces the cost of strategic deployment, but also postpones the benefits which society will obtain from larger-scale application of competitive PV.

The anticipated cost improvements can only materialize if producers invest and experiment with new production processes and technology options. For this to happen, industry must be confident that the global market growth will be sustained. While it is not difficult to give guarantees around individual projects, it is far more difficult to guarantee that strategic deployment policies will be maintained; indeed, they are bound to be reviewed periodically. However, the more countries that are engaged, the less exposed producers will be to interruptions of policy processes in individual countries (Wilson, 1989; Grubb and Vigotti, 1997).

9. Research, Development, and Demonstration

Innovation is frequently pictured as a linear process, taking a new technology from R&D to demonstration and strategic deployment until the technology can finally compete in mass markets (Foxon and Kemp, 2004). Tidal, wave, and solar concentration technologies are at an early stage of the innovation process and require extensive demonstration projects to explore options and improve solutions. More advanced technologies, such as wind and solar PV, also need R&D to improve their performance. Market experience from strategic deployment programmes then refines the research results and at the same time helps to identify new research needs.

Margolis and Kammen (1999b) estimate that private returns on R&D across various sectors are between 20 and 30 per cent, while social rates of return are around 50 per cent. This shows that private investors only appropriate a fraction of social returns because technology 'spillover' in the energy sector is large. Investors also face difficulties in evaluating intangible R&D output (Alic et al., 2003) and therefore under-invest in

---

[12] D-Ram semiconductor sales show an average annual growth rate of 33 per cent, in units shipped of 43 per cent and in shipped memory density of 98 per cent for the period 1974–98 (*Source*: Firsthand, Understanding Semi Conductor Cycles, http://advisors.firsthandfunds.com/documents/investor_ed/semiconductors.pdf).

R&D (Azar and Dowlatabadi, 1999). As a result, R&D-intensive companies are systematically under-priced by the market. This is likely to reduce the incentive to perform basic research. Lev (2004) observed among companies that are members of the industrial research institute that they reduced the allocation of R&D funds to basic research every year from 1993 to 2003, in favour of modifications and extensions of current products. Furthermore, energy technologies are usually sold to markets that are closely regulated. A path-breaking research success might induce a change in the market design or regulation, such that the public appropriates the profits, not the private innovator. This would further reduce the incentive to fund R&D privately. Therefore it is generally accepted that public support is required to achieve the optimal R&D level.

The importance of R&D is also supported by macroeconomic analysis. Jorgenson and Wilcoxen (1990) attribute about 50 per cent of economic growth to technology change. Goulder and Schneider (1999) argue that increasing R&D expenditures in carbon-free technologies could crowd out R&D in the rest of the economy and therefore reduce overall growth rates. However, Azar and Dowlatabadi (1999) refer to Mansfield's (1968) counter-argument: radical technological change will trigger more research overall and therefore increase economy-wide productivity rates.

Industry-funded R&D focuses on the areas of existing activity of the firm. Jelen and Black (1983) observed that companies fund internal RD&D in rough proportion to sales revenues. The market volume of renewable energy technologies is still small and therefore industry R&D is likely to be small. Furthermore, even forward-looking companies do not plan for more than a decade and are therefore likely to focus on improvements that can be leveraged in the short term (Anderson and Bird, 1992).

This suggests that public funding will be the main driver for longer-term developments in new technology and production processes for existing renewables, exploration of untried renewable technologies, superconductivity to provide the option for efficient long-distance electricity transport, and non-hydro storage technologies. The innovation process is not linear but entails various feedback loops between market experience and research activities. Cost and efficiency improvements in existing renewable technologies (Luther, 2004) therefore require a parallel increase in strategic deployment efforts and public research funding. The optimal mix between R&D support and support for strategic deployment is unclear. Twenty-two per cent of the Japanese PV programme was spent on R&D in the period 1973–95 (Gruebler *et al.*,

Figure 5 IEA Country Public R&D Expenditure on Energy Technologies

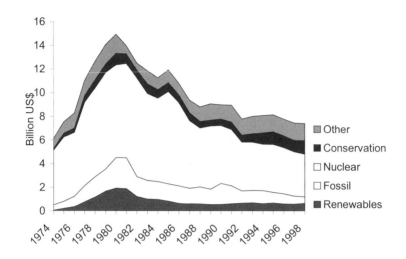

Source: IEA database of R&D.

Figure 6 Public R&D Expenditure on Renewable Energy Technologies in IEA Countries

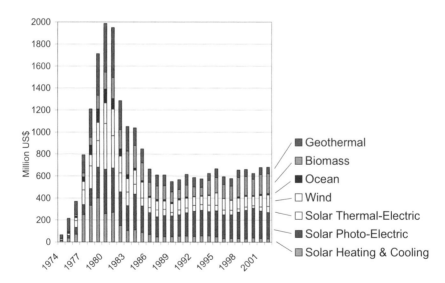

Note: US$ of 2000.
Source: IEA.

1999). The Japanese, German, and US PV programmes devoted 31 per cent of support in 2002 to RD&D (PVPS, 2003).

Figure 5 shows that, in recent decades, only a small fraction of public energy R&D funds of IEA countries have been allocated to renewable energy technologies, less than 8 per cent in the period 1987–2002.[13] Given public expectations and policy commitments, it is surprising that renewable energy technologies continue to be funded at a low level relative to nuclear and fossil energy. This picture is even more disturbing if we consider that private R&D expenditure in the energy sector is extremely low. In the USA, as a typical example, 0.5 per cent of sales revenue in the electricity sector is devoted to R&D, compared to 3.3 per cent in the car industry, 8 per cent in electronics, and 15 per cent in pharmaceuticals (based on Alic *et al.*, 2003).

Figure 6 shows the allocation of public R&D funds to different renewable technologies over time. Total funding has dropped after the initial interest created through the oil shock in the 1970s, and has stayed constant since.

However, the aggregate picture hides the large uncertainty to which individual research streams are exposed. Funding levels for individual technologies in individual countries have changed by more than 30 per cent in about half the observation years.[14] This 'roller-coaster' of research funding limits the ability of laboratories to attract, develop, and maintain human capital for successful R&D.

10. Policy Instruments

This chapter has surveyed five key features of energy-technology systems: an uneven playing field; specific barriers in the market; non-market structures; lock-out phenomena; and the overall economics of strategic deployment for technology learning. They provide economic arguments for government policies to unlock new technologies, if the expectation is that the unlocked technologies offer a valuable option for future energy supply. In the absence of such policies, new renewable technologies will be introduced, if at all, with large delays. Carbon constraints alone will not do the trick. With further reductions in CO_2 quotas, it is likely that renewable

[13] Margolis and Kammen (1999*a*) show that total investment in R&D in the USA increased from US$100 billion in 1976 to US$200 billion in 1996, while US energy R&D decreased from US$7.6 billion to US$4.3 billion. Renewable fuels make up 4 per cent of the United States' energy supply, yet receive only 1 per cent of federal tax expenditures and direct fiscal spending, excluding revenue outlays for the Alcohol Fuels Excise Tax (Herzog *et al.*, 2001).

[14] Based on own analysis of R&D data provided by IEA. Kammen (2004) concludes that national R&D programmes have frequently exhibited 'roller-coaster funding cycles'.

technologies are necessary to satisfy energy demand. Without strategic deployment, the carbon price will rise until it is high enough to finance new renewable technologies. With the application of these technologies, their costs, and therefore also the carbon price, will fall again. Such a peak in the carbon price is likely to result in distortions in other economic sectors and to increase the total costs of climate policy to society.

Governments have successfully supported technology improvements through market experience in other sectors, as the example of deep-water oil drilling showed (section 3). Governments reduced extraction taxes to compensate private oil companies for higher field-development costs of deep-water oil fields. Tax levels in the electricity sector are lower than in oil extraction, and a tax reduction would not suffice to make new renewable technologies cost competitive. A financial premium is needed, either funded from the general budget or through electricity consumers. General taxation creates economic distortions (Duke, 2002). It is economically preferable and also more commonplace to incorporate 'learning invest-ment' costs for energy technologies into the price of electricity. As environmental externalities are not fully included in electricity prices, the modest addition to electricity prices makes consumption decisions more efficient.

A variety of policy instruments are used to deliver financial support to renewable energy projects.

Up-front capital subsidies or investment tax deductions provide public financial support for the initial investment. The Japanese PV programme has successfully combined direct investment aid and capital grants with stable energy prices guaranteed at the level of retail tariffs (net-metering). This is a simple way to support distributed small-scale projects and creates few transaction costs. However, if too much of the project funding is based on up-front payments or tax deductions, India's experience with 100 per cent depreciation from corporate taxes shows that investors might pay insufficient attention to turbine siting, durability, and maintenance (Jagadeesh, 2000). As technologies improve and the scale of deployment increases, experience shows that it is increasingly important for incentives to support the value of power produced, rather than just the investment: to reward performance, not merely the fact of installing equipment.

Labelling of electricity and relying on consumer choice has been proposed as an alternative to obligatory schemes. While this option might be attractive in certain respects, it seems to have little impact on the deployment of renewable energy technologies (EWEA, 2004). Most consumers prefer renewable energy but are happy to free-ride, if their neighbours incur the costs (Rader and Norgaard, 1996; Swezey and Bird,

2001). With few consumers opting to buy renewable energy at higher tariffs, they are supplied by existing rather than new capacity.

Weitzman (1974) analysed the basic options for governments to set either price or quantity targets. Both approaches are currently applied in different countries to support new technologies. In the quantity approach, electricity suppliers are obliged to provide a certain percentage of power from renewables—'renewable portfolio standards' either through own production or purchases—generally implemented with some form of tradable 'renewable energy credits'. The major benefit attributed to trading of renewable energy certificates is price reductions from competition. This argument ignores the multi-layer market structure. Producers, installers, and planners compete to supply to project developers or investors, irrespective of the funding regime to which project developers are exposed. A drawback of renewable portfolio standards is that, so far, no mechanism has been found to isolate markets for renewable energy certificates from future policy decisions. The setting of the overall quota involves trade-offs between investment security and inherent uncertainties about rates of installation and qualifying technologies. As a result, the quota value may be quite unstable and difficult to predict and revenue streams of renewable energy projects are exposed to uncertainties from both the market and future government decisions. With such regulatory risk, investors apply higher discount rates when evaluating future revenues, and require higher total payments for projects to break even (see also Moore and Ihle, 1999).

Regulatory risk can be reduced if policies provide legally enforceable long-term guarantees. The German feed-in tariff and the British auctions for long-term renewable contracts under the Non Fossil Fuel Obligation (NFFO) in the 1990s defined electricity prices for most of the project lifespan. Although the tariff is fixed for the lifespan of a project, it can be adjusted year by year to represent technology advances for new projects coming online. Fixed prices have the additional benefit of insulating investors from the regulatory risk caused by future changes to electricity market design. For renewable energy plants, other than bio energy, fixed off-take prices do not distort the efficient operation of the plant, because the system operator does not require marginal prices to give priority to technologies with zero fuel costs. The increased investment security associated with long-term guarantees reduces the cost of financing (Butler and Neuhoff, 2004). Danish and German experience shows that it is still possible to find arrangements within the fixed-price feed-in mechanism to allow the system operator to reduce short-term output from wind turbines if required for system purposes (spill wind). Mechanisms, such as the feed-in tariff, offer two more levers to optimize technology policy. First, the tariff can be technology specific—enabling the parallel advancement of various renewable technologies in the market. Second, the tariff can be conditioned on the local wind resources. This adjustment minimizes the subsidy paid for a specific site, as it reduces the tariff below the level paid to the marginal unit in the system. It can also be used to develop a large range of sites, thereby increasing public acceptance and retaining high-wind sites for larger future turbine sizes.

As an alternative support mechanism in the USA, production tax-credits are used to offer investors tax benefits during the project's life. However, tax schemes are frequently modified; investors face risk, and discount the benefits, meaning higher payments are needed to ensure projects break even (Crooks, 1997).

Overall, the experience of different policy instruments is mixed. There is some indication that mechanisms that expose investors to regulatory risk or uncertainty about future market designs are either more expensive for the ratepayers, or do not result in significant investment. Mechanisms that do not provide technology-specific support premiums inevitably focus investment on the most cost effective technology available and do not encourage improvements, through market experience, in other renewable energy technologies. For example, Bird and Swezey (2004) report that wind accounts for 94 per cent of new renewables installed under green marketing programmes. The optimal policy instrument or mix of instruments might depend on the local and technology circumstances. A harmonization of instruments does not seem to be required, as the mechanisms predominantly affect local project developers and investors. These local actors then contract out technology and construction services and negotiate the best possible price. Therefore, a global market for renewable technologies is compatible with a mix of support mechanisms, as we can already see today.

11. International

Cost reductions in renewable technologies or their production process occur on an international scale.[15] Therefore, strategic deployment not

---

[15] Bottazzi and Peri (2004) use a panel data analysis over all industries to show that internationally generated ideas have a very significant impact in helping innovation in a country. As a consequence, a positive shock to innovation in a large country has, both in the short and in the long run, a significant positive effect on the innovation of all other countries.

only reduces technology costs for users in one country, it also has a positive impact in other countries. Global welfare increases with the number and scale of strategic deployment programmes.[16] Such joint learning experience can be facilitated if standards are harmonized. Standardization in the telecoms sector has allowed transfer of mobile equipment between most markets. Currently, wind-turbine producers face difficulties, as their power electronic equipment has to satisfy different requirements in many markets.

The objective is, therefore, to achieve coherence in energy and technology policy. This is not the same as convergence of policy instruments (Rowlands, 2004), which is perhaps not even desirable. Alic *et al.* (2003) argue that policy-makers should channel funds for technology development and diffusion through multiple agencies and programmes to promote competition and support a diversity of options rather than particular technological choices. Proponents of tradable renewable energy certificates argue that international trading of certificates allows developers to access the best wind and solar resources. This might reduce short-term costs, which are easily quantifiable and therefore typically emphasized. It ignores the fact that one objective of strategic deployment is to foster local industry, and institutional and stakeholder learning.

Renewable technologies are traded in competitive markets, which already successfully interface with a variety of support mechanisms in different countries. Costs of strategic deployment programmes can be added to the tariff bills of national consumers without significant distortions.[17]

How many countries will autonomously develop or expand strategic deployment programmes for renewable energy technologies? Results from R&D not only 'spill over' between companies but also between countries. This might induce national governments to free-ride on foreign R&D and deployment efforts, undermining the objective of large-scale deployment of renewable energy technologies (Barreto and Klaassen, 2004). However, the benefits from unlocking renewable technologies are

---

[16] Barreto and Klaassen (2004) use the ERIS model to show that, with global learning, optimal investment in renewable technologies is increased.

[17] In 2003, the average EU retail tariff based on class Da and Dd for Italy was 181.2 €/MWh with standard deviation of 47.0 €/MWh. The average tariff for large industrial customers was 58.8 €/MWh with standard deviation of 12.36 €/MWh (Eurostat, *Statistics in Focus*, Theme 8, 21/2003). This compares to a less than 4 €/MWh price increase to cover costs of the current German deployment programme. In 2003, 6.1 per cent of electricity was produced from renewables with average remuneration of 91.3 €/MWh. The costs above wholesale price level (~30€/MWh) are shared among all consumers with the exception of exempt industrial customers (6 per cent in 2003) (http://www.vdn-berlin.de/aktuelledaten_eeg.asp).

a multiple of the costs of the learning investment. Therefore, it can be advantageous for individual countries to finance learning investment, even if they only capture a fraction of the global benefits. Furthermore, national industry policy and national institutional learning provide additional arguments to pursue or expand a strategic deployment programme.

National politicians or administrations will be more successful in pursuing strategic deployment programmes, if these programmes are coherent with similar initiatives in other countries (Barreto and Klaassen, 2004). A joint public declaration or non-committing statement made by the Johannesburg Renewable Energy Coalition, the G8 (2001), or similar institutions (Johansson *et al.*, 2004), could express support for stretching targets for increases in R&D budgets or strategic deployment funding. This could provide a reference point for national policy debate and focus the attention of national administrations on energy technology policy.

An international agreement that supports the strategic deployment of several renewable energy technologies would have the advantage that the nationally championed technology of each country could be included. This is likely to increase the number of participating countries. However, it would require a lengthy international process to foster such an agreement, as demonstrated by negotiations of the Kyoto Protocol and the difficulties experienced with the EU policy-making process in defining a renewable quota (Rowlands, 2004).

It might be easier to foster agreements for individual technologies. For example, the Concentrating Solar Power Global Market Initiative of several European, North American, and North African countries aims at deploying 5 GW of solar concentration in the next 10 years. The resulting learning by doing is expected to reduce costs and allow competition with mid-range generation capacity.[18]

In the past, Implementing Agreements of the International Energy Agency focused on R&D and particularly on information provision and exchange. These exist not only in fields such as bioenergy, climate technology initiative, PV power systems, solar heating and cooling, and wind turbine systems, but also in fossil technologies, energy efficiency, and other topics (in all, 41 Agreements). Total spending under the collaborative programme is only $120–150m per year, of which renewables

---

[18] See http://www.solarpaces.org

get a minor share. In principle, there are no objections to using the credibility provided by the IEA to support internationally coordinated deployment programmes.

Partnerships with developing countries could provide mutual benefits. OECD countries would benefit from larger markets and lower production costs; developing countries would obtain access to new technologies, new employment opportunities, and reduced fossil fuel costs. All participants would benefit from reduced emissions. One step towards facilitating such cooperation would be the expansion of export credit guarantees for renewable energy technologies.

12. Conclusion

Resource assessments suggest that renewables could satisfy a much larger share of global energy demand. This would enhance our security and environment. However, the market share of renewables will not increase unless new energy and technology policies address the following barriers.

- Traditional energy technologies are not exposed to full security and environmental costs, and they offer energy below the level of total social costs. Levelling the playing field implies reallocation of rent between stakeholders and is, therefore, a slow process. In the meantime, subsidies for renewable technologies might be required to ensure efficient investment decisions, while subsidies for conventional technologies should be reduced.

- Markets and tariff structures are designed and optimized for fossil generation technologies. They do not address the specific requirements of renewables: flexible operation, long-term contractual arrangements to reduce financing costs, particularly in an environment with high regulatory risk, and simple procedures with low transaction costs for their small-scale nature.

- Renewables are at different stages of development, and fit into different markets. Therefore, policy support must address the specific stage and market of each renewable. For emerging and innovative technologies, this means increasing substantially the collective investment in RD&D and, for those entering the market, increasing the level of deployment incentives. Several countries applying strategic deployment in parallel will create industry confidence in continuous market growth.

The discovery of a new energy technology that suddenly resolves all energy challenges is a frequently cited dream, but has not happened in the past and is unlikely to occur in the future. In contrast, we have consistently observed that technologies become more cost effective with improvements through market experience. However, this does not happen autonomously. Most renewable energy technologies are locked out from large-scale market experience because the playing field is uneven and various barriers and technology spillover prevent industry from financing the learning investment. It is in the power of governments to unlock these technologies.

11

Policy Uncertainty and Supply Adequacy in Electric Power Markets

Gert Brunekreeft and Tanga McDaniel

1. Introduction

Supply adequacy in the power markets takes on added importance with liberalization. Relevant episodes illustrating inadequacies in the electricity supply industry include the California power crisis of 2001, which raised questions of whether liberalized power markets include the incentives needed to induce investment in new assets, and the recent blackouts in both the USA and Europe, which raised concerns about the adequacy of the high-voltage transmission networks. The OECD (2003) reports that, globally, new electricity investment to 2030 will amount to some dazzling $10 trillion.

The USA-based North American Electric Reliability Council (NERC) defines reliability as:

the degree of performance of the elements of the bulk electric system that results in electricity being delivered to customers within accepted standards and in the amount desired. Reliability may be measured by the frequency, duration, and magnitude of adverse effects on the electric supply (or service to customers).

Reliability is divided into two functional attributes: adequacy and security. We focus on adequacy, which is defined by the Union for the Coordination of Transmission of Electricity (UCTE, 2003*b*, p. 7) as: 'the capability of the power system to supply the load in all the steady states in which the power system may exist *considering standard conditions*'. This reflects the long-term concern of whether there is sufficient investment. We use the term 'supply adequacy' to cover both generation and network adequacy.

In this chapter we focus on policy uncertainty, which we interpret broadly as the effect on investment incentives as a consequence of uncertain government policy. A narrow definition would be the uncertain effect of economic regulation alone. Concerning new investment in generation assets, a primary problem is that governments cannot credibly commit to doing nothing if capacity becomes scarce and price soars. Tangential to this issue is the uncertainty created by the threat of intervention in (subsets of) markets where there is currently no regulation. We attempt to identify key sources of policy uncertainty, to analyse effects on supply adequacy, and to give recommendations for reducing the impact of uncertainty on investment.

As a benchmark, we assume that risks which are symmetric, non-systematic, diversifiable, and without (future) spin-offs do not affect investment. The benchmark allows us to identify types of uncertainty which do have an effect, namely: asymmetry, which affects expected returns; incompletely diversifiable or systematic risk which, through the capital asset pricing model (CAPM), affects the cost of capital; and uncertainties that create real option values. As Armstrong *et al.* (1994, p. 186) discuss: 'The correct way to model this [regulatory] risk is probably to see it as a factor that lowers expected future cash flows, thus reducing expected profitability, without altering the cost of capital *per se*.' We note that the risk must be asymmetric to reduce expected profits. Asymmetry is introduced if profits are (possibly) capped from above but not below because of price ceilings.

We concentrate on the effects of policy uncertainty in two areas: generation adequacy and network adequacy. Here, generation adequacy includes fuel policy, and network adequacy covers both the transmission and distribution networks. Two points are of particular interest. First, for generation *political reality* dictates that if generation capacity becomes scarce and prices rise, political pressure is likely to force intervention by the regulator or responsible government body. We argue these policy expectations may well be self-fulfilling. Second, rate-of-return regulation, including a used-and-useful clause, is better equipped to handle policy uncertainty than price-cap regulation. With growing concern on long-term investment instead of short-term efficiency, we would expect to see adjustment towards variations of rate-of-return regulation. We also discuss the argument for regulatory independence as a means of increasing the regulator's credibility.

The remainder of the chapter is organized as follows: section 2 discusses policy uncertainty as it relates to supply adequacy; section 3 presents some empirical evidence on adequacy; section 4 focuses on policy recommendations; and section 5 concludes.

2. Policy Uncertainty

2.1 Self-fulfilling Policy Expectations and Market Obstacles for Generation Reliability

We suggest that policy expectations generally (and, in the context of generation, investment in particular) can be self-fulfilling. To illustrate, assume political reality dictates the government interferes in the market at some point and government cannot commit to refrain from interference. A justification for these assumptions is that capping high wholesale prices is likely to occur owing to the inability to distinguish between the exercise of market power and real scarcity prices.[1] A rational investor has to anticipate and internalize this possibility. If the anticipated interference manifests as an asymmetric upward price-cap, expected returns would decrease *ceteris paribus* as compared to a situation where the government could credibly commit to do nothing. The result would be a decline in new investment leading to scarcity, price spikes, and an increased probability of involuntary rationing. This would in turn increase the likelihood of an actual interference. A rational government also has these beliefs. Knowing it cannot commit to non-interference, and anticipating rational behaviour by the investors, the government's anticipation of scarcity and the necessity to do something would be self-fulfilling. The reverse argument also holds. If both the government and the investors believe there will be sufficient capacity, the probability of an intervention will be low (or absent), and investors will be willing to invest such that there will be sufficient capacity. Thus, multiple equilibria can exist: low-capacity equilibria with interference and high-capacity equilibria without interference.

Cabral (2000, ch. 17) describes the existence of multiple fulfilled-expectations equilibria in the context of network effects. The underlying problem in that literature is that an individual's decision to adopt a

---

[1] This argument has been put forth by the OECD, as noted by Roques *et al.* (2004, p. 40).

technology with network externalities depends on the expectation of whether others will also adopt the technology. Similarly, Armstrong *et al.* (1994, p. 188) discuss the problem of circularity that occurs if a regulator determines the regulatory asset base (RAB) relying on the firm's stock-exchange value. If the market expects the stock-exchange value to be high, the firm's market value will be high, the RAB will be high, and allowed revenues will be high; thus expectations self-fulfil.

It is therefore plausible that a high-capacity equilibrium might not be reached. As such, if the government cannot credibly commit to doing nothing, actually acting is the (second) best option. The current situation both in the USA and lately in Europe seems to be just this 'better safe than sorry' policy which is in line with Oren's (2004, p. 24) discussion of rationales for capacity mechanisms:

Legitimate concerns for failure of the energy markets to reflect scarcity rents or failure of the capital market to produce proper levels of investment in response to such rents may justify some intervention. In some cases regulatory intervention in adequacy assurance is needed to compensate for regulatory interference in the energy market.

Policy expectations can inhibit markets from achieving reliability as can technology. For example, Stoft (2002, p. 111) discusses the following two demand-side flaws. First, the lack of real-time metering and billing limits price responsiveness, and price as a scarcity signal or a rationing device does not work well. Even if consumers were more price responsive, there would be the free-rider problem captured by the second flaw: the system operator's inability to control the real-time flow to specific customers. In other words, selective curtailment of demand is not feasible. These two problems together imply that involuntary rationing will be unavoidable when markets do not clear.[2] Stoft (2002, p. 113) also explains that independent system operators (ISOs) in the USA commit to operating reserves of about 10 per cent of load, and pay 'whatever is necessary', and with prices 'exceeding a few thousand dollars per mega-watt-hour, system operators understandably begin to have second thoughts'. As a consequence the ISOs have requested Federal Energy Regulatory Commission (FERC) approval for price caps; these have been set at $1,000/MWh.

There is not a unique reason for the market's limited capacity to secure generation adequacy. Would there be a need for policy to augment investment incentives if political uncertainties were resolved and technology more

[2] Neuhoff and De Vries (2004) connect this to retail competition and argue that end-user switching impedes long-term contracting, resulting in inefficiently low capacity.

advanced, or would energy prices alone signal the need for *timely* investments? Despite some support for an 'energy-only' market, a prevailing view is that extra-market incentives are required to meet current reliability criteria, and this position seems to be supported by evidence. Hogan (2005) refers to the 'missing money' problem which leads many commentators to support extra-market incentives.[3] Missing money is a problem if price caps are set such that peaking plant are unable to cover costs when capacity is short. However, even in the absence of price caps, money for peaking plant may be insufficient. With annualized costs for peaking plant in an order of magnitude of €40,000 per MW, a plant would have to run 40 hours per year to meet cost with a price of €1,000/MWh (cf. similar but slightly higher values for the USA in Stoft (2002)). Bijvoet *et al.* (2003) estimate the value of lost load (VOLL) in the Netherlands on average at a rather high €8.6/kWh (and even €16.4 /kWh for households). If the shutdown price is set at a VOLL of €8,000/MWh, the running time would only be 5 hours. Using real data for New England, Joskow (2003) illustrates the energy-only cost-recovery problem.[4] New England has a cap of $1,000/MWh on wholesale prices (installed after May 2000), which is considerably below the €8,000/MWh mentioned above. Joskow shows that the price cap was binding only 6 hours per year on average. He calculates the scarcity rents earned over this period at $10,000/MW-year, far less than the cost of reserve capacity which he estimates at approximately $70,000.

The Brattle Group (2004, p. 10) concludes: 'we see unique institutional factors that contribute to a fundamental mistrust of markets. For example, the California power crisis has put pressure on most regulators in the United States to intervene directly with security of supply' and 'In contrast, the British energy regulator (Ofgem) believes that markets will provide security of supply naturally.'

This distrust of spot markets is in line with the self-fulfilling expectation brought on by regulatory commitment problems. Consider the case of San Diego just before the California crisis of 2001. Under California Assembly Bill 1890, which laid the foundation for the reformed California market in 1996, retail rates were frozen for 6 years in order that load serving entities (LSEs) could recoup stranded costs. A company recovering costs before the 2002 deadline could raise rates. San Diego met this criterion in 1999 and doubled retail rates over the period that wholesale prices soared in late 2000. As discussed in Bushnell and Mansur (2004) the

[3] Hogan is an advocate of energy-only markets.
[4] With annualized costs of $60,000–$80,000/MW-year.

political response was to step in and (retroactively) freeze rates for small and medium-sized customers. Ironically, the initial rate freeze was to satisfy producers' worries that retail prices would fall in a more competitive environment, leaving them unable to recoup existing investment costs. The San Diego example illustrates the uncertainties associated with regulatory discretion which responds to political opposition to retail price spikes and also with policy 'stickiness'. Following the crisis in 2000, what was intended to be a revenue floor became a binding cap, but once enacted there was significant lag before regulation was revised.

2.2 Real Option Value of Waiting: Primary Fuels

Three recent, important policy drivers include import dependence for primary fuels, emission trading, and renewed interest in nuclear. Commissioned by the European Commission, the Clingendael Institute (2004) analysed the geo-political risk in the supply of primary fuels and noted increasing import dependence. One reason is the increasing share of gas as a primary fuel for electricity production. The concerns for supply security are that strategic dependence on the exporters is disturbing, and supply security is threatened by low investment in the exporting countries. Policies addressing security will also affect policies for: primary fuel diversification (which covers both fuel sources and importation from different regions); integrated strategic reserves development (sufficiently large reserves will flatten out short-run interruptions); demand-side management to reduce energy dependency; and development of indigenous energy sources (in particular, renewables such as wind and hydro).

The first round of the European emission trading system (ETS) of tradable carbon-dioxide (CO_2) emission rights started on 1 January 2005. Rights can be traded and thus have a price. During 2005, the CO_2 allowance price tended to be surprisingly high, peaking at about €32/ tCO_2, and subsequently raising electricity prices by as much as €10–15/ MWh. Currently, politicians are under great public pressure to interfere, which adds uncertainty to the market. Two additional uncertainties concern the commitment to announced allocations and the number of rights allocated between incumbents and new entrants. Although the initial allocation is decided by the European Commission, details of national allocation plans are to be decided by national governments, with substantial discretion. IPA (2005) discusses the delay in new UK investments resulting from uncertainties over new entrant allocations. Current expectation is that new entrants will be allocated rights for zero price; projects which may be uneconomic if this is not the case are on hold.

Helm *et al.* (2003) argue national governments will have difficulty credibly committing to long-term targets as they will be tempted to renege *ex post.* This pressure will increase, if it turns out the targets cannot be achieved and hence scarcity of CO_2 allowances starts to bind. As a remedy against non-commitment, they favour an independent energy agency with a duty to fulfil targets set by the government. Their insights carry over to more general forms of regulatory credibility, and Helm *et al.* argue on the same line for an independent agency to handle supply security. The CO_2 ETS uncertainty could alternatively speed up new investment. Investors know they will receive allowances free of charge if the new plant is in operation before 2012, whereas it is yet unknown what will happen after 2012.

Renewables and nuclear policy add to uncertainty as well. Renewables are part of environmental policy and also enhance supply security of primary fuels, since wind and hydro are indigenous. However, a variety of arguments indicate the limits of the promotion of renewables. As such, it seems reasonable to expect some hesitation to invest further. Both the share of nuclear capacity and the policy towards a nuclear phase-out differ strongly in various countries, reflecting controversies. For instance, in the Netherlands and the UK, the nuclear option has been reopened. Sweden, with a 50 per cent share of nuclear generation capacity, has an uncertain policy on nuclear, while (with political unease) Finland recently approved a new nuclear plant. In 1998, the German parliament passed a law to phase out nuclear power, which has a share of about 30 per cent in national electricity generation. Yet, following the change in government in autumn 2005, keeping the nuclear option open is debatable again. A highly relevant argument in the debate is how to achieve the Kyoto targets in CO_2 reduction without the nuclear capacity. Nuclear power is receiving renewed emphasis in the USA as well, under the 2005 Energy Policy Act, with incentives for the development and siting of advanced nuclear technologies.

The primary effect of these types of policy uncertainty is to create real option values. The real options model, as developed by Dixit and Pindyck (1994) says that project valuations and thereby the investment decision should include the potential spin-offs on future prospects and/or other projects. Brealey and Myers (2003) discuss four different real options: the option to expand, the option to wait and learn, the option to shrink or abandon, and the option to vary the mix of production methods. Of these, the second is the most important for our purposes. Uncertainty around environmental or nuclear policy creates a real option value *if* it is profitable to wait and see. The CO_2 ETS is good environmental policy, but its uncertainty will affect investment in two ways. First, we should expect a delay of investment. Second, as the relative cost of various technologies is uncertain, a stronger diversification in different technologies is likely. Overall policy uncertainty on primary fuels tends to delay investment as a wait-and-see effect.

2.3 Cost of Capital: Regulation of the Network

The 'buffering hypothesis' put forth by Peltzman (1976, p. 230) explains the effect of market risk on the regulated firm:

> Regulation should reduce conventional measures of owner risk. By buffering the firm against demand and cost changes, the variability of profits and stock prices should be lower than otherwise. To the extent that the cost and demand changes are economy-wide, regulation should reduce systematic as well as diversifiable risk.[5]

The crucial factor is how much of the shocks can be passed through to customers. Profit-maximizing prices of a firm with market power pass through only part of the demand and cost shocks, absorbing the remainder; consequently, profits vary with demand and cost shocks. Under an extreme notion of rate-of-return regulation (i.e. with a zero regulatory gap), the firm passes through all of the shocks in order to stick to the allowed rate of return. The investment in the rate-of-return regulated firm gives moderate, but safe returns.

The story changes for firms regulated with a price cap. Restricting attention to systematic, non-diversifiable risks, Wright *et al.* (2003) examine the case of price caps in detail. They conclude that the cost of capital is higher under price-cap regulation than for an unregulated firm if there is cost uncertainty.[6] This is intuitive because, if costs change while prices stay the same, the variability in profits will be strong. With demand uncertainty, the cost of capital is lower under price-cap regulation than without regulation. In this case, the price cap works as the buffer under rate-of-return regulation. The fact that the firm is not allowed to increase the price (to adjust to a demand increase) and, with a binding cap, does not wish to decrease the price (to adjust to a demand decrease) means that the volatility of profits is less under the price cap than it would be if the firm would freely adjust to demand changes.

In practice, rate-of-return and price-cap regulation are quite similar. As has been explained by Joskow (1989), in the USA rate hearings to adjust

---

[5] Brennan and Schwartz (1982) confirm the claim with a formal and numerical approach.
[6] Except for the case of complete cost-pass-through.

utility tariffs can be triggered by either the firm or the regulatory commission, but as long as tariffs fall within a reasonable range nothing happens, and the endogenous regulatory lag can be quite long. Grout and Zalewska (2003) present a study on the effect of different regulatory regimes on risk as measured by CAPM. They study the effect of profit-sharing regimes in the UK during the second half of the 1990s. Profit sharing should here be seen as an explicit modification of price-cap regulation in order to reallocate high profits made by the firms under the price-cap regulation. The authors define profit sharing as a weighted average of the outcome under rate-of-return regulation and the outcome under price-cap regulation where the weight is the profit-sharing factor. The econometric analysis confirms that profit sharing lowers the risk and thus the cost of capital.

As underinvestment becomes a more serious threat, rate-of-return regulation will become more attractive *ceteris paribus*. We would expect to observe an increasing tendency to shorten and/or endogenize the regulatory lag. Modifying the price-cap rules with an explicit profit-sharing rule may be an interesting hybrid. The task is to design a profit-sharing rule which reduces risk while at the same time retaining the virtues of a price-cap rule. After 15 years of low investment activity, the distribution price control 2005–10 in the UK illustrates well. In response to very substantial requests for investment allowances by the network operators, the UK regulator, Ofgem, fearing to frustrate required new investment, installed a menu of sliding scales. Firms with high investment requirements should self-select a larger cost-pass-through element.

2.4 *Time Inconsistency and the Non-commitment Problem*

The inability of regulators credibly to commit to an implicitly or explicitly agreed rate of return creates uncertainty over the regulator's behaviour. The problem, as mentioned earlier, is that investors will expect asymmetric capping of revenues and a subsequent decrease in expected returns. The cost of capital, however, might be unaffected in this case.

The policy question is how to achieve consistency in the regulated rate of return. A seminal contribution on this topic is Myers' (1972) study of the 'fair' rate of return in regulation. Myers argues in favour of a competitive benchmark implying the use of a 'conscious' regulatory lag (thereby arguing for a price-cap regulation *avant la lettre*). The emphasis is on making the concept of a fair rate of return operational and centred on short-run efficiency effects.[7] He notes that the risk for firms might be higher than under rate-of-return regulation without lags and that *ex ante* price capping might allow (excessively) high profits.

The electric power industry in the USA provides a critical illustration of regulatory uncertainty, which may or may not indicate opportunism. The power industry in the USA has long been regulated by rate-of-return regulation, whereby costly and time consuming rate hearings are required to revise electric tariffs. These rate hearings establish an endogenous regulatory gap and cause prices to be sticky (especially upward). In the 1970s, fuel prices rose, demand growth stagnated, and rate hearings were triggered. Joskow (1989) argues the increasing energy prices put regulators under pressure to disallow price rises. In effect, a used-and-useful clause was applied *ex post* to, especially, nuclear power plants. The used-and-useful clause mandates that project costs can only be passed through if their economic value is higher than the accounting costs. Lyon and Mayo (2000) estimate that some $19 billion of investment was not allowed; while they attribute the bulk of these disallowances to management imprudence, substantial disallowances concerned excess capacity. In our view, the distinction is crucially important: scrutiny of managerial imprudence is in line with regulatory consistency, but breaching the regulatory contract in the face of excess capacity is opportunistic behaviour. Joskow (1989, p. 161) notes critically that: 'utilities learned that if they built large new generating plants, they might very well not recover their investment: commissions might resist large rate increases even if the increases were fully justified'.

For firms subject to a disallowance, Lyon and Mayo (2000) find that the propensity to invest did decline (and moderately so for nuclear investment by other utilities in the same state). This characterizes the non-commitment problem: if the regulator cannot credibly commit to its announced policy, it will frustrate investment.[8] Stated with some reservation, Lyon and Mayo's analysis suggests a used-and-useful rule applied against bad management is consistent regulatory policy and does not have adverse spillover effects; at the same time, when application of the rule is a breach of regulatory contract it increases uncertainty (asymmetrically) and adversely affects investment. The distinction between a regulator's consistency and opportunism is ultimately for the investors to decide.

---

[7] Note that the traditional rate of regulation in the USA did have a regulatory lag but that this has not been conscious but rather *ad hoc* (cf. Joskow, 1974, 1989).

[8] They also find that the reputational spillover effect on non-nuclear investment is small or even positive, which is counter-intuitive. The argument may be that the spillover effect (which reduces investment) is compensated by better investment opportunities in non-nuclear assets.

Gilbert and Newbery (1994) offer an interesting perspective on the used-and-useful rule under rate-of-return regulation (UUROR). In essence, the used-and-useful clause may strike a good balance between pure rate-of-return and price-cap regulation. Under pure rate-of-return regulation the regulator has been constrained constitutionally to allow a fair return on investment. This may lower firms' risk, but it is well known that it induces overinvestment. Under price-cap regulation the regulator is not (constitutionally) constrained to allow a fair rate of return. In this case, regulators may be tempted to deviate from previously announced policies and will have difficulty committing not to do so. Anticipating this, firms will tend to underinvest. By permitting the regulator to disallow extreme and unreasonable outcomes, UUROR decreases the regulator's incentives to cheat and thereby increases his credibility. At the same time, proper application of the used-and-useful clause mitigates the goldplating incentives of pure rate-of-return regulation.

3. Evidence of Supply Adequacy

3.1 Generation Adequacy

Empirical evidence, while inconclusive, suggests some reason for concern about future generation adequacy. In most cases we will adopt the generation reserve margin as an indicator of adequacy, which is defined as the difference between installed capacity and peak demand as a ratio of installed capacity.[9] The OECD (2002, pp. 22–3) provides reserve margins for OECD countries for the period 1985–99. Over that period the reserve margin was stable at approximately 33 per cent in Europe. In the Asia Pacific region margins fluctuated between 25 per cent and 35 per cent. Notably, the US reserve margin dropped steadily from 30 per cent to a low 16 per cent in 1999.

Figure 1 shows the reserve margin across the contiguous USA between 1991 and 2002.[10] The picture is typical—a significant decline with recent recovery. Margins were at their lowest during the period after plans for

[9] We note that numbers on generation adequacy presented by different institutions may be difficult to compare since indicators such as reserve margin, capacity margin, and reserve factors are quite often defined in varying terms. Moreover, installed capacity is not always fully adjusted for capacity that is not (or only partly) available, reserves and planned outages, and mothballed and import capacity.

[10] We label the graph with 'capacity margin' as in the source, although the figure depicts 'reserve margins' according to our definition. The numbers are calculated as: (capacity resources – net internal demand)/capacity resources.

Figure 1 USA Reserve Margin 1991–2002

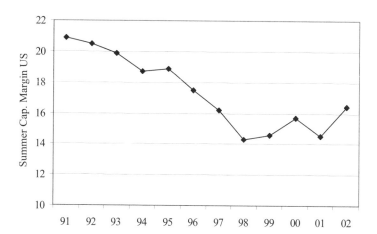

Source: EIA Electricity Power Annual (2002 Table 3.2).

deregulation were under way, but before definitive commitments were made (i.e. 1997–9 or the time between FERC orders 888 and 2000). Rebounding occurred around the time of FERC's order 2000. The data are what we would expect if policy uncertainty was affecting investment. Numbers from the EIA (2002, table 3.2) and the OECD (2003, p. 372) suggest substantial capacity additions from 2000 onward, most notably in gas plant. The picture is suggestive of industry waiting to see how the deregulation process would unfold. FERC orders 888 and 2000 dealt primarily with open and transparent transmission access and rules for creating Regional Transmission Operators (RTOs), but within the 1996–2000 period, policies on competition at the wholesale and retail levels also began to take shape. To some extent the later increase in margins was due to merchant investments that were later untenable. Joskow (2003) describes this period as a boom–bust cycle in electricity that was not unlike the high-tech bubble of the same time. As the bubble burst many proposed projects were abandoned.

Figure 2 shows 'remaining capacity' in the UCTE area.[11] The UCTE compares remaining capacity with a reserve of 5 per cent of installed capacity, which is considered to be reasonable; this is depicted by the

[11] The UCTE covers a large part of Europe except the Nordic countries, Great Britain, and Ireland. Remaining capacity is defined as guaranteed capacity less peak load. Guaranteed capacity is installed capacity minus non-usable capacity (including wind) and reserves (some 6 per cent of installed capacity).

Figure 2 UCTE Forecast of Remaining Capacity

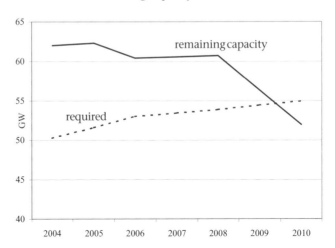

Source: UCTE (2003*b*).

dotted line in Figure 2. If remaining capacity falls below the 5 per cent reserve margin, scarcity problems may occur. The estimates of UCTE suggest that margins should increase slightly in the next 2 or 3 years, but fall noticeably after 2007.

Forecasts for 2007 and beyond are typically pessimistic, which may be a systematic effect at least partly due to a lack of information on new, unknown, or undeclared additions and decommissions. These calculations exclude future capacity additions but also decommissions. Additions and decommissions do not cancel each other, however, since capacity should grow as demand grows, and in normal circumstances there will be relatively more additions. Hence, the decline of the estimated reserve margin may be indicative of what is required but should not be interpreted as conclusive evidence that there will be a shortage. We have examined NERC and UCTE forecasts in more detail. Using the NERC's Reliability Assessment Studies (from 1997 to 2004) and UCTE's System Adequacy Forecast (from 2001 to 2006), we conclude that the forecasts are indeed systematically pessimistically biased: projected reserve margins further in the future are systematically lower. Normalizing the projected reserve margin on the year the projections were made, we conducted a non-linear regression:

$$y = \beta_1 + \beta_2 x + \beta_3 x^2$$

where y is the normalized projected reserve margin and x is the difference between the year for which the projection was made and the year in which the projection was made. Hence, if the projection was made in 2000 for the year 2005, then x is 5. The claim is that y falls with x. The results of the regressions are (with t-statistics in parenthesis):

$$\beta_1 = 1.007727 \ (37.690)$$
$$\beta_2 = 0.020444 \ (1.377)$$
$$\beta_3 = -0.005240 \ (-3.245)$$

For the overall test, F= 24.8 and R^2 = 0.33. Of the parameters, both β_1 and β_3 are significant, while β_2 is not significant. We should note that, rather than revealing a bias, the regression might indicate a decline of real reserve margins if there happens to be a monotonic downward trend. Checking real numbers in the sources (the $x = 0$ or 1 values in these studies) quickly reveals that for 1997 and beyond there is no such trend. In fact, and quite surprisingly, if anything the reserve margin increased. Thus, we conclude that the projected reserve margins are systematically biased downward.

This means that a picture as in Figure 2, which at first glance may be worrying, will be the same next year, with only the scales adjusted. NERC and UCTE are aware of this problem. UCTE adjusted its studies by distinguishing between a 'conservative' and 'best-estimate' scenario. The conservative scenario only includes 'known' capacity additions; the best-estimate scenario includes 'reasonably probable' projects. If, in addition, there are 'unknown' projects (perhaps because market parties treat these confidentially or because these projects have not been planned yet) we find that future reserve margins may in fact be sufficient. This does not mean that NERC and UCTE should include unknown projects in their projections, but rather that interpretations of these forecasts should be made with reservation.

The numbers above are highly aggregated and the details matter. Estimations of the reserve margins in the Netherlands (TenneT, 2004) indicate strong reliance on imports, for example. Reserve margins including import capacity are at safe levels, but excluding import capacity the reserve margin drops to 4 per cent in 2011. High import dependence is concerning for strategic reasons, since interconnector capacity is scarce and because not all countries can rely on imports at the same time. Likewise, heavy reliance on imports rather than inland generation capacity may result in problematic unplanned exchanges at the interconnectors. Yet, after initial worries, 2005 data suggest that new generation capacity is sufficient. For Germany, capacity numbers highlight the growing importance of renewables which have an impact on generation adequacy (cf. Brunekreeft and Twelemann, 2005). Wind energy has low reliability and scheduled availability is usually 20 per cent or lower. Consequently, while German generation capacity looks sufficient in the aggregate, remaining capacity (taking proper account of wind) is rather low.[12] Hence, wind turbines may be good for the environment but do little for generation adequacy according to these definitions. As in the Netherlands, though, plans for new investment are promising. Although no agency knows exactly, numbers floating around in the media suggest plans for about 25 GW of new generation investment in conventional fuels, roughly half gas (based on old gas contracts) and half coal and lignite (cf. Brunekreeft and Bauknecht, 2006). The investment announcements stem from incumbents and new entrants, for instance distributors/retailers who, faced with increasing wholesale power prices, integrate backward. An interesting question is how much of these announcements is credible and how much is cheap talk. The incumbents, in particular, may have incentives to announce new generation capacity to keep others from doing so. This kind of cheap talk, or preemptive announcement, seems to have two effects. First, it may unduly keep third parties out of the market. Second, it might flatten out investment cycles. The former effect is discussed in, for example, Farrell (1987). The latter effect would result if system operators are overly pessimistic when projecting future capacity; i.e. pessimistic reporting by the system operator (SO) signals high future prices, which should incentivize investors. Overly pessimistic reporting would incentivize too much investment, which the cheap talk announcements might temper.

Roques *et al.* (2004, pp. 12 ff.) provide a detailed analysis of market response to scarcity signals in the England and Wales (EW) market. At the introduction of NETA (which among other things replaced a system of capacity payments with an energy-only market) in 2001, there was excess capacity in EW and post-NETA wholesale prices have been (very) low. Capacity margins have dropped substantially as plant has been mothballed and new projects postponed. Following a low reserve margin and further plant-closure announcements, NGT, the Transmission System Operator (TSO), announced in May 2003 that the reserve margin might fall as low as 16.2 per cent in the winter 2003/4. Forward prices responded

---

[12] On the other hand, as wind is indigenous it adds to supply security by reducing dependence on gas imports.

immediately, which subsequently brought back mothballed capacity to the system, restoring the reserve margin.[13] Thus it appears that the market handled the first stress test well. Yet, this response was short term and relied on mothballed capacity; there is no indication in this case about new investment.

Capacity margins in the Nordic countries have also grown thin and, as noted by von der Fehr *et al.* (2004, p. 12), investment has been very low. They call this occurrence 'one of the most important successes of regulatory reforms in the Nordic countries'. They note that the reduction is simply a reduction of excess capacity and that the wholesale prices and the rate of return on capital in the electricity supply industry (ESI) had been very low (5.5 per cent). Since 2000, the rate of return has been increasing and has almost caught up with the average value of manufacturing industries. This is an important point. It may well be that the recent decline in reserve margins reflects reductions in excess capacity, rather than an indication of insufficient investment incentives.

3.2 Network Adequacy

The evidence on network adequacy is similar but less clear. Whereas network capacity is largely demand driven and may be adequate, interconnector capacity has become short, increased trading congests network corridors, networks are ageing, and investment levels have been low. Figure 3 shows network capacity over peak demand for the USA. The substantial downward trend in the USA is striking, but it is not *a priori* clear what this trend tells us. First, Hirst (2004) notes that this has been a trend since the early 1980s and thus it is unlikely to be (solely) the effect of liberalization. Second, an existing grid can be optimized in use and design, facilitating higher network load. Third, planned grid expansions are often delayed by environmental permission obstacles. Fourth, since the 1980s power plants have become smaller. One should expect that with decentralization of power generation, capacity of the high-voltage grid can be reduced *ceteris paribus*. Fifth, generation and transmission capacity can be traded off to some extent. Lastly, grid capacity did grow in the last two decades, but peak load grew faster: lumpiness and scale economies in construction caused networks to be 'oversized', while utilization has improved.[14]

[13] Since the actual prices were lower than futures prices, which had predominantly been determined by mothballed and subsequently reactivated plant, one wonders whether traders have been fooled and whether (and how long) gaming by the producers is possible.
[14] These caveats notwithstanding, networks are ageing and need substantial investment to be modernized.

Figure 3 Network Capacity in the USA

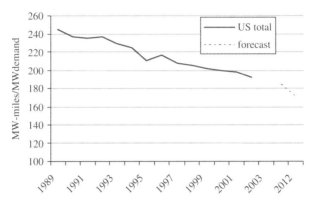

Note: Capacity over the system's peak load.
Source: Hirst (2004).

Other arguments for a slowdown in grid growth are directly or indirectly related to liberalization and regulation. Under the 'gold-plating' hypothesis, rate-of-return regulation resulted in excess capacity with inefficiently high reliability. Thus, reduced capacity margins partly reflect a reduction in excess capacity. Also, demand growth up to the late 1970s and early 1980s had been large but fell steeply after that. The sudden decrease in demand growth exaggerated excess capacity.

In both Europe and the USA, network capacity has been affected by increased trading—an indirect effect of deregulation. UCTE data suggest that cross-border exchanges in the UCTE area increased from about 200 TWh in 1999 to 300 TWh in 2003. The European Commission (CEC, 2002b) outlines substantial congestion on European interconnectors. Bialek (2004) argues that increased trade and reliance on the existing networks causes many of the current reliability problems. Vertically integrated firms may lack strong incentives to increase interconnector capacity as this would increase competition. Moreover, approval procedures are cumbersome and lengthy. Sometimes two sides of one interconnector may be authorized to give approval; this is typically a problem if energy prices increase on the exporting side of the interconnector. Further, regulation and, in particular, regulatory uncertainty, impede new investment. Recent policies in both the USA and Europe address network investment. The 2005 Energy Policy Act, the first formal renewal of energy guidelines in the USA in 13 years, includes provisions that substantially increase federal powers and oversight regarding network investment. Under the Act reliability standards become mandatory as opposed to voluntary, provisions are made for expedited siting of transmission capacity (including on private land), and federal utilities must participate in Regional Transmission Organizations. In Europe, Art. 6(6) of the regulation for cross-border exchanges prescribes that cross-border congestion revenues should be used to lower network charges or be reinvested in network investment lowering congestion. As these congestion revenues are substantial, there is scope for considerable new network investment in the near future. A good example is the recent approval of the interconnector between Norway and the Netherlands, NorNed.

There is also concern that the price-cap regulation impedes network investment. The arguments here are threefold. The first argument relates to accounting. Depending on accounting rules (i.e. whether historic or current cost accounting is employed), a significant new investment requires higher charges and hence a revision of the price cap. Second, as pointed out in section 2, price-cap regulation worsens the ability of regulators to commit to pre-announced policies. Third, there is justified concern that price-cap regulation impedes quality of supply (QoS) investment, which is an important indicator of network adequacy (and reliability). With fixed prices, quality will be lower than optimal (Spence, 1975). In the short run, price caps set a rather straightforward incentive to cut costs at the expense of quality. In the long run, as prices and demand adjust, these effects are mitigated. Because the classical form of rate-of-return regulation induces excessive quality, one might expect quality to go down in many cases as a result of implementing price-cap regulation.

CPB (2004) studied QoS in electricity networks in the UK and Norway and found similar developments. Figure 4 shows the development for the price-capped electricity networks in the UK since liberalization expressed in duration of supply interruptions. There is no clear pattern in unplanned outages but planned outages have gone down. The first is good news and suggests that the quality degradation under price caps may be moderate. The reduction in planned outages may be caused by reduced maintenance, and thus the associated short-run gain in quality may be bought at the expense of future lower quality. This explanation is convincing but one expects to see it manifest in higher unplanned outages at some point. Perhaps it is too early to see this effect. Also the reduction in planned outages could be the result of better managed maintenance.

Figure 4 Duration of Supply Interruptions in the UK

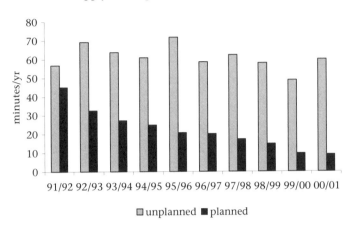

Source: CPB (2004, p. 77).

A last indication of the network adequacy is the investment activity. The OECD (2003) report suggests significant investment activity. Under the EU-TEN programme, 23,000 MW of additional transmission capacity inside or to the EU is planned, which is substantial. Figures for Germany (Brunekreeft and Twelemann, 2005) suggest that the 'downward' trend in investment seems to have stabilized and investment may in fact be increasing again. The picture in the UK looks the same (JESS, 2003, p. 37). In the Nordic countries investment is low, but according to von der Fehr *et al.* (2004, p. 17), there is no lack of initiative, but 'it would seem that regulatory and political will, rather than commercial will, is going to be decisive'.

4. Good Policy

4.1 *How to Secure Generation Adequacy?*

Determining an optimal capacity level (including capacity reserves) must take account of outside options (e.g. imports), the cost of peaking capacity, and the VOLL—which will vary internationally and regionally depending on the social cost of outages. The optimal capacity level trades off a reduction in lost load (greater capacity) and an increase in the cost of meeting load (smaller capacity) (Stoft, 2002).

The energy-only view of optimal investment suggests that energy prices alone are sufficient to induce adequate generation investment.[15] The energy-only paradigm might also include VOLL pricing since efficient bargaining dictates that trading should only occur when willingness to pay exceeds the cost of production. During periods of scarcity the system operator purchases power on behalf of consumers; capping the purchase price at VOLL would ensure that he never paid more than consumers' maximum reservation value. While this is economically attractive and theoretically produces optimal investment, it is a high-risk means of securing investment since political reality is such that high but intermittent price spikes will yield erratic profit cycles for producers (Stoft, 2002) and possibly invite regulatory intervention.

In addition to (though not necessarily independent from) problems of political uncertainties, examples in section 2 show that energy prices have so far not been high enough for sufficient duration to cover the cost of peaking plant. There is also some debate over the public-good aspect of operating reserves. Joskow and Tirole (2004) use the case of a system collapse, resulting from the outage of a given generator or transmission line, as an illustration. Also, the public-good view is embodied in Stoft's second demand-side flaw discussed earlier. Since the SO cannot enforce bilateral contracts between producers and load that rely on the transmission network, individual customers cannot be shut down (or left on line) when there is load shedding. Thus, the consumer cannot pay for the property right to a given level of reliability.

An alternative to an energy-only market is to institute a capacity market with the aim of increasing the regulator's credibility. Capacity markets use either price or quantity methods to set incentives for investment. Price incentives take the form of capacity payments, such as accompanied the former power Pool in EW. With capacity payments, generators declared available during a dispatch time period receive a payment (even if they are not dispatched).[16] Even though capacity margins remained high throughout the life of the Pool in EW, the capacity payment was widely criticized for being open to manipulation. This method is arguably transparent, however, and uncertainties surrounding market power can be minimized if there are outside options to deal with anti-competitive behaviour. That was the case in England and Wales since the regulator could refer companies to the Monopolies and Merger Commission (now

---

[15] Texas is an energy-only market with bilateral contracting between LSEs and producers. LSEs must also contract for ancillary services. Relative to California, Texas has surplus generating capacity (adding 4.3 GW of new capacity in 2003) and has added over 850 miles of new transmission lines since 1999. As discussed earlier, EW is now an energy-only market.

[16] Argentina, Colombia, and Spain use capacity payments.

the Competition Commission). In the USA, market monitoring units accompany newly established RTOs and these units can monitor and investigate potential manipulation of market rules. On the other hand, Stoft (2002) discusses risk and market power as two side-effects of reliability policy. Since capacity payments relying on VOLL pricing have high but uncertain, infrequent price spikes, investors would face high risk, and high price spikes invite market power abuse. Consequently, one would expect political uncertainty to be high under this method.

Quantity methods to procure reserve capacity are either centralized or decentralized, the former involving contracts between the SO and producers and/or load, and the latter involving contracts between producers and load.[17] One advantage of quantity alternatives relative to pricing alternatives is that the SO has some control over the magnitude and duration of price spikes. As discussed in Stoft (2002), the social/political acceptability of price spikes depends on their size and duration. A mechanism that produces low spikes more often has three benefits: (i) it is likely to be more acceptable, (ii) it would be less risky for investors, and (iii) it would be less susceptible to market power. Two such methods include operating reserve pricing and capacity obligations.

Under operating reserve pricing the SO determines the amount of capacity to be held in reserve, leaving the market to provide sufficient capacity for the energy market. The SO has two instruments: a maximum willingness to pay for reserves and the level of reserve capacity. The price the SO has to pay for reserve capacity is inversely related to the size of the reserve level. This holds for two reasons: (i) the more power contracted as reserve, the less there is available to be bid in the energy market, and (ii) the SO can always reduce the reserve requirement (up to available capacity). The opportunity cost to a generator of contracting with the SO is the price he could obtain in the energy market. If the gap between demand and available capacity is large, the opportunity cost is small, so the SO can maintain a large reserve without paying much for it. As the gap gets smaller, the SO can release reserve capacity into the energy market (i.e. reduce the size of the reserve) while maintaining the price he is willing to pay. At some point, however, as the capacity gap closes, the opportunity cost for generators rises above the SO's willingness to pay, and the SO can only attract more reserves by paying more for them. The price in periods when reserves are dispatched would optimally be set at the cost of the marginal generator who is not included as part of the reserve.

---

[17] Our explanation of quantity alternatives closely follows Stoft (2002) and de Vries (2004).

The SO can make this price higher (lower) by decreasing (increasing) the reserve level. A lower reserve level increases the duration of price spikes necessary for new investments.

Reserve pricing can be augmented by long-term contracts. This would strengthen the price signals to investors and lessen arbitrariness and discretion in setting the reserve capacity level. The Dutch Ministry of Economic Affairs has recently recommended that the SO, TenneT, make broader use of (auctioning) long-term contracts to secure adequacy.[18] TenneT worked out a 'safety net' approach: expanding reserve requirements increases shortage on the day-ahead market and should be expected to increase power prices which in turn triggers new investment. Following announcements of substantial decentralized generation investment, TenneT decided to set the size of the 'safety net' at zero, thereby indicating that intervention is momentarily unnecessary. Market-friendly extensions of reserve capacity pricing discussed by Vázquez *et al.* (2002) and Oren (2004) would allow the use of (call) options to procure reserve capacity.

US capacity markets aimed at securing long-term adequacy are decentralized, requiring individual LSEs to obtain resources to meet their obligations (usually through bilateral contracts with generators).[19] The additional market for their capacity should induce generators to invest in capacity beyond that required to meet peak load, and because contractual obligations can be traded in secondary markets price discovery is improved. ICAP (installed capacity) markets are used in the PJM, New York, and New England. In PJM, for example, capacity obligations are set such that the system as a whole maintains a loss-of-load expectation of 1 day in 10 years. Under this mechanism, generally LSEs pay a penalty if they have not contracted with generators for the required surplus power or met shortfalls through interruptible contracts with consumers. The penalty becomes the indifference price between contracting for surplus power or being short, and so sets the price for capacity contracts when they are scarce (de Vries, 2004). If the length of the contract period is too short, generators will renege on their contractual obligations during times when the spot price is above the penalty price. Requiring yearly contracts and annualizing the penalty surpasses this

[18] The Brattle Group study of 2004 recommended focusing contracts on peaking plant since a large part of peaking capacity in the Netherlands is likely to retire over the next 5 years; for the longer-term reserve capacity, quick-response spinning reserves normally provided by base load are not required and slow-response capacity provided by peak plant is cheaper.

[19] ICAP requirements in the USA are approximately 118 per cent of peak load (Stoft, 2002).

problem (Stoft, 2002). Vázquez *et al.* (2002) criticize capacity obligations because only the price is determined by competition, while the quantity that producers are allowed to sell is administered—a problem if there is a large amount of non-thermal generation on the system.

Relative to energy-only markets or VOLL pricing, capacity mechanisms reduce the level but increase the duration of price spikes, giving generators a more consistent revenue stream and lowering investment risk. Moreover, in an energy-only market the price signal for new investment occurs as *demand* approaches *available supply*. With capacity targets this price signal occurs much sooner since the market becomes tight as *demand plus target* approaches *available supply*, so the investment signal arises in advance of capacity need. The size of the target will determine how soon scarcity is reached and thus the timing of the investment signal. There is a trade-off with capacity mechanisms; capacity will be adequate, but prices will be higher on average than with energy-only markets. Generators' arbitrage opportunities between the energy and capacity market will determine the 'adequacy premium'.

4.2 Policy for Network Adequacy

The time inconsistency problem, as set out in section 2.4, lies at the heart of network investment. The policy question is about who regulates the regulator or, in other words, 'good market governance'. Hancher *et al.* (2003, p. 356) define good governance as: 'the search for the best set of all laws, regulations, processes and practices that affect the functioning of a regulatory framework and the market'. Amidst a list of aspects, we think two stand out for the regulation of the complex network industries: independence and flexible powers.

Helm *et al.* (2003, p. 444) note two basic remedies for the time inconsistency problem: delegation to an independent agency, and reduction in the number of regulatory objectives. Much of the background literature on time inconsistency is on monetary policy, where the objective translates into a committed inflation target.[20] Some revision of this literature is required to target better the specifics of the ESI, but an independent agent in charge of economic regulation is recommendable.

Independence has been well formulated by Ocana (2003, p. 17) as meaning 'that the regulatory agency is protected from short-term political interference'. Indeed, a regulator with the authority to create and divide rents will be subject to capture by politics. The politician is likely to have

---

[20] See Blackburn and Christensen (1989) for a good survey.

different aims from the regulator. Politicians, subject to re-elections, will tend to have a higher 'political discount factor', and will therefore have a stronger tendency to 'make hay while the sun shines'.[21] Also, politicians will typically have multiple objectives (economic and social concerns), whereas, as Helm *et al.* (2003, p. 444) point out, with delegation the number of objectives per agency can be reduced. This means that a regulator could be mandated to have an economic objective while leaving social objectives to the politicians (who would apply different instruments than economic regulation).[22]

The effect of political interference can go two ways, depending on ownership. If the state is owner of the regulated industry it will have an interest in high prices and subsequent profits. On the other hand, if the regulated industry is fully private, the state may follow consumer interests and pursue low prices. In that case, the industry runs into the hold-up problem as outlined above.

Independence of regulators requires careful formulation of regulators' authority, and control of the use of powers is a key issue. As mentioned above, it is in general desirable to delegate a small number of clear and unambiguous objectives. This also allows assessing the agency's use of powers along the objectives. This, however, is simply not straightforward for regulation of electricity networks. There is no single one-size-fits-all objective. Too detailed formulation is likely to become unworkable for complex and dynamic sectors like network industries. It seems an impossible task to design a complete regulatory contract, without having to modify it frequently. Not only will legal adjustment be slow and costly, but the regulator will also be vulnerable to legal challenge. It appears inevitable to formulate a mandate in more general terms (social welfare or consumer interests) and preferably different from the political objectives. Yet, this will in general require that the regulator should be given the authority to interpret the law: i.e. the regulator should have flexible powers. Hence, for the regulation in the ESI, independence requires flexible powers to interpret the law.

The story of the regulated (electricity) charges in the Netherlands illustrates this well.[23] The regulator for energy markets in the Netherlands is DTe, which is a chamber of the competition agency, NMa, which is a supervisory body of the Ministry of Economics. Under RPI – X regulation

---

[21] The terms are derived in analogy to the management–shareholder relation as set out in Vickers and Yarrow (1988, p. 21), who use the term 'managerial discount factor'.

[22] The term 'political unbundling' suggests itself.

[23] The interested reader may be referred to Hancher *et al.* (2003) and Nillesen and Pollitt (2004) for more detail.

DTe decided correctly to apply individual X_is to firms for the first regulation period (2001–3), after which it could reasonably be expected that firms would have caught up and a non-individual yardstick could then be applied in the second regulation period. The X_is determined by DTe in the first round were high and subsequently appealed by the firms. Appeals against DTe decisions are the responsibility of the Court of Appeal for Trade and Industry (CBB), which makes judicial reviews rather than testing for substance. CBB decided the law did not allow individual X-factors and the regulation had to be revised. This suggests a system flaw. On the one hand, one would like to give DTe flexible powers to interpret the law; on the other hand, one would like to constrain DTe's authority. Since there is no substance review, the judicial review by the Appeal Court restricted DTe's power to interpret the law, at the expense of good substance.[24]

Two approaches mitigate the apparent incompatibility of independence and flexible powers. First, the design of a governance system of checks and balances. Second, changing the regulator's incentives. A system of checks and balances between regulators and the competition commission (CC) has been developed in the UK (see Green, 1999, and Geroski, 2004), but the process can become complex.[25] Green (1999) discusses that regulators have to abide by the CC's recommendations following a referral. The inevitable result is that the regulators start to anticipate and mimic the CC's procedures, thereby undermining the system of checks and balances. A strong system of checks and balances requires different institutions to have different mandates and possibly to accentuate different interests (for a similar argument, see Laffont and Martimort, 1999). However, this prompts the question of who decides in case of disagreement. The following suggestion strikes a balance. First, regulators should have a clearly specified mandate. In the context of the time-inconsistency problems that delay investment, we propose that social welfare might be a more appropriate objective than consumer surplus (which reduces weights on shareholders' interests).[26] A court can judicially review whether the regulator acts according to the objectives set

---

[24] The ruling had several consequences. First, the law was modified retrospectively to allow individual X-factors. Second, the X-factors had to be adjusted again. Finally, in May 2003, the final X-factors were agreed with the sector; this was only months before the end of the regulatory period.

[25] See Vol. 12 (2004) of *Utilities Policy* which is a special issue on the UK.

[26] As pointed out by Helm *et al.* (2003), one is tempted to argue that given delegation, the government should be responsible for social objectives and not the regulator.

by the legislator. Second, a system of checks and balances of different institutions can guarantee a check on substance.

Geroski (2004) describes a two-tier approach for the UK with the sector regulators in the first tier and the CC in the second tier. According to Geroski (p. 78, italics added), the CC is: 'an investigative body with the expertise to decide on issues of *substance*'. Interestingly, the CC has determinative powers for most regulators, but in the case of the regulation of airport landing charges it can only make non-binding recommendations. Where CC decisions are determinative, firms can appeal for judicial review by the Competition Appeal Tribunal.

An alternative approach is to change the regulator's incentives. The approach of increasing independence is akin to an 'incentive mechanism'; the idea is to reduce incentives to behave opportunistically (or myopically) by increasing the 'regulatory discount factor'. Further, the analysis of UUROR by Gilbert and Newbery (1994), as set out above, represents an incentive change. As they explain, specifying that assets should be 'used and useful' reduces the regulator's incentive to deviate from the (optimal) regulatory contract after the investment. Overall, rate-of-return regulation provides a better commitment to a fair rate of return than price-cap regulation. As explained in section 2.3, profit-sharing can be a promising hybrid. Lastly, suppose that complete regulatory independence from political interference is an illusion and suppose further that it is correct that the state's incentives to capture the regulator depend on ownership of the regulated industry. If the state is owner, the state will want to have high prices, while if the industry is privately owned the state will press for low prices. The logical conclusion must be that private–public ownership might strike a balance on the incentives of the state. This view adds another dimension to the privatization debate.

5. Concluding Remarks

This chapter identifies and analyses key sources of policy uncertainty which impede investment incentives in the electric power industry. New investment critically determines long-term system reliability, which is captured by the term supply adequacy, covering both generation and network adequacy. The benchmark in this chapter is that symmetric, non-systematic, diversifiable risk without (future) spin-offs has no effect on investment. We have thus constrained attention to asymmetric uncertainty, non-diversifiable risk, and uncertainties creating a real option value. We use the term policy uncertainty in a broad sense to cover the effects of uncertain regulation where it already exists, the effects of market risks under different types of regulation, and, importantly, the mere possibility of an intervention where no policy exists or where policy is vague.

For generation adequacy the short-run outlook is optimistic, as are stress tests, but the long-run perspective gives cause for concern. Calculations suggest that hands-off, energy-only markets and resulting prices might simply not suffice to attract sufficient new investment in peaking plant. This is supported by three observations. First, it has not yet happened that prices have been high enough and for sufficient duration to cover estimated costs of peaking generation capacity. Second, as discussed by Joskow and Tirole (2004), high prices are extremely sensitive to the discretion of the TSOs. Third, extreme situations are likely to trigger intervention. Hence, the mere possibility of an intervention already asymmetrically caps revenues. Following this line, we put forth the argument that policy expectations can be self-fulfilling, leading to multiple potential equilibria: low-capacity equilibria with interference and high-capacity equilibria without interference.

If the scenario of fulfilled policy expectations is plausible, the second-best option of actually doing something seems inevitable. Hence, a 'better safe than sorry' policy may simply be realistic. To this end, a myriad of capacity mechanisms have been proposed and debated in the literature. Part of this debate centres on the relative merits of price and quantity methods for incentivizing investment. Stoft (2002) notes capacity payments produce higher, more erratic price spikes, implying that quantity measures appear less susceptible to market power abuses. As such, one would also expect quantity measures to invite less regulatory interference. Capacity mechanisms should be flexible and 'market-friendly', including well-defined long-term and secondary contract markets. Reserve pricing fits this description and can include hedging instruments that might be exercised centrally by the system operator or bilaterally between producers and load. A disadvantage relative to capacity 'obligations' is that the SO has discretion over both the quantity of reserves and the willingness to pay for reserves. With obligations, only the quantity is determined by the SO. On the other hand, centralized mechanisms are less risky to LSEs, who are reluctant to sign long-term bilateral contracts with producers when retail competition is active. A challenge for policy is to address ways of lowering regulatory discretion and minimizing distortions from capacity markets on energy and retail markets.

Empirically, with the exceptions of the interconnectors, network investment seems adequate. Declines in network capacity and investment have been observed but this may reflect a reduction of excess capacity and, moreover, the decline may have stabilized. With respect to policy uncertainty there are two lines of argument. First, price-cap regulation is likely to increase market risk compared to no regulation and rate-of-return regulation. Second, regulators may be unable credibly to commit to a consistent regulatory policy and to refrain from opportunistic behaviour. The 'time-inconsistency' (or 'hold-up', or 'non-commitment') problem has received extensive attention in the literature. This is particularly relevant for significant new investment under price caps. Gilbert and Newbery (1994) argue that the so-called used-and-useful rate-of-return regulation may be a way to increase the regulator's credibility, thereby improving investment incentives. Overall, we would expect to see increased use of rate-of-return regulation compared to price-caps if underinvestment in the network gains importance and short-run efficiency gains are exhausted.

Lastly, we discussed the institutional prospects to improve the credibility of the regulators in order to improve the investment climate. Given the key importance of independence from political interference and flexible powers to interpret the law, a system of checks and balances with an institution with jurisdiction on substance is recommended.

12

Effect of Liberalizing UK Retail Energy Markets on Consumers

*Catherine Waddams Price**

1. Introduction

Retail energy markets in the UK were opened between 1996 and 1998 and from 1990 to 2004 retail energy prices in the UK fell. This was partly because feedstock costs were falling world wide, but the government claims that at least some of the price decrease results from the introduction of supplier choice and the removal of price controls. However, the new energy paradigm, described elsewhere in this book, will involve rising costs, in which residential consumers face increasing energy prices, and these will be experienced within a market structure very different from that which prevailed 10 years ago, before retail competition was introduced. This chapter examines the development of the market as it has been deregulated and the effect of those structural changes on consumers, particularly low-income households; and it analyses how far the experience of the market as energy prices fell will be reflected in the impact as prices rise. The analysis focuses on the changes in market structure and

* The support of the Economic and Social Research Council (ESRC) is gratefully acknowledged. This chapter incorporates results from several projects undertaken by the author with others on the deregulation of the UK energy markets. The author is grateful to her co-authors, to Morten Hviid for his advice, and to Laurence Mathieu for research assistance, and to two referees, the editor of the *Oxford Review of Economic Policy*, and participants at seminars at the Universities of Brescia and Tilburg for very helpful comments on earlier versions of this chapter. As usual, she retains responsibility for any sins of omission or commission which remain.

regulation during the last decade, rather than the earlier change in ownership at privatization.

The government demonstrated its concern with the distributional consequences of energy policy by its 2000 reform of the duties of the energy regulator, Ofgem. Not only was the regulator given a new duty to take account of needs of low-income consumers, but formal procedures for the government to provide both social and environmental guidance to the regulator were introduced (Utilities Act, 2000). One outcome of these somewhat non-specific provisions has been an interdepartmental government initiative to eliminate fuel poverty in vulnerable households by 2010 (DTI, 2001*b*). A household is defined as being in fuel poverty if it spends, or needs to spend, more than 10 per cent of its income on household energy requirements; vulnerable households are those containing children or those who are elderly, disabled, or long-term sick. The government has reiterated and strengthened its policy, for example in the Energy White Paper (DTI, 2003) and in its updates to the Fuel Poverty programme (Defra, 2004*b*).

Although fuel poverty is defined in terms of the need to spend more than 10 per cent of household income on energy, authoritative figures on heating *need* are hard to link with other household characteristics, so much analysis relates to households who *do* spend more than a tenth of their income on fuel. Such households are a subset[1] of the fuel poor group that can be classified as 'expenditure fuel poor' (EFP). EFP is generally associated with low income and larger household size (Bennett *et al.*, 2002).

Ofgem claims that its 'main contribution to tackling fuel policy is its work to reduce consumers' energy costs. . . . We ensure competition works for the benefit of all gas and electricity customers, including the vulnerable' (Ofgem, 2003). The government estimates that a total of about 3m households were removed from fuel poverty between 1996 and 2002 as a result of lower energy prices, higher incomes, and improved housing stock, and Ofgem claims that around 1m of these were the result of pressures of regulation and competition. Table 1 shows how residential energy prices have fallen in real terms since 1990, but are now increasing. As fuel bills rise once more, so do the numbers in fuel poverty, expected to reach 3m again by the end of 2006 (energywatch, 2006).

The regulator emphasizes the role of competition in reducing prices and fuel poverty. Competition, and its intensity, may affect both the

---

[1] This assumes that every household which spends more than 10 per cent of income on fuel does, indeed, need to do so.

Table 1. Price Index of Retail Fuels, Relative to Overall Retail Price Index

	Electricity	Gas
1990	100	100
1996	99	93
2000	77	78
2002	75	82
2005	82	94
Fourth quarter 2005	85	99

Source: DTI (2006); based on average consumption levels.

Figure 1 Percentage of Fuel Expenditure in Income

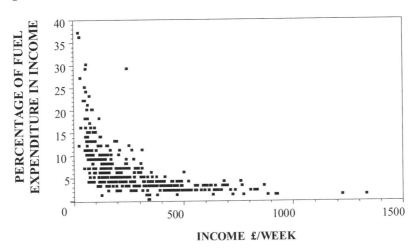

level and the structure of prices. A change in the price *level* affects different households differently because demand for domestic energy increases with income, but at a decreasing rate, as shown in Figure 1.

Low-income groups spend a higher proportion of their income on energy, so that even if all fuel prices change in a similar pattern, the impact on different households varies; an increase or decrease in prices has a proportionately greater effect on low-income than higher-income groups. Low-income groups might also be adversely affected if the *relative* prices which they paid increased compared with others. This second point is discussed in more detail later, and we note that changing market structure may affect price levels or price structures or both.

The next section reviews the reform of the energy industry, focusing on the past 10 years, and section 3 assesses the expected effect of such reforms in the light of the government's own claims that deregulation has benefited low-income consumers (DTI, 2000). Section 4 examines the competitiveness of the market: first, at deregulation; then by looking at indicators of market power and the potential competitive constraint of consumer switching. Section 5 considers price structures from evidence of entrants' and incumbents' behaviour. Section 6 assesses the likely consequence of the current market structure as the sector faces the challenges of climate change and rising costs, and the implications for the government's own targets on fuel poverty; and section 7 concludes.

2. UK Energy Supply and Retail Reform

The residential electricity and gas supply industries each comprises four vertical stages: generation; national high-voltage/pressure transmission; regional and local low-voltage/pressure distribution; and the retail function of sales and billing to final consumers. Key dates in the reform process are shown in Table 2. Gas was privatized in 1986 and electricity in 1990/91. The gas supply industry was originally privatized with transmission, distribution, and retail integrated ('from beachhead to meter'), but regulatory pressure resulted in the separation of transmission and distribution from retail by 1997. The electricity industry in England and Wales was restructured by separating generation from transmission at privatization, but full operating separation of distribution from retail was not enabled by licence separation until 2001. Electricity distribution and retail has traditionally been divided between 14 geographical regions—12 in England and two in Scotland (the supply chain in the two Scottish regions remains vertically integrated). By May 2006 the company which is the incumbent supplier in each of the 14 regions also owned the (monopoly) distribution system in seven of the 14 areas, although they are operated and accounted for separately.

Household energy markets were opened to competition between 1996 and 1999. In gas, competition had become well established for large consumers in the years immediately preceding; as effective competition was established in the industrial market, prices fell much faster than in the (still monopolized) residential market. Primary legislation was required to enable the introduction of competition into the residential gas market. Because the concept of retail competition while the transmission and distribution pipelines remained monopolized was so novel, competition was introduced very gradually in the residential gas market between 1996 and 1998. Following the experience in gas, electricity

Table 2. Key Dates in Retail Energy Market Reform

	Gas	Electricity
Privatization	1986	1990/91
Separation of generation from transmission	pre-privatization	1990/91
Separation of distribution from retail	1997	2001
First consumers can choose suppliers	May 1996	Sept 1998
All consumers can choose suppliers	May 1998	May 1999
Reform of generation market in England and Wales (NETA)		2001
Last price caps removed from incumbents	April 2002	April 2002
Reform of generation market in Scotland (BETTA)		April 2005

markets (where the entry timetable had been included in the privatization legislation) were opened much more quickly between August 1998 and May 1999. Entry into the gas market was assisted by the incumbent's handicap of commitment to long-term contracts which had been struck at prices above those prevailing on the spot market when entrants were obtaining their supplies. Since the product itself is homogeneous, competition focused on price rather than service, and the process was widely seen as determining which of the many entrants would survive in the medium term, when the market was expected to be supplied by 'a handful' of companies.

Residential consumers pay for energy in one of three ways. The traditional method is to await a quarterly meter reading, from which a bill is generated, and pay in arrears, known as 'standard credit'. Because of the poor state of the British housing stock and the potentially large bills generated by such infrequent billing, especially after a winter quarter, prepayment was introduced for some consumers, requiring them to charge a card or key at a local payment outlet and insert it into the meter to release a flow of energy. This method was introduced chiefly for those in debt to the retail company or with poor credit ratings, and is used predominantly by low-income households, particularly for gas. About 11 per cent of gas consumers and 14 per cent of electricity consumers use prepayment (Ofgem, 2006a). The third method of payment is by monthly automated debit from a customer's bank account, known as direct debit; as competition was introduced, retail companies have introduced discounts for direct-debit payers. Of the three methods of payment, automated direct debit is cheapest for the companies; prepayment is the most expensive because it involves the cost of handling frequent cash payments.

352

Before competition was introduced, tariff structures largely reflected those established by the incumbents' nationalized predecessors, namely a fixed rate per consumer for being attached to the distribution system (a standing charge) and a single per-unit charge for energy consumed. There were other structures: in the most common alternative the standing charge is replaced by a much higher per-unit rate for the first units consumed, followed by a lower charge for subsequent units. Sometimes such a two-part tariff is combined with a standing charge. One effect of introducing competition was to increase the variety of tariffs, as well as introduce some innovative charging systems (the effects of which are discussed below).

When the companies were monopolies it was generally agreed that the standing charge did not cover all the consumer-related costs, and that the differences between the tariffs did not reflect fully the differences in the costs of supplying those using different payment methods. As part of its argument to retain its monopoly, the incumbent gas supplier had argued that the standing charge would rise dramatically if competition were to be introduced (MMC, 1994).

Some other aspects of tariffs did not reflect costs fully either—for example, the higher costs of rural distribution networks were recovered from all consumers. However, there is little pressure to remove such cross-subsidies so long as distribution remains a monopoly. Cross-subsidies became an issue in the retail market precisely because competition was expected to attract entrants to compete most vigorously where profitability was greatest. This raised concerns for low-income consumers, who were more likely to use prepayment meters and to use small amounts of energy, and for whom tariffs were thought to have been low relative to costs before competition was introduced.

Incumbent firms in domestic energy markets were subject to price caps immediately after privatization, but entrants were not. As consumers started to switch supplier, regulation was gradually withdrawn, and the final markets were fully deregulated in April 2002. Wholesale electricity markets were also reformed in 2001. This chapter does not discuss these wholesale market changes, which are described and analysed elsewhere in this volume by Richard Green, but focuses on the effects of retail market changes.

The most successful entrants into both the gas and electricity markets have been incumbents in similar markets: the regional electricity suppliers entered the gas markets and the national gas incumbent and incumbents from other areas entered each regional electricity market.

Some other companies entered in the early stages, mostly from other parts of the energy industry, such as Calor gas, oil, and coal supply companies. But by 2004, six big players had emerged in both the gas and electricity markets; one is the gas incumbent and the other five are merged electricity incumbents. Of these, two are owned by German companies, one by the French government, and the other two are British plcs. A very small number of niche players remain, each with a tiny market share. Any entrant must offer the full range of payment methods in any market which it supplies.

3. Expected Effects of Opening the Market

One major argument for reforming retail energy markets was that competitive markets would provide better incentives for companies to keep costs and prices at low levels than regulated monopoly could achieve. But the validity of such an argument depends on the competitiveness of the market which emerges from the process, relative to the effectiveness of regulation of the monopoly supplier. Even if costs are reduced by the competitive process, if the unregulated market includes significant levels of market power, consumers as a whole may be worse off if price levels rise. In some cases, total surplus might increase, but suppliers might benefit at the expense of consumers.

Introducing competition might also change the relative prices which are paid by different consumer groups. Retailing energy includes some fixed and common costs which need to be recovered through a mark-up above marginal cost, from at least some markets. As nationalized monopolies, the energy sector had pursued a policy of broadly uniform pricing. Prepayment charges were usually somewhat higher than those for credit consumers, but we have seen that cost differences were not fully reflected in price differentials. Consumers using the more expensive prepayment methods were partially subsidized by credit consumers, and payment by direct debit was a comparative novelty in the 1990s as competition was introduced, and so there was no tradition of discount for such payment. Such cross-subsidy between payment methods had developed from a general concept of universal service among the nationalized industries, indicating that households should receive such essential services at a similar price, regardless of differences in retail costs. By happy coincidence it may also have been an efficient pricing structure, in the sense of maximizing the sum of the producer and consumer surplus,[2] if it resulted in Ramsey prices. These are the prices which distort the demand as little as possible from the 'first best' efficient allocation (i.e. that which results from prices equal to marginal cost). If prices need to be raised above marginal cost to cover joint or common costs, then Ramsey pricing requires that the mark-up should be greatest in markets where demand is least price responsive, i.e. will change least in response to those mark-ups. The energy demand of low-income households is more price responsive that that of richer groups (Baker *et al.*, 1989).

Ramsey pricing would therefore require that mark-ups above marginal cost should be smallest for payment methods predominantly used by low-income consumers, i.e. prepayment. Since these are the more expensive payment methods, a lower mark up on their higher marginal costs would result in prices that were more uniform than the cost differences, along the lines of those applied by the nationalized energy suppliers.

When they were first privatized, each incumbent was a monopoly in its part of the residential market, and subject to a cap on its average prices in that market. Some forms of such caps can motivate a private monopolist to impose the same pattern of prices as Ramsey pricing, but the form applied to gas prices (and to some extent electricity) might have led to prices above Ramsey prices for high-cost consumers (Bradley and Price, 1988). Rather surprisingly, these newly privatized monopolies did not much alter the pricing patterns they had inherited from their nationalized predecessors (Giulietti and Waddams Price, 2005). Such conservatism probably reflected a combination of ignorance about the pattern of their own costs, and concern not to attract adverse publicity by increasing the prices for low-income consumers at a time when these industries were in the political limelight and formal regulatory restrictions were being relaxed.

Armstrong and Vickers (2001) show that, in general, firms will choose efficient two-part tariffs in a competitive market. If these were already in place under prices which reflected a Ramsey scheme in nationalized industries, significant price rebalancing would not necessarily result from market liberalization. This result also suggests that competition authorities (including regulators) confronting market power should focus on controlling the level rather than the structure of prices from an efficiency perspective. Of course, if the authorities also have a distributive role, intervention in price structures may be appropriate on these grounds.

---

[2] The same result would hold if the welfare objective were to maximize consumer surplus subject to the firm breaking even.

Having considered what we might expect to happen as regulated markets are opened to competition, in the next section we examine how competitive the market has been at different times since it first opened. First, we consider indications of competitiveness when price caps were removed in 2002; then we consider more recent indications. And we assess how far consumer switching may act as a constraint on the exercise of market power. In section 5 we consider whether, regardless of *level*, prices have been rebalanced in such a way as to benefit some households more than others. The final sections discuss the likely impact of future price increases in light of these findings.

4. Market Power in the Deregulated Retail Energy Market

Deregulation of retail energy markets is justified if competition reduces costs and prices below the level which regulated monopoly can achieve. Competition might also introduce innovation which regulation would not generate.[3] But if regulation is withdrawn prematurely, firms may be able to exercise market power, either individually or jointly, to raise prices. Figure 2 shows the likely deregulation trade-off diagrammatically in a market with constant marginal costs.

If a regulated monopolist can convince the regulator that efficient costs are at MC_R, greater than their true level, MC_E, the regulator will cap prices at p_R (with quantity q_R). If deregulation is accompanied by competition which reduces prices to the efficient level, MC_E, consumers will be charged the lower price of p_C. However, if suppliers exercise some market power, prices might be higher, up to the monopoly price P_M. The effect of deregulation on consumers as a whole, therefore, depends crucially on how competitive the market becomes. Monitoring the process is handicapped by uncertainty about upstream costs in the volatile energy markets. The rest of this section examines evidence on the competitiveness of the retail market at various stages of its deregulation, and an assessment of consumers' gains from the process. How upstream prices relate to costs, and market power in the wholesale market, are not examined here. Richard Green's chapter in this book and Dieter Helm's book (Helm, 2004*a*) both provide good discussions of this aspect.

---

[3] This is analogous to the fundamental trade-off of privatization outlined by Jones *et al.* (1990).

Figure 2 The 'Fundamental Trade-off of Privatization'

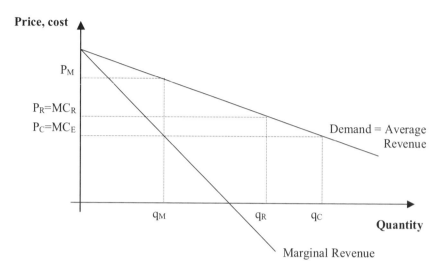

4.1 *Competitiveness of the Retail Market at Deregulation*

By April 2002, the regulator believed that retail energy markets were sufficiently competitive to remove price caps. Analysis of the relation between annual electricity bills and cost and demand factors at that time (Salies and Waddams Price, 2004) showed that the market was developing rather differently for credit and prepayment consumers. In the credit markets there seemed to be quite vigorous competition; the spread of prices there could be interpreted as a disequilibrium situation with entrants undercutting incumbents; incumbents maintained a price higher than that of entrants, a policy which is profitable because some consumers will not switch, even for quite large gains (this is discussed further below). However, once some incumbent power had been accounted for, prices for credit payment methods seemed to be largely related to costs, indicating a market with strong competitive elements. In contrast, the prepayment tariffs were much less closely related to costs; the incumbent's prices were not significantly higher than those of entrants, suggesting somewhat lackadaisical competition and unenthusiastic entry.

4.2 *Market Concentration Measures*

Though prices at deregulation confirm dynamic competition in the credit markets and less vigorous rivalry in prepayment markets, incumbents have

Table 3. Percentage of Customers Supplied by Energy Retailers, September 2005

Supplier	Gas market	National electricity market	In region where retailer is incumbent[a]
British Gas	53	22	n.a.
Powergen	14	20	51
npower	9	15	49
EDF Energy	5	13	58
Southern and Scottish Energy	10	16	69
Scottish Power	9	13	59
Others	0	1	n.a.

Notes: [a] group percentage, unweighted average across regions; n.a. = not applicable
Source: Ofgem (2006*b*).

slowly lost market share across all markets. Even so, most incumbents retained more than 50 per cent of the market in their home areas (and British Gas does so on a national basis) at the end of 2005. However a significantly smaller proportion of prepayment consumers has switched suppliers (Ofgem, 2006*c*), so incumbents have a higher than average market share for these consumers.

Table 3 is based on a regional definition of retail electricity markets, following Ofgem's own 2004 analysis. The high national shares among electricity suppliers reflect consolidation since privatization. In gas, concentration is falling slowly but is still very high. These high levels of concentration confer considerable individual market power on the incumbents, and we see from Table 4 that incumbents still charge higher prices than entrants, both in gas and electricity, with little difference now between payment methods.

Ofgem acknowledges the possibility of coordinated effects in energy markets, which can arise where firms recognize that it is in their mutual interests not to compete actively against each other (Ofgem, 2004*b*). The energy sector exhibits characteristics which could give rise to coordinated effects. Gas and electricity are homogeneous products, facilitating coordination. Electricity incumbents have broadly similar market profiles, though the gas incumbent's national market presence gives it a somewhat different structure. There is repeated interaction between the firms, both in each of the 14 regional electricity markets and in the national gas market, strengthened by the high proportion of consumers switching to dual fuel supply. Bernheim and Whinston (1990) show that such multi-market contact can facilitate collusion, especially when costs vary between firms in different markets. Such extensive multi-market contact can also help overcome the difficulties of punishing any deviant firms which Ofgem (2004*b*) identifies.

The regulator itself assists transparency in the market, another condition for coordinated effects, by publishing tariff schedules. While such information may reduce consumers' search costs (see below), it also provides information to firms about each others' behaviour. Indeed, the very market analyses which the regulator publishes are themselves likely to help the participating firms understand better the actions of competitors and the implications for themselves (Ordover and Saloner, 1989, Albæk *et al.*, 1997). Moreover, energy prices can be changed quickly, another condition for coordinated effects. As noted above, there has been little successful entry from outside the group of incumbent firms, so entry does not seem to be a competitive constraint, perhaps because of the importance of brand knowledge identified by the regulator (Ofgem, 2004*b*).

The UK Competition Commission identifies three conditions for coordinated effects: a sufficiently high market concentration for firms to be aware of each others' actions; an ability to change prices quickly so deviant behaviour can be punished; and weak competitive constraints from entrants or fringe players outside the core group (Competition Commission, 2003). All seem to be satisfied in retail energy markets. There is, therefore, both theoretical justification and empirical evidence that these markets are prone to abuse of dominant power by incumbents who retain very high market shares, and to coordinated effects among a small group of similar firms which interact repeatedly in 15 closely related markets.

4.3 *Competitive Constraints from Consumer Behaviour*

How far can such individual and joint dominance be challenged by consumers, particularly by exercising their recently acquired power to switch suppliers? Consumers confer individual market power on the incumbent by tolerating higher prices from the incumbent, as demonstrated in Table 4. Giulietti *et al.* (2005) explored this tolerance by asking consumers what savings they would require to switch supplier. This effectively identifies the incumbent's demand curve. At any particular mark-up above the prices charged by competitors, the incumbent can choose to retain more customers by narrowing the gap, but making less profit on consumers who are retained; or to maintain or raise its premium, realizing more profit from retained consumers, but losing the profit on those who switch away. If entrants are charging marginal costs (or the competitive price), the information provided by consumers about

Table 4. Maximum and Median Price Premia of Incumbent over Entrants, May 2006, % Mark-up for Consumer with Medium Demand (20,500 kWh per year for gas and 3,300 kWh per year for electricity)

Incumbent supplier	Direct-debit premia		Quarterly credit premia		Pre-payment premia	
	Maximum	Median	Maximum	Median	Maximum	Median
British Gas	15	8	20	15	17	11
Powergen	18	12	19	9	16	4
npower	21	13	22	13	26	16
EDF Energy	9	2	2	0	7	0
Southern and Scottish Energy	15	3	11	3	15	6
Scottish Power	3	0	8	2	9	3

Sources: energywatch price sheets for April 2006 and own calculations with SSE price rises from 1 May incorporated (average SSE domestic bills will increase by 16.5 per cent for gas and 9.4 per cent for electricity from 1 May 2006).

the margins they would tolerate enables estimation of the profit-maximizing mark-up for the incumbent. When the survey was undertaken, very soon after the market opened in 1998, consumer responses suggested that it was profitable for the gas incumbent to maintain a price around one-third above that of its competitors, even though it would lose about 45 per cent of the market. By September 2005, Table 4 shows that around 47 per cent of residential gas consumers had, indeed, switched away from the incumbent, and Table 3 that the maximum savings available to a typical consumer by switching from the incumbent (at the same payment method and consumption level) are 15–20 per cent of the bill, suggesting that this model derived from consumer reaction in the very early days of competition provided a good indication of developments.

Consumers were also asked whether they expected the incumbent to match entrants' prices. Much of the incumbent's market power arises from consumers not switching because they (incorrectly) expect the incumbent to match. Over time we might expect consumers to become wise to the fact that matching was not occurring, but when the same group of consumers were asked the same question 18 months later, a *higher* proportion of the group of consumers who had not switched by that time believed that the incumbent would match (perhaps partly to justify their continued inactivity in the market (Waddams Price, 2004)). Awareness of choice in the market had also declined. Both of these trends suggest that the market power of incumbents is robust over time.

Another potential measure of the market's competitiveness, the con-vergence of prices, was examined by Giulietti *et al.* (2004). Preliminary results suggest that differences in trend values of electricity prices have not shrunk as the market has matured. This persistence in price differ-ences confirms that the market is not exhibiting the characteristics which would be expected in an increasingly competitive market, even after the removal of price caps.

One way in which consumers impose a competitive constraint on suppliers is by choosing the best value in the market. For a homogeneous good like energy this will usually be the cheapest offering. In an analysis of low-income households, interviewed in 2000, the gains which con-sumers had made by switching electricity were calculated from the difference in bills between the supplier to whom they had changed and the incumbent. Preliminary analysis showed that almost a third of switching households moved to a supplier which charged more than the incumbent at their current consumption level and payment method (Wilson and Waddams Price, 2005). The sample was designed to include a disproportionate number of prepayment respondents and, as already observed, the entrants' prices offered less reduction on the incumbent's charges for prepayment. However, similar 'errors' are shown in a more recent survey, conducted among a group representative of all consumers in 2005 (Chang *et al.*, 2006). Even though both gains and losses were generally small, this evidence suggests that consumers may not exert an effective competitive constraint on incumbents.

4.4 *Potential Consumer Gains from Liberalizing Energy Markets*

The process of opening residential energy markets to competition has been costly, and commentators questioned beforehand whether the benefits would outweigh the costs (see, for example, Green and MacDaniel, 1998). Given the novel element of being able to choose supplier in this market, the inevitable inertia of many consumers, and some concerns about whether the marketing methods of incumbents were over zealous, research into early switching behaviour suggests that, even if consumers switch to the best possible alternatives, the potential gains are small on aggregate, and are unlikely to outweigh the costs of establishing the scheme and companies' marketing expenditure.

Giulietti *et al.* (2005) analysed potential welfare gains assuming in the gas market that consumers who had switched had achieved the greatest available savings for their payment method and consumption level;[4] we have already seen that such a favourable assumption is optimistic. Calculations of the overall effect of competition both on switchers and non-switchers depended on assumptions about suppliers' behaviour in equilibrium and, in particular, whether coordinated effects enabled entrants to maintain prices above marginal costs. In the most optimistic scenario, entrants set a competitive price level which the incumbent matches, resulting in consumer gains of around a thousand million pounds a year, very similar to the estimated costs of companies in persuading the relevant number of consumers in this model to switch. In more pessimistic scenarios, where incumbents raised their prices above those which would have prevailed under regulation, consumers as a whole lost up to a hundred million pounds per year. The signs reported above of both incumbent and joint dominance, and of continuing incumbent price premia in the markets suggest that such pessimism may be appropriate.

Higher price levels would have a greater impact on low-income households, because they spend a higher proportion of their income on energy, as shown in section 1 above. We return to this issue in the final sections of the chapter. In the next section we examine concerns that deregulation would have an impact on low-income households because it might lead to rebalancing between different tariff elements and payment methods.

5. Relative Prices as the Retail Energy Market is Opened: Empirical Evidence from Incumbents and Entrants

We would expect companies operating in energy markets, either as incumbents or entrants, to choose prices according to their view of costs, the competitive conditions in the market, and the regulatory constraints imposed upon them. We have seen that there was remarkably little change in relative prices immediately after companies were privatized, even though the average price caps imposed on most companies enabled them to rebalance, at least to some extent, within the regulatory cap.

As the companies anticipated competition, their pricing behaviour should give us information about their understanding of relative costs in

---

[4] The authors were not able to calculate whether consumers increased consumption as a result of switching to a lower tariff, but since short-term elasticities are comparatively small, this omission has only second-order effects.

the market, and enable forecasts of likely changes in relative prices. This deregulation process can be divided into two phases: the entry of new firms into markets where the incumbent is still regulated; and after deregulation, where there are no *ex ante* constraints on any of the firms' behaviour. The sections below examine the evidence from each of these phases, first with respect to different payment methods, and then in terms of fixed and variable charges.

5.1 *Payment Method*

REGULATED INCUMBENTS

If prices are not cost reflective we would expect incumbents to change their prices in anticipation of competition, and they did, indeed, start to rebalance their prices as they foresaw the end of their monopoly. This was most dramatic in the gas industry, where the incumbent announced changes within 48 hours of the government's confirmation that competition would be introduced in the residential market. Charges for prepayment were raised and for direct debit lowered, maintaining the same average revenue within the regulatory cap. Similar rebalancing occurred in electricity, but more gradually, leading up to market opening, since competition had been anticipated in the privatization Act of 1989; the form of regulation also restricted rebalancing more in electricity than in gas. There was some effect on consumer bills in the period leading up to market opening, particularly for gas prepayment consumers, as shown in Table 5.

The initial reaction of the incumbents to the threat of competition suggested further price rebalancing in favour of higher-income direct-debit payers. Suppliers maintained that prices of other payment methods, particularly prepayment, did not adequately reflect their costs, and they needed to lower prices to direct-debit customers to meet the better deals which they expected entrants to offer in these markets. Between the dates of privatization and 1996, when the first energy consumers were given a choice of supplier, the *relative* bills of direct-debit customers fell, with corresponding rises for those paying by standard credit and using prepayment meters. There was particular concern for households using prepayment, who have lower than average income.

Table 5 shows the change in relative bills between privatization and 1996 at constant consumption levels (Waddams Price and Hancock, 1998). All the aggregate changes are small, with the largest gains, for direct-debit gas consumers, representing only about 4 per cent of an

Table 5. Net Aggregate Increases in Bills as a Result of Rebalancing in Anticipation of Market Opening, £s per year

Household group	Gas, 1986–96	Electricity, 1990–96
All	0.0	0.0
Pensioner households	1.7	1.2
Income quintile		
Lowest	0.7	−1.1
2nd	0.4	0.9
3rd	−0.4	0.3
4th	−0.7	−0.6
Highest	0.2	0.7
Payment method		
Prepayment	3.1	0.1
Quarterly credit	8.9	1.7
Direct debit	−14.2	−4.1
Household numbers	15,906	6,717

Source: Waddams Price and Hancock (1998).

annual bill. Nevertheless, these early changes by incumbents, before there was any entry, caused concern about potential losers as competition developed. Pensioner households were marginal net losers, largely because they use less energy and suffered from relative increases in standing charge; and households using prepayment and quarterly credit paid more in both industries relative to those using direct-debit payment. One of the government's aims, expressed in its 1998 White Paper (HM Government, 1998), and echoed by the regulator (Ofgem, 2003) was that all household groups should receive a fair share of gains from competition, and this early rebalancing suggested that vulnerable households might gain less. However, it indicated few obvious differences in gains by different income quintiles.

RELATIVE PRICES FOR DIFFERENT PAYMENT METHODS CHARGED BY FIRMS AS INCUMBENTS AND ENTRANTS

Before deregulation, when their prices were capped in their home markets, we could deduce the views of incumbents on the costs of supplying different markets by examining how they behaved as entrants, where they were not subject to regulatory price constraints. All companies are required to offer prepayment tariffs in regions where they are active, but there is no requirement that such prices should be competitive with those of the incumbent. Indeed, early prepayment offers in June 1999 showed very little discount against the incumbent compared with direct-debit payment (Otero and Waddams Price, 2001). For prepayment, most

Table 6 Ratio of Direct Debit to Prepayment Charges for Customers Consuming 3,300 kWh/annum

	In own (incumbent) region	Average as entrant
1999	0.93	0.86
2006	0.94	0.92

Source: Otero and Waddams Price (2001, updated).

entrants' prices are above that of the entrant, while for direct debit most are below the incumbent's price.

This discrepancy can be interpreted as an indication of companies' perceived relative costs. Unlike incumbents, entrants were free to choose prices for different payment methods, and would be expected to target markets with the highest profit margins. Table 6 shows the average ratio of direct debit to prepayment charges[5] levied by companies in 1999 as incumbents in their own region, and as entrants elsewhere. Relative prices were analysed to abstract from unobserved differences in generation, transmission, and distribution costs. The latter were the same for all suppliers in any one region, and the former were the same for each company.

In 1999 companies judged the appropriate discount for direct debit relative to prepayment to be much higher where they were entrants than the regulated discount imposed on them as incumbents by the price cap. Eleven out of 13 entrants chose to give a significantly deeper discount to direct-debit customers, where they were entrants, than they offered in their home area, where prices were regulated. The average discount where they were entrants was 14 per cent, but as incumbent, only half as much (Otero and Waddams Price, 2001).

In entering other markets, a supplier incurs some costs in attracting consumers from another firm to switch. The expected profitability of a consumer who switches depends on the mark-up of price over cost once transferred, less the cost of recruitment. The supplier's cost of inducing switching is higher for prepayment consumers because of the more complex arrangements necessitated by the prepayment meter, and this would account for some of the difference in relative prices offered out of area, where these switching costs would be incurred, compared with in area, where there are no such costs for continuing consumers. (Of course they would be incurred where consumers switch back to the incumbent, but 'switched-back' consumers will be a minority, around 20 per cent, of

[5] For a household with average consumption levels.

the total consumers served in the region where the supplier is incumbent.) However, it seems unlikely that this differential switching cost for the supplier accounts for the full difference in relative prices in and out of area; rather, these differences suggest a belief by the firms that the regulator had capped prepayment prices at an unprofitably low level relative to direct debit in the home region. In this case, incumbents might be expected to raise the relative charges for prepayment as soon as the caps were removed.

To check whether this had occurred, a similar analysis of relative charges was repeated for May 2006, 4 years after all price caps were removed, and in a market with rising energy prices. By this time only five of the 13 incumbent electricity companies remained, after merger and exit, and the relative charges in and out of area are shown in the bottom row of Table 6. Far from the 'in area' ratios moving towards those which companies had chosen as entrants in 1999, Table 6 shows the reverse. Discounts for direct debit now average only 8 per cent for entrants and 6 per cent for incumbents. There is no statistically significant difference between these average discounts.

In their home areas, two of the five major consolidated electricity incumbents have lowered the price for prepayment *relative* to direct debit, and the other three incumbents show virtually no change. Where they are entrants, too, the picture is unclear. Comparing the tariffs charged by entrants in May 2006 with those in 1999, two of the six[6] major suppliers have reduced the relative cost of prepayment, one has increased it slightly, and three show no significant change. Most are maintaining slightly lower relative prices for prepayment where they are incumbent than where they are entrants.

There is some evidence that concern of the regulator, pressure groups, and the media may be acting as a 'surrogate cap' on the relative prices which companies charge for tariffs used mainly by lower-income households, both as incumbents and entrants. Companies themselves have suggested that they feel considerable informal pressure from the regulator, and from the consumer watchdog and the public and media more generally, not to make changes which operate against the interests of what are perceived as a vulnerable group (Sharratt, 2003). The consumer watchdog, energywatch, has been quick to publicize any such changes, and since it also publishes complaints data, companies may feel vulnerable to its criticism. Moreover, although the regulator no longer controls

---

[6] British Gas is the major entrant to the electricity market which is not an incumbent.

prices, it does still issue supply licences and exercises responsibility for implementing the government's social and environmental programmes, and so companies are clearly conscious of its influence. If this is the reason for the 'reversal' in rebalancing, continued vigilance would be needed to prevent changes which might adversely affect low-income consumers once such moves are no longer in the limelight.

Another interpretation of the reverse in changing relative prices is that companies have found out more about their own costs since they first entered the market, and the more recent ratios show improved understanding. In this case, companies will want to retain the new relative prices, both in and out of area, regardless of regulatory influence (formal or informal).

5.2 *Fixed and Variable Charges*

One result of market reform was the introduction of new tariff structures. Although standing charges had been expected to increase with the introduction of competition, several suppliers abolished them; they had always been unpopular with consumers and politically sensitive (Gibson and Price, 1983); some retailers introduced, instead, differential running rates, with the fixed costs of connection being recovered through a higher running rate for the first few units. It is ironic that British Gas, which was so vehement in 1993 that the effect of competition would be to raise the standing charge to the detriment of consumers of small quantities, was one of these (MMC, 1994).

We examine the impact of two contrasting tariff innovations on different households. British Gas had introduced its new tariff structure while its prices were still regulated, and so the regulator was concerned to assess the effect of the change on different household groups, subject to it being revenue neutral for the firm. The effect was small losses (on average £1.76 a year) for 85 per cent of consumers, while 15 per cent would gain, on average, £9.67 per annum. Gains and losses depended on consumption levels: users of very small amounts of gas would gain, while those who consumed higher amounts would lose. As consumption increases with income, the effect of replacing the standing charge with a two-part tariff was progressive, since the proportion of gainers in each income decile decreased as income increased (see Table 7). Nevertheless, more than three-quarters of the poorest decile lost (on average £2.01) from removal of standing charges. The effect on the government's target of reducing fuel poverty was somewhat perverse, since fuel poor house-

Table 7. Proportion of Winners and Losers from British Gas Trading Abolishing the Standing Charge in April 2000 in each Income Decile[a]

	Income deciles										
	1	2	3	4	5	6	7	8	9	10	All
Winners (%)	24	22	21	19	16	15	12	10	7	6	15
	(5.33)	(6.21)	(7.34)	(8.10)	(8.72)	(9.30)	(10.04)	(10.86)	(10.97)	(11.21)	(9.67)
Losers (%)	76	78	79	81	84	85	88	90	93	94	85
	(2.01)	(1.99)	(1.96)	(1.91)	(1.88)	(1.85)	(1.81)	(1.80)	(1.75)	(1.72)	(1.76)

Note: [a] Average annual gains and losses in pounds per annum are presented in parentheses.

holds generally consume large amounts of fuel in absolute terms, as well as relative to their income, and would predominantly lose from this change.

In contrast, the second innovative tariff, Staywarm, abolished the variable charge. It was selective, introduced by one of the then electricity incumbents, TXU, and consisted purely of a standing charge, in the sense that payment depended only on the size of home and household, and was completely independent of the household's actual energy consumption. Eligibility has been narrowed considerably since the scheme was first introduced, and now applies only to those households with occupants over 60 years old who use relatively little energy. The scheme is particularly interesting in the context of energy conservation, since it transfers responsibility for reducing consumption from the consumer (who has no financial interest in lower energy use) to the supplier.

Analysis of the initial Staywarm scheme, which was then available to all households on certain income-related benefits, showed that in its original form it did benefit the fuel poor, and particularly households in the three lowest income deciles (see Bennett *et al.*, 2002). The restrictions introduced since then may reflect its very success in assisting low-income households, requiring subsidies from other users which were not sustainable in a competitive market.

Overall, the changes in the relative prices charged for different payment methods and different levels of fuel consumption do not show a clear pattern of rebalancing, but rather a variety of different approaches in the newly competitive energy markets. This suggests that there is little evidence of continuing disadvantage to low-income consumers from rebalancing of prices in the first decade of competition. The next section assesses likely future effects on consumers in the unregulated retail energy market.

Table 8. Percentage of Household Expenditure on Fuel by Income Decile, 2004/5

	Income deciles										
	1	2	3	4	5	6	7	8	9	10	Avge
Electricity	3.1	3.0	2.3	2.0	1.8	1.7	1.6	1.5	1.3	1.1	1.6
Gas	2.5	2.6	2.1	1.9	1.7	1.5	1.4	1.4	1.2	1.1	1.5
Other fuels	0.4	0.3	0.4	0.3	0.3	0.4	0.2	0.2	0.2	0.3	0.3
Total fuel expenditure	6.1	5.9	4.8	4.2	3.8	3.6	3.3	3.1	2.7	2.4	3.4

Sources: Office of National Statistics (2005) and own calculations based on averages in each category.

6. Impact of Rising Wholesale Energy Prices in Deregulated Retail Markets

While low-income households have not suffered more than others from tariff rebalancing in the competitive market, they are more vulnerable to increases in the level of prices, because they devote a higher proportion of their income to energy expenditure. In 2004/5 the average expenditure by the poorest tenth of households was over 6 per cent of income, while that of the richest tenth was only 2 per cent (see Table 8).

Energywatch (2006) estimates that 3m people will be in fuel poverty by the end of 2006, double the number in 2003, and Help the Aged (reported in the *Guardian*, 3 November 2004) states that every 10 per cent rise in fuel bills adds another half million. The effect of such rises in price levels depends partly on how competitive the market becomes, and again we have seen mixed evidence. When the final price caps were removed in April 2002, the prepayment market seemed uncompetitive (prices did not reflect costs closely); direct debit and standard credit markets showed more vigorous competition, though with incumbents still able to charge a considerable premium. Most incumbents retain more than half their home markets, and levy a considerable price premium. Such incumbent power would be constrained if consumers actively switched to cheaper suppliers, but many believed (with little justification to date) that the incumbent would match the lower entrants' prices, and many of those who did switch, did so to more expensive suppliers. These signs suggest considerable remaining incumbency advantage. But this was in an era of falling energy prices; households may be less tolerant of incumbent mark-ups as their attention is caught by sharply increasing bills.

Even if incumbents' power to keep their prices above those of entrants is eroded, new concerns arise from consolidation in the industry. There are now only six significant players, who share an interest in keeping prices well above costs; market conditions make this a relatively easy exercise, without necessitating explicit collusion. Consumer switching would not constrain prices raised by coordinated effects, since there is no 'better deal' to switch to.

Introducing competition and deregulating the markets could affect vulnerable consumers much more adversely than price rebalancing if it leads to the exercise of 'joint dominance' among these suppliers. Either single or joint dominance in the retail market may lead to price rises which are above the competitive level, with particularly adverse effects on vulnerable households and the government's fuel poverty strategy. Plans to improve the housing conditions and heating infrastructure available, especially in vulnerable households, would clearly deliver important benefits to such households; but such measures may do little to protect them from fuel poverty if unconstrained supplier power in retail energy markets simultaneously raises prices well above costs, which are themselves likely to be rising in the wholesale market.

7. Conclusion

When it confirmed that it would continue the previous government's policy of liberalizing the energy markets, the incoming Labour government of 1997 was anxious to alleviate fears that such action might prove distributionally regressive. In a series of policy papers it sought to reassure consumers and lobbyists that low-income consumers would not be disadvantaged, and changed the duties of the regulator to include the interests of low-income consumers and the need to take account of social guidance provided by the government. It also instituted a policy to eliminate fuel poverty. Concerns about the social impact of opening energy markets initially centred on expectations that companies would rebalance their tariffs to make them more cost reflective. Most commentators thought this would disadvantage low-income consumers. These fears seemed justified by early company actions in markets where they were not regulated and free to choose relative prices. But as price caps were removed from incumbent suppliers, this trend has not continued, as feared, and seems in some cases to have reversed. Whether this is the result of 'informal' regulation from fear of adverse publicity, or reflects a new understanding of the costs and markets by the firms concerned, is unclear. If it is the former, then further rebalancing would eventually be expected, when the industries slipped further from the public limelight. If the latter, the original fears will prove unfounded.

However, other concerns have arisen from the increasing concentration of the retail market, and the possibility that the introduction of competition has left considerable market power in the hands of retail suppliers. Both measures of unilateral dominance (high remaining market shares for incumbents) and joint dominance suggest that the fewer remaining suppliers retain considerable market power. This chapter has summarized a number of indicators which suggest that the industry may be exercising such power, so that prices charged to final consumers are above the competitive level. If this is the case, low-income consumers would suffer more from the excess price than those in higher income groups, because they devote a higher proportion of their income to energy. The concern for vulnerable households may, therefore, have been well founded, if for the wrong reason.

These arguments might suggest that *ex ante* regulation should be reimposed on these markets. However, such a conclusion would be premature. While some of the analysis above suggests that deregulation has not yet yielded net benefits, much as predicted by Green and McDaniel (1998), it would seem more sensible to stay with the current model a little longer, to see whether *ex post* competition policy can provide sufficient discipline on the market to yield consumer benefits, particularly as rising energy prices may stimulate more consumer switching. While deregulation might have seemed a less attractive policy with the benefit of the hindsight now available, reimposing price caps and removing consumer choice at this stage would bring with it new costs and disturbances in the market. The regulator will need to continue its market monitoring (notwithstanding some of the disadvantages of its transparency, discussed above), and assess how far consumers themselves can curb supplier power through their switching behaviour as prices rise. The jury is still out on how successful liberalization will prove in the longer term, with rising costs, both for the market as a whole and for vulnerable consumers in particular.

371

13

Nuclear Energy

Malcolm Grimston

1. Introduction

One of the most startling recent characteristics of the energy debate in many developed countries is the speed and extent to which nuclear power, for many years effectively ignored as a major option, has returned to the agenda—'with a vengeance' in the words of UK Prime Minister Tony Blair.[1]

From its emergence in the late 1950s and early 1960s nuclear energy underwent a period of rapid growth. By the late 1980s nuclear power stations were generating about a sixth of global electricity production and were deployed in over 30 countries. Nuclear energy received a major boost as a result of the oil price hikes in the 1970s, when concerns about security of energy supplies reached epidemic proportions.

However, the technology lost its shine, especially after the Three Mile Island accident in 1979. A variety of factors—falling global fossil fuel prices, cost and schedule overruns on nuclear projects, growing public concerns about nuclear energy as a result of the accidents at Three Mile Island and Chernobyl (Ukraine, 1986) and a failure to make progress on radioactive waste management—combined to undermine the case made for nuclear energy by its early enthusiasts. By 2000 plant construction had practically stalled in Western Europe and North America, although it continued at reduced rates in central and eastern Europe and the Asia Pacific region. Several countries had enacted legislation or introduced policy barriers to

[1] http://news.bbc.co.uk/1/hi/uk_politics/4987196.stm, BBC News Online (2006), Blair backs nuclear power plans (26 May 2006).

nuclear new build and some—Germany, Sweden, Belgium, Nether-lands—had policies of closing existing plants before the end of their economic lifetimes.

The middle years of the first decade of the twenty-first century saw a global reappraisal of the challenges associated with energy production and of the potential role that nuclear might play.

- Energy demand was expected to double between 2000 and 2050.

- The oil price increased eight-fold between 1998 and 2006.

- Oil and gas were heavily concentrated in a limited number of countries.

- Both the European Union and the USA were getting increasingly concerned about dependence on imported energy.

- Fears about climate change were increasing, based both on perceptions of an increased frequency of climate-related disasters and observations that the world was getting a higher proportion of its traded energy from fossil fuels than it was at the time of the Rio Convention in 1992, which established climate change as a major political issue.

- The nuclear industry claimed to have a new range of products available which would be much cheaper and quicker to build and much more reliable in operation than traditional 1970s-style plants.

Proponents of nuclear energy pointed to its status as an energy resource that did not depend on limited fossil reserves, which was more resistant to fuel price inflation and which did not contribute to greenhouse gas emissions in everyday operation (though there are some emission implications arising from mining and processing fuel, building reactors, etc.). Finland and France ordered new reactors, many other countries embarked on programmes of lifetime extension, phase-out timetables were relaxed or abandoned, and several governments began to consider removing regulatory barriers to investment and offering incentives to promote nuclear new build.

By early 2007 this change of heart had not translated into a major programme of new nuclear orders, but for the first time in two decades this looked a realistic possibility.

2. Background

Nuclear fission was effectively 'discovered' in Berlin in December 1938. That the new phenomenon, a way of harnessing Einstein's famous equation $E = mc^2$ to produce enormous quantities of energy, should emerge in Germany on the eve of the Second World War led to intense scientific and technological effort in the USA and the UK. In December 1942 Enrico Fermi started the world's first fission reactor in a Chicago squash court and atomic devices were exploded in Japan in August 1945.

The ending of the war did not seem to result in any slowing of the pace of research. By the end of 1945 the Canadians were running a research reactor, the French agency CEA (Commissariat à l'Energie Atomique) had been set up, and the UK government announced the intention to build an Atomic Energy Research Establishment at Harwell in Oxfordshire. A production group was established at Risley in Cheshire and work at Windscale in Cumberland, for plutonium production, started in 1947.

In the early days of the UK programme, secrecy was obsessive. Few MPs were aware of the work until the second half of the 1950s and though the decision to build a British bomb was announced to Parliament in 1948, there was little or no public or press debate. However, alongside the early military research, a desire was emerging to harness the new source of energy for more overtly beneficial purposes. Practical issues, such as growing concerns over global energy supplies and the power of the coal mining unions, coupled with political pressures (especially in the USA there was a perceived need to put a positive face on nuclear technology in order to stave off opposition to nuclear weapons, leading to Eisenhower's 'Atoms for Peace' programme) and even moral considerations on the part of some of the scientists who had unleashed the dreadful potential of atomic weapons and felt a need to see that potential turned to positive ends, combined to give research into atomic energy considerable impetus. In 1949 the UK government decided that the next plutonium-producing reactors, to replace the early 'Windscale piles', should also be capable of generating electricity. The first of four such reactors which were built at Calder Hall, near Windscale on the Sellafield site, was opened in 1956 by the Queen (a symbol of nuclear energy's prestigious status). Four more were constructed at Chapelcross, 70 miles away in Dumfries and Galloway, and opened in 1959. Calder Hall and Chapelcross operated as power reactors until closure in 2003 and 2005 respectively, though their military role was curtailed earlier.

The United Kingdom Atomic Energy Authority (UKAEA) was set up in 1954 and was to be responsible for all aspects of radioactive research, development and manufacture for nearly 20 years. In effect, the UKAEA not only implemented policy with respect to nuclear matters; alongside the Central Electricity Generating Board (CEGB) it also played a major role in determining that policy until the emergence of the new market paradigm for producing electricity over 30 years later.

3. Nuclear Energy in the UK

3.1 *The First UK Nuclear Power Programme*

In 1955 the first phase of the UK nuclear power programme was announced, envisaging a programme of some 2,000 MW capacity (Ministry of Fuel and Power, 1955). It was based on the Calder Hall concept, involving gas-cooled, graphite-moderated reactors in which the fuel was kept in a non-oxidizing magnesium alloy (*Magnox*) can. Apart from Calder Hall and Chapelcross, the Magnox programme eventually consisted of nine stations, each consisting of two reactors, with combined capacity of over 4,000 MW. Construction of the first two began in 1956; the last was commissioned in 1971. The Suez crisis of 1956, causing problems such as petrol rationing, further strengthened the determination to develop a source of energy that was less vulnerable to foreign disruption and led to plans to treble the Magnox programme to 6,000 MW. The first Magnox station to cease generating electricity closed in March 1989; the last will come out of service around 2010.

During this period there were five industrial consortia competing to build Magnox stations. All of the 11 Magnoxes built in the UK, including Calder Hall and Chapelcross, were built to different designs. One was refuelled from below, one had heat exchangers external to the reactor building, two were built with concrete 'pressure vessels' (which protect the reactor core), while the rest used steel, and so on. Each of the 11 took a different size of fuel element. This practice of building a series of prototypes has not served the UK nuclear industry well, severely limiting both learning-curve benefits and economies of scale during manufacture and servicing.

Notwithstanding bizarre and somewhat unhelpful comments such as 'too cheap to meter' emanating from the USA,[2] at the start of the Magnox programme it was estimated that electricity generated from Magnox stations would be more expensive than that generated by burning coal. Nuclear energy was none the less to be pursued, for a number of reasons. It represented an added degree of fuel diversity, and therefore potentially security, in a world in which coal (and coal mining unions) remained dominant, in which global oil supplies were questionable (especially in the run-up to and after the Suez crisis in 1956) and the UK was unaware of the hydrocarbon resource lying under its territorial waters, and in which the environmental effects of burning coal remained starkly apparent. In

---

[2] 'Our children will enjoy in their homes electrical energy too cheap to meter' (Strauss, 1954).

1952, less than 5 years before the opening of Calder Hall, the last of the great London smogs, caused by burning coal in the capital, had killed 3,900 people in a fortnight. It was believed that, in due course, as the cost of other fuels rose and nuclear technology became cheaper, nuclear power would become more competitive than other options, with the exception of hydropower.

By the mid-1960s the UK was generating more nuclear electricity than the rest of the world put together. Two Magnox stations were exported, to Italy and Japan. However, the Magnox reactors were relatively inefficient, both thermally and in terms of use of uranium, with a result that relatively large quantities of operational and, in due course, decommissioning waste were created. In addition, a great deal of waste arose from the research projects of the 1940s, 1950s, and 1960s. Some nominal financial provision was made to discharge these liabilities in due course, but, as discussed later, this provision, inadequate as it undoubtedly was, was never made available, leaving a large liability to future taxpayers in the form of what have become known as the 'legacy wastes'.

In 1957 a fire broke out at Windscale Pile 1 which in some senses (e.g. releases of radioactive materials) still ranks as the world's second most serious incident in a nuclear reactor, albeit not a power reactor. Reports commissioned after the fire made several criticisms of the UKAEA management structure at the time. In 1959 what was to become the Nuclear Installations Inspectorate (NII) was set up. It is now part of the Health and Safety Executive and acts as the independent governmental watchdog on the industry. Though the Windscale fire did relatively little real damage, it did perhaps mark the end of the honeymoon, the early acceptance or even enthusiasm which had accompanied developments in the nuclear field thus far. At the same time, opposition to the arms race and the atmospheric testing of atomic weapons was growing. In 1957 there were protests by the likes of Albert Schweitzer, J. B. Priestley, the Japanese government, and an influential group of West German physicists. The forerunner of the Campaign for Nuclear Disarmament (CND) was formed in the UK and in the following year the first march on the weapons establishment at Aldermaston took place.

3.2 *The Second UK Nuclear Power Programme*

By the late 1950s, with the Magnox programme under construction, the UKAEA turned its attention to its successor. This heralded a time of many different research programmes. In 1957 it was decided to build an improved version of the Magnox design at Windscale. The 33 MW prototype advanced gas-cooled reactor (AGR) started operating in 1962. A small fast reactor at Dounreay (Caithness) went critical (i.e. started up) in 1959 and an international project to develop a gas-cooled high-temperature reactor ('Dragon') began at Winfrith (Dorset) in 1959. Construction of another reactor concept, with some similarities to the Canadian Candu programme and called the steam-generating heavy-water reactor (SGHWR), began in 1963, also at Winfrith. There was also enthusiastic research into nuclear fusion. The impression that in the UK, as in other countries, decisions on policy, as well as how to implement that policy, had been delegated to the nuclear community was strengthened. Politicians seemed to feel that nuclear energy was both essential (for concrete reasons and as a proof of the technological credentials of the nation) but at the same time too complicated for anyone but the 'experts' to provide governance. It is hard to avoid a feeling that a vast amount of research resource was made available without proper democratic or commercial oversight, resulting in the development of a wide range of dead-end technologies at the end of which the wrong one (at least with the benefit of hindsight) was chosen.

Following the success of the Windscale prototype, the chosen successor to Magnox was the AGR, a decision which in effect cut the UK off from the global nuclear mainstream for 25 years, most of the rest of the world pursuing light water technology (mainly pressurized water reactor, PWR, or boiling water reactor, BWR). In 1964 the Minister of Power, Fred Lee, announced the decision, telling Parliament, 'we have hit the jackpot . . . we have the greatest breakthrough of all time' (Official Report, 1965). It was apparently assumed that scaling up the prototype by a factor of 20 would be a relatively straighforward technical matter.

This decision and the decision to give the work for the first three AGR stations to the three surviving construction consortia in the nuclear field were not without their critics. There were those who preferred the essentially American PWR, the first of which had begun generating electricity at Shippingport in 1957 and which had been developed for use in nuclear submarines. (Several countries, such as France, did follow that route and the PWR is the leading design type in use in the world today.) Others felt that the wrong version of AGR was chosen as the first to be constructed.

Such issues notwithstanding, the AGR programme was a disappointment. The first station, Dungeness B in Kent, ordered in 1965, only began working properly in 1993 and ran heavily over cost as well. The second design, built at Hinkley Point (B) in Somerset and Hunterston (B), Strathclyde, has been considerably more successful but the third design,

Heysham I (Lancashire) and Hartlepool (County Durham), also took some time to start performing adequately. A fourth design, based on the Hinkley Point/Hunterston design, was built at Torness (Lothian) and Heysham II in the late 1970s, as something of a stopgap. Seven AGR stations, four different designs. Closure of the AGR programme is currently projected to span the period 2011 to 2023, though lifetime extension looks likely in at least some cases.

3.3 A Third Phase?

The inconsistent performance of the AGR programme led to considerable debate over the third phase of Britain's nuclear power programme. Despite a decision in 1966 to build a one-quarter scale (250 MW) prototype fast reactor at Dounreay, which operated from 1973 to 1994, and the relative technical success of the Dragon programme, which was abandoned in 1974, the choice lay between continuing with the AGR, developing the SGHWR, or adopting the PWR. SGHWR was favoured in an announcement by the Secretary of State for Energy in 1974, Sizewell (Suffolk) and Torness being chosen for the first stations, but within 2 years rumours were circulating that the decision was to be reversed. Demand for electricity was not growing as rapidly as expected, obviating the need for new plant of any description, and the task of scaling up the 100 MW prototype SGHWR at Winfrith in Dorset to a 600 MW commercial design was proving problematic and expensive. A government direction to the CEGB to build a new coal-fired plant, Drax B, further damaged the case for new nuclear investment at that stage.

In 1978 the SGHWR was duly abandoned, following a critical report by the National Nuclear Corporation (NNC) the previous July, the last two AGRs were ordered, and the PWR became the favoured technology for development of a third nuclear programme in Britain—a strange compromise but one forced by the bitter rivalry between the AGR and PWR camps in the industry. The first PWR, Sizewell B, began operating in 1995 and planning permission for a second, Hinkley Point C, was granted in 1990 but not pursued.

The early 1970s saw a major reorganization of the UK nuclear industry. In 1971 the UKAEA Production Group became British Nuclear Fuels plc (BNFL), responsible for procurement and manufacture of fuel and for reprocessing of spent fuel, and in 1973 the Weapons Group was transferred to the Ministry of Defence, in effect breaking the formal (if not perceived) link between nuclear power and nuclear weapons in Britain. The remaining construction companies merged to become the National Nuclear Corporation, NNC. The commercial power stations, with the exception of

Calder Hall and Chapelcross, remained part of the CEGB in England and Wales or the South of Scotland Electricity Board (SSEB) in Scotland. By the mid-1970s the nuclear power industry in Britain had taken on the shape that it was to retain until the privatizations of the 1990s. Nirex, the agency charged with finding a solution to managing radioactive waste, was formed in 1983.

4. A New UK Government

When Margaret Thatcher was elected as Prime Minister in 1979 she took power as a firm advocate of nuclear energy, not least because she had seen the National Union of Mineworkers (NUM) destroy the previous Conservative administration (1970–4) and was determined to break its powers. To do that, in a country where coal was responsible for some 80 per cent of electricity generation, would require a number of measures, of which having a large-scale alternative way of generating electricity was one. The final two AGRs were under construction, the UK had decided to rejoin the global nuclear mainstream by buying in PWR technology from the USA, and oil prices were in the throes of the second major hike within a decade. In December 1979 Energy Secretary David Howell made a statement implying support for building 15,000 MW of PWR capacity, a family of 10 reactors. This was never quite a commitment, the actual wording being:

Looking ahead, the electricity supply industry have advised that even on cautious assumptions they would need to order at least one new nuclear power station a year in the decade from 1982, or a programme of the order of 15,000 megawatts over ten years. The precise level of future ordering will depend on the development of electricity demand and the performance of the industry but we consider this a reasonable prospect against which the nuclear and power plant industries can plan. Decisions about the choice of reactor for later orders will be taken in due course.

None the less the implications looked clear enough, and Sizewell was chosen as the site for the lead plant of such a programme. A Public Inquiry was held between 1983 and 1985 and the decision to build followed in 1987. Hinkley Point was identified as the site for the second reactor, to be followed by Wylfa (north Wales) and then by Sizewell again. Note the hint once again that changes to the technology might be expected as the programme rolled out.

However, the global nuclear industry was coming to terms with the accident at Three Mile Island in Pennsylvania in March 1979. In the UK the direct implications of Three Mile Island were limited since Britain did not yet use light water technology, but the incident was influential in persuading the NII that, if the UK were indeed to pursue light water technology for its next programme of reactors, a 'belt-and-braces' approach to safety licensing would have to be followed.

At the same time a competing policy agenda was emerging as the Thatcher government embarked on its programme of privatization and, later, the introduction of competition into what had once been regarded as natural state-owned monopolies—telecommunications, gas, electricity, transportation. By 1982 Howell had been replaced as Energy Secretary by Nigel Lawson, who, in a speech entitled 'The Market for Energy' (Lawson, 1982), signalled a move in government policy towards treating electricity as an industrial commodity.

I do not see the government's task as being to try to plan the future shape of energy production and consumption. It is not even primarily to try to balance UK demand and supply for energy. Our task is rather to set a framework which will ensure that the market operates in the energy sector with a minimum of distortion and energy is produced and consumed efficiently.

The tension between a competitive market approach to the provision of energy and governmental predilection towards certain fuels is obvious.

5. New Paradigm, Old Nuclear

The challenges to nuclear energy within the new competitive market paradigm were considerable. Nuclear energy had grown up within centrally organized and controlled electricity supply industries. The plants that evolved were large, expensive to build, inflexible in output—features that could be regarded as essentially unproblematic in a planned electricity system in which nuclear plants could command a guaranteed market as baseload providers. A much higher proportion of their costs were associated with initial investment (as opposed to operation and maintenance and to fuel costs) than was the case with traditional coal-fired stations and even more than with the new gas-fired technology, combined-cycle gas turbine (CCGT), which emerged during the 1980s.

In the CEGB/SSEB days, the costs associated with a nuclear power station could be passed on to the captive customer over the lifetime of the station (assuming the regulator was satisfied that the costs were justified). The economic risk associated with this investment was therefore relatively limited as far as the investor was concerned (i.e. the government,

Figure 1 Average Electricity Generation Cost Structure for Nuclear, Coal-fired, and Natural Gas Combined-cycle Plants (10 per cent discount rate and 25-year planning horizon)

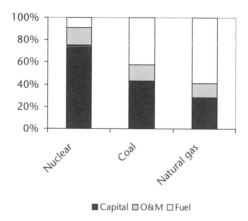

■Capital ▢O&M ▢Fuel

Note: O&M is operation and maintenance.
Source: Rogner *et al.* (2000).

but it could have been a private utility, as found, for example, in much of the USA), the main risk being borne by the consumer (or taxpayer).

Companies in competition have no captive customers and so generally require higher rates of return on capital than those operating as monopolies, because they face higher economic risks. In particular, there is no longer a guaranteed market for electrical output at suitable prices.

For nuclear power, this is particularly detrimental. The higher rates of return demanded in the competitive market of themselves damage the relative competitiveness of highly capital-intensive projects compared to those with lower capital costs (notably natural gas). In addition, however, projects which take longer to recoup initial investment are more risky than those in which initial costs can be amortized more rapidly. As a result, investors are likely to require a higher expected rate of return from nuclear projects than from those powered by natural gas, so further increasing the economic advantage enjoyed by gas-fired projects.

Individual considerations that may appear especially risky for nuclear power in competitive markets include:

- the long timescale for construction, during which external events, changes in government regulation, etc. may necessitate mid-project redesign, delay, or abandonment;
- perceived risks of project cost overruns;

381

- the risk of government interference, either owing to unhelpful external events or because of political considerations, including the election of a new government with a less favourable attitude to nuclear technology, e.g. Germany in 1998;

- the absence, in some countries, of coherent, long-term government policy and support;

- the perceived risk of technical problems reducing availability factors, especially when considering innovative reactor concepts;

- the availability of energy investment alternatives with lower initial investment costs and therefore lower risks in times of stable fuel prices, notably natural gas;

- the need to cover first-time engineering and licensing costs for the first of any innovative reactor design.

The period up to electricity privatization, then, was characterized by two issues particularly unhelpful to the prospects of nuclear new build. The first involved the inherently unattractive profile of traditional 1970s-style nuclear technology within competitive markets; the second was the greater clarity that commercial discipline brought to the true economics of nuclear energy, revealing a number of cross-subsidies and other less than crystal-clear accounting practices. When these were combined with the emergence of CCGT, a major new technology, and the collapse in hydrocarbon prices—oil but also gas—then nuclear energy began to look highly unattractive.

Despite the changing agenda, Sizewell B, the first of the supposed programme of PWRs (now chopped back to four), was approved in a Public Inquiry in 1987. The Public Inquiry into the second of the programme, Hinkley Point C, began in October 1988.

However, negotiations over transferring the nuclear stations to the private sector failed, mainly for market reasons, although the accident at Chernobyl, Ukraine, in April 1986 added to antinuclear sentiment among the public. The Magnox reactors were removed from privatization in July 1989, to be followed by the abandonment of privatization of the AGRs and the embryonic Sizewell B on 9 November 1989 (the same day on which the Berlin Wall fell—that nuclear successfully vied for front-page coverage illustrates what an obsession the industry had become for the British media). At the same time a 5-year 'moratorium' was placed on new nuclear build, though in concessions to the incoming chairman of state-owned Nuclear Electric plc, John Collier, the construction of Sizewell B was to continue, as was the Public Inquiry into Hinkley Point C. The latter concluded with permission to build Hinkley C being granted, but by then this was the emptiest of gestures—nobody was interested in putting the money up. Once again the UK was left with a prototype, and an expensive one at that—the costs of 'Britifying' what the industry regarded as a perfectly good American design added some £700m to the basic £1.3 billion cost in money of the day.

In effect, each of the three nuclear programmes—Magnox, AGRs, and PWRs, including the assumption of new build—was withdrawn from privatization for different reasons. In the case of Magnox, the stations were nearing the end of their lifetimes, but insufficient provision had been made to manage their back-end costs (waste management and decommissioning, both of which are considerably higher per unit of installed Magnox capacity than was to be the case with later designs). Given the considerable uncertainties in the estimates of these back-end costs, private companies (notably National Power, the larger of the two successor companies to the CEGB's generating arm which were to be privatized and which was expected to take the nuclear plants) asked for price or other financial guarantees which the government was not prepared to offer.

In the case of the AGRs the problem was the disappointing performance of these stations. Once again, the private sector wanted guarantees that would allow profit to be made even if performance did not improve; once again, government was unprepared to distort the market to this extent.

For the remaining PWRs, National Power wanted government support for a construction programme, knowing that it could not necessarily pass any cost overruns through to its customers within a competitive market. Whether such support were to come in the form of large direct subsidies or of long-term price guarantees, the level of interference in the emerging market was unacceptable to the government.

As the nuclear stations were pulled from privatization, so a 5-year moratorium on new nuclear build was imposed and a new White Paper was promised following a Nuclear Review in 1994 (DTI, 1995). The first half of the 1990s saw considerable improvement in the output from the AGRs plus the completion of Sizewell B. When the White Paper was published, privatization of the more modern nuclear stations was once again mooted. A new company, British Energy plc, was set up to own and manage the AGRs from Nuclear Electric plc and Scottish Nuclear Ltd, plus Sizewell B, and was privatized in 1996. It subsequently bought interests in coal- and gas-fired power capacity and in renewables such as offshore wind. British Energy also acquired stakes in nuclear power stations in the USA and Canada.

BNFL took over responsibility for the Magnox programme in 1998 and also bought major nuclear plant designers and builders Westinghouse

(USA) and ABB (Sweden/Switzerland). In 1996 the UKAEA was split into a business arm, privatized as AEA Technology, and a state-owned company to manage the organization's long-term liabilities: in 2002 the government announced plans to create a single Liabilities Management Agency (now known as the Nuclear Decommissioning Authority, NDA) to take over responsibility for the nuclear liabilities of BNFL, UKAEA, and the Ministry of Defence. (BNFL was to be in effect broken up in 2006, Westinghouse being sold to Mitsubishi of Japan and the intended sale being announced of its decommissioning and fuel cycle arm, British Nuclear Group.)

However, new build remained off the agenda. The 1990s were a time of unusual comfort with respect to UK energy policy. The coal mining unions had been broken and fragmented during the 1984 strike, the regional electricity companies (RECs) were building new CCGT capacity which produced cheap electricity from plentiful North Sea gas reserves, carbon-dioxide (CO_2) emissions were falling at a faster rate than required in the Rio Convention (and subsequent Kyoto Protocol). Security of supply, low prices and falling environmental impact were all being achieved with very little central effort. The nuclear debate retired from the front line, or even the battlefield, the main issues being the rate at which Magnox stations should be closed, the desirability of commissioning and operating new plant such as the Mixed Oxide Plant (SMP) and Thermal Oxide Reprocessing Plant (THORP) at Sellafield and some work on finding a waste disposal site (effectively abandoned in 1997). The continued operation of the AGRs and Sizewell B seemed relatively uncontroversial and there was no discernible lobby for building new plants to replace the Magnoxes, beyond a few surviving advocates for a further twin PWR station at Sizewell. Indeed, by this point it was hard to identify a 'nuclear industry' in the sense that the term was used 20 years previously—a clear body of companies, government departments, and other interested entities, which had a particular vested interest in more nuclear power stations being built. British Energy was essentially an electricity generating company, UKAEA was developing a long-term remediation programme for its own sites, and even BNFL was increasingly turning to the global clean-up market.

6. Managing and Funding the Legacy Liabilities

A further barrier to the development of nuclear energy, at least insofar as it has played very badly with the public, is the slow (and in some cases almost undetectable) progress in identifying routes for funding the disposal of radioactive waste resulting from plant operation and decommissioning and in finding sites where this can be done.

As is the case in most countries, the UK has a low-level waste disposal facility. This is located at Drigg, near the Sellafield site in Cumbria. Debate has focused more on intermediate and high-level wastes. Intermediate-level waste includes the metal cans in which the uranium or other fuel is contained when it is in the core of the reactor plus some components of the core itself, alongside some wastes that arise during reprocessing.

In the UK and countries such as France, Germany, and Japan, 'spent fuel' (fuel which has been used in a reactor for energy production) is 'reprocessed'. This involves separating the spent fuel into reusable uranium, plutonium (another potential reactor fuel), and the extremely radioactive 'fission products' which make up high-level waste. In some other countries the spent fuel itself is regarded as highly radioactive waste for direct disposal.

Before 1983 intermediate-level waste was disposed of at sea but the London Dumping Convention of that year banned this practice. Since then intermediate-level waste has generally been stored on the sites at which it arises as an 'interim' measure, while high-level waste is mainly stored at the Sellafield site where fuel is reprocessed. Liquid high-level waste is gradually being 'vitrified', i.e. turned into glass blocks.

Long-term governmental policy in almost all countries is to dispose of intermediate- and high-level wastes deep underground. Proponents argue that deep disposal has a number of advantages over indefinite surface storage. First, deep disposal would allow this generation to deal with its own waste rather than leaving it to the future and hence serve 'intergenerational equity' considerations. Second, the likelihood of accidental or deliberate damage is less if the waste is deep underground rather than on or near the surface, a factor which has gained more weight since the terrorist attacks of September 2001 in the USA. Third, the doses to workers are significantly less. Fourth, the hundreds of metres of rock between a deep repository and the surface act as a very secure barrier against the waste escaping.

However, critics argue that unless the geology of a potential site is understood in great detail, and the behaviour of groundwater can be predicted for several centuries or longer, there is a danger that the waste could leach out in unpredicted ways and make its way into water supplies. As a result the last decade has seen the establishment of the concepts of monitorable and retrievable disposal—the repository would remain un-sealed and subject to checks after it was full until such a point as operators could convince the relevant authorities that it was safe to seal it. Until that point, and perhaps even afterwards, the waste could be removed if leakage was occurring or a better technology had emerged.

In several countries there have been well-organized and protracted objections to particular proposals. The search for suitable sites has therefore often been a frustrating and unsuccessful one. In the UK a series of investigations—Billingham in the early 1980s, four sites around the country in the mid-1980s, a site near Sellafield in the mid-1990s—have all been abandoned. In 2003 the government set up a Committee on Radioactive Waste Management (CoRWM) to re-examine all options and recommend a way forward. In Germany major demonstrations have accompanied attempts to move radioactive material round the country, notably to an interim storage site at Gorleben, and in the USA a protracted legal battle has accompanied proposals to dispose of waste in Yucca Mountain, Nevada.

Other countries have had more success. In Finland, Olkiluoto has been chosen as the site for deep geological disposal with the agreement of the local community and construction is under way. Swedish plans are also well advanced. The process in each of these countries has been characterized by a stepwise consultative approach, high levels of trust between regulators and local communities, the embedding of the waste issue in national energy priorities (notably the argument for building a fifth reactor in Finland), and promises to local communities that, should they show willingness to find out more, they could withdraw from the process at any point, promises which were honoured as many communities did indeed decide they did not wish to proceed. The UK, by contrast, has tended to proceed in a secretive fashion, refusing to publish the list of potential sites and failing to make the reasons for its proposals transparent. The mistrust that has been generated has been a major barrier to cool and reflective discussions about the merits of particular sites.

The issue has been exacerbated by one notable outcome of the way in which privatization proceeded, viz. its effect on the provisions made for discharging nuclear liabilities. The UK, as noted earlier, was in effect first to exploit nuclear energy on a commercial scale. The Magnox stations were relatively inefficient by the standards of later designs (especially light water reactors), producing more spent fuel per unit of electricity generated and also more decommissioning wastes. In principle, moneys were being put aside in the accounts of the CEGB and SSEB to discharge the waste management and decommissioning liabilities when they became due (expected to be some decades after the end of the lifetime of the reactors). However, unlike practice in countries such as the USA, Sweden, and

Switzerland, where a levy on nuclear-generated electricity went into segregated state-administered funds to deal with the back-end, in the UK these virtual provisions were not ring-fenced. In practice, the money was reinvested in the business—grid strengthening, new power stations— with the expectation that income from these assets would be used for nuclear decommissioning and waste management in due course.

Whether the provision was sufficient is doubtful but that was to become irrelevant, since the basis of this expectation was shattered by privatization. The nuclear stations, and all of their associated liabilities, were retained in state hands while the assets which had been built using the virtual liabilities were sold off. It would have been possible (and perhaps right) for the government to divert a considerable proportion (or all) of the proceeds from privatization into a waste and decommissioning fund, but the proceeds were not enormous and were required for other uses as a hotly contested general election approached. In 1988 the replacement costs of power stations in England and Wales were estimated at £22.6 billion; in 1991 shares equivalent to 60 per cent of the equity in National Power and its smaller rival PowerGen (and excluding the nuclear plants) were sold for £2.9 billion, equivalent to just £4.8 billion for the entire share capital of the companies (Newbery and Pollitt, 1997).

Instead, a 'Non-fossil Fuel Obligation' was imposed on the newly privatized RECs in England and Wales, whereby they were mandated to buy a certain proportion of their electricity from non-fossil sources—in effect nuclear at first, but with an increasing proportion of renewables. (In Scotland the two privatized utilities, Scottish Power and Scottish Hydro, were contracted on vestment to take the entire output of the state-owned Scottish Nuclear Ltd for 15 years.) If the price of non-fossil electricity were to be higher than that of fossil-generated power, a non-fossil fuel levy (NFFL) on all electricity bills would cover the difference.

This was not an operating subsidy on nuclear energy—the avoidable operating costs of nuclear stations were falling as the output from the AGRs increased—but was designed to recreate the provisions for back-end costs that had been lost at the time of privatization. The nuclear part of the levy raised some £7 billion between 1990 and 1996 (Mitchell, 1998), considerably more than the nominal provision it replaced so as to reflect higher estimates of the costs involved.

History, however, was repeating itself. Much of the income from the NFFL was spent by Nuclear Electric on the construction of Sizewell B. As noted earlier, by the time of the promised White Paper on nuclear energy in 1995, the performance of the AGRs had improved very considerably and Sizewell B was ready to come on line, having been constructed essentially to the time and cost agreed in 1989. Although nuclear new build was not recommended, privatization of the AGRs and Sizewell B was, and the sale of British Energy was duly completed in 1996, raising some £1.5 billion, considerably less than the cost of Sizewell B alone. In addition the company carried £600m of debt and was apportioned its estimated nuclear liabilities of £3.7 billion. A segregated Nuclear Decommissioning Fund was finally set up with initial endowment of £228m and requirements that British Energy make annual contributions to the fund (NAO, 1998). The Magnox liabilities were retained in state hands and transferred to BNFL.

The outcome, temporarily exacerbated by British Energy's financial crisis in 2002 which resulted in the government taking back responsibility for contributions to British Energy's Nuclear Decommissioning Fund, was a very large liability for back-end costs remaining with the taxpayer and without any provisions made to discharge it. The total legacy liability managed by the Nuclear Decommissioning Agency was estimated at some £70 billion in 2006 (Blakely, 2006), though this included military and research wastes as well as the Magnox stations and other former BNFL facilities involved, for example, in reprocessing and fuel manufacture.

Although these sums cannot be regarded as a subsidy towards new nuclear build—the costs will have to be met whatever policy is pursued towards new plants—policy-makers will be keen to reduce the risk that taxpayers in the future do not pick up unprovided-for costs associated with any new reactors. Measures requiring the building up of a segregated fund from the early years of a nuclear project would seem essential within a competitive marketplace. The good news for the industry is that, if provision is put aside throughout the lifetime of the plant, the levelized cost per unit of electricity generated should be modest, below 5 per cent of total costs.

7. Different Experiences

Perhaps more than any other fuel, the deployment (or non-deployment) of nuclear energy varies enormously from country to country. While the same broad trends can be detected in most countries of North America and Western Europe—relative enthusiasm or at least neutrality in the 1960s and 1970s, growth of relative antagonism in the 1980s and 1990s, and a swing back in the mid-2000s—the expression of these trends has differed considerably. In many countries which had never developed nuclear energy, policy decisions or laws were adopted in the 1990s to prevent them from ever doing so, followed in some cases, such as Australia, by government moves to re-examine the nuclear option (BBC News, 2006). In Italy initial enthusiasm towards nuclear energy resulted in the construction of just four nuclear power stations, all of which were closed by 1990 (the last three as a result of a post-Chernobyl referendum). In 2005, however, Prime Minister Berlusconi said that Italy should not rule out a return to nuclear generation. In France, by contrast, bullish enthusiasm cooled to a commitment to replacing existing capacity in due course, followed by an order for a new plant at Flamanville in 2006.

The reasons for the loss of confidence in nuclear investment were several. The recession caused by the oil shocks of the 1970s reduced electricity demand well below that projected in the early 1970s, leaving many countries with significant overcapacity. The subsequent fall in fossil fuel prices further improved the relative economics of these fuels when compared to nuclear energy, while concerns about the security of oil supplies receded as tensions emerged within OPEC.

However, the poor economic performance of nuclear projects when judged against the early promises was undoubtedly a major factor, as were the accidents at Three Mile Island (1979) and Chernobyl (1986).

At Three Mile Island a technical fault coupled with a sub-optimal subsequent response by operators led to nearly half of the fuel in the reactor melting down in an emergency that lasted for several hours and required evacuation of local residents. Eventually the event was controlled without significant releases of radioactivity but it had considerable effects on the attitudes of the public, regulators, and policy-makers. Many plants being built at the time of the accident were redesigned in mid-construction, leading to major overruns in time and cost. In the most extreme case, the Shoreham nuclear station at Long Island, New York, was closed in 1989, before commercial operation began, because it was refused an operating licence on the grounds that it could not comply with evacuation requirements introduced after construction had started. The Long Island Lighting Company was effectively bankrupted by the affair.

The full effects of Three Mile Island were not felt immediately—many plants were completed after the accident (the peak year for nuclear plants being commissioned was 1984 when 33 plants with capacity over 31 GW came on line globally). However, no orders made after 1977 in the USA, the largest user of nuclear energy globally, were completed and many other countries cancelled proposals for new plants. Sixty-five new stations entered commercial operation in 1984 and 1985, but just 28 between 1991 and 1995 inclusive.

Figure 2 Age of Nuclear Power Capacity (GW) Worldwide as of May 2006

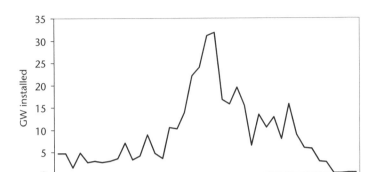

7.1 *France*

In 1973 France generated 43 per cent of its electricity using oil, a further 32 per cent using hydropower, and 10 per cent using coal.[3] Nuclear energy, on 8 per cent, was a relatively small player. France, like the UK, had started by using gas-cooled technology for its first three commercial reactors (the first was commissioned in 1962), but soon came to believe that the PWR was more efficient. An American design was purchased and became the basis of the next phase of the programme.

OPEC increased oil prices sharply in that year. France had little by way of indigenous hydrocarbon reserves and the government decided to pursue rapid nuclear development in order to preserve French independence. Prime Minister Pierre Messmer outlined the pro-nuclear case in a speech on national television on 6 March 1974.

France has not been favoured by nature in energy resources. There is almost no petrol on our territory, we have less coal than England and Germany and much less gas than Holland. Our great chance is electrical energy of nuclear origin because we have had good experience with it since the end of World War II. In this effort that we will make to acquire a certain independence, or at least reduced dependence in energy, we will give priority to electricity and in electricity to nuclear electricity.

The Messmer Plan, as it became known, foresaw the launch of 13 nuclear power plants, each with a capacity of 1,000 MW, within 2 years.

---

[3] http://www.fundinguniverse.com/company-histories/Electriciteacute;-de-France-Company-History.html

In the 6 years to 1979, nuclear energy's share of Electricité de France (EdF)'s total output rose from 8 to 20 per cent, reaching 49 per cent in 1983 and 75 per cent by 1990. The share produced by oil and coal fell from 53 per cent in 1973 to 11 per cent in 1990. EdF's total nuclear capacity had reached 54,000 MW by the end of 1990, with another 6,800 MW under construction, giving France a nuclear capacity greater than those of West Germany, the UK, Spain, and Sweden combined.

The programme came to enjoy all-party support. The newly elected Socialist government of François Mitterrand initially froze reactor construction in 1981 but soon changed its position and allowed construction to continue, albeit at a reduced rate.

EdF, unlike the authorities in the UK, built its reactors to a standardized design which allowed both series economies of scale in construction and considerable 'learning effect' benefits. However, the programme was not without its challenges. The sheer size of the nuclear energy programme, caused in part by overestimates of energy demand and the fixation with energy independence, left EdF with high levels of overcapacity. By 1988 EdF's nuclear units were operating at an average load factor of 61 per cent, compared with smaller nuclear operators like Switzerland (84 per cent) and Finland (92 per cent). For a heavily capital-intensive source of electricity like nuclear energy, even if it is technically capable of load-following, the savings made by doing so in terms of fuel costs are much lower than is the case with low-capital, high-fuel-cost sources such as coal, oil, or gas. One partial solution was export to neighbouring countries, e.g. through the interconnector with the UK. In theory this was installed to allow each country to draw on the other's power grid in times of shortage, but in practice it became a one-way cable for the export of electricity from France to Britain. By 1990 France was exporting large amounts of power to Switzerland, Italy, the UK, Germany, the Netherlands, Belgium, Luxembourg, and Spain. The emergence of cross-border electricity markets in Europe as a result of increased liberalization represents a considerable opportunity for France to export surplus output and so maximize its return on investment.

One can perhaps identify two key features in the relative success of the French programme:

- political leadership, based on a publicly attractive message about energy independence, determined to develop nuclear energy very quickly;

- standardization of plant design, made more manageable because of the very short period of time (often a matter of months) between orders which reduced the temptation to meddle with each new plant to be built.

7.2 Belgium

Belgium commissioned its first nuclear reactor, a small (11 MW) prototype, at Mol in 1962. This had the distinction of being the first PWR built in Europe. In 1965 a 305 MW joint Franco-Belgian plant was opened at Chooz in France (on the Belgian border) and a decision was taken to build two more plants in Belgium and another joint venture with the French. These were commissioned in 1974/5. In 1974 a further four reactors were ordered, the last of which came into production in 1985. The seven plants are located on two sites, at Doel and Tihange.

Public concern about nuclear energy had been growing since protests at Doel in 1979. In 1988 proposals for an eighth Belgian reactor at Doel, a 1400 MW PWR which was to have been jointly owned by Electrabel and EdF, were abandoned, followed in 1992 by an indefinite moratorium on new build. None the less, with 56 per cent of its electricity coming from nuclear energy in 2005, Belgium remains one of the countries most dependent on nuclear reactors for its power production.

In 1999 the Belgian government, then a Liberal/Socialist/Green coalition, introduced policies banning further reprocessing, limiting the lifetime of the existing plants to 40 years and preventing construction of new ones. These restrictions passed into law in January 2003, though with a clause allowing life extension if regulators regarded it as necessary.

7.3 Spain

Spain's first commercial nuclear plant, Zorita, was connected to the grid in December 1968 and was followed by Garoña (1971) and Vandellòs-1 (1972). The first National Energy Plan (1975) predicted a grandiose role for nuclear energy, some 24,000 MW by 1985 and 35,000 MW by 1992. However, by the time a new version of the National Energy Plan was approved in July 1979 planned nuclear capacity for 1990 had fallen to 12,700 MW. Between 1981 and 1985 five reactors were connected to the grid, with a total capacity of 4,700 MW. The third version of the National Energy Plan, published in 1984 by the recently elected Socialist government, included the capping of nuclear power at 10 reactors with combined capacity 7,800 MW. Only two new nuclear power plants were to be completed, Vandellòs-2 and Trillo-1, both PWRs of around 1,000 MW output.

As elsewhere, the causes of the reduced ambitions for nuclear energy included poor economic performance of the nuclear projects, falling oil prices and growing public concerns, especially in the Basque country where major protests against two reactors in Lemoniz near Bilbao resulted in construction being halted in 1982 and subsequent cancellation.

In 1989 a fire in a turbine at Vandellòs-1 seriously damaged the connections from the turbine to the plant's cooling system. Plans to restart the plant were abandoned after 8 months following major demonstrations. In 2005 the remaining nine plants generated 20 per cent of Spain's electricity.

The Socialist government elected in 2004 had concluded a pact with the Green Party to phase out Spain's remaining nine reactors by 2024. Zorita closed in May 2006.

7.4 Sweden

In 1956 a Swedish commission recommended development of a nuclear power programme (also producing heat for district heating) and a 50 MW test reactor was commissioned in 1960. After initial dabbling with heavy-water technology, a 460 MW BWR unit was ordered for Oskarshamm, the first European light-water reactor designed and built without licence from US vendors. It entered commercial operation in 1972, the first of six reactors to be commissioned in the 1970s, followed by a further six in the first half of the 1980s using a mixture of BWR and PWR technology.

After the Three Mile Island accident, Sweden held a referendum on nuclear energy, as a result of which the Swedish parliament decided in 1980 that no further nuclear power plants should be built and that a nuclear power phase-out should be completed by 2010. (The referendum had three phase-out options but no options allowing continuation or expansion.) However, the rate of closure has been slow, being limited to the two reactors at Barsebäck, in 1999 and 2005. Sweden has policies not to develop any further hydropower resources—in 2005 47 per cent of Sweden's electricity came from nuclear energy and 44 per cent from hydro—and to become independent of fossil fuels.

7.5 USA

The USA produced the first nuclear electricity (in 1951), the first PWR (the 60 MW prototype at Shippingport, commissioned in 1957), and the first BWR (1960).

Development of commercial nuclear energy through the 1960s was modest but was given a major boost by the oil price hikes of the 1970s. Output of nuclear electricity increased rapidly after 1973, when 83 TWh were produced, 4.5 per cent of US electricity generation. By 2005 some 782 TWh of nuclear-generated electricity were being produced from 103 licensed nuclear power units (68 PWRs and 35 BWRs), representing 19 per cent of US electricity generation, although 20 of the 51 States had no nuclear capacity.

This degree of growth was in a sense deceptive, since many plant orders were cancelled during this period, including all of those placed since 1977. The accident at Three Mile Island 2 in Pennsylvania in 1979 exacerbated the growing public concerns about the technology (the motion picture *The China Syndrome*, about safety problems at a nuclear plant, was released a fortnight before the accident and included the line that in the event of a major accident 'an area the size of Pennsylvania would be left uninhabitable'). Furthermore, the regulatory response to the accident led to significant redesign of plants already being built, adding enormously to the time and cost of construction, and introduced changes to regulations about evacuation routes which, in the most extreme example, prevented the Shoreham plant in New York State from ever getting a full operating licence. Construction of the last nuclear reactor commissioned so far in the USA, Watts Bar I in Tennessee, began in 1973, but the plant did not enter commercial operation until 1996.

8. The Nuclear Industry Responds

For some time, then, it seemed accepted wisdom that liberalization of power markets had 'done for' nuclear energy. As competitive markets became embedded in the electricity sector of developed countries, so orders for new nuclear stations dried up. Nuclear plants, or at least the large, heavily capital-intensive plants that had evolved in the command-and-control electricity supply systems of the 1960s and 1970s, looked unattractive in liberalized markets. To summarize the common perception of nuclear power stations, they were very expensive to build—even if they came in to time and cost, which they did not usually do, a nuclear plant was kilowatt for kilowatt at least four or five times as expensive as CCGT. In a competitive marketplace investors need strong reasons to believe that they will at least get their money back. If one source of electricity is more expensive to build than another, then inevitably it carries greater economic risk, since it will need more or less guaranteed prices for a much longer period of time to provide an acceptable rate of return. In theory, of course, electricity users could sign very long-term contracts with owners of the nuclear plant, but experience of liberalized markets suggests that contracts of 20 or 30 years (or anywhere near) simply do not exist. Furthermore, when long-term contracts (even 5 years or so) are signed, if the short-term markets get severely out of kilter with the prices at which longer-term contracts have been struck then one or other party to those contracts goes broke.

However, the early years of the twentieth century saw a gradual change in these perceptions and of other perceptions in the energy field. As far as the nuclear industry was concerned, the first years of the decade represented something of a false dawn of optimism. Energy security was rising up the political agenda, something which might have been expected to strengthen the case for considering new nuclear stations. The petrol protests of September 2000, the series of major power outages in California in 2000 and 2001, and the trebling of global oil prices between late 1998 and mid-2000 served to persuade the Blair government to launch an energy review as its first act following the June 2001 general election. However, by the time this study reported and the subsequent White Paper was published (DTI, 2003) many of the concerns that prompted the review seemed to have receded and the final document was not radical. Nuclear new build was in effect dismissed ('We do not propose nuclear new build') but the nuclear option was to be 'kept open'.

The UK nuclear industry itself did little to strengthen the case for new build. In 1999 BNFL was at the centre of a scandal involving the falsification of quality assurance data concerning the export of mixed oxide fuel pellets to Japan. Then in 2002 British Energy had to appeal for government support to stave off bankruptcy.

Between 1998 and 2002 the wholesale price of electricity fell significantly, owing to forced divestment of generating capacity by the larger generating companies and the introduction of New Electricity Trading Arrangements (NETA).

The wholesale price fell below the operating costs of most generators in the marketplace. However, some of the big generating companies, notably E.ON Powergen and RWE Innogy, also owned domestic supply businesses carved out of the former RECs. Owing to the relative unwillingness of household consumers to 'shop around', compared to industrial and commercial electricity users, household power prices fell much more slowly than wholesale prices. In effect the household market behaved as if the local supply company still had a franchise over a

Figure 3 Wholesale Power Prices 1990–2002

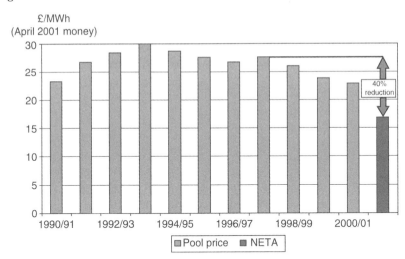

£/MWh
(April 2001 money)

Source: Ofgem.

majority of its customers and so could pass costs through to a considerable extent. For the vertically integrated electricity companies, then, the
collapse in the wholesale price was not a particularly serious matter—they
still had their income from supply activities, which on paper were making
a bigger profit as the generating arms made bigger paper losses.

British Energy did own South Wales Electricity's supply business for a
few months but sold it on to Scottish & Southern Electricity (SSE) in 2000
(BBC News, 2000). British Energy was therefore heavily exposed to the
collapse in wholesale prices, as were other companies such as AES Drax.
Government, unwilling to allow British Energy to declare bankruptcy
and therefore be left with the direct responsibility both of ensuring secure
supplies of electricity and of dealing with the nuclear plants safely,
offered loans to British Energy in return for major restructuring which
saw the company sell its North American assets and convert most of its
share capital into bonds. The government also took over ultimate
responsibility for payments into the company's decommissioning fund.

The company was to recover and in due course regain its place in the FTSE-
100 index of leading companies. But though the crisis was not principally
caused by British Energy's dependence on nuclear energy, opponents of
nuclear energy lost no opportunity of painting the event as 'proof' that
nuclear energy could not be economic.

9. The Pendulum Swings

By mid-decade a number of developments had acted to increase the attractiveness of nuclear energy. On the back of an eight-fold increase in the global oil price over the period from late 1998, energy from fossil fuels became much more expensive. Recognition that measures to combat emissions of greenhouse gases were having very little effect, coupled with a string of extreme weather events worldwide, increased concerns about climate change. The depletion of the UK's own gas and oil reserves led to fears about security of energy supplies, exacerbated by President Putin's decision to cut off Russian gas supplies to Ukraine early in 2006. Proponents of nuclear energy pointed to its status as a source of electricity that did not depend on limited fossil fuel supplies which, in the case of gas, would increasingly have to be imported; which was more resistant to fuel price inflation (as the fuel costs were a much lower proportion of overall costs than was the case with electricity generated using coal or gas); and which had much lower emissions of greenhouse gases across the whole fuel cycle, there being some emissions as a result of uranium mining and processing, plant construction, etc., but none as a result of normal operation.

External pressures on traditional electricity production were accompanied by features of liberalization of power markets which also began to work in nuclear power's favour. First, the UK (in common with other countries which had liberalized their electricity industries in the 1990s) was reaching a stage where very large investment in some kind of generating plant was necessary. As noted earlier, one of the reasons for liberalization was that 'capacity margins'—the spare plant which must be kept available in case there is an unexpected surge in demand or significant numbers of plants breaking down at once—tended to be overgenerous where security of supply dominated thinking and the cost of whatever level of surplus capacity was retained could be passed on to captive customers (or charged to the taxpayer). In the UK, unusually, the early years of liberalization were accompanied by new plant investment, the market having been set up to encourage RECs to invest in their own (gas-fired) generating capacity. But once the RECs lost the last elements of a captive market (electricity consumers were allowed to shop around from their supplies in three tranches—greater than 1MW in 1990, greater than 100 kW in 1994, and all consumers in 1998/9, roughly a third of the market in each tranche), investment in all kinds of electricity generating capacity practically stopped. No major plants were ordered between 2000 and Centrica's 885 MW CCGT

Figure 4 New Installed Capacity since 1991, UK (MW, cumulative)

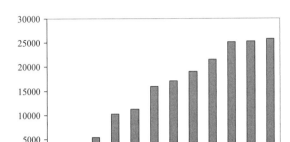

Source: Shuttleworth and MacKerron (2002).

at Langage, near Plymouth, approved in 2006 and set to start operating in the winter of 2008/9.

As the first decade of the twenty-first century proceeded, concerns began to re-emerge about the adequacy of future capacity margins, as power stations reached the end of their lives and demand continued to grow at modest rates. A remarkable string of major outages in developed countries in the summer and autumn of 2003—Italy, USA and southeastern Canada, London, Birmingham, Copenhagen and south Sweden, Italy again—served to remind people and politicians of both the possibility and the effects of such events, though most of these were actually caused by failures of transmission systems rather than shortages of available plant.

It may be in the interest of generators in competitive marketplaces for there to be the odd power cut or at least serious fear thereof, since that

Figure 5 Projected Decline in UK Nuclear Capacity

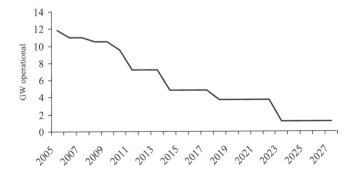

keeps power prices very high. But eventually new investment becomes attractive and new plant will be built. The argument that it would cost a great deal of money to build a new programme of nuclear stations was true but the alternatives looked just as expensive when judged over station lifetimes.

Second, new nuclear designs were emerging with features more in line with the requirements of competitive electricity markets—quicker and cheaper to build and more reliable in operation, at least on paper, with recent experience of projects in Asia Pacific appearing promising. There are as many ways of making energy from uranium as there are from water, and just because 1970s nuclear technology is not well suited to liberalized markets—why should it be?—does not mean that other potential approaches are the same. It was claimed that simplification of design and use of passive rather than engineered safety systems should halve the cost of nuclear plants without any negative implications (and quite possibly positive ones) for safety or plant reliability. Passive designs contain significantly fewer pumps, pipes, valves, and cables, so there are fewer items to install, inspect, and maintain than in a traditional plant. From a safety perspective such plants rely on naturally occurring phenomena, such as gravity, natural circulation, and condensation, guaranteeing (it is claimed) a safe shutdown of the plant even in the highly unlikely event of an accident. A small number of competing international designs were emerging, as described later.

Third, liberalization was finally breaking down the 'Little National' approach which had so dogged nuclear energy. The UK bought a perfectly good design from the USA for Sizewell B but then spent another £700m in 'Britifying' it. The growth of a cross-border approach to plant design (not of course just in the nuclear field), component manufacture, and skills was introducing efficiencies which were largely absent in the command-control days.

Fourth, the performance of nuclear power plants globally improved steadily. Market discipline was one likely factor contributing towards this.

Fifth, the growth of cross-border power markets with a handful of very large pan-European players—EdF, Enel, RWE, E.ON—offered a new model of funding and operating nuclear stations. Instead of needing a large number of plants in a small market in order to benefit from economies of scale, a programme of say 10 AP1000 or EPR-1600 reactors spread around Europe could enjoy such economies without introducing great inflexibilities on individual national markets.

So two new ways of funding nuclear plants were emerging. One was the Finnish model—TVO, which ordered a new station at Olkiluoto, was a

Figure 6 Average World Nuclear Energy 'Availability Factor' (%)

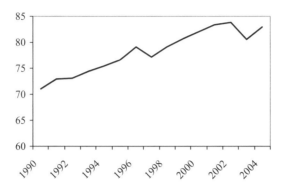

consortium of major electricity users and suppliers who didn't want to get too dependent on Russian gas. Members contracted to take electricity at cost in proportion to their initial investment, thereby in effect creating lifetime contracts for the output within a mature liberalized market. The other was that which served as the basis of the new French plant at Flamanville—a consortium of big European electricity generators with deep enough pockets to invest in both long- and short-term power sources.

In addition, concerns were growing about the UK's environmental record. Between 1990 and 1997 the 'dash for gas' and increased nuclear output had delivered considerable reductions in CO_2 emissions from electricity production, allowing the UK to meet its Rio commitment of emitting no more CO_2 in 2000 than it had in 1990 with a considerable comfort margin. The UK's Kyoto commitment of a 12.5 per cent reduction in emissions of the 'basket' of six greenhouse gases by 2008/12 also looked secure. However, Labour had been elected in 1997 with a manifesto commitment to cut CO_2 emissions by 20 per cent from 1990 levels by 2010 and Prime Minister Tony Blair had played a high profile role internationally in calling for further reductions. That UK CO_2 emissions had actually risen since 1997 was something of an embarrassment.

New nuclear plants could not help with the 2010 commitment but could reduce emissions subsequently.

10. New Plant Technologies

Most important among the new international designs of nuclear plant that emerged in the first years of the twenty-first century were:

Figure 7 UK CO$_2$ Emissions, 1997–2004 (1990 level 165.4)

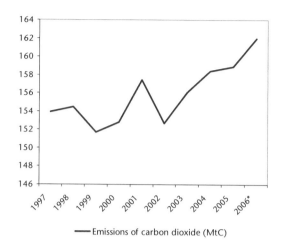

Note: * 2006 projected from first 6 months.

- Mitsubishi-Westinghouse AP1000 and AP600—advanced passive PWRs.
- AECL (Atomic Energy of Canada Ltd)—Advanced CANDU reactor (ACR).
- Areva—European Pressurized Water Reactor (EPR).
- On a slightly longer timescale, the Pebble Bed Modular concept, being developed by Eskom (South Africa) and Chinergy (China).

Westinghouse estimated that AP1000, which had a licence in the USA, would cost around $1,000 to $1,200 per kW installed (Westinghouse, 2004). The plant would be constructed modularly, which would improve construction quality while reducing construction time to about 36 months from the time concrete was first poured until the time that fuel was loaded into the core. This shortened construction period would reduce the amount of time that investment capital would be tied up before the plant began to generate electricity and hence cash flow.

The EPR is an evolutionary PWR of 1,600 MW output, incorporating characteristics of 'traditional' French and German reactors with innovative features, including better thermal efficiency (37 per cent) and fuel burn-up (15 per cent improvement on previous designs). In mid-decade it had the advantage of being ahead of the field, one being under construction in Finland, and steps were being taken to license it in the

USA. However, investment costs appeared higher than those of competitors (around $1,500 per kW) and some commentators felt that the large size of the units might lead to inflexibilities in relatively small markets.

AECL's ACR was based on evolutionary changes to CANDU, including light water cooling and use of enriched uranium fuel. Some of these changes had been applied to modern CANDU projects in China and South Korea. Its capital costs were expected to be within the $1,000 to $1,200 range for a mature programme. CANDU was a well-established design but neither the USA nor Western Europe had much experience of heavy water reactors.

More innovative was the pebble bed modular reactor (PBMR) being developed by Eskom of South Africa, based on German technological research in the 1980s and 1990s. A similar concept was being pursued in China. PBMR has a number of features that look attractive on paper. It can be built in relatively small units, perhaps 110 MW output, increasing its load-following possibilities and allowing for better economics during construction. (Individual units can be built quickly, so although a PBMR plant would probably still be in the 1,000 MW range, its early units could be generating while later ones were still under construction.) It is cooled with helium gas, removing the need for a secondary circuit to boil water and hence increasing its thermal efficiency (about 45 per cent). The fuel is in the form of small spheres, made up of large numbers of relatively highly enriched (8 per cent) uranium fragments each covered in an impermeable silicon/carbon barrier, coated with graphite, which would appear to offer considerable safety advantages. However, until the pilot plants are built it will be difficult to make firm estimates of cost and other issues.

Various recent studies have considered the relative economics of nuclear new build. They are summarized in Table 1.

Perhaps the main message that can be taken from such an exercise is that almost any answer can be obtained if the input assumptions are appropriate. Estimates of the cost of capital and of gas and coal prices are particularly important. Until a number of examples have actually been built it will prove difficult to assess the various claims being made.

However, for policy-makers the issue may be a little less acute than was the case in the days of centrally planned electricity supply systems. Decisions on which nuclear technology to build, if any, will be more market-based than was the case previously and will be financed largely or wholly by private investors. The stance of government will remain important but will be more one of setting market parameters than of direct involvement.

Table 1. Studies of Comparative Costs of New Generating Plants

	MIT (2003) $	DGEMP (2003) €	T&L (2003) €	RAE (2004) £	UofC (2004) $	CERI (2004) Can$
Capital cost per kW						
Nuclear	2,000	1,280	1,900	1,150	1,500	2,347
Gas	500	523	600	300	590	711
Coal	1,300	1,281	860	820	1,189	1,600
Construction period, years						
Nuclear	5	5	5	5	5	5
Gas	2	2	2	2	2	2
Coal	4	3	3	4	4	4
Cost of capital of D rate (%)						
Nuclear	11.5	8	5	7.5	12.5	8
Gas	9.6	8	5	7.5	9.5	8
Coal	9.6	8	5	7.5	9.5	8
Gas price	3.50/MBTU	3.30/MBTU	3.00/Gj	2.18/Gj	3.39/MBTU	6.47/Mcf
Electricity price per MWh						
Nuclear	67	28	24	23	51	53
Gas	38	35	32	22	33	72
Coal	42	34	28	25	35	48
Electricity price, nuclear = 100						
Nuclear	100	100	100	100	100	100
Gas	57	125	133	96	65	136
Coal	63	121	117	109	69	89

Notes: MIT—Massachusetts Institute of Technology; DGEMP—French Ministry of the Economy, Finance and Industry; T&L–Tarjanne and Luostarinen; RAE—Royal Academy of Engineering; UofC—University of Chicago; CERI—Canadian Energy Research Institute for Canadian Nuclear Association.
Source: World Nuclear Association (2005).

10.1 *The Generation IV Nuclear Energy Initiative*[4]

There are a number of other advanced reactors under study or on the drawing board. Most of these schemes require substantial development and may not be commercially proven before 2020–30. In addition to basic research, such concepts may need a series of pilot and demonstration plants to allow study in depth of such factors as the effects of different types of fuel, detailed study of the resulting waste and the means of disposing of it, and the potential effect of the fuel cycle associated with the envisaged reactor or assembly on weapons proliferation.

[4] Generation I nuclear reactors are defined as the early programmes such as Magnox; Generation II as the PWRs, BWRs, and AGRs of the 1970s and 1980s; Generation III as the advanced reactors available today or in the near future, such as EPR, AP-1000, ACR, and PBMR.

To explore opportunities for such research, 10 countries (Argentina, Brazil, Canada, France, Japan, South Korea, South Africa, Switzerland, the UK, and the USA) formed the 'Generation IV International Forum' (GIF).[5] The technological goals for the Generation IV study were:

- to provide sustainable energy generation that meets clean air objectives and promotes long-term availability of systems as well as effective fuel utilization for worldwide energy production;
- to minimize and manage nuclear waste and notably reduce the burden of the long-term stewardship of waste;
- to increase the assurance that the waste streams are very unattractive for diversion into weapons;
- to excel in safety and reliability;
- to have a very low likelihood and degree of reactor core damage;
- to eliminate the need for offsite emergency response;
- to have a clear life-cycle cost advantage over other energy sources;
- to have financial risks comparable to other energy projects.

In 2002 the US Department of Energy, which initiated the programme, provided Congress with a 'roadmap' for evaluating potential nuclear energy concepts, selecting the most promising line for further development and defining the required research and development to bring the project to commercialization within the proposed time (USDOE, 2002). The roadmap addresses the full fuel cycle, not just reactors.

Among the concepts considered are:

- a high-temperature gas reactor under development by General Atomic Corporation in conjunction with France, Japan, and Russia;
- advanced light-water reactor systems, such as IRIS, a modular design of 100 to 300 MW unit capacity, longer core reloading schedule (5–8 years) and enhanced safety features and proliferation resistance;
- renewed interest in fast reactors (FRs), though not necessarily as breeders;[6]

[5] http://gif.inel.gov/, 'Nuclear Energy Systems for the Future', Generation IV International Forum.

[6] It is claimed that new designs of FR are simpler and safer than thermal reactors, and that they can destroy plutonium and other actinides better and more effectively than via a mixed oxide fuel route making use of light water reactors. This may become important in view of the need to destroy surplus weapons-grade plutonium as well as material from civil reprocessing. Much of the work on FRs has made use of sodium cooling, but more recently another coolant, a lead/bismuth eutectic, originally developed for Russian submarine reactors, has caused interest. However, widespread use of plutonium fuels could lead to concerns over proliferation.

- substantial advances in the design and use of powerful accelerators, making it possible to consider accelerator driven systems (ADS);[7]

- a number of other, perhaps more specialized, reactors which are under development, including high temperature reactors providing high temperature heat for the production of hydrogen from hydrocarbons and for use in water desalination,[8] both such uses being likely to become important during this century;

- very small reactors, possibly down to 15 MW, with sealed fuel lasting the lifetime of the reactor for use as the energy source in isolated areas— the Russians have been in the forefront of the concept as a possible way of providing electricity for isolated regions such as Siberia's mining operations.

In 2004 the USDOE sought a partner to develop the Next Generation Nuclear Plant (NGNP), a Generation IV reactor of some kind, as its leading concept for developing advanced power systems both for electricity and hydrogen production on a very large scale. A pilot plant demonstrating technical feasibility was envisaged by 2020 at Idaho National Laboratory, with international collaboration. If successful, the NGNP would be 'smaller, safer, more flexible and more cost-effective than any commercial nuclear plant in history. The NGNP will secure a major role for nuclear energy for the long-term future and also provide the USA with a practical path toward replacing imported oil with domestically produced, clean, and economic hydrogen (USDOE, 2004). The DOE goals for a commercial NGNP were electricity at less than 1.5¢ per kWh, hydrogen at less than 40¢ per litre petrol equivalent, and overnight capital cost below $1,000 per kW, dropping to half of this in due course.

10.2 *Fusion*

Looking even further into the future, there may come a time when nuclear fusion is a serious contender. Fusion works on a different principle from fission; instead of breaking up relatively large atoms to

---

[7] In such systems assemblies containing fissile material operate in subcritical mode—i.e. they do not produce sufficient neutrons to keep the nuclear reaction going and therefore require additional neutrons from an outside source, such as an accelerator. It is possible that such subcritical reactors may have advantages over critical FRs, especially as regards fuel composition, although the external source of neutrons may be very expensive. ADSs are also attracting interest as a possible way of 'transmuting' long-lived radioactive waste and thereby making it more manageable.

[8] The use of nuclear energy in desalination has been demonstrated through the BN350 fast reactor in Kazakhstan and is the subject of an 11-member International Atomic Energy Agency technical cooperation project.

make energy, in fusion the smallest atoms, generally various types of hydrogen, are built up into bigger ones, creating significantly more energy per reaction. It is the energy of the stars.

Fusion has a number of apparently attractive features. It would in effect run on water and lithium (a plentiful resource). There would be no fission products nor long-lived 'actinides', so waste management would be very much easier. The stations themselves would become radioactive over a period of time but research is going on to develop materials which could be reused in further fusion reactors after being stored for a few decades. And because there would only be a few grammes of radioactive material in the reactor at any one time the possibility of a big accident like Chernobyl could not arise.

However, there are considerable technical challenges still to be overcome. The 'plasma' in which fusion takes place must be heated to 100–200m degrees Centigrade (about 10 times the temperature of the sun). No solid substance can be used to contain such temperatures so the plasma has to be trapped in a magnetic field, or 'bottle', requiring massive electrical fields. Converting the energy released into electricity could also be a difficult practical issue.

Fusion research has been carried out for some decades, notably in the UK (the Joint European Torus, JET, was established in 1978), the USA, and Japan. This research has confirmed that fusion can be made to happen on earth. The next stage will be to determine if a way can be found of harnessing this energy to make electricity before a commercial demonstration reactor can be built to determine the economics of fusion. In 1985 the then Soviet Union suggested building a next generation reactor with Europe, Japan, and the USA. Between 1988 and 1990 initial designs were drawn up for an international thermonuclear experimental reactor (ITER). In 1998 the ITER Council approved the first comprehensive design of a fusion reactor based on well-established physics and technology, at an expected cost of US$6 billion.

The USA pulled out of the project but rejoined in 2003, when China also joined it. After a further period of indecision the partners agreed in mid-2005 to site ITER at Cadarache, in southern France, but with major concessions to the Japanese who had proposed Rokkasho as an alternative. The EU and France are to contribute half of the €10 billion total cost (about half of which will go on construction and half on 20 years of operation) with the other partners—Japan, China, South Korea, the USA, and Russia—putting in 10 per cent each. Japan will provide high-tech components, host a €1 billion materials testing facility, and have the right to host a subsequent demonstration fusion reactor. India joined the ITER project in late 2005 (http://www.iter.org/).

Even if fusion is now 30 years away, having been 40 years away in the 1950s, the uncertainties inherent in such a large and complex programme mean that it will be some time before a realistic assessment of the practical role that fusion might play can be made. Even if an economic technology should emerge from ITER and the subsequent commercial prototype, it will presumably take some decades before fusion is making a major contribution to global electricity production.

11. Fission—A Global Reappraisal?

11.1 *Western Europe and North America*

The global factors affecting energy policy in the UK also had their effect in other countries to a greater or lesser extent and resulted in a marked increase in interest in nuclear life extension and new build. The first decade of the twenty-first century saw new reactors being ordered in Finland and France (both Areva EPR-1600s) and the Netherlands reversed its policy of early closure of its commercial nuclear station at Borssele.

In May 2003 two referenda regarding the future of nuclear power in Switzerland were held. 'Electricity without nuclear' asked for a decision on a phase-out, and 'Moratorium plus' asked about an extension of an existing law forbidding new build. Both were rejected, 'Moratorium plus' with 58.4 per cent opposed and 'Electricity without nuclear' with 66.3 per cent opposed. The former 10-year moratorium on the construction of new nuclear power plants was the result of a 1990 vote which had passed with 54.5 per cent in favour.

In September 2005 the Belgian government decided partially to overturn the previous decision to limit the lifetime of nuclear plants, extending the phase-out period for another 20 years with possible further extensions, although remaining silent on new build. The reason given for revoking the previous phase-out timetable was that it was unrealistic to expect to replace the electricity being generated by nuclear plants by alternative means. In Spain no firm timetable was set for closure of the other plants (after Zorita in 2006) as concerns grew about Spain's growing energy dependency and burgeoning greenhouse gas emissions.

Sweden's nuclear phase-out has always been controversial. Swedish businesses in particular have expressed fears that they will lose international competititiveness and the output of the remaining nuclear power plants has been considerably increased in recent years to compensate for the closure of the two Barsebäck units in 1999 and 2005. In a March 2005 opinion poll carried out by the Analysis Group, 49 per cent of Swedes wanted existing reactors replaced at the end of their lifetimes and a total of 83 per cent wanted them to be operated until the end of their lifetimes rather than being phased out earlier (The Analysis Group, 2005). In 2006 the Centre Party, an opposition party that was actually the first to argue for nuclear phase-out in the 1970s, announced that it was dropping its opposition to nuclear power, claiming that it was unrealistic to expect phase-out in the short term.

Even in Italy, which had phased out nuclear energy in the late 1980s, the Berlusconi government was talking about new build before it lost power in 2006.[9]

In the late 1990s and early 2000s the price paid for nuclear stations changing hands in the USA began to grow significantly. For example, Amergen, a joint venture between British Energy and Peco (now Exelon), bought Three Mile Island I (790 MW), Clinton (Illinois, 930 MW) and Oyster Creek (New Jersey, 650 MW) for prices in the tens of millions of US dollars. In 2001, however, its $23m bid for the 522 MW Vermont Yankee (which included $60m-worth of fuel) was rejected on price grounds, the plant being sold to Entergy for $180m the following year and being revalued at $239m by state authorities in 2006 (Ceccarrossi, 2006). By 2003 Constellation Energy was paying over $400m for the 495 MW RE Ginna plant (North Carolina) which began operation in 1969. Another signal that nuclear energy's fortunes were improving was the growth in interest in lifetime extension from March 2000 onwards. By May 2006 42 plants had received lifetime licence extensions to 60 years (from the initial 40 years), with nine more applications having been lodged and 27 more expected over the following 6 years (Nuclear Energy Institute, 2006).

Nuclear new build returned to the agenda with the election of George W. Bush in 2001. The much-delayed Energy Policy Act (US Government, 2005), which eventually entered law in 2005, included financial incentives for nuclear plants (including indemnification against regulatory change for the first four to be ordered). In May 2006, for example, the President said, 'For the sake of economic security and national security, the United States of America must aggressively move forward with the construction of nuclear power plants' (Gerstenzang, 2006). In 2004 seven companies (Constellation, EdF, Entergy, Exelon, Southern, Westinghouse,

---

[9] 'Italy should not dismiss nuclear power—Berlusconi', Reuters (20 January 2005).

Figure 8 Nuclear Reactors under Construction as of March 2006

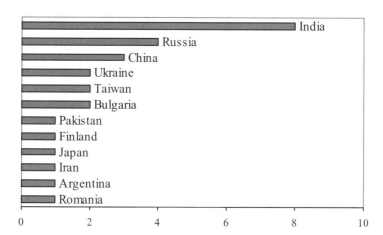

Source: IAEA (2006).

and GE Energy) announced plans to form a consortium to work with the US Department of Energy to demonstrate and test a new licensing process for obtaining a combined construction and operating licence for advanced nuclear power reactors (NuStart Energy, 2004). Whether the USA moves to new nuclear construction or not is likely to be a major influence on nuclear development in other countries.

Similarly, in Canada in June 2006 Ontario energy minister Dwight Duncan announced plans to spend up to C$20 billion over 20 years in refurbishing existing reactors (eight of the province's 19 plants were out of action in the mid-2000s) and building at least two new ones, as part of a basket of measures which also included delaying the closure of Ontario's coal-fired power stations (Bloomberg, 2006). Ontario Power Generation is state-owned and liberalization of the electricity system was effectively abandoned in 2002.

However, in a number of countries attitudes to nuclear energy did not seem to change. Those like Austria and Ireland maintained their long-standing opposition. The election of a Christian Democrat Chancellor, Angela Merkel (in coalition with the leftist SPD), in Germany did not result in a reversal of the phase-out policy of the previous SPD/Green coalition (elected in 1998), although by late 2006 the Chancellor was indicating that a rethink might be necessary.

11.2 *Developing Countries*

Even when investment in nuclear energy stalled in Europe and the USA it continued elsewhere, notably in the Asia Pacific region, but also in the former Communist bloc of central and eastern Europe. For example, the four new connections to grid in 2005 were in China, South Korea, and Japan (two).

In the first decade of the new century countries such as Egypt, Indonesia, and Venezuela signalled an intention to build their first nuclear plants, while China announced plans to build 30 new plants by 2020 and in mid-2006 declared an intention to build six in the south-eastern province of Fujian (Taylor, 2006).

12. Conclusions

As perceptions of problems associated with other fuels grow so it is natural that nuclear energy should be reappraised as a major option in many countries. New designs have attractive features in theory but these are as yet largely undemonstrated in practice. Further, the economics of the new plants, even if they do prove more attractive, are not the only issue. Public perceptions over issues such as waste management, plant safety, and possibly terrorist action will need to be addressed. Potential investors in nuclear technology will need to feel some confidence that unpredictable regulatory changes will not pull the rug from under their feet through no fault of their own, while government will need to be sure that future taxpayers are not left with large bills if nuclear generating companies declare bankruptcy. It looks more likely that government support for nuclear energy in competitive markets, if it is forthcoming, will be of the kind of stream-lined planning and licensing procedures and some kind of indemnity against regulatory change, rather than a firm commitment to nuclear build at all costs.

Part 4: International Policy

14

The Investment Implications of Global Energy Trends

Fatih Birol

1. Introduction

Although events that are short term in nature, such as spiking oil prices, typically dominate newspaper headlines, it is crucial that we keep our eyes open to the medium- and longer-term threats that environment, security and economic demands place on our energy system. To assist in this, the International Energy Agency (IEA)'s *World Energy Outlook* seeks to provide an analytical basis for understanding the drivers of energy markets and emerging energy challenges.

In even-numbered years, the *World Energy Outlook* series provides projections for demand and supply of oil, gas, coal, nuclear power, electricity, and renewables for the world and each major region over a time horizon through to 2030. It draws lessons for energy security, trade, and investment, quantifies energy-related carbon-dioxide (CO_2) emissions, and assesses policies designed to reduce them. In odd-numbered years the series provides analysis of a topical issue or challenge confronting the energy sector.

This chapter draws on the two most recent editions in the series, the *World Energy Outlook 2005—Middle East and North Africa Insights* (IEA, 2005) and the *World Energy Outlook 2006* (IEA, 2006d), which were released during an extremely volatile and uncertain period in modern energy history. These reports highlighted that converting the world's energy resources into available supplies will require massive investments, and that, in some cases, financing for new energy infrastructure will be hard to come by. The chapter starts by providing insight into the methodology used by the two studies, before presenting the key findings and then discussing the major uncertainties and challenges that they identified.

2. Methodology

2.1 *Energy Projection Methodology*

The *World Energy Outlook* series adopts a scenario approach to analyse the possible evolution of energy markets. The central projections are derived from a Reference Scenario. They are based on a set of assumptions about government policies, macroeconomic conditions, population growth, energy prices, and technology. The Reference Scenario in the latest edition takes into account only those government policies and measures that were already enacted—though not necessarily implemented—as of mid-2006. These projections should not be interpreted as a forecast of how energy markets are likely to develop. The Reference Scenario projections should, rather, be considered a baseline vision of how the global energy system will evolve if governments take no further action to affect its evolution beyond that to which they have already committed themselves. The study also includes a World Alternative Policy Scenario, which takes into account a range of new policies to address environmental problems and enhance energy security that are currently under consideration by countries around the world.

The IEA's World Energy Model (WEM)—a large-scale mathematical model that has been developed over several years—is the principal tool used to generate the detailed sector-by-sector and region-by-region projections for both scenarios.[1] Input data to the WEM are sourced primarily from IEA databases which are updated on a continual basis. These databases cover energy production, trade, stocks, transformation, consumption, prices, and taxes as well as greenhouse-gas emissions. The geographical coverage of IEA's statistics includes the 30 OECD member countries and over 100 non-OECD countries worldwide. The WEM also draws on input from numerous secondary sources.

The main exogenous assumptions used by the WEM include economic growth, demographics, and international fossil-fuel prices. The assumptions made by the current *Outlook* for these variables are as follows.

---

[1] See www.worldenergyoutlook.org for a detailed description of the World Energy Model.

- Global economic growth—the primary driver of energy demand—is assumed to average 3.4 per cent per year over the period 2004–30. The rate will drop from 4 per cent in 2004–15 to 2.9 per cent from 2015 to 2030, as developing countries' economies mature and population growth slows. The economies of China, India, and other Asian countries are expected to continue to grow most rapidly.

- The world's population is assumed to expand from 6.4 billion in 2004 to over 8.1 billion in 2030—an increase of 1 per cent per year on average. Population growth will slow progressively over the projection period, mainly due to falling fertility rates in developing countries. The share of the world's population living in developing regions will, none the less, increase from 76 per cent today to 80 per cent in 2030.

- In the Reference Scenario, the average IEA crude oil import price is assumed to fall back from current highs to $47 (in year-2005 dollars) in 2012.[2] The price is assumed to rise slowly thereafter, reaching $55 in 2030. Gas prices are assumed to move broadly in line with oil prices. Steam coal prices are assumed to fall back to around $55/tonne in the next few years, and to rise slowly thereafter, to $60 in 2030. The Deferred Investment Case sees a crude oil price $19 higher than the Reference Scenario in 2030.

The *World Energy Outlook* projections of energy demand and supply are subject to a wide range of uncertainties, including macroeconomic conditions, resource availability, technological developments, and investment flows, as well as government energy and environmental policies. The near-term energy outlook depends heavily on the prospects for economic growth—especially in China—and on oil-price trends.

2.2 *Investment Projection Methodology*

The estimates of investment requirements cover the period 2005–30 and are derived from the projections of energy supply and demand from the *World Energy Outlook 2006* Reference Scenario. The quantification of capital requirements, notably the compilation of unit capital cost estimates and capacity needs for each fuel, component, and region, involved compiling and processing large quantities of data. A significant contribution to this work has been made by a number of organizations in the energy sector and in the financial community.

---

[2] For comparison, in 2005 the average IEA crude oil price was $5.97 per barrel lower than first-month West Texas Intermediate (WTI).

Table 1. Key Global Energy Supply and Infrastructure Inputs

		Units	2002	2030
Oil	Production	mb/d	77	121
	Refining capacity	mb/d	82	121
	Tanker capacity	million DWT	271	522
Gas	Production	bcm	2,622	4,900
	Transmission pipelines	thousand km	1,139	2,058
	Distribution pipelines	thousand km	5,007	8,523
	Underground storage working volume	bcm	328	685
Coal	Production	Mt	4,791	7,029
	Port capacity	Mt	2,212	2,879
Electricity	Generation capacity	GW	4,105	7,052
	Transmission network	thousand km	3,550	7,231

Note: DWT == dead weight tonnes.
Source: *World Energy Outlook 2003*.

The calculation of the investment requirements involved the following steps for each fuel and region.

- New-build capacity needs for production, transportation and (where appropriate) transformation were calculated on the basis of projected supply trends, estimated rates of retirement of the existing supply infrastructure, and decline rates for oil and gas production.

- Unit capital cost estimates were compiled for each component in the supply chain. These costs were then adjusted for each year of the projection period using projected rates of change based on a detailed analysis of the potential for technology-driven cost reductions and on country-specific factors.

- Incremental capacity needs were multiplied by unit costs to yield the amount of investment needed.

The estimates of investment in the current decade take account of projects that have already been decided and expenditures that have already been incurred. Table 1 details developments in key aspects of the global supply infrastructure for each fuel that were taken into account in determining investment requirements.

3. Key Findings

3.1 *Global Energy Trends*

In the *World Energy Outlook 2006* Reference Scenario, world primary energy demand is projected to expand at an average annual rate of 1.6 per cent per

Figure 1 World Primary Energy Demand by Region

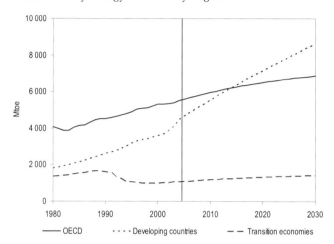

Source: World Energy Outlook 2006.

year between 2004 and 2030. This will see demand reach 17.1 billion tonnes of oil equivalent (toe), compared to 11.2 billion toe in 2004.

Over 70 per cent of the increase in world primary energy demand will come from the developing countries (Figure 1). The increase in the share of the developing regions in world energy demand results from their more rapid rates of economic and population growth, as well as industrialization and urbanization. Despite relatively strong growth in energy use in developing regions, *per capita* consumption there will remain much lower than in the rest of the world. In addition, it is projected that by 2030, 1.4 billion people, mainly in Sub-Saharan Africa and India, will still be without electricity. This is just marginally less than the 1.6 billion people who lack access today.

As a consequence of these projections, energy-related emissions of CO_2 are expected to grow marginally faster than energy use. CO_2 emissions will be 55 per cent higher in 2030 than now. The average carbon content of energy, which fell markedly during the past three decades, will actually increase slightly. Over three-quarters of the projected increase in emissions will come from developing countries, which will remain big users of coal—the most carbon-intensive of fuels.

TRENDS BY FUEL

By 2030, oil will remain the single largest fuel in the global primary energy mix, even though its share will fall marginally, from 35 per cent in 2004 to

33 per cent. Demand for oil is projected to grow by 1.3 per cent per year, from about 84 mb/d now, to 91 mb/d in 2010, and 116 mb/d in 2030. Oil use will become increasingly concentrated in the transport sector, which will account for two-thirds of the increase in total oil use.

Demand for natural gas will grow at a steady rate of 2 per cent per year. By 2030, gas consumption will be 68 per cent higher than now, but will remain the third largest energy source, behind oil and coal. The power sector will be the main driver of demand in all regions. This trend will be particularly marked in developing countries, where electricity demand is expected to rise most rapidly.

Coal use is projected to increase by 1.8 per cent per year to 2030. By that time, coal demand, at almost 9 billion tonnes, will be almost 60 per cent higher than at present. China and India, which both have ample coal reserves, will account for more than three-quarters of the increase in global coal use over the projection period.

Nuclear power—which could make a major contribution to reducing dependence on imported gas and curbing CO_2 emissions—increases from 368 GW in 2005 to 416 GW in 2030, but its share in the primary energy mix still falls, on the assumption that few new reactors are built and existing ones are retired. Interest in building nuclear reactors has, however, increased as a result of higher fossil-fuel prices, which have made nuclear power relatively more competitive. As nuclear power plants are capital-intensive, governments will have to play a stronger role in facilitating private investment for nuclear power to make a major contribution.

Hydropower production will expand by 2 per cent per year over the projection period, a slightly faster rate than that of global primary energy demand. Most of the increase in output will occur in developing countries, where there are still considerable unexploited resources and where public opposition is less of an impediment to new projects.

The role of biomass and waste, the use of which is concentrated in developing countries, will gradually diminish as they are replaced with modern fuels. Other renewables—a group that includes geothermal, solar, wind, tidal, and wave energy—will grow faster than any other primary energy source but their share of world demand will still be small in 2030 because they start from a very low base.

3.2 *Energy Investment Projections*

The projected increase in global energy demand will call for cumulative infrastructure investment of $20 trillion (in year-2005 dollars) over the period 2005–30. This investment will be needed to expand supply

Figure 2 Cumulative Energy Investment, 2003–30

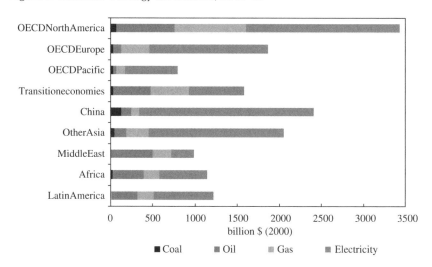

Source: World Energy Outlook 2003.

capacity and to replace existing and future supply facilities that will be closed.

The electricity sector will account for the majority of future energy investment spending. Collectively, power generation, transmission, and distribution will absorb almost $11 trillion, or 56 per cent, of the total. If investment in the fuel chain to meet the fuel needs of power stations is included, electricity's share rises to two-thirds. More than half of the investment in the electricity industry will go to transmission and distribution networks. Total investments in the oil and gas sectors will each amount to almost $4 trillion, or around 20 per cent of global energy investment. Exploration and development will take more than 70 per cent of total investment in oil. The share is lower for gas, at 56 per cent, because transportation infrastructure needs for gas are bigger. Coal investment will amount to only $560 billion, or 3 per cent. Coal is about a sixth as capital-intensive as gas in producing and transporting a given amount of energy.

Developing countries, where production and demand will increase most rapidly, will require about half of global investment in the energy sector as a whole (Figure 2). China, alone, will need to invest $3.7 trillion—18 per cent of the world total and more than in all the other developing Asian countries put together. Investment needs amount to $1.5 trillion in the Middle East and $1.4 trillion in Africa. Russia and other transition economies will account for 9 per cent of global investment and OECD countries for the remaining 36 per cent. Investment needs will be largest in OECD North America—$4.1 trillion. Over 40 per cent of total non-OECD investment in the oil-, gas-, and coal-supply chains will go to provide fuels for export to OECD countries.

More than half of all this investment will go simply to maintain the present level of supply. Most of the world's current production capacity for oil, gas and coal will need to be replaced by 2030. Indeed, much of the new production capacity brought on stream in the early years of the projection period will itself need to be replaced before 2030. Some electricity-generation, transmission, and distribution infrastructure will also need replacing or refurbishing.

The projected global energy investment of $20 trillion equates to approximately 1 per cent of expected global GDP on average over the next 25 years.

There is considerable uncertainty that the necessary investment in the Middle East upstream oil sector will take place in a timely manner. This is despite the fact that the region's share in total upstream oil investment spending, at less than 16 per cent, is small relative to its contribution to the increase in global production capacity, owing to very low exploration and development costs.

To analyse the consequences of reduced investment, the *World Energy Outlook 2006* included a 'Deferred Investment Case' in which MENA countries were assumed to adopt policies that restrict or slow upstream oil investment. It found that the resulting crude oil price is $19 higher in 2030—or $33 in money of the day—when compared to the Reference Scenario and both natural gas and coal prices also rise. MENA oil production falls by 7 mb/d in 2030 compared with the Reference Scenario. These findings imply that it will be in the interests of both consumer and producer countries to facilitate capital flows to the Middle East upstream oil sector.

4. Financing Energy Investment

How is the $20 trillion of capital that is expected to be needed for energy investment to be mobilized? Globally, capital is available on the necessary scale. But ease of access to capital varies among sectors and regions. Access to capital for particular energy projects might be constrained by an absolute insufficiency of financial resources, underdeveloped financial markets or the expectation of inadequate returns on investment relative to the risks, when compared to alternative use of the capital. These potential constraints are of particular significance for developing countries and the transition economies. Financial resources in those regions are more limited, yet their energy investment needs will be especially large compared with OECD countries—both in absolute terms and relative to the size of their economies.

More of the capital needed for energy projects will have to come from private and foreign sources than in the past. There has already been a marked trend away from financing energy investments from public budgets. Many governments have privatized energy businesses, both to raise money and to limit the future call on the public budget, and have opened up their markets to foreign involvement. Foreign direct investment is expected to remain an important source of private capital in non-OECD regions, particularly for oil and gas projects. These private capital flows are very sensitive to macroeconomic conditions and to the nature and stability of government policies.

The risks faced by investors in energy projects are formidable and are changing. Those risks, which include those of a geological, technical, geopolitical, market, fiscal, and regulatory nature, vary by fuel, by the stage of the fuel chain in question, and by region (Table 2). But the energy sector has, in most cases, been able to mobilize the required financing in the past. It will be able to do so in the future only if financing mechanisms are in place, investment returns are high enough, and investment conditions are appealing.

In developing regions, however, few governments could fund fully the necessary investment, even if they wanted to. Poorly developed financial markets often limit opportunities for borrowing from domestic private lenders. Exchange-rate risks, economic and political instability, and uncertain legal and regulatory regimes impede inward capital flows. Governments with heavy demands on their domestic budgets may be tempted to over-tax exploitation of national natural resources, inhibiting investment.

5. Conclusions

Serious concerns about energy security emerge from the projected trends from the *World Energy Outlook* series. The world's vulnerability to supply disruptions will increase as all the large consuming countries—now including China and India—grow increasingly dependent on imports from an ever-smaller group of distant, producer countries, some of them politically unstable. Climate-destabilizing CO_2 emissions will continue to rise, calling into question the sustainability of the current energy system. Many of the

Table 2. Risks in Energy Investment

Type of risk	Examples
Economic risk	
Market risk	Inadequate price and/or demand to cover investment and production costs
	Increase in input cost
Construction risk	Cost overruns
	Project completion delays
Operation risk	Insufficient reserves
	Unsatisfactory plant performance
	Lack of capacity of operating entities
	Cost of environmental degradation
Macroeconomic risk	Abrupt depreciation or appreciation of exchange rates
	Changes in inflation and interest rates
Political risk	
Regulatory risk	Changes in price controls and environmental obligations
	Cumbersome administrative procedures
Transfer-of-profit risk	Foreign exchange convertibility
	Restrictions on transferring funds
Expropriation/ nationalization risk	Changing title of ownership of the assets
Legal risk	
Documentation/ contract risk	Terms and validity of contracts, such as purchase/supply, credit facilities, lending agreements, and security/collateral agreements
Jurisdictional risk	Choice of jurisdiction
	Enforcement risk
	Lack of a dispute-settlement mechanism
***Force majeure* risk**	Natural disaster
	Civil unrest/war
	Strikes

Source: *World Energy Outlook 2003*.

world's poorest people will still be deprived of modern energy services. And huge amounts of new energy infrastructure will need to be financed.

In terms of the investment challenge, fortunately, no individual or organization has sole responsibility for mobilizing the level of finance required. But all of us who have a role need to recognize that the task is daunting. We all need to contribute constructively and sagely to easing the way. If the problem goes unsolved, someone, somewhere in the world, will go without the energy they need.

The role of governments in securing energy investment will have to continue to change, with greater emphasis being given to creating the right enabling conditions. Governments that have promoted competitive energy markets have introduced new investment risks—alongside benefits to consumers. Many uncertainties remain about how to make competitive markets function in such a way that security of supply is ensured in a cost-effective manner, so governments need to monitor developments closely and assess the need for changes to market rules and regulations. They also need to create more stable, transparent, and predictable regulatory conditions in order to enable players in competitive markets to evaluate those risks and to ensure that market structures do not impede investments that are economically viable. In many non-OECD regions, there is still a long way to go to ensure that basic principles of good governance, both in the energy sector and more generally, are applied properly and respected.

It is clear that the greatest part of this investment challenge lies in financing electrification projects in developing countries. To extend electricity supplies to the energy poor and give them better access to other forms of modern energy, stronger government policies, and coordinated international action will be essential. Developed countries have a clear interest in facilitating investment flows to such projects as this will not only significantly reduce human suffering and improve the quality of life but could also help reduce regional and global instability. It is encouraging to see that this link was been reflected by the agenda of the 2005 G8 Summit which, among other issues, covered the role of modern energy services in overcoming poverty in Africa.

The growing importance of China and India and their impact on world energy markets will be the focus of the next edition of the *World Energy Outlook* series, provisionally titled *China and India Energy Outlook: Implications for the World*. Issues of key importance include the prospects for oil and gas demand/supply balances and import requirements, for indigenous coal supply, for the fuel mix in power generation, for energy-investment flows, and for local, regional, and global pollution levels. A central component of *World Energy Outlook 2007* will be an assessment of the implications of energy trends in China and India for global energy markets and for the world economy. In particular, it will analyse the impact of rising energy needs in these countries on international energy prices, on investment needs and financing arrangements, and on energy-related greenhouse gas and other emissions. It will also examine the effects of higher energy-import needs in China and India on energy and non-energy international trade flows. Analysing the main factors driving coal use in China and India will be a key component of the analysis, including the development and deployment of cleaner coal technologies. *World Energy Outlook 2007* will highlight the impact of coal use for global climate security. The ability of potential energy-security and climate-change policies to rein in energy demand will also be explored. It is scheduled to be published in November 2007.

15

Climate Change Negotiations: Past and Future

Scott Barrett

1. Introduction

In the history of large-scale, international negotiations, no issue has attracted as much attention as global climate change (the previous record holder was the Law of the Sea negotiations). For over 15 years, numerous negotiating sessions have been held, involving huge delegations, supported in turn by countless domestic meetings among specialized agencies and ministries, colossal efforts by the Intergovernmental Panel on Climate Change to synthesize the scientific evidence, and the further attentions of environmental groups, businesses, and academics. The input into this process has been unprecedented.

The output has been less impressive. So far, all this effort has achieved very little. Two agreements have entered into force—the Framework Convention on Climate Change and the Kyoto Protocol—but neither will do much to mitigate or forestall climate change. Certainly, neither agreement has had much effect so far. Atmospheric concentrations of carbon dioxide (CO_2) have increased every year since the Framework Convention was negotiated in 1992. The trend did not change after the Kyoto Protocol was adopted in 1997.

True, there has been limited progress outside of the international negotiation process: some countries have adopted significant domestic policies; Europe has established an emissions trading arrangement; and a few states in the USA have drafted legislation to limit their emissions.

However, all these efforts combined will reduce global emissions only slightly from the business-as-usual trajectory. The European emissions trading programme, for example, covers only about half of the emission reductions required to meet the Kyoto targets—and these targets will have little effect on the climate in any event.

My assessment of the Kyoto Protocol may seem premature; the agreement has not been implemented yet. But it cannot be assumed that the parties to Kyoto will comply with the agreement. Alternatively, they may comply only by trading 'hot air', in which case global emissions will fall by little if at all. Even the most positive assessment of Kyoto has to concede that the agreement will achieve little if anything in the long run unless it can get the United States to join and to get major developing countries such as China and India to consent to capping their emissions. Kyoto was meant to be a first step, but, as I shall explain, the prospects for Kyoto to be broadened and deepened appear poor.

A common view is that, should Kyoto fail, the United States will be to blame. The United States has certainly blocked progress. The Clinton administration negotiated the agreement, despite receiving a clear warning from the Senate that the treaty would not be ratified, and then failed to make the case that the Senate ought to ratify it (Clinton never even sent the treaty to the Senate). President George W. Bush rejected the agreement outright (and in a most tactless manner); worse, he and his administration failed to acknowledge the real nature of the climate problem—and the responsibility of the United States to address it. However, that the United States should behave in this way also points to a failure of the agreement itself. The whole point of a treaty, after all, is to change the behaviour of states, even big, powerful states like the USA. (This can be done: in 2003, the Bush administration reversed its decision on steel tariffs, fearing that trade restrictions would be imposed in response to a ruling that the tariffs violated the World Trade Organization's rules.) From this perspective, the bigger failure by the United States has been not to offer the world an alternative to Kyoto—one that the USA would accept and that takes the problem seriously.[1] US leadership is essential to moving forward on this global issue (as on so many others), and so far US leadership has been lacking.

At the recent meetings held in Montreal in late 2005, the parties to the Kyoto Protocol and the parties to the Framework Convention (the latter

[1] The Asia Pacific Partnership, consisting of China, India, Japan, and South Korea (all parties to Kyoto) and Australia and the United States (non-parties) might ultimately evolve into an alternative model. In contrast to Kyoto, the Partnership focuses on technologies, not emission caps. What this model now lacks is ambition and a strategy.

including the USA) agreed on a two-track negotiation process. The Kyoto parties would meet to negotiate new emission ceilings for the countries now subject to emission constraints (China and India would remain unbound). The parties to the Framework Convention (including the USA) would open a nonbinding 'dialogue on long-term cooperative action'. A kind of process for moving forward has thus been initiated. But where will it lead? Where should it lead?

My guess is that the problems inherent in Kyoto will force a redirection in the negotiations, with a shift away from the single-track Kyoto approach (with one emission-limitation treaty being succeeded by another and so on in linear fashion) towards a multi-track approach. This shift should be welcomed: as I shall explain, a multi-track approach is to be preferred even if Kyoto worked exactly as intended. However, the multi-track approach cannot overcome the more profound limitations of Kyoto. These derive not only from the structure of that agreement but from the nature of the climate challenge itself and from the political and legal setting in which international agreements are negotiated, brought into force (or not), and implemented. There is no easy remedy to the climate problem.

We can, however, do better. My ultimate aim in this paper is to look forward—to propose a future course for the negotiations that, while necessarily imperfect for the reasons just mentioned, represents a kind of 'second best'. However, before doing this, we need first to look backwards. The need for a change in course can only be understood against the background of the current situation, and the brief history that preceded it.

2. Framework Convention

The first climate agreement, the Framework Convention on Climate Change, was adopted in 1992, and now has 188 parties. The achievement is perhaps best understood by listing the countries that have so far failed to participate: Andorra, Brunei, the Holy See, Iraq, and Somalia. Quite plainly, this is not an agreement suffering from free riding.

To be sure, one reason for this nearly universal support is that the agreement does not require that parties reduce their emissions of greenhouse gases. And yet the consensus achieved by the agreement is impressive none the less. It demonstrates broad support for the goal of stabilizing atmospheric concentrations of greenhouse gases. Indeed, the only environmental agreement with a participation level this high is the Vienna Convention for the Protection of the Ozone Layer, which is encouraging since the Vienna Convention provided the framework for the very successful ozone regime, one of the greatest achievements of international cooperation ever (Barrett, 2005). If there were a problem with the existing climate regime, it would seem not to be the Framework Convention.

Indeed, the Convention's goal of stabilizing 'greenhouse gas concentrations in the atmosphere at a level that would prevent dangerous anthropogenic interference with the climate system' seems unassailable (who could be in favour of dangerous interference with the climate?), and that is the other reason that the participation level is so high. However, I believe this is the wrong goal. As I explain below, stabilization will require a monumental effort and great sacrifice, introducing dangers of its own; predicting the concentration level that avoids 'dangerous interference' with the climate system is an impossible task; stabilization is a global target, and yet countries can only take on individual obligations; and stabilization is only one of the means by which the challenge of climate change should be addressed.

2.1 *Stabilizing Concentrations*

To stabilize concentrations implies an atmospheric balance, with the quantity of molecules being added to the atmosphere equalling the quantity being subtracted. Today, only a fraction of the gases added to the atmosphere are removed (by ocean absorption and biomass growth), with the result that concentrations (measured in parts per million or ppm) have been increasing. If emissions were stabilized today (and not much were done to 'capture' CO_2 from the atmosphere), CO_2 concentrations (currently about 380 ppm) would continue to rise. Limiting concentrations to a level close to twice the pre-industrial level (that is, twice 280 ppm; or, roughly, 550 ppm) would require something like '50 years of flat emissions, followed by a linear decline of about two thirds in the following 50 years, and a very slow decline thereafter that matches the declining ocean sink' (Pacala and Socolow, 2004, p. 968). Current projections are that emissions will more than double over the next 50 years, in the absence of climate policy (Pacala and Socolow, 2004). This means that, just to stabilize concentrations in the long run at twice the pre-industrial level, global emissions must be cut by more than half by 2050, and reduced by much more after this.

We are not remotely close to achieving any such goal. The Kyoto Protocol does not limit global emissions. It only aims to limit the emissions of about 30 of the world's more than 190 countries by only about 5 per cent (from the 1990 level) over a period of just 5 years. Even if Kyoto worked as originally intended, the emissions of the countries unconstrained by the agreement will rise (China is adding a new coal-fired electricity plant almost every week, and India's growth in coal use is not far behind), as will global emissions. Making matters worse (and as I explain later), Kyoto is unlikely to work as intended. The gap between the goal of stabilizing concentrations and present circumstances and trends is so wide that it raises awkward questions. If stabilization at a level like 550 ppm is so hard to achieve, does that mean that it is not worth meeting? Or does it mean that the institutions being developed are simply not up to the task?

2.2 Dangerous Interference

The answer to the first question depends in part on whether stabilization at a level like 550 ppm is needed to avoid dangerous interference with the climate. Put more broadly, do we know what level is dangerous?

The European Union has set the goal of limiting climate change to 2°C, and to meet this has recommended a concentrations goal of 550 ppm. However, climate sensitivity means that, at 550 ppm, mean global temperature could rise from 1.5° to 4.5°C. Put differently, the 2°C goal would require limiting concentrations to between 380 and 700 ppm (Caldeira *et al.*, 2003, p. 2052). 550 ppm is just the midpoint of this range. But why choose the midpoint? If it is absolutely essential to limit climate change to 2°C, shouldn't concentrations be limited to the current level?

The concept of 'dangerous interference' implies a discontinuity (presumably, temperature increases below this level are 'safe'), and abrupt climate change is very possible. O'Neill and Oppenheimer (2002) have identified three discontinuous changes that would be very serious indeed: the destruction of large-scale coral reef ecosystems; the disintegration of the West Antarctic Ice Sheet; and the collapse of the thermohaline circulation that warms Western Europe. They then suggest that all three changes can probably be avoided by limiting long-term warming to 1°C; that the last two can probably be avoided by limiting change to 2°C; and that the last one can probably be avoided by limiting change to 3°C above the 1990 global mean temperature. Their analysis thus demonstrates that there are substantial uncertainties, and that even the 2°C limit is unlikely to avoid at least some abrupt change. But why then should this particular target be the focus of attention?

Here is another way to frame the problem: there is reason to believe that climate change may be abrupt, and that the probability of triggering a threshold increases as mean global temperature (and the concentration level that causes temperature to change) rises. So a 'premium' should be added to the damages associated with 'gradual' climate change—a premium that is positive today and that increases as the concentration level increases. (Note the difference: a discontinuity implies a zero premium for concentrations below the threshold concentration level and an infinite premium above it.) The magnitude of the premium should reflect climate change risk—the probability of abrupt climate change occurring, and the damage associated with that change (destruction of the coral reefs is to be distinguished from disintegration of the West Antarctic Ice Sheet, which would increase sea level by as much as 5–6 metres).

This is to focus on global effects. Gradual climate change, however, may benefit some countries, even while others are harmed or even devastated. Which countries' interests ought to shape policy? Only those harmed the most by climate change? Or all countries? (In the latter case, the focus would be on the total, or average, effect.) A focus on dangerous interference fails to acknowledge these distributional considerations.

Another difficulty is that mitigation, at least on the scale needed to reduce emissions substantially, will be costly. It will also introduce new risks. Stabilization of concentrations would require, among other things, an expansion in civilian nuclear power globally, creating problems for storage and proliferation. A focus on the consequences of 'dangerous' interference ignores the costs and even the dangers associated with avoiding this level of interference—there are two sides to that particular coin. Expressing policy in terms of a premium, by contrast, allows climate change damages to be balanced against mitigation costs.

2.3 Collective versus Individual Limits

Another problem with setting a goal in terms of atmospheric concentrations is that reaching it has to be a collective responsibility, and yet the international system is decentralized and cannot enforce a collective goal. There is no world government; there are, instead, nearly 200 sovereign countries. An agreement like the Framework Convention can express the desirability of reaching a collective goal, but under the rules of international law, countries are free to participate in such an agreement or not as they please. Should some countries not participate, adherence to the goal implies that the other countries would need to pick up the slack. But this in turn means that, if the global goal is to be met irrespective of which countries participate, every country has an incentive not to participate. What is required is an arrangement that creates precisely the opposite incentive.

2.4 *Beyond Mitigation*

Another problem with the goal of stabilizing concentrations is that it ignores other means for reducing climate change risk.

The first of these is adaptation, much of which will be undertaken automatically. If climate change reduces agricultural yields in a region, for example, farmers will have incentives to change the timing of planting, or the crops that are planted, or other inputs like irrigation. Similarly, bioengineering companies will have incentives to develop new seed varieties that can be expected to perform better in the changing environment. Other forms of adaptation will require public intervention: an example being augmentation of the Thames Barrier protecting London from flooding. In contrast to mitigation, however, adaptation will rarely require international cooperation. Adaptation can thus partially substitute for the failure of collective action in promoting mitigation.

Developing countries are likely to be especially vulnerable to climate change, partly because their economies are more climate-dependent, and partly because they lack the resources (financial and institutional) that could make their social and economic systems resilient to climate shocks. There are reasons why industrialized countries should want to assist developing countries to adapt, but this possibility also raises the issue of the opportunity costs of mitigation. Consider, for example, the vulnerability of developing countries in tropical zones to malaria. One way to assist these countries is for the industrialized countries to limit their emissions, so that malaria, in both its endemic and epidemic forms, does not significantly worsen over time. Another way, however, is for industrialized countries to invest in, say, the development of a malaria vaccine. The former investment would limit *increases* in malaria prevalence decades from now. The latter would limit prevalence *overall* and possibly much sooner. Other investments, such as bed nets, could reduce malaria mortality substantially *today*. So, if the concern is with poor countries, and their inability to adapt to climate change, which kind of investment should be made? Of course, both kinds are needed. But a pound spent on mitigation cannot be spent addressing malaria directly. Choices have to be made (Schelling, 2002). A focus on atmospheric concentrations alone misses this fundamental truth.

The second means for reducing climate change risk is geoengineering—such as blasting aerosols into the stratosphere to scatter solar radiation back into space. Geoengineering could reduce climate change risk by counteracting the effect of rising atmospheric concentrations. It is analogous to the practice of adding ground limestone to lakes, so as to avoid the consequences of acid deposition—an intervention that has been used in Sweden to very good effect.

Like many of the other options available, however, geoengineering would introduce new risks. For example, stratospheric aerosols might destroy ozone. As well, because it does not reduce atmospheric concentrations, geoengineering would fail to address the related environmental problem of ocean acidification (though it may also have the environmental advantage of increasing plant growth). On the other hand, geoengineering may offer environmental benefits—some schemes, for example, would lower harmful UV radiation. Indeed, Hyde *et al.* (2003, p. 91) claim that this benefit alone, calculated only for the United States, far exceeds the cost of preventing global warming. Geoengineeering also has two important things going for it. The first is that it is potentially able to alter temperature quickly—a particular benefit should climate change appear to be abrupt. The second is that geoengineering essentially requires financing a large project, an intervention that is much less susceptible to free-riding behaviour than mitigation, which requires constraining the activities of millions of entities worldwide. Geoengineering need not be undertaken now, but research on geoengineering options should be undertaken now, to determine the consequences of deploying such technologies some time in the future.

The remainder of this chapter focuses on the mitigation challenge, beginning with an assessment of the Kyoto Protocol.

3. Kyoto Protocol

As mentioned in the introduction, Kyoto cannot sustain even the little that it sets out to achieve, and the reason is that Kyoto cannot be effectively enforced. Enforcement has two dimensions in this context: compliance and participation. I discuss both of these in turn below.[2]

3.1 Compliance

A strong and effective compliance mechanism is key to the success of the implementation of the treaty. (Richard Kinley, acting head of the United Nations Climate Change Secretariat)[3]

Compliance is the problem of getting the parties to an agreement to do what they agreed to do. The 1997 agreement did not incorporate a compliance mechanism, though it did require that parties approve 'appropriate and effective procedures and mechanisms' for compliance at the first meeting of the parties. However, according to Article 18 of the agreement, 'any procedures and mechanism . . . entailing binding consequences shall be adopted by means of an amendment to this Protocol'. Under the rules of international law, an amendment is binding only on the countries that ratify it (and on the countries that accede to the original agreement after the amendment enters into law). Since any party to Kyoto could decline to ratify a subsequent compliance amendment, each can avoid being punished for failing to comply. In other words, Kyoto contains no formal mechanism giving parties an incentive to comply. At the recent meeting in Montreal, the parties agreed to consider adopting a compliance amendment, with a view to making a decision by the end of 2007. (Interestingly, it was Saudi Arabia that asked that an amendment be agreed!) As matters now stand, however, the Kyoto emission limits are more 'political' than 'legal'.

A compliance mechanism was negotiated at meetings held in Bonn in 2001. Under this mechanism, a party that fails to meet its emission ceiling in the first control period (2008–12) has to make up for the shortfall and reduce its emissions by an additional 30 per cent of this amount in the *next* control period (presumably, 2013–17). This additional amount was meant to reflect 'interest' on the shortfall (removing the incentive for countries to 'borrow' emission reductions from the future) plus a penalty

---

[2] See Schelling (2002), Victor (2001), and Barrett (2005) for critical assessments of the Kyoto Protocol, including discussions of the enforcement challenge. For a more encouraging view, see Böhringer and Finus (2005).

[3] Framework Convention on Climate Change Secretariat Press Release, 'Groundbreaking Kyoto Protocol Compliance System Launched', 3 March 2006; http://64.233.161.104/ search?q=cache:bchp1LXEZIwJ:unfccc.int/files/press/news_room/press_releases_and_advisories/ application/pdf/20060303_compliance_committee_1st_meeting.pdf +groundbreaking+ kyoto+compliance&hl=en&gl=us&ct=clnk&cd=1

(for failing to comply). Countries found to be in non-compliance would also be prohibited from making use of the protocol's trading mechanism—an additional penalty.

Unfortunately, it is difficult to see how this could possibly work, and not only because it cannot be binding (except by means of an amendment, as noted previously) for the first control period.

Hovi and Kallbekken (2004) offer one interesting scenario. Suppose a country such as Russia failed to comply. Under the enforcement plan, Russia would then be prohibited from selling permits. But that would raise the price of permits, harming countries that had complied (as explained by Hovi and Kallbekken (2004), Norway would be particularly affected by the imposition of non-compliance penalties against third parties). This then invites the question of whether these countries, with representatives on the compliance committee, would really want to impose the punishment. If they would suffer by doing so, the threat may not be credible.[4]

There are, however, more fundamental problems with this approach to compliance. First, the mechanism relies on self-punishment. That is, it fails to say what would happen to a country that failed to comply with the compliance procedure itself. (If a country fails to comply with the punishment imposed for the second period, will it be expected to pay another penalty in the third period? And if it does not comply with *that* penalty, must it then comply in the fourth period? Is there no end to this process?) Second, the emission limits for the second control period have yet to be negotiated. A country that believes it may fail to comply in the first control period could thus hold out for easy targets in the second control period—so that the punishment, if triggered, would not actually bite. Finally, and perhaps most importantly, a country can always avoid the punishment by not ratifying a follow-on protocol for 2013–17, or by withdrawing from the agreement at a later date (both steps are permitted by international law). This is why participation is important.

3.2 *Participation*

As of April 2006, Kyoto has been ratified by 161 states (plus the European Union as a whole) making up 61.6 per cent of the emissions of industrialized countries (Annex I emissions). This would appear to be a

---

[4] The situation is reminiscent of the Stability and Growth Pact, which was meant to punish fiscal indiscipline among the Euro members. When this treaty was put to the test, its punishments, though severe, were revealed to lack credibility. The agreement collapsed. See Barrett (2005, pp. 400–1).

success in terms of participation. However, closer analysis suggests a different interpretation.

The failure of the USA to participate, noted in the introduction, is particularly striking, but it is really part of a general pattern. The USA failed to participate (at least in part) because the costs to the USA of participating were high. Other countries agreed to participate (at least in part) because the costs to them of participating were low (as is true of some EU states), zero (as is true of all the non-Annex I states), or even negative (as is true of the states given 'hot air' allowances). After the USA announced that it would not participate, the Annex I countries likely to have the hardest time complying (Canada and Japan) agreed to participate only on the condition that their initial reduction obligations be diluted (by a technical renegotiation, giving credit for 'sinks'). Russia's ratification brought Kyoto into force, but Russia was also given a more generous allowance (on top of its original gift of 'hot air') as part of the same deal, and made its participation conditional on European support for Russia's entry into the World Trade Organization (what will Russia need to be given in return for participating in a post-Kyoto agreement?). Rules allowing free trade in emission entitlements were also agreed around this time. The combination of these changes is potent. Ironically, though Russia's accession brought the agreement into force, if the trading mechanism is used fully, Russia's participation ensures that Kyoto will fail to reduce emissions by much. Indeed, it may not reduce global emissions at all (Buchner *et al.*, 2001).

Another potential problem with this approach to participation is trade leakage. If the Annex I countries limit their emissions, comparative advantage in the emitting industries will shift towards other countries, causing the emissions of these countries to rise. Kyoto fails to address this problem, suggesting either that the Annex I countries will be less inclined to comply by limiting their own emissions or that their efforts to reduce emissions will be partially undermined.

3.3 *Prospects*

Kyoto's participation level (at least as regards the Annex I countries) is now fixed, but what are the prospects for compliance? There are three possible futures. One is that all the parties will comply by meeting their own emission limits without trading. The second is that the parties will comply but only by making generous use of the trading arrangement. The third is that at least some countries will fail to comply.

According to the most recent data available from the UNFCCC Secretariat,[5] which for most countries is current through 2003, the 15 members of the European Union that negotiated Kyoto as a block (the EU-15) are as a whole about 4 per cent below the 1990 level, whereas Kyoto says that they must be 8 per cent below. Only four of the EU-15 countries are currently within their Kyoto limits—France, Greece, Sweden, and the United Kingdom. Many other EU countries are a long way off. Austria and Denmark are each about 26 per cent above their caps; Finland is 42 per cent off. (Under Kyoto, if all of the EU-15 member states meet their collective target, it will not matter whether each of the 15 states meets its own target. However, should the EU-15 fail to meet its collective target, then each member state is obligated to meet its individual target.) Outside the EU, the situation is no better. Japan is off even its (revised) base year figure, and New Zealand is even further wide of its mark. An official document of the Government of Canada says that Canada's emissions in 2010 will be about 45 per cent above its (revised) Kyoto target (Government of Canada, 2005).

Canada's predicament is particularly difficult. It is hard to see how Canada could cut its emissions by almost half over such a short period of time, and justify the cost to its citizens, when its big neighbour and major trading partner was doing nothing to reduce emissions. It is also hard to see how Canada could make full use of the trading mechanism just for the sake of complying. This, after all, would mean paying for 'hot air'. That is, it would mean paying to comply rather than paying to reduce global emissions—the real aim of the agreement, and the reason, presumably, that Canada signed up to Kyoto in the first place.

Now, to be sure, Canada's situation is extreme, but other countries will also find compliance difficult, and as non-compliance by one country begins to be seen as inevitable, and perhaps even justified, non-compliance by others may appear less objectionable. Remember as well that Article 18 essentially implies that the Kyoto targets are more 'political' than 'legal'.

How might events unfold? Here is one scenario: all the parties required to reduce their emissions make sincere efforts to comply, but some nevertheless fail to comply fully. What matters in the end, their political leaders may argue, are the steps each country has taken to limit emissions relative to other countries, both in and out of the treaty, rather than the more 'technical' matter of compliance. An outcome like this is all the

[5] UNFCCC Subsidiary Body for Implementation, 'National Greenhouse Gas Inventory Data for the Period 1990-2003 and Status of Reporting', FCCC/SBI/2005/17, 12 October 2005.

more to be expected because the need to get countries like the USA, China, and India to reduce their emissions will increasingly come to dominate the two-track negotiation process, and none of these countries is likely to accept emission caps, at least not as part of an international agreement, and at least not any time soon (though technically separate, the two tracks will plainly be co-determined). It is as well to recall that, in the recent Montreal negotiations, the countries most eager to engage with the United States and other countries in a 'dialogue on long-term cooperative action' were the countries that must reduce their emissions under Kyoto. The United States resisted the appeal until the last moment, and insisted that such negotiations be understood not to lead to any new commitments.

The Kyoto parties may want to continue to negotiate emission limits in some form, but future negotiations are as likely to be open to other approaches. Along with this change, the belief that there will be strong international enforcement will have to be reconsidered. This does not mean that the only alternative is pure unilateralism. It means that the burden for enforcement will need to shift to the domestic level; and that, at the international level, enforcement of obligations undertaken within a multilateral framework will need to depend less on explicit punishments, and more on alternatives such as 'naming and shaming'. Pledges for action—whether to meet emission limits or to implement policies and measures—undertaken in a multilateral framework, can improve somewhat over pure unilateralism (see Levy, 1993), though they are unlikely to change behaviour very substantially.

To sum up, the gap between the targets so often mentioned as being needed for stabilizing concentrations and the arrangements developed thus far for meeting these is enormous. It is time for a reassessment. The overall objective needs to change, as must our means for meeting it. We should focus on reducing climate change risk rather than meeting some arbitrary concentration level. We should focus on a range of measures and instruments rather than short-term emissions targets for a subset of countries. My discussion turns now to just one part of this new model—the connection between R&D and mitigation.

4. R&D and Technology Diffusion

There are really only two ways to reduce emissions very substantially—by constraining economic activity or by developing and diffusing technologies that decouple economic activity and emissions. It is very unlikely that countries will accept substantial reductions in the standard of living or growth prospects. The possibility of reducing emissions very substantially thus depends on the development and diffusion of very new kinds of technologies. The focus in the longer term needs to be on zero-emission technologies.

Kyoto tries to create a short-term 'pull' incentive for technology development and diffusion. In limiting emissions, it seeks to raise the cost of emitting carbon dioxide, creating a market for carbon-saving technologies and thus an incentive for the invention and diffusion of such technologies. This is a good way to design a domestic environmental policy (an example being the acid rain trading programme in the United States), but not an international agreement. A substantial pull incentive requires robust enforcement—and as I have already explained, Kyoto is unable to provide this. As well, Kyoto provides no incentive for *long-term* technological innovation. It is completely silent on post-2012 emission controls, and provides no incentive for investment that can lower the cost of reducing emissions substantially in the future. Again, even if Kyoto worked as intended, it would not stimulate the innovation that is really needed.

4.1 *R&D*

Having a robust 'pull' incentive is essential, but so is a 'push' programme for R&D, and Kyoto fails entirely to address this need.

The knowledge gained from basic research is in part a global public good. For some problems, we can rely on individual countries to undertake the needed research unilaterally. For climate change, however, no country has a strong enough incentive to invest. Hence, a new R&D protocol, or system of protocols, is needed.

How much R&D funding is needed? This is a hard question to answer, not least because an assumption needs to be made about how R&D expenditure will translate into new technologies (and associated reductions in marginal abatement costs or the costs of backstop technologies). David Popp has made a first attempt to estimate this value. In a model in which the 'optimal' carbon tax is about $10 per ton of carbon in 2005 (and rising after that), he finds that, today, $13 billion more should be spent on R&D that improves energy efficiency generally, and just over $1 billion more on R&D that lowers the cost of the backstop technology (Popp, 2005, p. 15). These calculations are for gradual climate change.

Concerns about abrupt and catastrophic climate change would warrant even greater expenditure.

Perhaps surprisingly, financing of R&D should not be undermined by free-riding behaviour, even though the knowledge output of R&D is a global public good. This is because the R&D needed to achieve 'breakthroughs' is a threshold global public good. As more countries contribute to the project, the remaining amount needed to finance completion dwindles (Barrett 2006). The new international thermonuclear experimental reactor (ITER) being developed to produce net fusion energy, for example, has been fully financed (by the European Union, Russia, Japan, China, India, South Korea, and the United States). However, the willingness to finance R&D for climate change will depend on the prospects of new technologies actually being diffused globally so as to reduce atmospheric concentrations, and the diffusion of new technologies encounters the same obstacles, more or less, as Kyoto (Barrett, 2006).

4.2 Technology Diffusion

What would help diffusion? There are three possibilities.

First, it is possible, though very unlikely, that R&D will discover a 'silver bullet' technology that produces climate-friendly energy at lower cost than fossil fuels. This is the best outcome that can be hoped for. For reasons of cost only, substitution would be universally attractive. There would be no need for enforcement.

Second, and much more likely, R&D may lower the cost of reducing emissions. This would not improve the prospects for international cooperation, but to the extent that countries had some incentive to reduce emissions unilaterally, it would make the cooperation that is achievable more effective in reducing emissions. Without changing the basic incentive problem for mitigation, however, this approach will only be 'incremental'. Popp (2005) shows that the main effect of R&D is to lower abatement costs, not to increase the level of abatement.

The third possibility is to think strategically about diffusion (Barrett, 2005, 2006). If a technology could be developed that had certain key features—such as economies of scale, network externalities, and domestic-related benefits—then it may spread even without the need for international enforcement. This is how the catalytic converter coupled with the use of unleaded petrol became a global standard.

The demand for a particular kind of automobile (internal combustion, electric, fuel cell, and so on) depends on the availability of the required energy source. Likewise, the availability of the energy source distributed throughout the established road network depends on the stock of automobiles requiring that form of energy. These characteristics coupled with international travel create a tendency for standardization, both in the technology and its fuel source. The effect is reinforced by economies of scale (in production both of the automobile and the energy), which favour adoption of the same technology–energy combination. Local environmental benefits from adoption of a particular technology provide an additional motivation for domestic regulation.

The tendency to standardize implies a threshold in adoption. It only pays every country to adopt the combination if enough others do so, or can be expected to do so. Using a treaty to push countries over a threshold is fairly easy (in Barrett (2005) I call this a 'tipping treaty'). The harder challenge is to find a technology–fuel combination that has the characteristics needed to create the tipping effect.

So, is there a technology–energy combination that has these features? A shift to a breakthrough automobile technology such as hydrogen is very likely to be characterized by increasing returns, because of knowledge spillovers, economies of scale, and, especially, the need to combine a new automobile technology with a supporting energy infrastructure. However, increasing returns are likely to be less important for the production of the hydrogen fuel.

Increasing returns also do not feature largely in electricity generation. The light water standard may dominate nuclear reactor design (Cowan, 1990), but nuclear power is not generally favoured over alternative sources of generation. There may exist other possibilities for this sector— Hoffert *et al.* (2002), for example, explain that renewable energy would become economically more attractive if the electricity transmission grid were re-engineered so that power could be redistributed between continents and time zones. According to Caldeira *et al.* (2005), development of high-temperature superconductor or carbon nanotube cables or even wireless power transmission could make creation of a global electricity grid feasible sometime in the future.

So there does not exist a technology today that has the desired characteristics for global diffusion. What that means, however, is that R&D needs to be directed. It needs not only to develop technologies that produce energy without greenhouse gas emissions; it needs to develop technologies that can be diffused globally without the need for enforcement. This is another sense in which R&D and mitigation must be chosen jointly.

Agreements establishing technology standards may also have political economy advantages. Technology standards create trade restrictions, which are legal and easy to enforce. Moreover, they allow the transfer of technologies with little in the way of transactions costs (in contrast to the Kyoto Protocol's Clean Development Mechanism, which finances project-based 'offsets'). Finally, if the technologies are produced at home, domestic politics will favour financing their use abroad.

The need to transfer technology is manifest. Poor countries such as China and India are growing very rapidly, and it is important that the investment underlying this new growth be climate-friendly. Indeed, from this perspective also, Kyoto got the design exactly wrong. Kyoto allows the poor countries to grow like the rich countries and *then* to transition on to a new development path, relying on a different kind of technology. Rich countries, by contrast, are required to invest in emission reductions that would necessitate the scrapping of a still-productive installed base of capital. It would have been much better to get the fast growing, poor countries on to a new, more climate-friendly development path (financed partly by the rich countries) as a matter of urgency. The rich countries could then move on to the same path more gradually as their own capital stock was retired.

4.3 *Economic Perspectives*

Economists emphasize the need for cost-effectiveness, and the proposal I have outlined does not fully satisfy that criterion. That failure, however, may be the price that must be paid to sustain greater cooperation (Barrett and Stavins, 2003). Kyoto was designed to be cost-effective, but it cannot sustain significant mitigation. To sustain significant mitigation, it may be necessary to sacrifice cost-effectiveness.

As well, the logic of cost-effectiveness presumes a context that may not be appropriate. While it is true that governments can be bad at picking technology winners, in a world characterized by technological lock-in (path dependence), markets cannot be relied upon to pick the best technologies either, even when the price signals are right (David, 1985). The idea that we need only set the optimal carbon tax and let the market do the rest is simplistic. Even without lock-in, carbon taxes are not guaranteed to sustain an efficient outcome when abatement costs are non-convex (Hoel, 1998).

5. Conclusion

How might we view the climate negotiations a century from now? There is a reason for posing this question. One of the main justifications for sticking with Kyoto is that so much has been invested in this process that we cannot abandon it for an alternative. But what has been invested so far is sunk. Moreover, even if we change tack and adopt a different approach, this earlier effort would not have been wasted. If it is looked upon as an investment in learning—learning about the nature of the problem and of how we can best address it—then it will be seen as having been worthwhile and perhaps even a necessary first step.

Indeed, this is not the first time that a treaty has been painstakingly negotiated only to stall at the starting gate, or to enter into force but not be implemented, or to enter into force and be implemented but fail to make a material difference. A striking example is the approach taken to limit the deliberate release of oil at sea by tankers. As explained by Ronald Mitchell (1994), though negotiations on this issue began in 1926, it was not until 1954 that a first agreement was adopted, and it was not until 1978 that a formula was found to address this problem successfully. Climate change is a much more challenging problem, and it is perhaps unrealistic to expect that our first attempt to address it would succeed.

In this chapter, I have pointed out the flaws in the existing arrangements, and suggested some possible ways forward. An approach that focused more on R&D and technologies would, in my view, improve upon the current approach, but it is not an easy or perfect remedy. Addressing global climate change is very much a challenge for which the perfect can be the enemy of the good.

16

European Energy Policy: Securing Supplies and Meeting the Challenge of Climate Change

*Dieter Helm**

1. The Energy Challenges Facing Europe

For the past two decades Europe has focused overwhelmingly on the completion of the European energy market, and in particular on liberalization of electricity and gas markets (CEC, 1998, 1996). This process is close to completion, subject to the last phases of market opening and a number of 'difficult' cases. Europe's energy is now supplied overwhelmingly by private companies competing in liberalized markets.

Though the internal energy market has yielded considerable benefits, it has been hampered by the fact that, in an important sense, there is no integrated European market yet, but rather a string of national markets with bilateral connections. Thus physical trade has been limited and, as a result, Europeans have not reaped the full benefits of a fully integrated internal market, and competitiveness has suffered.

This major gap did not matter so much in the 1980s and 1990s because most member states had excess capacity, and world energy prices were very low. But now it does matter, because the energy sector in Europe has changed fundamentally since the 1980s and 1990s. The decades of

---

* This chapter was prepared for the UK Presidency of the EU. For further analysis of the issues, see Helm (2004*a*, ch. 20), Helm and Hepburn (2005), and Helm (2005*c*,*d*).

440

abundant low-priced fossil fuels, combined with the overhang of the power stations built in (or before) the 1970s and early 1980s, has given way to a new set of challenges.

There are three main challenges: *the oil shock, security of supply*, and *climate change*. These will require a major wave of investment, and need to be met in ways which do not undermine Europe's competitiveness. Europe's energy policy should focus on this new energy reality, rather than on continuing to find ever more effective solutions to yesterday's problems of excess supply and low prices.

Let us take each in turn.

1.1 *The Oil Shock*

- The oil price shock, from 2000, has ushered in sustained higher prices. The peak of world oil production is now within the planning horizon of the sector. Few new big reserves are being found, while the growth of demand from China, India, and other fast-developing countries will underpin prices. By 2030, the International Energy Agency (IEA) forecasts that world energy demand will rise by 60 per cent from current levels (IEA, 2004).

- The gas price shock follows that of oil, and gas continues to be priced in contracts which are indexed to the oil price. With European supplies heavily concentrated in Russia and Norway, and new LNG supplies at a premium to pipeline gas, this linkage is likely to remain for the foreseeable future.

- Electricity prices have risen to reflect gas costs, since in most European countries, gas is the marginal fuel. The tightening supply/demand balance has also begun to be reflected in prices, which will have to sustain new investment.

The European economy has developed in the last two decades on the basis of low prices; it will need to adapt to a very different set of assumptions.

1.2 *Security of Supply*

Since the oil embargoes of the 1970s, much of Europe has not faced any serious threat to the security of its energy supplies. The North Sea has provided oil and gas, while world markets in coal and oil have been benign. With the exception of the first Gulf War, the only threats have been internal and temporary, and focused largely on labour problems.

These conditions have now changed, and security of supply is threatened in a number of ways:

- the external dependency on gas, notably from Russia, and the reliance on long pipelines through sometimes politically difficult territories;
- the external dependency on oil supplies, with production increasingly concentrated in the Middle East;
- terrorist threats to key energy installations;
- network failures, owing to the decades of asset-sweating in the low-return years of the 1980s and 1990s;
- ageing oil refineries and power stations, and low investment in the last two decades;
- poor interconnections between European electricity and gas grids;
- lack of effective Europe-wide mechanisms for addressing security-of-supply risks and coordination of infrastructure investment.

Addressing the multi-dimensional security-of-supply problems will require a major investment programme across Europe and much greater cooperation between member countries, and between the EU and its partners, notably Russia.[1]

1.3 Climate Change

Climate change was recognized in the EU back in the 1980s, but the constraints have only begun to bite in this decade. The EU has endorsed the ambition of stabilizing emissions of greenhouse gases, adopting specific Kyoto targets, and introduced the world's most advanced emissions trading scheme (CEC, 2003*b*). It has also adopted a directive on renewables (CEC, 2001*c*).

These initiatives pose major challenges to Europe's energy sector, in particular:

- the Kyoto targets, which in the context of global warming trends are modest, are nevertheless proving very hard for most member countries to achieve;
- the majority of European electricity assets are based upon fossil fuels, and most are old and coming up to replacement;

---

[1] The EU White Paper on security of supply sets out some of these issues (CEC, 2000).

- renewables technologies have proved expensive relative to fossil fuels, adding to pressure on competitiveness;[2]

- the first generation of nuclear power stations are coming towards the end of their lives, taking out significant zero carbon emissions capacity, and some countries are considering a new wave of investment.

The challenge of climate change arises at the historical point when much plant needs replacing anyway. This provides an opportunity to use this point of the investment cycle to invest in substantial non-carbon sources. Thus, both security of supply and the climate change challenges need to be met with major new investment.

2. Meeting the Challenges: Security of Supply

2.1 *The Critical Role of Interconnection—Creating the European Electricity Grid*

Each member state has built up its own national electricity network in the twentieth century. These nationally integrated networks enable the shocks to demand and supply to be managed, so that spare capacity on the national system allows peak demand to be met. The greater the interconnection, the lower the margin of spare capacity needed. Thus, historically, the move from town to regional and then to country-wide networks led to a reduction in the overall costs of the system for a given level of security of supply. Risk is reduced through the diversification of sources of supply, and there is a portfolio effect.

To date, interconnection between member countries has been limited largely to bilateral links. The internal energy market is not much more than a series of national markets with limited cross-border trade. As a result, each country carries a high burden in spare capacity, physical trading is limited, and the resulting security of supply is lower. (Competition is also inevitably limited, too.)

Each new interconnection adds security, and this has a system-wide—European—benefit, as well as between the two countries thereby connected. Electricity networks are system-wide in their effects, and it makes economic sense to think of them from a system (European) perspective. The European gains are in addition to the national ones, and these need to be reflected in the determination of investments—and their finance.

[2] See, for example, NAO (2005) on renewables in the UK.

Europe should, therefore, identify the missing links in the European electricity networks, creating a framework or plan for a fully integrated network over the next decade. There should then be a priority ordering for investments, and infrastructure finance to support these investments should be considered.

2.2 Gas Storage and Mutual Support—A Regional IEA for European Gas

Unlike electricity, gas can be stored, both directly and through liquefied natural gas (LNG) capacity. Storage provides insurance against physical interruptions to supply, and the ability to smooth out extraordinary price movements. It provides a bargaining counter, too, against dominant suppliers.

As with electricity networks, storage has advantages *to the system as a whole* as well as to individual member countries and companies. These aspects have long been recognized in oil markets, with major countries carrying strategic reserves in the event of major shocks to world oil markets, under the auspices of the IEA, created as a result of the oil shocks of the 1970s.

In contrast to oil, gas is a *regional* energy source, and it makes sense to consider security of supply on a regional level, too. The EU could provide the forum for the cooperation between members on gas storage. This could either be through the ceding of formal powers of control, or through an inter-government agreement. The latter, having worked well for oil, would probably be adequate for gas in Europe.

2.3 Exchanging Information—A European Capacity Statement

As the internal energy market develops through greater physical interconnection (and, as a result, the level of the capacity margin can be reduced), each new power station investment has a greater effect on the European market as a whole, and there are, in consequence, greater benefits to coordination and cooperation.

In each member country, some form of planning is typically used. At one extreme, there is formal capacity planning; at the other, regular statements collating information on investment planning. Member countries also have security-of-supply institutional structures—whether ministerial, regulator, or grid operator based. In all of these, the exchange of information is central.

The EU should consider the creation of a centre for information exchange on capacity planning and prospective investments, and issue a 10-year statement on a rolling basis, summarizing prospective levels of capacity and investment across the EU. Such an exchange could also provide the basis for collating other information relevant to the security of supply.

2.4 *Negotiating with Russia—A Framework for Cooperation*

For the foreseeable future, one company in one country will dominate the European gas—and, therefore, energy—scene. That company is GazProm, itself with close political ties to the Russian government. It is therefore inevitable that there will be a core political element in securing Russian gas supplies, complicated by the fact that a number of governments will be involved in transit issues in relation to pipelines.

This concentration of monopoly power requires a response, if European countries and companies are to maximize their negotiating power. Such a response could have several dimensions. There should at minimum be an exchange of information for all substantive gas contracts, so that each is aware of the total contracted position, and European authorities can gauge the total energy security exposure among EU countries. This could be a further dimension of the information exchange proposed above.

It is also inevitable—and desirable—that transit of gas will require a developing framework of political agreements, and this inevitably has a European dimension.[3]

3. Europe's Lead in Tackling Climate Change

3.1 *Building on the EU Emissions Trading Scheme (EU ETS)*

The EU has pioneered emissions trading on a regional level as a market-driven solution to meeting the Kyoto targets at minimum cost. Getting the EU ETS up and running is a major success, and the market architecture is now in place to widen and deepen the scheme.

Building on the EU ETS does, however, pose a number of difficult problems. So far, it is a time-limited scheme, and allowances have only been granted until 2008, with negotiations under way for 2008–12. For companies, this is largely *outside* the investment horizon and well outside the R&D horizon. To build on the EU ETS requires active consideration *now* of its evolution after 2012, so that markets can factor the implied cost of carbon into the major investment programme now beginning to get under way across the European energy sector.

---

[3] Transit is already covered by the CEC (2003c).

As part of the considerations for 2008–12, and as the EU builds up its position in the post-Kyoto international negotiations, there are a number of new policy initiatives which need to be considered. These include:

- longer-term carbon contracts after 2012, let by governments or EU institutions, which can be sold back into the market after 2012 as the formal national allocation plans eventually emerge (see Helm and Hepburn, chapter 3);
- the integration of air transport and road and rail travel into the EU ETS;
- developing proposals to bring in other, non-EU countries as part of the post-Kyoto negotiations;
- the use of Clean Development Mechanisms and Joint Implementation on a wider scale.

It is also important that the competition aspects of the internal energy market are brought to bear on the emissions trading market, to prevent abuse or anti-competitive behaviour, and the EU sectoral inquiry into the energy sector should take emissions trading into account.[4]

3.2 Building on Europe's Renewables

Almost all member countries have pursued policies aimed at boosting investment in renewables, and these are set within the framework of the EU directive on renewable energy. To date, these policies have overwhelmingly focused on wind technology.

In taking this approach to energy policy forward, the EU should consider widening the scope of renewables towards a definition that includes a number of emissions-reduction technologies, and to consider how, over time, the renewables obligation and the EU ETS may converge to provide the least-cost carbon reduction outcomes for the EU.

There is considerable scope for cooperation across the EU in R&D. For some large-scale technologies—such as hydrogen, clean coal, and nuclear—the economies of scale are likely to be considerable, and the EU is currently at a competitive disadvantage to the USA because of its fragmented approach.

---

[4] European Commission (2005). The final report on the inquiry was published in early 2007 (CEC, 2007b).

3.3 *Taking Nuclear Forward on a European Basis*

As a number of EU members consider new nuclear build programmes, there are several European dimensions which will affect their costs and the timing. At the European level, it makes sense to have a Europe-wide licensing regime, with mutual recognition of safety standards, and to consider a Europe-wide safety inspectorate.

There are also technology gains from cooperation, and the choice of reactor, its manufacture, and construction display the kinds of cost structures familiar in the airline industry.

As a new investment phase begins to develop momentum, there is a case for the EU to modernize its nuclear legislation, and to consider how best to create the conditions which minimize the costs of the inevitable regulatory burden. A nuclear task force to identify barriers and areas for improved cooperation would be timely.

3.4 *Negotiating a Post-Kyoto Framework*

An extremely important factor shaping the future of European energy markets is what happens at the end of the Kyoto period in 2012. The negotiations under the United Nations Framework Convention on Climate Change (UNFCCC) are now getting under way, and the EU is a natural focus for these discussions.

What, however, is missing is the ability at the European level to model the impact of various outcomes on the European energy market. The EU needs to develop this modelling capability quickly, bringing together the appropriate expertise. During the two decades of low prices and abundant supplies in the 1980s and 1990s, there was little need for much expertise in energy markets. That has now changed, and the Commission will need to build up its expertise quickly ahead of these negotiations—and consistent with the considerations above on information exchanges.

4. Providing an Investment-friendly Framework

Meeting security of supply and addressing climate change requires a massive investment programme, and this—fortunately, as noted above—coincides with a turning point in the investment cycle, when much of the capacity built in the 1970s comes to the end of its life. What is required is an investment-friendly policy and regulatory framework.

4.1 *Recognizing that Energy Investments are 'Sunk Costs' and Need Long-term Contracts*

The core problems with energy investments are that they are typically long-lived and specific to the energy systems in which they are embedded. This means that energy investments are very vulnerable to changes in future circumstances (political intervention, technology change, and other investments). They are, in the economist's sense, 'sunk'.

In such circumstances, investors seek protection from these kinds of risk through long-term contracts in competitive markets, and through regulation in monopoly infrastructures. European energy policy has not been particularly conducive to the former, and the latter is as yet immature. There is considerable variance between member states on both. It is not, therefore, surprising that companies have sought to increase their size through a massive merger wave to gain some protection for their sunk costs.

European energy policy needs to adapt to the new investment agenda, and in large measure this means a combination of changes in the regulation of monopolies and the treatment of long-term contracts. While competition policy has focused on short-term spot market competition and freedom to switch suppliers in the short run, it needs to take full account of the impacts on longer-term investment (see 4.5 below).

4.2 *Investment-friendly Interconnector Regimes*

Interconnectors are risky investments. They are sunk costs and, in crossing boundaries, have political risk and are high in transaction costs (such as national planning and national regulations). There is a strong case for taking these investments out of purely national hands, and treating them as 'European', analogous to the way 'European' mergers are considered.

Such investments yield gains above and beyond the immediate parties, and these need to be captured in returns to investors. This could be by preferential treatment for funding, or tax exemptions.

4.3 *Developing Longer-term Energy Markets*

The focus on longer-term energy markets, rather than spot markets, requires a rethink of the architecture of market design. This has proved very effective with the EU ETS, but the presence of a whole host of different types of energy markets across the EU provides a barrier to trade and to the realization of the benefits of the internal energy market. There are different energy and capacity markets, ranging from pools to voluntary trading markets, and specific longer-term tariffs. (Even within countries, electricity markets can vary—for example the England and Wales system has radically changed twice in the last 15 years, and a different approach is to be adopted in the all-Ireland market.)

The EU should initiate a work programme to identify the costs of this plurality of market designs, and bring forward proposals for a gradual harmonization in trading arrangements, analogous to the harmonized approach to the EU ETS.

4.4 *Minimizing Regulatory Burdens*

Regulatory burdens on energy in the EU are considerable. Each country has its own regulatory systems, and as energy companies increasingly operate on a pan-European basis, there are considerable costs involved. In some countries, regulation is designed still with a pre-liberalization agenda in mind, and it can prove an obstacle to competition and entry.

It is recommended that the EU initiate a regulatory review to compare the regulation of energy in each member state and identify as a priority any regulations which inhibit competition. Such a cooperative exercise should seek to help each member reduce its own regulatory burden.

In specific areas—such as nuclear regulation—there is a strong case for a European approach to regulation, as discussed above.

4.5 *Combining Liberalization, Regulation, and Investment*

Liberalization is a fact which is likely to remain in European energy markets for decades to come. The challenge is to design a policy and regulatory framework which promotes investment *within the liberalization context*. As discussed above, allowing investors to recover sunk costs may require an element of longer-term contracting, while it is important to ensure that regulated third-party access to new infrastructure permits the investor to pass on the full capacity costs. Inevitably, this requires a considerable rethink across the Commission as to how to interpret competition rules in the context of investment, and it is important to signal to the market how this might work—though it does not mean that regulated third-party access should be curtailed as currently happens with exemptions. It is recommended that, given the importance of these issues, and the confusion that exists among investors, that the Commission consider issuing further guidelines on competition matters in relation to interconnectors and infrastructure investments, and in respect of new large-scale power projects, notably nuclear.

5. Enhancing Competitiveness

Security of supply and climate change are important drivers for energy policy. The consequences show up in the costs to businesses and households, and the ways in which different parts of the international trading system deal with these will greatly impact on international competitiveness. Europe's energy policy must be designed with these international competitiveness dimensions in mind.

5.1 *The Portfolio Advantages of Interconnection*

Perhaps the greatest single contribution to enhancing the efficiency of the European energy market and reducing costs is the physical interconnection of the member states' individual markets, as discussed above. The portfolio effects are likely to be large.

In the USA, and in South-East Asia the benefits are being recognized. China's energy sector is being planned with interconnection in mind. In the USA, progress is slow, hampered by the conflicts between federal and state level regulation. Europe has an enormous opportunity to gain competitive advantage through interconnection and the creation of the European electricity and gas grids—completing the *physical* internal energy market.

5.2 *Longer-term Price Stability and Longer-term Contracts*

In a world of excess supply and low prices, short-term contracting is cost-reducing and gives competitive advantage. In the 1990s, those European countries which liberalized fast gained these competitive advantages over those which stuck to longer-term contracts. However, going forward, competitive advantage may derive from longer-term contracting.[5]

It is important for the EU to avoid undermining further longer-term contracting arrangements as the underlying market conditions change. Rather than prohibiting or breaking up long-term contracts, the EU should seek ways of encouraging a competitive longer-term market to develop.

5.3 *Stabilizing the Carbon Price*

For investors in the energy sector, the carbon price is extremely uncertain, and the short-term nature of the EU ETS has led to considerable volatility.

---

[5] Indeed, this has already been witnessed as gas margins have tightened in the North Sea in late 2005.

Stabilizing the carbon price, and hence reducing uncertainty, would reduce risk and hence improve competitiveness. Most of this risk is political, and at the EU level. Competitiveness would be enhanced by a clear framework for the post-2012 climate change regime.

6. Modernizing European Energy Policy: Specific Proposals for Action

This chapter has argued that the EU has a considerable opportunity to modernize its energy policy, in the new context of the oil shock and higher prices, greater threats to security of supply which come from external dependency, and the challenge of climate change.

It has been argued that, given the need to replace much of the old energy capacity anyway, the energy policy framework needs at its core the theme of investment—investment to enhance security of supply and make the transition to a lower carbon European economy. This can, properly designed, enhance competitiveness too.

The chapter has made a number of proposals, notably:

- the completion of the physical interconnection of the electricity grid, with a ten-year plan, and appropriate investment and regulatory incentives;

- the creation of a European gas security and storage regime, analogous on a regional level to the IEA for oil;

- the deepening and widening of the EU ETS and the consideration of longer-term carbon contracts;

- reform of the market and regulatory frameworks, including the application of competition policy, to encourage investment and facilitate longer-term contracting;

- a European information exchange on future capacity plans, feeding into the 10-year statement detailed above, providing a European focus for the coordination of investment and security of supply, and substantially increasing energy expertise.

Bibliography

Abrego, L., and Perroni, C. (2002), 'Investment Subsidies and Time-consistent Environmental Policy', *Oxford Economic Papers*, **54**, 617–35.

ACCC (2000), 'Determination: Applications for Authorisation: VoLL, Capacity Mechanisms and Price Floor', File no. C1999/865, Canberra, Australian Competition and Consumer Commission.

Adelman, M. A. (1980), 'The Clumsy Cartel', *The Energy Journal*, **1**(1), 43–53.

— (1982), 'OPEC as a Cartel', in J. Griffin and D. Teece (eds), *OPEC Behavior and World Oil Prices*, London, Allen & Unwin, 37–57.

— (1990), 'Mineral Depletion, with Special Reference to Petroleum', *Review of Economics and Statistics*, **72**(1), 1–10.

— (1993), 'Modelling World Oil Supply', *The Energy Journal*, **14**(1), 1–32.

— Watkins, G. C. (1995), 'Reserve Asset Values and the Hotelling Valuation Principle: Further Evidence', *Southern Economic Journal*, January.

Admire Rebus (2003), 'Renewable Electricity Market Development in the European Union', final report, www.admire-rebus.net

Albæk, S., Møllgaard, P., and Overgaard, P. B. (1997), 'Government-assisted Oligopoly Coordination? A Concrete Case', *Journal of Industrial Economics*, **45**(4), 429–43.

Alderfer, R. B., Eldridge, M. M., and Starrs, T. J. (2000), 'Making Connections, Case Studies of Interconnection Barriers and their Impacts on Distributed Power Projects', NREL/SR-200-28053.

Alic, J. A., Mowery, D. C., and Rubin, E. S. (2003), 'US Technology and Innovation Policies: Lessons for Climate Change', prepared for the Pew Center on Global Climate Change.

Allaz, B., and Vila, J. L. (1993), 'Cournot Competition, Forward Markets and Efficiency', *Journal of Economic Theory*, **59**, 1–16.

Alsema, E. A. (2000), 'Energy Pay-back Time and CO2 Emissions of PV Systems', *Progress in Photovoltaics: Research and Applications*, **8**, 17–25.

Al Turki, S. (1994), 'Autocorrelation in Static Economic Models and their Dynamic Respecifications: An Application to OPEC Behaviour', *Journal of King Saud University, Administrative Sciences*.

Al-Yousef, N. A. (1998), 'The Role of Saudi Arabia in the World Oil Market 1974–1997', Ph.D. thesis, University of Surrey, Guildford.

Anderson, D., and Bird, C. D. (1992), 'Carbon Accumulations and Technical Progress—A Simulation Study of Costs', *Oxford Bulletin of Economics and Statistics*, **54**(1), 1–27.

Andrews-Speed, P., Liao, X., and Dannreuther, R. (2002), 'The Strategic Implications of China's Energy Needs', Adelphi Paper 346, Oxford University Press.

Ansolabehere, S., Deutch, J., Driscoll, M., Gray, P. E., Holdren, J. P., Joskow, P. L., Lester, R. K., Moniz, E. J., and Todreas, N. E. (2003), 'The Future of Nuclear Power', an interdisciplinary MIT study, Boston, MA.

Armstrong, M., and Vickers, J. (2001), 'Competitive Price Discrimination', *RAND Journal of Economics*, **32**(4), 579–605.

— Cowan, S., and Vickers, J. (1994), *Regulatory Reform; Economic Analysis and British Experience*, Cambridge, MA, MIT Press.

Arthur, W. B. (1989), 'Competing Technologies, Increasing Returns, and Lock-in by Historical Events', *The Economic Journal*, **99**(394), 116–31.

Azar, C., and Dowlatabadi, H. (1999), 'A Review of Technical Change in Assessment of Climate Policy', *Annual Review of Energy Economics*, **24**, 513–44.

Bagwell, K., and Staiger, R. (1997), 'Collusion over the Business Cycle', *RAND*, **28**, 82–106.

Baker, P., Blundell, R., and Micklewright, J. (1989), 'Modelling Household Energy Expenditures Using Micro-data', *The Economic Journal*, **99**, 720–38.

Balabanoff, S. (1995), 'Oil Price Changes and Economic Activity in the US and Germany', *OPEC Review*, **21**(3).

Ballard, C. L., and Fullerton, D. (1992), 'Distortionary Taxes and the Provision of Public Goods', *Journal of Economic Perspectives*, **6**(3), 117–31.

Balzer, H. (2006), 'Vladimir Putin on Russian Energy Policy', *Energy Politics*, **9**, 31–9.

Barnett, H., and Morse, C. (1963), *Scarcity and Growth: The Economics of Natural Resource Availability*, Baltimore, Johns Hopkins/R.FF.

Barreto, L., and Klaassen, G. (2004), 'Emission Trading and the Role of Learning-by-Doing Spillovers in the "Bottom-up" Energy-system ERIS Model', *International Journal of Energy Technology and Policy*, **2**(1/2), 70–95.

Barrett, S. (2005), *Environment and Statecraft: The Strategy of Environmental Treaty-making*. Oxford, Oxford University Press (paperback edition).

— (2006), 'Climate Treaties and "Breakthrough" Technologies', *American Economic Review*, Papers and Proceedings, **96**(2), 22–5.

— Stavins, R. (2003), 'Increasing Participation and Compliance in International Climate Change Agreements', *International Environmental Agreements: Politics, Law, and Economics*, **3**(4), 349–76.

Barro, R., and Gordon, D. (1983), 'A Positive Theory of Monetary Policy in a Natural-rate Model', *Journal of Political Economy*, **91**, 589–610.

Barsky, R., and Kilian, L. (2004), 'Oil and the Macroeconomy since the 1970s', *Journal of Economic Perspectives*, **18**(4), 115–34.

BBC News (2000), 'Swalec Bought for £210 million', *BBC News Online*, 7 August, available at http://news.bbc.co.uk/1/hi/wales/869317.stm

— (2006), 'Australia in Nuclear Power Review', *BBC News Online*, 6 June, available at http://news.bbc.co.uk/1/hi/world/asia-pacific/5051022.stm

Bennett, M., Cooke, D., and Waddams Price, C. (2002), 'Left Out in the Cold? The Impact of New Energy Tariffs on the Fuel Poor and Low Income Households', *Fiscal Studies*, **23**(2), 167–94.

Bergek, A., and Jacobsson, S. (2003), 'The Emergence of a Growth Industry: A Comparative Analysis of the German, Dutch and Swedish Wind Turbine Industries', in S. Metcalfe and U. Cantner (eds), *Change, Transformation and Development*, Heidelberg, Physica-Verlag, 197–228.

Berman, M., and Tuck, B. (1994), 'New Crude Oil Reserve Formation: Responsiveness to Changes in Real Prices and the Reserves to Production Ratio', *OPEC Review*, Autumn.

Bernheim, D., and Whinston, M. D. (1990), 'Multimarket Contact and Collusive Behaviour', *RAND Journal of Economics*, **21**(1), 1–26.

Bhattacharyya, S. C. (1995), 'Domestic Petroleum Product Pricing Policy: Old Issues in New Perspective. Energy Sources', **17**.

Bialek, J. W. (2004), 'Recent Blackouts in US and Continental Europe: Is Liberalisation to Blame?', Working Paper CMI EP 34, University of Cambridge.

Bidwell, M. (2005), 'Reliability Options', *Electricity Journal*, June, 11–25.

Bijvoet, C. C., Nooij de, M., and Koopmans, C.C. (2003), 'Kosten van Stroomstoringen', *ESB*, 3 October, 460–3.

Bindemann, K. (1999), 'Vertical Integration in the Oil Industry: A Review of the Literature', *Journal of Energy Literature*, **5**, 1 June.

Bird, L., and Swezey, B. (2004), 'Capacity Estimates of Renewable Energy Developed to Serve Green Power Markets', National Renewable Energy Laboratory.

Blackburn, K., and Christensen, M. (1989), 'Monetary Policy and Policy Credibility: Theories and Evidence', *Journal of Economic Literature*, **27**, 1–45.

Blakely, R. (2006), 'Cost of Britain's Nuclear Legacy Surges to £70 billion', *Times Online*, 30 March, available at http://business.timesonline.co.uk/article/0,,9078-2110926,00

Bleakley, T., Gee, D. S., and Hulme, R. (1997), 'The Atomization of Big Oil', *The McKinsey Quarterly*, No. 2.

Bloomberg (2006), 'Ontario to Build Reactors, Delay Coal Plant Closings', 13 June, available at http://www.bloomberg.com/apps/news?pid=10000082&sid=a1HtD5lnInZY&refer=canada

Blumstein, C., Friedman, L., and Green, R. J. (2002), 'The History of Electricity Restructuring in California', *Journal of Industry Competition and Trade*, **2**(1–2), 9–38.

Bohi, D., and Toman, M. (1996), *The Economics of Energy Security*, Boston, Kluwer Academic Publishers.

Böhringer, C., and Finus, M. (2005). 'The Kyoto Protocol: Success or Failure?', in D. R. Helm (ed.), *Climate-change Policy*, Oxford, Oxford University Press, 253–81.

Boiteux, M. (1960), 'Peak Load Pricing', *Journal of Business*, **33**, 157–79 (translated from the original in French published in 1951).

Borch, K. (1962), 'Equilibrium in Reinsurance Markets', *Econometrica*, **30**, 424–44.

Bottazzi, L., and Peri, G. (2004), 'The Dynamics of R&D and Innovation in the Short Run and in the Long Run', Centre for Economic Policy Research, DP4479.

Bower, J., and Bunn, D. W. (2000), 'Model-based comparisons of Pool and Bilateral Markets for Electricity', *The Energy Journal*, **21**(3), 1–29.

Bradley, I., and Price, C. (1988), 'Economic Regulation of Private Monopolies through Price Constraints', *Journal of Industrial Economics*, 99–106, September.

Bradley, P. G., and Watkins, G. C. (1994), 'Detecting Resource Scarcity: The Case of Petroleum', Conference Proceedings, Vol. II, IAEE 17th Annual International Conference, Stavanger, Norway, May.

Brattle Group (2004), *Long-term Reserve Contracts in the Netherlands*, London, Brattle Group.

Braunholtz, S. (2003), *Public Attitudes towards Wind Farms*, Mori Scotland and Scottish Executive, www.scotland.gov.uk

Brealey, R. A., and Myers, S. C. (2003), *Principles of Corporate Finances*, 7th edn, McGraw Hill.

Brennan, M. J., and Schwartz, E. S. (1982), 'Consistent Regulatory Policy under Uncertainty', *Bell Journal of Economics*, **13**(2), 506–21.

Brock, W. A., and Scheinkman, J. (1985), 'Price Setting Supergames with Capacity Constraints', *Review of Economic Studies*, **52**, 371–82.

Brown, E. C. (1948), 'Barriers Income Taxation and Investment Incentives', ch. 4, Part III in *Income, Employment and Public Policy, Essays in Honor of Alvin H. Hansen*, New York, W. W. Norton & Co.

Brown, S. (1970), 'The Next 25 Years in the Electricity Supply Industry', Lecture Delivered to the Institute of Electrical and Electronic Technical Engineers, 16 November.

Brunekreeft, G., and Bauknecht, D. (2006), 'Energy Policy and Investment in the German Power Market', in F. P. Sioshansi and W. Pfaffenberger (eds), *International Experience in Restructured Electricity Markets: What Works, What Does Not and Why?*, Elsevier Scientific (2006).

— Twelemann, S. (2005), 'Regulation, Competition and Investment in the German Electricity Market: RegTP or REGTP', *Energy Journal* (Special Issue European Energy Liberalisation), 99–126.

Buchner, B., Carraro, C., and Cersosimo, I. (2001), 'On the Consequences of the US Withdrawal from the Kyoto/Bonn Protocol', Fondazione Eni Enrico Mattei, Venice, Italy.

Bushnell, J. (2005), 'Electricity Resource Adequacy: Matching Policies with Goals', CSEM Working Paper No. 146, August, available at http://www.ucei.berkeley.edu/PDF/csemwp146.pdf

— Mansur, E. (2004), 'Consumption under Noisy Price Signals: A Study of Electricity Retail Rate Deregulation in San Diego', *Power Working Paper-082r*, Berkeley, CA, University of California Energy Institute.

Butler, L., and Neuhoff, K. (2004), 'Comparison of Feed in Tariff, Quota and Auction Mechanisms to Support Wind Power Development', CMI Working Paper 70.

Cabral, L. M. B. (2000), *Introduction to Industrial Organization*, Cambridge, MA, MIT Press.

Caldeira, K., Day, D., Fulkerson, W., Hoffert, M., and Lane, L. (2005), 'Climate Change Technology Exploratory Research', Washington, DC, Climate Policy Center.

Caldeira, K., Jain, A. K., and Hoffert, M. I. (2003), 'Climate Sensitivity, Uncertainty and the Need for Energy without CO_2 Emission', *Science*, **299**, 2052–4.

Campbell, C. J. (1997), *The Coming Oil Crisis*, Brentwood, Multiscience Publishing Company for Petroconsultants.

— (2003), *The Essence of Oil & Gas Depletion*, Collected Papers and Excerpts, Multi-Science Publishing Co.

— Laherre, J. H. (1998), 'The End of Cheap Oil', *Scientific American*, March.

Carbon Trust (2003), 'Building Options for UK Renewable Energy', available at www.thecarbontrust.co.uk

— (2004), *The European Emissions Trading Scheme: Implications for Industrial Competitiveness,* London, The Carbon Trust.

CEC (1996), 'Directive 96/92/EC of the European Parliament and of the Council of 19 December 1996 Concerning Common Rules for the Internal Market in Electricity', Brussels, Commission of the European Communities.

— (1998), 'Directive 98/30/EC of the European Parliament and of the Council of 22 June 1998 Concerning Common Rules for the Internal Market in Natural Gas', *Official Journal of the European Union*, L204, 21 July, 1–12, Brussels, Commission of the European Communities.

— (2000), *Towards a European Strategy for the Security of Energy Supply*, Green Paper, COM (2000) 769, Brussels, Commission of the European Communities.

— (2001*a*), 'Directive 2001/80/EC of the European Parliament and of the Council of 23 October 2001 on the Limitation of Emissions of Certain Pollutants into the Air from Large Combustion Plants', *Official Journal of the European Communities*, L309, Brussels, Commission of the European Communities.

— (2001*b*), 'Proposal for a Directive of the European Parliament and of the Council Establishing a Scheme for Greenhouse Gas Emission Allowance Trading within the Community and Amending Council Directive 96/61/EC', COM (2001) 581 final, Brussels, Commission of the European Communities.

— (2001*c*), 'Directive 2001/77/EC of the European Parliament and of the Council of 27 September 2001 on the Promotion of Electricity Produced from Renewable Energy Sources in the Internal Electricity Market', Brussels, Commission of the European Communities.

— (2002*a*), 'Amended Proposal for a Directive of the European Parliament and of the Council Establishing a Scheme for Greenhouse Gas Emission Allowance Trading within the Community and Amending Council Directive 96/61/EC', COM (2002) 680 final, Brussels, Commission of the European Communities.

— (2002*b*), 'Second Benchmarking Report on the Implementation of the Internal Electricity and Gas Market', Commission Staff Working Paper, October 2002, SEC(2002)1038, Brussels, Commission of the European Communities.

— (2003*a*), 'Directive 2003/55/EC of the European Parliament and the Council of June 26 2003 Concerning Common Rules for the Internal Market in Natural Gas and Repealing Directive 98/30/EC', Acceleration Directive, *Official Journal of the European Union*, L176, 15 July, 57–78, Brussels, Commission of the European Communities.

CEC (2003*b*), 'Directive 2003/87/EC of the European Parliament and of the Council of 13 October 2003 Establishing a Scheme for Greenhouse Gas Emission Allowance Trading within the Community and Amending Council Directive 96/61/EC', Brussels, Commission of the European Communities.

— (2003*c*), 'Regulation (EC) No 1228/2003 of the European Parliament and of the Council of 26 June 2003 on Conditions for Access to the Network for Cross-border Exchanges in Electricity', Brussels, Commission of the European Communities.

— (2004), 'Council Directive 2004/67/EC of 26 April 2004 Concerning Measures to Safeguard Security of Natural Gas Supply', Security of Gas Supply Directive, *Official Journal of the European Union*, 29 April, L127/92, Brussels, Commission of the European Communities.

— (2005*a*), 'Regulation (EC) No 1775/2005 of the European Parliament and of the Council of 28 September 2005 on Conditions for Access to the Natural Gas Transmission Networks', *Official Journal of the European Union*, L289, 3 November, 1–13, Brussels, Commission of the European Communities.

— (2005*b*), 'Report on Progress in Creating the Internal Gas and Electricity Market', Communication from the Commission to the Council and the European Parliament, COM(2005) 568 final, 15 November, Brussels, Commission of the European Communities.

— (2005*c*), *Energy Sector Inquiry Issues Paper*, 15 November, Directorate General for Competition, Brussels, Commission of the European Communities.

— (2006*a*), *A European Strategy for Sustainable, Competitive and Secure Energy*, Green Paper, COM(2006)105 final, Brussels, Commission of the European Communities, March.

— (2006*b*), *Energy Sector Inquiry Draft Preliminary Report,* 16 February, Directorate General for Competition, Brussels, Commission of the European Communities.

— (2007*a*), 'Communication from the Commission to the European Council and the European Parliament: An Energy Policy for Europe', COM(2007) 1 final, 10 January.

— (2007*b*), 'Communication from the Commission to the Council and the European Parliament: Prospects for the Internal Gas and Electricity Market', COM(2006) 841 final, 10 January.

Ceccarossi, K. (2006), 'VY Assessment Raises by 25 per cent to $239 million', *Brattleboro Reformer*, 6 June, available at html http://www.wcax.com/Global/story.asp?S=5002331&nav=4QcS

Cedigaz (2005), *Natural Gas in the World: Trends and Figures in 2005*, Paris, www.cedigaz.org

— (2006), *The 2005 Natural Gas Year in Review*, first estimates, Paris, www.cedigaz.org

Chang, Y. T., Waddams Price, C., and Wilson, C. M. (2006), 'Consumer Search and Switching: Much Still to Gain', mimeo.

Chao, H. P., and Wilson, R. (1987), 'Priority Service: Pricing, Investment and Market Organization', *American Economic Review*, **77**, 89–116.

Chapman, D., and Khanna, N. (2001), 'An Economic Analysis of Aspects of Petroleum and Military Security in the Persian Gulf', *Contemporary Economic Policy*, **19**(4), 371–81.

Clingendael (2004), *Study of Energy Supply Security and Geopolitics*, Clingendael Institute, Report prepared for DG TREN, January, The Hague, http://www.clingendael.nl/publications/2004/200401000_ciep_study.pdf

Commission de Regulation de l'Energie and Autorita per l'Energia Ellectrica e il Gas (2004), 'Report on the Events of September 28th 2003 Culminating in the Separation of the Italian Power System from the other UCTE Networks', 22 April.

Competition Commission (2003), *Merger References: Competition Commission Guidelines*.

Compte, O., Jenny, F., and Rey, P. (2002), 'Capacity Constraints, Mergers, and Collusion', *European Economic Review*, **46**(1), 1–29.

Considine, J. I., and Kerr, W. A. (2002), *The Russian Oil Economy*, Cheltenham, Edward Elgar.

Correljé, A., and van der Linde, C. (2006), 'Energy Supply Security and Geopolitics: A European Perspective', *Energy Policy*, **34**, 532–43.

Cowan, R. (1990), 'Nuclear Power Reactors: A Study in Technological Lock-in', *Journal of Economic History*, **50**(3), 541–67.

CPB (2004), 'Better Safe than Sorry? Reliability Policy in Network Industries', CPB Document No. 73, The Hague.

Cramton, P., and Stoft, S. (2006), 'The Convergence of Market Designs for Adequate Generating Capacity', MIT Center for Energy and Environmental Policy Research, Working Paper 06-007, April, available at http://web.mit.edu/ceepr/www/2006-007.pdf

Crawford, V., and Sobel, J. (1982), 'Strategic Information Transmission', *Econometrica*, **50**(6), 1431–51.

Crémer, J., and Salehi-Isfahani, D. (1991), *Models of the Oil Market*, New York, Harwood Academic Publishers.

Crew, M. A., and Kleinforder, P. R. (1976), 'Peak Load Pricing with Diverse Technology', *Bell Journal of Economics*, **7**(1), 207–31.

Crooks, A. C. (1997), 'Cooperatives and New Uses for Agricultural Products: An Assessment of the Fuel Ethanol Industry, USDA Rural Business-Cooperative Service', RBS Research Report 148.

Dahl, C. A., and Yucel, M. (1991), 'Testing Alternative Hypothesis of Oil Producer Behaviour', *Energy Journal*, **12**(4).

Dal Bó, E. (2006), 'Regulatory Capture: a Review', *Oxford Review of Economic Policy*, **22**(2), 203–25.

Dargay, J., and Gately, D. (1995), 'The Imperfect Price Reversibility of Non-Transport Oil Demand in the OECD', *Energy Economics*, **17**(1).

Dasgupta, P., and Heal, G. (1979), *The Economic Theory and Exhaustible Resources*, England, Cambridge University Press.

— Stiglitz, J. (1988), 'Learning-by-doing, Market Structure and Industrial and Trade Policies', *Oxford Economic Papers*, **40**, 256–68.

David, P. (1985), 'Clio and the Economics of QWERTY', *American Economic Review Papers and Proceedings*, **75**(2), 332–7.

Davis, J., Ossowski, R., Daniel, J., and Barnett, S. (2001), 'Stabilization and Savings Funds for Non-renewable Resources', Occasional Paper 205, Washington, DC, International Monetary Fund.

De Chazeau, M. G., and Kahn, A. E. (1959), *Integration and Competition in the Petroleum Industry*, New Haven, Yale University Press.

Defra (2004*a*), *Energy Efficiency, the Government's Plan for Action*, London, Department for Environment, Food and Rural Affairs, April.

— (2004*b*), *Fuel Poverty in England: The Government's Plan for Action*, London, Department for Environment, Food and Rural Affairs.

Dekimpe, M. G., Parker, P. M., and Sarvary, M. (2000), '"Globalization": Modeling Technology Adoption Timing Across Countries', *Technology Forecasting and Social Change*, **63**, 25–42.

de Moor, A. (2001), 'Towards a Grand Deal on Subsidies and Climate Change', *Natural Resources Forum*, **25**.

Department of Energy (1987), *Sizewell B Public Inquiry: Report by Sir Frank Layfield. Vol. 5 The Economic Case*, London, HMSO.

— (1989), 'The Demand for Energy', in D. R. Helm, J. Kay, and D. Thompson (eds), *The Market for Energy*, Oxford, Oxford University Press.

Department for Transport (2004), *The Future of Air Transport*, White Paper, Cm 6046.

Desta, M. G. (2003), 'OPEC, The WTO, Regionalism and Unilateralism', *Journal of World Trade*, **37**(3).

Devlin, J., and Lewin, M. (2002), 'Issues in Oil Revenue Management', Paper to the World Bank/ESMAP Workshop in Petroleum Revenue Management, Washington, DC, 23–24 October.

de Vries, L. (2004), 'Securing the Public Interest in Electricity Generation Markets: The Myths of the Invisible Hand and the Copper Plate', TU Delft, Netherlands.

Dixit, A. K., and Pindyck, R. S. (1994), *Investment under Uncertainty*, Princeton, NJ, Princeton University Press.

Doran, C. (1980), 'OPEC Structure and Cohesion: Exploring the Determinants of Cartel Policy', *Journal of Politics*, **42**(1), 82–101.

DTI (1995), *The Prospects for Nuclear Power in the UK*, Cm 2860, London, Department of Trade and Industry.

— (2000), *The Social Effects of Energy Liberalisation, the UK Experience*, London, Department of Trade and Industry.

— (2001*a*), 'Draft Social and Environmental Guidance to the Gas and Electricity Markets Authority: A Consultation Document', London, Department of Trade and Industry, May.

— (2001*b*), *UK Fuel Poverty Strategy*, London, Department of Trade and Industry.

— (2003), *Our Energy Future—Creating a Low Carbon Economy*, White Paper, CM 5761, London, The Stationery Office.

— (2006), 'Quarterly Energy Prices', available at http://www.dti.gov.uk/energy/

Duke, R. (2002), 'Clean Energy Technology Buydowns: Economic Theory, Analytic Tools, and the Photovoltaics Case', Ph.D. Dissertation, Princeton University.

Duke, R., and Kammen, D. M. (1999), 'The Economics of Energy Market Transformation Programs', *Energy Journal*, **20**(4), 15–64.

— Jacobson, A., and Kammen, D. M. (2002), 'Photovoltaic Module Quality in the Kenyan Solar Home Systems Market', *Energy Policy*, **30**, 477–99.

ECSSR (2000), *Caspian Energy Resources*, Abu Dhabi, ECSSR.

EIA (2002), US Department of Energy, Energy Information Association, www.eia.doe.gov.

— (2005*a*), 'Non-OPEC Fact Sheet', Country Analysis Briefs, available at http://www.eia.doe.gov/emeu/cabs/nonopec.html

— (2005*b*), *International Energy Outlook 2005*, Washington, DC, Energy Information Administration.

— (2006), *International Energy Outlook 2006*, Washington, DC, Energy Information Administration.

Ellerman, A. D., Schmalensee, R., Joskow, P. L., Montero, J. P., and Bailey, E. (2000) *Markets for Clean Air: The US Acid Rain Program*, Cambridge, Cambridge University Press.

— Joskow, P. L., and Harrison, D. (2003) *Emissions Trading in the U.S. Experience, Lessons and Considerations for Greenhouse Gases*, Arlington, Pew Center on Global Climate Change.

energywatch (2006), 'SSE Price Rise Can Only Increase the Fuel Poverty Spiral', 31 March, available at http://www.energywatch.org.uk/media/news/show_release.asp?article_id=956

ESMAP (2003), 'Cross-border Oil and Gas Pipelines: Problems and Prospects', ESMAP Technical Paper 035, Washington, DC, Joint UNDP/ESMAP.

Espejo, R., Schuhmann, W., Schwaninger, M., and Bilello, U. (1996), *Organizational Transformation and Learning—A Cybernetic Approach to Management*, Chichester, John Wiley & Sons.

EU Commission (2000), *Towards a European Strategy for Security of Energy Supply*, Green Paper.

Eurelectric (2005), *Europrog*, Brussels.

European Commission (2005), 'Communication by Ms Neelie Kroes in agreement with Mr Piebalgs. Subject: Sector inquiry pursuant to Article 17 of Regulation 1/2003 EC in the European Electricity and Gas Markets COMP/B-1/39172 (electricity sector inquiry) and COMP/B-1/39173 (gas sector inquiry)', 13 June.

European Union (2003), 'Directive 2003/87/EC of the European Parliament and of the Council of 13 October 2003 Establishing a Scheme for Greenhouse Gas Emission Allowance Trading within the Community and Amending Council Directive 96/61/EC', Brussels, Commission of the European Communities.

Evans, J. E., and Green, R. J. (2005), 'Why Did British Electricity Prices Fall After 1998?', Department of Economics Working Paper 05-13, University of Birmingham.

EWEA (2004), *Wind Energy, The Facts, An Analysis of Wind Energy in the EU-25*, European Wind Energy Association, funded by EU Commission, DG TREN.

Fabra, N. (2006), 'Collusion with Capacity Constraints over the Business Cycle', *International Journal of Industrial Organization*, **24**(1), 69–81.

Farrell, J. (1987), 'Cheap Talk, Coordination, and Entry', *Rand Journal of Economics*, **18**(1), 34–9.

— Rabin, M. (1996), 'Cheap Talk', *Journal of Economic Perspectives*, **10**(3), 103–18.

Fasano, U. (2000), 'Review of the Experience with Oil Stabilization and Savings Funds in Selected Countries', IMF Working Paper WP/00/112, Washington, DC, International Monetary Fund.

Fattouh, B. (2006*a*), 'The Origins and Evolution of the Current International Oil Pricing System: A Critical Assessment', in R. Mabro (ed.), *Oil in the Twenty-First Century: Issues, Challenges, and Opportunities*, Oxford, Oxford University Press.

— (2006*b*), 'Spare Capacity and Oil Price Dynamics', *Middle East Economic Survey*, **49**(5).

— (2007), 'OPEC's Dilemma', *Oxford Energy Forum*, forthcoming.

— Mabro, R. (2006), 'The Investment Challenge', in R. Mabro (ed.), *Oil in the Twenty-First Century: Issues, Challenges, and Opportunities*, Oxford, Oxford University Press.

FCO (2004), 'UK International Priorities: The Energy Strategy', Foreign and Commonwealth Office, October.

Federico, G., and Rahman, D. (2003), 'Bidding in an Electricity Pay-as-Bid Auction', *Journal of Regulatory Economics*, **24**(2), 175–211.

FERC (2002), 'Notice of Proposed Rulemaking, Docket No. RM01-12-000, issued July 31, 2002' (the 'Standard Market Design'), Washington, DC, Federal Energy Regulatory Commission.

— (2005), *State of the Markets Report*, US Federal Energy Regulatory Commission, available at http://www.ferc.gov/EventCalendar/Files/20050615093455-06-15-05-som2004.pdf

Fesharaki, F. (1990), 'The International Oil Market: The Future Relations between Producers and Consumers', in D. C. Pirages and C. Sylvester (eds), *Transformations in the Global Political Economy*, London, Macmillan.

Foxon, T., and Kemp, R. (2004), 'Innovation Impacts of Environmental Policies', in *International Handbook on Environment and Technology Management*, forthcoming.

Frankel, P. (1946), *The Essentials of Petroleum*, London, Chapman & Hall.

Fried, E. R., and Schultze, C. L. (1975), *Higher Oil Prices and the World Economy: The Adjustment Problem*, Washington, DC, The Brookings Institution.

— Trezise, P. H. (1993), *Oil Security: Retrospect and Prospect*, Washington, DC, The Brookings Institution.

G8 (2001), 'Renewable Energy: Development that Lasts', G8 Renewable Energy Task Force Chairman Report.

Gabriel, S. (2006), 'Germany Remains at the Forefront of Climate Protection', downloaded from Federal Ministry for the Environment, Nature Conservation and Nuclear Safety web site on 26 July 2006, http://www.bmu.de/english/emissions_trading/current/doc/37401.php

Garcia, P. A. M. (2005), 'OPEC in the 21st Century: What Has Changed and What Have We Learned?', *Oxford Energy Forum*, 60, Oxford, Oxford Institute for Energy Studies.

Garnaut, R., and Clunies Ross, A. (1983), *Taxation of Mineral Rents*, Oxford, Oxford University Press.

Garriba, S. (2006), 'Dealing with Gas Supply Disruption in Italy during Winter 2005–06 and its Aftermaths', paper to the IEA Gas Security Workshop, Paris, 12 June.

Gately, D. (1984), 'A Ten-year Retrospective: OPEC and the World Oil Market', *Journal of Economic Literature*, **22**(3), 1100–14.

— (1995), 'Strategies for Opec Pricing and Output Decisions', *Energy Journal*, **16**(3).

— (2001), 'How Plausible is the Consensus Projection of Oil Below $25 and Persian Gulf Oil Capacity and Output Doubling by 2020?', The Energy Journal, **22**(4), 1–27.

— (2004), 'OPEC's Incentives For Faster Output Growth', *Energy Journal*, **25**(2), 75–96.

Gazprom (2005), *Gazprom Annual Report 2005*, www.gazprom.com

Geroski, P. A. (2004), 'Appealing to the UK Competition Commission', *Utilities Policy*, **12**, 77–81.

— Ulph, A. M., and Ulph, D. T. (1987), 'A Model of the Crude Oil Market in which Market Conduct Varies', *The Economic Journal*, **97**(Conference), 77–86.

Gerstenzang, J. (2006), 'Expand Nuclear Power, Bush Says', *Los Angeles Times*, 25 May, available at http://www.latimes.com/news/nationworld/nation/la-na-bush25may25,1,2545903.story?coll=la-headlines-nation&ctrack=1&cset=true

Gibson, M., and Price, C. (1983), 'Gas Supply', *Public Money*, 6–7, December.

Gilbert, R. J., and Newbery, D. M. (1994), 'The Dynamic Efficiency of Regulatory Constitutions', *Rand Journal of Economics*, **25**(4), 538–54.

Giulietti, M., and Waddams Price, C. (2005), 'Incentive Regulation and Efficient Pricing', *Annals of Public and Co-operative Economics*, 1/2005, January.

— Otero, J., and Waterson, M. (2004), 'Supply Competition and Price Behaviour in the UK Electricity Supply Industry', Centre for Management under Regulation, Discussion Paper.

— Waddams Price, C., and Waterson, M. (2005), 'Consumer Choice and Industrial Policy: A Study of UK Energy Markets', *The Economic Journal*, **115**, 949–68.

Glachant, J.-M., and Pignon, V. (2005) 'Nordic Congestion's Arrangement as a Model for Europe? Physical Constraints and Economic Incentives', *Utilities Policy*, **13**(2), 153–62.

Gordon, R. L. (1994), 'Energy, Exhaustion, Environmentalism, and Etatism', *Energy Journal*, **15**(1).

Goulder, L. H. (1995), 'Environmental Taxation and the "Double Dividend": A Reader's Guide', *International Tax and Public Finance*, **2**, 157–84.

— Schneider, S. H. (1999), 'Induced Technological Change and the Attractiveness of CO_2 Emissions Abatement Policies', *Resource and Energy Economics*, **21**, 211–53.

Government of Canada (2005), *Moving Forward on Climate Change: A Plan for Honouring our Kyoto Commitment*, http://www.climatechange.gc.ca/english/newsroom/2005/plan05.asp

Green, R. J. (1999), 'Checks and Balances in Utility Regulation—The UK Experience', *Public Policy for the Private Sector*, World Bank Series No. 185, May 1999, World Bank.

— (2001), 'Markets for Electricity in Europe', *Oxford Review of Economic Policy*, **17**(3), 329–45.

Green, R. J. (2004*a*), 'Did English Generators Play Cournot? Capacity Withholding in the Electricity Pool', CMI Working Paper EP41, University of Cambridge.

— (2004*b*), 'Retail Competition and Electricity Contracts', CMI Working Paper EP33, University of Cambridge.

— (2007), 'Nodal Pricing of Electricity: How Much Does it Cost to Get it Wrong?' *Journal of Regulatory Economics*, forthcoming.

— McDaniel, T. M. (1998), 'Competition in Electricity Supply: Will 1998 Be Worth It?', *Fiscal Studies*, **19**(3), 273–94.

— —(1999), 'Expected Revenues in the Balancing Market: Equivalence between Pay-as-bid and SMP', DAE Working Paper 0002, University of Cambridge.

— Newbery, D. M. (1997) 'Competition in the Electricity Industry in England and Wales' *Oxford Review of Economic Policy*, **13**(1), 27–46.

Griffin, J. M. (1985), 'OPEC Behaviour: A Test of Alternative Hypotheses', *American Economic Review*, **75**(5), 954–63.

— Nielson, W. S. (1994), 'The 1985–1986 Oil Price Collapse and Afterwards: What Does Game Theory Add?', *Economic Inquiry*, **32**(4), 543–61.

Grout, P. A., and Zalewska, A. (2003), 'Do Regulatory Changes Affect Market Risk?', LIFE Working Paper 03-022, LIFE, Maastricht University.

Grubb, M., and Vigotti, R., (1997), *Renewable Energy Strategies for Europe—Electricity Systems and Primary Electricity Sources*, vol. II, London, Earthscan.

Gruebler, A., Nakicenovic, N., and Victor, D. G. (1999), 'Modelling Technological Change: Implications for the Global Environment', *Annual Review of Energy and the Environment*, **24**, 545–69.

Gulen G. (1996), 'Is OPEC a Cartel ? Evidence from Cointegration and Causality Tests', *Energy Journal*, **17**(2).

Hallouche, H. (forthcoming), *Algeria's Gas Future: Between A Growing Economy And A Growing Export Market*, Oxford Institute for Energy Studies.

Haltiwanger, J.. and Harrington, J. (1991), 'The Impact of Cyclical Demand Movements on Collusive Behavior', *RAND Journal of Economics*, **22**, 89–106.

Hamilton, J. D. (1983), 'Oil and the Macro-economy since World War II', *Journal of Political Economy*, **91**.

Hancher, L., Larouche, P., and Lavrijssen, S. (2003), 'Principles of Good Market Governance', *Journal of Network Industries*, **4**, 355–89.

Hart, O. (1995), *Firms, Contracts and Financial Structure*, Oxford, Clarendon Press.

Hartshorn, J. E. (1980), 'From Multinational to National Oil: The Structural Change', *Journal of Energy and Development*, **6**(Spring).

— (1993), *Oil Trade: Politics and Prospects*, Cambridge, Cambridge University Press.

Heal, G. M., and Chichilnisky G. (1991), *Oil and the International Economy*, Oxford, Clarendon Press.

Helm, D. R. (2003) 'The Assessment: Climate Change Policy' *Oxford Review of Economic Policy*, **19**(3), 349–61.

— (2004*a*), *Energy, the State, and the Market: British Energy Policy since 1979*, revised edn, Oxford, Oxford University Press.

Helm, D. R. (2004*b*), *The New Regulatory Agenda*, London, Social Market Foundation.

— (ed.) (2005*a*), *Climate-change Policy*, Oxford, Oxford University Press.

— (2005*b*), 'Climate Change and Energy Policy', ch. 15 in D. R. Helm (ed.), *Climate-change Policy*, Oxford, Oxford University Press.

— (2005*c*), 'A New British Energy Policy', Social Market Foundation, London, November.

— (2005*d*), 'The Assessment: The New Energy Paradigm', *Oxford Review of Economic Policy*, **21**(1), 1–18.

— (2006*a*), 'Regulatory Reform, Capture, and the Regulatory Burden', *Oxford Review of Economic Policy*, **22**(2), 169–85.

— (2006*b*), *From Review to Reality: The Search for a Credible Energy Policy*, London, Social Market Foundation.

— (2006*c*), 'Energy Policy and Climate Change', Beesley Lecture, November.

— Hepburn, C., and Mash, R. (2003), 'Credible Carbon Policy', *Oxford Review of Economic Policy*, **19**(3), 438–50, reprinted in Helm (2005*a*).

— — —(2004), 'Time-inconsistent Environmental Policy and Optimal Delegation', Royal Economic Society, Conference Paper.

— Kay, J., and Thompson D. (1988), 'Energy Policy and the Role of the State in the Market for Energy', *Fiscal Studies*, **9**(1).

Hepburn, C., Neuhoff, K., Grubb, M., Matthes, F., and Tse, M. (2006), 'Auctioning of EU ETS Phase II Allowances: Why and How?', *Climate Policy*, **6**(1), 137–60.

Herig, C. (2000), 'PV is On When the Power is Out', National Association of Regulatory Utility Commissioners Committee on Energy Resources and the Environment, 2000 Annual Convention, San Diego.

Herzog, A. V., Lipman, T. E., Edwards, J. L., and Kammen, D. M. (2001), 'Renewable Energy: A Viable Choice', *Environment*, **43**(10).

Hirst, E. (2004), *US Transmission Capacity: Present Status and Future Prospects*, June, Washington, DC.

HM Government (1998), 'A Fair Deal for Consumers. Modernising the Framework for Utility Regulation', CM 3898, The Stationery Office.

— (2004), 'Review of the UK Climate Change Programme', Consultation Paper, December.

— (2006), *The Energy Challenge*, report on the Energy Review, July.

HMSO (1990), *The Hinkley Point Public Inquiries. A Report by Michael Barnes to the Secretaries of State for Energy and the Environment*, London, HMSO.

Hoel, M. (1998), 'Emission Taxes versus Other Environmental Policies', *Scandinavian Journal of Economics*, **100**(1), 79–104.

Hoff, T., and Cheney, M. (2000), 'The Potential for Photovoltaics and Other Distributed Resources in Rural Electric Cooperatives', *Energy Journal*, **21**(3), 113–27.

Hoffert, M. I, Caldeira, K., Benford, G., Criswell, D. R., Green, C., Herzog, H., Jain, A. T., Kheshgi, H. S., Lackner, K. S., Lewis, J. S., Lightfoot, H. D., Manheimer, W., Mankins, J. C., Mauel, M. E., Perkins, L. J., Schlesinger, M. E., Volk, T., and Wigley, T. M. L. (2002),

'Advanced Technology Paths to Global Climate Stability: Energy for a Greenhouse Planet', *Science*, **298**, 981–7.

Hogan, W. W. (1992), 'Contract Networks for Electric Power Transmission', *Journal of Regulatory Economics*, **4**(2), 211–42.

— (1998), 'Independent System Operator: Pricing and Flexibility in a Competitive Electricity Market', mimeo, Harvard University.

— (2005), 'On an "Energy-only" Electricity Market Design for Resource Adequacy', Working Paper, Center for Business and Government, Harvard University.

Honoré, A. (2006), 'Future Gas Demand in Europe, the Importance of the Power Sector', January, available at http://www.oxfordenergy.org/pdfs/NG10.pdf

— (forthcoming), 'European Gas Demand, Supply and Pricing: Cycles, Seasons and the Impact of Prices Arbitrage', forthcoming in 2007, Oxford Institute for Energy Studies and Oxford University Press.

Horn, M. (2004), 'OPEC's Optimal Crude Oil Price', *Energy Policy*, **32**, 269–80.

Horsnell, P. (1997), *Oil in Asia: Markets, Trading, Refining and Deregulation*, Oxford, Oxford University Press.

— (2004), 'Why Oil Prices Have Moved Higher', *Oxford Energy Forum*, 58, August.

Hotelling, H. (1931), 'The Economics of Exhaustible Resources', *Journal of Political Economy*, **39**(2), 137–75.

Hovi, J., and Kallbekken, S. (2004). 'The Price of Non-compliance with the Kyoto Protocol: The Remarkable Case of Norway', Working Paper 2004:07, CICERO, Oslo.

Hunt, L. C. (2003), *Energy in a Competitive Market: Essays in Honour of Colin Robinson*, Cheltenham, Edward Elgar.

Huntington, H. G. (1998), 'Crude Oil Prices and US Economic Performance: Where does the Asymmetry Reside?', *Energy Journal*, **19**(4).

Hyde, R. A., Teller, E., and Wood, L. L. (2003), 'Active Climate Stabilization: Practical Physics-Based Approaches to Preventing Climate Change', in *The Carbon Dioxide Dilemma: Promising Technologies and Policies*, Washington, DC, The National Academy of Sciences.

Hynilicza, E., and Pindyck, R. S. (1976), 'Pricing Policies for a Two-Part Exhaustible Resource Cartel: The Case of OPEC', *European Economic Review*, **8**, 139–54.

IAEA (2006), 'Power Reactor Information System', available at http://www.iaea.org/programmes/a2/

IEA (various years), *Energy Policies of IEA Countries, Review*, Paris, International Energy Agency.

— (2000, 2002, 2003, 2004, 2005), *World Energy Outlook* (for respective years), Paris, International Energy Agency, Organization for Economic Cooperation and Development.

— (1999), *World Energy Outlook, Looking at Energy Subsidies: Getting the Price Right*, Paris, International Energy Agency, Organization for Economic Cooperation and Development.

— (2000), *Experience Curves for Technology Policy*, Paris, International Energy Agency.

IEA (2003*a*), *World Energy Investment Outlook: 2003 Insights*, Paris, International Energy Agency, Organization for Economic Cooperation and Development.

— (2003*b*), *Creating Markets for Energy Technologies*, Paris, International Energy Agency.

— (2003*c*), *Renewables for Power Generation, Status and Prospects*, Paris, International Energy Agency.

— (2004), *World Energy Outlook 2004*, Paris, International Energy Agency, Organization for Economic Cooperation and Development.

— (2005), *World Energy Outlook 2005—Middle East and Africa Insights*, Paris, International Energy Agency, Organization for Economic Cooperation and Development.

— (2006*a*), *Natural Gas Information*, Paris, International Energy Agency, Organization for Economic Cooperation and Development.

— (2006*b*), *Electricity Information*, Paris, International Energy Agency, Organization for Economic Cooperation and Development.

— (2006*c*), *Optimising Russian Natural Gas: Reform and Climate Policy*, Paris, International Energy Agency, Organization for Economic Cooperation and Development.

— (2006*d*), *World Energy Outlook 2006*, Paris, International Energy Agency, Organization for Economic Cooperation and Development.

IGU (2005), *Gas for Power in Europe*, Brussels, International Gas Union.

Ilex (2004), 'Impact of the EU ETS on Electricity Prices: A Report to DTI', Oxford, Ilex Energy Consulting.

IMF (2005), 'Will the Oil Market Continue to be Tight?', in *World Economic Outlook: Globalization and External Imbalances*, April, ch. 4.

IPA (2005), 'Implications of the EU Emissions Trading Scheme for the UK Generation Sector: Final Report to DTI', IPA Energy Consulting, 11 November.

Irwin, D., and Klenow, P. (1994), 'Learning-by-Doing Spillovers in the Semiconductor Industry', *Journal of Political Economy*, **102**, 1200–27.

Isoard, S., and Soria, A. (1997), 'Learning Curves and Returns to Scale Dynamics: Evidence from the Emerging Renewable Energy Technologies', IPTS Working Paper Series WP 97/05.

ISO New England (2004), 'Final Report on Electricity Supply Conditions in New England During the January 14–16 2004 Cold Snap', October, available at http://www.iso-ne.com

— (2005), *2004 Annual Market Report*, available at http://www.iso-ne.com

— (2006), 'FERC Filing on Proposed LICAP Settlement', available at http://www.iso-ne.com/regulatory/ferc/filings/2006/mar/er03-563-000_030_055_3-7-06_corrected.pdf

Jagadeesh, A. (2000), 'Wind Energy Development in Tamil Nadu and Andhra Pradesh, India: Institutional Dynamics and Barriers—A Case Study', *Energy Policy*, **28**, 157–68.

Jamasb, T. (2002), 'Reform and Regulation of the Electricity Sectors in Developing Countries', DAE Working Paper 0226 (CMI EP 08), Department of Applied Economics, University of Cambridge, available at http://www.electricitypolicy.org.uk/pubs/wp/ep08.pdf

Jamasb, T., and Pollitt, M. (2005), 'Deregulation and R&D in Network Industries: The Case of the Electricity Industry', Cambridge Working Papers in Economics CWPE 0533 / Electricity Policy Research Group Working Paper EPRG 05/02, August, Faculty of Economics, University of Cambridge.

Jelen, F. C., and Black, L. (1983), *Cost and Optimization Engineering*, New York, McGraw Hill.

Jensen, S. G. (2004), 'Reducing Costs of Emerging Renewable Energy Technologies—An Analysis of the Dynamic Development with Wind Power as Case Study', *International Journal of Energy Technology and Policy*, **2**(1/2), 179–202.

— Skytte, K. (2003), 'Simultaneous Attainment of Energy Goals by Means of Green Certificates and Emission Permits', *Energy Policy*, **31**, 63–71.

JESS (2003), *Joint Energy Security of Supply Working Group (JESS); Third Report*, November 2003, London.

Johansson, T. B., Fritsche, U. R., Flavin, C., Sawin, J., Assmann, D., and Herberg, T. C. (2004), 'Policy Recommendations for Renewable Energies', International Conference for Renewables, Bonn.

Johany, A. (1980), *The Myth of the OPEC Cartel: The Role of Saudi Arabia*, New York, John Wiley and Sons.

Jones, D. W., Leiby, P. N., and Paik, I. K. (2004), 'Oil Price Shocks and the Macroeconomy: What has been Learned since 1996', *Energy Journal*, **25**(2).

Jones, L., Tandon, P., and Vogelsang, I. (1990), *Selling Public Enterprises A Cost Benefit Methodology*, Cambridge, MA, MIT Press.

Jorgenson, D. W., and Wilcoxen, P. J. (1990), 'Environmental Regulation and US Economic Growth', *RAND Journal of Economics*, **21**(2), 314–40.

Joskow, P. L. (1974), 'Inflation and Environmental Concern: Structural Change in the Process of Public Utility Price Regulation', *Journal of Law and Economics*, **17**(1), 291–327.

— (1976), 'Contributions to the Theory of Marginal Cost Pricing', *Bell Journal of Economics*, **7**(1), 197–206.

— (1987), 'Contract Duration and Relationship Specific Investments', *American Economic Review*, **77**, 168–75.

— (1989), 'Regulatory Failure, Regulatory Reform, and Structural Change in the Electric Power Industry', *Brookings Papers on Economic Activity; Microeconomics*, 125–208.

— (2001), 'California's Electricity Crisis', *Oxford Review of Economic Policy*, **17**(3), 365–88.

— (2003), 'The Difficult Transition to Competitive Electricity Markets in the US', MIT, May.

— (2005), 'The Difficult Transition to Competitive Electricity Markets in the United States', in J. Griffin and S. Puller (eds), *Electricity Deregulation: Where To From Here?*, Chicago, IL, University of Chicago Press.

— (2006), 'Markets for Power in the US: An Interim Assessment', *Energy Journal*, **27**(1), 1–36.

Joskow, P. L., and Tirole, J. (2004), 'Reliability and Competitive Electricity Markets', *Working Paper*, CMI EP 53, University of Cambridge.

— —(2005), 'Retail Electricity Competition', *RAND Journal of Economics*, forthcoming.

— —(2006), 'Reliability and Competitive Electricity Markets', *RAND Journal of Economics* (forthcoming), available at http://econ-www.mit.edu/faculty/download_pdf.php?id=917

Kammen, D. M. (2004), 'Renewable Energy Options for the Emerging Economy: Advances, Opportunities and Obstacles', Background Paper for 'The 10–50 Solution: Technologies and Policies for a Low-Carbon Future', Pew Center & NECP Conference, Washington, DC.

Kaplan, A. (1999), 'Generating Interest, Generating Power: Commercializing Photovoltaics in the Utility Sector', *Energy Policy*, **27**, 317–29.

Keats Martinez, K, and Neuhoff, K. (2005), 'Allocation of Carbon Emission Certificates in the Power Sector: How Generators Profit from Grandfathered Rights', *Climate Policy*, **5**(5), 61–78.

Kemp, A. G. (1988), *Petroleum Rent Collection Around the World*, Halifax, Institute for Research in Public Policy.

— Kasim, A. S. (2006), 'A Regional Model of Oil and Gas Exploration in the UKCS', *Scottish Journal of Political Economy*, **53**(2), 198–221.

— —(2005), 'Are Decline Rates Really Exponential? Evidence from the UK Continental Shelf', *Energy Journal*, **26**(1), 27–58.

King, D. (2005), 'Science Informing Policy on Climate Change', ch. 2 in D. R. Helm (ed.), *Climate-change Policy*, Oxford, Oxford University Press.

Klare, M. (2004), *Blood and Oil*, London, Hamish Hamilton.

Klemperer, P. (2004), *Auctions: Theory and Practice*, Princeton, NJ, Princeton University Press.

Kline, D. (2001), 'Positive Feedback, Lock-in, and Environmental Policy', *Policy Science*, **34**, 95–107.

Klinski, S. (2004), 'Rechtliche und administrative Hemmnisse des Ausbaus erneuerbare Energien in Deutschland', Ergebnisse des 1. Teilberichts (Results of the Interim Report), March.

Kohl, W. L. (2002), 'OPEC Behaviour, 1998-2001', *Quarterly Review of Economics and Finance*, **42**(2), 209–233.

Koyama, K. (2001), 'Japan's Energy Strategies towards the Middle East', unpublished Ph.D. thesis, University of Dundee.

Kuhn, T. S. (1962), *The Structure of Scientific Revolutions. International Encyclopedia of Unified Science*, Chicago, IL, University of Chicago Press, 2nd edn 1970.

Kydland, F., and Prescott, E. (1977), 'Rules rather than Discretion: The Inconsistency of Optimal Plans', *Journal of Political Economy*, **85**, 473–91.

Laffont, J.-J., and Martimort, D. (1999), 'Separation of Regulators against Collusive Behavior', *RAND Journal of Economics*, **30**(2), 232–62.

Lakatos, I., and Musgrave, A. (eds) (1970), *Criticism and the Growth of Knowledge*, Cambridge, Cambridge University Press.

Lawson, N. (1982), 'Energy Policy', ch. 1 in D. R. Helm, J. Kay, and D. Thompson (eds), *The Market for Energy*, Oxford, Oxford University Press.

Lee, K. N. S., and Ratti, R. A. (1995), 'Oil Shocks and the Macro Economy: The Role of Price Variability', *Energy Journal*, **16**(4).

Leiby, P. N., Bowman, D., and Jones, D. W. (2002), 'Improving Energy Security through an International Cooperative Approach to Emergency Oil Stockpiling', Oak Ridge National Laboratory Web Site.

Leland, H. E., and Pyle, D. H. (1977), 'Informational Asymmetries, Financial Structure, and Financial Intermediation', *Journal of Finance*, **32**, 371–87.

Lev, B. (2004), 'Sharpening the Intangibles' Edge', *Harvard Business Review*, June, 109–16.

Levy, M. A. (1993), 'European Acid Rain: The Power of Tote-Board Diplomacy', in P. M. Haas, R. O. Keohane, and M. A. Levy (eds), *Institutions for the Earth: Sources of Effective International Environmental Protection*, Cambridge, MA, MIT Press.

Libecap, G. D., and Smith, J. L. (2004), 'Political Constraints on Government Cartelization: The Case of Oil Production Regulation in Texas and Saudi Arabia', in P. Grossman (ed.), *How Cartels Endure and How They Fail: Studies of Industrial Collusion*, Cheltenham, UK, Edward Elgar.

Lindahl, M. (1996), 'Should Oil States Hedge Oil Revenues?', *IAEE Newsletter*, Winter.

Lohmann, H. (2006), 'The German Path to Natural Gas Liberalisation: Is it a Special Case?', Oxford Institute for Energy Studies, September.

Luciani, G., and Salustri, M. (1998), 'Vertical Integration as a Strategy for Oil Security', in P. J. Stevens (ed.), *Strategic Positioning in the Oil Industry: Trends and Options*, Abu Dhabi, The Emirates Center for Strategic Studies and Research.

Lund, D. (2002), 'Petroleum Tax Reform Proposals in Norway and Denmark', *Energy Journal*, **23**(4).

Luther, J. (2004), 'Research and Development, The Basis for Wide-spread Employment of Renewable Energy', Thematic Background Paper, International Conference for Renewable Energies, Bonn.

Lux, T. (1995), 'Herd Behaviour, Bubbles and Crashes', *The Economic Journal*, **105**.

Lynch, M. C. (1995), 'Shoulder against Shoulder: The Evolution of Oil Industry Strategy', *Journal of Energy and Development*, **19**(1).

— (2003), 'Causes of Oil Price Volatility', *Journal of Energy and Development*, **28**(1).

Lyon, T. P., and Mayo, J. W. (2000), 'Regulatory Opportunism and Investment Behavior: Evidence from the US Electric Utility Industry', mimeo, June.

Mabro, R. (1984), 'On Oil Price Concepts', WPM3, Oxford, Oxford Institute for Energy Studies.

— (1986), 'The Netback Pricing System and the Price Collapse of 1986', WPM 10, Oxford, Oxford Institute for Energy Studies.

— (1991), 'OPEC and the Price of Oil', *Energy Journal*, **13**, 1–17.

— (1992), 'OPEC and the Price of Oil', Oxford Institute for Energy Studies, Oxford.

— (1998*a*). 'OPEC Behavior 1960–1998: A Review of the Literature', *Journal of Energy Literature*, **4**(1), 3–27.

470

Mabro, R. (1998*b*), 'The Oil Price Crisis of 1998', SP10, Oxford, Oxford Institute for Energy Studies.

—— (2003), 'Saudi Arabia's Oil Policies', *Middle East Economic Survey*, **44**.

—— (2005), 'The International Oil Price Regime: Origins, Rationale, and Assessment', *Journal Of Energy Literature*, **11**(1).

McCabe, P. J. (1998), 'Energy Resources—Cornucopia or Empty Barrel?', *AAPG Bulletin*, **82**(11), November.

McClellan, K. (2005), 'Securing Investment for Climate-friendly Projects: Uses and Limitations of Carbon Trading', in K. Tang (ed.), *The Finance of Climate Change*, London, Riskbooks, 65–76.

McDonald, A., and Schrattenholzer, L. (2001), 'Learning Rates for Energy Technologies', *Energy Policy*, **29**, 255–61.

MacKerron, G.. and Pearson P. (eds), (1996), *The International Energy Experience*, London, Imperial College Press.

—— —— (2000), *The UK Energy Experience: A Model or a Warning?*, London, Imperial College Press.

McKibbin, W. J., and Wilcoxen, P. J. (2002), 'The Role of Economics in Climate Change Policy', *Journal of Economic Perspectives*, **16**(2), 107–29.

Mansfield, E. (1968), *Industrial Research and Technological Innovation*, New York, Norton.

Marcel, V. (2006), *Oil Titans: National Oil Companies in the Middle East*, London, Chatham House and the Brookings Institute.

Margolis, R. M., and Kammen, D. M. (1999*a*), 'Underinvestment: The Energy Technology and R&D Policy Challenge', *Science*, **285**, 690–2.

—— —— (1999*b*), 'Evidence of Under-investment in Energy R&D in the United States and the Impact of Federal Policy', *Energy Policy*, **27**, 575–84.

Marsiliani, L., and Renström, T. I. (2000), 'Time Inconsistency in Environmental Policy: Tax Earmarking as a Commitment Solution', *The Economic Journal*, **110**, C123–38.

Mead, W. J. (1979), 'The Performance of Government Energy Regulation', *American Economic Review*, **69**, 352–6.

Mendlesohn, R. (2005), 'The Social Costs of Greenhouse Gases: Their Values and Policy Implications', ch. 6 in D. R. Helm (ed.), *Climate-change Policy*, Oxford, Oxford University Press.

Ministry of Economic Affairs, Netherlands (2004), *Innovation in Energy Policy, Energy Transition: State of Affairs and the Way Ahead*.

Ministry of Fuel and Power (1955), 'A Programme of Nuclear Power', Cmnd 9389, London, HMSO.

Mitchell, C. (1998), *Renewable Energy in the UK: Policies for the Future*, Council for the Protection of Rural England.

Mitchell, J. V. (1994), *An Oil Agenda for Europe*, London, Royal Institute for International Affairs.

—— Beck, P., and Grubb, M. (1996), *The New Geopolitics of Energy*, London, Royal Institute of International Affairs.

Mitchell, R. (1994), *Intentional Oil Pollution at Sea: Environmental Policy and Treaty Compliance*, Cambridge, MA, MIT Press.

Mkandawire, T. (2001), 'Thinking about Developmental States in Africa', *Cambridge Journal of Economics*, **25**.

MMC (1981), 'Central Electricity Generating Board: A Report on the Operation by the Board of its System for the Generational and Supply of Electricity in Bulk', HC315, 1980–81, Monopolies and Mergers Commission, London, HMSO, May.

— (1994), 'Gas and British Gas, plc', volume 2, Cm 2316, Monopolies and Mergers Commission, London, HMSO.

Montero, J.-P. (1999) 'Voluntary Compliance with Market-Based Environmental Policy: Evidence from the US Acid Rain Program', *Journal of Political Economy*, **107**(5), 998–1033.

Moore, C., and Ihle, J. (1999), 'Renewable Energy Policy outside the United States', *Renewable Energy Policy Project*, No. 14, October.

Mork, K. A. (1994), 'Business Cycles and the Oil Market', *Energy Journal*, **15**(Special Issue), 15–38.

Musial, W., and Butterfield, S. (2004), 'Future for Offshore Wind Energy in the United States', National Renewable Energy Laboratory, CP-500-36313.

Myers, S. C. (1972), 'The Application of Finance Theory to Public Utility Rate Cases', *Bell Journal of Economics*, **3**(1), 58–97.

Nagel, E. (1961), *The Structure of Science*, New York, Routledge.

NAO (1998), *The Sale of British Energy*, National Audit Office, available at http://www.nao.org.uk/pn/9798694.htm

— (2005), 'Renewables Energy, Report by the Comptroller and Auditor General', HC210, Session 2004–05, February.

National Grid Transportation (2005), *Ten-Year Statement*, National Grid Transportation.

Natural Resources Canada and US Department of Energy (2004), 'The August 14 2003 Blackout One Year Later: Actions taken in the United States and Canada to Reduce Blackout Risk', report to US-Canada Power System Outage Task Force, August.

NEMMCO (2004), *An Introduction to Australia's National Electricity Market*, Melbourne, National Electricity Market Management Company.

NEPDG (2001), *National Energy Policy: Reliable, Affordable and Environmentally Sound Energy for America's Future*, National Energy Policy Development Group, Washington, DC, US Government Printing Office.

Neuhoff, K. (2004), 'Large Scale Deployment of Renewables for Electricity Generation', Cambridge Working Papers in Economics, 0460.

— De Vries, L. (2004), 'Insufficient Incentives for Investment in Electricity Generation', *Utilities Policy*, **12**, 253–67.

Neumann, T., Ender, C., Molly, J. P., Neddermann, B., Winkler, W., and Strack, M. (2002), 'Weiterer Ausbau der Windenergienutzung im Hinblick auf den Klimaschutz—Teil 2', Deutsches Windenergie-Institut.

Newbery, D. M. (1985), 'Pricing Policy', ch. 5 in R. Belgrave and M. Cornell (eds), *Energy Self-Sufficiency for the UK?*, Joint Studies in Public Policy, Gower, 77–120.

Newbery, D. M. (1996), 'The Restructuring of the UK Energy Industry: What have we Learned?', in G. MacKerron and P. Pearson (eds), *The International Energy Experience*, London, Imperial College Press.

— (2000), 'Markets, Regulation and Environment—A Summing Up', in G. MacKerron and P. Pearson (eds), *The UK Energy Experience: A Model or a Warning?*, London, Imperial College Press.

— (2002) 'Problems of Liberalising the Electricity Industry', *European Economic Review*, **46**, 919–27.

— Pollitt, M. G. (1997), 'The Restructuring and Privatisation of Britain's CEGB—Was it Worth It?', *Journal of Industrial Economics*, **45**(3), 269–303.

— Nuttall, W. J., and Roques, F. (2004), 'Generation Adequacy and Investment Incentives in Britain: From the Pool to NETA', CMI Working Paper EP58, Department of Applied Economics, University of Cambridge.

Newton-Smith, W. H. (1981), *The Rationality of Science*, London, Routledge.

New York ISO (2005*a*), '2004 State of the Markets Report', prepared by David Patton, July, available at http://www.nyiso.com/public/webdocs/documents/market_advisor_reports/2004_patton_final_report.pdf

— (2005*b*), 'NYISO's Demand Response Program', presentation by Aaron Breidenbaugh, 15 March.

NGC (2004), *Seven Year Statement*, Warwick, National Grid Company.

Nillesen, P. H. L., and Pollitt, M. G. (2004), 'The Consequences for Consumer Welfare of the 2001–2003 Electricity Distribution Price Review in the Netherlands', Working Paper, CMI EP 50, University of Cambridge.

Norberg-Bohm, V. (2000), 'Creating Incentives for Environmentally Enhancing Technological Change: Lessons from 30 years of US Energy Technology Policy', *Technological Forecasting and Social Change*, **65**, 125–48.

Nordel (2004) *Annual Report 2003*, available at http://www.nordel.org, Vällingby, Nordel.

Nuclear Energy Institute (2006), 'Nuclear Statistics; Lifetime Extension', Washington, DC, available at http://www.nei.org/index.asp?catnum=2&catid=343

NuStart Energy (2004), 'Seven Companies to Investigate Licensing, Design Certification of Advanced Nuclear Reactors', 30 March, available at http://www.nustartenergy.com/DisplayArticle.aspx?ID=20040330-1

Ocana, C. (2003), 'Trends in the Management of Regulation: A Comparison of Energy Regulators in Member Countries of the OECD', *International Journal of Regulation and Governance*, **3**(1), 13–32.

OECD (2002), *Security of Supply in Electricity Markets*, Paris, Organization for Economic Cooperation and Development.

— (2003), *World Energy Investment Outlook*, Paris, Organization for Economic Cooperation and Development

— IEA, and UNEP (2002), *Reforming Energy Subsidies*, Paris, Organization for Economic Cooperation and Development, International Energy Agency, and United Nations Environment Programme.

Offer (1991) *Pool Price Enquiry*, Birmingham, Office of Electricity Regulation.

—   (1999) *Pool Price: A Consultation by Offer, February 1999*, Birmingham, Office of Electricity Regulation.

Office of National Statistics (2005), *Family Spending: A Report on the 2004–05 Expenditure and Food Survey*.

Official Report (1965), *Official Report*, 25 May 1965, Vol. 713, c. 237–8.

Ofgem (2003), 'Ofgem's Work to Reduce Fuel Poverty', Factsheet 27, http://www.ofgem.gov.uk/temp/ofgem/cache/cmsattach/3191_factsheet27_fuelpoverty03.pdf

—   (2004*a*), *Report on Support Investigations into Recent Blackouts in London and West Midlands*, London, Office of Gas and Electricity Markets, February.

—   (2004*b*), *Domestic Competitive Market Review 2004, A Review Document*, April, London, Office of Gas and Electricity Markets.

—   (2006a), 'Monitoring Company Performance, Quarter 4 and Annual 2005' (Social Action Plan), http://www.ofgem.gov.uk/temp/ofgem/cache/cmsattach/14238_sapq4.pdf?wtfrom=/ofgem/work/index.jsp&section=/areasofwork/socialactionplan

—   (2006b), 'Domestic Retail Market Report—September 2005', http://www.ofgem.gov.uk/temp/ofgem/cache/cmsattach/13816_2306.pdf?wtfrom=/ofgem/work/index.jsp&section=/areasofwork/retailcompetition

—   (2006c), 'Domestic Retail Market Report—June 2005', appendices, http://www.ofgem.gov.uk/temp/ofgem/cache/cmsattach/13823_2406b.pdf?wtfrom=/ofgem/work/index.jsp&section=/areasofwork/retailcompetition

Ogawa. Y. (2002), 'Proposals on Measures for Reducing Asian Premium of Crude Oil', monograph, Tokyo IEEJ. November.

Ollinger. M. (1994), 'The Limits of Growth of the Multidivisional Firm: A Case Study of the US Oil Industry from 1930–90', *Strategic Management Journal*, **15**.

O'Neill, B. C., and Oppenheimer, M. (2002), 'Dangerous Climate Impacts and the Kyoto Protocol', *Science*, **296**, 1971–2.

OPEC (2003), *Statistical Bulletin*, Vienna, OPEC.

Ordover, J. A., and Saloner, G. (1989), 'Predation, Monopolization, and Antitrust', in R. Schmalensee and R. Willig (eds), *Handbook of Industrial Organization*, Volume I, Amsterdam, Elsevier Science.

Oren, S. (2004), 'Ensuring Generation Adequacy in Competitive Electricity Markets', mimeo, UC Berkeley, April.

—   (2005), 'Generation Adequacy Via Call Options: Safe Passage to the Promised Land', University of California Energy Institute Working Paper EPE-016, September, available at http://www.ucei.berkeley.edu/pwrpubs/epe016.html and http://stoft.com/metaPage/lib/Oren-2005-09-call-options-obligations.pdf.

Otero, J., and Waddams Price, C. (2001), 'Price Discrimination in a Regulated Market with Entry: The Residential UK Electricity Market', *Bulletin of Economic Research*, **53**(3), 161–75.

Oxera (2003), 'The Non-market Value of Generation Technologies', funded by British Nuclear Fuels, available at www.oxera.co.uk/oxera/public.nsf/images/DKIG-5NCERA/$file/OXERAReport.pdf.

— (2005), 'Where has the Innovation Gone? R&D in UK Utility Regulation', *Agenda*, November, Oxford, Oxera Consulting.

Pacala, S., and Socolow, R. (2004), 'Stabilization Wedges: Solving the Climate Problem for the Next 50 Years with Current Technologies', *Science*, **305**, 968–72.

Paga, E., and Birol, F. (1994), 'Empirical Analysis of Oil Demand in Developing Countries', *OPEC Review*, **18**(1).

Parra, F. (2004), *Oil Politics: A Modern History of Petroleum*, London, I.B. Taurus.

Parry, I. (2003), 'Fiscal Interactions and the Case for Carbon Taxes over Grandfathered Carbon Permits', *Oxford Review of Economic Policy*, **19**(3), 385–99, reprinted in Helm (2005*a*).

Pearce, D. W. (2003), 'The Social Cost of Carbon', *Oxford Review of Economic Policy*, **19**(3), 362–84, reprinted in Helm (2005*a*).

Peltzman, S. (1976), 'Toward a More General Theory of Regulation', *Journal of Law and Economics*, **19**(2), 211–40.

Penrose, E. T. (1965), 'Vertical Integration with Joint Control of Raw Material Production: Crude Oil in the Middle East', *Journal of Development Studies*, **1**(3), April.

— (1968), *The Large International Firm in Developing Countries: The International Petroleum Industry*, USA, Greenwood Press.

Pershing, J., and Mackenzie, J. (2004), 'Removing Subsidies, Leveling the Playing Field for Renewable Energy Technologies', Thematic Background Paper, International Conference for Renewable Energies, Bonn.

Phlips, L. (1995), *Competition Policy: A Game-Theoretic Perspective*, Cambridge, Cambridge University Press.

Pindyck, R. S. (1978), 'Gains to Producers from the Cartelization of Exhaustible Resources', *Review of Economics and Statistics*, **60**, 238–51.

PIU (2002), *The Energy Review*, Performance and Innovation Unit, London, Cabinet Office, February.

Pizer, W. A. (2002), 'Combining Price and Quantity Controls to Mitigate Global Climate Change', *Journal of Public Economics*, **85**(3), 409–34.

PJM (2004) *State of the Market 2003*, Norristown, Pennsylvania, PJM.

— (2006), *2005 State of the Market Report*, PJM Interconnection, available at http://www.pjm.com/markets/market-monitor/som.html

Plourde, A., and Watkins, G. C. (1994), 'How Volatile are Crude Prices?', *OPEC Review*, Winter.

Popp, D. (2005), 'R&D Subsidies and Climate Policy: Is there a "Free Lunch"?', mimeo, The Maxwell School, Syracuse University.

Popper, K. (1968), *The Logic of Scientific Discovery*, London, Hutchison.

PowerGen (2001), *Powergen Environment Report 2000*, Coventry, PowerGen plc.

Public Utility Commission of Texas (2006), *Investigation into the April 17 2006 Rolling Blackouts in the Electric Reliability Council of Texas Region: Preliminary Report*, April.

PVPS—Photovoltaic Power System Program (2003), 'Trends in Photovoltaic Applications, Survey Report of Selected IEA Countries between 1992 and 2002', Report IEA-PVPS T1-12.

Rader, N., and Norgaard, R. (1996), 'Efficiency and Sustainability in Restructured Electricity Markets: The Renewables Portfolio Standard', *Electricity Journal*, **9**(6), 37–49.

RCEP (2000), *Energy: The Changing Climate*, 22nd Report, Royal Commission on Environmental Pollution, London, HMSO, June.

Roberts, M. J., and Spence, M. (1976), 'Effluent Charges and Licenses under Uncertainty', *Journal of Public Economics*, **5**, 193–208.

Robinson, C. (1993), 'Energy Policy, Errors, Illusions and Market Realities', Institute of Economic Affairs, London, Occasional Paper 90.

Roeber, J. (1993), 'The Evolution of Oil Markets: Trading Instruments and their Role in Oil Price Formation', Royal Institute of International Affairs, London.

Rogner, H.-H., Langlois, L., and Cleveland, J. (2000), 'The Economic Future of Nuclear Power in Competitive Markets', available at http://www.onlineopinion.com.au/view.asp?article=1238

Romer, D. (1996), *Advanced Macroeconomics*, McGraw–Hill.

Roques, F., Newbery, D. M., and Nuttall, W. J. (2004), 'Generation Adequacy and Investment Incentives in the UK: from the Pool to NETA', Working Paper, CMI EP 58, University of Cambridge.

Ross, S. (1977), 'The Determination of Financial Structure: The Incentive Signalling Approach', *Bell Journal of Economics*, **8**, 23–40.

Rotemberg, J., and Saloner, G. (1986), 'A Supergame Theoretic Model of Price Wars during Booms', *American Economic Review*, **70**, 390–407.

Roth, F. I., and Ambs, L. L. (2004), 'Incorporating Externalities into a Full Cost Approach to Electric Power Generation Life-cycle Costing', *Energy*, **29**(12–15), 2125–44.

Rowlands, I. H. (2004), 'The European Directive on Renewable Electricity: Conflicts and Compromises', *Energy Policy*, **33**(8), 965–74.

Salant, S. (1976), 'Exhaustible Resources and Industrial Structure: A Nash-Cournot Approach to the World Oil Market', *Journal of Political Economy*, **84**, 1079–93.

Salehi-Isfahani, D. (1995), 'Models of the Oil Market Revisited', *Journal of Energy Literature*, **1**(1).

Salies, E., and Waddams Price, C. (2004), 'Charges, Costs and Market Power: The Deregulated UK Electricity Retail Market', forthcoming in *The Energy Journal*, **25**(3), 19–35.

Sanden, B., and Azar, C. (2005), 'Near-term Technologies for Long-term Climate Targets—Economy-wide versus Technology-specific Approaches', *Energy Policy*, **33**, 1557–76.

Sawin, J. L. (2004), 'Mainstreaming Renewable Energy in the 21st Century', Worldwatch Paper 169.

Schelling, T. C. (2002), 'What Makes Greenhouse Sense?' *Foreign Affairs*, **81**(3), 2–9.

Scherer, F. M. (1980), *Industrial Market Structure and Economic Performance*, 2nd edn, Boston, Houghton Mifflin.

Seymour I. (1980), *OPEC Instrument of Change*, London, Macmillan.

Seymour, A. and Mabro, R. (1994), *Energy Taxation and Economic Growth*, Vienna, The OPEC Fund for International Development.

Sharratt, D. (2003), 'Social Obligations and Economic Regulation: Coincidence or Conflict—A Report on the UK Energy Supply Industry'.

Shell (2005), *The Shell Global Scenarios to 2025*, available at http://www.shell.com/static/royal-en/downloads/scenarios/exsum_23052005.pdf

Shuttleworth, G., and MacKerron, G. (2002), 'Guidance and Commitment: Persuading the Private Sector to Meet the Aims of Energy Policy', London, NERA, available at http://www.nera.com/wwt/publications/5740.pdf

Sijm, J., Neuhoff, K., and Chen, Y. (2006), 'CO_2 Cost Pass-through and Windfall Profits in the Power Sector', *Climate Policy*, **6**(1), 47–70.

Singh, H. (2000), 'Call Options for Energy: A Market-based alternative to ICAP', mimeo, October, available at http://stoft.com/metaPage/lib/Singh-2000-10-Options-ICAP.pdf

Sioshansi, F. P., and Pfaffenberger, W. (2006), *Electricity Market Reform: An International Perspective*, Elsevier.

Skeet, I. (1988), *OPEC: Twenty-Five Years of Price and Politics*, Cambridge, Cambridge University Press.

Smith, J. C., DeMeo, E. A., Parson, B., and Milligan, M. (2004), 'Wind Power Impacts on Electric Power System Operating Costs: A Summary and Perspective on Work to Date', National Renewable Energy Laboratory, CP-500-35946.

Smith, J. L. (2005), 'Inscrutable OPEC? Behavioral Tests of the Cartel Hypothesis', *Energy Journal*, **26**(1), 51–82.

Soligo, R., and Jaffe, A. (2006), 'Market Structure in the New Gas Economy: Is Cartelization Possible?'.

Sonntag-O'Brien, V., and Usher, E. (2004), 'Mobilising Finance For Renewable Energies', International Conference for Renewable Energies, Bonn.

Spence, A. M. (1975), 'Monopoly, Quality and Regulation', *Bell Journal of Economics*, 417–29.

Staiger, B., and Wolak, F. (1992), 'Collusive Pricing with Capacity Constraints in the Presence of Demand Uncertainty', *RAND Journal of Economics*, **70**, 390–407.

Stern, J. P. (2004), 'UK Gas Security: Time to Get Serious', *Energy Policy*, **32**, 1967–79.

— (2005), *The Future of Russian Gas and Gazprom*, Oxford, Oxford University Press.

— (2006a), *The Russian–Ukrainian Gas Crisis of January 2006*, Oxford Institute for Energy Studies, available at http://www.oxfordenergy.org/pdfs/comment_0106.pdf

— (2006b), 'Natural Gas Security Problems in Europe: The Russian–Ukrainian Gas Crisis of 2006', *Asia-Pacific Review*, **13**(1), 32–59.

— (2006c), *The New Security Environment for European Gas: Worsening Geopolitics and Increasing Global Competition for LNG'*, Oxford Institute for Energy Studies, October, available at http://www.oxfordenergy.org/pdfs/NG15.pdf

Stevens, P. J. (1996), 'Pipeline Regulation and the North Sea Infrastructure', in G. MacKerron and P. Pearson, *The UK Energy Experience: A Model or a Warning?*, London, Imperial College Press.

Stevens, P. J. (1998), 'Introduction—Strategic Positioning in the Oil Industry: Trends and Options', in P. J. Stevens (ed.), *Strategic Positioning in the Oil Industry: Trends and Options*, Abu Dhabi, The Emirates Center for Strategic Studies and Research.

— (1999), 'Oil Company Mergers: Why and the What Effect?', *Pipeline*, 22 April.

— (2000), *Energy Economics, Vol. 1*, Cheltenham, Edward Elgar.

— (2002), Micro-managing Global Oil Markets: Is it Getting more Difficult?', *Journal of Energy and Development*, **26**(2).

— (2003*a*), 'Resource Impact: Curse or Blessing? A Literature Survey', *Journal of Energy Literature*, **9**(1), June.

— (2003*b*), 'Economists and the Oil Industry: Facts versus Analysis, the Case of Vertical Integration', in L. C. Hunt, *Energy in a Competitive Market: Essays in Honour of Colin Robinson*, Cheltenham, Edward Elgar.

— (2004a), 'The Future Price of Crude Oil', *Middle East Economic Survey*, **47**(37), 13 September.

— (2004b), 'National Oil Companies: Good or Bad? A Literature Survey', *On-Line Journal*, **14**(10), www.cepmlp.org

— (2005), 'Resource Curse: How to Avoid It', *Journal of Energy and Development*, **31**(1).

Stoft, S. E. (2002), *Power System Economics: Designing Markets for Electricity*, Chichester, Wiley.

Strauss, L. (1954), 'Speech to the National Association of Science Writers, New York City, 16 September', *New York Times*, 17 September.

Strbac, G. (2002), 'Quantifying the System Costs of Additional Renewables in 2020', Report to UK Department of Trade and Industry.

Swezey, B., and Bird, L. (2001), 'Utility Green Pricing Programs: What Defines Success?', National Renewable Energy Laboratory, TP-620-29831.

Swiss Federal Office of Energy (2003), 'Report on the Blackout in Italy on 28 September 2003', 25 November.

Tang, L., and Hammoudeh, S. (2002), 'An Empirical Exploration of the World Oil Price under the Target Zone Model', *Energy Economics*, **24**, 577–96.

Taylor, J. (2006), 'China Plans Six Nuclear Power Plants', ABC News, 19 May, available at http://www.abc.net.au/news/newsitems/200605/s1643151.htm

Teece, D. (1982), 'OPEC Behaviour: An Alternative View', in J. Griffin and D. Teece, *OPEC Behaviour and World Oil Prices*, London, Allen & Unwin.

TenneT (2004), *Rapport Monitoring Leveringszekerheid 2003–2011*, 3 June, TenneT, Arnhem.

Terzian, P. (1985), *OPEC: The Inside Story*, London, Zed Books Ltd.

The Analysis Group (2005), '25 years after the Referendum: No Support for Nuclear Phase-out in Sweden', available at http://www.analys.se/engsite/engopin/engopin_0503.html

The Energy Contract Company (March 2006), *2006 UK Gas Market Review*, Twickenham.

Tol, R. S. J. (2003), 'The Marginal Cost of Carbon Dioxide Emissions: An Assessment of the Uncertainties', Working Paper FNU 19.

— (2005), 'The Marginal Damage Costs of Carbon-dioxide Emissions', ch. 7 in D. R. Helm (ed.), *Climate-change Policy*, Oxford, Oxford University Press.

Turvey, R. (1968), *Optimal Pricing and Investment in Electricity Supply: An Essay in Applied Welfare Economics*, Cambridge, MA, MIT Press.

UCTE (2003a), 'Interim Report of the Investigation Committee on the 28 September 2003 Blackout in Italy', Brussels, Union for the Coordination of Transmission of Electricity, 27 October.

— (2003b), *UCTE System Adequacy Forecast 2004–2010*, report, December 2003, UCTE.

UNFCCC (1997), 'Kyoto Protocol to the United Nations Framework Convention on Climate Change', Bonn, available at http://unfccc.int/resource/docs/convkp/kpeng.pdf

United Nations Environment Programme (2004), 'Financial Risk Management Tools for Renewable Energy Projects', study available at www.uneptie.org/energy/act/fin/index.htm

UNPD (2003), *World Population Prospects: The 2002 Revision*, United Nations Population Division, New York, United Nations.

Unruh, G. C. (2002), 'Escaping Carbon lock-in', *Energy Policy*, **30**, 317–25.

US–Canada Power System Outage Task Force (2004), 'Final Report on the August 14, 2003 Blackout in the United States and Canada: Causes and Recommendations', April.

USDOE (2002), 'A Technology Roadmap for Generation IV Nuclear Energy Systems', US Department of Energy, available at http://gif.inel.gov/roadmap/pdfs/gen_iv_roadmap.pdf

— (2004), 'DOE Releases Final Request for Proposals to Establish World Class Nuclear Technology Lab in Idaho', Washington, DC, 26 May, available at http://energy.gov/news/1360.htm

US Government (2005), *Energy Policy Act of 2005*, Washington, DC, available at http://www.fedcenter.gov/_kd/Items/actions.cfm?action=Show&item_id=2969&destination=ShowItem

Utilities Act (2000), Chapter 27, The Stationery Office.

Van der Linde, C. (2000), *The State and the International Oil Market*, Boston, Kluwer Academic Publishers.

— Correljé, A., de Jong, J., and Tönjes, C. (2006), 'The Paradigm Change in International Natural Gas Markets and the Impact on Regulation', Clingendael International Energy Programme, April, available at http://www.clingendael.nl/publications/2006/20060600_ciep_misc_wgc-regulation-report.pdf

Vázquez, C., Rivier, M., and Pérez-Arriaga, I. J. (2002), 'A Market Approach to Long-term Security of Supply', *IEEE Transactions on Power Systems*, **17**(2), 349–57.

Vickers, J., and Yarrow, G. (1988), *Privatization: An Economic Analysis*, Cambridge, MA, MIT Press.

Victor, D. G. (2001), *The Collapse of the Kyoto Protocol and the Struggle to Slow Global Warming*. Princeton, NJ, Princeton University Press.

von der Fehr, N.-H., Amundsen, E. S., and Bergman, L., 2004, 'The Nordic Market: Signs of Stress?', mimeo, 12 July.

— — — (2005), 'The Nordic Market: Signs of Stress?', *Energy Journal*, **26**, special issue, 71–98.

Waddams Price, C. (2004), 'Spoilt for Choice? The Costs and Benefits of Opening UK Residential Energy Markets', Center for the Study of Electricity Markets Working Paper 123, University of California.

— Hancock, R. (1998), 'Distributional Effects of Liberalising UK Residential Utility Markets', *Fiscal Studies*, **19**(3), 295–319.

Waelde, T. W. (ed.) (1996), *The Energy Charter Treaty: An East–West Gateway for Investment and Trade*, London, Kluwer Law International.

Walsh, C. E. (2003), *Monetary Theory and Policy*, 2nd edn, Cambridge, MA, MIT Press.

Watanabe, C., Zhu, B., Griffy-Brown, C., and Asgari, B. (2001), 'Global Technology Spillover and its Impact on Industry's R&D Strategies', *Technovation*, **21**, 281–91.

Watkins, G. C. (1992), 'The Hotelling Principle: Autobahn or Cul de Sac?', *Energy Journal*, **13**(1), 1–24.

WBGU (2004), *World in Transition: Towards Sustainable Energy Systems*, London, Earthscan

Weitzman, M. L. (1974), 'Prices vs Quantities', *Review of Economic Studies*, **41**(4), 477–91.

Westinghouse (2004), 'The Westinghouse AP1000: Proven, Advanced and Economical', available at http://www.prnewswire.com/cgi-bin/micro_stories.pl?ACCT= 127481&TICK=WE&STORY=/www/story/09-13-2004/0002249393&EDATE= Sep+13,+2004

Williamson, O. (1979), 'Transaction-cost Economics: The Governance of Contractual Relations', *Journal of Law and Economics*, **22**, 3–61.

Wilson, C. M., and Waddams Price, C. (2005), 'Irrationality in Consumers' Switching Decisions: When More Firms May Mean Less Benefit', CCP Working Paper No. 5, available at http://www.ccp.uea.ac.uk/public_files/workingpapers/CCP05-4.pdf

Wilson, J. Q. (1989), *Bureaucracy: What Government Agencies Do and Why They Do It*, Library of Congress, Basic Books.

Wirl, F., and Kujundzic, A. (2004), 'The Impact of OPEC Conference Outcomes on World Oil Prices 1984–2001', *Energy Journal*, **25**(1), 45–62.

Wolak, F. (2004), 'What's Wrong with Capacity Markets', mimeo, available at http:// stoft.com/metaPage/lib/WolaK-2004-06-contract-adequacy.pdf

Wolfram, C. (1999), 'Measuring Duopoly Power in the Deregulated UK Electricity Market', *American Economic Review*, **89**, 805–26.

World Nuclear Association (2005), 'The New Economics of Nuclear Power', available at http://www.world-nuclear.org/economics.pdf

Wright, P. (2006), *Gas Prices in the UK: Markets and Insecurity of Supply*, Oxford, Oxford Institute for Energy Studies and Oxford University Press.

Wright, S., Mason, R., and Miles, D. (2003), *A Study into Certain Aspects of the Cost of Capital for Regulated Utilities in the UK*, Report, 13 February, London, Smithers & Co.

Yergin, D. (1991), *The Prize*, Simon & Schuster.

Yohe, G. W. (2003), 'More Trouble for Cost–Benefit Analysis', *Climatic Change*, **56**(3), 235–44.

Index

481

The new energy paradigm